HUMPHRY CLINKER

AN AUTHORITATIVE TEXT
CONTEMPORARY RESPONSES
CRITICISM

D0650329

W.W. NORTON & COMPANY, INC.
also publishes

THE NORTON ANTHOLOGY OF AMERICAN LITERATURE
edited by Ronald Gottesman et al.

THE NORTON ANTHOLOGY OF ENGLISH LITERATURE
edited by M. H. Abrams et al.

THE NORTON ANTHOLOGY OF MODERN POETRY
edited by Richard Ellmann and Robert O'Clair

THE NORTON ANTHOLOGY OF POETRY
edited by Alexander W. Allison et al.

THE NORTON ANTHOLOGY OF SHORT FICTION
edited by R. V. Cassill

THE NORTON ANTHOLOGY OF WORLD MASTERPIECES
edited by Maynard Mack et al.

THE NORTON FACSIMILE OF
THE FIRST FOLIO OF SHAKESPEARE
prepared by Charlton Hinman

THE NORTON INTRODUCTION TO LITERATURE
edited by Carl E. Bain, Jerome Beaty, and J. Paul Hunter

THE NORTON INTRODUCTION TO THE SHORT NOVEL
edited by Jerome Beaty

THE NORTON READER
edited by Arthur M. Eastman et al.

THE NORTON SAMPLER
edited by Thomas Cooley

and the

NORTON CRITICAL EDITIONS

➤➤➤ A NORTON CRITICAL EDITION ◄◄◄

TOBIAS SMOLLETT

HUMPHRY CLINKER

AN AUTHORITATIVE TEXT
CONTEMPORARY RESPONSES
CRITICISM

➤➤➤ ◄◄◄

Edited by

JAMES L. THORSON
UNIVERSITY OF NEW MEXICO

➤➤➤ ◄◄◄

W • W • NORTON & COMPANY
New York • London

Library of Congress Cataloging in Publication Data
Smollett, Tobias George, 1721–1771.
Humphry Clinker: an authoritative text,
contemporary responses, criticism.

(A Norton critical edition)
Originally published as: The expedition of
Humphry Clinker. 1771.
Bibliography: p.
1. Smollett, Tobias George, 1721–1771. Expedition
of Humphry Clinker—Addresses, essays, lectures.
I. Thorson, James L.   II. Title.
PR3694.H8   1982   823'.6   81–18724
                                  AACR2

W. W. Norton & Company, Inc., 500 Fifth Avenue,
New York, N.Y. 10110
W. W. Norton & Company Ltd., 37 Great Russell Street,
London WC1B 3NU

ISBN 0-393-01592-0   CLOTH
ISBN 0-393-95283-5   PAPER

1 2 3 4 5 6 7 8 9 0

Acknowledgments

Byron Gassman: from *Tobias Smollett: Bicentennial Essays Presented to Lewis M. Knapp*, edited by G. S. Rousseau and P.-G. Boucé. Copyright © 1971 by Oxford University Press, Inc. Reprinted by permission.

Wolfgang Iser: "The Generic Control of the Aesthetic Response: An Examination of Smollett's *Humphry Clinker*." Reprinted by kind permission of *Southern Humanities Review*.

Lewis M. Knapp: from *The Age of Johnson*, ed. by Frederick W. Hilles, pp. 149–58. Copyright © 1949 by Yale University Press. Reprinted by permission.

William Park: "Fathers and Sons: *Humphry Clinker*." Reprinted by kind permission of *Literature and Psychology* and Professor William Park.

Thomas Rowlandson: Frontispiece photographed from Bodleian Library press mark 12 Θ 1675 and reprinted by permission of the Bodleian Library.

John Sekora: from *Luxury: The Concept in Western Thought, Eden to Smollett*, pp. 215–38; notes pp. 326–28. Copyright © 1977 by The Johns Hopkins University Press. Reprinted by permission.

John F. Sena: "Ancient Design and Modern Folly: Architecture in *The Expedition of Humphry Clinker*." Reprinted by kind permission of John M. Sena and the *Harvard Library Bulletin*.

Mary Wagoner: "On the Satire in *Humphry Clinker*." Reprinted by kind permission of *Papers on Language & Literature* and Mary Wagoner.

Acknowledgments

Contents

List of Illustrations

Preface

When Tobias George Smollett (1721–71) published *The Expedition of Humphry Clinker* in June, 1771, reaction to the new work by the controversial writer was mixed, but the excellence of the novel was quickly recognized by the public and by many critics. Its popular and critical success in the more than two hundred years since its first publication has been firmly established, and it is often called one of the very best English novels in the epistolary form.

Samuel Richardson (1689–1761) was the first author to utilize the formal fiction of presenting a novel in the form of a series of letters. His first novel, *Pamela* (1740), was largely made up of letters from the besieged but virtuous young title character to her parents. Henry Fielding (1707–54), with whom Smollett is often compared, retained Richardson's form in his parody of *Pamela*, called *Shamela* (1741), but he did not use the device in *Joseph Andrews* (1742) or in his later comic masterpiece *Tom Jones* (1748).

Richardson returned to the epistolary form in the extensive *Clarissa, or, The History of a Young Lady* (1747, dated 1748) but added considerable sophistication to it by including the letters of two pairs of correspondents, Clarissa Harlowe and her young friend, Anna Howe, and the vile rapist Robert Lovelace and his correspondent, Belford. The form was used in *Clarissa* to communicate psychological nuance and shade of emotion as well as to portray tragic events in a masterful way, but for all of his accomplishments, Richardson did not explore the capacity of the epistolary novel for humor.

In 1766 Christopher Anstey (1724–1805) brought out *The New Bath Guide: or, Memoires of the B__R__D Family. In a series of Poetical Epistles.* The book consists largely of versified observations of Bath and the customs which pertain to that spa rather than the telling of a progressive story. It uses humor, some of it rather broad, in many of its letters and shifts the point of view among members of the party of visitors.

Smollett may well have taken some hints from Anstey's *New Bath Guide*, but the idea of using an epistolary form had occurred to him before. Smollett's major contribution to travel literature is *Travels through France and Italy* (1766). In it, the traveler's observations are related through a series of familiar letters, though the volume is not simply the unedited letters of a traveler. The author forms his experiences and observations into a literary structure.

When Smollett wrote *Humphry Clinker,* he wove several threads into the fabric of his new work. In the manner of travel literature, he included descriptions of the cities and countryside visited, but many of the descriptions, particularly in the early portions of the novel, do as much to characterize the observer as to present what is being observed. One correspondent is Matthew Bramble, an irascible Welsh squire of fifty-five, whose search for health is one of the stimuli for the tour. His somewhat younger sister, Tabitha Bramble, is trying desperately to avoid being an old maid. Her letters back to their home at Brambleton Hall, an imaginary country seat near the real market town of Abergavenny, Wales, reveal her concerns with her dowry, which she accurately perceives as her most attractive feature to a potential husband. Two young people, a tutor-sick scholar, Jeremy Melford, apparently on leave from his studies at Jesus College, Oxford, and his sister Lydia, just released from a boarding school for young ladies at Gloucester, are nephew and niece to the oddly matched older pair of siblings. Jery and Liddy are orphans, children of Matt's sister, and the valetudinarian has decided to take them along on the trip to improve their knowledge of the United Kingdom and to improve his own acquaintance with his nephew, who is likely to become his heir. Win Jenkins, the Welsh maid to Miss Tabby, is the last of the important correspondents.

Each of the writers has an appropriate person to whom to send his or her letters. Matt Bramble writes to his confidant, friend, and physician, Dr. Lewis. Tabby writes for the most part to Mrs. Gwyllim, the housekeeper at Brambleton Hall, and Win Jenkins to Mary Jones, another maid at the Hall. Both Win and Tabby reveal more of themselves than they intend as Smollett has a high old time with their malapropisms, misspellings, and inadvertant double-entendres. Lydia corresponds mainly with her schoolmate, Laetitia Willis, and Jery with his college chum, Sir Watkin Phillips, a baronet in residence at Jesus College, Oxford. But what of the Humphry Clinker of the title? Suffice it to say that he comes into the story rather belatedly as a substitute postilion; readers will discover the rest of his story in the novel.

While travel observations make up part of the substance of the book, there is also a good bit of storytelling. Matthew Bramble seeks and finally finds his health; Lydia finds out the identity and suitability of the mysterious Wilson, whom she has fallen in love with; Tabby finds a very unlikely husband; Jery finds some maturity; and Humphry Clinker finds his identity, his father, and a place in the world. The novel presents a number of important themes. The critical essays included in this edition suggest what some of them are, but the book will provide a rich field for further thematic exploration.

Tobias Smollett, as the title page of the first edition of *The Expedition of Humphry Clinker* proclaimed, was the author of *The Adventures of Roderick Random* (1748), but he was many other things as well. He was born in 1721, the third and last child of Archibald and Barbara Smollett, who were the less affluent branch of a prominent Scottish family. His father died soon after the author's birth, and Tobias was subsequently educated at Dumbarton Grammar School and Glasgow University. In the 1730's he was apprenticed to two surgeons in Glasgow, but in 1739 he was released from his contract and went to London with his play, *The Regicide*, in his luggage.

To his chagrin, the play did not bring him instant fame and fortune, and after spending some months in London, he obtained a commission as a naval surgeon and sailed in H.M.S. *Chichester* in 1740 to take part in the ill-fated British expedition to Carthagena, then a Spanish colony. Smollett visited Jamaica and returned to England in 1744, when he set up a surgical practice in London. He had, in the interim, married a Jamaican heiress, Anne Lassells, though her inheritance was not enough to give the Smolletts complete financial independence.

Smollett published some poems in 1746 and 1747, and in 1748 launched the work that was to establish his early literary reputation, *Roderick Random*. The young title character of not overwhelming virtue and his traveling companion Strap have numerous adventures during their extensive wanderings. Told with great verve and humor, it was extremely popular at the time of its appearance, and it continues to be eminently readable and highly considered by many critics. In 1748 Smollett also published his translation from the French of Le Sage's (1648–1747) picaresque tale, *Gil Blas*, which he had been working on for some time and which had influenced his own work. He published *The Adventures of Peregrine Pickle*, another novel in the picaresque vein, in 1751, after having brought out *The Regicide* by subscription in 1749, but none of these ventures made him very much money. The author was to plunge into a wide variety of literary and journalistic projects over the next two decades in order to try to gain financial security.

Smollett published *The Adventures of Ferdinand Count Fathom* in 1753, but the novel, which featured an utterly reprehensible title character, had little success, either critically or commercially. In 1755, he published a translation from the Spanish of Miguel de Cervantes's (1547–1616) *Don Quixote*. His claims as a translator from Spanish have been largely discredited, but the work was to have an important influence on Smollett nevertheless.

He worked on *A Complete History of England* during the middle 1750's, and founded, edited, and wrote a great deal of *The Critical Review* from 1756 until he withdrew from active participation in the periodical in 1763. He edited the seven volumes of *A Compendium of Authentic and Diverting Voyages*, which came out in 1757, and in 1760 he started *The British Magazine* and published his novel *The Adventures of Sir Launcelot Greaves* serially in it. He took an important part in editing and translating *The Complete Works of Voltaire* (1761) in more than thirty volumes, in compiling and writing the five volumes of the *Continuation of the Complete History of England* (1763–65), and in editing and writing much of *The Briton*. This periodical supported the Scottish Lord Bute's ministry during 1762–63. Smollett and his wife undertook a trip to France and Italy in 1763 after the death of their only daughter at the age of fifteen. They returned to England in 1765, and in the next year he published *Travels through France and Italy*. In 1766, he made a pilgrimage to his native Scotland and returned to London via Bath. In 1768, he published *The Present State of All Nations* in eight volumes and left England to seek health in Italy. In 1769, he published *The History and Adventures of an Atom*, a political satire on England purportedly set in Japan. In June 1771, while the Smolletts were living near Leghorn, Italy, *The Expedition of Humphry Clinker* was published. Smollett died about three months later, in September 1771, in Italy, where he was buried.

The text of the present edition has been newly established from the Zimmerman Library copy of the three-volume first edition of 1771 (Volume I, mis-dated 1671) at the University of New Mexico. It has been read against the editor's copy of the same edition and also against the Bodleian Library copy. None of the other early editions of the work is bibliographically significant, but they have all been examined by the editor. The "long *s*" characteristic of eighteenth-century editions has silently been changed to the modern *s*, and the conventional continuation of quotation marks down the left-hand margin in extended direct discourse has been eliminated. The eighteenth-century use of parentheses rather than closing and re-opening quotation marks for "he/she said" has been retained. A few obvious typographical errors have been corrected, but since Tabitha Bramble's and Win Jenkins's letters are filled with creative spellings which are part of Smollett's joke, the editor has used extremely conservative principles in emendation.

The illustrations in this edition are those designed by Thomas Rowlandson for the 1793 two-volume edition of the novel. They were originally engraved by C. Grignion and have been photographed from the Zimmerman Library copy of their first edition by Karl P. Koenig. The topics for the illustrations were selected by Rowlandson with no care to spreading them out through the text, as most of them appear in the first half of the novel. The cover picture is also by Rowlandson, and it first appeared in the 1790 edition of the novel. It is reproduced from the Bodleian Library copy of the 1790 edition, shelf mark 12 Θ 1675, and is reproduced with the permission of the Bodleian Library, Oxford.

Smollett provided two notes for the first edition, and they have been retained and identified, but all other notes to the text of *Humphry Clinker* are the editor's. Most of the places mentioned in the novel are real, and where the geographical relationships are clear in the text or by reference to the map provided by Charles Seavey, the editor has tried not to belabor the obvious. The same restraint has been exercised on words which are defined in context. Where persons mentioned in the text can be identified, they have been noted. Smollett often italicized proverbial sayings and literary quotations in his text, and these typographical distinctions have been retained and sources identified as far as possible. Notes in the Contemporary Responses section are generally the editor's, but notes in the Criticism section are those of the writers of the essays unless otherwise indicated.

The editor owes particular thanks to the Bodleian Library, Oxford, and to the Principal and Fellows of Jesus College, Oxford, who extended hospitality and help as well as a Visiting Senior Research Fellowship while some of the research for this edition was being done. The University of New Mexico has been generous with sabbatical leaves and leaves without pay, which also facilitated the research. The Research Allocations Committee and the English Department of the University of New Mexico provided grants to allow Zimmerman Library to acquire copies and microfilms of early editions of the novel. Many of the identifications of quotations, persons, and places in the novel have been made by earlier scholars, and individual discoveries have been attributed to earlier students in many of the notes. The editor's personal thanks are owed to Professor O. M. Brack, Jr., who generously shared his knowledge of Smollett's work, to Professor Donald Farren and many other members of the staff at Zimmerman Library, and to Professor Ernest Baughman for his help with folklore problems. Mrs. K. T. Martin and the English department office staff, particularly Carol Belcher-Morgan, were most helpful in accomplishing many tedious tasks. Thanks also to Emily Garlin and Barry Wade, my helpful editors at W. W. Norton, and to Margaret White Wilson and Esther Fleming, who helped with the proofreading. The editor is especially thankful to Connie C. Thorson, who contributed the bibliographical essay and the bibliography and whose other help was immeasurable.

JAMES L. THORSON

The Text of
HUMPHRY CLINKER

THE

EXPEDITION

OF

HUMPHRY CLINKER.

By the AUTHOR of

RODERICK RANDOM.

IN THREE VOLUMES.
VOL. I.

———Quorſum hæc tam putida tendunt,
Furcifer ? ad te, inquam——— HOR.

LONDON,
Printed for W. JOHNSTON, in Ludgate-Street;
and B. COLLINS, in Saliſbury.
MDCLXXI.

Note

The epigraph is taken from Horace's *Satires* II. vii. 21–22. This is the Saturnalian satire in which Horace's servant Davus is taking the seasonal privilege of lecturing to his master, but the impatient Horace is telling him to get to the point. Horace says, "What is the point of this rot," and Davus responds, "It is aimed at you." The first volume of the first edition is mis-dated 1671 though it appeared in 1771.

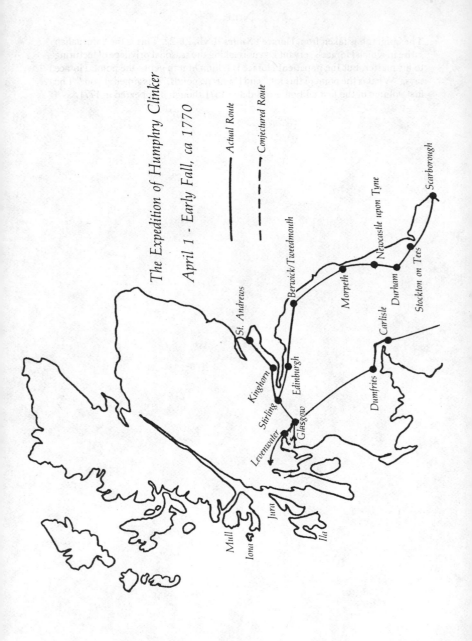

The Expedition of Humphry Clinker

April 1 - Early Fall, ca 1770

———— Actual Route
- - - - Conjectured Route

Scarborough

Newcastle upon Tyne

Morpeth

Stockton on Tees

Durham

Carlisle

Berwick/Tweedmouth

St. Andrews

Dumfries

Kinghorn

Edinburgh

Stirling

Glasgow

Levenwater

Jura

Mull

Iona

Ila

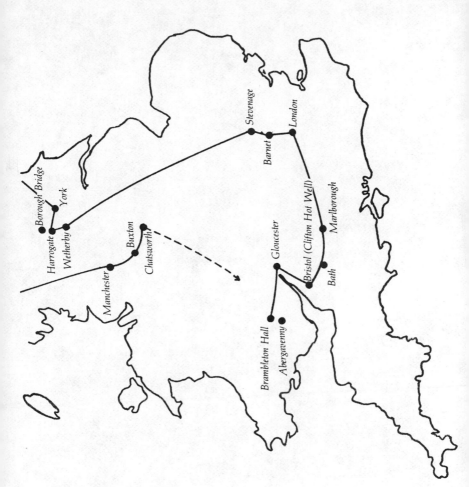

Borough Bridge
York
Harrogate
Wetherby
Manchester
Buxton
Chatsworth
Stevenage
Barnet
London
Gloucester
Bristol (Clifton Hot Well)
Marlborough
Bath
Brambleton Hall
Abergavenny

Volume I

To Mr. Henry Davis, Book-seller, in London.

Abergavenny,[1] Aug. 4.

Respected Sir,

I have received your esteemed favour of the 13th ultimo, whereby it appeareth, that you have perused those same Letters, the which were delivered unto you by my friend the reverend Mr. Hugo Behn; and I am pleased to find you think they may be printed with a good prospect of success; in as much as the objections you mention, I humbly conceive, are such as may be redargued,[2] if not entirely removed—And, first, in the first place, as touching what prosecutions may arise from printing the private correspondence of persons still living, give me leave, with all due submission, to observe, that the Letters in question were not written and sent under the seal of secrecy; that they have no tendency to the *mala fama*,[3] or prejudice of any person whatsoever; but rather to the information and edification of mankind: so that it becometh a sort of duty to promulgate them *in usum publicum*.[4] Besides, I have consulted Mr. Davy Higgins, an eminent attorney of this place, who, after due inspection and consideration, declareth, That he doth not think the said Letters contain any matter which will be held actionable in the eye of the law. Finally, if you and I should come to a right understanding, I do declare *in verbo sacerdotis*,[5] that, in case of any such prosecution, I will take the whole upon my own shoulders, even *quoad*[6] fine and imprisonment, though, I must confess, I should not care to undergo flagellation: *Tam ad turpitudinem, quam ad amaritudinem pœna spectans*[7]—Secondly, concerning the personal resentment of Mr. Justice Lismahago, I may say, *non flocci facio*[8]—I would not willingly vilipend[9] any Christian, if, peradventure, he deserveth that epithet: albeit, I am much surprised that more care is not taken to exclude from the commission all such vagrant foreigners as may be justly suspected of disaffection to our happy constitution, in church and state—God forbid that I should be so uncharitable, as to affirm positively, that the said Lismahago is no better than a Jesuit in disguise; but this I will assert and maintain, *totis viribus*,[1] that, from the day he qualified, he has never been once seen *intra templi parietes*, that is to say, within the parish church.

---

1. Abergavenny is a real market town in Wales, near where the fictional seat of Matthew Bramble, Brambleton Hall, is supposedly located. No further notes will be provided for real places mentioned in the text which can be found on the map, pp. xix–xx.
2. Refuted.
3. Ill Fame.

4. For the good of the public.
5. On my sacred word.
6. As far as.
7. As much for the shame as the bitterness of the penalty.
8. I care not a straw, or rush.
9. To treat as of little value, to belittle.
1. With all of [my] power.

Thirdly, with respect to what passed at Mr. Kendal's table, when the said Lismahago was so brutal in his reprehensions, I must inform you, my good sir, that I was obliged to retire, not by fear arising from his minatory[2] reproaches, which, as I said above, I value not of a rush; but from the sudden effect produced by a barbel's row, which I had eaten at dinner, not knowing, that the said row is at certain seasons violently cathartic, as Galen observeth in his chapter περί ιχθυς.[3]

Fourthly, and lastly, with reference to the manner in which I got possession of these Letters, it is a circumstance that concerns my own conscience only; sufficeth it to say, I have fully satisfied the parties in whose custody they were; and, by this time, I hope I have also satisfied you in such ways, that the last hand may be put to our agreement, and the work proceed with all convenient expedition; in which hope I rest,

respected sir,

your very humble servant,

JONATHAN DUSTWICH.

P.S. I propose, *Deo volente*,[4] to have the pleasure of seeing you in the great city, towards All-hallow-tide, when I shall be glad to treat with you concerning a parcel of MS. sermons, of a certain clergyman deceased; a cake of the right leaven, for the present taste of the public. *Verbum sapienti*,[5] &c.

J.D.

To the Revd. Mr. JONATHAN DUSTWICH, at ———.

SIR,

I received yours in course of post, and shall be glad to treat with you for the MS. which I have delivered to your friend Mr. Behn; but can by no means comply with the terms proposed. Those things are so uncertain —Writing is all a lottery—I have been a loser by the works of the greatest men of the age—I could mention particulars, and name names; but don't chuse it—The taste of the town is so changeable. Then there have been so many letters upon travels lately published—What between Smollett's, Sharp's, Derrick's, Thickness's, Baltimore's, and Baretti's, together with Shandy's Sentimental Travels,[6] the public seems to be cloyed with

---

2. Menacing.
3. Concerning fish. Galen was a Greek physician and writer of the second century whose works were still studied, especially by pedants. "Barbel's row," just above is the roe, or egg mass, of the fish called barbel from its beard-like feelers.
4. God willing.
5. A word to the wise. . . .
6. This list of books is authentic. It includes

Smollett's own *Travels through France and Italy* (1766); Samuel Sharp's *Letters from Italy* (1766); Samuel Derrick's *A Collection of Travels through various parts of the world* (1762); Philip Thickness's *Useful Hints to those who make the tour of France* (1768); *A Tour in the East in the Years 1763 and 1764* (1767) by Frederick Calvert, Baron Baltimore; Guiseppe Baretti's *An Account of the Manners and Customs of Italy* (1768) and *A Jour-*

that kind of entertainment—Nevertheless, I will, if you please, run the risque of printing and publishing, and you shall have half the profits of the impression—You need not take the trouble to bring up your sermons on my account—No body reads sermons but Methodists and Dissenters —Besides, for my own part, I am quite a stranger to that sort of reading; and the two persons, whose judgment I depended upon in these matters, are out of the way; one is gone abroad, carpenter of a man of war; and the other has been silly enough to abscond, in order to avoid a prosecution for blasphemy—I'm a great loser by his going off—He has left a manual of devotion half finished on my hands, after having received money for the whole copy—He was the soundest divine, and had the most orthodox pen of all my people; and I never knew his judgment fail, but in flying from his bread and butter on this occasion.

By owning you was not put in bodily fear by Lismahago, you preclude yourself from the benefit of a good plea, over and above the advantage of binding him over. In the late war, I inserted in my evening paper, a paragraph that came by the post, reflecting upon the behaviour of a certain regiment in battle.[7] An officer of said regiment came to my shop, and, in the presence of my wife and journeyman, threatened to cut off my ears——As I exhibited marks of bodily fear, more ways than one, to the conviction of the byestanders, I bound him over; my action lay, and I recovered. As for flagellation, you have nothing to fear, and nothing to hope, on that head—There has been but one printer flogged at the cart's tail these thirty years; that was Charles Watson; and he assured me it was no more than a flea-bite. C—— S—— has been threatened several times by the House of L——;[8] but it came to nothing. If an information should be moved for, and granted against you, as the editor of those Letters, I hope you will have honesty and wit enough to appear and take your trial ——If you should be sentenced to the pillory, your fortune is made—As times go, that's a sure step to honour and preferment. I shall think myself happy if I can lend you a lift; and am, very sincerely,

yours,

London, Aug. 10th.   HENRY DAVIS.

Please my kind service to your neighbour, my cousin Madoc—I have sent an Almanack and Court-kalendar, directed for him at Mr. Sutton's, bookseller, in Gloucester, carriage paid, which he will please to accept as a small token of my regard. My wife, who is very fond of toasted cheese, presents her compliments to him, and begs to know if there's any of that

nal from London to Genoa (1770); and Lawrence Sterne's A Sentimental Journey through France and Italy (1768). In this last volume, Smollett was satirized as "the learned Dr. Smelfungus."
7. The allusion is probably to the flight of "The Blues" at the Battle of Dettingen in June, 1743. See also p. 98 and note 4, below.
8. John Sekora has confirmed the identification of this printer as Charles Green Say, who worked in Ludgate Street in London. L—— is Lords.

kind, which he was so good as to send us last Christmas, to be sold in London.

H.D.

The
Expedition
of
Humphry Clinker

To Dr. Lewis.

Doctor,

The pills are good for nothing—I might as well swallow snow-balls to cool my reins[9]—I have told you over and over, how hard I am to move; and at this time of day, I ought to know something of my own constitution. Why will you be so positive? Prithee send me another prescription—I am as lame and as much tortured in all my limbs as if I was broke upon the wheel: indeed, I am equally distressed in mind and body—As if I had not plagues enough of my own, those children of my sister are left me for a perpetual source of vexation—what business have people to get children to plague their neighbours? A ridiculous incident that happened yesterday to my niece Liddy, has disordered me in such a manner, that I expect to be laid up with another fit of the gout—perhaps, I may explain myself in my next. I shall set out to-morrow morning for the Hot Well at Bristol, where I am afraid I shall stay longer than I could wish. On the receipt of this, send Williams thither with my saddle-horse and the *demi pique*.[1] Tell Barns to thresh out the two old ricks, and send the corn to market, and sell it off to the poor at a shilling a bushel under market price.—I have received a sniveling letter from Griffin, offering to make a public submission and pay costs. I want none of his submissions; neither will I pocket any of his money—The fellow is a bad neighbour, and I desire to have nothing to do with him: but as he is purse-proud, he shall pay for his insolence: let him give five pounds to the poor of the parish, and I'll withdraw my action; and in the mean time you may tell Prig to stop proceedings.—Let Morgan's widow have the Alderney cow, and forty shillings to clothe her children: but don't say a syllable of the matter to any living soul—I'll make her pay when she is able. I desire you will lock up all my drawers, and keep the keys till meeting; and be sure

9. Kidneys. The statement is an adaptation of Falstaff's "My belly's as cold as if I had swallowed snow-balls for pills to cool the reins." Shake-speare, *Merry Wives of Windsor* II. v. 24.
1. A saddle only half the height of the tall battle saddle.

you take the iron chest with my papers into your own custody—Forgive all this trouble from,

Dear Lewis,

Your affectionate

Gloucester, April 2.   M. BRAMBLE.

To MRS. GWYLLIM, house-keeper at Brambleton-hall.

MRS. GWILLIM,

When this cums to hand, be sure to pack up in the trunk male[2] that stands in my closet, to be sent me in the Bristol waggon without loss of time, the following articles, viz. my rose collard neglejay, with green robins, my yellow damask, and my black velvet suit, with the short hoop; my bloo quilted petticot, my green manteel, my laced apron, my French commode,[3] Macklin head and lappets,[4] and the litel box with my jowls. Williams may bring over my bum-daffee, and the viol with the easings of Dr. Hill's dock-water,[5] and Chowder's lacksitif. The poor creature has been terribly constuprated ever since we left huom. Pray take particular care of the house while the family is absent. Let there be a fire constantly kept in my brother's chamber and mine. The maids, having nothing to do, may be sat a spinning. I desire you'll clap a pad-luck on the wind-seller, and let none of the men have excess to the strong bear—don't forget to have the gate shit every evening before dark.——The gardnir and the hind may lie below in the landry, to partake the house, with the blunderbuss and the great dog; and I hope you'll have a watchfull eye over the maids. I know that hussy, Mary Jones, loves to be rumping with the men. Let me know if Alderney's calf be sould yet, and what he fought —if the ould goose be sitting; and if the cobler has cut Dicky, and how the pore anemil bore the operation.—No more at present, but rests,

Yours,

Glostar, April 2.   TABITHA BRAMBLE.

2. A trunk large enough to require that duty be paid on it when crossing international borders. The word should be spelled *mail*. In the letters of Tabitha Bramble and Win Jenkins the language is often scrambled. Footnotes will be provided when the word they are trying to approximate needs explanation.
3. A tall, elaborate headdress already considerably out of style.
4. A cap made of lace of the variety made in Mechlin in Belgium, with streamers at the side and back.
5. The "viol with the easings of Dr. Hill's

dockwater" is Tabitha's approximation of the essence of waterdock, a common herb, which was prepared and sold in vials by the physician and writer John Hill (1716?–75) whom some called a quack. "Bum-daffee" is probably bumtaffy, as it is spelled later in the novel, and is apparently a stomach remedy based on essense of rum. Later in the novel, Win Jenkins is threatened with having to take a dose of bumtaffee if she does not take the waters of Bath, and she chooses the bathing over the medicine. W. Arthur Boggs has suggested that it refers to Daffey's Elixir, a laxative.

To Mrs. MARY JONES, at Brambleton-hall.

DEAR MOLLY,

Heaving this importunity, I send my love to you and Saul, being in good health, and hoping to hear the same from you; and that you and Saul will take my poor kitten to bed with you this cold weather.—We have been all in a sad taking here at Glostar—Miss Liddy had like to have run away with a player-man, and young master and he would adone themselves a mischief; but the squire applied to the mare, and they were bound over.—Mistress bid me not speak a word of the matter to any Christian soul—no more I shall: for, we servints should see all and say nothing—But what was worse than all this, Chowder has had the misfortune to be worried by a butcher's dog, and came home in a terrible pickle—Mistriss was taken with the asterisks, but they soon went off. The doctor was sent for to Chowder, and he subscribed a repository, which did him great service—thank God he's now in a fair way to do well —pray take care of my box and the pillyber,[6] and put them under your own bed; for, I do suppose, madam Gwyllim will be a prying into my secrets, now my back is turned. John Thomas is in good health, but sulky. The squire gave away an ould coat to a poor man; and John says as how tis robbing him of his parquisites.[7]—I told him, by his agreement he was to receive no vails;[8] but he says as how there's a difference betwixt vails and parquisites; and so there is for sartain. We are all going to the Hot Well, where I shall drink your health in a glass of water, being,

Dear Molly,

Your humble servant to command,

Glostar, April 2d.   WIN. JENKINS.

To Sir WATKIN PHILLIPS, Bar[t].[9] of Jesus college, Oxon.[1]

DEAR PHILLIPS,

As I have nothing more at heart than to convince you I am incapable of forgetting, or neglecting the friendship I made at college, I now begin that correspondence by letters, which you and I agreed, at parting, to

6. A misspelling of pillow-bear, an archaic term for pillowcase.
7. Perquisites are the fringe benefits associated with a position.
8. Gratuities.
9. The usual abbreviation for Baronet, a member of the hereditary order which ranked below Baron, the lowest step in the peerage. The name is probably adapted from Sir Watkin Williams Wynn (1692–1749), a Baronet, who matriculated as a fellow-commoner at Jesus College in 1710, was a prominent Tory and Jacobite member of Parlia-

ment from Denbighshire from 1716 until his death, received the D.C.L. from Oxford in 1732, and was a benefactor of Jesus College. Smollett noted in his *History of England* that in the House of Commons, Wynn was regarded as "a brave open hospitable gentleman."
1. Jesus College, Oxford, founded by Queen Elizabeth in 1571 at the behest of Dr. Hugh Price, maintained close ties with Wales through the eighteenth century, and so is most appropriate as the college of the young Welshman Jeremy Melford.

cultivate. I begin it sooner than I intended, that you may have it in your power to refute any idle reports which may be circulated to my prejudice at Oxford, touching a foolish quarrel, in which I have been involved on account of my sister, who had been some time settled here in a boarding-school.—When I came hither with my uncle and aunt (who are our guardians) to fetch her away, I found her a fine, tall girl, of seventeen, with an agreeable person; but remarkably simple, and quite ignorant of the world. This disposition, and want of experience, had exposed her to the addresses of a person—I know not what to call him, who had seen her at a play; and, with a confidence and dexterity peculiar to himself, found means to be recommended to her acquaintance. It was by the greatest accident I intercepted one of his letters; as it was my duty to stifle this correspondence in its birth, I made it my business to find him out, and tell him very freely my sentiments of the matter. The spark did not like the stile I used, and behaved with abundance of mettle. Though his rank in life (which, by the bye, I am ashamed to declare) did not entitle him to much deference; yet as his behaviour was remarkably spirited, I admitted him to the privilege of a gentleman, and something might have happened, had not we been prevented.—In short, the business took air, I know not how, and made abundance of noise—recourse was had to justice—I was obliged to give my word and honour, &c. and to-morrow morning we set out for Bristol Wells, where I expect to hear from you by the return of the post.——I have got into a family of originals, whom I may one day attempt to describe for your amusement. My aunt, Mrs. Tabitha Bramble,[2] is a maiden of forty-five, exceedingly starched, vain, and ridiculous.—My uncle is an odd kind of humorist, always on the fret, and so unpleasant in his manner, that rather than be obliged to keep him company, I'd resign all claim to the inheritance of his estate.—Indeed his being tortured by the gout may have soured his temper, and, perhaps, I may like him better on further acquaintance: certain it is, all his servants and neighbours in the country, are fond of him, even to a degree of enthusiasm, the reason of which I cannot as yet comprehend. Remember me to Griffy Price, Gwyn, Mansel, Basset, and all the rest of my old Cambrian[3] companions.——Salute the bed-maker in my name—give my service to the cook, and pray take care of poor Ponto, for the sake of his old master, who is, and ever will be,   Dear Phillips,

Your affectionate friend,

and humble servant,

Gloucester, April 2.   JER. MELFORD.

2. Mrs. was commonly used as a title of respect before the names of unmarried women in the eighteenth century, as it is here.
3. Welsh. The names just above are all typically Welsh, and Francis Mansel (1519–1665) was a Principal and benefactor of Jesus College in the seventeenth century, during whose tenure the college buildings were notably extended.

To Mrs. JERMYN, at her house in Gloucester.

DEAR MADAM,

Having no mother of my own, I hope you will give me leave to disburthen my poor heart to you, who have always acted the part of a kind parent to me, ever since I was put under your care.—Indeed, and indeed, my worthy governess may believe me, when I assure her, that I never harboured a thought that was otherwise than virtuous; and, if God will give me grace, I shall never behave so as to cast a reflection on the care you have taken in my education. I confess I have given just cause of offence by my want of prudence and experience. I ought not to have listened to what the young man said; and it was my duty to have told you all that passed, but I was ashamed to mention it; and then he behaved so modest and respectful, and seemed to be so melancholy and timorous, that I could not find in my heart to do any thing that should make him miserable and desperate. As for familiarities, I do declare, I never once allowed him the favour of a salute;[4] and as to the few letters that passed between us, they are all in my uncle's hands, and I hope they contain nothing contrary to innocence and honour.—I am still persuaded that he is not what he appears to be: but time will discover—mean while I will endeavour to forget a connexion, which is so displeasing to my family. I have cried without ceasing, and have not tasted any thing but tea, since I was hurried away from you; nor did I once close my eyes for three nights running.——My aunt continues to chide me severely when we are by ourselves; but I hope to soften her in time, by humility and submission. —My uncle, who was so dreadfully passionate in the beginning, has been moved by my tears and distress; and is now all tenderness and compassion; and my brother is reconciled to me, on my promise to break off all correspondence with that unfortunate youth: but, notwithstanding all their indulgence, I shall have no peace of mind 'till I know my dear and ever honoured governess has forgiven her poor, disconsolate, forlorn,

Affectionate humble servant,

till death,

Clifton, April 6.   LYDIA MELFORD.

4. A kiss as a formal salutation.

To Miss Lætitia Willis, at Gloucester.

MY Dearest Letty,

I am in such a fright, lest this should not come safe to hand by the conveyance of Jarvis the carrier, that I beg you will write me, on the receipt of it, directing to me, under cover, to Mrs. Winifred Jenkins, my aunt's maid, who is a good girl, and has been so kind to me in my affliction, that I have made her my confidant; as for Jarvis, he was very shy of taking charge of my letter and the little parcel, because his sister Sally had like to have lost her place on my account: indeed I cannot blame the man for his caution; but I have made it worth his while.—My dear companion and bed-fellow, it is a grievous addition to my other misfortunes, that I am deprived of your agreeable company and conversation, at a time when I need so much the comfort of your good humour and good sense; but, I hope, the friendship we contracted at boarding-school, will last for life——I doubt not but on my side it will daily increase and improve, as I gain experience, and learn to know the value of a true friend.—O, my dear Letty! what shall I say about poor Mr. Wilson? I have promised to break off all correspondence, and, if possible, to forget him: but, alas! I begin to perceive that will not be in my power. As it is by no means proper that the picture should remain in my hands, lest it should be the occasion of more mischief, I have sent it to you by this opportunity, begging you will either keep it safe till better times, or return it to Mr. Wilson himself, who, I suppose, will make it his business to see you at the usual place. If he should be low-spirited at my sending back his picture, you may tell him I have no occasion for a picture, while the original continues engraved on my——But no; I would not have you tell him that neither; because there must be an end of our correspondence——I wish he may forget me, for the sake of his own peace; and yet if he should, he must be a barbarous——But 'tis impossible—poor Wilson cannot be false and inconstant: I beseech him not to write to me, nor attempt to see me for some time; for, considering the resentment and passionate temper of my brother Jery, such an attempt might be attended with consequences which would make us all miserable for life—let us trust to time and the chapter of accidents; or rather to that Providence which will not fail, sooner or later, to reward those that walk in the paths of honour and virtue.—I would offer my love to the young ladies; but it is not fit that any of them should know you have received this letter.—If we go to Bath, I shall send you my simple remarks upon that famous center of polite amusement, and every other place we may chance to visit; and I flatter myself that my dear Miss Willis will be punctual in answering the letters of her affectionate,

Clifton, April 6.   Lydia Melford.

To Dr. LEWIS.

DEAR LEWIS,

I have followed your directions with some success, and might have been upon my legs by this time, had the weather permitted me to use my saddle horse. I rode out upon the Downs last Tuesday, in the forenoon, when the sky, as far as the visible horizon, was without a cloud; but before I had gone a full mile, I was overtaken instantaneously by a storm of rain that wet me to the skin in three minutes—whence it came the devil knows; but it has laid me up (I suppose) for one fortnight. It makes me sick to hear people talk of the fine air upon Clifton-Downs: how can the air be either agreeable or salutary, where the dæmon of vapours descends in a perpetual drizzle? My confinement is the more intolerable, as I am surrounded with domestic vexations.—My niece has had a dangerous fit of illness, occasioned by that cursed incident at Gloucester, which I mentioned in my last.——She is a poor good-natured simpleton, as soft as butter, and as easily melted—not that she's a fool—the girl's parts are not despicable, and her education has not been neglected; that is to say, she can write and spell, and speak French, and play upon the harpsichord; then she dances finely, has a good figure, and is very well inclined; but, she's deficient in spirit, and so susceptible—and so tender forsooth!—truly, she has got a languishing eye, and reads romances ——Then there's her brother, 'squire Jery, a pert jackanapes, full of college-petulance and self-conceit; proud as a German count, and as hot and hasty as a Welch mountaineer. As for that fantastical animal, my sister Tabby, you are no stranger to her qualifications—I vow to God, she is sometimes so intolerable, that I almost think she's the devil incarnate come to torment me for my sins; and yet I am conscious of no sins that ought to entail such family-plagues upon me—why the devil should not I shake off these torments at once? I an't married to Tabby, thank Heaven! nor did I beget the other two: let them choose another guardian: for my part, I an't in a condition to take care of myself; much less to superintend the conduct of giddy headed boys and girls. You earnestly desire to know the particulars of our adventure at Gloucester, which are briefly these, and I hope they will go no further:—Liddy had been so long cooped up in a boarding-school, which, next to a nunnery, is the worst kind of seminary that ever was contrived for young women, that she became as inflammable as touch-wood;[5] and going to a play in holiday-time, —'sdeath, I'm ashamed to tell you! she fell in love with one of the actors —a handsome young fellow that goes by the name of Wilson. The rascal soon perceived the impression he had made, and managed matters so as to see her at a house where she went to drink tea with her governess.

5. Tinder.

—This was the beginning of a correspondence, which they kept up by means of a jade of a milliner, who made and dressed caps for the girls at the boarding-school. When we arrived at Gloucester, Liddy came to stay at lodgings with her aunt, and Wilson bribed the maid to deliver a letter into her own hands; but it seems Jery had already acquired so much credit with the maid, (by what means he best knows) that she carried the letter to him, and so the whole plot was discovered. The rash boy, without saying a word of the matter to me, went immediately in search of Wilson; and, I suppose, treated him with insolence enough. The theatrical hero was too far gone in romance to brook such usage: he replied in blank verse, and a formal challenge ensued. They agreed to meet early next morning and decide the dispute with sword and pistol. I heard nothing at all of the affair, 'till Mr. Morley came to my bed-side in the morning, and told me he was afraid my nephew was going to fight, as he had been over-heard talking very loud and vehement with Wilson at the young man's lodgings the night before, and afterwards went and bought powder and ball at a shop in the neighbourhood. I got up immediately, and upon inquiry found he was just gone out. I begged Morley to knock up the mayor, that he might interpose as a magistrate, and in the mean time I hobbled after the squire, whom I saw at a distance walking at a great pace towards the city gate—in spite of all my efforts, I could not come up 'till our two combatants had taken their ground, and were priming their pistols. An old house luckily screened me from their view; so that I rushed upon them at once, before I was perceived. They were both confounded, and attempted to make their escape different ways; but Morley coming up with constables at that instant, took Wilson into custody, and Jery followed him quietly to the mayor's house. All this time I was ignorant of what had passed the preceding day; and neither of the parties would discover a tittle of the matter. The mayor observed that it was great presumption in Wilson, who was a stroller,[6] to proceed to such extremities with a gentleman of family and fortune; and threatened to commit him on the vagrant act.—The young fellow bustled up with great spirit, declaring he was a gentleman, and would be treated as such; but he refused to explain himself further. The master of the company being sent for, and examined, touching the said Wilson, said the young man had engaged with him at Birmingham about six months ago; but never would take his salary; that he had behaved so well in his private character, as to acquire the respect and good-will of all his acquaintance, and that the public owned his merit, as an actor, was altogether extraordinary.———After all, I fancy, he will turn out to be a run-away prentice from London.—The manager offered to bail him for any sum, provided he would give his word and honour that he would keep the peace; but the young gentleman was on his high ropes, and would by no

6. An itinerant actor.

means lay himself under any restrictions: on the other hand, Hopefull was equally obstinate; till at length the mayor declared, that if they both refused to be bound over, he would immediately commit Wilson as a vagrant to hard labour. I own I was much pleased with Jery's behaviour on this occasion: he said, that rather than Mr. Wilson should be treated in such an ignominious manner, he would give his word and honour to prosecute the affair no further while they remained at Gloucester —Wilson thanked him for his generous manner of proceeding, and was discharged. On our return to our lodgings, my nephew explained the whole mystery; and I own I was exceedingly incensed.——Liddy being questioned on the subject, and very severely reproached by that wild-cat my sister Tabby, first swooned away, then dissolving in a flood of tears, confessed all the particulars of the correspondence, at the same time giving up three letters, which was all she had received from her admirer. The last, which Jery intercepted, I send you inclosed, and when you have read it, I dare say you won't wonder at the progress the writer had made in the heart of a simple girl, utterly unacquainted with the characters of mankind. Thinking it was high time to remove her from such a dangerous connexion, I carried her off the very next day to Bristol; but the poor creature was so frightened and fluttered, by our threats and expostulations, that she fell sick the fourth day after our arrival at Clifton, and continued so ill for a whole week, that her life was despaired of. It was not till yesterday that Dr. Rigge declared her out of danger. You cannot imagine what I have suffered, partly from the indiscretion of this poor child, but much more from the fear of losing her entirely. This air is intolerably cold, and the place quite solitary—I never go down to the well without returning low-spirited; for there I meet with half a dozen poor emaciated creatures, with ghostly looks, in the last stage of a consumption,[7] who have made shift to linger through the winter, like so many exotic plants languishing in a hot-house; but, in all appearance, will drop into their graves before the sun has warmth enough to mitigate the rigour of this ungenial spring.—If you think the Bath water will be of any service to me, I will go thither as soon as my niece can bear the motion of the coach.——Tell Barns I am obliged to him for his advice; but don't choose to follow it. If Davis voluntarily offers to give up the farm, the other shall have it; but I will not begin at this time of day to distress my tenants, because they are unfortunate, and cannot make regular payments: I wonder that Barns should think me capable of such oppression —As for Higgins, the fellow is a notorious poacher, to be sure; and an impudent rascal to set his snares in my own paddock; but, I suppose, he thought he had some right (especially in my absence) to partake of what nature seems to have intended for common use—you may threaten him in my name, as much as you please, and if he repeats the offence, let me

7. Pulmonary tuberculosis.

know it before you have recourse to justice.——I know you are a great sportsman, and oblige many of your friends: I need not tell you to make use of my grounds; but it may be necessary to hint, that I'm more afraid of my fowling piece than of my game. When you can spare two or three brace of partidges, send them over by the stage coach, and tell Gwyllim that she forgot to pack up my flannels and wide shoes in the trunk-mail——I shall trouble you as usual, from time to time, 'till at last I suppose you will be tired of corresponding with

Your assured friend,

Clifton, April 17. M. Bramble.

To Miss Lydia Melford.

Miss Willis has pronounced my doom——you are going away, dear Miss Melford!——you are going to be removed, I know not whither! what shall I do? which way shall I turn for consolation? I know not what I say —all night long have I been tossed in a sea of doubts and fears, uncertainty and distraction, without being able to connect my thoughts, much less to form any consistent plan of conduct——I was even tempted to wish that I had never seen you; or that you had been less amiable, or less compassionate to your poor Wilson; and yet it would be detestable ingratitude in me to form such a wish, considering how much I am indebted to your goodness, and the ineffable pleasure I have derived from your indulgence and approbation——Good God! I never heard your name mentioned without emotion! the most distant prospect of being admitted to your company, filled my whole soul with a kind of pleasing alarm! as the time approached, my heart beat with redoubled force, and every nerve thrilled with a transport of expectation; but, when I found myself actually in your presence;——when I heard you speak;—when I saw you smile; when I beheld your charming eyes turned favourably upon me; my breast was filled with such tumults of delight, as wholly deprived me of the power of utterance, and wrapt me in a delirium of joy!——encouraged by your sweetness of temper and affability, I ventured to describe the feelings of my heart——even then you did not check my presumption——you pitied my sufferings, and gave me leave to hope ——you put a favourable—perhaps too favourable a construction, on my appearance—certain it is, I am no player in love——I speak the language of my own heart; and have no prompter but nature.——Yet there is something in this heart, which I have not yet disclosed——I flattered myself—But, I will not——I must not proceed—Dear Miss Liddy! for Heaven's sake, contrive, if possible, some means of letting me speak to you before you leave Gloucester; otherwise, I know not what will—But I begin to rave again——I will endeavour to bear this trial with fortitude —while I am capable of reflecting upon your tenderness and truth, I surely have no cause to despair—yet I am strangely affected. The sun seems to deny me light—a cloud hangs over me, and there is a dreadful weight upon my spirits! While you stay in this place, I shall continually hover about your lodgings, as the parted soul is said to linger about the grave where its mortal consort lies.—I know, if it is in your power, you will task your humanity—your compassion—shall I add, your affection? —in order to assuage the almost intolerable disquiet that torments the heart of your afflicted,

Gloucester, March 31.   WILSON.

To Sir WATKIN PHILLIPS, of Jesus college, Oxon.

Hot-well, April 18.

DEAR PHILLIPS,

I give Mansel credit for his invention, in propagating the report that I had a quarrel with a mountebank's merry Andrew[8] at Gloucester: but I have too much respect for every appendage of wit, to quarrel even with the lowest buffoonery; and therefore I hope Mansel and I shall always be good friends. I cannot, however, approve of his drowning my poor dog Ponto, on purpose to convert Ovid's pleonasm into a punning epitaph. —*deerant quoque Littora Ponto*:[9] for, that he threw him into the Isis,[1] when it was so high and impetuous, with no other view than to kill the fleas, is an excuse that will not hold water—But I leave poor Ponto to his fate, and hope Providence will take care to accommodate Mansel with a drier death.

As there is nothing that can be called company at the Well, I am here in a state of absolute rustication:[2] This, however, gives me leisure to observe the singularities in my uncle's character, which seems to have interested your curiosity. The truth is, his disposition and mine, which, like oil and vinegar, repelled one another at first, have now begun to mix by dint of being beat up together. I was once apt to believe him a complete Cynic; and that nothing but the necessity of his occasions could compel him to get within the pale of society—I am now of another opinion. I think his peevishness arises partly from bodily pain, and partly

8. A mountebank was an itinerant quack who sold medicines from a raised platform with the aid of a show which often featured a clown or Merry Andrew.
9. From Ovid's *Metamorphoses* I. 292. The whole line is "Omnia pontus erat, deerant quoque litora ponto,": "There was nothing but the sea, and the sea had no shores." A pleonasm is a redundancy; if there were nothing but the sea, it could certainly not have shores. Latin played a very important part in the Oxford curriculum in the eighteenth century, and there are many examples of punning and word games in Latin in the literature of the period.
1. A small river that runs through Oxford, where it becomes the Thames. There is considerable local confusion about the relationship of the two names for the same river, and no agreement about where the name changes.
2. To be rusticated from Oxford was to be sent down from the university, usually as punishment, but Jery is playing with the term to indicate the lack of appropriate society for himself. His status at the university is never made altogether clear, but he is probably on leave to attend his uncle on the expedition.

from a natural excess of mental sensibility; for, I suppose, the mind as well as the body, is in some cases endued with a morbid excess of sensation.

I was t'other day much diverted with a conversation that passed in the Pump-room, betwixt him and the famous Dr. L——n,[3] who is come to ply at the Well for patients. My uncle was complaining of the stink, occasioned by the vast quantity of mud and slime, which the river leaves at low ebb under the windows of the Pump-room. He observed, that the exhalations arising from such a nuisance, could not but be prejudicial to the weak lungs of many consumptive patients, who came to drink the water. The Doctor overhearing this remark, made up to him, and assured him he was mistaken. He said, people in general were so misled by vulgar prejudices, that philosophy was hardly sufficient to undeceive them. Then humming thrice, he assumed a most ridiculous solemnity of aspect, and entered into a learned investigation of the nature of stink. He observed, that stink, or stench, meant no more than a strong impression on the olfactory nerves; and might be applied to substances of the most opposite qualities; that in the Dutch language, *stinken* signified the most agreeable perfume, as well as the most fetid odour, as appears in Van Vloudel's translation of Horace, in that beautiful ode, *Quis multa gracilis*, &c.—The words *liquidis perfusus odoribus*, he translates *van civet & moschata gestinken:*[4] that individuals differed *toto cælo*[5] in their opinion of smells, which, indeed, was altogether as arbitrary as the opinion of beauty; that the French were pleased with the putrid effluvia of animal food; and so were the Hottentots in Africa, and the Savages in Greenland; and that the Negroes on the coast of Senegal would not touch fish till it was rotten; strong presumptions in favour of what is generally called *stink*, as those nations are in a state of nature, undebauched by luxury, unseduced by whim and caprice: that he had reason to believe the stercoraceous[6] flavour, condemned by prejudice as a stink, was, in fact, most agreeable to the organs of smelling; for, that every person who pretended to nauseate the smell of another's excretions, snuffed up his own with particular complacency; for the truth of which he appealed to all the ladies and gentlemen then present: he said, the inhabitants of Madrid and Edinburgh found particular satisfaction in breathing their own atmosphere, which was always impregnated with stercoraceous effluvia: that the learned Dr. B—, in his treatise on the Four Digestions,[7]

3. Dr. Dietrich Wessel Linden, a German physician who practiced in England and wrote a number of works on the medicinal effects of the waters of various spas. Smollett, also a physician, probably thought him a quack.
4. Smollett has Linden refer inaccurately to Joost van den Vondel's translation of Horace's *Odes* I. v. (Amsterdam, 1735). The original reads "Quis multa gracilis te puer in rosa perfusus liquidis urget odoribus?": "What slender youth inundated

with liquid perfumes, presses thee amid many roses?" Van den Vondel's translation, though misquoted, uses the Dutch verb *stinkende*.
5. Entirely.
6. Pertaining to dung or feces.
7. Probably Dr. Edward Barry, Bart. (1696–1776), who wrote *A Treatise on the Three Different Digestions, and Discharges of the Human Body and the Diseases of their Principal Organs* (1759).

explains in what manner the volatile effluvia from the intestines, stimulate and promote the operations of the animal oeconomy: he affirmed, the last Grand Duke of Tuscany, of the *Medicis* family, who refined upon sensuality with the spirit of a philosopher, was so delighted with that odour, that he caused the essence of ordure to be extracted, and used it as the most delicious perfume: that he himself, (the doctor) when he happened to be low-spirited, or fatigued with business, found immediate relief and uncommon satisfaction from hanging over the stale contents of a close-stool,[8] while his servant stirred it about under his nose; nor was this effect to be wondered at, when we consider that this substance abounds with the self-same volatile salts that are so greedily smelled to by the most delicate invalids, after they have been extracted and sublimed by the chemists.——By this time the company began to hold their noses; but the doctor, without taking the least notice of this signal, proceeded to shew, that many fetid substances were not only agreeable but salutary; such as *assafetida*,[9] and other medicinal gums, resins, roots, and vegetables, over and above burnt feathers, tan-pits, candle-snuffs, &c. In short, he used many learned arguments to persuade his audience out of their senses; and from *stench* made a transition to *filth*, which he affirmed was also a mistaken idea, in as much as objects so called, were no other than certain modifications of matter, consisting of the same principles that enter into the composition of all created essences, whatever they may be: that in the filthiest production of nature, a philosopher considered nothing but the earth, water, salt, and air of which it was compounded; that, for his own part, he had no more objection to drinking the dirtiest ditch water, than he had to a glass of water from the Hot Well, provided he was assured there was nothing poisonous in the concrete.[1] Then addressing himself to my uncle, "Sir, (said he) you seem to be of a dropsical habit, and probably will soon have a confirmed *ascites*:[2] if I should be present when you are tapped, I will give you a convincing proof of what I assert, by drinking without hesitation the water that comes out of your abdomen."——The ladies made wry faces at this declaration, and my uncle, changing colour, told him he did not desire any such proof of his philosophy: "But I should be glad to know (said he) what makes you think I am of a dropsical habit?" "Sir, I beg pardon, (replied the doctor) I perceive your ancles are swelled, and you seem to have the *facies leucophlegmatica* .[3] Perhaps, indeed, your disorder may be *oedematous*,[4] or gouty, or it may be the *lues venerea*:[5] If you have any reason to flatter yourself it is this last, sir, I will undertake to cure you with three small pills, even if the disease should have attained its utmost inveteracy. Sir, it

---

8. A stool with a hole containing a chamber pot.
9. A compound of resin with an obnoxious odor commonly used for various medical purposes.
1. Compound.

2. Dropsy.
3. Dropsical appearance.
4. Swollen.
5. Venereal infection.

is an arcanum[6] which I have discovered, and prepared with infinite labour.—Sir, I have lately cured a woman in Bristol—a common prostitute, sir, who had got all the worst symptoms of the disorder; such as *nodi, tophi,* and *gummata, verrucæ, cristæ Galli,* and a *serpiginous* eruption,[7] or rather a pocky itch all over her body.——By that time she had taken the second pill, sir, by Heaven! she was as smooth as my hand, and the third made her as sound and as fresh as a new born infant." "Sir, (cried my uncle peevishly) I have no reason to flatter myself that my disorder comes within the efficacy of your nostrum. But, this patient you talk of, may not be so sound at bottom as you imagine." "I can't possibly be mistaken: (rejoined the philosopher) for I have had communication with her three times—I always ascertain my cures in that manner." At this remark, all the ladies retired to another corner of the room, and some of them began to spit.—As to my uncle, though he was ruffled at first by the doctor's saying he was dropsical, he could not help smiling at this ridiculous confession, and, I suppose, with a view to punish this original, told him there was a wart upon his nose, that looked a little suspicious. "I don't pretend to be a judge of those matters; (said he) but I understand that warts are often produced by the distemper; and that one upon your nose seems to have taken possession of the very keystone of the bridge, which I hope is in no danger of falling."[8] L——n seemed a little confounded at this remark, and assured him it was nothing but a common excrescence of the cuticula, but that the bones were all sound below; for the truth of this assertion he appealed to the touch, desiring he would feel the part. My uncle said it was a matter of such delicacy to meddle with a gentleman's nose, that he declined the office—upon which, the Doctor turning to me, intreated me to do him that favour. I complied with his request, and handled it so roughly, that he sneezed, and the tears ran down his cheeks, to the no small entertainment of the company, and particularly of my uncle, who burst out a-laughing for the first time since I have been with him; and took notice, that the part seemed to be very tender. "Sir, (cried the Doctor) it is naturally a tender part; but to remove all possibility of doubt, I will take off the wart this very night."

So saying, he bowed with great solemnity all round, and retired to his own lodgings, where he applied caustic to the wart; but it spread in such a manner as to produce a considerable inflammation, attended with an enormous swelling; so that when he next appeared, his whole face was overshadowed by this tremendous nozzle; and the rueful eagerness with which he explained this unlucky accident, was ludicrous beyond all description.——I was much pleased with meeting the original of a character, which you and I have often laughed at in description; and what

---

6. Miraculous remedy.
7. Knots, tufts, and gummy spots, warts, cock's combs, and a skin disease spreading over the body.

8. The collapse of the bridge of the nose signals the final stages of syphilis.

surprizes me very much, I find the features in the picture, which has been drawn for him, rather softened than over-charged.—

As I have something else to say; and this letter has run to an unconscionable length, I shall now give you a little respite, and trouble you again by the very first post. I wish you would take it in your head to retaliate these double strokes upon

Yours always,

J. MELFORD.

To Sir WATKIN PHILLIPS, of Jesus college, Oxon.

Hot Well, April 20.

DEAR KNIGHT,

I now sit down to execute the threat in the tail of my last. The truth is, I am big with the secret, and long to be delivered. It relates to my guardian, who, you know, is at present our principal object in view.

T'other day, I thought I had detected him in such a state of frailty, as would but ill become his years and character. There is a decent sort of a woman, not disagreeable in her person, that comes to the Well, with a poor emaciated child, far gone in a consumption. I had caught my uncle's eyes several times directed to this person, with a very suspicious expression in them, and every time he saw himself observed, he hastily withdrew them, with evident marks of confusion—I resolved to watch him more narrowly, and saw him speaking to her privately in a corner of the walk. At length, going down to the Well one day, I met her half way up the hill to Clifton, and could not help suspecting she was going to our lodgings by appointment, as it was about one o'clock, the hour when my sister and I are generally at the Pump-room.—This notion exciting my curiosity, I returned by a back way, and got unperceived into my own chamber, which is contiguous to my uncle's apartment. Sure enough, the woman was introduced, but not into his bed-chamber; he gave her audience in a parlour; so that I was obliged to shift my station to another room, where, however, there was a small chink in the partition, through which I could perceive what passed.—My uncle, though a little lame, rose up when she came in, and setting a chair for her, desired she would sit down: then he asked if she would take a dish of chocolate, which she declined, with much acknowledgment. After a short pause, he said, in a croaking tone of voice, which confounded me not a little, "Madam, I am truly concerned for your misfortunes; and if this trifle can be of any service to you, I beg you will accept it without ceremony." So saying, he put a bit of paper into her hand, which she opening with great trepidation, exclaimed in an extacy, "Twenty pounds! O, sir!" and sinking down upon a settee, fainted away—Frightened at this fit, and, I suppose, afraid of calling for assistance, lest her situation should give rise to unfavourable conjectures, he ran about the room in distraction, making frightful grimaces; and, at length, had recollection enough to throw a little water in her face; by which application she was brought to herself: but, then her feeling took another turn. She shed a flood of tears, and cried aloud, "I know not who you are: but, sure——worthy sir! —generous sir!—the distress of me and my poor dying child—Oh! if the widow's prayers—if the orphan's tears of gratitude can ought avail —gracious Providence!—Blessings! shower down eternal blessings——" Here she was interrupted by my uncle, who muttered in a voice still more and more discordant, "For Heaven's sake be quiet, madam—consider —the people of the house——'sdeath! can't you——" All this time she was struggling to throw herself on her knees, while he seizing her by the wrists, endeavoured to seat her upon the settee, saying, "Pr'ythee—good now——hold your tongue——" At that instant, who should burst into the room but our aunt Tabby! of all antiquated maidens the most diabolically capricious—Ever prying into other people's affairs, she had seen the woman enter, and followed her to the door, where she stood listening, but probably could hear nothing distinctly, except my uncle's last exclamation; at which she bounced into the parlour in a violent rage, that dyed the tip of her nose of a purple hue,—"Fy upon you, Matt! (cried she) what doings are these, to disgrace your own character, and disparage your family?—" Then, snatching the bank-note out of the stranger's hand, she went on—"How now, twenty pounds!—here is temptation with a witness!——Good-woman, go about your business—Brother, brother, I know not which most to admire; your concupissins, or your extravagance! —" "Good God, (exclaimed the poor woman) shall a worthy gentleman's character suffer for an action, that does honour to humanity?" By this time, uncle's indignation was effectually roused. His face grew pale, his teeth chattered, and his eyes flashed—"Sister, (cried he, in a voice like thunder) I vow to God, your impertinence is exceedingly provoking." With these words, he took her by the hand, and, opening the door of communication, thrust her into the chamber where I stood, so affected by the scene, that the tears ran down my cheeks. Observing these marks of emotion, "I don't wonder (said she) to see you concerned at the back-slidings of so near a relation; a man of his years and infirmities: These are fine doings, truly—This is a rare example, set by a guardian, for the benefit of his pupils—Monstrous! incongrous! sophistical!"—I thought it was but an act of justice to set her to rights; and therefore explained the mystery—But she would not be undeceived. "What! (said she) would you go for to offer, for to arguefy me out of my senses? Did'n't I hear him whispering to her to hold her tongue? Did'n't I see her in tears? Did'n't I see him struggling to throw her upon the couch? O filthy! hideous! abominable! Child, child, talk not to me of charity.——Who gives twenty pounds in charity?—But you are a stripling—You know nothing of the world—Besides, charity begins at home—Twenty pounds would buy me a complete suit of flowered silk, trimmings and all—" In short, I quitted the room, my contempt for her, and my respect for her brother, being increased in the same proportion. I have since been informed, that the person, whom my uncle so generously relieved, is the widow of an ensign, who has nothing to depend upon but the pension of fifteen pounds a year. The people of the Well-house give her an excellent character. She lodges in a garret, and works very hard at plain-work,[9] to support her daughter, who is dying of a consumption. I must own, to my shame, I feel a strong inclination to follow my uncle's example, in relieving this poor widow; but, betwixt friends, I am afraid of being detected in a weakness, that might entail the ridicule of the company upon,

Dear Philips,

yours always,

J. MELFORD.

Direct your next to me at Bath; and remember me to all our fellow-jesuits.[1]

To Dr. LEWIS.

Hot Well, April 20.

I understand your hint. There are mysteries in physick, as well as in religion; which we of the profane have no right to investigate—A man must not presume to use his reason, unless he has studied the categories, and can chop logic by mode and figure[2]—Between friends, I think, every man of tolerable parts ought, at my time of day, to be both physician and lawyer, as far as his own constitution and property are concerned. For my own part, I have had an hospital these fourteen years within myself, and studied my own case with the most painful attention; consequently may be supposed to know something of the matter, although I have not taken regular courses of physiology *et cetera et cetera.*—In short, I have for some time been of opinion, (no offence, dear Doctor) that the sum of all your medical discoveries amounts to this, that the more you study the less you know.—I have read all that has been written on the Hot Wells, and what I can collect from the whole, is, that the water contains nothing but a little salt, and calcarious[3] earth, mixed in such inconsiderable proportion,

---

9. Simple needlework, as distinct from embroidery.
1. The slight joke here turns on the usual name applied to members of the Roman Catholic religious order the Society of Jesus and the joking reference of students at Jesus College, Oxford, to themselves as jesuits. The joke still persists at Oxford.
2. Terms used in formal logic.
3. Chalky.

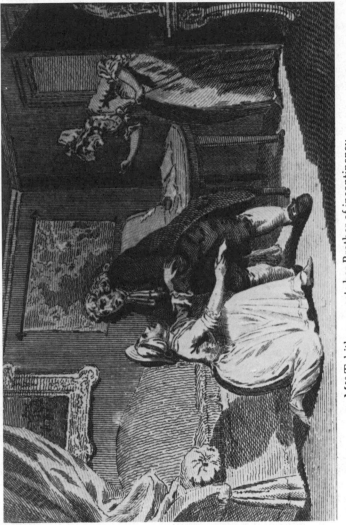

Mrs Tabitha suspects her Brother of incontinency.

as can have very little, if any, effect on the animal oeconomy. This being the case, I think, the man deserves to be fitted with a cap and bells, who, for such a paltry advantage as this spring affords, sacrifices his precious time, which might be employed in taking more effectual remedies, and exposes himself to the dirt, the stench, the chilling blasts, and perpetual rains, that render this place to me intolerable. If these waters, from a small degree of astringency, are of some service in the *diabetes, diarrhœa,* and *night sweats,* when the secretions are too much encreased, must not they do harm in the same proportion, where the humours are obstructed, as in the *asthma, scurvy, gout,* and *dropsy?*—Now we talk of the *dropsy,* here is a strange, fantastical oddity, one of your brethren, who harrangues every day in the Pump-room, as if he was hired to give lectures on all subjects whatsoever—I know not what to make of him——Sometimes he makes shrewd remarks; at other times, he talks like the greatest simpleton in nature—He has read a great deal; but without method or judgment, and digested nothing. He believes every thing he has read; especially if it has any thing of the marvelous in it; and his conversation is a surprizing hotch-potch of erudition and extravagance.——He told me t'other day, with great confidence, that my case was dropsical; or, as he called it, *leucophlegmatic:* A sure sign, that his want of experience is equal to his presumption; for, you know, there is nothing analagous to the dropsy in my disorder—I wish those impertinent fellows, with their ricketty understandings, would keep their advice for those that ask it ——*Dropsy,* indeed! Sure I have not lived to the age of fifty-five, and had such experience of my own disorder, and consulted you and other eminent physicians, so often, and so long, to be undeceived by such a —But, without all doubt, the man is mad; and, therefore, what he says is of no consequence. I had, yesterday, a visit from Higgins; who came hither under the terror of your threats, and brought me in a present a brace of hares; which he owned he took in my ground; and I could not persuade the fellow that he did wrong, or that I would ever prosecute him for poaching—I must desire you will wink hard at the practices of this rascallion; otherwise I shall be plagued with his presents; which cost me more than they are worth.—If I could wonder at any thing Fitzowen does, I should be surprized at his assurance, in desiring you to solicit my vote for him, at the next election for the county: for him, who opposed me on the like occasion, with the most illiberal competition—You may tell him civilly, that I beg to be excused. Direct your next for me at Bath, whither I propose to remove to-morrow; not only on my own account, but for the sake of my niece, Liddy, who is like to relapse. The poor creature fell into a fit yesterday, while I was cheapening a pair of spectacles, with a Jew-pedlar.—I am afraid there is something still lurking in that little heart of her's; which I hope a change of objects will remove. Let me know what you think of this half-witted Doctor's impertinent, ridiculous, and absurd notion of my disorder—So far from being dropsical, I am as lank in the belly as a grey-hound; and, by measuring my ancle with a pack-thread, I find the swelling subsides every day—From such doctors, good Lord deliver us!—I have not yet taken any lodgings in Bath; because there we can be accommodated at a minute's warning, and I shall choose for myself—I need not say your directions for drinking and bathing will be agreeable to,

Dear Lewis,

yours ever,

MAT. BRAMBLE.

P. S. I forgot to tell you, that my right ancle pits, a symptom, as I take it, of its being *oedematous*, not *leucophlegmatic*.[4]

To Miss LETTY WILLIS, at Gloucester.

Hot Well, April 21.

MY DEAR LETTY,

I did not intend to trouble you again, till we should be settled at Bath; but having the occasion of Jarvis, I could not let it slip, especially as I have something extraordinary to communicate—O, my dear companion! What shall I tell you? for several days past there was a Jew-looking man, that plied at the Wells with a box of spectacles; and he always eyed me so earnestly, that I began to be very uneasy. At last, he came to our lodgings at Clifton, and lingered about the door, as if he wanted to speak to somebody——I was seized with an odd kind of fluttering, and begged Win to throw herself in his way: but the poor girl has weak nerves, and was afraid of his beard. My uncle, having occasion for new glasses, called him up stairs, and was trying a pair of spectacles, when the man, advancing to me, said, in a whisper—O gracious! what d'ye think he said? —"I am Wilson!" His features struck me that very moment——it was Wilson, sure enough! but so disguised, that it would have been impossible to know him, if my heart had not assisted in the discovery. I was so surprised, and so frightened, that I fainted away; but soon recovered; and found myself supported by him on the chair, while my uncle was running about the room, with the spectacles on his nose, calling for help. I had no opportunity to speak to him; but our looks were sufficiently expressive. He was payed for his glasses, and went away. Then I told Win who he was, and sent her after him to the Pump-room; where she spoke to him, and begged him in my name to withdraw from the place, that he might not incur the suspicion of my uncle or my brother, if he did not want to

---

4. Matt's distinction here is specious, as the two terms mean almost exactly the same thing in the usage of the period. "To pit" is to have the flesh give way easily to the touch and to retain the impression of the finger.

see me die of terror and vexation. The poor youth declared, with tears in his eyes, that he had something extraordinary to communicate; and asked, if she would deliver a letter to me: but this she absolutely refused, by my order.—Finding her obstinate in her refusal, he desired she would tell me, that he was no longer a player, but a gentleman; in which character he would very soon avow his passion for me, without fear of censure or reproach—Nay, he even discovered his name and family; which, to my great grief, the simple girl forgot, in the confusion occasioned by her being seen talking to him by my brother; who stopt her on the road, and asked what business she had with that rascally Jew—She pretended she was cheapening a stay hook; but was thrown into such a quandary, that she forgot the most material part of the information; and when she came home, went into an hysteric fit of laughing. This transaction happened three days ago, during which he has not appeared; so that I suppose he is gone. Dear Letty! you see how Fortune takes pleasure in persecuting your poor friend. If you should see him at Gloucester—or if you have seen him, and know his real name and family, pray keep me no longer in suspence—And yet, if he is under no obligation to keep himself longer concealed, and has a real affection for me, I should hope he will, in a little time, declare himself to my relations. Sure, if there is nothing unsuitable in the match, they won't be so cruel as to thwart my inclinations—O what happiness would then be my portion! I can't help indulging the thought, and pleasing my fancy with such agreeable ideas; which, after all, perhaps, will never be realised—But, why should I despair? who knows what will happen?—We set out for Bath to-morrow, and I am almost sorry for it; as I begin to be in love with solitude, and this is a charming romantic place. The air is so pure; the Downs are so agreeable; the furze in full blossom; the ground enamelled with daisies, and primroses, and cowslips; all the trees bursting into leaves, and the hedges already clothed with their vernal livery; the mountains covered with flocks of sheep, and tender bleating wanton lambkins playing, frisking and skipping from side to side; the groves resound with the notes of black-bird, thrush, and linnet; and all night long sweet Philomel[5] pours forth her ravishingly delightful song. Then, for variety, we go down to the *nymph of Bristol spring*, where the company is assembled before dinner; so good-natured, so free, so easy; and there we drink the water so clear, so pure, so mild, so charmingly maukish.[6] There the sun is so chearful and reviving; the weather so soft; the walk so agreeable; the prospect so amusing; and the ships and boats going up and down the river, close under the windows of the Pump-room, afford such an enchanting variety of moving pictures, as require a much abler pen than mine to describe. To make this place a perfect paradise to me, nothing is wanting but an agreeable companion and sincere friend;

---

5. The nightingale.   6. Mawkish; having a sickly, insipid flavor.

such as my dear miss Willis hath been, and I hope still will be, to her ever faithful

LYDIA MELFORD.

Direct for me, still under cover, to Win; and Jarvis will take care to convey it safe. Adieu.

To Sir WATKIN PHILLIPS, of Jesus college, Oxon.

Bath, April 24.

DEAR PHILLIPS,

You have, indeed, reason to be surprised, that I should have concealed my correspondence with miss Blackerby from you, to whom I disclosed all my other connexions of that nature; but the truth is, I never dreamed of any such commerce, till your last informed me, that it had produced something which could not be much longer concealed. It is a lucky circumstance, however, that her reputation will not suffer any detriment, but rather derive advantage from the discovery; which will prove, at least, that it is not quite so rotten, as most people imagined—For my own part, I declare to you, in all the sincerity of friendship, that, far from having any amorous intercourse with the object in question, I never had the least acquaintance with her person; but, if she is really in the condition you describe, I suspect Mansel to be at the bottom of the whole. His visits to that shrine were no secret; and this attachment, added to some good offices, which you know he has done me, since I left *Alma-mater*, give me a right to believe him capable of saddling me with this scandal, when my back was turned——Nevertheless, if my name can be of any service to him, he is welcome to make use of it; and if the woman should be abandoned enough to swear his bantling[7] to me, I must beg the favour of you to compound with the parish:[8] I shall pay the penalty without repining; and you will be so good as to draw upon me immediately for the sum required——On this occasion, I act by the advice of my uncle; who says, I shall have good-luck if I pass through life without being obliged to make many more compositions of the same kind. The old gentleman told me last night, with great good-humour, that betwixt the age of twenty and forty, he had been obliged to provide for nine bastards, sworn to him by women whom he never saw—Mr. Bramble's character, which seems to interest you greatly, opens and improves upon me every day.—His singularities afford a rich mine of entertainment: his understanding, so far as I can judge, is well cultivated:

7. Brat.
8. To pay a sum of money to the parish authorities, who would then see to the raising of the illegitimate child.

his observations on life are equally just, pertinent, and uncommon. He affects misanthropy, in order to conceal the sensibility of a heart, which is tender, even to a degree of weakness. This delicacy of feeling, or soreness of the mind, makes him timorous and fearful; but then he is afraid of nothing so much as of dishonour; and although he is exceedingly cautious of giving offence, he will fire at the least hint of insolence or ill-breeding. —Respectable as he is, upon the whole, I can't help being sometimes diverted by his little distresses; which provoke him to let fly the shafts of his satire, keen and penetrating as the arrows of Teucer[9]—Our aunt, Tabitha, acts upon him as a perpetual grind-stone—She is, in all respects, a striking contrast to her brother—But I reserve her portrait for another occasion.

Three days ago we came hither from the Hot Well, and took possession of the first floor of a lodging-house, on the South Parade; a situation which my uncle chose, for its being near the Bath, and remote from the noise of carriages. He was scarce warm in the lodgings when he called for his night cap, his wide shoes, and flannel; and declared himself invested with the gout in his right foot; though, I believe, it had as yet reached no farther than his imagination. It was not long before he had reason to repent his premature declaration; for our aunt Tabitha found means to make such a clamour and confusion, before the flannels could be produced from the trunk, that one would have imagined the house was on fire. All this time, uncle sat boiling with impatience, biting his fingers, throwing up his eyes, and muttering ejaculations; at length he burst into a kind of convulsive laugh, after which he hummed a song; and when the hurricane was over, exclaimed, "Blessed be God for all things!" This, however, was but the beginning of his troubles. Mrs. Tabitha's favourite dog Chowder, having paid his compliments to a female turnspit,[1] of his own species, in the kitchen, involved himself in a quarrel with no fewer than five rivals, who set upon him at once, and drove him up stairs to the dining-room door, with hideous noise: there our aunt and her woman, taking arms in his defence, joined the concert; which became truly diabolical. This fray being with difficulty suppressed, by the intervention of our own foot-man and the cook-maid of the house, the 'squire had just opened his mouth, to expostulate with Tabby, when the town-waits,[2] in the passage below, struck up their musick, (if musick it may be called) with such a sudden burst of sound, as made him start and stare, with marks of indignation and disquiet. He had recollection enough to send his servant with some money to silence those noisy intruders; and they were immediately dismissed, though not without some opposition on the part of Tabitha, who thought it but reasonable that he should have more

9. A noted archer in the Trojan war.
1. A small dog trained to walk on a treadmill to turn a cooking spit.

2. Quasi-official greeters who sang to newcomers to Bath for tips.

musick for his money. Scarce had he settled this knotty point, when a strange kind of thumping and bouncing was heard right overhead, in the second story, so loud and violent as to shake the whole building. I own I was exceedingly provoked at this new alarm; and before my uncle had time to express himself on the subject, I ran up stairs, to see what was the matter. Finding the room-door open, I entered without ceremony, and perceived an object, which I cannot now recollect without laughing to excess—It was a dancing-master, with his scholar, in the act of teaching. The master was blind of one eye, and lame of one foot, and led about the room his pupil; who seemed to be about the age of three-score, stooped mortally, was tall, raw-boned, hard-favoured, with a woollen night-cap on his head; and he had stript off his coat, that he might be more nimble in his motions—Finding himself intruded upon, by a person he did not know, he forthwith girded himself with a long iron sword, and advancing to me, with a peremptory air, pronounced, in a true Hibernian accent, "Mister What d'ye callum, by my saoul and conscience, I am very glad to sea you, if you are after coming in the way of friendship; and indeed, and indeed now, I believe you are my friend sure enough, gra;[3] though I never had the honour to sea your face before, my dear; for becaase you come like a friend, without any ceremony at all, at all—" I told him the nature of my visit would not admit of ceremony; that I was come to desire he would make less noise, as there was a sick gentleman below, whom he had no right to disturb with such preposterous doings. "Why, look-ye now; young gentleman, (replied this original) perhaps, upon another occasion, I might shivilly request you to explain the maining of that hard word, *prepasterous:* but there's a time for all things, honey—" So saying, he passed me with great agility, and, running down stairs, found our footman at the dining-room door, of whom he demanded admittance, to pay his respects to the stranger. As the fellow did not think proper to refuse the request of such a formidable figure, he was immediately introduced, and addressed himself to my uncle in these words: "Your humble servant, good sir—I'm not so *prepasterous,* as your son calls it, but I know the rules of shivility—I'm a poor knight of Ireland, my name is sir Ulic Mackilligut, of the county of Galway; being your fellow-lodger, I'm come to pay my respects, and to welcome you to the South Parade, and to offer my best services to you, and your good lady, and your pretty daughter; and even to the young gentleman your son, though he thinks me a *prepasterous* fellow—You must know I am to have the honour to open a ball next door to-morrow with lady Mac Manus; and being rusted in my dancing, I was refreshing my memory with a little exercise; but if I had known there was a sick person below, by Christ! I would have sooner danced a hornpipe upon my own head, than walk the softest minuet over yours."—My

3. An obsolete Irish interjection meaning "my dear."

uncle, who was not a little startled at his first appearance, received his compliment with great complacency, insisted upon his being seated, thanked him for the honour of his visit, and reprimanded me for my abrupt expostulation with a gentleman of his rank and character. Thus tutored, I asked pardon of the knight, who, forthwith starting up, embraced me so close, that I could hardly breathe; and assured me, he loved me as his own soul. At length, recollecting his night-cap,[4] he pulled it off in some confusion; and, with his bald-pate uncovered, made a thousand apologies to the ladies, as he retired—At that instant, the Abbey bells began to ring so loud, that we could not hear one another speak; and this peal, as we afterwards learned, was for the honour of Mr. Bullock, an eminent cow-keeper of Tottenham, who had just arrived at Bath, to drink the waters for indigestion.[5] Mr. Bramble had not time to make his remarks upon the agreeable nature of this serenade, before his ears were saluted with another concert that interested him more nearly. Two negroes, belonging to a Creole[6] gentleman, who lodged in the same house, taking their station at a window in the stair-case, about ten feet from our dining-room door, began to practise upon the French-horn;[7] and being in the very first rudiments of execution, produced such discordant sounds, as might have discomposed the organs of an ass ——You may guess what effect they had upon the irritable nerves of uncle; who, with the most admirable expression of splenetic surprize in his countenance, sent his man to silence those dreadful blasts, and desire the musicians to practise in some other place, as they had no right to stand there and disturb all the lodgers in the house. Those sable performers, far from taking the hint, and withdrawing, treated the messenger with great insolence; bidding him carry his compliments to their master, colonel Rigworm, who would give him a proper answer, and a good drubbing into the bargain; in the mean time they continued their noise, and even endeavoured to make it more disagreeable; laughing between whiles, at the thoughts of being able to torment their betters with impunity. Our 'squire, incensed at the additional insult, immediately dispatched the servant, with his compliments to colonel Rigworm; requesting that he would order his blacks to be quiet, as the noise they made was altogether intolerable—To this message, the Creole colonel replied, that his horns had a right to sound on a common staircase; that there they should play for his diversion; and that those who did not like the noise, might look for lodgings else-where. Mr. Bramble no sooner received this reply, than his eyes began to glisten, his face grew pale, and

4. Gentlemen normally wore wigs, which often required the head to be clean-shaven. A cloth nightcap was worn when the wig was not.

5. The bells of the Abbey Church at Bath were rung to honor new arrivals when they paid the bell-ringers. Tottenham was, at the time of the novel, a separate village near London of less than the highest social stature.

6. A person born in the West Indies, but of foreign or mixed descent, possibly Spanish or French.

7. French horns and other brass instruments were often played by members of the retinues of wealthy travelers in this period.

his teeth chattered. After a moment's pause, he slipt on his shoes, without speaking a word, or seeming to feel any further disturbance from the gout in his toes. Then, snatching his cane, he opened the door and proceeded to the place where the black trumpeters were posted. There, without further hesitation, he began to belabour them both; and exerted himself with such astonishing vigour and agility, that both their heads and horns were broken in a twinkling, and they ran howling down stairs to their master's parlour-door. The 'squire, following them half way, called aloud, that the colonel might hear him, "Go, rascals, and tell your master what I have done; if he thinks himself injured, he knows where to come for satisfaction. As for you, this is but an earnest of what you shall receive, if ever you presume to blow a horn again here, while I stay in the house." So saying, he retired to his apartment, in expectation of hearing from the West Indian; but the colonel prudently declined any farther prosecution of the dispute. My sister Liddy was frighted into a fit, from which she was no sooner recovered, than Mrs. Tabitha began a lecture upon patience; which her brother interrupted with a most significant grin, exclaiming, "True, sister, God increase my patience and your discretion. I wonder (added he) what sort of sonata we are to expect from this overture, in which the devil, that presides over horrid sounds, hath given us such variations of discord—The trampling of porters, the creaking and crashing of trunks, the snarling of curs, the scolding of women, the squeaking and squalling of fiddles and hautboys out of tune, the bouncing of the Irish baronet over-head, and the bursting, belching, and brattling of the French-horns in the passage (not to mention the harmonious peal that still thunders from the Abbey steeple) succeeding one another without interruption, like the different parts of the same concert, have given me such an idea of what a poor invalid has to expect in this temple, dedicated to Silence and Repose, that I shall certainly shift my quarters to-morrow, and endeavour to effectuate my retreat before Sir Ulic opens the ball with my lady Mac Manus; a conjunction that bodes me no good." This intimation was by no means agreeable to Mrs. Tabitha, whose ears were not quite so delicate as those of her brother —She said it would be great folly to move from such agreeable lodgings, the moment they were comfortably settled. She wondered he should be such an enemy to musick and mirth. She heard no noise but of his own making: it was impossible to manage a family in dumb-shew. He might harp as long as he pleased upon her scolding; but she never scolded, except for his advantage; but he would never be satisfied, even tho'f she should sweat blood and water in his service—I have a great notion that our aunt, who is now declining into the most desperate state of celibacy, had formed some design upon the heart of Sir Ulic Mackilligut, which she feared might be frustrated by our abrupt departure from these lodgings. Her brother, eyeing her askance, "Pardon me, sister, (said he) I should be a savage, indeed, were I insensible of my own felicity, in having such a mild, complacent, good-humoured, and considerate companion and house-keeper; but as I have got a weak head, and my sense of hearing is painfully acute, before I have recourse to plugs of wool and cotton, I'll try whether I can't find another lodging, where I shall have more quiet and less musick." He accordingly dispatched his man upon this service; and next day he found a small house in Milsham-street,[8] which he hires by the week. Here, at least, we enjoy convenience and quiet within doors, as much as Tabby's temper will allow; but the 'squire still complains of flying pains in the stomach and head, for which he bathes and drinks the waters. He is not so bad, however, but that he goes in person to the pump, the rooms, and the coffee-houses; where he picks up continual food for ridicule and satire. If I can glean any thing for your amusement, either from his observation or my own, you shall have it freely, though I am afraid it will poorly compensate the trouble of reading these tedious insipid letters of,

> Dear Phillips,
>
> yours always,
>
> J. MELFORD.

To Dr. LEWIS.

Bath, April 23.

DEAR DOCTOR,

If I did not know that the exercise of your profession has habituated you to the hearing of complaints, I should make a conscience of troubling you with my correspondence, which may be truly called *the lamentations of Matthew Bramble.*[9] Yet I cannot help thinking, I have some right to discharge the overflowings of my spleen upon you, whose province it is to remove those disorders that occasioned it; and let me tell you, it is no small alleviation of my grievances, that I have a sensible friend, to whom I can communicate my crusty humours, which, by retention, would grow intolerably acrimonious.

You must know, I find nothing but disappointment at Bath; which is so altered, that I can scarce believe it is the same place that I frequented about thirty years ago. Methinks I hear you say, "Altered it is, without all doubt; but then it is altered for the better; a truth which, perhaps, you would own without hesitation, if you yourself was not altered for the worse." The reflection may, for aught I know, be just. The inconveniences which I overlooked in the high-day of health, will naturally strike

8. There was and is a Milsom Street in Bath, but no Milsham Street.
9. An adaptation of the title of the Old Testament book traditionally entitled "The Lamentations of Jeremiah."

with exaggerated impression on the irritable nerves of an invalid, surprised by premature old age, and shattered with long-suffering—But, I believe, you will not deny, that this place, which Nature and Providence seem to have intended as a resource from distemper and disquiet, is become the very center of racket and dissipation. Instead of that peace, tranquility and ease, so necessary to those who labour under bad health, weak nerves, and irregular spirits; here we have nothing but noise, tumult, and hurry; with the fatigue and slavery of maintaining a ceremonial, more stiff, formal, and oppressive, than the etiquette of a German elector.[1] A national hospital it may be; but one would imagine, that none but lunatics are admitted; and, truly, I will give you leave to call me so, if I stay much longer at Bath.—But I shall take another opportunity to explain my sentiments at greater length on this subject—I was impatient to see the boasted improvements in architecture, for which the upper parts of the town have been so much celebrated, and t'other day I made a circuit of all the new buildings. The Square, though irregular, is, on the whole, pretty well laid out, spacious, open, and airy; and, in my opinion, by far the most wholsome and agreeable situation in Bath, especially the upper side of it; but the avenues to it are mean, dirty, dangerous, and indirect. Its communication with the Baths, is through the yard of an inn, where the poor trembling valetudinarian[2] is carried in a chair, betwixt the heels of a double row of horses, wincing under the curry-combs of grooms and postilions, over and above the hazard of being obstructed, or overturned by the carriages which are continually making their exit or their entrance—I suppose after some chairmen shall have been maimed, and a few lives lost by those accidents, the corporation will think, in earnest, about providing a more safe and commodious passage. The Circus[3] is a pretty bauble; contrived for shew, and looks like Vespasian's amphitheatre turned outside in. If we consider it in point of magnificence, the great number of small doors belonging to the separate houses, the inconsiderable height of the different orders, the affected ornaments of the architrave,[4] which are both childish and misplaced, and the areas projecting into the street, surrounded with iron rails, destroy a good part of its effect upon the eye; and, perhaps, we shall find it still more defective, if we view it in the light of convenience. The figure of each separate dwelling house, being the segment of a circle, must spoil the symmetry of the rooms, by contracting them towards the street windows, and leaving a larger sweep in the space behind. If, instead of the areas and iron rails, which seem to be of very little use, there had

---

1. One of the German princes qualified to vote in the election of the Holy Roman Emperor.
2. Invalid.
3. The Circus was one of the architectural wonders of Bath. It was designed by John Wood the elder (1705?–54), begun in the year of his death, and completed by his son in 1764. It consisted of three sections of buildings laid out in arcs which made up a circle, or circus, broken only by the three streets which entered the circular space in the middle. Matt's negative opinion expressed here was in the minority.
4. A molded or decorated band surrounding a panel or an opening.

been a corridore with arcades all round, as in Covent-Garden,[5] the appearance of the whole would have been more magnificent and striking; those arcades would have afforded an agreeable covered walk, and sheltered the poor chairmen and their carriages from the rain, which is here almost perpetual. At present, the chairs stand soaking in the open street, from morning to night, till they become so many boxes of wet leather, for the benefit of the gouty and rheumatic, who are transported in them from place to place. Indeed this is a shocking inconvenience that extends over the whole city; and, I am persuaded, it produces infinite mischief to the delicate and infirm; even the close chairs, contrived for the sick, by standing in the open air, have their frize[6] linings impregnated, like so many spunges, with the moisture of the atmosphere, and those cases of cold vapour must give a charming check to the perspiration of a patient, piping hot from the Bath, with all his pores wide open.

But, to return to the Circus: it is inconvenient from its situation, at so great a distance from all the markets, baths, and places of public entertainment. The only entrance to it, through Gay-street, is so difficult, steep, and slippery, that, in wet weather, it must be exceedingly dangerous, both for those that ride in carriages, and those that walk a-foot; and when the street is covered with snow, as it was for fifteen days successively this very winter,[7] I don't see how any individual could go either up or down, without the most imminent hazard of broken bones. In blowing weather, I am told, most of the houses in this hill are smothered with smoke, forced down the chimneys, by the gusts of wind reverberated from the hill behind, which (I apprehend likewise) must render the atmosphere here more humid and unwholesome than it is in the square below; for the clouds, formed by the constant evaporation from the baths and rivers in the bottom, will, in their ascent this way, be first attracted and detained by the hill that rises close behind the Circus, and load the air with a perpetual succession of vapours: this point, however, may be easily ascertained by means of an hygrometer, or a paper of salt of tartar exposed to the action of the atmosphere. The same artist,[8] who planned the Circus, has likewise projected a Crescent; when that is finished, we shall probably have a Star; and those who are living thirty years hence, may, perhaps, see all the signs of the Zodiac exhibited in architecture at Bath. These, however fantastical, are still designs that denote some ingenuity and knowledge in the architect; but the rage of

5. The handsome theater in London built in 1731–32.

6. A heavy napped woolen cloth, usually spelled "frieze."

7. Bath had an unusually severe snowstorm in January 1767. The events in the novel which can be dated take place in the 1760's, but Smollett apparently did not try to tie the events into a particular year. See, for instance, p. 47, note 9, below.

8. The elder John Wood planned many of the features of Bath mentioned in the text. His son, John Wood the younger, who survived until 1782, completed many of them and added more of his own. The Royal Crescent was started in 1767 and finished in 1775, four years after the publication of the novel. For an analysis of Matt's architectural criticism, see the essay by John Sena reprinted below.

building has laid hold on such a number of adventurers, that one sees new houses starting up in every out-let and every corner of Bath; contrived without judgment, executed without solidity, and stuck together, with so little regard to plan and propriety, that the different lines of the new rows and buildings interfere with, and intersect one another in every different angle of conjunction. They look like the wreck of streets and squares disjointed by an earthquake, which hath broken the ground into a variety of holes and hillocks; or, as if some Gothic devil had stuffed them altogether in a bag, and left them to stand higgledy piggledy, just as chance directed. What sort of a monster Bath will become in a few years, with those growing excrescences, may be easily conceived: but the want of beauty and proportion is not the worst effect of these new mansions; they are built so slight, with the soft crumbling stone found in this neighbourhood, that I should never sleep quietly in one of them, when it blowed (as the sailors say) a cap-full of wind; and, I am persuaded, that my hind,[9] Roger Williams, or any man of equal strength, would be able to push his foot through the strongest part of their walls, without any great exertion of his muscles. All these absurdities arise from the general tide of luxury, which hath overspread the nation, and swept away all, even the very dregs of the people. Every upstart of fortune, harnessed in the trappings of the mode, presents himself at Bath, as in the very focus of observation—Clerks and factors from the East Indies, loaded with the spoil of plundered provinces; planters, negro-drivers, and hucksters, from our American plantations, enriched they know not how; agents, commissaries, and contractors, who have fattened, in two successive wars, on the blood of the nation; usurers, brokers, and jobbers of every kind; men of low birth, and no breeding, have found themselves suddenly translated into a state of affluence, unknown to former ages; and no wonder that their brains should be intoxicated with pride, vanity, and presumption. Knowing no other criterion of greatness, but the ostentation of wealth, they discharge their affluence without taste or conduct, through every channel of the most absurd extravagance; and all of them hurry to Bath, because here, without any further qualification, they can mingle with the princes and nobles of the land. Even the wives and daughters of low tradesmen, who, like shovel-nosed sharks, prey upon the blubber of those uncouth whales of fortune, are infected with the same rage of displaying their importance; and the slightest indisposition serves them for a pretext to insist upon being conveyed to Bath, where they may hobble country-dances and cotillons among lordlings, 'squires, counsellors, and clergy. These delicate creatures from Bedfordbury, Butcher-row, Crutched-Friers, and Botolph-lane,[1] cannot breathe in the gross air of the Lower Town, or conform to the vulgar rules of a common lodging-

9. Farm laborer.
1. Lower-class neighborhoods near the Strand in London.

house; the husband, therefore, must provide an entire house, or elegant apartments in the new buildings. Such is the composition of what is called the fashionable company at Bath; where a very inconsiderable proportion of genteel people are lost in a mob of impudent plebeians, who have neither understanding nor judgment, nor the least idea of propriety and decorum; and seem to enjoy nothing so much as an opportunity of insulting their betters.

Thus the number of people, and the number of houses continue to increase; and this will ever be the case, till the streams that swell this irresistible torrent of folly and extravagance, shall either be exhausted, or turned into other channels, by incidents and events which I do not pretend to foresee. This, I own, is a subject on which I cannot write with any degree of patience; for the mob is a monster I never could abide, either in its head, tail, midriff, or members: I detest the whole of it, as a mass of ignorance, presumption, malice, and brutality; and, in this term of reprobation, I include, without respect of rank, station, or quality, all those of both sexes, who affect its manners, and court its society.

But I have written till my fingers are crampt, and my nausea begins to return—By your advice, I sent to London a few days ago for half a pound of Gengzeng;[2] though I doubt much, whether that which comes from America is equally efficacious with what is brought from the East Indies. Some years ago, a friend of mine paid sixteen guineas for two ounces of it; and, in six months after, it was sold in the same shop for five shillings[3] the pound. In short, we live in a vile world of fraud and sophistication; so that I know nothing of equal value with the genuine friendship of a sensible man; a rare jewel! which I cannot help thinking myself in possession of, while I repeat the old declaration, that I am, as usual,

Dear Lewis,

Your affectionate

M. BRAMBLE.

After having been agitated in a short hurricane, on my first arrival, I have taken a small house in Milsham-street, where I am tolerably well lodged, for five guineas a week. I was yesterday at the Pump-room, and drank about a pint of the water, which seems to agree with my stomach; and to-morrow morning I shall bathe, for the first time; so that in a few posts you may expect farther trouble; mean while, I am glad to find that the inoculation has succeeded so well with poor Joyce, and that her face will be but little marked———If my friend Sir Thomas was a single man, I

2. More commonly ginseng, a Chinese plant utilized for medicinal purposes. It was purported to cure impotence, though Matt says that he is taking it for his stomach.

3. The guinea was a gold coin, first minted in the seventeenth century for trade with Africa. Because England was on a silver (sterling) standard, the value of a guinea fluctuated against the pound until it was standardized at twenty-one shillings in 1717. The pound sterling contains twenty shillings, so the guinea is 5 percent more valuable than the pound.

would not trust such a handsome wench in his family; but as I have recommended her, in a particular manner, to the protection of lady G ——,[4] who is one of the best women in the world, she may go thither without hesitation, as soon as she is quite recovered, and fit for service ——Let her mother have money to provide her with necessaries, and she may ride behind her brother on Bucks; but you must lay strong injunctions on Jack, to take particular care of the trusty old veteran, who has faithfully earned his present ease, by his past services.

To Miss WILLIS, at Gloucester.

Bath, April 26.

MY DEAREST COMPANION,

The pleasure I received from yours, which came to hand yesterday, is not to be expressed. Love and friendship are, without doubt, charming passions; which absence serves only to heighten and improve. Your kind present of the garnet bracelets, I shall keep as carefully as I preserve my own life; and I beg you will accept, in return, of my heart-housewife, [5] with the tortoise-shell memorandum-book, as a trifling pledge of my unalterable affection.

Bath is to me a new world——All is gayety, good-humour, and diversion. The eye is continually entertained with the splendour of dress and equipage; and the ear with the sound of coaches, chaises, chairs, and other carriages. *The merry bells ring round,*[6] from morn till night. Then we are welcomed by the city-waits in our own lodgings: we have musick in the Pump-room every morning, cotillons every fore-noon in the rooms, balls twice a week, and concerts every other night, besides private assemblies and parties without number——As soon as we were settled in lodgings, we were visited by the Master of the Ceremonies;[7] a pretty little gentleman, so sweet, so fine, so civil, and polite, that in our country he might pass for the prince of Wales; then he talks so charmingly, both in verse and prose, that you would be delighted to hear him discourse; for you must know he is a great writer, and has got five tragedies ready for the stage. He did us the favour to dine with us, by my uncle's invitation; and next day 'squired my aunt and me to every part of Bath; which, to be sure, is an earthly paradise. The Square, the Circus, and the Parades, put you in mind of the sumptuous palaces represented in prints and pictures; and the new buildings, such as Princes-row, Harlequin's-row, Bladud's-row,

4. Lady Griskin, probably a completely fictional character.
5. A pocket case for needles, pins, and other small items.
6. From John Milton's "L'Allegro," where the bells call villagers to an occasional dance.
7. Samuel Derrick (1724–69) filled the position of master of the ceremonies at Bath after the death of Beau Nash in 1761. In addition to introducing people at the assemblies of the spa, he was a writer of great perseverence but small talent. He was a friend of Smollett, Dr. Samuel Johnson, and James Boswell.

and twenty other rows, look like so many enchanted castles, raised on hanging terraces.

At eight in the morning, we go in dishabille[8] to the Pump-room; which is crowded like a Welsh fair; and there you see the highest quality, and the lowest trades folks, jostling each other, without ceremony, hail-fellow well-met. The noise of the musick playing in the gallery, the heat and flavour of such a crowd, and the hum and buz of their conversation, gave me the head-ach and vertigo the first day; but, afterwards, all these things became familiar, and even agreeable.—Right under the Pump-room windows is the King's Bath; a huge cistern, where you see the patients up to their necks in hot water. The ladies wear jackets and petticoats of brown linen, with chip hats,[9] in which they fix their handkerchifs to wipe the sweat from their faces; but, truly, whether it is owing to the steam that surrounds them, or the heat of the water, or the nature of the dress, or to all these causes together, they look so flushed, and so frightful, that I always turn my eyes another way—My aunt, who says every person of fashion should make her appearance in the bath, as well as in the abbey church, contrived a cap with cherry-coloured ribbons to suit her complexion, and obliged Win to attend her yesterday morning in the water. But, really, her eyes were so red, that they made mine water as I viewed her from the Pump-room; and as for poor Win, who wore a hat trimmed with blue, what betwixt her wan complexion and her fear, she looked like the ghost of some pale maiden, who had drowned herself for love. When she came out of the bath, she took assafœtida drops, and was fluttered all day; so that we could hardly keep her from going into hysterics: but her mistress says it will do her good; and poor Win curtsies, with the tears in her eyes. For my part, I content myself with drinking about half a pint of the water every morning.

The pumper, with his wife and servant, attend within a bar; and the glasses, of different sizes, stand ranged in order before them, so you have nothing to do but to point at that which you chuse, and it is filled immediately, hot and sparkling from the pump. It is the only hot water I could ever drink, without being sick—Far from having that effect, it is rather agreeable to the taste, grateful to the stomach, and reviving to the spirits. You cannot imagine what wonderful cures it performs—My uncle began with it the other day; but he made wry faces in drinking, and I'm afraid he will leave it off—The first day we came to Bath, he fell into a violent passion; beat two black-a-moors, and I was afraid he would have fought with their master; but the stranger proved a peaceable man. To be sure, the gout had got into his head, as my aunt observed: but, I believe, his passion drove it away; for he has been remarkably well ever since. It is

8. To be in an informal state of dress, or partial undress. Dishabille also denoted a kind of loose dressing gown, which may apply here, but it much more likely means informal dress, as befits the early morning at a resort.
9. Hat made of woody fiber or straw.

a thousand pities he should ever be troubled with that ugly distemper; for, when he is free from pain, he is the best-tempered man upon earth; so gentle, so generous, so charitable, that every body loves him; and so good to me, in particular, that I shall never be able to shew the deep sense I have of his tenderness and affection.

Hard by the Pump-room, is a coffee-house for the ladies; but my aunt says, young girls are not admitted, inasmuch as the conversation turns upon politics, scandal, philosophy, and other subjects above our capacity; but we are allowed to accompany them to the booksellers shops, which are charming places of resort; where we read novels, plays, pamphlets, and news-papers, for so small a subscription as a crown a quarter; and in these offices of intelligence, (as my brother calls them) all the reports of the day, and all the private transactions of the Bath, are first entered and discussed. From the bookseller's shop, we make a tour through the milliners and toy-men; and commonly stop at Mr. Gill's,[1] the pastry-cook, to take a jelly, a tart, or a small bason of vermicelli. There is, moreover, another place of entertainment on the other side of the water, opposite to the Grove; to which the company cross over in a boat—It is called Spring Garden; a sweet retreat, laid out in walks and ponds, and parterres of flowers; and there is a long-room for breakfasting and dancing. As the situation is low and damp, and the season has been remarkably wet, my uncle won't suffer me to go thither, lest I should catch cold: but my aunt says it is all a vulgar prejudice; and, to be sure, a great many gentlemen and ladies of Ireland frequent the place, without seeming to be the worse for it. They say, dancing at Spring Gardens, when the air is moist, is recommended to them as an excellent cure for the rheumatism. I have been twice at the play; where, notwithstanding the excellence of the performers, the gayety of the company, and the decorations of the theatre, which are very fine,[2] I could not help reflecting, with a sigh, upon our poor homely representations at Glouces-ter—But this, in confidence to my dear Willis—You know my heart, and will excuse its weakness.——

After all, the great scenes of entertainment at Bath, are the two public rooms;[3] where the company meet alternately every evening—They are spacious, lofty, and, when lighted up, appear very striking. They are generally crowded with well-dressed people, who drink tea in separate parties, play at cards, walk, or sit and chat together, just as they are disposed. Twice a-week there is a ball; the expence of which is defrayed by a voluntary subscription among the gentlemen; and every subscriber has three tickets. I was there Friday last with my aunt, under the care of

1. Apparently Mr. Gill kept an establishment for food in Bath, but its location has not been verified. It is also mentioned in Christopher Anstey's *New Bath Guide* (1766).
2. The theater, located in Orchard Street near the South Parade, had been opened in 1750.
3. The two sets of public rooms, to which an invitation was not necessary, were located in Terrace Walk. One was managed by Mr. Wilshire and the other by Mr. Simpson.

my brother, who is a subscriber; and Sir Ulic Mackilligut recommended his nephew, captain O Donaghan, to me as a partner; but Jerry excused himself, by saying I had got the head-ach; and, indeed, it was really so, though I can't imagine how he knew it. The place was so hot, and the smell so different from what we are used to in the country, that I was quite feverish when we came away. Aunt says it is the effect of a vulgar constitution, reared among woods and mountains; and, that as I become accustomed to genteel company, it will wear off.—Sir Ulic was very complaisant, made her a great many high-flown compliments; and, when we retired, handed her with great ceremony to her chair. The captain, I believe, would have done me the same favour; but my brother, seeing him advance, took me under his arm, and wished him good-night. The Captain is a pretty man, to be sure; tall and strait,[4] and well made; with light-grey eyes, and a Roman nose; but there is a certain boldness in his look and manner, that puts one out of countenance—But I am afraid I have put you out of all patience with this long unconnected scrawl; which I shall therefore conclude, with assuring you, that neither Bath nor London, nor all the diversions of life, shall ever be able to efface the idea of my dear Letty, from the heart of her ever affectionate

LYDIA MELFORD.

To Mrs. MARY JONES, at Brambleton-hall.

DEAR MOLLY JONES,

Heaving got a frank,[5] I now return your fever, which I received by Mr. Higgins, at the Hot Well, together with the stockings, which his wife footed for me; but now they are of no survice. No body wears such things in this place—O Molly! you that live in the country have no deception of our doings at Bath. Here is such dressing, and fidling, and dancing, and gadding, and courting, and plotting—O gracious! if God had not given me a good stock of discretion, what a power of things might not I reveal, consarning old mistress and young mistress; Jews with beards, that were no Jews; but handsome Christians, without a hair upon their sin, strolling with spectacles, to get speech of Miss Liddy. But she's a dear sweet soul, as innocent as the child unborn. She has tould me all her inward thoughts, and disclosed her passion for Mr. Wilson; and that's not his name neither; and thof he acted among the player-men, he is meat for their masters; and she has gi'en me her yellow trollopea;[6] which Mrs. Drab, the manty-maker,[7] says will look very well when it is scowred and smoaked with

4. Erect.
5. An envelope, or cover, could be signed by an official, or franked, and it would then be carried free through the mail.
6. The tralopee, sometimes called the slamerkin, was a loose dress of the period. An association with the adjectival form of "trollop" appears also.
7. Dressmaker, from "mantua," another design of dress.

silfur—You knows as how, yallow fitts my fizzogmony. God he knows
what havock I shall make among the mail-sex, when I make my first
appearance in this killing collar, with a full soot of gaze, as good as new,
that I bought last Friday of madam Friponeau, the French mullaner
—Dear girl, I have seen all the fine shews of Bath; the Prades, the Squires,
and the Circlis, the Crashit, the Hottogon,[8] and Bloody Buildings,[9] and
Harry King's row; and I have been twice in the Bath with mistress, and
na'r a smoak upon our backs, hussy——The first time I was mortally
afraid, and flustered all day; and afterwards made believe that I had got
the heddick; but mistress said, if I didn't go, I should take a dose of
bumtaffy; and so remembring how it worked Mrs. Gwyllim a pennorth, I
chose rather to go again with her into the Bath, and then I met with an
axident. I dropt my petticoat, and could not get it up from the bottom
—But what did that signify? they mought laff, but they could see nothing;
for I was up to the sin in water. To be sure, it threw me into such a
gumbustion, that I know not what I said, nor what I did, nor how they got
me out, and rapt me in a blanket—Mrs. Tabitha scoulded a little when
we got home; but she knows as I know what's what—Ah Laud help you!
—There is Sir Yury Micligut, of Balnaclinch, in the cunty of Kalloway—I
took down the name from his gentleman, Mr. O Frizzle, and he has got
an estate of fifteen hundred a year—I am sure he is both rich and
generous——But you nose, Molly, I was always famous for keeping
secrets; and so he was very safe in trusting me with his flegm for mistress;
which, to be sure, is very honourable; for Mr. O Frizzle assures me, he
values not her portion a brass varthing—And, indeed, what's poor ten
thousand pounds to a Baron Knight of his fortune? and, truly, I told Mr. O
Frizzle, that was all she had to trust to—As for John Thomas, he's a
morass fellor[1]—I vow, I thought he would a fit with Mr. O Frizzle,
because he axed me to dance with him at Spring Garden—But God he
knows I have no thoughts eyther of wan or t'other.

As for house news, the worst is, Chowder has fallen off greatly from his
stomick—He eats nothing but white meats, and not much of that; and
wheezes, and seems to be much bloated. The doctors think he is
threatened with a dropsy—Parson Marrofat, who has got the same
disorder, finds great benefit from the waters; but Chowder seems to like
them no better than the squire; and mistress says, if his case don't take a
favourable turn, she will sartinly carry him to Aberga'nny,[2] to drink
goat's-whey—To be sure, the poor dear honymil is lost for want of

---

8. "Crashit" seems to be the Crescent; the Octagon
Chapel in Milsom Street, finished in 1767, was
considered a curiosity and a fashionable place of
worship.
9. Probably Bladud's Buildings, named after the
legendary founder of Bath. They were located in
Broad Street. "Harry King's Row" is Win's approximation of Harlequin's Row, which was so
named because of the mixture of brick and stone
which gave it a motley appearance.
1. Win probably means that the man is a morose
fellow, one who is sullenly ill-humored.
2. The town in Wales is now usually pronounced
Abergavénny by the local inhabitants, but was
apparently popularly pronounced as Win spells it
during the eighteenth century. The current holders
of the title Lord Abergavenny use the elided pronunciation.

axercise; for which reason, she intends to give him an airing once a-day upon the Downs, in a post-chaise——I have already made very creditable correxions in this here place; where, to be sure, we have the very squintasense of satiety——Mrs. Patcher, my lady Kilmacullock's woman, and I are sworn sisters. She has shewn me all her secrets, and learned me to wash gaze, and refrash rusty siks and bumbeseens, by boiling them with winegar, chamberlye,[3] and stale beer. My short sack[4] and apron luck as good as new from the shop, and my pumpydoor[5] as fresh as a rose, by the help of turtle-water——But this is all Greek and Latten to you, Molly——If we should come to Aberga'ny, you'll be within a day's ride of us; and then we shall see wan another, please God ——If not, remember me in your prayers, as I shall do by you in mine; and take care of my kitten, and give my kind sarvice to Sall; and this is all at present, from your beloved friend and sarvent,

Bath, April 26. WINIFRED JENKINS.

To Mrs. GWYLLIM, house-keeper at Brambleton-hall.

I am astonished, that Dr. Lewis should take upon him to give away Alderney, without my privity and concurrants——What signifies my brother's order? My brother is little better than Noncompush.[6] He would give away the shirt off his back, and the teeth out of his head; nay, as for that matter, he would have ruinated the family with his ridiculous charities, if it had not been for my four quarters[7]——What between his willfullness and his waste, his trumps,[8] and his frenzy, I lead the life of an indented slave. Alderney gave four gallons a-day, ever since the calf was sent to market. There is so much milk out of my dairy, and the press must stand still: but I won't loose a cheese paring; and the milk shall be made good, if the sarvents should go without butter. If they must needs have butter, let them make it of sheeps' milk; but then my wool will suffer for want of grace; so that I must be a looser on all sides——Well, patience is like a stout Welsh poney; it bears a great deal, and trots a great way; but it will tire at the long run. Before its long, perhaps I may shew Matt, that I was not born to be the household drudge to my dying day——Gwyn rites from Crickhowel, that the price of flannel is fallen three-farthings an ell; and that's another good penny out of my pocket——When I go to market to

3. Human urine, which was used in some washing processes to save soap.
4. The short sack, or sac dress, was another popular fashion of the day.
5. A long cloak with slits for the arms rather than sleeves which was probably given to the maid by her mistress, as were many of the clothes worn by servants.
6. *Non compos mentis* is the legal phrase which means "not of sound mind."
7. Probably the quarterly returns from an annuity in Tabitha's name, which she adds to the family income, though there is no other evidence in the novel that she contributes to the expenses of the family or the trip.
8. Lewis Knapp and others have conjectured that "trumps" is a misprint for "frumps," which are sulks, but given the vagaries of Tabitha's spelling, the editor has retained the spelling of the first edition.

sell, my commodity stinks; but when I want to buy the commonest thing, the owner pricks it up under my nose; and it can't be had for love nor money—I think every thing runs cross at Brambleton-hall—You say the gander has broke the eggs; which is a phinumenon I don't understand; for when the fox carried off the old goose last year, he took her place, and hatched the eggs, and partected the goslings like a tender parent—Then you tell me the thunder has soured two barrels of beer in the seller. But how the thunder should get there, when the seller was double-locked, I can't comprehend. Howsomever, I won't have the beer thrown out, till I see it with my own eyes. Perhaps, it will recover—At least it will serve for vinegar to the sarvents. You may leave off the fires in my brother's chamber and mine, as it is unsartain when we return.——I hope, Gwyllim, you'll take care there is no waste; and have an eye to the maids, and keep them to their spinning. I think they may go very well without beer in hot weather—It serves only to inflame the blood, and set them a-gog after the men. Water will make them fair, and keep them cool and tamperit. Don't forget to put up in the portmantel, that cums with Williams, along with my riding-habit, hat, and feather, the viol of purl water,[9] and the tincktur for my stomach; being as how I am much troubled with flutterencies. This is all at present, from

Yours,

Bath, April 26.   TABITHA BRAMBLE.

To Dr. LEWIS.

DEAR DICK,

I have done with the waters; therefore your advice comes a day too late —I grant that physick is no mystery of your making. I know it is a mystery in its own nature; and, like other mysteries, requires a strong gulp of faith to make it go down—Two days ago, I went into the King's Bath,[1] by the advice of our friend Ch——,[2] in order to clear the strainer of the skin, for the benefit of a free perspiration; and the first object that saluted my eye, was a child full of scrophulous ulcers, carried in the arms of one of the guides, under the very noses of the bathers. I was so shocked at the sight, that I retired immediately with indignation and disgust—Suppose the matter of those ulcers, floating on the water, comes in contact with my skin, when the pores are all open, I would ask you what must be the consequence?——Good Heaven, the very thought makes my blood run cold! we know not what sores may be running into the water while we are

<hr>

9. A drink used as an appetizer, made from beer or ale and bitter herbs.
1. The largest of the public baths in Bath at the time.

2. Rice Charleton (1710–89) was a physician at Bath who wrote several treatises on the use of the waters.

bathing, and what sort of matter we may thus imbibe; the king's-evil, the scurvy, the cancer, and the pox;[3] and, no doubt, the heat will render the *virus*[4] the more volatile and penetrating. To purify myself from all such contamination, I went to the duke of Kingston's private Bath,[5] and there I was almost suffocated for want of free air; the place was so small, and the steam so stifling.

After all, if the intention is no more than to wash the skin, I am convinced that simple element is more effectual than any water impregnated with salt and iron; which, being astringent, will certainly contract the pores, and leave a kind of crust upon the surface of the body. But I am now as much afraid of drinking, as of bathing; for, after a long conversation with the Doctor, about the construction of the pump and the cistern, it is very far from being clear with me, that the patients in the Pumproom don't swallow the scourings of the bathers. I can't help suspecting, that there is, or may be, some regurgitation from the bath into the cistern of the pump. In that case, what a delicate beveridge is every day quaffed by the drinkers; medicated with the sweat, and dirt, and dandriff; and the abominable discharges of various kinds, from twenty different diseased bodies, parboiling in the kettle below. In order to avoid this filthy composition, I had recourse to the spring that supplies the private baths on the Abbey-green; but I at once perceived something extraordinary in the taste and smell; and, upon inquiry, I find that the Roman baths in this quarter, were found covered by an old burying ground, belonging to the Abbey; thro' which, in all probability, the water drains in its passage: so that as we drink the decoction of living bodies at the Pump-room, we swallow the strainings of rotten bones and carcasses at the private bath —I vow to God, the very idea turns my stomach!—Determined, as I am, against any farther use of the Bath waters, this consideration would give me little disturbance, if I could find any thing more pure, or less pernicious, to quench my thirst; but, although the natural springs of excellent water are seen gushing spontaneous on every side, from the hills that surround us, the inhabitants, in general, make use of well water, so impregnated with nitre, or alum, or some other villainous mineral, that it is equally ungrateful to the taste, and mischievous to the constitution. It must be owned, indeed, that here, in Milsham-street, we have a precarious and scanty supply from the hill; which is collected in an open bason in the Circus, liable to be defiled with dead dogs, cats, rats, and

3. The king's evil, or scrofula, was a tubercular infection of the lymph glands, usually around the neck. It took its name from the folk belief that it could be cured by the touch of the ruling sovereign. Scurvy is a disease, caused by malnutrition, whose symptoms include swollen and bleeding gums and livid spots on the skin. "The pox" probably refers to syphilis, though it often referred to smallpox as well.

4. This word was not used in its modern sense until relatively recently, and here refers to a poisonous substance produced by the body as the result of a disease.

5. A group of small private baths and steam baths completed in 1764.

every species of nastiness, which the rascally populace may throw into it, from mere wantonness and brutality.——

Well, there is no nation that drinks so hoggishly as the English ——What passes for wine among us, is not the juice of the grape. It is an adulterous mixture, brewed up of nauseous ingredients, by dunces, who are bunglers in the art of poison-making; and yet we, and our forefathers, are and have been poisoned by this cursed drench, without taste or flavour—The only genuine and wholesome beveridge in England, is London porter, and Dorchester table-beer;[6] but as for your ale and your gin, your cyder, and your perry,[7] and all the trashy family of made wines, I detest them as infernal compositions, contrived for the destruction of the human species.——But what have I to do with the human species? except a very few friends, I care not if the whole was——.

Heark ye, Lewis, my misanthropy increases every day—The longer I live, I find the folly and the fraud of mankind grow more and more intolerable—I wish I had not come from Brambleton-hall; after having lived in solitude so long, I cannot bear the hurry and impertinence of the multitude; besides, every thing is sophisticated[8] in these crowded places. Snares are laid for our lives in every thing we eat or drink: the very air we breathe, is loaded with contagion. We cannot even sleep, without risque of infection. I say, infection—This place is the rendezvous of the diseased —You won't deny, that many diseases are infectious; even the consumption[9] itself, is highly infectious. When a person dies of it in Italy, the bed and bedding are destroyed; the other furniture is exposed to the weather, and the apartment white-washed, before it is occupied by any other living soul. You'll allow, that nothing receives infection sooner, or retains it longer, than blankets, feather-beds, and matrasses—'Sdeath! how do I know what miserable objects have been stewing in the bed where I now lie!—I wonder, Dick, you did not put me in mind of sending for my own matrasses—But, if I had not been an ass, I should not have needed a remembrancer——There is always some plaguy reflection that rises up in judgment against me, and ruffles my spirits—Therefore, let us change the subject—

I have other reasons for abridging my stay at Bath—You know sister Tabby's complexion—If Mrs. Tabitha Bramble had been of any other race, I should certainly have looked upon her as the most—But, the truth is, she has found means to interest my affection; or, rather, she is beholden to the force of prejudice, commonly called the ties of blood. Well, this amiable maiden has actually commenced a flirting correspondence with an Irish baronet of sixty-five. His name is Sir Ulic Mackilligut.

6. Porter is dark-brown ale, in this case brewed in London. It takes its name from porters, who favored the drink, and it is reputed to make the drinker strong. The strong beer of Dorchester, in Dorset, was widely distributed and prized.

7. A fermented beverage similar to cider, made from the juice of pears.
8. Adulterated or mixed with other substances.
9. Pulmonary tuberculosis, which was infectious, as Matt notices.

He is said to be much out at elbows; and, I believe, has received false intelligence with respect to her fortune. Be that as it may, the connexion is exceedingly ridiculous, and begins already to excite whispers. For my part, I have no intention to dispute her free-agency; though I shall fall upon some expedient to undeceive her paramour, as to the point which he has principally in view. But I don't think her conduct is a proper example for Liddy, who has also attracted the notice of some coxcombs in the Rooms; and Jerry tells me, he suspects a strapping fellow, the knight's nephew, of some design upon the girl's heart. I shall, therefore, keep a strict eye over her aunt and her, and even shift the scene, if I find the matter grow more serious—You perceive what an agreeable task it must be, to a man of my kidney, to have the cure of such souls as these—But, hold, you shall not have another peevish word (till the next occasion) from

yours,

Bath, April 28.   MATT. BRAMBLE.

To Sir WATKIN PHILLIPS of Jesus college, Oxon.

DEAR KNIGHT,

I think those people are unreasonable, who complain that Bath is a contracted circle, in which the same dull scenes perpetually revolve, without variation—I am, on the contrary, amazed to find so small a place, so crowded with entertainment and variety. London itself can hardly exhibit one species of diversion, to which we have not something analogous at Bath, over and above those singular advantages that are peculiar to the place. Here, for example, a man has daily opportunities of seeing the most remarkable characters of the community. He sees them in their natural attitudes and true colours; descended from their pedestals, and divested of their formal draperies, undisguised by art and affectation—Here we have ministers of state, judges, generals, bishops, projectors, philosophers, wits, poets, players, chemists, fiddlers, and buffoons.[1] If he makes any considerable stay in the place, he is sure of meeting with some particular friend, whom he did not expect to see; and to me there is nothing more agreeable, than such casual rencounters —Another entertainment, peculiar to Bath, arises from the general mixture of all degrees assembled in our public rooms, without distinction of rank or fortune. This is what my uncle reprobates, as a monstrous jumble of heterogeneous principles; a vile mob of noise and imperti-

---

1. Jery quotes from John Dryden's *Absalom and Achitophel* (1681), where the italicized words apply to Zimri, a satirical portrait of the Duke of Buckingham.

nence, without decency or subordination. But this chaos is to me a source of infinite amusement.

I was extremely diverted, last ball-night, to see the Master of the Ceremonies leading, with great solemnity, to the upper end of the room, an antiquated Abigail,[2] dressed in her lady's cast-clothes; whom he (I suppose) mistook for some countess just arrived at the Bath. The ball was opened by a Scotch lord, with a mulatto heiress from St. Christopher's;[3] and the gay colonel Tinsel danced all the evening with the daughter of an eminent tinman from the borough of Southwark—Yesterday morning, at the Pump-room, I saw a broken-winded Wapping[4] landlady squeeze through a circle of peers, to salute her brandy-merchant, who stood by the window, prop'd upon crutches; and a paralytic attorney of Shoe-lane,[5] in shuffling up to the bar, kicked the shins of the chancellor of England,[6] while his lordship, in a cut bob,[7] drank a glass of water at the pump. I cannot account for my being pleased with these incidents, any other way than by saying, they are truly ridiculous in their own nature, and serve to heighten the humour in the farce of life, which I am determined to enjoy as long as I can.—

Those follies, that move my uncle's spleen,[8] excite my laughter. He is as tender as a man without a skin; who cannot bear the slightest touch without flinching. What tickles another would give him torment; and yet he has what we may call lucid intervals, when he is remarkably facetious —Indeed, I never knew a hypochondriac so apt to be infected with good-humour. He is the most risible misanthrope I ever met with. A lucky joke, or any ludicrous incident, will set him a-laughing immoderately, even in one of his most gloomy paroxysms; and, when the laugh is over, he will curse his own imbecillity. In conversing with strangers, he betrays no marks of disquiet—He is splenetic with his familiars only; and not even with them, while they keep his attention employed; but when his spirits are not exerted externally, they seem to recoil and prey upon himself ——He has renounced the waters with execration; but he begins to find a more efficacious, and, certainly, a much more palatable remedy in the pleasures of society. He has discovered some old friends, among the

2. This proper name was used for any lady's maid after 1610, when Beaumont and Fletcher produced their play *The Scornful Lady*, whose characters included a notable lady's maid with this name.
3. Saint Christopher, now usually known as Saint Kitts Island, is in the Leeward Islands, in the Caribbean. It was a British colony in the eighteenth century.
4. Both Wapping and Southwark were unfashionable sections of metropolitan London. Southwark lies to the south of the Thames, and Wapping is located east of the City near the Thames.
5. This lane was near, but not in, the City, and would not have been a good address for an attorney.
6. The lord chancellor of England from 1761 to

1766 was Robert Henley, first Earl of Northington. He represented the city of Bath in Parliament and frequented it when not in London. He suffered from severe gout.
7. This is a short, uncurled wig which was worn most often by members of the lower classes, though here it is worn by the chancellor, which reflects the confusion of classes Matt finds so repugnant.
8. The spleen was commonly believed to be the seat of ill humor, which also went under the name of hypochondria, and Jery goes on just below to call his uncle a hypochondriac; but both terms could also refer to various degrees of mental disturbance.

invalids of Bath; and, in particular, renewed his acquaintance with the celebrated James Quin,[9] who certainly did not come here to drink water. You cannot doubt, but that I had the strongest curiosity to know this original; and it was gratified by Mr. Bramble, who has had him twice at our house to dinner.

So far as I am able to judge, Quin's character is rather more respectable than it has been generally represented. His *bons mots* are in every witling's mouth; but many of them have a rank flavour, which one would be apt to think was derived from a natural grossness of idea. I suspect, however, that justice has not been done the author, by the collectors of those *Quiniana;* who have let the best of them slip through their fingers, and only retained such as were suited to the taste and organs of the multitude. How far he may relax in his hours of jollity, I cannot pretend to say; but his general conversation is conducted by the nicest rules of propriety; and Mr. James Quin is, certainly, one of the best bred men in the kingdom. He is not only a most agreeable companion; but (as I am credibly informed) a very honest man; highly susceptible of friendship, warm, steady, and even generous in his attachments; disdaining flattery, and incapable of meanness and dissimulation. Were I to judge, however, from Quin's eye alone, I should take him to be proud, insolent, and cruel. There is something remarkably severe and forbidding in his aspect; and, I have been told, he was ever disposed to insult his inferiors and dependants.——Perhaps that report has influenced my opinion of his looks——You know we are the fools of prejudice. Howsoever that may be, I have as yet seen nothing but his favourable side; and my uncle, who frequently confers with him in a corner, declares he is one of the most sensible men he ever knew—He seems to have a reciprocal regard for old Square-toes,[1] whom he calls by the familiar name of Matthew, and often reminds of their old tavern-adventures: on the other hand, Matthew's eyes sparkle whenever Quin makes his appearance—Let him be never so jarring and discordant, Quin puts him in tune; and, like treble and bass in the same concert, they make excellent musick together—T'other day, the conversation turning upon Shakespeare, I could not help saying, with some emotion, that I would give an hundred guineas to see Mr. Quin act the part of Falstaff; upon which, turning to me with a smile, "And I would give a thousand, young gentleman, (said he) that I could gratify your longing." My uncle and he are perfectly agreed in their estimate of life; which, Quin says, would stink in his nostrils, if he did not steep it in claret.

9. Quin (1693–1766) was one of the most celebrated actors of his age before he retired to Bath in 1751, after which he indulged his appetites for food, drink, and conversation. Smollett had satirized Quin in his earlier novels, *Roderick Random* and *Peregrine Pickle*, but here treats him more generously. He died on January 21, 1766, but Smollett apparently wished to praise him anyway.
1. Square-toed shoes were worn in England until about the 1730's, when round toes came into fashion. The term which Jery uses for Matt was commonly applied to old-fashioned people from the 1730's on.

I want to see this phenomenon in his cups; and have almost prevailed upon uncle to give him a small turtle at the Bear.[2] In the mean time, I must entertain you with an incident, that seems to confirm the judgment of those two cynic philosophers. I took the liberty to differ in opinion from Mr. Bramble, when he observed, that the mixture of people in the entertainments of this place was destructive of all order and urbanity; that it rendered the plebeians insufferably arrogant and troublesome, and vulgarized the deportment and sentiments of those who moved in the upper spheres of life. He said, such a preposterous coalition would bring us into contempt with all our neighbours; and was worse, in fact, than debasing the gold coin of the nation. I argued, on the contrary, that those plebeians who discovered such eagerness to imitate the dress and equipage of their superiors, would likewise, in time, adopt their maxims and their manners, be polished by their conversation, and refined by their example; but when I appealed to Mr. Quin, and asked if he did not think that such an unreserved mixture would improve the whole mass?—"Yes, (said he) as a plate of marmalade would improve a pan of sirreverence."[3]

I owned I was not much conversant in high-life, but I had seen what were called polite assemblies in London and elsewhere; that those of Bath seemed to be as decent as any; and that, upon the whole, the individuals that composed it, would not be found deficient in good manners and decorum. "But let us have recourse to experience, (said I) —Jack Holder, who was intended for a parson, has succeeded to an estate of two thousand a year, by the death of his elder brother. He is now at the Bath, driving about in a phaeton and four, with French horns. He has treated with turtle and claret at all the taverns in Bath and Bristol, till his guests are gorged with good chear: he has bought a dozen suits of fine clothes, by the advice of the Master of the Ceremonies, under whose tuition he has entered himself: he has lost some hundreds at billiards to sharpers, and taken one of the nymphs of Avon-street into keeping; but, finding all these channels insufficient to drain him of his current cash, his counsellor has engaged him to give a general tea-drinking to-morrow at Wiltshire's room.[4] In order to give it the more eclat, every table is to be furnished with sweet-meats and nosegays; which, however, are not to be touched till notice is given by the ringing of a bell, and then the ladies may help themselves without restriction. This will be no bad way of trying the company's breeding—"

"I will abide by that experiment, (cried my uncle) and if I could find a place to stand secure, without the vortex of the tumult, which I know will ensue, I would certainly go thither and enjoy the scene." Quin proposed that we should take our station in the musick-gallery; and we took his

2. Quin was known to be fond of turtle, and the Bear was one of the luxurious inns of Bath at the time.

3. Human excrement.
4. One of the two large public rooms mentioned earlier by Liddy.

advice. Holder had got thither before us, with his horns perdue;[5] but we were admitted. The tea-drinking passed as usual; and the company having risen from the tables, were sauntring in groupes, in expectation of the signal for attack, when the bell beginning to ring, they flew with eagerness to the desert, and the whole place was instantly in commotion. There was nothing but justling, scrambling, pulling, snatching, struggling, scolding, and screaming. The nosegays were torn from one another's hands and bosoms; the glasses and china went to wreck; the tables and floor were strewed with comfits. Some cried; some swore; and the tropes and figures of Billingsgate[6] were used without reserve in all their native zest and flavour; nor were those flowers of rhetoric unattended with significant gesticulation. Some snapped their fingers; some forked them out; some clapped their hands, and some their back-sides; at length, they fairly proceeded to pulling caps, and every thing seemed to presage a general battle; when Holder ordered his horns to sound a charge, with a view to animate the combatants, and inflame the contest; but this manœuvre produced an effect quite contrary to what he expected. It was a note of reproach that roused them to an immediate sense of their disgraceful situation. They were ashamed of their absurd deportment, and suddenly desisted. They gathered up their caps, ruffles, and handkerchiefs; and great part of them retired in silent mortification.

Quin laughed at this adventure; but my uncle's delicacy was hurt. He hung his head in manifest chagrin, and seemed to repine at the triumph of his judgment—Indeed, his victory was more complete than he imagined; for, as we afterwards learned, the two amazons who singularized themselves most in the action, did not come from the purlieus of Puddle-dock,[7] but from the courtly neighbourhood of St. James's palace. One was a baroness, and the other, a wealthy knight's dowager—My uncle spoke not a word, till we had made our retreat good to the coffee-house; where, taking off his hat and wiping his forehead, "I bless God (said he) that Mrs. Tabitha Bramble did not take the field to-day!" "I would pit her for a cool hundred (cried Quin) against the best shake-bag[8] of the whole main." The truth is, nothing could have kept her at home but the accident of her having taken physick before she knew the nature of the entertainment. She has been for some days furbishing up an old suit of black velvet, to make her appearance as Sir Ulic's partner at the next ball.

I have much to say of this amiable kinswoman; but she has not been properly introduced to your acquaintance. She is remarkably civil to Mr. Quin; of whose sarcastic humour she seems to stand in awe; but her

5. His horn players and their instruments are hidden.
6. Originally an area in London, the seat of a fish market, but the term became synonymous with the coarse and vulgarly abusive language used there.
7. An area along the Thames near Blackfriars bridge.
8. In cockfighting, a shake-bag is a bird which has been excited by shaking it in a bag before releasing it into the pit, or pitting it.

caution is no match for her impertinence. "Mr. Gwynn, (said she the other day) I was once vastly entertained with your playing the Ghost of Gimlet at Drury-lane, when you rose up through the stage, with a white face and red eyes, and spoke of *quails upon the frightful porcofine*[9]—Do, pray, spout a little the Ghost of Gimlet." "Madam, (said Quin, with a glance of ineffable disdain) the Ghost of Gimlet is laid, never to rise again —" Insensible of this check, she proceeded: "Well, to be sure, you looked and talked so like a real ghost; and then the cock crowed so natural. I wonder how you could teach him to crow so exact, in the very nick of time; but, I suppose, he's game——An't he game, Mr. Gwynn?" "Dung-hill,[1] madam." "Well, dung-hill, or not dunghill, he has got such a clear counter-tenor, that I wish I had such another at Brambleton-hall, to wake the maids of a morning. Do you know where I could find one of his brood?" "Probably in the work-house of St. Giles's parish, madam; but I protest I know not his particular mew."[2] My uncle, frying with vexation, cried, "Good God, sister, how you talk! I have told you twenty times, that this gentleman's name is not Gwynn.——" "Hoity toity, brother mine, (she replied) no offence, I hope—Gwynn is an honourable name, of true old British extraction——I thought the gentleman had been come of Mrs. Helen Gwynn,[3] who was of his own profession; and if so be that were the case, he might be of king Charles's breed, and have royal blood in his veins—" "No, madam, (answered Quin, with great solemnity) my mother was not a whore of such distinction—True it is, I am sometimes tempted to believe myself of royal descent; for my inclinations are often arbitrary—If I was an absolute prince, at this instant, I belive I should send for the head of your cook in a charger—She has committed felony, on the person of that John Dory;[4] which is mangled in a cruel manner, and even presented without sauce—*O tempora! O mores!*"[5]

This good-humoured sally turned the conversation into a less disagree-able channel—But, lest you should think my scribble as tedious as Mrs. Tabby's clack, I shall not add another word, but that I am as usual

Yours,

Bath, April 30.   J. MELFORD.

---

9. Misquoted and mispronounced from *Hamlet* (Gimlet) I. v. 20. It refers to Hamlet's hair stand-ing on end "Like quills upon the fretful porpentine [porcupine]."
1. In cockfighting, "game" means "brave" and "dunghill" means "cowardly."
2. Saint Giles was a less than prosperous parish in London, and a mew was a courtyard or alley not on

one of the main streets.
3. Eleanor or Nell Gwyn (1650–87) was a popular actress and mistress of Charles II.
4. A popular variety of flatfish, similar to the turbot.
5. A famous classical tag from Cicero's oration on Catiline: "Oh, what times! Oh, what standards!"

To Dr. LEWIS.

DEAR LEWIS,

I received your bill upon Wiltshire, which was punctually honoured; but as I don't choose to keep so much cash by me, in a common lodging-house, I have deposited 250 *l.* in the bank of Bath, and shall take their bills for it in London, when I leave this place, where the season draws to an end—You must know, that now being a-foot, I am resolved to give Liddy a glimpse of London. She is one of the best hearted creatures I ever knew, and gains upon my affection every day—As for Tabby, I have dropt such hints to the Irish baronet, concerning her fortune, as, I make no doubt, will cool the ardour of his addresses. Then her pride will take the alarm; and the rancour of stale maidenhood being chafed, we shall hear nothing but slander and abuse of Sir Ulic Mackilligut—This rupture, I foresee, will facilitate our departure from Bath; where, at present, Tabby seems to enjoy herself with peculiar satisfaction. For my part, I detest it so much, that I should not have been able to stay so long in the place if I had not discovered some old friends; whose conversation alleviates my disgust—Going to the coffee-house one forenoon, I could not help contemplating the company, with equal surprize and compassion—We consisted of thirteen individuals; seven lamed by the gout, rheumatism, or palsy; three maimed by accident; and the rest either deaf or blind. One hobbled, another hopped, a third dragged his legs after him like a wounded snake, a fourth straddled betwixt a pair of long crutches, like the mummy of a felon hanging in chains; a fifth was bent into a horizontal position, like a mounted telescope, shoved in by a couple of chairmen; and a sixth was the bust of a man, set upright in a wheel machine, which the waiter moved from place to place.

Being struck with some of their faces, I consulted the subscription-book; and, perceiving the names of several old friends, began to consider the groupe with more attention. At length I discovered rear-admiral Balderick, the companion of my youth, whom I had not seen since he was appointed lieutenant of the Severn. He was metamorphosed into an old man, with a wooden leg and a weatherbeaten face; which appeared the more antient from his grey locks, that were truly venerable—Sitting down at the table, where he was reading a news-paper, I gazed at him for some minutes, with a mixture of pleasure and regret, which made my heart gush with tenderness; then, taking him by the hand, "Ah, Sam, (said I) forty years ago I little thought—" I was too much moved to proceed. "An old friend, sure enough! (cried he, squeezing my hand, and surveying me eagerly thro' his glasses) I know the looming of the vessel, though she has been hard strained since we parted; but I can't heave up the name—" The moment I told him who I was, he exclaimed, "Ha! Matt, my old fellow cruizer, still afloat!" And, starting up, hugged me in his arms. His transport, however, boded me no good; for, in saluting me, he thrust the spring of his spectacles into my eye, and, at the same time, set his wooden stump upon my gouty toe; an attack that made me shed tears in sad earnest——After the hurry of our recognition was over, he pointed out two of our common friends in the room: the bust was what remained of colonel Cockril, who had lost the use of his limbs in making an American campaign; and the telescope proved to be my college chum, sir Reginald Bently; who, with his new title, and unexpected inheritance, commenced fox-hunter, without having served his apprenticeship to the mystery; and, in consequence of following the hounds through a river, was seized with an inflammation in his bowels, which has contracted him into his present attitude.

Our former correspondence was forthwith renewed, with the most hearty expressions of mutual good-will; and as we had met so unexpectedly, we agreed to dine together that very day at the tavern. My friend Quin, being luckily unengaged, obliged us with his company; and, truly, this was the most happy day I have passed these twenty years. You and I, Lewis, having been always together, never tasted friendship in this high goût,[6] contracted from long absence. I cannot express the half of what I felt at this casual meeting of three or four companions, who had been so long separated, and so roughly treated by the storms of life. It was a renovation of youth; a kind of resuscitation of the dead, that realized those interesting dreams, in which we sometimes retrieve our antient friends from the grave. Perhaps my enjoyment was not the less pleasing for being mixed with a strain of melancholy, produced by the remembrance of past scenes, that conjured up the ideas of some endearing connexions, which the hand of Death has actually dissolved.

The spirits and good-humour of the company seemed to triumph over the wreck of their constitutions. They had even philosophy enough to joke upon their own calamities; such is the power of friendship, the sovereign cordial of life——I afterwards found, however, that they were not without their moments, and even hours of disquiet. Each of them apart, in succeeding conferences, expatiated upon his own particular grievances; and they were all malcontents at bottom——Over and above their personal disasters, they thought themselves unfortunate in the lottery of life. Baldrick complained, that all the recompence he had received for his long and hard service, was the half-pay of a rear-admiral. The colonel was mortified to see himself over-topped by upstart generals, some of whom he had once commanded; and, being a man of a liberal turn, could ill put up with a moderate annuity, for which he had sold his commission. As for the baronet, having run himself considerably in debt, on a contested election, he has been obliged to relinquish his seat in parliament, and his seat in the country at the same time, and put his

---

6. French for relish, savour, or taste.

Matthew Bramble recognises some ancient Friends.

estate to nurse; but his chagrin, which is the effect of his own misconduct, does not affect me half so much as that of the other two; who have acted honourable and distinguished parts on the great theatre, and are now reduced to lead a weary life in this stewpan of idleness and insignificance. They have long left off using the waters, after having experienced their inefficacy. The diversions of the place they are not in a condition to enjoy. How then do they make shift to pass their time? In the forenoon, they crawl out to the Rooms or the coffee-house, where they take a hand at whist, or descant upon the General Advertiser;[7] and their evenings they murder in private parties, among peevish invalids, and insipid old women—This is the case with a good number of individuals, whom nature seems to have intended for better purposes.

About a dozen years ago, many decent families, restricted to small fortunes, besides those that came hither on the score of health, were tempted to settle at Bath, where they could then live comfortably, and even make a genteel appearance, at a small expence: but the madness of the times has made the place too hot for them, and they are now obliged to think of other migrations—Some have already fled to the mountains of Wales, and others have retired to Exeter. Thither, no doubt, they will be followed by the flood of luxury and extravagance, which will drive them from place to place to the very Land's End; and there, I suppose, they will be obliged to ship themselves to some other country. Bath is become a mere sink of profligacy and extortion. Every article of house-keeping is raised to an enormous price; a circumstance no longer to be wondered at, when we know that every petty retainer of fortune piques himself upon keeping a table, and thinks 'tis for the honour of his character to wink at the knavery of his servants, who are in a confederacy with the market-people; and, of consequence, pay whatever they demand. Here is now a mushroom of opulence, who pays a cook seventy guineas a week for furnishing him with one meal a day. This portentous frenzy is become so contagious, that the very rabble and refuse of mankind are infected. I have known a negro-driver, from Jamaica, pay over-night to the master of one of the rooms, sixty-five guineas for tea and coffee to the company, and leave Bath next morning, in such obscurity, that not one of his guests had the slightest idea of his person, or even made the least inquiry about his name. Incidents of this kind are frequent; and every day teems with fresh absurdities, which are too gross to make a thinking man merry.—But I feel the spleen creeping on me apace; and therefore will indulge you with

7. The out-of-date name for the popular newspaper which became the *Public Advertiser* in 1752.

a cessation, that you may have no unnecessary cause to curse your correspondence with,

Dear Dick,

yours ever,

Bath, May 5. MAT. BRAMBLE.

To Miss LÆTITIA WILLIS, at Gloucester.

MY DEAR LETTY,

I wrote you at great length by the post, the twenty-sixth of last month, to which I refer you for an account of our proceedings at Bath; and I expect your answer with impatience. But, having this opportunity of a private hand, I send you two dozen of Bath rings;[8] six of the best of which I desire you will keep for yourself, and distribute the rest among the young ladies, our common friends, as you shall think proper——I don't know how you will approve of the mottoes; some of them are not much to my own liking; but I was obliged to take such as I could find ready manufactured—I am vexed, that neither you nor I have received any further information of a certain person—Sure it can't be wilful neglect! —O my dear Willis! I begin to be visited by strange fancies, and to have some melancholy doubts; which, however, it would be ungenerous to harbour without further inquiry—My uncle, who has made me a present of a very fine set of garnets, talks of treating us with a jaunt to London; which, you may imagine, will be highly agreeable: but I like Bath so well, that I hope he won't think of leaving it till the season is quite over; and yet, betwixt friends, something has happened to my aunt, which will probably shorten our stay in this place.

Yesterday, in the forenoon, she went by herself to a breakfasting in one of the rooms; and, in half an hour, returned in great agitation, having Chowder along with her in the chair. I believe some accident must have happened to that unlucky animal, which is the great source of all her troubles. Dear Letty! what a pity it is, that a woman of her years and discretion, should place her affection upon such an ugly, ill-conditioned cur, that snarls and snaps at every body. I asked John Thomas, the footman who attended her, what was the matter? and he did nothing but grin. A famous dog-doctor was sent for, and undertook to cure the patient, provided he might carry him home to his own house; but his mistress would not part with him out of her own sight——She ordered the cook to warm cloths, which she applied to his bowels, with her own hand. She gave up all thoughts of going to the ball in the evening; and when Sir Ulic

---

8. Finger rings from resorts, with mottoes engraved on them, were often presented to acquaintances as souvenirs of a visit.

came to drink tea, refused to be seen; so that he went away to look for another partner. My brother Jery whistles and dances. My uncle sometimes shrugs up his shoulders, and sometimes bursts out a-laughing. My aunt sobs and scolds by turns; and her woman, Win Jinkins, stares and wonders with a foolish face of curiosity; and, for my part, I am as curious as she, but ashamed to ask questions.

Perhaps time will discover the mystery; for if it was any thing that happened in the Rooms, it can't be long concealed——All I know is, that last night at supper, miss Bramble spoke very disdainfully of Sir Ulic Mackilligut, and asked her brother if he intended to keep us sweltering all the summer at Bath? "No, sister Tabitha, (said he, with an arch smile) we shall retreat before the Dog-days[9] begin; though I make no doubt, that with a little temperance and discretion, our constitutions might be kept cool enough all the year, even at Bath." As I don't know the meaning of this insinuation, I won't pretend to make any remarks upon it at present: hereafter, perhaps, I may be able to explain it more to your satisfaction——In the mean time, I beg you will be punctual in your correspondence, and continue to love your ever faithful

Bath, May 6.   LYDIA MELFORD.

To Sir WATKIN PHILLIPS, of Jesus college, Oxon.

So then Mrs. Blackerby's affair has proved a false alarm, and I have saved my money? I wish, however, her declaration had not been so premature; for though my being thought capable of making her a mother, might have given me some credit, the reputation of an intrigue with such a cracked pitcher does me no honour at all——In my last I told you I had hopes of seeing Quin, in his hours of elevation at the tavern which is the temple of mirth and good-fellowship; where he, as priest of Comus,[1] utters the inspirations of wit and humour——I have had that satisfaction. I have dined with his club at the Three Tuns,[2] and had the honour to sit him out. At half an hour past eight in the evening, he was carried home with six good bottles of claret under his belt; and it being then Friday, he gave orders, that he should not be disturbed till Sunday at noon——You must not imagine that this dose had any other effect upon his conversation, but that of making it more extravagantly entertaining——He had lost the use of his limbs, indeed, several hours before we parted, but he retained all his other faculties in perfection; and as he gave vent to every whimsical idea as it rose, I was really astonished at the brilliancy of his thoughts, and the force of his expression. Quin is a real voluptuary in the articles of eating and drinking; and so confirmed an epicure, in the

9. The hottest days of the year, in July and August. The name comes from the rising of the "dog-star," Sirius.

1. The ancient Roman god of drinking and revelry.
2. A well-known coaching inn at Bath.

common acceptation of the term, that he cannot put up with ordinary fare. This is a point of such importance with him, that he always takes upon himself the charge of catering; and a man admitted to his mess, is always sure of eating delicate victuals, and drinking excellent wine—He owns himself addicted to the delights of the stomach, and often jokes upon his own sensuality; but there is nothing selfish in this appetite ——He finds that good chear unites good company; exhilerates the spirits, opens the heart, banishes all restraint from conversation, and promotes the happiest purposes of social life.—But Mr. James Quin is not a subject to be discussed in the compass of one letter; I shall therefore, at present, leave him to his repose, and call another of a very different complexion.

You desire to have further acquaintance with the person of our aunt, and promise yourself much entertainment from her connexion with Sir Ulic Mackilligut: but in this hope you are baulked already; that connexion is dissolved. The Irish baronet is an old hound, that, finding her carrion, has quitted the scent—I have already told you, that Mrs. Tabitha Bramble is a maiden of forty-five. In her person, she is tall, raw-boned, aukward, flat-chested, and stooping; her complexion is sallow and freckled; her eyes are not grey, but greenish, like those of a cat, and generally inflamed; her hair is of a sandy, or rather dusty hue; her forehead low; her nose long, sharp, and, towards the extremity, always red in cool weather; her lips skinny, her mouth extensive, her teeth straggling and loose, of various colours and conformation; and her long neck shrivelled into a thousand wrinkles—In her temper, she is proud, stiff, vain, imperious, prying, malicious, greedy, and uncharitable. In all likelihood, her natural austerity has been soured by disappointment in love; for her long celibacy is by no means owing to her dislike of matrimony: on the contrary, she has left no stone unturned to avoid the reproachful epithet of old maid.

Before I was born, she had gone such lengths in the way of flirting with a recruiting officer, that her reputation was a little singed. She afterwards made advances to the curate of the parish, who dropped some distant hints about the next presentation to the living,[3] which was in her brother's gift; but finding that was already promised to another, he flew off at a tangent; and Mrs. Tabby, in revenge, found means to deprive him of his cure. Her next lover was lieutenant of a man of war, a relation of the family, who did not understand the refinements of the passion, and expressed no aversion to grapple with cousin Tabby in the way of marriage; but before matters could be properly adjusted, he went out on a cruise, and was killed in an engagement with a French frigate. Our aunt,

3. A "living" in the Anglican church was the income attached to a particular parish, such as the income from certain church-owned lands. The "presentation," or right to give the living to a properly ordained clergyman, was often in the hands of a gentleman of the neighborhood, as here Matthew Bramble has the right of presentation.

though baffled so often, did not yet despair—She layed all her snares for Dr. Lewis, who is the *fidus Achates*[4] of my uncle. She even fell sick upon the occasion, and prevailed with Matt to interpose in her behalf with his friend; but the Doctor, being a shy cock, would not be caught with chaff, and flatly rejected the proposal: so that Mrs. Tabitha was content to exert her patience once more, after having endeavoured in vain to effect a rupture betwixt the two friends; and now she thinks proper to be very civil to Lewis, who is become necessary to her in the way of his profession.

These, however, are not the only efforts she has made towards a nearer conjunction with our sex. Her fortune was originally no more than a thousand pounds; but she gained an accession of five hundred by the death of a sister, and the lieutenant left her three hundred in his will. These sums she has more than doubled, by living free of all expence, in her brother's house; and dealing in cheese and Welsh flannel, the produce of his flocks and dairy. At present her capital is increased to about four thousand pounds; and her avarice seems to grow every day more and more rapacious: but even this is not so intolerable, as the perverseness of her nature, which keeps the whole family in disquiet and uproar. She is one of those geniuses who find some diabolical enjoyment in being dreaded and detested by their fellow-creatures.

I once told my uncle, I was surprised that a man of his disposition could bear such a domestic plague, when it could be so easily removed—The remark made him sore, because it seemed to tax him with want of resolution—Wrinkling up his nose, and drawing down his eyebrows, "A young fellow, (said he) when he first thrusts his snout into the world, is apt to be surprised at many things, which a man of experience knows to be ordinary and unavoidable—This precious aunt of yours is become insensibly a part of my constitution—Damn her! She's a *noli me tangere*[5] in my flesh, which I cannot bear to be touched or tampered with." I made no reply; but shifted the conversation. He really has an affection for this original; which maintains its ground in defiance of common sense, and in despite of that contempt which he must certainly feel for her character and understanding. Nay, I am convinced, that she has likewise a most virulent attachment to his person; though her love never shews itself but in the shape of discontent; and she persists in tormenting him out of sheer tenderness—The only object within doors upon which she bestows any marks of affection, in the usual stile, is her dog Chowder; a filthy cur from Newfoundland,[6] which she had in a present from the wife of a skipper in Swansey[7]—One would imagine she had distinguished this beast with her

4. Aeneas's faithful friend in Virgil's *Aeneid*, hence any faithful friend.
5. Literally "do not touch me," but a tender ulcer, usually on the face.
6. Chowder may be a native of Newfoundland, but he seems to be a small mixed-breed dog rather

than the large black species now called Newfoundland.
7. Swansea is a principal seaport of south Wales, and a logical place for the wife of a captain of a ship to locate.

favour on account of his ugliness and ill-nature; if it was not, indeed, an instinctive sympathy between his disposition and her own. Certain it is, she caresses him without ceasing; and even harrasses the family in the service of this cursed animal, which, indeed, has proved the proximate cause of her breach with Sir Ulic Mackilligut.

You must know, she yesterday wanted to steal a march of poor Liddy, and went to breakfast in the Room without any other companion than her dog, in expectation of meeting with the Baronet, who had agreed to dance with her in the evening——Chowder no sooner made his appearance in the Room, than the Master of the Ceremonies, incensed at his presumption, ran up to drive him away, and threatened him with his foot; but the other seemed to despise his authority, and displaying a formidable case of long, white, sharp teeth, kept the puny monarch at bay ——While he stood under some trepidation, fronting his antagonist, and bawling to the waiter, Sir Ulic Mackilligut came to his assistance; and seeming ignorant of the connexion between this intruder and his mistress, gave the former such a kick in the jaws, as sent him howling to the door——Mrs. Tabitha, incensed at this outrage, ran after him, squalling in a tone equally disagreeable; while the Baronet followed her on one side, making apologies for his mistake; and Derrick on the other, making remonstrances upon the rules and regulations of the place.

Far from being satisfied with the Knight's excuses, she said she was sure he was no gentleman; and when the Master of the Ceremonies offered to hand her into the chair, she rapped him over the knuckles with her fan. My uncle's footman being still at the door, she and Chowder got into the same vehicle, and were carried off amidst the jokes of the chairmen and other populace——I had been riding out on Clerkendown, and happened to enter just as the *fracas* was over——The Baronet, coming up to me with an affected air of chagrin, recounted the adventure; at which I laughed heartily, and then his countenance cleared up. "My dear soul, (said he) when I saw a sort of a wild baist, snarling with open mouth at the Master of the Ceremonies, like the red cow going to devour Tom Thumb,[8] I could do no less than go to the assistance of the little man; but I never dreamt the baist was one of Mrs. Bramble's attendants——O! if I had, he might have made his breakfast upon Derrick and wellcome——But, you know, my dear friend, how natural it is for us Irishmen to blunder, and to take the wrong sow by the ear——However, I will confess judgment, and cry her mercy; and, 'tis to be hoped, a penitent sinner may be forgiven." I told him, that as the offence was not involuntary of his side, it was to be hoped he would not find her implacable.

8. This mythical tale of a tiny man was represented in illustrated form in chapbooks during the early eighteenth century, and then was raised to the stage in Henry Fielding's *Tom Thumb* (1730) and *The Tragedy of Tragedies* (1731).

But, in truth, all this concern was dissembled. In his approaches of gallantry to Mrs. Tabitha, he had been misled by a mistake of at least six thousand pounds, in the calculation of her fortune; and in this particular he was just undeceived. He, therefore, seized the first opportunity of incurring her displeasure decently, in such a manner as would certainly annihilate the correspondence; and he could not have taken a more effectual method, than that of beating her dog. When he presented himself at our door, to pay his respects to the offended fair, he was refused admittance; and given to understand, that he should never find her at home for the future. She was not so inaccessible to Derrick, who came to demand satisfaction for the insult she had offered to him, even in the verge of his own court. She knew it was convenient to be well with the Master of the Ceremonies, while she continued to frequent the Rooms; and, having heard he was a poet, began to be afraid of making her appearance in a ballad or lampoon.—She therefore made excuses for what she had done, imputing it to the flutter of her spirits; and subscribed handsomely for his poems: so that he was perfectly appeased, and overwhelmed her with a profusion of compliment. He even solicited a reconciliation with Chowder; which, however, the latter declined; and he declared, that if he could find a precedent in the annals of the Bath, which he would carefully examine for that purpose, her favourite should be admitted to the next public breakfasting—But, I believe, she will not expose herself or him to the risque of a second disgrace—Who will supply the place of Mackilligut in her affections, I cannot foresee; but nothing in the shape of man can come amiss. Though she is a violent church-woman, of the most intolerant zeal, I believe in my conscience she would have no objection, at present, to treat on the score of matrimony with an Anabaptist, Quaker, or Jew; and even ratify the treaty, at the expence of her own conversion. But, perhaps, I think too hardly of this kinswoman; who, I must own, is very little beholden to the good opinion of

Yours,

Bath, May 6. J. MELFORD.

To Dr. LEWIS.

You ask me, why I don't take the air a-horseback, during this fine weather?—In which of the avenues of this paradise would you have me take that exercise? Shall I commit myself to the high-roads of London or Bristol, to be stifled with dust, or pressed to death in the midst of post-chaises, flying-machines,[9] waggons, and coal-horses; besides the troops of fine gentlemen that take to the high-way, to shew their horsemanship;

---

9. Not an anachronism, but the name then current for express coaches.

and the coaches of fine ladies, who go thither to shew their equipages? Shall I attempt the Downs, and fatigue myself to death in climbing up an eternal ascent, without any hopes of reaching the summit? Know then, I have made divers desperate leaps at those upper regions; but always fell backward into this vapour-pit, exhausted and dispirited by those ineffectual efforts; and here we poor valetudinarians pant and struggle, like so many Chinese gudgeons, gasping in the bottom of a punch-bowl. By Heaven, it is a kind of inchantment! If I do not speedily break the spell, and escape, I may chance to give up the ghost in this nauseous stew of corruption—It was but two nights ago, that I had like to have made my public exit, at a minute's warning. One of my greatest weaknesses is that of suffering myself to be over-ruled by the opinion of people, whose judgment I despise—I own, with shame and confusion of face, that importunity of any kind I cannot resist. This want of courage and constancy is an original flaw in my nature, which you must have often observed with compassion, if not with contempt. I am afraid some of our boasted virtues may be traced up to this defect.——

Without further preamble, I was persuaded to go to a ball, on purpose to see Liddy dance a minuet with a young petulant jackanapes, the only son of a wealthy undertaker [1] from London, whose mother lodges in our neighbourhood, and has contracted an acquaintance with Tabby. I sat a couple of long hours, half stifled, in the midst of a noisome crowd; and could not help wondering, that so many hundreds of those that rank as rational creatures, could find entertainment in seeing a succession of insipid animals, describing the same dull figure for a whole evening, on an area, not much bigger than a taylor's shop-board. If there had been any beauty, grace, activity, magnificent dress, or variety of any kind, howsoever absurd, to engage the attention, and amuse the fancy, I should not have been surprised; but there was no such object: it was a tiresome repetition of the same languid, frivolous scene, performed by actors that seemed to sleep in all their motions——The continual swimming of those phantoms before my eyes, gave me a swimming of the head; which was also affected by the fouled air, circulating through such a number of rotten human bellows——I therefore retreated towards the door, and stood in the passage to the next room, talking to my friend Quin; when an end being put to the minuets, the benches were removed to make way for the country-dances; and the multitude rising at once, the whole atmosphere was put in commotion. Then, all of a sudden, came rushing upon me an Egyptian gale, so impregnated with pestilential vapours, that my nerves were overpowered, and I dropt senseless upon the floor.

1. The modern meaning of "undertaker" to denote one who arranges funerals was coming into common usage at this time, and Smollett uses it in the modern sense on p. 85, below. Here, however, it probably has one of its older meanings of either a person who undertook to influence the action of Parliament, presumably for money, or a person who undertook to collect a particular tax, also for personal gain. Both of these senses have a negative connotation.

You may easily conceive what a clamour and confusion this accident must have produced, in such an assembly—I soon recovered, however, and found myself in an easy chair, supported by my own people—Sister Tabby, in her great tenderness, had put me to the torture, squeezing my head under her arm, and stuffing my nose with spirit of hartshorn, till the whole inside was excoriated. I no sooner got home, than I sent for doctor Ch——, who assured me, I needed not be alarmed, for my swooning was entirely occasioned by an accidental impression of fetid effluvia upon nerves of uncommon sensibility. I know not how other people's nerves are constructed; but one would imagine they must be made of very coarse materials, to stand the shock of such a horrid assault. It was, indeed, *a compound of villainous smells,*[2] in which the most violent stinks, and the most powerful perfumes, contended for the mastery. Imagine to yourself a high exalted essence of mingled odours, arising from putrid gums, imposthumated lungs, sour flatulencies, rank arm-pits, sweating feet, running sores and issues, plasters, ointments, and embrocations, hungary-water, spirit of lavender, assafœtida drops, musk, hartshorn, and sal volatile; besides a thousand frowzy steams, which I could not analyse. Such, O Dick! is the fragrant æther we breathe in the polite assemblies of Bath—Such is the atmosphere I have exchanged for the pure, elastic, animating air of the Welsh mountains——*O Rus, quando te aspiciam!*[3] —I wonder what the devil possessed me—

But few words are best: I have taken my resolution—You may well suppose I don't intend to entertain the company with a second exhibition —I have promised, in an evil hour, to proceed to London, and that promise shall be performed; but my stay in the metropolis shall be brief. I have, for the benefit of my health, projected an expedition to the North, which, I hope, will afford some agreeable pastime. I have never travelled farther that way than Scarborough; and, I think, it is a reproach upon me, as a British freeholder, to have lived so long without making an excursion to the other side of the Tweed. Besides, I have some relations settled in Yorkshire, to whom it may not be improper to introduce my nephew and his sister—At present, I have nothing to add, but that Tabby is happily disentangled from the Irish Baronet; and that I will not fail to make you acquainted, from time to time, with the sequel of our adventures: a mark of consideration, which, perhaps, you would willingly dispense with in

Your humble servant,

Bath, May 8.

MATT. BRAMBLE.

2. Matt applies Falstaff's complaint about the unsavory smell of a laundry basket in which he had been hidden (*The Merry Wives of Windsor* III. v. 93) to the assembly at Bath.

3. From Horace's *Satire* II. vi. 60, when the country mouse, appalled by what he sees when visiting the city mouse, exclaims, "Oh my countryside, when will I see you again?"

To Sir WATKIN PHILLIPS, of Jesus college, Oxon.

DEAR PHILLIPS,

A few days ago we were terribly alarmed by my uncle's fainting at the ball—He has been ever since cursing his own folly, for going thither at the request of an impertinent woman. He declares, he will sooner visit a house infected with the plague, than trust himself in such a nauseous spital for the future, for he swears the accident was occasioned by the stench of the crowd; and that he would never desire a stronger proof of our being made of very gross materials, than our having withstood the annoyance, by which he was so much discomposed. For my part, I am very thankful for the coarseness of my organs, being in no danger of ever falling a sacrifice to the delicacy of my nose. Mr. Bramble is extravagantly delicate in all his sensations, both of soul and body. I was informed by Dr. Lewis, that he once fought a duel with an officer of the horse-guards, for turning a-side to the Park wall, on a necessary occasion, when he was passing with a lady under his protection. His blood rises at every instance of insolence and cruelty, even where he himself is no way concerned; and ingratitude makes his teeth chatter. On the other hand, the recital of a generous, humane, or grateful action, never fails to draw from him tears of approbation, which he is often greatly distressed to conceal.

Yesterday, one Paunceford[4] gave tea, on particular invitation—This man, after having been long buffetted by adversity, went abroad; and Fortune, resolved to make him amends for her former coyness, set him all at once up to the very ears in affluence. He has now emerged from obscurity, and blazes out in all the tinsel of the times. I don't find that he is charged with any practices that the law deems dishonest, or that his wealth has made him arrogant and inaccessible; on the contrary, he takes great pains to appear affable and gracious. But they say, he is remarkable for shrinking from his former friendships, which were generally too plain and home-spun to appear amidst his present brilliant connexions; and that he seems uneasy at sight of some old benefactors, whom a man of honour would take pleasure to acknowledge—Be that as it may, he had so effectually engaged the company at Bath, that when I went with my uncle to the coffee-house in the evening, there was not a soul in the room but one person, seemingly in years, who sat by the fire, reading one of the papers. Mr. Bramble, taking his station close by him, "There is such a crowd and confusion of chairs in the passage to Simpson's, (said he) that we could hardly get along—I wish those minions of fortune would fall upon more laudable ways of spending their money.—I suppose, sir, you like this kind of entertainment as little as I do?" "I can't say, I have any

4. In the incident of Paunceford which follows, Smollett turns his own treatment by Alexander Campbell, whom he had helped, into the fictional ingratitude of Paunceford toward his benefactor, Serle. See pp. 290–292 of Lewis Knapp's biography (listed in the Bibliography, below).

great relish for such entertainments," answered the other, without taking his eyes off the paper—Mr. Serle, (resumed my uncle) I beg pardon for interrupting you; but I can't resist the curiosity I have to know if you received a card on this occasion?"

The man seemed surprised at this address, and made some pause, as doubtful what answer he should make. "I know my curiosity is impertinent, (added my uncle) but I have a particular reason for asking the favour." "If that be the case, (replied Mr. Serle) I shall gratify you without hesitation, by owning, that I have had no card. But, give me leave, sir, to ask in my turn, what reason you think I have to expect such an invitation from the gentleman who gives tea?" "I have my own reasons; (cried Mr. Bramble, with some emotion) and am convinced, more than ever, that this Paunceford is a contemptible fellow." "Sir, (said the other, laying down the paper) I have not the honour to know you; but your discourse is a little mysterious, and seems to require some explanation. The person you are pleased to treat so cavalierly, is a gentleman of some consequence in the community; and, for aught you know, I may also have my particular reasons for defending his character—" "If I was not convinced of the contrary, (observed the other) I should not have gone so far—" "Let me tell you, sir, (said the stranger, raising his voice) you have gone too far, in hazarding such reflections——"

Here he was interrupted by my uncle; who asked peevishly, if he was Don Quixote enough, at this time of day, to throw down his gauntlet as champion for a man who had treated him with such ungrateful neglect. "For my part, (added he) I shall never quarrel with you again upon this subject; and what I have said now, has been suggested as much by my regard for you, as by my contempt of him—" Mr. Serle, then pulling off his spectacles, eyed uncle very earnestly, saying, in a mitigated tone, "Surely I am much obliged——Ah, Mr. Bramble! I now recollect your features, though I have not seen you these many years." "We might have been less strangers to one another, (answered the 'squire) if our correspondence had not been interrupted, in consequence of a misunderstanding, occasioned by this very——, but no matter—Mr. Serle, I esteem your character; and my friendship, such as it is, you may freely command." "The offer is too agreeable to be declined; (said he) I embrace it very cordially; and, as the first fruits of it, request that you will change this subject, which, with me, is a matter of peculiar delicacy."

My uncle owned he was in the right, and the discourse took a more general turn. Mr. Serle passed the evening with us at our lodgings; and appeared to be intelligent, and even entertaining; but his disposition was rather of a melancholy hue. My uncle says he is a man of uncommon parts, and unquestioned probity: that his fortune, which was originally small, his been greatly hurt by a romantic spirit of generosity, which he has often displayed, even at the expence of his discretion, in favour of worthless individuals——That he had rescued Paunceford from the

lowest distress, when he was bankrupt, both in means and reputation
—That he had espoused his interests with a degree of enthusiasm, broke
with several friends, and even drawn his sword against my uncle, who
had particular reasons for questioning the moral character of the said
Paunceford: that, without Serle's countenance and assistance, the other
never could have embraced the opportunity, which has raised him to this
pinnacle of wealth: that Paunceford, in the first transports of his success,
had written, from abroad, letters to different correspondents, owning his
obligations to Mr. Serle, in the warmest terms of acknowledgment, and
declaring he considered himself only as a factor for the occasions of his
best friend: that, without doubt, he had made declarations of the same
nature to his benefactor himself, though this last was always silent and
reserved on the subject; but for some years, those tropes and figures of
rhetoric had been disused: that, upon his return to England, he had been
lavish in his caresses to Mr. Serle, invited him to his house, and pressed
him to make it his own: that he had overwhelmed him with general
professions, and affected to express the warmest regard for him, in
company of their common acquaintance; so that every body believed his
gratitude was as liberal as his fortune; and some went so far as to
congratulate Mr. Serle on both.

All this time Paunceford carefully and artfully avoided particular
discussions with his old patron, who had too much spirit to drop the most
distant hint of balancing the account of obligation: that, nevertheless, a
man of his feelings could not but resent this shocking return for all his
kindness; and, therefore, he withdrew himself from the connexion,
without coming to the least explanation, or speaking a syllable on the
subject to any living soul; so that now their correspondence is reduced to
a slight salute with the hat, when they chance to meet in any public place;
an accident that rarely happens, for their walks lie different ways. Mr.
Paunceford lives in a palace, feeds upon dainties, is arrayed in sumptuous
apparel, appears in all the pomp of equipage, and passes his time among
the nobles of the land. Serle lodges in Stall-street,[5] up two pair of stairs
backwards, walks a-foot in a Bath-rug, eats for twelve shillings a-week,
and drinks water as a preservative against the gout and gravel——Mark
the vicissitude. Paunceford once resided in a garret; where he subsisted
upon sheeps'-trotters[6] and cow-heel, from which commons he was
translated to the table of Serle, that ever abounded with good-chear; until
want of oeconomy and retention, reduced him to a slender annuity in his
decline of years, that scarce affords the bare necessaries of life
—Paunceford, however, does him the honour to speak of him still, with
uncommon regard; and to declare what pleasure it would give him to
contribute in any shape to his convenience: "But you know, (he never

5. A street in central Bath.
6. The shank and feet of sheep, cooked for cheap food.

fails to add) he's a shy kind of a man—And then such a perfect philosopher, that he looks upon all superfluities with the most sovereign contempt."

Having given you this sketch of 'squire Paunceford, I need not make any comment on his character, but leave it at the mercy of your own reflection; from which, I dare say, it will meet with as little quarter as it has found with

yours always,

Bath, May 10.   J. MELFORD.

To Mrs. MARY JONES, at Brambleton-hall.

DEAR MOLLY,

We are all upon the ving—Hey for London, girl!—Fecks! we have been long enough here; for we're all turned tipsy turvy——Mistress has excarded Sir Ulic for kicking of Chowder; and I have sent O Frizzle away, with a flea in his ear—I've shewn him how little I minded his tinsy[7] and his long tail—A fellor, who would think for to go, for to offer, to take up with a dirty trollop under my nose——I ketched him in the very fect, coming out of the house-maids garret.—But I have gi'en the dirty slut a siserary.[8] O Molly! the sarvants at Bath are devils in garnet—They lite the candle at both ends—Here's nothing but ginketting, and wasting, and thieving, and tricking, and trigging; and then they are never content —They won't suffer the 'squire and mistress to stay any longer; because they have been already above three weeks in the house; and they look for a couple of ginneys a-piece at our going away; and this is a parquisite they expect every month in the season; being as how no family has a right to stay longer than four weeks in the same lodgings; and so the cuck swears, she will pin the dish-clout to mistress's tail; and the house-maid vows, she'll put cowitch in master's bed, if so be he don't discamp without furder ado——I don't blame them for making the most of their market, in the way of vails and parquisites; and I defy the devil to say I am a tail-carrier, or ever brought a poor sarvant into trouble——But then they oft to have some conscience, in vronging those that be sarvants like themselves—For you must no, Molly, I missed three-quarters of blond lace, and a remnant of muslin, and my silver thimble; which was the gift of true love: they were all in my work-basket, that I left upon the table in the sarvants-hall, when mistresses bell rung; but if they had been under lock and kay, 'twould have been all the same; for there are double keys to all the locks in Bath; and they say as how the very teeth an't safe in your

7. A common corruption of tinsel, cheap ostentation. The tail, further on in the line, refers to his braided hair, which he wears to appear stylish.

8. A severe rebuke or scolding. The word is a corruption of *certiorari*, a writ issued by a superior court.

head, if you sleep with your mouth open—And so says I to myself, *them things could not go without hands; and so I'll watch their waters:* and so I did with a vitness; for then it was I found Bett consarned with O Frizzle. And as the cuck had thrown her slush at me, because I had taken part with Chowder, when he fit with the turnspit, I resolved to make a clear kitchen, and throw some of her fat into the fire. I ketched the chare-woman going out with her load in the morning, before she thought I was up, and brought her to mistress with her whole cargo—Marry, what do'st think she had got in the name of God? Her buckets were foaming full of our best bear, and her lap was stuffed with a cold tongue, part of a buttock of beef, half a turkey, and a swinging lump of butter, and the matter of ten mould kandles, that had scarce ever been lit. The cuck brazened it out, and said it was her rite to rummage the pantry; and she was ready for to go before the mare: that he had been her potticary[9] many years, and would never think of hurting a poor sarvant, for giving away the scraps of the kitchen——I went another way to work with madam Betty, because she had been saucy, and called me skandelus names; and said O Frizzle couldn't abide me, and twenty other odorous falsehoods. I got a varrant from the mare, and her box being sarched by the constable, my things came out sure enuff; besides a full pound of vax candles, and a nite-cap of mistress, that I could sware to on my cruperal oaf[1]—O! then madam Mopstick came upon her merry bones; and as the 'squire wouldn't hare of a pursecution, she scaped a skewering: but the longest day she has to live, she'll remember your

humble sarvant,

Bath, May 15.   WINIFRED JENKINS.
If the hind should come again, before we be gone, pray send me the shift and apron, with the vite gallow manky[2] shoes; which you'll find in my pillowber——Sarvice to Saul——

To Sir WATKIN PHILLIPS, Bar[t]. of Jesus college, Oxon.

You are in the right, dear Phillips; I don't expect regular answers to every letter—I know a college-life is too circumscribed to afford materials for such quick returns of communication. For my part, I am continually shifting the scene, and surrounded with new objects; some of which are striking enough. I shall therefore conclude my journal for your amuse-ment; and though, in all appearance, it will not treat of very important or

9. It appears that the mayor of Bath was an apothecary, or druggist, but the editor has not identified him.
1. Win's approximation of "corporal oath," one made while touching the *Holy Bible.* "Merry

bones," just below, should be "marrowbones," or "knees."
2. White calamanco material, which was a glossy wool fabric.

interesting particulars, it may prove, perhaps, not altogether uninstructive and unentertaining.

The musick and entertainments of Bath are over for this season; and all our gay birds of passage have taken their flight to Bristol-well, Tunbridge, Brighthelmstone,[3] Scarborough, Harrowgate, &c. Not a soul is seen in this place, but a few broken-winded parsons, waddling like so many crows along the North Parade. There is always a great shew of the clergy at Bath: none of your thin, puny, yellow, hectic figures, exhausted with abstinence and hard study, labouring under the *morbi eruditorum*;[4] but great overgrown dignitaries and rectors, with rubicund noses and gouty ancles, or broad bloated faces, dragging along great swag bellies; the emblems of sloth and indigestion—

Now we are upon the subject of parsons, I must tell you a ludicrous adventure, which was atchieved the other day by Tom Eastgate, whom you may remember on the foundation of Queen's.[5] He had been very assiduous to pin himself upon George Prankley, who was a gentleman-commoner of Christ-church,[6] knowing the said Prankley was heir to a considerable estate, and would have the advowson of a good living, the incumbent of which was very old and infirm. He studied his passions, and flattered them so effectually, as to become his companion and counsellor; and, at last, obtained of him a promise of the presentation, when the living should fall. Prankley, on his uncle's death, quitted Oxford, and made his first appearance in the fashionable world at London; from whence he came lately to Bath, where he has been exhibiting himself among the bucks and gamesters of the place. Eastgate followed him hither; but he should not have quitted him for a moment, at his first emerging into life. He ought to have known he was a fantastic, foolish, fickle fellow, who would forget his college-attachments the moment they ceased appealing to his senses. Tom met with a cold reception from his old friend; and was, moreover, informed, that he had promised the living to another man, who had a vote in the county, where he proposed to offer himself a candidate at the next general election. He now remembered nothing of Eastgate, but the freedoms he had used to take with him, while Tom had quietly stood his butt,[7] with an eye to the benefice; and those freedoms he began to repeat in common place sarcasms on his person and his cloth, which he uttered in the public coffee-house, for the entertainment of the company. But he was egregiously mistaken in giving his own wit credit for that tameness of Eastgate, which had been entirely owing to prudential considerations. These being now removed, he retorted his repartee with interest, and found no great difficulty in turning the laugh upon the aggressor; who, losing his temper, called him

3. The older name for Brighton, just becoming a popular place of resort.
4. Maladies of the learned.
5. That is, he held a scholarship from Queen's College, Oxford.
6. A student who paid his own bills.
7. The object of his contempt or target of his jokes.

names, and asked, *If he knew whom he talked to?* After much altercation, Prankley, shaking his cane, bid him hold his tongue, otherwise he would dust his cassock for him. "I have no pretensions to such a valet; (said Tom) but if you should do me that office, and overheat yourself, I have here a good oaken towel at your service."

Prankley was equally incensed and confounded at this reply. After a moment's pause, he took him aside towards the window; and, pointing to the clump of firs on Clerken-down, asked in a whisper, if he had spirit enough to meet him there, with a case of pistols, at six o'clock to-morrow morning. Eastgate answered in the affirmative; and, with a steady countenance, assured him, he would not fail to give him the rendezvous at the hour he mentioned. So saying, he retired; and the challenger stayed some time in manifest agitation. In the morning, Eastgate, who knew his man, and had taken his resolution, went to Prankley's lodgings, and roused him by five o'clock—

The 'squire, in all probability, cursed his punctuality in his heart, but he affected to talk big; and having prepared his artillery over-night, they crossed the water at the end of the South Parade. In their progress up the hill, Prankley often eyed the parson, in hopes of perceiving some reluctance in his countenance; but as no such marks appeared, he attempted to intimidate him by word of mouth. "If these flints do their office, (said he) I'll do thy business in a few minutes." "I desire you will do your best; (replied the other) for my part, I come not here to trifle. Our lives are in the hands of God; and one of us already totters on the brink of eternity—" This remark seemed to make some impression upon the 'squire, who changed countenance, and with a faultering accent observed, "That it ill became a clergyman to be concerned in quarrels and blood-shed—" "Your insolence to me (said Eastgate) I should have bore with patience, had not you cast the most infamous reflections upon my order, the honour of which I think myself in duty bound to maintain, even at the expence of my heart's blood; and surely it can be no crime to put out of the world a profligate wretch, without any sense of principle, morality, or religion——" "Thou may'st take away my life, (cried Prankley, in great perturbation) but don't go to murder my character. —What! has't got no conscience?" "My conscience is perfectly quiet (replied the other); and now, sir, we are upon the spot—Take your ground as near as you please; prime your pistol; and the Lord, of his infinite mercy, have compassion upon your miserable soul!"

This ejaculation he pronounced in a loud solemn tone, with his hat off, and his eyes lifted up; then drawing a large horse-pistol, he presented, and put himself in a posture of action. Prankley took his distance, and endeavoured to prime, but his hand shook with such violence, that he found this operation impractible—His antagonist, seeing how it was with him, offered his assistance, and advanced for that purpose; when the poor 'squire, exceedingly alarmed at what he had heard and seen, desired the action might be deferred till next day, as he had not settled his affairs. "I ha'n't made my will (said he); my sisters are not provided for; and I just now recollect an old promise, which my conscience tells me I ought to perform—I'll first convince thee, that I'm not a wretch without principle, and then thou shalt have an opportunity to take my life, which thou seem'st to thirst after so eagerly—"

Eastgate understood the hint; and told him, that one day should break no squares;[8] adding, "God forbid that I should be the means of hindering you from acting the part of an honest man, and a dutiful brother—" By virtue of this cessation, they returned peaceably together. Prankley forthwith made out the presentation of the living, and delivered it to Eastgate, telling him at the same time, he had now settled his affairs, and was ready to attend him to the Fir-grove; but Tom declared he could not think of lifting his hand against the life of so great a benefactor—He did more: when they next met at the coffee-house, he asked pardon of Mr. Prankley, if in his passion he had said any thing to give him offence; and the 'squire was so gracious as to forgive him with a cordial shake of the hand, declaring that he did not like to be at variance with an old college-companion—Next day, however, he left Bath abruptly; and then Eastgate told me all these particulars, not a little pleased with the effects of his own sagacity, by which he has secured a living worth 160l. per annum.

Of my uncle, I have nothing at present to say; but that we set out to-morrow for London *en famille*. He and the ladies, with the maid and Chowder in a coach; I and the man-servant a-horseback. The particulars of our journey you shall have in my next, provided no accident happens to prevent,

Yours ever,

Bath, May 17.   J. MELFORD.

To Dr. LEWIS.

DEAR DICK,

I shall to-morrow set out for London, where I have bespoke lodgings, at Mrs. Norton's in Golden-square.[9] Although I am no admirer of Bath, I shall leave it with regret; because I must part with some old friends, whom, in all probability, I shall never see again. In the course of coffee-house conversation, I had often heard very extraordinary encomiums passed on the performances of Mr. T——,[1] a gentleman residing in this

8. This idiom apparently means that it will make no difference, but it is not listed in dictionaries of slang.
9. Golden Square is located north of Piccadilly Circus, and was the home of several surgeons, including John Norton. Smollett lived in Brewer Street, near the square, in 1765, and may have resided with the Nortons.
1. Probably John Taylor (1745?–1806), a landscape painter who sometimes signed his paintings "John Taylor of Bath."

place, who paints landscapes for his amusement. As I have no great confidence in the taste and judgment of coffee-house connoisseurs, and never received much pleasure from this branch of the art, those general praises made no impression at all on my curiosity; but, at the request of a particular friend, I went yesterday to see the pieces, which had been so warmly commended—I must own I am no judge of painting, though very fond of pictures. I don't imagine that my senses would play me so false, as to betray me into admiration of any thing that was very bad; but, true it is, I have often over-looked capital beauties, in pieces of extraordinary merit.—If I am not totally devoid of taste, however, this young gentleman of Bath is the best landscape-painter now living: I was struck with his performances in such a manner, as I had never been by painting before. His trees not only have a richness of foliage and warmth of colouring, which delights the view; but also a certain magnificence in the disposition, and spirit in the expression, which I cannot describe. His management of the *chiaro oscuro*, or light and shadow, especially gleams of sun-shine, is altogether wonderful, both in the contrivance and execution; and he is so happy in his perspective, and marking his distances at sea, by a progressive series of ships, vessels, capes, and promontories, that I could not help thinking, I had a distant view of thirty leagues upon the back-ground of the picture. If there is any taste for ingenuity left in a degenerate age, fast sinking into barbarism, this artist, I apprehend, will make a capital figure, as soon as his works are known—

Two days ago, I was favoured with a visit by Mr. Fitz-owen; who, with great formality, solicited my vote and interest at the general election. I ought not to have been shocked at the confidence of this man; though it was remarkable, considering what had passed between him and me on a former occasion— —These visits are mere matter of form, which a candidate makes to every elector; even to those who, he knows, are engaged in the interest of his competitor, lest he should expose himself to the imputation of pride, at a time when it is expected he should appear humble. Indeed, I know nothing so abject as the behaviour of a man canvassing for a seat in parliament— —This mean prostration, (to borough-electors, especially) has, I imagine, contributed in a great measure to raise that spirit of insolence among the vulgar; which, like the devil, will be found very difficult to lay. Be that as it may, I was in some confusion at the effrontery of Fitz-owen; but I soon recollected myself, and told him, I had not yet determined for whom I should give my vote, nor whether I should give it for any.—The truth is, I look upon both candidates in the same light; and should think myself a traitor to the constitution of my country, if I voted for either. If every elector would bring the same consideration home to his conscience, we should not have such reason to exclaim against the venality of p——ts.[2] but we are all a

2. Parliaments.

pack of venal and corrupted rascals; so lost to all sense of honesty, and all tenderness of character, that, in a little time, I am fully persuaded, nothing will be infamous but virtue and public-spirit.

G. H———,[3] who is really an enthusiast in patriotism, and represented the capital in several successive parliaments, declared to me t'other day, with the tears in his eyes, that he had lived above thirty years in the city of London, and dealt in the way of commerce with all the citizens of note in their turns; but that, as he should answer to God, he had never, in the whole course of his life, found above three or four whom he could call thoroughly honest: a declaration, which was rather mortifying than surprising to me; who have found so few men of worth in the course of my acquaintance, that they serve only as exceptions; which, in the grammarian's phrase, confirm and prove a general canon———I know you will say, G. H———saw imperfectly through the mist of prejudice, and I am rankled by the spleen——Perhaps, you are partly in the right; for I have perceived that my opinion of mankind, like mercury in the thermometer, rises and falls according to the variations of the weather.

Pray settle accompts with Barnes; take what money of mine is in his hands, and give him acquittance. If you think Davis has stock or credit enough to do justice to the farm, give him a discharge for the rent that is due: this will animate his industry; for I know that nothing is so discouraging to a farmer, as the thoughts of being in arrears with his landlord. He becomes dispirited, and neglects his labour; and so the farm goes to wreck. Tabby has been clamouring for some days about the lamb's skin, which Williams, the hind, begged of me, when he was last at Bath. Pr'ythee take it back, paying the fellow the full value of it, that I may have some peace in my own house; and let him keep his own counsel, if he means to keep his place——O! I shall never presume to despise or censure any poor man, for suffering himself to be henpecked; conscious how I myself am obliged to truckle to a domestic dæmon; even though (blessed be God) she is not yoked with me for life, in the matrimonial waggon——She has quarrelled with the servants of the house about vails; and such intolerable scolding ensued on both sides, that I have been fain to appease the cook and chamber-maid by stealth. Can't you find some poor gentleman of Wales, to take this precious commodity off the hands of

yours,

Bath, May 19.   M. BRAMBLE.

---

3. George Heathcote (1700–68) was a member of Parliament and had been lord mayor of London. He published "A Letter" in 1749 complaining about the corruption of the age.

To Dr. LEWIS.

DOCTER LEWS,

Give me leaf to tell you, methinks you mought employ your talons better, than to encourage servants to pillage their masters—I find by Gwyllim, that Villiams has got my skin; for which he is an impotent rascal. He has not only got my skin, but, moreover, my butter-milk to fatten his pigs; and, I suppose, the next thing he gets, will be my pad[4] to carry his daughter to church and fair: Roger gets this, and Roger gets that; but I'd have you to know, I won't be rogered[5] at this rate by any ragmatical fellow in the kingom—And I am surprised, docter Lews, you would offer to put my affairs in composition with the refuge and skim of the hearth. I have toiled and moyled to a good purpuss, for the advantage of Matt's family, if I can't safe as much owl as will make me an under petticoat. As for the butter-milk, ne'er a pig in the parish shall thrust his snout in it, with my good-will. There's a famous physician at the Hot Well, that prescribes it to his patience, when the case is consumptive; and the Scots and Irish have begun to drink it already, in such quantities, that there is not a drop left for the hogs in the whole neighbourhood of Bristol. I'll have our butter-milk barrelled up, and sent twice a-week to Aberginny, where it may be sold for a halfpenny the quart; and so Roger may carry his pigs to another market—I hope, Docter, you will not go to put any more such phims[6] in my brother's head, to the prejudice of my pockat; but rather give me some raisins (which hitherto you have not done) to subscribe myself

your humble servant,

Bath, May 19.   TAB. BRAMBLE.

To Sir WATKIN PHILLIPS, of Jesus college, Oxon.

DEAR PHILLIPS,

Without waiting for your answer to my last, I proceed to give you an account of our journey to London, which has not been wholly barren of adventure. Tuesday last, the 'squire took his place in a hired coach and four, accompanied by his sister and mine, and Mrs. Tabby's maid, Winifrid Jenkins, whose province it was to support Chowder on a cushion in her lap. I could scarce refrain from laughing, when I looked into the vehicle, and saw that animal sitting opposite to my uncle, like any other passenger. The 'squire, ashamed of his situation, blushed to the

---

4. A gentle road horse.
5. The obvious meaning of this phrase is that Tabby will not have Roger's name used as an excuse for everything that goes wrong. However,
the word "roger" had also taken on a vulgar meaning by about 1750. To "roger" was to have sexual intercourse with, to screw.
6. Whims.

eyes: and, calling to the postilions[7] to drive on, pulled the glass up in my face. I, and his servant John Thomas, attended them on horseback.

Nothing worth mentioning occured, till we arrived on the edge of Marlborough Downs. There one of the fore horses fell, in going down hill at a round trot; and the postilion behind, endeavouring to stop the carriage, pulled it on one side into a deep rut, where it was fairly overturned. I had rode on about two hundred yards before; but, hearing a loud scream, galloped back and dismounted, to give what assistance was in my power. When I looked into the coach, I could see nothing distinctly, but the nether end of Jenkins, who was kicking her heels and squalling with great vociferation. All of a sudden, my uncle thrust up his bare pate, and bolted through the window, as nimble as a grashopper, having made use of poor Win's posteriors as a step to rise in his ascent —The man (who had likewise quitted his horse) dragged this forlorn damsel, more dead than alive, through the same opening. Then Mr. Bramble, pulling the door off its hinges with a jerk, laid hold on Liddy's arm, and brought her to the light; very much frighted, but little hurt. It fell to my share to deliver our aunt Tabitha, who had lost her cap in the struggle; and being rather more than half frantic, with rage and terror, was no bad representation of one of the sister Furies that guard the gates of hell——She expressed no sort of concern for her brother, who ran about in the cold, without his periwig, and worked with the most astonishing agility, in helping to disentangle the horses from the carriage: but she cried, in a tone of distraction, "Chowder! Chowder! my dear Chowder! my poor Chowder is certainly killed!"

This was not the case—Chowder, after having tore my uncle's leg in the confusion of the fall, had retreated under the seat, and from thence the footman drew him by the neck; for which good office, he bit his fingers to the bone. The fellow, who is naturally surly, was so provoked at this assault, that he saluted his ribs with a hearty kick, exclaiming, "Damn the nasty son of a bitch, and them he belongs to!" A benediction, which was by no means lost upon the implacable virago his mistress —Her brother, however, prevailed upon her, to retire into a peasant's house, near the scene of action, where his head and her's were covered, and poor Jenkins had a fit——Our next care was to apply some sticking plaster to the wound in his leg, which exhibited the impression of Chowder's teeth; but he never opened his lips against the delinquent ——Mrs. Tabby, alarmed at this scene, "You say nothing, Matt (cried she); but I know your mind—I know the spite you have to that poor unfortunate animal! I know you intend to take his life away!" "You are mistaken, upon my honour! (replied the 'squire, with a sarcastic smile) I should be incapable of harbouring any such cruel design against an object

7. A postilion was a servant who rode one of the coach horses to aid the driver in directing the team.

so amiable and inoffensive; even if he had not the happiness to be your favourite."

John Thomas was not so delicate. The fellow, whether really alarmed for his life, or instigated by the desire of revenge, came in, and bluntly demanded, that the dog should be put to death; on the supposition, that if ever he should run mad hereafter, he, who had been bit by him, would be infected—My uncle calmly argued upon the absurdity of his opinion, observing, that he himself was in the same predicament, and would certainly take the precaution he proposed, if he was not sure he ran no risque of infection. Nevertheless, Thomas continued obstinate; and, at length declared, that if the dog was not shot immediately, he himself would be his executioner——This declaration opened the flood-gates of Tabby's eloquence, which would have shamed the first-rate oratress of Billingsgate.[8] The footman retorted in the same stile; and the 'squire dismissed him from his service, after having prevented me from giving him a good horse-whipping for his insolence.

The coach being adjusted, another difficulty occured—Mrs. Tabitha absolutely refused to enter it again, unless another driver could be found to take the place of the postilion; who, she affirmed, had overturned the carriage from malice aforethought—After much dispute, the man re-signed his place to a shabby country fellow, who undertook to go as far as Marlborough, where they could be better provided; and at that place we arrived about one o'clock, without farther impediment. Mrs. Bramble, however, found new matter of offence; which, indeed, she had a particu-lar genius for extracting at will from almost every incident in life. We had scarce entered the room at Marlborough, where we stayed to dine, when she exhibited a formal complaint against the poor fellow who had superseded the postilion. She said, he was such a beggarly rascal, that he had ne'er a shirt to his back; and had the impudence to shock her sight by shewing his bare posteriors, for which act of indelicacy he deserved to be set in the stocks. Mrs. Winifred Jenkins confirmed the assertion, with respect to his nakedness, observing, at the same time, that he had a skin as fair as alabaster.

"This is a heinous offence, indeed, (cried my uncle) let us hear what the fellow has to say in his own vindication." He was accordingly summoned, and made his appearance, which was equally queer and pathetic. He seemed to be about twenty years of age, of a middling size, with bandy legs, stooping shoulders, high forehead, sandy locks, pinking eyes, flat nose, and long chin—but his complexion was of a sickly yellow: his looks denoted famine; and the rags that he wore, could hardly conceal what decency requires to be covered——My uncle, having surveyed him attentively, said, with an ironical expression in his countenance, "An't you ashamed, fellow, to ride postilion without a shirt to cover your backside from the view of the ladies in the coach?" "Yes, I am, an please your noble honour; (answered the man) but necessity has no law, as the saying is——And more than that, it was an accident—My breeches cracked behind, after I had got into the saddle—" "You're an impudent varlet, (cried Mrs. Tabby) for presuming to ride before persons of fashion without a shirt—" "I am so, an please your worthy ladyship; (said he) but I'm a poor Wiltshire lad.—I ha'n't a shirt in the world, that I can call my own, nor a rag of clothes, an please your ladyship, but what you see—I have no friend, nor relation upon earth to help me out—I have had the fever and ague these six months, and spent all I had in the world upon doctors, and to keep soul and body together; and, saving your ladyship's good presence, I han't broke bread these four and twenty hours—"

Mrs. Bramble, turning from him, said, she had never seen such a filthy tatterdemalion, and bid him begone; observing, that he would fill the room full of vermin—Her brother darted a significant glance at her, as she retired with Liddy into another apartment; and then asked the man if he was known to any person in Marlborough?—When he answered, that the landlord of the inn had known him from his infancy; mine host was immediately called, and being interrogated on the subject, declared that the young fellow's name was Humphry Clinker.[9] That he had been a love begotten babe, brought up in the work-house, and put out apprentice by the parish to a country black-smith, who died before the boy's time was out: that he had for some time worked under his ostler, as a helper and extra postilion, till he was taken ill of the ague, which disabled him from getting his bread: that, having sold or pawned every thing he had in the world for his cure and subsistence, he became so miserable and shabby, that he disgraced the stable, and was dismissed; but that he never heard any thing to the prejudice of his character in other respects. "So that the fellow being sick and destitute, (said my uncle) you turned him out to die in the streets." "I pay the poors' rate,[1] (replied the other) and I have no right to maintain idle vagrants, either in sickness or health; besides, such a miserable object would have brought a discredit upon my house—"

"You perceive (said the 'squire, turning to me) our landlord is a Christian of bowels—Who shall presume to censure the morals of the age, when the very publicans exhibit such examples of humanity? ——Heark ye, Clinker, you are a most notorious offender——You stand convicted of sickness, hunger, wretchedness, and want—But, as it does not belong to me to punish criminals, I will only take upon me the task of

---

9. "To dine with Duke Humphry" was a proverbial phrase for doing without a meal, and
"clinker" was a slang term for a piece of excrement.
1. Pay the tax levied to support poorhouses.

Humphry Clinker introduced to the Bramble family.

giving you a word of advice—Get a shirt with all convenient dispatch, that your nakedness may not henceforward give offence to travelling gentlewomen, especially maidens in years—"

So saying, he put a guinea into the hand of the poor fellow, who stood staring at him in silence, with his mouth wide open, till the landlord pushed him out of the room.

In the afternoon, as our aunt stept into the coach, she observed, with some marks of satisfaction, that the postilion, who rode next to her, was not a shabby wretch like the ragamuffin who had drove them into Marlborough. Indeed, the difference was very conspicuous: this was a smart fellow, with a narrow brimmed hat, with gold cording, a cut bob, a decent blue jacket, leather breeches, and a clean linen shirt, puffed above the waist-band. When we arrived at the castle on Spin-hill,[2] where we lay, this new postilion was remarkably assiduous, in bringing in the loose parcels; and, at length, displayed the individual countenance of Humphry Clinker, who had metamorphosed himself in this manner, by relieving from pawn part of his own clothes, with the money he had received from Mr. Bramble.

Howsoever pleased the rest of the company were with such a favourable change in the appearance of this poor creature, it soured on the stomach of Mrs. Tabby, who had not yet digested the affront of his naked skin——She tossed her nose in disdain, saying, she supposed her brother had taken him into favour, because he had insulted her with his obscenity: that a fool and his money were soon parted; but that if Matt intended to take the fellow with him to London, she would not go a foot further that way——My uncle said nothing with his tongue, though his looks were sufficiently expressive; and next morning Clinker did not appear, so that we proceeded without further altercation to Salt-hill,[3] where we proposed to dine—There, the first person that came to the side of the coach, and began to adjust the foot-board, was no other than Humphry Clinker—When I handed out Mrs. Bramble, she eyed him with a furious look, and passed into the house—My uncle was embarrassed, and asked him peevishly, what had brought him hither? The fellow said, his honour had been so good to him, that he had not the heart to part with him; that he would follow him to the world's end, and serve him all the days of his life, without fee or reward—

Mr. Bramble did not know whether to chide or laugh at this declaration——He foresaw much contradiction on the side of Tabby; and, on the other hand, he could not but be pleased with the gratitude of Clinker, as well as with the simplicity of his character—"Suppose I was inclined to take you into my service, (said he) what are your qualifications? what are

2. Speen Hill, in Berkshire, near the town of Speenhamland, had a coaching inn called The Castle on it. The hill was approximately halfway on the hundred-mile trip from Bath to London.

3. Salt Hill stands between Maidenhead and Slough, about halfway between Speen Hill and London.

you good for?" "An please your honour, (answered this original) I can read and write, and do the business of the stable indifferent well—I can dress a horse, and shoe him, and bleed and rowel him; and, as for the practice of sow-gelding, I won't turn my back on e'er a he in the county of Wilts——Then I can make hog's-puddings and hob-nails, mend kettles, and tin saucepans—" Here uncle burst out a-laughing; and enquired, what other accomplishments he was master of—"I know something of single-stick,[4] and psalmody, (proceeded Clinker) I can play upon the Jew's-harp, sing Black-ey'd Susan, Arthur-o'Bradley,[5] and divers other songs; I can dance a Welsh jig, and Nancy Dawson;[6] wrestle a fall with any lad of my inches, when I'm in heart; and, under correction, I can find a hare when your honour wants a bit of game." "Foregad! thou art a complete fellow, (cried my uncle, still laughing) I have a good mind to take thee into my family——Pr'ythee, go and try if thou can'st make peace with my sister—Thou ha'st given her much offence by shewing her thy naked tail."

Clinker accordingly followed us into the room, cap in hand, where, addressing himself to Mrs. Tabitha, "May it please your ladyship's worship (cried he) to pardon and forgive my offences, and, with God's assistance, I shall take care that my tail shall never rise up in judgment against me, to offend your ladyship again——Do, pray, good, sweet, beautiful lady, take compassion on a poor sinner—God bless your noble countenance; I am sure you are too handsome and generous to bear malice—I will serve you on my bended knees, by night and by day, by land and by water; and all for the love and pleasure of serving such an excellent lady—"

This compliment and humiliation had some effect upon Tabby; but she made no reply; and Clinker, taking silence for consent, gave his attendance at dinner. The fellow's natural aukwardness and the flutter of his spirits were productive of repeated blunders in the course of his attendance—At length, he spilt part of a custard upon her right shoulder; and, starting back, trod upon Chowder, who set up a dismal howl ——Poor Humphry was so disconcerted at this double mistake, that he dropt the china dish, which broke into a thousand pieces; then, falling down upon his knees, remained in that posture gaping, with a most ludicrous aspect of distress——Mrs. Bramble flew to the dog, and, snatching him in her arms, presented him to her brother, saying, "This is all a concerted scheme against this unfortunate animal, whose only crime is its regard for me—Here it is: kill it at once; and then you'll be satisfied."

Clinker, hearing these words, and taking them in the literal acceptation, got up in some hurry, and, seizing a knife from the side-board, cried,

4. Fencing with a short stick or cudgel.
5. The first of these songs was a ballad by John Gay, and the second was one of several about this fabled character, perhaps "Arthur O'Bradley's Wedding."
6. This is a hornpipe dance named after a dancer in Gay's *The Beggar's Opera* (1728).

Direful consequences of Clinker's awkwardness.

"Not here, an please your ladyship—It will daub the room—Give him to me, and I'll carry him in the ditch by the roadside—" To this proposal he received no other answer, than a hearty box on the ear, that made him stagger to the other side of the room. "What! (said she to her brother) am I to be affronted by every mangy hound that you pick up in the highway? I insist upon your sending this rascallion about his business immediately ——" "For God's sake, sister, compose yourself, (said my uncle) and consider, that the poor fellow is innocent of any intention to give you offence—" "Innocent as the babe unborn"—(cried Humphry.) "I see it plainly, (exclaimed this implacable maiden) he acts by your direction; and you are resolved to support him in his impudence—This is a bad return for all the services I have done you; for nursing you in your sickness, managing your family, and keeping you from ruining yourself by your own imprudence——But now you shall part with that rascal or me, upon the spot, without farther loss of time; and the world shall see whether you have more regard for your own flesh and blood, or for a beggarly foundling, taken from the dunghill—"

Mr. Bramble's eyes began to glisten, and his teeth to chatter. "If stated fairly, (said he, raising his voice) the question is, whether I have spirit to shake off an intolerable yoke, by one effort of resolution, or meanness enough to do an act of cruelty and injustice, to gratify the rancour of a capricious woman—Heark ye, Mrs. Tabitha Bramble, I will now propose an alternative in my turn—Either discard your four-footed favourite, or give me leave to bid you eternally adieu—For I am determined, that he and I shall live no longer under the same roof; and now *to dinner with what appetite you may*—"[7] Thunderstruck at this declaration, she sat down in a corner; and, after a pause of some minutes, "Sure I don't understand you, Matt! (said she)" "And yet I spoke in plain English—" answered the 'squire, with a peremptory look. "Sir, (resumed this virago, effectually humbled) it is your prerogative to command, and my duty to obey. I can't dispose of the dog in this place; but if you'll allow him to go in the coach to London, I give you my word, he shall never trouble you again—"

Her brother, entirely disarmed by this mild reply, declared, she could ask him nothing in reason that he would refuse; adding, "I hope, sister, you have never found me deficient in natural affection." Mrs. Tabitha immediately rose, and, throwing her arms about his neck, kissed him on the cheek: he returned her embrace with great emotion. Liddy sobbed, Win Jenkins cackled, Chowder capered, and Clinker skipped about, rubbing his hands for joy of this reconciliation.

Concord being thus restored, we finished our meal with comfort; and in the evening arrived at London, without having met with any other

7. Matt's words are borrowed from Henry VIII's speech to Wolsey after warning him in *Henry VIII* III. ii. 202–3.

adventure. My aunt seems to be much mended by the hint she received from her brother. She has been graciously pleased to remove her displeasure from Clinker, who is now retained as a footman; and in a day or two will make his appearance in a new suit of livery; but as he is little acquainted with London, we have taken an occasional valet, whom I intend hereafter to hire as my own servant. We lodge in Golden-square, at the house of one Mrs. Norton, a decent sort of a woman, who takes great pains to make us all easy. My uncle proposes to make a circuit of all the remarkable scenes of this metropolis, for the entertainment of his pupils; but as both you and I are already acquainted with most of those he will visit, and with some others he little dreams of, I shall only communicate what will be in some measure new to your observation. Remember me to our Jesuitical friends, and believe me ever,

Dear knight,

yours affectionately,

London, May 24.   J. MELFORD.

To Dr. LEWIS.

DEAR DOCTOR,

London is literally new to me; new in its streets, houses, and even in its situation; as the Irishman said, "London is now gone out of town."[8] What I left open fields, producing hay and corn, I now find covered with streets, and squares, and palaces, and churches. I am credibly informed, that in the space of seven years, eleven thousand new houses have been built in one quarter of Westminster, exclusive of what is daily added to other parts of this unweildy metropolis. Pimlico and Knightsbridge are now almost joined to Chelsea and Kensington; and if this infatuation continues for half a century, I suppose the whole county of Middlesex will be covered with brick.[9]

It must be allowed, indeed, for the credit of the present age, that London and Westminster are much better paved and lighted than they were formerly. The new streets are spacious, regular, and airy; and the houses generally convenient. The bridge at Blackfriars[1] is a noble monument of taste and public-spirit—I wonder how they stumbled upon a work of such magnificence and utility. But, notwithstanding these improvements, the capital is become an overgrown monster; which, like a dropsical head, will in time leave the body and extremities without

8. James Bramston (1694?–1744), in *The Art of Politicks* (1729), a satire based loosely on Horace's *Art of Poetry*. The line in its context has exactly the same meaning that Matt intends here.
9. As any recent visitor to London can attest, the urban sprawl which Matt foresaw has indeed taken place.
1. This bridge was designed by the Scottish architect Robert Mylne. Construction began in 1760, and the bridge was opened to traffic near the end of the decade.

nourishment and support. The absurdity will appear in its full force, when we consider, that one sixth part of the natives of this whole extensive kingdom, is crowded within the bills of mortality.[2] What wonder that our villages are depopulated, and our farms in want of day-labourers? The abolition of small farms, is but one cause of the decrease of population. Indeed, the incredible increase of horses and black cattle, to answer the purposes of luxury, requires a prodigious quantity of hay and grass, which are raised and managed without much labour; but a number of hands will always be wanted for the different branches of agriculture, whether the farms be large or small. The tide of luxury has swept all the inhabitants from the open country—The poorest 'squire, as well as the richest peer, must have his house in town, and make a figure with an extraordinary number of domestics. The plough-boys, cow-herds, and lower hinds, are debauched and seduced by the appearance and discourse of those coxcombs in livery, when they make their summer excursions. They desert their dirt and drudgery, and swarm up to London, in hopes of getting into service, where they can live luxuriously and wear fine clothes, without being obliged to work; for idleness is natural to man——Great numbers of these, being disappointed in their expectation, become thieves and sharpers; and London being an immense wilderness, in which there is neither watch nor ward of any signification, nor any order or police, affords them lurking-places as well as prey.

There are many causes that contribute to the daily increase of this enormous mass; but they may be all resolved into the grand source of luxury and corruption—About five and twenty years ago, very few, even of the most opulent citizens of London, kept any equipage, or even any servants in livery. Their tables produced nothing but plain boiled and roasted, with a bottle of port and a tankard of beer. At present, every trader in any degree of credit, every broker and attorney, maintains a couple of footmen, a coachman, and postilion. He has his town-house, and his country-house, his coach, and his postchaise. His wife and daughters appear in the richest stuffs, bespangled with diamonds. They frequent the court, the opera, the theatre, and the masquerade. They hold assemblies at their own houses: they make sumptuous entertainments, and treat with the richest wines of Bourdeaux, Burgundy, and Champagne. The substantial tradesman, who wont to pass his evenings at the ale-house for fourpence half-penny, now spends three shillings at the tavern, while his wife keeps card-tables at home; she must likewise have fine clothes, her chaise, or pad, with country lodgings, and go three times a-week to public diversions. Every clerk, apprentice, and even

2. The London Company of Parish Clerks began publishing a weekly list of births, deaths, and marriages within the 109 parishes that made up metropolitan London in 1592. The boundaries were revised with the passage of time, but to be "within the bills of mortality" was to be within metropolitan London.

waiter of tavern or coffee-house, maintains a gelding by himself, or in partnership, and assumes the air and apparel of a petit maitre[3]——The gayest places of public entertainment are filled with fashionable figures; which, upon inquiry, will be found to be journeymen taylors, serving-men, and abigails, disguised like their betters.

In short, there is no distinction or subordination left——The different departments of life are jumbled together—The hod-carrier, the low mechanic, the tapster, the publican, the shop-keeper, the pettifogger, the citizen, and courtier, *all tread upon the kibes of one another:*[4] actuated by the demons of profligacy and licentiousness, they are seen every where, rambling, riding, rolling, rushing, justling, mixing, bouncing, cracking, and crashing in one vile ferment of stupidity and corruption—All is tumult and hurry; one would imagine they were impelled by some disorder of the brain, that will not suffer them to be at rest. The foot-passengers run along as if they were pursued by bailiffs. The porters and chairmen trot with their burthens. People, who keep their own equi-pages, drive through the streets at full speed. Even citizens, physicians, and apothecaries, glide in their chariots like lightning. The hackney-coachmen make their horses smoke, and the pavement shakes under them; and I have actually seen a waggon pass through Piccadilly at the hand-gallop. In a word, the whole nation seems to be running out of their wits.

The diversions of the times are not ill suited to the genius of this incongrous monster, called *the public.* Give it noise, confusion, glare, and glitter; it has no idea of elegance and propriety—What are the amuse-ments at Ranelagh?[5] One half of the company are following one another's tails, in an eternal circle; like so many blind asses in an olive-mill, where they can neither discourse, distinguish, nor be distinguished; while the other half are drinking hot water, under the denomination of tea, till nine or ten o'clock at night, to keep them awake for the rest of the evening. As for the orchestra, the vocal musick especially, it is well for the performers that they cannot be heard distinctly. Vauxhall[6] is a composition of baubles, overcharged with paltry ornaments, ill con-ceived, and poorly executed; without any unity of design, or propriety of disposition. It is an unnatural assembly of objects, fantastically illumi-nated in broken masses; seemingly contrived to dazzle the eyes and divert the imagination of the vulgar—Here a wooden lion, there a stone statue; in one place, a range of things like coffee-house boxes, covered a-top; in another, a parcel of ale-house benches; in a third, a puppet-shew

3. French for "little master," but implying an excessive regard for dress. Petite maîtres, or beaux, were commonly of the upper class, but were often aped by their inferiors, as here.
4. An allusion to the graveyard scene in *Hamlet* (V. i. 152–53), where Hamlet uses these words to note the crowded burial ground and the equality of people in death.
5. A famous public garden devoted to entertain-ments, located in Chelsea. It was open from 1742 to 1803.
6. Another "pleasure-garden," this one located near Vauxhall bridge, and more properly named Spring Gardens. It operated from 1661 to 1859.

representation of a tin cascade; in a fourth, a gloomy cave of a circular form, like a sepulchral vault half lighted; in a fifth, a scanty slip of grass-plat, that would not afford pasture sufficient for an ass's colt. The walks, which nature seems to have intended for solitude, shade, and silence, are filled with crowds of noisy people, sucking up the nocturnal rheums of an aguish climate;[7] and through these gay scenes, a few lamps glimmer like so many farthing candles.

When I see a number of well-dressed people, of both sexes, sitting on the covered benches, exposed to the eyes of the mob; and, which is worse, to the cold, raw, night-air, devouring sliced beef, and swilling port, and punch, and cyder, I can't help compassionating their temerity, while I despise their want of taste and decorum; but, when they course along those damp and gloomy walks, or crowd together upon the wet gravel, without any other cover than the cope of Heaven, listening to a song, which one half of them cannot possibly hear, how can I help supposing they are actually possessed by a spirit, more absurd and pernicious than any thing we meet with in the precincts of Bedlam?[8] In all probability, the proprietors of this, and other public gardens of inferior note, in the skirts of the metropolis, are, in some shape, connected with the faculty of physic, and the company of undertakers; for, considering that eagerness in the pursuit of what is called pleasure, which now predominates through every rank and denomination of life, I am persuaded, that more gouts, rheumatisms, catarrhs, and consumptions are caught in these nocturnal pastimes, *sub dio,*[9] than from all the risques and accidents to which a life of toil and danger is exposed.

These, and other observations, which I have made in this excursion, will shorten my stay at London, and send me back with a double relish to my solitude and mountains; but I shall return by a different route from that which brought me to town. I have seen some old friends, who constantly resided in this virtuous metropolis, but they are so changed in manners and disposition, that we hardly know or care for one another —In our journey from Bath, my sister Tabby provoked me into a transport of passion; during which, like a man who has drank himself pot-valiant, I talked to her in such a stile of authority and resolution, as produced a most blessed effect. She and her dog have been remarkably quiet and orderly, ever since this expostulation. How long this agreeable calm will last, Heaven above knows—I flatter myself, the exercise of travelling has been of service to my health; a circumstance, which encourages me to proceed in my projected expedition to the North. But I must, in the mean time, for the benefit and amusement of my pupils,

86 • *Humphry Clinker*

explore the depths of this chaos; this mishapen and monstrous capital, without head or tail, members or proportion.

Thomas was so insolent to my sister on the road, that I was obliged to turn him off abruptly, betwixt Chippenham and Marlborough, where our coach was overturned. The fellow was always sullen and selfish; but, if he should return to the country, you may give him a character for honesty and sobriety; and, provided he behaves with proper respect to the family, let him have a couple of guineas in the name of

yours always,

London, May 29. MATT. BRAMBLE.

To Miss LÆTITIA WILLIS, at Gloucester.

MY DEAR LETTY,

Inexpressible was the pleasure I received from yours of the 25th, which was last night put into my hands by Mrs. Brentwood, the milliner, from Gloucester——I rejoice to hear that my worthy governess is in good health, and, still more, that she no longer retains any displeasure towards her poor Liddy. I am sorry you have lost the society of the agreeable miss Vaughan; but, I hope, you won't have cause much longer to regret the departure of your school companions, as I make no doubt but your parents will, in a little time, bring you into the world, where you are so well qualified to make a distinguished figure. When that is the case, I flatter myself you and I shall meet again, and be happy together; and even improve the friendship which we contracted in our tender years ——This at least I can promise——It shall not be for the want of my utmost endeavours, if our intimacy does not continue for life.

About five days ago we arrived in London, after an easy journey from Bath; during which, however, we were overturned, and met with some other little incidents, which had like to have occasioned a misunderstanding betwixt my uncle and aunt; but now, thank God, they are happily reconciled: we live in harmony together, and every day make parties to see the wonders of this vast metropolis, which, however, I cannot pretend to describe; for I have not as yet seen one hundredth part of its curiosities, and I am quite in a maze of admiration.

The cities of London and Westminster are spread out into an incredible extent. The streets, squares, rows, lanes, and alleys, are innumerable. Palaces, public buildings, and churches, rise in every quarter; and, among these last, St. Paul's appears with the most astonishing preeminence. They say it is not so large as St. Peter's at Rome; but, for my own part, I can have no idea of any earthly temple more grand and magnificent.

But even these superb objects are not so striking as the crowds of people that swarm in the streets. I at first imagined, that some great assembly was just dismissed, and wanted to stand aside till the multitude should pass; but this human tide continues to flow, without interruption or abatement, from morn till night. Then there is such an infinity of gay equipages, coaches, chariots, chaises, and other carriages, continually rolling and shifting before your eyes, that one's head grows giddy looking at them; and the imagination is quite confounded with splendour and variety. Nor is the prospect by water less grand and astonishing than that by land: you see three stupendous bridges, [1] joining the opposite banks of a broad, deep, and rapid river; so vast, so stately, so elegant, that they seem to be the work of the giants: betwixt them, the whole surface of the Thames is covered with small vessels, barges, boats, and wherries, passing to and fro; and below the three bridges, such a prodigious forest of masts, for miles together, that you would think all the ships in the universe were here assembled. All that you read of wealth and grandeur, in the Arabian Night's Entertainment, and the Persian Tales, [2] concerning Bagdad, Diarbekir, Damascus, Ispahan, and Samarkand, is here realized.

Ranelagh looks like the inchanted palace of a genie, adorned with the most exquisite performances of painting, carving, and gilding, enlightened with a thousand golden lamps, that emulate the noon-day sun; crowded with the great, the rich, the gay, the happy, and the fair; glittering with cloth of gold and silver, lace, embroidery, and precious stones. While these exulting sons and daughters of felicity tread this round of pleasure, or regale in different parties, and separate lodges, with fine imperial tea and other delicious refreshments, their ears are entertained with the most ravishing delights of musick, both instrumental and vocal. There I heard the famous Tenducci, [3] a thing from Italy—It looks for all the world like a man, though they say it is not. The voice, to be sure, is neither man's nor woman's; but it is more melodious than either; and it warbled so divinely, that, while I listened, I really thought myself in paradise.

At nine o'clock, in a charming moonlight evening, we embarked at Ranelagh for Vauxhall, in a wherry, so light and slender, that we looked like so many fairies sailing in a nut-shell. My uncle, being apprehensive of catching cold upon the water, went round in the coach, and my aunt would have accompanied him, but he would not suffer me to go by water if she went by land; and therefore she favoured us with her company, as she perceived I had a curiosity to make this agreeable voyage——After all, the vessel was sufficiently loaded; for, besides the waterman, there

1. London, Westminster, and Blackfriars Bridges.
2. A translation of Petis de la Croix's *Contes Persanes* appeared in 1709 and was often reprinted.

3. Giusto Ferdinando Tenducci (1736?–1800) was a *castrato* whose singing was very popular. He was Italian, but he spent many years in England.

was my brother Jery, and a friend of his, one Mr. Barton, a country
gentleman, of a good fortune, who had dined at our house—The pleasure
of this little excursion was, however, damped, by my being sadly frighted
at our landing; where there was a terrible confusion of wherries, and a
crowd of people bawling, and swearing, and quarrelling: nay, a parcel of
ugly-looking fellows came running into the water, and laid hold on our
boat with great violence, to pull it a-shore; nor would they quit their hold
till my brother struck one of them over the head with his cane. But this
flutter was fully recompensed by the pleasures of Vauxhall; which I no
sooner entered, than I was dazzled and confounded with the variety of
beauties that rushed all at once upon my eye. Image to yourself, my dear
Letty, a spacious garden, part laid out in delightful walks, bounded with
high hedges and trees, and paved with gravel; part exhibiting a wonderful assemblage of the most picturesque and striking objects, pavilions,
lodges, groves, grottoes, lawns, temples, and cascades; porticoes,
colonades, and rotundos; adorned with pillars, statues, and painting: the
whole illuminated with an infinate number of lamps, disposed in different
figures of suns, stars, and constellations; the place crowded with the
gayest company, ranging through those blissful shades, or supping in
different lodges on cold collations, enlivened with mirth, freedom, and
good-humour, and animated by an excellent band of musick. Among the
vocal performers I had the happiness to hear the celebrated Mrs.——,[4]
whose voice was so loud and so shrill, that it made my head ake through
excess of pleasure.

In about half an hour after we arrived we were joined by my uncle, who
did not seem to relish the place. People of experience and infirmity, my
dear Letty, see with very different eyes from those that such as you and I
make use of—Our evening's entertainment was interrupted by an
unlucky accident. In one of the remotest walks we were surprised with a
sudden shower, that set the whole company a-running, and drove us in
heaps, one upon another, into the rotunda; where my uncle, finding
himself wet, began to be very peevish and urgent to be gone. My brother
went to look for the coach, and found it with much difficulty; but as it
could not hold us all, Mr. Barton stayed behind. It was some time before
the carriage could be brought up to the gate, in the confusion, notwithstanding the utmost endeavours of our new footman, Humphry Clinker,
who lost his scratch periwig,[5] and got a broken head in the scuffle. The
moment we were seated, my aunt pulled off my uncle's shoes, and
carefully wrapped his poor feet in her capuchin;[6] then she gave him a

4. It has been suggested that this blank should be
filled with the name of Kitty Clive (1711–85), a
popular singer and actress of the time, but not
enough information is present in the text to be
sure.
5. A short wig, often the color of the hair of the
person who wore it. It would have been appropriate for Humphry, a servant, to wear such an
unprepossessing wig.
6. The cloak with a hood that went by this name
was originally of French design and took its name
from the monks whose habit it resembled. It was
popular in the early 1750's, but was out of fashion,
as are most of Tabitha's clothes, by the later

mouth-full of cordial, which she always keeps in her pocket, and his clothes were shifted as soon as we arrived at lodgings; so that, blessed be God, he escaped a severe cold, of which he was in great terror.

As for Mr. Barton, I must tell you in confidence, he was a little particular;[7] but, perhaps, I mistake his complaisance; and I wish I may, for his sake—You know the condition of my poor heart; which, in spite of hard usage—And yet I ought not to complain: nor will I, till farther information.

Besides Ranelagh and Vauxhall, I have been at Mrs. Cornelys'[8] assembly, which, for the rooms, the company, the dresses, and decorations, surpasses all description; but as I have no great turn for card-playing, I have not yet entered thoroughly into the spirit of the place: indeed I am still such a country hoyden, that I could hardly find patience to be put in a condition to appear, yet I was not above six hours under the hands of the hair-dresser, who stuffed my head with as much black wool as would have made a quilted petticoat;[9] and, after all, it was the smallest head in the assembly, except my aunt's—She, to be sure, was so particular with her rumpt[1] gown and petticoat, her scanty curls, her lappet-head, deep triple ruffles, and high stays, that every body looked at her with surprise: some whispered, and some tittered; and lady Griskin, by whom we were introduced, flatly told her, she was twenty good years behind the fashion.

Lady Griskin is a person of fashion, to whom we have the honour to be related. She keeps a small rout[2] at her own house, never exceeding ten or a dozen card-tables, but these are frequented by the best company in town—She has been so obliging as to introduce my aunt and me to some of her particular friends of quality, who treat us with the most familiar good-humour: we have once dined with her, and she takes the trouble to direct us in all our motions. I am so happy as to have gained her good-will to such a degree, that she sometimes adjusts my cap with her own hands; and she has given me a kind invitation to stay with her all the winter. This, however, has been cruelly declined by my uncle, who seems to be (I know not how) prejudiced against the good lady; for, whenever my aunt happens to speak in her commendation, I observe that he makes wry faces, though he says nothing.——Perhaps, indeed, these grimaces may be the effect of pain arising from the gout and rheumatism, with which he

1760's, when the story is set.

7. Being "particular," in the usage of the period, is to bestow marked attentions on a person, so to be a little particular would be to be warmer or more personal in the attentions than Lydia wants.

8. Theresa Cornelys (1723–97), born Therese Imer, promoted subscription assemblies and masquerades at Carlisle House in Soho Square during the 1760's.

9. The preparation of the hair for dress occasions during the period consisted of stuffing the coiffure with additional hair, often human, in order to make the hairpiece larger. Styles in hair dressing changed quickly, and Lydia is willing only grudgingly to conform with the extravagant style.

1. Having a bustle or false rump. "Particular" in Lydia's sense here means individualized to the point of being eccentric or excessively noticeable.

2. An evening assembly, from the French *raout*. It could be a dance, a card party, a masquerade, or simply a gathering for conversation.

is sadly distressed—To me, however, he is always good-natured and generous, even beyond my wish. Since we came hither, he has made me a present of a suit of clothes, with trimmings and laces, which cost more money than I shall mention; and Jery, at his desire, has given me my mother's diamond drops, which are ordered to be set a-new; so that it won't be his fault if I do not glitter among the stars of the fourth or fifth magnitude. I wish my weak head may not grow giddy in the midst of all this gallantry and dissipation; though, as yet, I can safely declare, I could gladly give up all these tumultuous pleasures, for country solitude, and a happy retreat with those we love; among whom, my dear Willis will always possess the first place in the breast of her

ever affectionate,

London, May 31. LYDIA MELFORD.

To Sir WATKIN PHILLIPS, of Jesus college, Oxon.

DEAR PHILLIPS,

I send you this letter, franked by our old friend Barton; who is as much altered as it was possible for a man of his kidney to be—Instead of the careless, indolent sloven we knew at Oxford, I found him a busy talkative politician; a petit-maître in his dress, and a ceremonious courtier in his manners. He has not gall enough in his constitution to be enflamed with the rancour of party, so as to deal in scurrilous invectives; but, since he obtained a place, he is become a warm partizan of the ministry,[3] and sees every thing through such an exaggerating medium, as to me, who am happily of no party, is altogether incomprehensible—Without all doubt, the fumes of faction not only disturb the faculty of reason, but also pervert the organs of sense; and I would lay a hundred guineas to ten, that if Barton on one side, and the most conscientious patriot in the opposition on the other, were to draw, upon honour, the picture of the k——or m——,[4] you and I, who are still uninfected, and unbiassed, would find both painters equally distant from the truth. One thing, however, must be allowed for the honour of Barton, he never breaks out into illiberal abuse, far less endeavours, by infamous calumnies, to blast the moral character of any individual on the other side.

Ever since we came hither, he has been remarkably assiduous in his attention to our family; an attention, which, in a man of his indolence and avocations, I should have thought altogether odd, and even unnatural, had not I perceived that my sister Liddy has made some impression upon his heart. I can't say that I have any objection to his trying his fortune in this pursuit: if an opulent estate and a great stock of good-nature are

3. Probably the ministry of the Marquis of Rockingham, who was prime minister in 1765–66.　　4. King or minister.

sufficient qualifications in a husband, to render the marriage-state happy for life, she may be happy with Barton; but, I imagine, there is something else required to engage and secure the affection of a woman of sense and delicacy: something which nature has denied our friend—Liddy seems to be of the same opinion. When he addresses himself to her in discourse, she seems to listen with reluctance, and industriously avoids all particular communication; but in proportion to her coyness, our aunt is coming. Mrs. Tabitha goes more than half way to meet his advances; she mistakes, or affects to mistake, the meaning of his courtesy, which is rather formal and fulsome; she returns his compliments with hyperbolical interest, she persecutes him with her civilities at table, she appeals to him for ever in conversation, she sighs, and flirts, and ogles, and by her hideous affectation and impertinence, drives the poor courtier to the very extremity of his complaisance: in short, she seems to have undertaken the siege of Barton's heart, and carries on her approaches in such a desperate manner, that I don't know whether he will not be obliged to capitulate. In the mean time, his aversion to this inamorata struggling with his acquired affability, and his natural fear of giving offence, throws him into a kind of distress which is extremely ridiculous.

Two days ago, he persuaded my uncle and me to accompany him to St. James's,[5] where he undertook to make us acquainted with the persons of all the great men in the kingdom; and, indeed, there was a great assemblage of distinguished characters, for it was a high festival at court. Our conductor performed his promise with great punctuality. He pointed out almost every individual of both sexes, and generally introduced them to our notice, with a flourish of panegyrick——Seeing the king approach, "There comes (said he) the most amiable fovereign that ever swayed the sceptre of England; the *deliciæ humani generis*;[6] Augustus, in patronizing merit; Titus Vespasian in generosity; Trajan in beneficence; and Marcus Aurelius, in philosophy." "A very honest kindhearted gentleman (added my uncle); he's too good for the times. A king of England should have a spice of the devil in his composition." Barton, then turning to the duke of C—,[7] proceeded,—"You know the duke; that illustrious hero, who trod rebellion under his feet, and secured us in possession of every thing we ought to hold dear, as Englishmen and Christians. Mark what an eye, how penetrating, yet pacific! what dignity in his mein! what humanity in his aspect——Even malice must own, that he is one of the greatest officers in Christendom." "I think he be (said Mr.

5. Saint James's Palace was the royal residence and the place where royal audiences were held.

6. The delight of mankind, originally said of Titus by the classical historian Suetonius. The following classical figures were noted for the qualities ascribed to them in the text.

7. William Augustus, Duke of Cumberland, was the hero of the battle of Culloden in 1746, when the uprising in support of the Jacobite pretender to the throne, Prince Charles Edward, was defeated. Cumberland was given the nickname of "the Butcher" by the Scots for his ruthless suppressions after the victory. He was the third son of King George II and the younger brother of the reigning monarch, George III.

Bramble); but who are these young gentlemen that stand beside him?"
"Those! (cried our friend) those are his royal nephews; the princes of the
blood. Sweet young princes! the sacred pledges of the Protestant line; so
spirited, so sensible, so princely—" "Yes; very sensible! very spirited!
(said my uncle, interrupting him) but see the queen! ha, there's the
queen!——There's the queen! let me see—Let me see——Where are
my glasses? ha! there's meaning in that eye——There's sentiment
—There's expression—Well, Mr. Barton, what figure do you call next?"
The next person he pointed out, was the favourite *yearl*;[8] who stood
solitary by one of the windows—"Behold yon northern star, (said he)
Shorn of his beams——"[9] "What! the Caledonian luminary, that lately
blazed so bright in our hemisphere! methinks, at present, it glimmers
through a fog; like Saturn without his ring, bleak, and dim, and distant
——Ha, there's the other great phœnomenon, the grand pensionary,[1]
that weather-cock of partiotism that veers about in every point of the
political compass, and still feels the wind of popularity in his tail. He too,
like a portentous comet, has risen again above the court-horizon; but how
long he will continue to ascend, it is not easy to foretel, considering his
great eccentricity—Who are those two satellites[2] that attend his motions?" When Barton told him their names, "To their characters (said
Mr. Bramble) I am no stranger. One of them, without a drop of red blood
in his veins, has a cold intoxicating vapour in his head; and rancour
enough in his heart to inoculate and affect a whole nation. The other is (I
hear) intended for a share in the ad——n,[3] and the pensionary vouches
for his being duly qualified—The only instance I ever heard of his
sagacity, was his deserting his former patron, when he found him
declining in power, and in disgrace with the people. Without principle,
talent, or intelligence, he is ungracious as a hog, greedy as a vulture, and
thievish as a jackdaw; but, it must be owned, he is no hypocrite. He
pretends to no virtue, and takes no pains to disguise his character—His
ministry will be attended with one advantage, no man will be disappointed by his breach of promise, as no mortal ever trusted to his word. I
wonder how lord——first discovered this happy genius, and for what
purpose lord——has now adopted him: but one would think, that as
amber has a power to attract dirt, and straws, and chaff, a minister is
endued with the same kind of faculty, to *lick up every knave and*

8. The third Earl of Bute, John Stuart (1713–99)
was prime minister in 1762–63. He was widely
believed to be prejudiced in favor of fellow Scots,
and apparently employed Smollett as writer and
editor of *The Briton*. Caledonian, just below,
means Scot.
9. From Milton's *Paradise Lost* I. 596, where the
line compares Satan's diminished glory to the sun
shining through the mist.
1. Probably William Pitt, who was given an annual

pension of £3,000 when he left office, but who later
returned to power.
2. John Sekora (see Bibliography) has convinc-
ingly identified the two satellites as John Wilkes
(1727–97) and Earl Temple, Richard Grenville
Temple (1711–79). Wilkes was the editor and
main writer of *The North Briton*, a newspaper
which opposed Smollett's *The Briton*. Both were
political allies of Pitt.
3. Administration.

blockhead in his way———"[4] His elogium was interrupted by the arrival of
the old duke of N———;[5] who, squeezing into the circle with a busy face of
importance, thrust his head into every countenance, as if he had been in
search of somebody, to whom he wanted to impart something of great
consequence—My uncle, who had been formerly known to him, bowed
as he passed; and the duke, seeing himself saluted so respectfully by a
well-dressed person, was not slow in returning the courtesy—He even
came up, and, taking him cordially by the hand, "My dear friend, Mr. A
———,[6] (said he) I am rejoiced to see you—How long have you been come
from abroad?—How did you leave our good friends, the Dutch? The king
of Prussia don't think of another war, ah?———He's a great king! a great
conqueror! a very great conqueror! Your Alexanders and Hannibals were
nothing at all to him, sir———Corporals! drummers! dross! mere trash
———Damned trash, heh?—" His grace being by this time out of breath,
my uncle took the opportunity to tell him he had not been out of
England, that his name was Bramble, and that he had the honour to sit in
the last parliament but one of the late king, as representative for the
borough of Dymkymraig. "Odso! (cried the duke) I remember you
perfectly well, my dear Mr. Bramble———You was always a good and
loyal subject———a staunch friend to administration———I made your
brother an Irish bishop—" "Pardon me, my lord (said the 'squire) I once
had a brother, but he was a captain in the army—" "Ha! (said his grace)
he was so—He was, indeed! But who was the bishop then? Bishop
Blackberry———Sure it was bishop Blackberry—Perhaps some relation of
yours—" "Very likely, my lord (replied my uncle); the Blackberry is the
fruit of the Bramble—But, I believe, the bishop is not a berry of our bush
—" "No more he is—No more he is, ha, ha, ha! (exclaimed the duke)
there you gave me a scratch, good Mr. Bramble, ha, ha, ha!—Well, I shall
be glad to see you at Lincoln's-inn-fields[7] —You know the way
———Times are altered. Though I have lost the power, I retain the
inclination—Your very humble servant, good Mr. Blackberry—" So
saying, he shoved to another corner of the room. "What a fine old
gentleman! (cried Mr. Barton) what spirits! what a memory!—He never
forgets an old friend." "He does me too much honour, (observed our
'squire) to rank me among the number—Whilst I sat in parliament, I
never voted with the ministry but three times, when my conscience told
me they were in the right: however, if he still keeps levee, I will carry my
nephew thither, that he may see, and learn to avoid the scene; for, I think,
an English gentleman never appears to such disadvantage, as at the levee
of a minister—Of his grace I shall say nothing at present, but that for

4. Slightly misquoted from Alexander Pope's *The Dunciad* III. 296, where the lines describe the slow progress of Dulness.
5. The Duke of Newcastle, Thomas Pelham-Holles (1693–1768), a prominent politician, eccentric,
and dispenser of ecclesiastical patronage.
6. Identified by John Sekora as John Almon (1707–1805).
7. Apparently the duke has his home in this area of London.

thirty years he was the constant and common butt of ridicule and execration. He was generally laughed at as an ape in politics, whose office and influence served only to render his folly the more notorious; and the opposition cursed him, as the indefatigable drudge of a first-mover,[8] who was justly stiled and stigmatized as the father of corruption:[9] but this ridiculous ape, this venal drudge, no sooner lost the places he was so ill qualified to fill, and unfurled the banners of faction, than he was metamorphosed into a pattern of public virtue; the very people who reviled him before, now extolled him to the skies, as a wise, experienced statesman, chief pillar of the Protestant succession, and corner stone of English liberty. I should be glad to know how Mr. Barton reconciles these contradictions, without obliging us to resign all title to the privilege of common sense." "My dear sir, (answered Barton) I don't pretend to justify the extravagations of the multitude; who, I suppose, were as wild in their former censure, as in their present praise: but I shall be very glad to attend you on Thursday next to his grace's levee; where, I'm afraid, we shall not be crowded with company; for, you know, there's a wide difference between his present office of president of the council, and his former post of first lord commissioner of the treasury."

This communicative friend having announced all the remarkable characters of both sexes, that appeared at court, we resolved to adjourn, and retired. At the foot of the stair-case, there was a crowd of laqueys and chairmen, and in the midst of them stood Humphry Clinker, exalted upon a stool, with his hat in one hand, and a paper in the other, in the act of holding forth to the people—Before we could inquire into the meaning of this exhibition, he perceived his master, thrust the paper into his pocket, descended from his elevation, bolted through the crowd, and brought up the carriage to the gate.

My uncle said nothing till we were seated, when, after having looked at me earnestly for some time, he burst out a-laughing, and asked if I knew upon what subject Clinker was holding forth to the mob——"If (said he) the fellow is turned mountebank, I must turn him out of my service, otherwise he'll make Merry Andrews of us all—" I observed, that, in all probability, he had studied medicine under his master, who was a farrier.

At dinner, the 'squire asked him, if he had ever practised physic? "Yes, an please your honour, (said he) among brute beasts; but I never meddle with rational creatures." "I know not whether you rank in that class the audience you was harranguing in the court at St. James's, but I should be glad to know what kind of powders you was distributing; and whether you had a good sale—" "Sale, sir! (cried Clinker) I hope I shall never be base enough to sell for gold and silver, what freely comes of God's grace. I

8. Sir Robert Walpole (1676–1745) virtually invented the post of prime minister, which he filled for over twenty years between 1715 and 1742. The Duke of Newcastle served as secretary of state under him from 1724 to 1742.
9. Walpole was notoriously venal and supposedly coined the political aphorism that "every man has his price."

distributed nothing, an like your honour, but a word of advice to my fellows in servitude and sin." "Advice! concerning what?" "Concerning profane swearing, an please your honour; so horrid and shocking, that it made my hair stand on end." "Nay, if thou can'st cure them of that disease, I shall think thee a wonderful doctor indeed—" "Why not cure them, my good master? the hearts of those poor people are not so stubborn as your honour seems to think——Make them first sensible that you have nothing in view but their good, then they will listen with patience, and easily be convinced of the sin and folly of a practice that affords neither profit nor pleasure—" At this remark, our uncle changed colour, and looked round the company, conscious that his *own withers were not altogether unwrung.* [1] "But, Clinker, (said he) if you should have eloquence enough to persuade the vulgar, to resign those tropes and figures of rhetoric, there will be little or nothing left to distinguish their conversation from that of their betters." "But then your honour knows, their conversation will be void of offence; and, at the day of judgment, there will be no distinction of persons."

Humphry going down stairs to fetch up a bottle of wine, my uncle congratulated his sister upon having such a reformer in the family; when Mrs. Tabitha declared, he was a sober civilized fellow; very respectful, and very industrious; and, she believed, a good Christian into the bargain. One would think, Clinker must really have some very extraordinary talent, to ingratiate himself in this manner with a virago of her character, so fortified against him with prejudice and resentment; but the truth is, since the adventure of Salt-hill, Mrs. Tabby seems to be entirely changed. She has left off scolding the servants, an exercise which was grown habitual, and even seemed necessary to her constitution; and is become so indifferent to Chowder, as to part with him in a present to lady Griskin, who proposes to bring the breed of him into fashion. Her ladyship is the widow of sir Timothy Griskin, a distant relation of our family. She enjoys a jointure of five hundred pounds a-year, and makes shift to spend three times that sum. Her character before marriage was a little equivocal; but at present she lives in the *bon ton*, keeps card-tables, gives private suppers to select friends, and is visited by persons of the first fashion—She has been remarkably civil to us all, and cultivates my uncle with the most particular regard; but the more she strokes him, the more his bristles seem to rise—To her compliments he makes very laconic and dry returns—T'other day, she sent us a pottle of fine strawberries, which he did not receive without signs of disgust, muttering from the Æneid, *timeo Danaos et Dona ferentes.* [2] She has twice called for Liddy, of a forenoon, to take an airing in the coach; but Mrs. Tabby was always so

1. These words are adapted from *Hamlet* III. ii. 253, where Hamlet proclaims his innocence, while Jery notes Matt's lack of innocence.

2. "I fear the Greeks, even bearing gifts"; from Virgil's *Aeneid* II. 49.

alert, (I suppose by his direction) that she never could have the niece without her aunt's company—I have endeavoured to sound Square-toes on this subject; but he carefully avoids all explanation.

I have now, dear Phillips, filled a whole sheet; and if you have read it to an end, I dare say, you are as tired as

Your humble servant,

London, June 2, J. MELFORD.

To Dr. LEWIS.

Yes. Doctor, I have seen the British Museum; which is a noble collection, and even stupendous, if we consider it was made by a private man, a physician,[3] who was obliged to make his own fortune at the same time: but great as the collection is, it would appear more striking if it was arranged in one spacious saloon, instead of being divided into different apartments, which it does not entirely fill—I could wish the series of medals was connected, and the whole of the animal, vegetable, and mineral kingdoms completed, by adding to each, at the public expence, those articles that are wanting. It would likewise be a great improvement, with respect to the library, if the deficiencies were made up, by purchasing all the books of character that are not to be found already in the collection—They might be classed in centuries, according to the dates of their publication, and catalogues printed of them and the manuscripts, for the information of those that want to consult, or compile from such authorities. I could also wish, for the honour of the nation, that there was a complete apparatus for a course of mathematics, mechanics, and experimental philosophy; and a good salary settled upon an able professor, who should give regular lectures on these subjects.

But this is all idle speculation, which will never be reduced to practice —Considering the temper of the times, it is a wonder to see any institution whatsoever established, for the benefit of the public. The spirit of party is risen to a kind of phrenzy, unknown to former ages, or rather degenerated to a total extinction of honesty and candour—You know I have observed, for some time, that the public papers are become the infamous vehicles of the most cruel and perfidious defamation: every rancorous knave——every desperate incendiary, that can afford to spend half a crown or three shillings, may skulk behind the press of a newsmonger, and have a stab at the first character in the kingdom, without running the least hazard of detection or punishment.

3. Sir Hans Sloane (1660–1753) was a physician, a naturalist, and a collector. After his death, Parliament authorized the purchase of his collection, which was opened to the public in 1759. Sloane's collection of books formed the nucleus of what is now the British Library, and the other collections, described below, started the British Museum.

I have made acquaintance with a Mr. Barton, whom Jery knew at Oxford; a good sort of a man, though most ridiculously warped in his political principles; but his partiality is the less offensive, as it never appears in the stile of scurrility and abuse. He is a member of parliament, and a retainer to the court; and his whole conversation turns upon the virtues and perfections of the ministers, who are his patrons. T'other day, when he was bedaubing one of those worthies, with the most fulsome praise, I told him I had seen the same nobleman characterised very differently, in one of the daily-papers; indeed, so stigmatized, that if one half of what was said of him was true, he must be not only unfit to rule, but even unfit to live: that those impeachments had been repeated again and again, with the addition of fresh matter; and that as he had taken no steps towards his own vindication, I began to think there was some foundation for the charge. "And pray, sir, (said Mr. Barton) what steps would you have him take?—Suppose he should prosecute the publisher, who screens the anonymous accuser, and bring him to the pillory for a libel; this is so far from being counted a punishment, *in terrorem*, that it will probably make his fortune. The multitude immediately take him into their protection, as a martyr to the cause of defamation, which they have always espoused—They pay his fine, they contribute to the increase of his stock, his shop is crowded with customers, and the sale of his paper rises in proportion to the scandal it contains. All this time the prosecutor is inveighed against as a tyrant and oppressor, for having chosen to proceed by the way of information, which is deemed a grievance; but if he lays an action for damages, he must prove the damage, and I leave you to judge, whether a gentleman's character may not be brought into contempt, and all his views in life blasted by calumny, without his being able to specify the particulars of the damage he has sustained."

"This spirit of defamation is a kind of heresy, that thrives under persecution. *The liberty of the press* is a term of great efficacy; and, like that of *the Protestant religion*, has often served the purposes of sedition —A minister, therefore, must arm himself with patience, and bear those attacks without repining—Whatever mischief they may do in other respects, they certainly contribute, in one particular, to the advantage of government; for those defamatory articles have multiplied papers in such a manner, and augmented their sale to such a degree, that the duty upon stamps and advertisements has made a very considerable addition to the revenue." Certain it is, a gentleman's honour is a very delicate subject to be handled by a jury, composed of men, who cannot be supposed remarkable either for sentiment or impartiality—In such a case, indeed, the defendant is tried, not only by his peers, but also by his party; and I really think, that of all patriots, he is the most resolute who exposes himself to such detraction, for the sake of his country—If, from the ignorance or partiality of juries, a gentleman can have no redress from law, for being defamed in a pamphlet or news-paper, I know but one other method of proceeding against the publisher, which is attended with some risque, but has been practised successfully, more than once, in my remembrance—A regiment of horse was represented, in one of the news-papers,[4] as having misbehaved at Dettingen; a captain of that regiment broke the publisher's bones, telling him, at the same time, if he went to law, he should certainly have the like salutation from every officer of the corps. Governor——took the same satisfaction on the ribs of an author, who traduced him by name in a periodical paper—I know a low fellow of the same class, who, being turned out of Venice for his impudence and scurrility, retired to Lugano, a town of the Grisons,[5] (a free people, God wot) where he found a printing press, from whence he squirted his filth at some respectable characters in the republic, which he had been obliged to abandon. Some of these, finding him out of the reach of legal chastisement, employed certain useful instruments, such as may be found in all countries, to give him the bastinado; which, being repeated more than once, effectually stopt the current of his abuse.

As for the liberty of the press, like every other privilege, it must be restrained within certain bounds; for if it is carried to a breach of law, religion, and charity, it becomes one of the greatest evils that ever annoyed the community. If the lowest ruffian may stab your good-name with impunity in England, will you be so uncandid as to exclaim against Italy for the practice of common assassination? To what purpose is our property secured, if our moral character is left defenceless? People thus baited, grow desperate; and the despair of being able to preserve one's character, untainted by such vermin, produces a total neglect of fame; so that one of the chief incitements to the practice of virtue is effectually destroyed.

Mr. Barton's last consideration, respecting the stamp-duty, is equally wise and laudable with another maxim which has been long adopted by our financiers, namely, to connive at drunkenness, riot, and dissipation, because they inhance the receipt of the excise; not reflecting, that in providing this temporary convenience, they are destroying the morals, health, and industry of the people——Notwithstanding my contempt for those who flatter a minister, I think there is something still more despicable in flattering a mob. When I see a man of birth, education, and fortune, put himself on a level with the dregs of the people, mingle with low mechanics, feed with them at the same board, and drink with them in the same cup, flatter their prejudices, harangue in praise of their virtues, expose themselves to the belchings of their beer, the fumes of their tobacco, the grossness of their familiarity, and the impertinence of their

---

4. During the War of the Austrian Succession, at Dettingen in 1743, the Royal Horse Guards (the Blues) were repulsed, though the British ultimately won the battle.
5. There is a slight geographical error here, as Lugano was not part of the canton of the Grisons.

conversation, I cannot help despising him, as a man guilty of the vilest prostitution, in order to effect a purpose equally selfish and illiberal.

I should renounce politics the more willingly, if I could find other topics of conversation discussed with more modesty and candour; but the dæmon of party seems to have usurped every department of life. Even the world of literature and taste is divided into the most virulent factions, which revile, decry, and traduce the works of one another. Yesterday, I went to return an afternoon's visit to a gentleman of my acquaintance, at whose house I found one of the authors of the present age, who has written with some success—As I had read one or two of his performances, which gave me pleasure, I was glad of this opportunity to know his person; but his discourse and deportment destroyed all the impressions which his writings had made in his favour. He took upon him to decide dogmatically upon every subject, without deigning to shew the least cause for his differing from the general opinions of mankind, as if it had been our duty to acquiese in the *ipse dixit* of this new Pythagoras. He rejudged the characters of all the principal authors, who had died within a century of the present time; and, in this revision, paid no sort of regard to the reputation they had acquired—Milton was harsh and prosaic; Dryden, languid and verbose; Butler and Swift, without humour; Congreve, without wit; and Pope destitute of any sort of poetical merit[6]—As for his cotemporaries, he could not bear to hear one of them mentioned with any degree of applause—They were all dunces, pedants, plagiaries, quacks, and impostors; and you could not name a single performance, but what was tame, stupid, and insipid. It must be owned, that this writer had nothing to charge his conscience with, on the side of flattery; for, I understand, he was never known to praise one line that was written, even by those with whom he lived on terms of good-fellowship. This arrogance and presumption, in depreciating authors, for whose reputation the company may be interested, is such an insult upon the understanding, as I could not bear without wincing.

I desired to know his reasons for decrying some works, which had afforded me uncommon pleasure; and, as demonstration did not seem to be his talent, I dissented from his opinion with great freedom. Having been spoiled by the deference and humility of his hearers, he did not bear contradiction with much temper; and the dispute might have grown warm, had it not been interrupted by the entrance of a rival bard, at whose appearance he always quits the place——They are of different cabals, and have been at open war these twenty years——If the other was dogmatical, this genius was declamatory: he did not discourse, but harangue; and his orations were equally tedious and turgid. He too

6. This catalogue includes the most highly reputed writers of the late seventeenth and early eighteenth centuries.

pronounces *ex cathedra* upon the characters of his cotemporaries; and though he scruples not to deal out praise, even lavishly, to the lowest reptile in Grub street who will either flatter him in private, or mount the public rostrum as his panegyrist, he damns all the other writers of the age, with the utmost insolence and rancour—One is a blunderbuss, as being a native of Ireland, another, a half-starved louse of literature, from the banks of the Tweed; a third, an ass, because he enjoys a pension from the government; a fourth, the very angel of dulness; because he succeeded in a species of writing in which this Aristarchus[7] had failed; a fifth, who presumed to make strictures upon one of his performances, he holds as a bug in criticism, whose stench is more offensive than his sting —In short, except himself and his myrmidons, there is not a man of genius or learning in the three kingdoms. As for the success of those, who have written without the pale of this confederacy, he imputes it entirely to want of taste in the public; not considering, that to the approbation of that very tasteless public, he himself owes all the consequence he has in life.

Those originals are not fit for conversation. If they would maintain the advantage they have gained by their writing, they should never appear but upon paper—For my part, I am shocked to find a man have sublime ideas in his head, and nothing but illiberal sentiments in his heart—The human soul will be generally found most defective in the article of candour—I am inclined to think, no mind was ever wholly exempt from envy; which, perhaps, may have been implanted, as an instinct essential to our nature. I am afraid we sometimes palliate this vice, under the specious name of emulation. I have known a person remarkably generous, humane, moderate, and apparently self-denying, who could not hear even a friend commended, without betraying marks of uneasiness; as if that commendation had implied an odious comparison to his prejudice, and every wreath of praise added to the other's character, was a garland plucked from his own temples. This is a malignant species of jealousy, of which I stand acquitted in my own conscience—Whether it is a vice, or an infirmity, I leave you to inquire.

There is another point, which I would much rather see determined; whether the world was always as contemptible, as it appears to me at present?—If the morals of mankind have not contracted an extraordinary degree of depravity, within these thirty years, then must I be infected with the common vice of old men, *difficilis, querulus, laudator temporis acti*;[8] or, which is more probable, the impetuous pursuits and avocations of youth have formerly hindered me from observing those rotten parts of human nature, which now appear so offensively to my observation.

7. A severe critic, from the name of the Greek critic who severely criticized Homer.

8. "Peevish, surly, and always praising the days of his youth": from Horace's *Ars Poetica* ll. 173–74.

We have been at court, and 'change,[9] and every where; and every where we find food for spleen, and subject for ridicule—My new servant, Humphry Clinker, turns out a great original; and Tabby is a changed creature——She has parted with Chowder; and does nothing but smile, like Malvolio in the play[1]——I'll be hanged if she is not acting a part which is not natural to her disposition, for some purpose which I have not yet discovered.

With respect to the characters of mankind, my curiosity is quite satisfied: I have done with the science of men, and must now endeavour to amuse myself with the novelty of things. I am, at present, by a violent effort of the mind, forced from my natural biass; but this power ceasing to act, I shall return to my solitude with redoubled velocity. Every thing I see, and hear, and feel, in this great reservoir of folly, knavery, and sophistication, contributes to inhance the value of a country life, in the sentiments of

yours always,

London, June 2.   MAT. BRAMBLE.

To Mrs. MARY JONES, at Brambleton-hall.

DEAR MARY JONES,

Lady Griskin's botler, Mr. Crumb, having got 'squire Barton to frank me a kiver, I would not neglect to let you know how it is with me, and the rest of the family.

I could not rite by John Thomas, for because he went away in a huff, at a minute's warming. He and Chowder could not agree, and so they fitt upon the road, and Chowder bitt his thumb, and he swore he would do him a mischief, and he spoke saucy to mistress, whereby the 'squire turned him off in gudgeon; and by God's providence we picked up another footman, called Umphry Klinker; a good sole as ever broke bread; which shews that a scalded cat may prove a good mouser, and a hound be staunch, thof he has got narro hare on his buttocks; but the proudest nose may be bro't to the grine-stone, by sickness and misfortunes.

O Molly! what shall I say of London? All the towns that ever I beheld in my born-days, are no more than Welsh barrows and crumlecks[2] to this wonderful sitty! Even Bath itself is but a fillitch, in the naam of God ——One would think there's no end of the streets, but the land's end. Then there's such a power of people, going hurry skurry! Such a racket of

9. The Royal Exchange, commonly contracted as here, was the stock exchange and also a fashionable shopping arcade.
1. In Shakespeare's *Twelfth Night*, the steward Malvolio is duped into smiling incessantly and is thought to be mad.
2. Burial mounds and circles of stones.

coxes![3] Such a noise, and haliballoo! So many strange sites to be seen! O gracious! my poor Welsh brain has been spinning like a top ever since I came hither! And I have seen the Park, and the paleass of Saint Gimses,[4] and the king's and the queen's magisterial pursing, and the sweet young princes, and the hillyfents, and pye-bald ass,[5] and all the rest of the royal family.

Last week I went with mistress to the Tower, to see the crowns and wild beastis; and there was a monstracious lion, with teeth half a quarter long; and a gentleman bid me not go near him, if I wasn't a maid; being as how he would roar, and tear, and play the dickens—Now I had no mind to go near him; for I cannot abide such dangerous honeymils, not I——but, mistress would go; and the beast kept such a roaring and bouncing, that I tho't he would have broke his cage and devoured us all; and the gentleman tittered for sooth; but I'll go to death upon it, I will, that my lady is as good a firchin, as the child unborn; and, therefore, either the gentleman told a fib, or the lion oft to be set in the stocks for bearing false witness again his neighbour; for the commandment sayeth, *Thou shalt not bear false witness again thy neighbour.*

I was afterwards of a party at Sadler's-wells,[6] where I saw such tumbling and dancing upon ropes and wires, that I was frightened, and ready to go into a fit—I tho't it was all inchantment; and, believing myself bewitched, began for to cry——You knows as how the witches in Wales fly upon broom-sticks; but here was flying without any broom-stick, or thing in the varsal world, and firing of pistols in the air, and blowing of trumpets, and swinging, and rolling of wheel-barrows upon a wire, (God bless us!) no thicker than a sewing-thread; that, to be sure, they must deal with the devil!——A fine gentleman, with a pig's-tail, and a golden sord by his side, came to comfit me, and offered for to treat me with a pint of wind; but I would not stay; and so, in going through the dark passage, he began to shew his cloven futt, and went for to be rude: my fellow-sarvant, Umpry Klinker, bid him be sivil, and he gave the young man a dowse in the chops; but, I fackins, Mr. Klinker wa'n't long in his debt——with a good oaken sapling he dusted his doublet, for all his golden cheese-toaster; and, sipping me under his arm, carried me huom, I nose not how, being I was in such a flustration—But, thank God! I'm now vaned from all such vanities; for what are all those rarities and vagaries to the glory that shall be revealed hereafter? O Molly! let not your poor heart be puffed up with vanity.

I had almost forgot to tell you, that I have had my hair cut and pippered, and singed, and bolstered, and buckled, in the newest fashion,

---

3. Coaches.
4. Saint James's Palace.
5. Elephants and a zebra were featured attractions at the menagerie in Saint James's Park.

6. A music hall built by a Mr. Sadler in the London borough of Islington. It featured somewhat less high-toned entertainment than Vauxhall and Ranelagh Gardens.

by a French freezer[7]—*Parley vow Francey*—*Vee madmansell*——I now carries my head higher than arrow[8] private gentlewoman of Vales. Last night, coming huom from the meeting, I was taken by lamp-light for an iminent poulterer's daughter, a great beauty—But as I was saying, this is all vanity and vexation of spirit—The pleasures of London are no better than sower whey and stale cyder, when compared to the joys of the new Gerusalem.

Dear Mary Jones! An please God when I return, I'll bring you a new cap, with a turkey-shell coom, and a pyehouse sermon, that was preached in the Tabernacle;[9] and I pray of all love, you will mind your vriting and your spilling; for, craving your pardon, Molly, it made me suet to disseyffer your last scrabble, which was delivered by the hind at Bath —O, voman! voman! if thou had'st but the least consumption of what pleasure we scullers have, when we can cunster the crabbidst buck off hand, and spell the ethnitch vords without lucking at the primmer. As for Mr. Klinker, he is qualified to be clerk to a parish—But I'll say no more —Remember me to Saul—poor sole! it goes to my hart to think she don't yet know her letters—But all in God's good time—It shall go hard, but I will bring her the A B C in ginger-bread; and that, you nose, will be learning to her taste.

Mistress says, we are going a long gurney to the North; but go where we will, I shall ever be,

Dear Mary Jones,

yours with true infection,

London, June 3.   WIN. JENKINS

To Sir WATKIN PHILLIPS, of Jesus college, Oxon.

DEAR WAT,

I mentioned in my last, my uncle's design of going to the duke of N ——'s[1] levee; which design has been executed accordingly. His grace has been so long accustomed to this kind of homage, that though the place he now fills does not imply the tenth part of the influence, which he exerted in his former office, he has given his friends to understand, that they cannot oblige him in any thing more, than in contributing to support the shadow of that power, which he no longer retains in substance; and therefore he has still public days, on which they appear at his levee.

My uncle and I went thither with Mr. Barton, who, being one of the duke's adherents, undertook to be our introducer—The room was pretty

7. Friseur, or hairdresser.
8. Any.
9. George Whitefield (1714–70), a Methodist evangelist, built a large chapel on Tottenham Court Road in 1756 which was enlarged in 1759. It was popularly known as "the Tabernacle."
1. Newcastle.

well filled with people, in a great variety of dress; but there was no more than one gown and cassock, though I was told his grace had, while he was minister, preferred almost every individual that now filled the bench of bishops in the house of lords; but, in all probability, the gratitude of the clergy is like their charity, which shuns the light—Mr. Barton was immediately accosted by a person, well stricken in years, tall, and raw-boned, with a hook-nose, and an arch leer, that indicated, at least, as much cunning as sagacity. Our conductor saluted him, by the name of captain C——, and afterwards informed us he was a man of shrewd parts, whom the government occasionally employed in secret services—But I have had the history of him more at large, from another quarter——He had been, many years ago, concerned in fraudulent practices, as a merchant, in France; and being convicted of some of them, was sent to the gallies, from whence he was delivered by the interest of the late duke of Ormond, to whom he had recommended himself in letter, as his name-sake and relation—He was in the sequel, employed by our ministry as a spy; and in the war of 1740, traversed all Spain, as well as France, in the disguise of a capuchin, at the extreme hazard of his life, in as much as the court of Madrid had actually got scent of him, and given orders to apprehend him at St. Sebastian's,[2] from whence he had fortunately retired but a few hours before the order arrived. This and other hair-breadth 'scapes he pleaded so effectually as a merit with the English ministry, that they allowed him a comfortable pension, which he now enjoys in his old age—He has still access to all the ministers, and is said to be consulted by them on many subjects, as a man of uncommon understanding and great experience—He is, in fact, a fellow of some parts, and invincible assurance; and, in his discourse, he assumes such an air of self-sufficiency, as may very well impose upon some of the shallow politicians, who now labour at the helm of administration. But, if he is not belied, this is not the only imposture of which he is guilty——They say, he is at bottom not only a Roman-catholic, but really a priest; and while he pretends to disclose to our state-pilots all the springs that move the cabinet of Versailles, he is actually picking up intelligence for the service of the French minister——Be that as it may, captain C——entered into conversation with us in the most familiar manner, and treated the duke's character without any ceremony—"This wise-acre (said he) is still a-bed; and, I think, the best thing he can do, is to sleep on till Christmas; for, when he gets up, he does nothing but expose his own folly.—Since Granville was turned out,[3] there has been no minister in this nation worth the meal that whitened his periwig—They are so ignorant, they scarce know a crab from a cauliflower; and then they are such dunces,

2. San Sebastian is a port in northern Spain, very near the French border.
3. Earl Granville, John Carteret (1690–1763) was

forced to resign his position as secretary of state in 1744.

that there's no making them comprehend the plainest proposition——In the beginning of the war, this poor half-witted creature told me, in a great fright, that thirty thousand French had marched from Acadie to Cape Breton[4]——Where did they find transports? (said I) "Transports! (cried he) I tell you, they marched by land——" By land to the island of Cape Breton? "What! is Cape Breton an island?" Certainly. "Ha! are you sure of that?" When I pointed it out in the map, he examined it earnestly with his spectacles; then, taking me in his arms, "My dear C——! (cried he) you always bring us good news—Egad! I'll go directly, and tell the king that Cape Breton is an island——"

He seemed disposed to entertain us with more anecdotes of this nature, at the expence of his grace, when he was interrupted by the arrival of the Algerine ambassador; a venerable Turk, with a long white beard, attended by his dragoman, or interpreter, and another officer of his household, who had got no stockings to his legs——Captain C——immediately spoke with an air of authority to a servant in waiting, bidding him go and tell the duke to rise, as there was a great deal of company come, and, among others, the ambassador from Algiers—Then, turning to us, "This poor Turk (said he) notwithstanding his grey beard, is a green-horn——He has been several years resident in London, and still is ignorant of our political revolutions. This visit is intended for the prime minister of England; but you'll see how this wise duke will receive it as a mark of attachment to his own person——" Certain it is, the duke seemed eager to acknowledge the compliment——A door opening, he suddenly bolted out, with a shaving-cloth under his chin, his face frothed up to the eyes with soap lather; and, running up to the ambassador, grinned hideous in his face——"My dear Mahomet! (said he) God love your long beard, I hope the dey will make you a horse-tail at the next promotion,[5] ha, ha, ha!——Have but a moment's patience, and I'll send to you in a twinkling——" So saying, he retreated into his den, leaving the Turk in some confusion. After a short pause, however, he said something to his interpreter, the meaning of which I had great curiosity to know, as he turned up his eyes while he spoke, expressing astonishment, mixed with devotion——We were gratified by means of the communicative captain C——, who conversed with the dragoman, as an old acquaintance. Ibrahim, the ambassador, who had mistaken his grace for the minister's fool, was no sooner undeceived by the interpreter, than he exlaimed to this effect——"Holy prophet! I don't wonder that this nation prospers, seeing it is governed by the counsel of ideots; a series of men, whom all good mussulmen revere as the organs of immediate inspiration!" Ibrahim was favoured with a particular audience of short duration; after which the

4. Acadie was the French name for the colony called Acadia in English which was in the area currently known as Nova Scotia. Cape Breton is an island just to the north of it.
5. The tail of a horse was used as an insignia of the rank of pasha in the Turkish army.

Turkish Ambassador introduced to the Duke of N——.

duke conducted him to the door, and then returned to diffuse his gracious looks among the crowd of his worshippers.

As Mr. Barton advanced to present me to his grace, it was my fortune to attract his notice, before I was announced—He forthwith met me more than half way, and, seizing me by the hand, "My dear sir Francis! (cried he) this is so kind—I vow to Gad! I am so obliged—Such attention to a poor broken minister—Well—Pray when does your excellency set sail?—For God's sake have a care of your health, and eat stewed prunes in the passage—Next to your own precious health, pray, my dear excellency, take care of the Five Nations—Our good friends the Five Nations[6] —The Toryrories, the Maccolmacks, the Out-o'the-ways, the Crickets, and the Kickshaws—Let 'em have plenty of blankets, and stinkubus,[7] and wampum; and your excellency won't fail to scour the kettle, and boil the chain, and bury the tree, and plant the hatchet—Ha, ha, ha!" When he had uttered this rhapsody, with his usual precipitation, Mr. Barton gave him to understand, that I was neither Sir Francis, nor St. Francis, but simply Mr. Melford, nephew to Mr. Bramble; who, stepping forward, made his bow at the same time. "Odso! no more it is Sir Francis—(said this wise statesman) Mr. Melford, I'm glad to see you—I sent you an engineer to fortify your dock—Mr. Bramble—your servant, Mr. Bramble —How d'ye, good Mr. Bramble? Your nephew is a pretty young fellow —Faith and troth, a very pretty fellow!—His father is my old friend —How does he hold it? Still troubled with that damned disorder, ha?" "No, my lord, (replied my uncle) all his troubles are over—He has been dead these fifteen years." "Dead! how—Yes, faith! now I remember: he is dead, sure enough—Well, and how—does the young gentleman stand for Haverford West? or—a—what d'ye—My dear Mr. Milfordhaven, I'll do you all the service in my power—I hope I have some credit left——" My uncle then gave him to understand, that I was still a minor; and that we had no intention to trouble him at present, for any favour whatsoever —"I came hither with my nephew (added he) to pay our respects to your grace; and I may venture to say, that his views and mine are at least as disinterested as those of any individual in this assembly." "My dear Mr. Brambleberry! you do me infinite honour—I shall always rejoice to see you and your hopeful nephew, Mr. Milfordhaven—My credit, such as it is, you may command—I wish we had more friends of your kidney—"

Then, turning to captain C——, "Ha, C——! (said he) what news, C ——? How does the world wag? ha!" "The world wags much after the old fashion, my lord (answered the captain): the politicians of London and Westminster have begun again to wag their tongues against your grace; and your short-lived popularity wags like a feather, which the next puff of

6. In 1722, the Tuscarora tribe joined the Five Nations (Seneca, Mohawk, Cayuga, Oneida, and Onondaga) to add themselves to the Iroquois confederation. Newcastle's mangling of the names and his calling Jery "Sir Francis" add to the negative portrait of the noble politician.
7. Bad liquor.

antiministerial calumny will blow away—" "A pack of rascals (cried the duke)—Tories, Jacobites, rebels; one half of them would wag their heels at Tyburn,[8] if they had their deserts—? So saying, he wheeled about; and, going round the levee, spoke to every individual, with the most courteous familiarity; but he scarce ever opened his mouth without making some blunder, in relation to the person or business of the party with whom he conversed; so that he really looked like a comedian, hired to burlesque the character of a minister—At length, a person of a very prepossessing appearance coming in, his grace ran up, and, hugging him in his arms, with the appellation of "My dear Ch——s!" led him forthwith into the inner apartment, or *Sanctum Sanctorum*[9] of this political temple. "That (said captain C——) is my friend C—T——,[1] almost the only man of parts who has any concern in the present administration—Indeed, he would have no concern at all in the matter, if the ministry did not find it absolutely necessary to make use of his talents upon some particular occasions—As for the common business of the nation, it is carried on in a constant routine by the clerks of the different offices, otherwise the wheels of government would be wholly stopt amidst the abrupt succession of ministers, every one more ignorant than his predecessor——I am thinking what a fine hovel we should be in, if all the clerks of the treasury, of the secretaries, the war-office, and the admiralty, should take it in their heads to throw up their places in imitation of the great pensioner—But, to return to C——T——; he certainly knows more than all the ministry and all the opposition, if their heads were laid together, and talks like an angel on a vast variety of subjects—He would really be a great man, if he had any consistency or stability of character—Then, it must be owned, he wants courage, otherwise he would never allow himself to be cowed by the great political bully,[2] for whose understanding he has justly a very great contempt. I have seen him as much afraid of that overbearing Hector, as ever schoolboy was of his pedagogue; and yet this Hector, I shrewdly suspect, is no more than a craven at bottom—Besides this defect, C——has another, which he is at too little pains to hide—There's no faith to be given to his assertions, and no trust to be put in his promises—However, to give the devil his due, he's very good-natured; and even friendly, when close urged in the way of solicitation—As for principle, that's out of the question—In a word, he is a wit and an orator, extremely entertaining, and he shines very often at the expence even of those ministers to whom he is a retainer—This is a mark of great imprudence, by which he has made them all his enemies, whatever face they may put upon the matter;

8. Tyburn hill, in London, was where public executions took place.
9. Literally, "holy of holies," but here the private retreat of Newcastle.
1. Charles Townshend (1725–67) was a notable

politician who was both brilliant and inconsistent. He held various posts in the government during the 1760s.
2. Probably William Pitt (1708–78), first Lord Chatham.

and sooner or later he'll have cause to wish he had been able to keep his own counsel—I have several times cautioned him on this subject; but 'tis all preaching to the desert—His vanity runs away with his discretion—" I could not help thinking the captain himself might have been the better for some hints of the same nature—His panegyric, excluding principle and veracity, puts me in mind of a contest I once over-heard, in the way of altercation, betwixt two apple-women in Spring-garden[3]——One of those viragos having hinted something to the prejudice of the other's moral character, her antagonist, setting her hands in her sides, replied —"Speak out, hussy—I scorn your malice—I own I'm both a whore and a thief; and what more have you to say?—Damn you, what more have you to say? bating that, which all the world knows, I challenge you to say black is the white of my eye—" We did not wait for Mr. T——'s coming forth; but after captain C——had characterised all the originals in waiting, we adjourned to a coffee-house, where we had buttered muffins and tea to breakfast, the said captain still favouring us with his company —Nay, my uncle was so diverted with his anecdotes, that he asked him to dinner, and treated him with a fine turbot, to which he did ample justice —That same evening I spent at the tavern with some friends, one of whom let me into C——'s character, which Mr. Bramble no sooner understood, than he expressed some concern for the connexion he had made, and resolved to disengage himself from it without ceremony.

We are become members of the Society for the Encouragement of the Arts,[4] and have assisted at some of their deliberations, which were conducted with equal spirit and sagacity—My uncle is extremely fond of the institution, which will certainly be productive of great advantages to the public, if, from its democratical form, it does not degenerate into cabal and corruption—You are already acquainted with his aversion to the influence of the multitude, which, he affirms, is incompatible with excellence, and subversive of order—Indeed his detestation of the mob has been heightened by fear, ever since he fainted in the room at Bath; and this apprehension has prevented him from going to the Little Theatre in the Hay-market,[5] and other places of entertainment, to which, however, I have had the honour to attend the ladies.

It grates old Square-Toes to reflect, that it is not in his power to enjoy even the most elegant diversions of the capital, without the participation of the vulgar; for they now thrust themselves into all assemblies, from a ridotto[6] at St. James's, to a hop at Rotherhithe.

---

3. A number of gardens went by this name, and fruit vendors could have been in any of them.
4. The full name is "The Society for the Encouragement of Arts, Manufactures, and Commerce." It was founded in 1754, and later became the Royal Society of Arts.
5. This theater, small by comparison to its neighbor, the Opera House, stood near the current site of the Haymarket Theatre.
6. A fairly formal gathering featuring music and dancing, here in the royal palace or its neighborhood. It is sharply contrasted with the informal dance, or hop, at Rotherhithe, often pronounced "Redriff," an area south of the Thames and inhabited largely by seafarers.

I have lately seen our old acquaintance Dick Ivy, who we imagined had died of dram-drinking; but he is lately emerged from the Fleet,[7] by means of a pamphlet which he wrote and published against the government with some success. The sale of this performance enabled him to appear in clean linen, and he is now going about soliciting subscriptions for his Poems; but his breeches are not yet in the most decent order.

Dick certainly deserves some countenance for his intrepidity and perseverance—It is not in the power of disappointment, nor even of damnation, to drive him to despair—After some unsuccessful essays in the way of poetry, he commenced brandy-merchant, and I believe his whole stock ran out through his own bowels; then he consorted with a milk-woman, who kept a cellar in Petty France: but he could not make his quarters good; he was dislodged and driven up stairs into the kennel by a corporal in the second regiment of footguards—He was afterwards the laureat of Blackfriars,[8] from whence there was a natural transition to the Fleet—As he had formerly miscarried in panegyric, he now turned his thoughts to satire, and really seems to have some talent for abuse. If he can hold out till the meeting of the parliament, and be prepared for another charge, in all probability Dick will mount the pillory, or obtain a pension, in either of which events his fortune will be made——Mean while he has acquired some degree of consideration with the respectable writers of the age; and as I have subscribed for his works, he did me the favour 'tother night to introduce me to a society of those geniuses; but I found them exceedingly formal and reserved—They seemed afraid and jealous of one another, and sat in a state of mutual repulsion, like so many particles of vapour, each surrounded by its own electrified atmosphere. Dick, who has more vivacity than judgment, tried more than once to enliven the conversation; sometimes making an effort at wit, sometimes letting off a pun, and sometimes discharging a conundrum; nay, at length he started a dispute upon the hackneyed comparison betwixt blank verse and rhyme, and the professors opened with great clamour; but, instead of keeping to the subject, they launched out into tedious dissertations on the poetry of the antients; and one of them, who had been a schoolmaster, displayed his whole knowledge of prosody, gleaned from Disputer and Ruddiman.[9] At last, I ventured to say, I did not see how the subject in question could be at all elucidated by the practice of the antients, who certainly had neither blank verse nor rhyme in their poems, which were measured by feet, whereas ours are reckoned by the number of syllables—This remark seemed to give umbrage to the

7. Fleet Street prison, where debtors were often imprisoned.
8. A section of London near the Thames which takes its name from the Dominican monks who had their monastery there from medieval times until the dissolution in the sixteenth century. Petty France, just above, was a section in Westminster and also a street there, both of which took their names from the settlement of French refugees in the area in 1635.
9. Johannes Despauterius (c. 1460–c. 1520) prepared a Latin grammar which was still in use, and Thomas Ruddiman (1674–1757) published *Rudiments of the Latin Tongue* (1714).

pedant, who forthwith involved himself in a cloud of Greek and Latin quotations, which nobody attempted to dispel—A confused hum of insipid observations and comments ensued; and, upon the whole, I never passed a duller evening in my life—Yet, without all doubt, some of them were men of learning, wit, and ingenuity. As they are afraid of making free with one another, they should bring each his butt, or whet-stone, along with him, for the entertainment of the company—My uncle says, he never desires to meet with more than one wit at a time—One wit, like a knuckle of ham in soup, gives a zest and flavour to the dish; but more than one serves only to spoil the pottage——And now I'm afraid I have given you an unconscionable mess, without any flavour at all; for which, I suppose, you will bestow your benedictions upon

your friend,

and servant,

London, June 5. J. MELFORD.

END OF THE FIRST VOLUME.

Volume II

To Dr. LEWIS.

DEAR LEWIS,

Your fable of the monkey and the pig, is what the Italians call *ben trovata:*[1] but I shall not repeat it to my apothecary, who is a proud Scotchman, very thin skinned, and, for aught I know, may have his degree in his pocket—A right Scotchman has always two strings to his bow, and is *in utrumque paratus*[2]—Certain it is, I have not 'scaped a scouring; but, I believe, by means of that scouring, I have 'scaped something worse, perhaps a tedious fit of the gout or rheumatism; for my appetite began to flagg, and I had certain croakings in the bowels, which boded me no good—Nay, I am not yet quite free of these remembrances, which warn me to be gone from this centre of infection——

What temptation can a man of my turn and temperament have, to live in a place where every corner teems with fresh objects of detestation and disgust? What kind of taste and organs must those people have, who really prefer the adulterate enjoyments of the town to the genuine pleasures of a country retreat? Most people, I know, are originally seduced by vanity, ambition, and childish curiosity; which cannot be gratified, but in the *busy haunts of men:*[3] but, in the course of this gratification, their very organs of sense are perverted, and they become habitually lost to every relish of what is genuine and excellent in it's own nature.

Shall I state the difference between my town grievances, and my country comforts? At Brambleton-hall, I have elbow-room within doors, and breathe a clear, elastic, salutary air——I enjoy refreshing sleep, which is never disturbed by horrid noise, nor interrupted, but in a-morning, by the sweet twitter of the martlet at my window—I drink the virgin lymph, pure and crystalline as it gushes from the rock, or the sparkling beveridge, home-brewed from malt of my own making; or I indulge with cyder, which my own orchard affords; or with claret of the best growth, imported for my own use, by a correspondent on whose integrity I can depend; my bread is sweet and nourishing, made from my own wheat, ground in my own mill, and baked in my own oven; my table is, in a great measure, furnished from my own ground; my five-year old mutton, fed on the fragrant herbage of the mountains, that might vie

---

1. This should probably be *ben trovato*, "well hit upon."
2. Prepared for either event, from Virgil's *Aeneid* II. 61.
3. Shakespeare has Benvolio talk "here in the public haunt of men" in *Romeo and Juliet* III. i. 53, and Milton's "L'Allegro," line 119, has the speaker being pleased by "the busy hum of men." It may be that Smollett has Matt conflate the two lines, or it may be an adaptation of either.

with venison in juice and flavour; my delicious veal, fattened with
nothing but the mother's milk, that fills the dish with gravy; my poultry
from the barn-door, that never knew confinement, but when they were at
roost; my rabbits panting from the warren; my game fresh from the
moors; my trout and salmon struggling from the stream; oysters from
their native banks; and herrings, with other sea-fish, I can eat in four
hours after they are taken—My sallads, roots, and pot-herbs, my own
garden yields in plenty and perfection; the produce of the natural soil,
prepared by moderate cultivation. The same soil affords all the different
fruits which England may call her own, so that my desert is every day
fresh-gathered from the tree; my dairy flows with nectarious tides of milk
and cream, from whence we derive abundance of excellent butter, curds,
and cheese; and the refuse fattens my pigs, that are destined for hams and
bacon—I go to bed betimes, and rise with the sun—I make shift to pass
the hours without weariness or regret, and am not destitute of amusements within doors, when the weather will not permit me to go abroad
—I read, and chat, and play at billiards, cards, or back-gammon—Without doors, I superintend my farm, and execute plans of improvement, the
effects of which I enjoy with unspeakable delight—Nor do I take less
pleasure in seeing my tenants thrive under my auspices, and the poor live
comfortably by the employment which I provide——You know I have
one or two sensible friends, to whom I can open all my heart; a blessing
which, perhaps, I might have sought in vain among the crowded scenes of
life: there are a few others of more humble parts, whom I esteem for their
integrity; and their conversation I find inoffensive, though not very
entertaining. Finally, I live in the midst of honest men, and trusty
dependants, who, I flatter myself, have a disinterested attachment to my
person—You, yourself, my dear Doctor, can vouch for the truth of these
assertions.

Now, mark the contrast at London—I am pent up in frowzy lodgings,
where there is not room enough to swing a cat; and I breathe the steams
of endless putrefaction; and these would, undoubtedly, produce a pes-
tilence, if they were not qualified by the gross acid of sea-coal, which is
itself a pernicious nuisance to lungs of any delicacy of texture: but even
this boasted corrector cannot prevent those languid, sallow looks, that
distinguish the inhabitants of London from those ruddy swains that lead
a country-life——I go to bed after mid-night, jaded and restless from the
dissipations of the day—I start every hour from my sleep, at the horrid
noise of the watchmen bawling the hour through every street, and
thundering at every door; a set of useless fellows, who serve no other
purpose but that of disturbing the repose of the inhabitants; and by five
o'clock I start out of bed, in consequence of the still more dreadful alarm
made by the country carts, and noisy rustics bellowing green pease under

my window.[4] If I would drink water, I must quaff the maukish contents of an open aqueduct, exposed to all manner of defilement; or swallow that which comes from the river Thames, impregnated with all the filth of London and Westminster—Human excrement is the least offensive part of the concrete, which is composed of all the drugs, minerals, and poisons, used in mechanics and manufacture, enriched with the putrefying carcases of beasts and men; and mixed with the scourings of all the wash-tubs, kennels, and common sewers, within the bills of mortality.

This is the agreeable potation, extolled by the Londoners, as the finest water in the universe—As to the intoxicating potion, sold for wine, it is a vile, unpalatable, and pernicious sophistication, balderdashed[5] with cyder, corn-spirit, and the juice of sloes. In an action at law, laid against a carman for having staved a cask of port, it appeared from the evidence of the cooper, that there were not above five gallons of real wine in the whole pipe, which held above a hundred, and even that had been brewed and adulterated by the merchant at Oporto. The bread I eat in London, is a deleterious paste, mixed up with chalk, alum, and bone-ashes;[6] insipid to the taste, and destructive to the constitution. The good people are not ignorant of this adulteration; but they prefer it to wholsome bread, because it is whiter than the meal of corn: thus they sacrifice their taste and their health, and the lives of their tender infants, to a most absurd gratification of a mis-judging eye; and the miller, or the baker, is obliged to poison them and their families, in order to live by his profession.—The same monstrous depravity appears in their veal, which is bleached by repeated bleedings, and other villanous arts, till there is not a drop of juice left in the body, and the poor animal is paralytic before it dies; so void of all taste, nourishment, and savour, that a man might dine as comfortably on a white fricasee of kid-skin gloves, or chip hats from Leghorn.[7]

As they have discharged the natural colour from their bread, their butchers-meat, and poultry, their cutlets, ragouts, fricassees, and sauces of all kinds; so they insist upon having the complexion of their pot-herbs mended, even at the hazard of their lives. Perhaps, you will hardly believe they can be so mad as to boil their greens with brass half-pence, in order to improve their colour; and yet nothing is more true—Indeed, without this improvement in the colour, they have no personal merit. They are produced in an artificial soil, and taste of nothing but the dunghills, from whence they spring. My cabbage, cauliflower, and 'sparagus in the country, are as much superior in flavour to those that are sold in Covent-garden, as my heath-mutton is to that of St. James's-market; which, in fact, is neither lamb nor mutton, but something

---

4. Vendors of vegetables who shouted their wares through the streets.
5. Made a jumbled mixture of.

6. Matt's complaints about adulteration were echoed in many publications during the period.
7. A hat made from woven wood or woody fiber.

betwixt the two, gorged in the rank fens of Lincoln and Essex, pale, coarse, and frowzy—As for the pork, it is an abominable carnivorous animal, fed with horse-flesh and distillers grains; and the poultry is all rotten, in consequence of a fever, occasioned by the infamous practice of sewing up the gut, that they may be the sooner fattened in coops, in consequence of this cruel retention.

Of the fish, I need say nothing in this hot weather, but that it comes sixty, seventy, fourscore, and a hundred miles by land-carriage; a circumstance sufficient, without any comment, to turn a Dutchman's stomach, even if his nose was not saluted in every alley with the sweet flavour of *fresh* mackarel, selling by retail—This is not the season for oysters; nevertheless, it may not be amiss to mention, that the right Colchester are kept in slime-pits, occasionally overflowed by the sea; and that the green colour, so much admired by the voluptuaries of this metropolis, is occasioned by the vitriolic scum, which rises on the surface of the stagnant and stinking water—Our rabbits are bred and fed in the poulterer's cellar, where they have neither air nor exercise, consequently they must be firm in flesh, and delicious in flavour; and there is no game to be had for love or money.

It must be owned, that Covent-garden affords some good fruit; which, however, is always engrossed by a few individuals of over grown fortune, at an exorbitant price; so that little else than the refuse of the market falls to the share of the community; and that is distributed by such filthy hands, as I cannot look at without loathing. It was but yesterday that I saw a dirty barrow-bunter[8] in the street, cleaning her dusty fruit with her own spittle; and, who knows but some fine lady of St. James's parish might admit into her delicate mouth those very cherries, which had been rolled and moistened between the filthy, and, perhaps, ulcerated chops of a St. Giles's huckster[9]—I need not dwell upon the pallid, contaminated mash, which they call strawberries; soiled and tossed by greasy paws through twenty baskets crusted with dirt; and then presented with the worst milk, thickened with the worst flour, into a bad likeness of cream: but the milk itself should not pass unanalysed, the produce of faded cabbage-leaves and sour draff,[1] lowered with hot water, frothed with bruised snails, carried through the streets in open pails, exposed to foul rinsings, discharged from doors and windows, spittle, snot, and tobacco-quids from foot-passengers, over-flowings from mud-carts, spatterings from coach-wheels, dirt and trash chucked into it by roguish boys for the joke's-sake, the spewings of infants, who have slabbered in the tin-measure, which is thrown back in that condition among the milk, for the benefit of the next customer; and, finally, the vermin that drops from the

8. A person employed in pushing a small two-wheeled cart, in this case filled with fruit for sale.

9. Street vendor in the Saint Giles area.

1. Dregs, as of a brewing process.

rags of the nasty drab that vends this precious mixture, under the respectable denomination of milk-maid.

I shall conclude this catalogue of London dainties, with that table-beer, guiltless of hops and malt, vapid and nauseous; much fitter to facilitate the operation of a vomit, than to quench thirst and promote digestion; the tallowy rancid mass, called butter, manufactured with candle-grease and kitchen-stuff; and their fresh eggs, imported from France and Scotland.——Now, all these enormities might be remedied with a very little attention to the article of police, or civil regulation; but the wise patriots of London have taken it into their heads, that all regulation is inconsistent with liberty; and that every man ought to live in his own way, without restraint——Nay, as there is not sense enough left among them, to be discomposed by the nuisances I have mentioned, they may, for aught I care, wallow in the mire of their own pollution.

A companionable man will, undoubtedly, put up with many inconveniences for the sake of enjoying agreeable society. A facetious friend of mine used to say, the wine could not be bad, where the company was agreeable; a maxim which, however, ought to be taken *cum grano salis:* [2] but what is the society of London, that I should be tempted, for its sake, to mortify my senses, and compound with such uncleanness as my soul abhors? All the people I see, are too much engrossed by schemes of interest or ambition, to have any room left for sentiment or friendship —Even in some of my old acquaintance, those schemes and pursuits have obliterated all traces of our former connexion——Conversation is reduced to party-disputes, and illiberal altercation—Social commerce, to formal visits and card-playing—If you pick up a diverting original by accident, it may be dangerous to amuse yourself with his oddities—He is generally a tartar at bottom; a sharper, a spy, or a lunatic. Every person you deal with endeavours to over-reach you in the way of business; you are preyed upon by idle mendicants, who beg in the phrase of borrowing, and live upon the spoils of the stranger—Your tradesmen are without conscience, your friends without affection, and your dependants without fidelity.—

My letter would swell into a treatise, were I to particularize every cause of offence that fills up the measure of my aversion to this, and every other crowded city—Thank Heaven! I am not so far sucked into the vortex, but that I can disengage myself without any great effort of philosophy—From this wild uproar of knavery, folly, and impertinence, I shall fly with double relish to the serenity of retirement, the cordial effusions of unreserved friendship, the hospitality and protection of the

2. With a grain of salt. Smollett may be having Matt quote from Jonathan Swift's *Tale of a Tub* II, or he may be merely having the same little learned joke.

rural gods; in a word, the *jucunda oblivia vitæ*,[3] which Horace himself had not taste enough to enjoy.——

I have agreed for a good travelling-coach and four, at a guinea a-day, for three months certain; and next week we intend to begin our journey to the North, hoping still to be with you by the latter end of October——I shall continue to write from every stage where we make any considerable halt, as often as any thing occurs, which I think can afford you the least amusement. In the mean time, I must beg you will superintend the œconomy of Barns, with respect to my hay and corn harvests; assured that my ground produces nothing but what you may freely call your own ——On any other terms I should be ashamed to subscribe myself

your unvariable friend,

London, June 8.   MATT. BRAMBLE.

To Sir WATKIN PHILLIPS, Bar[t]. of Jesus college, Oxon.

DEAR PHILLIPS,

In my last, I mentioned my having spent an evening with a society of authors, who seemed to be jealous and afraid of one another. My uncle was not at all surprised to hear me say I was disappointed in their conversation. "A man may be very entertaining and instructive upon paper, (said he) and exceedingly dull in common discourse. I have observed, that those who shine most in private company, are but secondary stars in the constellation of genius——A small stock of ideas is more easily managed, and sooner displayed, than a great quantity crowded together. There is very seldom any thing extraordinary in the appearance and address of a good writer; whereas a dull author generally distinguishes himself by some oddity or extravagance. For this reason, I fancy, an assembly of Grubs[4] must be very diverting."

My curiosity being excited by this hint, I consulted my friend Dick Ivy, who undertook to gratify it the very next day, which was Sunday last. ——He carried me to dine with S——,[5] whom you and I have long known by his writings.——He lives in the skirts of the town,[6] and every Sunday his house is open to all unfortunate brothers of the quill, whom he treats with beef, pudding, and potatoes, port, punch, and Calvert's entire butt beer.[7] ——He has fixed upon the first day of the week for the exercise of his

---

3. Pleasant oblivion to the troubles of life: from Horace's *Satires* II. vi. 62. This is also taken from the country mouse's praise of the country life at the expense of city life, but Matt points out Horace's own inability to stay away from the city.
4. Denizens of Grub Street, a street in London inhabited by hack writers, and lending its name to those who lived, albeit precariously, by the pen.
5. Smollett here takes the unusual step of presenting himself disguised only by his initial in his own

novel.
6. In Chelsea, where Smollett resided in Monmouth House from 1750 to 1763. He apparently did entertain a club of impecunious writers, but if the ones mentioned in this account represent real persons, they have remained unidentified.
7. The Calvert brothers ran an important brewery, where a dark-brown beer called "entire beer" or porter was made. (See note 6, p. 44, above.)

hospitality, because some of his guests could not enjoy it on any other, for reasons that I need not explain.[8] I was civilly received in a plain, yet decent habitation, which opened back wards into a very pleasant garden, kept in excellent order; and, indeed, I saw none of the outward signs of authorship, either in the house or the landlord, who is one of those few writers of the age that stand upon their own foundation, without patronage, and above dependence. If there was nothing characteristic in the entertainer, the company made ample amends for his want of singularity.

At two in the afternoon, I found myself one of ten mess-mates seated at table; and, I question, if the whole kingdom could produce such another assemblage of originals. Among their peculiarities, I do not mention those of dress, which may be purely accidental. What struck me were oddities originally produced by affectation, and afterwards confirmed by habit. One of them wore spectacles at dinner, and another, his hat flapped; though (as Ivy told me) the first was noted for having a seaman's eye, when a bailiff was in the wind; and the other was never known to labour under any weakness or defect of vision, except about five years ago, when he was complimented with a couple of black eyes by a player, with whom he had quarrelled in his drink. A third wore a laced stocking, and made use of crutches, because, once in his life, he had been laid up with a broken leg, though no man could leap over a stick with more agility. A fourth had contracted such an antipathy to the country, that he insisted upon sitting with his back towards the window that looked into the garden, and when a dish of cauliflower was set upon the table, he snuffed up volatile salts to keep him from fainting; yet this delicate person was the son of a cottager, born under a hedge, and had many years run wild among asses on a common. A fifth affected distraction—When spoke to, he always answered from the purpose—sometimes he suddenly started up, and rapped out a dreadful oath—sometimes he burst out a-laughing—then he folded his arms, and sighed—and then he hissed like fifty serpents.

At first, I really thought he was mad, and, as he sat near me, began to be under some apprehensions for my own safety, when our landlord, perceiving me alarmed, assured me aloud that I had nothing to fear. "The gentleman (said he) is trying to act a part, for which he is by no means qualified—if he had all the inclination in the world, it is not in his power to be mad. His spirits are too flat to be kindled into frenzy." "'Tis no bad p-p-puff, how-ow-ever (observed a person in a tarnished laced coat): aff-ffected m-madness w-will p-pass for w-wit w-with nine-ninet-teen out of t-twenty."—"And affected stuttering for humour: replied our landlord, tho', God knows, there is no affinity betwixt them." It seems, this wag, after having made some abortive attempts in plain speaking, had recourse to this defect, by means of which he frequently extorted the laugh of the company, without the least expence of genius; and that imperfection, which he had at first counterfeited, was now become so habitual, that he could not lay it aside.

A certain winking genius, who wore yellow gloves at dinner, had, on his first introduction, taken such offence at S——, because he looked and talked, and ate and drank like any other man, that he spoke contemptuously of his understanding ever after, and never would repeat his visit, until he had exhibited the following proof of his caprice. Wat Wyvil,[9] the poet, having made some unsuccessful advances towards an intimacy with S——, at last gave him to understand, by a third person, that he had written a poem in his praise, and a satire against his person; that if he would admit him to his house, the first should be immediately sent to press; but that if he persisted in declining his friendship, he would publish the satire without delay. S——replied, that he looked upon Wyvil's panegyrick, as in effect, a species of infamy, and would resent it accordingly with a good cudgel; but if he published the satire, he might deserve his compassion, and had nothing to fear from his revenge. Wyvil having considered the alternative, resolved to mortify S—by printing the panegyrick, for which he received a sound drubbing. Then he swore the peace against the aggressor, who, in order to avoid a prosecution at law, admitted him to his good graces. It was the singularity in S——'s conduct on this occasion, that reconciled him to the yellow-gloved philosopher, who owned he had some genius, and from that period cultivated his acquaintance.

Curious to know upon what subjects the several talents of my fellow-guests were employed, I applied to my communicative friend Dick Ivy, who gave me to understand, that most of them were, or had been, understrappers, or journeymen, to more creditable authors, for whom they translated, collated, and compiled, in the business of book-making; and that all of them had, at different times, laboured in the service of our landlord, though they had now set up for themselves in various departments of literature. Not only their talents, but also their nations and dialects were so various, that our conversation resembled the confusion of tongues at Babel. We had the Irish brogue, the Scotch accent, and foreign idiom, twanged off by the most discordant vociferation; for, as they all spoke together, no man had any chance to be heard, unless he could bawl louder than his fellows. It must be owned, however, there was nothing pedantic in their discourse; they carefully avoided all learned disquisitions, and endeavoured to be facetious; nor did their endeavours always miscarry——some droll repartee passed, and much laughter was excited; and if any individual lost his temper so far as to transgress the

---

9. Apparently a versifier named William Woty (1731?–91). Smollett had subscribed to his volume of verses *The Shrubs of Parnassus* (1760).

bounds of decorum, he was effectually checked by the master of the feast, who exerted a sort of paternal authority over this irritable tribe.

The most learned philosopher of the whole collection, who had been expelled the university for atheism, has made great progress in a refutation of lord Bolingbroke's metaphysical works, which is said to be equally ingenious and orthodox; but, in the mean time, he has been presented to the grand jury as a public nuisance, for having blasphemed in an alehouse on the Lord's day. The Scotchman gives lectures on the pronunciation of the English language, which he is now publishing by subscription.

The Irishman is a political writer, and goes by the name of my Lord Potatoe. He wrote a pamphlet in vindication of a minister, hoping his zeal would be rewarded with some place or pension; but finding himself neglected in that quarter, he whispered about, that the pamphlet was written by the minister himself, and he published an answer to his own production. In this, he addressed the author under the title of *your lordship* with such solemnity, that the public swallowed the deceit, and bought up the whole impression. The wise politicians of the metropolis declared they were both masterly performances, and chuckled over the flimsy reveries of an ignorant garretteer, as the profound speculations of a veteran statesman, acquainted with all the secrets of the cabinet. The imposture was detected in the sequel, and our Hibernian pamphleteer retains no part of his assumed importance, but the bare title of *my lord*, and the upper part of the table at the potatoe-ordinary in Shoe-lane. [1]

Opposite to me sat a Piedmontese, who had obliged the public with a humorous satire, intituled, *The Balance of the English Poets*, a perform-ance which evinced the great modesty and taste of the author, and, in particular, his intimacy with the elegancies of the English language. The sage, who laboured under the $\alpha\gamma\pi o\phi o\zeta\acute{\iota}\alpha$, or *horror of green fields*, had just finished a treatise on practical agriculture, though, in fact, he had never seen corn [2] growing in his life, and was so ignorant of grain, that our entertainer, in the face of the whole company, made him own, that a plate of hominy was the best rice pudding he had ever eat.

The stutterer had almost finished his travels through Europe and part of Asia, without ever budging beyond the liberties of the King's Bench, except in term-time, with a tipstaff for his companion; [3] and as for little Tim Cropdale, the most facetious member of the whole society, he had happily wound up the catastrophe of a virgin tragedy, [4] from the

---

1. An ordinary was a place where one could dine for a low, fixed price, and a potato-ordinary was probably one where the fare was potatoes, which were cheap but filling. Shoe Lane was near Fleet Street, the journalistic center of London.

2. Wheat, in English usage, whereas what is called "corn" in America is commonly referred to as "maize" in England.

3. The prison of the King's Bench, where Smollett himself was imprisoned for libel in 1760–61, was often used for debtors, who were permitted to range within definite bounds (liberties), except when they were required to appear before the court in term-time, when they would be accompanied by a bailiff or tipstaff.

4. Completed a play which was still unproduced, or virginal.

exhibition of which he promised himself a large fund of profit and reputation. Tim had made shift to live many years by writing novels, at the rate of five pounds a volume; but that branch of business is now engrossed by female authors,[5] who publish merely for the propagation of virtue, with so much ease and spirit, and delicacy, and knowledge of the human heart, and all in the serene tranquillity of high life, that the reader is not only inchanted by their genius, but reformed by their morality.

After dinner, we adjourned into the garden, where, I observed, Mr. S ———gave a short separate audience to every individual in a small remote filbert walk,[6] from whence most of them dropt off one after another, without further ceremony; but they were replaced by fresh recruits of the same clan, who came to make an afternoon's visit; and, among other's, a spruce bookseller, called Birkin, who rode his own gelding, and made his appearance in a pair of new jemmy[7] boots, with massy spurs of plate. It was not without reason, that this midwife of the Muses used exercise a-horseback, for he was too fat to walk a-foot, and he underwent some sarcasms from Tim Cropdale, on his unweildy size and inaptitude for motion. Birkin, who took umbrage at this poor author's petulance in presuming to joke upon a man so much richer than himself, told him, he was not so unweildy but that he could move the Marshalsea court for a writ, and even overtake him with it, if he did not very speedily come and settle accounts with him, respecting the expence of publishing his last Ode to the king of Prussia, of which he had sold but three, and one of them was to Whitefield the methodist. Tim affected to receive this intimation with good humour, saying, he expected in a post or two, from Potsdam, a poem of thanks from his Prussian majesty, who knew very well how to pay poets in their own coin; but, in the mean time, he proposed, that Mr. Birkin and he should run three times round the garden for a bowl of punch, to be drank at Ashley's[8] in the evening, and he would run boots against stockings. The bookseller, who valued himself upon his mettle, was persuaded to accept the challenge, and he forthwith resigned his boots to Cropdale, who, when he had put them on, was no bad representation of captain Pistol in the play.

Every thing being adjusted, they started together with great impetuosity, and, in the second round, Birkin had clearly the advantage, *larding the lean earth as he puff'd along.*[9] Cropdale had no mind to contest the victory further; but, in a twinkling, disappeared through the back-door of the garden, which opened into a private lane, that had communication with

---

5. A number of women wrote novels during the middle of the eighteenth century, including Sarah Fielding (1710–68), the sister of Henry Fielding (1707–54), and Charlotte Lenox (1720–1804).
6. A secluded walk through a garden set off by filbert or hazel trees or shrubs.
7. Spruce or neatly made.
8. Ashley's Punch House or Coffee House was located on Ludgate Hill, in the City of London. Punch was made of rum or wine and water, sugar, fruit juice, etc., in varying proportions.
9. Adapted from Prince Hal's description of the sweating Falstaff in *I Henry IV* II. ii. 116. Captain Pistol, just above, is Falstaff's swaggering companion in *II Henry IV*, *Henry V*, and *The Merry Wives of Windsor*.

the high road.—The spectators immediately began to hollow, "Stole away!"[1] and Birkin set off in pursuit of him with great eagerness; but he had not advanced twenty yards in the lane, when a thorn running into his foot, sent him hopping back into the garden, roaring with pain, and swearing with vexation. When he was delivered from this annoyance by the Scotchman, who had been bred to surgery,[2] he looked about him wildly, exclaiming, "Sure, the fellow won't be such a rogue as to run clear away with my boots!" Our landlord, having reconnoitred the shoes he had left, which, indeed, hardly deserved that name, "Pray, (said he) Mr. Birkin, wa'n't your boots made of calf-skin?" "Calf-skin or cow-skin, (replied the other) I'll find a slip of sheep-skin that will do his business—I lost twenty pounds by his farce, which you persuaded me to buy—I am out of pocket five pounds by his damn'd ode; and now this pair of boots, bran new, cost me thirty shillings, as per receipt.—But this affair of the boots is felony—transportation.—I'll have the dog indicted at the Old Bailey—I will, Mr. S——. I will be reveng'd, even though I should lose my debt in consequence of his conviction."

Mr. S——said nothing at present, but accommodated him with a pair of shoes; then ordered his servant to rub him down, and comfort him with a glass of rum-punch, which seemed, in a great measure, to cool the rage of his indignation. "After all, (said our landlord) this is no more than a *humbug* in the way of wit, though it deserves a more respectable epithet, when considered as an effort of invention. Tim, being (I suppose) out of credit with the cordwainer, fell upon this ingenious expedient to supply the want of shoes, knowing that Mr. Birkin, who loves humour, would himself relish the joke upon a little recollection. Cropdale literally lives by his wit, which he has exercised upon all his friends in their turns. He once borrowed my poney for five or six days to go to Salisbury, and sold him in Smithfield at his return. This was a joke of such a serious nature, that, in the first transports of my passion, I had some thoughts of prosecuting him for horse-stealing; and even when my resentment had in some measure subsided, as he industriously avoided me, I vowed, I would take satisfaction on his ribs with the first opportunity. One day, seeing him at some distance in the street, coming towards me, I began to prepare my cane for action, and walked in the shadow of a porter, that he might not perceive me soon enough to make his escape; but, in the very instant I had lifted up the instrument of correction, I found Tim Cropdale metamorphosed into a miserable blind wretch, feeling his way with a long stick from post to post, and rolling about two bald unlighted orbs instead of eyes. I was exceedingly shocked at having so narrowly escaped the concern and disgrace that would have attended such a misapplication

1. The cry from fox hunting when the game has apparently escaped.

2. Smollett had been apprenticed as a surgeon and practiced for some time.

of vengeance: but, next day, Tim prevailed upon a friend of mine to come and sollicit my forgiveness, and offer his note, payable in six weeks, for the price of the poney.—This gentleman gave me to understand, that the blind man was no other than Cropdale, who having seen me advancing, and guessing my intent, had immediately converted himself into the object aforesaid.—I was so diverted at the ingenuity of the evasion, that I agreed to pardon his offence, refusing his note, however, that I might keep a prosecution for felony hanging over his head, as a security for his future good behaviour—But Timothy would by no means trust himself in my hands till the note was accepted—then he made his appearance at my door as a blind beggar, and imposed in such a manner upon my man, who had been his old acquaintance and pot-companion,[3] that the fellow threw the door in his face, and even threatened to give him the bastinado. Hearing a noise in the hall, I went thither, and immediately recollecting the figure I had passed in the street, accosted him by his own name, to the unspeakable astonishment of the footman."

Birkin declared he loved a joke as well as another; but asked if any of the company could tell where Mr. Cropdale lodged, that he might send him a proposal about restitution, before the boots should be made away with. "I would willingly give him a pair of new shoes, (said he) and half a guinea into the bargain, for the boots, which fitted me like a glove; and I shan't be able to get the fellows of them till the good weather for riding is over." The stuttering wit declared, that the only secret which Cropdale ever kept, was the place of his lodgings; but, he believed, that, during the heats of summer, he commonly took his repose upon a bulk, or indulged himself, in fresco, with one of the kennel-nymphs,[4] under the portico of St. Martin's church. "Pox on him! (cried the bookseller) he might as well have taken my whip and spurs—In that case, he might have been tempted to steal another horse, and then he would have rid to the devil of course."

After coffee, I took my leave of Mr. S——, with proper acknowledgements of his civility, and was extremely well pleased with the entertainment of the day, though not yet satisfied, with respect to the nature of this connexion, betwixt a man of character in the literary world, and a parcel of authorlings, who, in all probability, would never be able to acquire any degree of reputation by their labours. On this head I interrogated my conductor, Dick Ivy, who answered me to this effect —"One would imagine S——had some view to his own interest, in giving countenance and assistance to those people, whom he knows to be bad men, as well as bad writers; but, if he has any such view, he will find himself disappointed; for if he is so vain as to imagine he can make them

---

3. Drinking partner.
4. The kennel is the gutter, and a kennel-nymph is a prostitute.

subservient to his schemes of profit or ambition, they are cunning enough to make him their property in the mean time. There is not one of the company you have seen to-day (myself excepted) who does not owe him particular obligations.—One of them he bailed out of a spunging-house,[5] and afterwards paid the debt—another he translated into his family, and cloathed, when he was turned out half naked from jail in consequence of an act for the relief of insolvent debtors—a third, who was reduced to a woollen night-cap, and lived upon sheeps trotters, up three pair of stairs backward in Butcher-row,[6] he took into present pay and free quarters, and enabled him to appear as a gentleman, without having the fear of sheriff's officers before his eyes. Those who are in distress he supplies with money when he has it, and with his credit when he is out of cash. When they want business, he either finds employment for them in his own service, or recommends them to booksellers to execute some project he has formed for their subsistence. They are always welcome to his table, (which, though plain, is plentiful) and to his good offices as far as they will go; and when they see occasion, they make use of his name with the most petulant familiarity; nay, they do not even scruple to arrogate to themselves the merit of some of his performances, and have been known to sell their own lucubrations as the produce of his brain. The Scotchman you saw at dinner once personated him at an ale-house in West-Smithfield,[7] and, in the character of S——, had his head broke by a cow-keeper, for having spoke disrespectfully of the Christian religion; but he took the law of him in his own person, and the assailant was fain to give him ten pounds to withdraw his action."

I observed, that all this appearance of liberality on the side of Mr. S——was easily accounted for, on the supposition that they flattered him in private, and engaged his adversaries in public; and yet I was astonished, when I recollected that I often had seen this writer virulently abused in papers, poems, and pamphlets, and not a pen was drawn in his defence.—"But you will be more astonished (said he) when I assure you, those very guests whom you saw at his table to-day, were the authors of great part of that abuse; and he himself is well aware of their particular favours, for they are all eager to detect and betray one another."—"But this is doing the devil's work for nothing (cried I). What should induce them to revile their benefactor without provocation?" "Envy (answered Dick) is the general incitement; but they are galled by an additional scourge of provocation. S——directs a literary journal,[8] in which their productions are necessarily brought to trial; and though many of them have been treated with such lenity and favour as they little deserved, yet

---

5. A house kept by a bailiff or other officer of the court or a sheriff for the confinement of debtors.
6. A row of tenements located just outside of the City, in the Strand.
7. An area to the northwest of the City of London,

West Smithfield was noted for its livestock markets.
8. *The Critical Review,* founded in 1756. During its early period, Smollett edited it and wrote most of it, but he stepped out in 1763.

the slightest censure, such as, perhaps, could not be avoided with any pretensions to candour and impartiality, has rankled in the hearts of those authors to such a degree, that they have taken immediate vengeance on the critic in anonymous libels, letters, and lampoons. Indeed, all the writers of the age, good, bad, and indifferent, from the moment he assumed this office, became his enemies, either professed or in petto,[9] except those of his friends who knew they had nothing to fear from his strictures; and he must be a wiser man than me, who can tell what advantage or satisfaction he derives from having brought such a nest of hornets about his ears."

I owned, that was a point which might deserve consideration; but still I expressed a desire to know his real motives for continuing his friendship to a set of rascals equally ungrateful and insignificant.—He said, he did not pretend to assign any reasonable motive; that, if the truth must be told, the man was, in point of conduct, a most incorrigible fool; that, though he pretended to have a knack at hitting off characters, he blundered strangely in the distribution of his favours, which were generally bestowed on the most undeserving of those who had recourse to his assistance; that, indeed, this preference was not so much owing to want of discernment as to want of resolution, for he had not fortitude enough to resist the importunity even of the most worthless; and, as he did not know the value of money, there was very little merit in parting with it so easily; that his pride was gratified in seeing himself courted by such a number of literary dependants; that, probably, he delighted in hearing them expose and traduce one another; and, finally, from their information, he became acquainted with all the transactions of Grub street, which he had some thoughts of compiling, for the entertainment of the public.

I could not help suspecting, from Dick's discourse, that he had some particular grudge against S———, upon whose conduct he had put the worst construction it would bear; and, by dint of cross-examination, I found he was not at all satisfied with the character which had been given in the Review of his last performance, though it had been treated civilly, in consequence of the author's application to the critic. By all accounts, S———is not without weakness and caprice; but he is certainly good-humoured and civilized; nor do I find, that there is any thing overbearing, cruel, or implacable in his disposition.

I have dwelt so long upon authors; that you will perhaps suspect I intend to enroll myself among the fraternity; but, if I were actually qualified for the profession, it is at best but a desperate resource against starving, as it affords no provision for old age and infirmity. Salmon,[1] at

9. In secret; literally, within the breast.
1. Thomas Salmon (1679–1767) was a writer of histories and travel literature, as was Smollett.

Unrewarded merit of writers is a favorite theme of many authors.

the age of fourscore, is now in a garret, compiling matter, at a guinea a sheet for a modern historian, who, in point of age, might be his grand-child; and Psalmonazar,[2] after having drudged half a century in the literary mill, in all the simplicity and abstinence of an Asiatic, subsists upon the charity of a few booksellers, just sufficient to keep him from the parish—I think Guy,[3] who was himself a bookseller, ought to have appropriated one wing or ward of his hospital to the use of decayed authors; though, indeed, there is neither hospital, college, nor work-house, within the bills of mortality, large enough to contain the poor of this society, composed, as it is, from the refuse of every other profession.

I know not whether you will find any amusement in this account of an odd race of mortals, whose constitution had, I own, greatly interested the curiosity of

Yours,

London, June 10.   J. MELFORD.

To Miss LÆTITIA WILLIS, at Gloucester

MY DEAR LETTY,

There is something on my spirits, which I should not venture to communicate by the post, but having the opportunity of Mrs. Brent-wood's return, I seize it eagerly, to disburthen my poor heart, which is oppressed with fear and vexation.—O Letty! what a miserable situation it is, to be without a friend to whom one can apply for counsel and consolation in distress! I hinted in my last, that one Mr. Barton had been very particular in his civilities: I can no longer mistake his meaning—he has formally professed himself my admirer; and, after a thousand assiduities, perceiving I made but a cold return to his addresses, he had recourse to the mediation of lady Griskin, who has acted the part of a very warm advocate in his behalf:—but, my dear Willis, her ladyship over-acts her part—she not only expatiates on the ample fortune, the great connexions, and the unblemished character of Mr. Barton, but she takes the trouble to catechise me; and, two days ago, peremptorily told me, that a girl of my age could not possibly resist so many considerations, if her heart was not pre-engaged.

This insinuation threw me into such a flutter, that she could not but observe my disorder; and, presuming upon the discovery, insisted upon my making her the confidante of my passion. But, although I had not such

2. George Psalmanazar (1679?–1763) was a fa-mous fraud, born in France, who passed himself off as a native of Formosa and published a *Description of Formosa* (1704). He was subse-quently exposed, and later converted sincerely to Christianity. He made his living as a hack writer.

Again, Smollett violates strict chronology by refer-ring to Psalmanazar as subsisting on charity, when he had died in 1763.
3. Thomas Guy (1645?–1724) was a bookseller who founded Guy's Hospital, still an important institution in London, in 1722.

command of myself as to conceal the emotion of my heart, I am not such a child as to disclose its secrets to a person who would certainly use them to its prejudice. I told her, it was no wonder if I was out of countenance at her introducing a subject of conversation so unsuitable to my years and inexperience; that I believed Mr. Barton was a very worthy gentleman, and I was much obliged to him for his good opinion; but the affections were involuntary, and mine, in particular, had as yet made no concessions in his favour. She shook her head with an air of distrust that made me tremble; and observed, that if my affections were free, they would submit to the decision of prudence, especially when enforced by the authority of those who had a right to direct my conduct. This remark implied a design to interest my uncle or my aunt, perhaps my brother, in behalf of Mr. Barton's passion; and I am sadly afraid that my aunt is already gained over. Yesterday in the forenoon, he had been walking with us in the Park, and stopping in our return at a toy-shop, he presented her with a very fine snuff-box, and me with a gold etuis,[4] which I resolutely refused, till she commanded me to accept it on pain of her displeasure: nevertheless, being still unsatisfied with respect to the propriety of receiving this toy, I signified my doubts to my brother, who said he would consult my uncle on the subject, and seemed to think Mr. Barton had been rather premature in his presents.

What will be the result of this consultation, Heaven knows; but I am afraid it will produce an explanation with Mr. Barton, who will, no doubt, avow his passion, and sollicit their consent to a connexion which my soul abhors; for, my dearest Letty, it is not in my power to love Mr. Barton, even if my heart was untouched by any other tenderness. Not that there is any thing disagreeable about his person, but there is a total want of that nameless charm which captivates and controuls the inchanted spirit—at least, he appears to me to have this defect; but if he had all the engaging qualifications which a man can possess, they would be excited in vain against that constancy, which, I flatter myself, is the characteristic of my nature. No, my dear Willis, I may be involved in fresh troubles, and I believe I shall, from the importunities of this gentleman and the violence of my relations; but my heart is incapable of change.

You know, I put no faith in dreams; and yet I have been much disturbed by one that visited me last night.—I thought I was in a church, where a certain person, whom you know, was on the point of being married to my aunt; that the clergyman was Mr. Barton, and that poor forlorn I stood weeping in a corner, half naked, and without shoes or stockings.—Now, I know there is nothing so childish as to be moved by those vain illusions; but, nevertheless, in spite of all my reason, this hath made a strong impression upon my mind, which begins to be very gloomy. Indeed, I have another more substantial cause of affliction—I

4. A small decorative case for needles, cosmetics, or other small articles.

have some religious scruples, my dear friend, which lie heavy on my conscience.—I was persuaded to go to the Tabernacle, where I heard a discourse that affected me deeply.—I have prayed fervently to be enlightened, but as yet I am not sensible of these inward motions, those operations of grace, which are the signs of a regenerated spirit; and therefore I begin to be in terrible apprehensions about the state of my poor soul. Some of our family have had very uncommon accessions, particularly my aunt and Mrs. Jenkins, who sometimes speak as if they were really inspired; so that I am not like to want for either exhortation or example, to purify my thoughts, and recall them from the vanities of this world, which, indeed, I would willingly resign, if it was in my power; but to make this sacrifice, I must be enabled by such assistance from above as hath not yet been indulged to

Your unfortunate friend,

June 10.   LYDIA MELFORD.

To Sir WATKIN PHILLIPS, of Jesus college, Oxon.

DEAR PHILLIPS,

The moment I received your letter, I began to execute your commission—With the assistance of mine host at the Bull and Gate,[5] I discovered the place to which your fugitive valet had retreated, and taxed him with his dishonesty—The fellow was in manifest confusion at sight of me, but he denied the charge with great confidence, till I told him, that if he would give up the watch, which was a family piece, he might keep the money and the clothes, and go to the devil his own way, at his leisure; but if he rejected this proposal, I would deliver him forthwith to the constable, whom I had provided for that purpose, and he would carry him before the justice without further delay. After some hesitation, he desired to speak with me in the next room, where he produced the watch, with all its appendages, and I have delivered it to our landlord, to be sent you by the first safe conveyance——So much for busines.

I shall grow vain, upon your saying you find entertainment in my letters; barren, as they certainly are, of incident and importance, because your amusement must arise, not from the matter, but from the manner, which you know is all my own—Animated, therefore, by the approbation of a person, whose nice taste and consummate judgment I can no longer doubt, I will chearfully proceed with our memoirs—As it is determined we shall set out next week for Yorkshire, I went to-day in the forenoon with my uncle to see a carriage, belonging to a coach-maker in our neighbourhood—Turning down a narrow lane, behind Longacre,[6] we

5. A well-known inn in Holborn.
6. A street which runs between Saint Martin's Lane and Drury Lane.

perceived a crowd of people standing at a door; which, it seems, opened into a kind of a methodist meeting, and were informed, that a footman was then holding forth to the congregation within. Curious to see this phœnomenon, we squeezed into the place with much difficulty; and who should this preacher be, but the identical Humphry Clinker. He had finished his sermon, and given out a psalm, the first stave of which he sung with peculiar graces[7]——But if we were astonished to see Clinker in the pulpit, we were altogether confounded at finding all the females of our family among the audience—There was lady Griskin, Mrs. Tabitha Bramble, Mrs. Winifred Jenkins, my sister Liddy, and Mr. Barton, and all of them joined in the psalmody, with strong marks of devotion.

I could hardly keep my gravity on this ludicrous occasion; but old Square-toes was differently affected—The first thing that struck him, was the presumption of his lacquey, whom he commanded to come down, with such an air of authority as Humphry did not think proper to disregard. He descended immediately, and all the people were in commotion. Barton looked exceedingly sheepish, lady Griskin flirted her fan, Mrs. Tabby groaned in spirit, Liddy changed countenance, and Mrs. Jenkins sobbed as if her heart was breaking—My uncle, with a sneer, asked pardon of the ladies, for having interrupted their devotion, saying, he had particular business with the preacher, whom he ordered to call a hackney-coach. This being immediately brought up to the end of the lane, he handed Liddy into it, and my aunt and I following him, we drove home, without taking any further notice of the rest of the company, who still remained in silent astonishment.

Mr. Bramble, perceiving Liddy in great trepidation, assumed a milder aspect, bidding her be under no concern, for he was not at all displeased at any thing she had done—"I have no objection (said he) to your being religiously inclined; but I don't think my servant is a proper ghostly director, for a devotee of your sex and character—if, in fact, (as I rather believe) your aunt is not the sole conductress of this machine—" Mrs. Tabitha made no answer, but threw up the whites of her eyes, as if in the act of ejaculation—Poor Liddy said she had no right to the title of a devotee; that she thought there was no harm in hearing a pious discourse, even if it came from a footman, especially as her aunt was present; but that if she had erred from ignorance, she hoped he would excuse it, as she could not bear the thoughts of living under his displeasure. The old gentleman, pressing her hand with a tender smile, said she was a good girl, and that he did not believe her capable of doing any thing that could give him the least umbrage or disgust.

When we arrived at our lodgings, he commanded Mr. Clinker to attend him up stairs, and spoke to him in these words—"Since you are

---

7. Musical embellishments.

called upon by the spirit to preach and to teach, it is high time to lay aside the livery of an earthly master; and, for my part, I am unworthy to have an apostle in my service——" "I hope (said Humphry) I have not failed in my duty to your honour—I should be a vile wretch if I did, considering the misery from which your charity and compassion relieved me—but having an inward admonition of the spirit——" "An admonition of the devil—(cried the 'squire, in a passion) What admonition, you blockhead? —What right has such a fellow as you to set up for a reformer?" "Begging your honour's pardon, (replied Clinker) may not the new light of God's grace shine upon the poor and the ignorant in their humility, as well as upon the wealthy, and the philosopher in all his pride of human learning?" "What you imagine to be the new light of grace, (said his master) I take to be a deceitful vapour, glimmering through a crack in your upper story—In a word, Mr. Clinker, I will have no light in my family but what pays the king's taxes,[8] unless it be the light of reason, which you don't pretend to follow."

"Ah, sir! (cried Humphry) the light of reason, is no more in comparison to the light I mean, than a farthing candle to the sun at noon —"[9]"Very true, (said uncle) the one will serve to shew you your way, and the other to dazzle and confound your weak brain—Heark-ye, Clinker, you are either an hypocritical knave, or a wrong-headed enthusiast; and, in either case, unfit for my service—If you are a quack in sanctity and devotion, you will find it an easy matter to impose upon silly women, and others of crazed understanding, who will contribute lavishly for your support—if you are really seduced by the reveries of a disturbed imagination, the sooner you lose your senses entirely, the better for yourself and the community. In that case, some charitable person might provide you with a dark room and clean straw in Bedlam, where it would not be in your power to infect others with your fanaticism; whereas, if you have just reflection enough left to maintain the character of a chosen vessel in the meetings of the godly, you and your hearers will be misled by a Will-i'the-wisp, from one error into another, till you are plunged into religious frenzy; and then, perhaps, you will hang yourself in despair ——" "Which the Lord of his infinite mercy forbid! (exclaimed the affrighted Clinker) It is very possible I may be under the temptation of the devil, who wants to wreck me on the rocks of spiritual pride—Your honour says, I am either a knave or a madman; now, as I'll assure your honour I am no knave, it follows that I must be mad; therefore, I beseech your honour, upon my knees, to take my case into consideration, that means may be used for my recovery—"

---

8. A levy against windows which was established in 1695 and only abolished only in 1851.
9. This is a fairly common comparison between the light of reason and the light of Revelation, probably adapted from Edward Young's couplet

How commentators each *dark* passage shun
And hold their farthing candle to the *sun.*
[Love of Fame VII. ii. 97–8]

The 'squire could not help smiling at the poor fellow's simplicity, and promised to take care of him, provided he would mind the business of his place, without running after the new-light of methodism: but Mrs. Tabitha took offence at his humility, which she interpreted into poorness of spirit and worldly mindedness—She upbraided him with the want of courage to suffer for conscience sake——She observed, that if he should lose his place for bearing testimony to the truth, Providence would not fail to find him another, perhaps more advantageous; and, declaring that it could not be very agreeable to live in a family where an inquisition was established, retired to another room in great agitation.

My uncle followed her with a significant look, then, turning to the preacher, "You hear what my sister says—If you cannot live with me upon such terms as I have prescribed, the vineyard of methodism lies before you, and she seems very well disposed to reward your labour—" "I would not willingly give offence to any soul upon earth (answered Humphry); her ladyship has been very good to me, ever since we came to London; and surely she has a heart turned for religious exercises; and both she and lady Griskin sing psalms and hymns like two cherubims ——But, at the same time, I'm bound to love and obey your honour—It becometh not such a poor ignorant fellow as me, to hold dispute with gentlemen of rank and learning—As for the matter of knowledge, I am no more than a beast in comparison of your honour; therefore I submit; and, with God's grace, I will follow you to the world's end, if you don't think me too far gone to be out of confinement—"

His master promised to keep him for some time longer on trial; then desired to know in what manner lady Griskin and Mr. Barton came to join their religious society. He told him, that her ladyship was the person who first carried my aunt and sister to the Tabernacle, whither he attended them, and had his devotion kindled by Mr. W——'s [1] preaching: that he was confirmed in this new way, by the preacher's sermons, which he had bought and studied with great attention: that his discourse and prayers had brought over Mrs. Jenkins and the house-maid to the same way of thinking; but as for Mr. Barton, he had never seen him at service before this day, when he came in company with lady Griskin——Humphry, moreover, owned that he had been encouraged to mount the rostrum, by the example and success of a weaver, who was much followed as a powerful minister: that on his first trial, he found himself under such strong impulsions, as made him believe he was certainly moved by the spirit; and that he had assisted in lady Griskin's, and several private houses, at exercises of devotion.

Mr. Bramble was no sooner informed, that her ladyship had acted as the primum mobile of this confederacy, than he concluded she had only made use of Clinker as a tool, subservient to the execution of some

---

1. George Whitefield (1714–70), the builder of the Tabernacle.

design, to the true secret of which he was an utter stranger—He observed, that her ladyship's brain was a perfect mill for projects; and that she and Tabby had certainly engaged in some secret treaty, the nature of which he could not comprehend. I told him I thought it was no difficult matter to perceive the drift of Mrs. Tabitha, which was to ensnare the heart of Barton, and that in all likelihood my lady Griskin acted as her auxiliary: that this supposition would account for their endeavours to convert him to methodism; an event which would occasion a connexion of souls that might be easily improved into a matrimonial union.

My uncle seemed to be much diverted by the thoughts of this scheme's succeeding; but I gave him to understand, that Barton was preengaged: that he had the day before made a present of an etuis to Liddy, which her aunt had obliged her to receive, with a view, no doubt, to countenance her own accepting of a snuff-box at the same time: that my sister having made me acquainted with this incident, I had desired an explanation of Mr. Barton, who declared his intentions were honourable, and expressed his hope that I would have no objections to his alliance: that I had thanked him for the honour he intended our family; but told him, it would be necessary to consult her uncle and aunt, who were her guardians: and their approbation being obtained, I could have no objection to his proposal; though I was persuaded that no violence would be offered to my sister's inclinations, in a transaction that so nearly interested the happiness of her future life: that he had assured me, he should never think of availing himself of a guardian's authority, unless he could render his addresses agreeable to the young lady herself; and that he would immediately demand permission of Mr. and Miss Bramble, to make Liddy a tender of his hand and fortune.

The 'squire was not insensible to the advantages of such a match, and declared he would promote it with all his influence; but when I took notice that there seemed to be an aversion on the side of Liddy, he said he would sound her on the subject; and if her reluctance was such as would not be easily overcome, he would civilly decline the proposal of Mr. Barton; for he thought that, in the choice of a husband, a young woman ought not to sacrifice the feelings of her heart for any consideration upon earth—"Liddy is not so desperate (said he) as to worship fortune at such an expence." I take it for granted, this whole affair will end in smoke; though there seems to be a storm brewing in the quarter of Mrs. Tabby, who sat with all the sullen dignity of silence at dinner, seemingly pregnant with complaint and expostulation. As she hath certainly marked Barton for her own prey, she cannot possibly favour his suit to Liddy; and therefore I expect something extraordinary will attend his declaring himself my sister's admirer. This declaration will certainly be made in form, as soon as the lover can pick up resolution enough to stand the brunt of Mrs. Tabby's disappointment; for he is, without doubt, aware of her designs upon his person——The particulars of the *denouement* you shall know in due season: mean while I am

always yours,

London, June 10. J. MELFORD.

To Dr. LEWIS.

DEAR LEWIS,

The deceitful calm was of short duration. I am plunged again in a sea of vexation, and the complaints in my stomach and bowels are returned; so that I suppose I shall be disabled from prosecuting the excursion I had planned—What the devil had I to do, to come a plague hunting with a leash of females in my train? Yesterday my precious sister (who, by the bye, has been for some time a professed methodist) came into my apartment, attended by Mr. Barton, and desired an audience with a very stately air—"Brother, (said she) this gentleman has something to propose, which I flatter myself will be the more acceptable, as it will rid you of a troublesome companion." Then Mr. Barton proceeded to this effect —"I am, indeed, extremely ambitious of being allied to your family, Mr. Bramble, and I hope you will see no cause to interpose your authority." "As for authority, (said Tabby, interrupting him with some warmth) I know of none that he has a right to use on this occasion—If I pay him the compliment of making him acquainted with the step I intend to take, it is all he can expect in reason—This is as much as I believe he would do by me, if he intended to change his own situation in life—In a word, brother, I am so sensible of Mr. Barton's extraordinary merit, that I have been prevailed upon to alter my resolution of living a single life, and to put my happiness in his hands, by vesting him with a legal title to my person and fortune, such as they are. The business at present, is to have the writings drawn; and I shall be obliged to you, if you will recommend a lawyer to me for that purpose—"

You may guess what an effect this overture had upon me; who, from the information of my nephew, expected that Barton was to make a formal declaration of his passion for Liddy; I could not help gazing in silent astonishment, alternately at Tabby, and her supposed admirer, which last hung his head in the most aukward confusion for a few minutes, and then retired on pretence of being suddenly seized with a vertigo——Mrs. Tabitha affected much concern, and would have had him make use of a bed in the house; but he insisted upon going home, that he might have recourse to some drops, which he kept for such emergencies, and his innamorata acquiesced—In the mean time I was exceedingly puzzled at this adventure, (though I suspected the truth) and did not know in what manner to demean myself towards Mrs. Tabitha, when Jery came in and told me, he had just seen Mr. Barton alight from his chariot[2] at lady Griskin's door—This incident seemed to threaten a visit from her ladyship, with which we were honoured accordingly, in less than half an hour—"I find (said she) there has been a match of cross purposes among you good folks; and I'm come to set you to rights—" So saying, she presented me with the following billet—

"Dear Sir,

I no sooner recollected myself from the extreme confusion I was thrown into, by that unlucky mistake of your sister, than I thought it my duty to assure you, that my devoirs to Mrs. Bramble never exceeded the bounds of ordinary civility; and that my heart is unalterably fixed upon miss Liddy Melford, as I had the honour to declare to her brother, when he questioned me upon that subject —Lady Griskin has been so good as to charge herself, not only with the delivery of this note, but also with the task of undeceiving Mrs. Bramble, for whom I have the most profound respect and veneration, though my affection being otherwise engaged, is no longer in the power of

Sir,

your very humble servant,

RALPH   BARTON."

Having cast my eyes over this billet, I told her ladyship, that I would no longer retard the friendly office she had undertaken; and I and Jery forthwith retired into another room. There we soon perceived the conversation grow very warm betwixt the two ladies; and, at length, could distinctly hear certain terms of altercation, which we could no longer delay interrupting, with any regard to decorum. When we entered the scene of contention, we found Liddy had joined the disputants, and stood trembling betwixt them, as if she had been afraid they would have proceeded to something more practical than words——Lady Griskin's face was like the full moon in a storm of wind, glaring, fiery, and portentuous; while Tabby looked grim and ghastly, with an aspect breathing discord and dismay.—Our appearance put a stop to their mutual revilings; but her ladyship turning to me, "Cousin, (said she) I can't help saying I have met with a very ungrateful return from this lady, for the pains I have taken to serve her family—" "My family is much obliged to your ladyship (cried Tabby, with a kind of hysterical giggle); but we have no right to the good offices of such an honourable go-between." "But, for all that, good Mrs. Tabitha Bramble, (resumed the

2. A light four-wheeled coach.

other) I shall be content with the reflection, that virtue is its own reward; and it shall not be my fault, if you continue to make yourself ridiculous —Mr. Bramble, who has no little interest of his own to serve, will, no doubt, contribute all in his power to promote a match betwixt Mr. Barton and his niece, which will be equally honourable and advantageous; and, I dare say, miss Liddy herself will have no objection to a measure so well calculated to make her happy in life———" "I beg your ladyship's pardon, (exclaimed Liddy, with great vivacity) I have nothing but misery to expect from such a measure; and I hope my guardians will have too much compassion, to barter my peace of mind for any consideration of interest or fortune—" "Upon my word, miss Liddy! (said she) you have profited by the example of your good aunt—I comprehend your meaning, and will explain it when I have a proper opportunity———In the mean time, I shall take my leave—Madam, your most obedient, and devoted humble servant," said she, advancing close up to my sister, and curtsying so low, that I thought she intended to squat herself down on the floor—This salutation Tabby returned with equal solemnity; and the expression of the two faces, while they continued in this attitude, would be no bad subject for a pencil like that of the incomparable Hogarth,[3] if any such should ever appear again, in these times of dulness and degeneracy.

Jery accompanied her ladyship to her house, that he might have an opportunity to restore the etuis to Barton, and advise him to give up his suit, which was so disagreeable to his sister, against whom, however, he returned much irritated—Lady Griskin had assured him that Liddy's heart was pre-occupied; and immediately the idea of Wilson recurring to his imagination, his family-pride took the alarm—He denounced vengeance against that adventurer, and was disposed to be very peremptory with his sister; but I desired he would suppress his resentment, until I should have talked with her in private.

The poor girl, when I earnestly pressed her on this head, owned, with a flood of tears, that Wilson had actually come to the Hot Well at Bristol, and even introduced himself into our lodgings as a Jew pedlar; but that nothing had passed betwixt them, further than her begging him to withdraw immediately, if he had any regard for her peace of mind: that he had disappeared accordingly, after having attempted to prevail upon my sister's maid, to deliver a letter; which, however, she refused to receive, though she had consented to carry a message, importing that he was a gentleman of a good family; and that, in a very little time, he would avow his passion in that character—She confessed, that although he had not kept his word in this particular, he was not yet altogether indifferent to her affection; but solemnly promised, she would never carry on any correspondence with him, or any other admirer, for the future, without the privity and approbation of her brother and me.

3. William Hogarth (1697–1764) was an extremely talented and popular artist and engraver.

Altercation between Mrs Tabitha and Lady Griskin.

By this declaration, she made her own peace with Jery; but the hot-headed boy is more than ever incensed against Wilson, whom he now considers as an impostor, that harbours some infamous design upon the honour of his family—As for Barton, he was not a little mortified to find his present returned, and his addresses so unfavourably received; but he is not a man to be deeply affected by such disappointments; and I know not whether he is not as well pleased with being discarded by Liddy, as he would have been with a permission to prosecute his pretensions, at the risque of being every day exposed to the revenge or machinations of Tabby, who is not to be slighted with impunity.—I had not much time to moralize on these occurrences; for the house was visited by a constable and his gang, with a warrant from justice Buzzard,[4] to search the box of Humphry Clinker, my footman, who was just apprehended as a highway-man—This incident threw the whole family into confusion. My sister scolded the constable for presuming to enter the lodgings of a gentleman on such an errand, without having first asked, and obtained permission; her maid was frightened into fits, and Liddy shed tears of compassion for the unfortunate Clinker, in whose box, however, nothing was found to confirm the suspicion of robbery.

For my own part, I made no doubt of the fellow's being mistaken for some other person, and I went directly to the justice, in order to procure his discharge; but there I found the matter much more serious than I expected—Poor Clinker stood trembling at the bar, surrounded by thief-takers;[5] and at a little distance, a thick, squat fellow, a postilion, his accuser, who had seized him in the street, and swore positively to his person, that the said Clinker had, on the 15th day of March last, on Blackheath,[6] robbed a gentleman in a post chaise, which he (the postilion) drove—This deposition was sufficient to justify his commitment; and he was sent accordingly to Clerkenwell prison,[7] whither Jery accompanied him in the coach, in order to recommend him properly to the keeper, that he may want for no convenience which the place affords.

The spectators, who assembled to see this highwayman, were sagacious enough to discern something very villanous in his aspect; which (begging their pardon) is the very picture of simplicity; and the justice himself put a very unfavourable construction upon some of his answers, which, he said, savoured of the ambiguity and equivocation of an old offender; but, in my opinion, it would have been more just and humane to impute them to the confusion into which we may suppose a poor country lad to be thrown on such an occasion. I am still persuaded he is innocent; and, in this persuasion, I can do no less than use my utmost endeavours

4. Angus Ross suggests that Buzzard may reflect Sir John Hawkins (1719–89), an author and magistrate.
5. During most of the eighteenth century, a reward of £40 was offered for evidence leading to the conviction of a male thief. This generous reward led to a new trade, that of catching thieves.
6. An area near London known for highwaymen.
7. Newgate Prison in Clerkenwell, a street and section of London.

that he may not be oppressed—I shall, to-morrow, send my nephew to
wait on the gentleman who was robbed, and beg he will have the
humanity to go and see the prisoner; that, in case he should find him quite
different from the person of the highwayman, he may bear testimony in
his behalf—Howsoever it may fare with Clinker, this cursed affair will be
to me productive of intolerable chagrin—I have already caught a
dreadful cold, by rushing into the open air from the justice's parlour,
where I had been stewing in the crowd; and though I should not be laid up
with the gout, as I believe I shall, I must stay at London for some weeks,
till this poor devil comes to his trial at Rochester; so that, in all
probability, my Northern expedition is blown up.

If you can find any thing in your philosophical budget, to console me in
the midst of these distresses and apprehensions, pray let it be communicated to

your unfortunate friend,

London, June 12.   MATT. BRAMBLE,

To Sir WATKIN PHILLIPS, Bart. of Jesus college, Oxon.

DEAR WAT,

The farce is finished, and another piece of a graver cast brought upon
the stage.——Our aunt made a desperate attack upon Barton, who had
no other way of saving himself, but by leaving her in possession of the
field, and avowing his pretensions to Liddy, by whom he has been
rejected in his turn.—Lady Griskin acted as his advocate and agent on
this occasion, with such zeal as embroiled her with Mrs. Tabitha, and a
high scene of altercation passed betwixt these two religionists, which
might have come to action, had not my uncle interposed. They are
however reconciled, in consequence of an event which hath involved us
all in trouble and disquiet. You must know, the poor preacher, Humphry
Clinker, is now exercising his ministry among the felons in Clerkenwell
prison.—A postilion having sworn a robbery against him, no bail could
be taken, and he was committed to jail, notwithstanding all the remonstrances and interest my uncle could make in his behalf.

All things considered, the poor fellow cannot possibly be guilty, and
yet, I believe, he runs some risque of being hanged.—Upon his examination, he answered with such hesitation and reserve, as persuaded most of
the people, who crowded the place, that he was really a knave, and the
justice's remarks confirmed their opinion. Exclusive of my uncle and
myself, there was only one person who seemed inclined to favour the
culprit.—He was a young man, well dressed, and, from the manner in
which he cross-examined the evidence, we took it for granted, that he
was a student in one of the inns of court.—He freely checked the justice

for some uncharitable inferences he made to the prejudice of the prisoner, and even ventured to dispute with his worship on certain points of law.

My uncle, provoked at the unconnected and dubious answers of Clinker, who seemed in danger of falling a sacrifice to his own simplicity, exclaimed, "In the name of God, if you are innocent, say so." "No, (cried he) God forbid, that I should call myself innocent, while my conscience is burthened with sin." "What then, you did commit this robbery?" resumed his master. "No, sure, (said he) blessed be the Lord, I'm free of that guilt."

Here the justice interposed, observing, that the man seemed inclined to make a discovery by turning king's evidence, and desired the clerk to take his confession; upon which Humphry declared, that he looked upon confession to be a popish fraud, invented by the whore of Babylon.[8] The Templar[9] affirmed, that the poor fellow was *non compos*; and exhorted the justice to discharge him as a lunatic.——"You know very well, (added he) that the robbery in question was not committed by the prisoner."

The thief-takers grinned at one another; and Mr. Justice Buzzard replied with great emotion, "Mr. Martin, I desire you will mind your own business; I shall convince you one of these days that I understand mine." In short, there was no remedy; the mittimus[1] was made out, and poor Clinker sent to prison in a hackney-coach, guarded by the constable, and accompanied by your humble servant. By the way, I was not a little surprised to hear this retainer to justice bid the prisoner to keep up his spirits, for that he did not at all doubt, but that he would get off for a few weeks confinement.— He said, his worship knew very well that Clinker was innocent of the fact, and that the real highwayman, who robbed the chaise, was no other than that very individual Mr. Martin, who had pleaded so strenuously for honest Humphry.

Confounded at this information, I asked, "Why then is he suffered to go about at his liberty, and this poor innocent fellow treated as a malefactor?" "We have exact intelligence of all Mr. Martin's transactions; (said he) but as yet there is not evidence sufficient for his conviction; and as for this young man, the justice could do no less than commit him, as the postilion swore point-blank to his identity." "So if this rascally postilion should persist in the falsity to which he is sworn, (said I) this innocent lad may be brought to the gallows."

The constable observed, that he would have time enough to prepare for his trial, and might prove an *alibi*; or, perhaps, Martin might be apprehended and convicted for another fact; in which case, he might be prevailed upon to take this affair upon himself; or, finally, if these chances

---

8. Many members of the dissenting sects identified the Whore of Babylon (*Revelations*) with the Roman Catholic church.

9. Jery assumes that Mr. Martin is a student at one of the inns of court and calls him a Templar, or resident of the Temple where the inns of court are located.

1. A legal writ committing a person to jail.

should fail, and the evidence stand good against Clinker, the jury might recommend him to mercy, in consideration of his youth, especially if this should appear to be the first fact of which he had been guilty.

Humphry owned, he could not pretend to recollect where he had been on the day when the robbery was committed, much less prove a circumstance of that kind so far back as six months, though he knew he had been sick of the fever and ague, which, however, did not prevent him from going about—then, turning up his eyes, he ejaculated, "The Lord's will be done! if it be my fate to suffer, I hope I shall not disgrace the faith, of which, though unworthy, I make profession."

When I expressed my surprize, that the accuser should persist in charging Clinker, without taking the least notice of the real robber, who stood before him, and to whom, indeed, Humphry bore not the smallest resemblance; the constable (who was himself a thief-taker) gave me to understand, that Mr. Martin was the best qualified for business of all the gentlemen on the road he had ever known; that he had always acted on his own bottom, without partner or correspondent, and never went to work, but when he was cool and sober; that his courage and presence of mind never failed him; that his address was genteel, and his behaviour void of all cruelty and insolence; that he never encumbered himself with watches or trinkets, nor even with bank-notes, but always dealt for ready money, and that in the current coin of the kingdom; and that he could disguise himself and his horse in such a manner, that, after the action, it was impossible to recognize either the one or the other—"This great man (said he) has reigned paramount in all the roads within fifty miles of London above fifteen months, and has done more business in that time, than all the rest of the profession put together; for those who pass through his hands are so delicately dealt with, that they have no desire to give him the least disturbance; but for all that, his race is almost run—he is now fluttering about justice, like a moth about a candle—there are so many lime-twigs[2] laid in his way, that I'll bett a cool hundred, he swings before Christmas."

Shall I own to you, that this portrait, drawn by a ruffian, heightened by what I myself had observed in his deportment, has interested me warmly in the fate of poor Martin, whom nature seems to have intended for a useful and honourable member of that community upon which he now preys for subsistence? It seems, he lived some time as a clerk to a timber-merchant, whose daughter Martin having privately married, was discarded, and his wife turned out of doors. She did not long survive her marriage; and Martin, turning fortune-hunter, could not supply his occasions any other way, than by taking to the road, in which he has

---

2. A twig smeared with birdlime to catch small birds, hence a trap. Highway robbery was a capital offense throughout the period.

travelled hitherto with uncommon success.—He pays his respects regularly to Mr. Justice Buzzard, the thief-catcher-general of this metropolis, and sometimes they smoke a pipe together very lovingly, when the conversation generally turns upon the nature of evidence.—The justice has given him fair warning to take care of himself, and he has received his caution in good part.—Hitherto he has baffled all the vigilance, art, and activity of Buzzard and his emissaries, with such conduct as would have done honour to the genius of a Cæsar or a Turenne;[3] but he has one weakness, which has proved fatal to all the heroes of his tribe, namely, an indiscreet devotion to the fair sex, and, in all probability, he will be attacked on this defenceless quarter.

Be that as it may, I saw the body of poor Clinker consigned to the gaoler of Clerkenwell, to whose indulgence I recommended him so effectually, that he received him in the most hospitable manner, though there was a necessity for equipping him with a suit of irons, in which he made a very rueful appearance. The poor creature seemed as much affected by my uncle's kindness, as by his own misfortune. When I assured him, that nothing should be left undone for procuring his enlargement, and making his confinement easy in the mean time, he fell down on his knees, and kissing my hand, which he bathed with his tears, "O 'squire! (cried he, sobbing) what shall I say?—I can't—no, I can't speak—my poor heart is bursting with gratitude to you and my dear —dear—generous—noble benefactor."

I protest, the scene became so pathetic, that I was fain to force myself away, and returned to my uncle, who sent me in the afternoon with a compliment to one Mr. Mead, the person who had been robbed on Blackheath. As I did not find him at home, I left a message, in consequence of which he called at our lodgings this morning, and very humanely agreed to visit the prisoner. By this time, lady Griskin had come to make her formal compliments of condolance to Mrs. Tabitha, on this domestic calamity; and that prudent maiden, whose passion was now cooled, thought proper to receive her ladyship so civilly, that a reconciliation immediately ensued. These two ladies resolved to comfort the poor prisoner in their own persons, and Mr. Mead and I 'squired them to Clerkenwell, my uncle being detained at home by some slight complaints in his stomach and bowels.

The turnkey, who received us at Clerkenwell, looked remarkably sullen; and when we enquired for Clinker, "I don't care, if the devil had him; (said he) here has been nothing but canting and praying since the fellow entered the place.—Rabbit him! the tap will be ruined—we han't sold a cask of beer, nor a dozen of wine, since he paid his garnish—the gentlemen get drunk with nothing but your damned religion.——For my

---

3. The famous Roman general (c. 100–44 B.C.) and marshall of France (1611–75).

part, I believe as how your man deals with the devil.—Two or three as bold hearts as ever took the air upon Hounslow,[4] have been blubbering all night; and if the fellow an't speedily removed by Habeas Corpus, or otherwise, I'll be damn'd if there's a grain of true spirit left within these walls—we shan't have a soul to do credit to the place, or make his exit like a true-born Englishman—damn my eyes! there will be nothing but snivelling in the cart—we shall all die like so many psalm-singing weavers."

In short, we found that Humphry was, at that very instant, haranguing the felons in the chapel; and that the gaoler's wife and daughter, together with my aunt's woman, Win Jenkins, and our house-maid, were among the audience, which we immediately joined. I never saw any thing so strongly picturesque as this congregation of felons clanking their chains, in the midst of whom stood orator Clinker, expatiating, in a transport of fervor, on the torments of hell, denounced in scripture against evil-doers, comprehending murderers, robbers, thieves, and whoremongers. The variety of attention exhibited in the faces of those ragamuffins, formed a groupe that would not have disgraced the pencil of a Raphael.[5] In one, it denoted admiration; in another, doubt; in a third, disdain; in a fourth, contempt; in a fifth, terror; in a sixth, derision; and in a seventh, indignation.—As for Mrs. Winifred Jenkins, she was in tears, overwhelmed with sorrow; but whether for her own sins, or the misfortune of Clinker, I cannot pretend to say. The other females seemed to listen with a mixture of wonder and devotion. The gaoler's wife declared he was a saint in trouble, saying, she wished from her heart, there was such another good soul, like him, in every gaol in England.

Mr. Mead, having earnestly surveyed the preacher, declared his appearance was so different from that of the person who robbed him on Black-heath, that he could freely make oath he was not the man: but Humphry himself was by this time pretty well rid of all apprehensions of being hanged; for he had been the night before solemnly tried and acquitted by his fellow-prisoners, some of whom he had already converted to methodism. He now made proper acknowledgements for the honour of our visit, and was permitted to kiss the hands of the ladies, who assured him, he might depend upon their friendship and protection. Lady Griskin, in her great zeal, exhorted his fellow-prisoners to profit by the precious opportunity of having such a saint in bonds among them, and turn over a new leaf for the benefit of their poor souls; and, that her admonition might have the greater effect, she reinforced it with her bounty.

---

4. Hounslow Heath was the notorious hangout for highwaymen during the period, so that "taking the air of Hounslow" means to have become a high-wayman.

5. Raphael (1483–1520) was one of the great artists of the Italian Renaissance.

Humphry Clinker in prison preaching to the Felons.

While she and Mrs. Tabby returned in the coach with the two maid-servants, I waited on Mr. Mead to the house of justice Buzzard, who, having heard his declaration, said his oath could be of no use at present, but that he would be a material evidence for the prisoner at his trial; so that there seems to be no remedy but patience for poor Clinker; and, indeed, the same virtue, or medicine, will be necessary for us all, the 'squire in particular, who had set his heart upon his excursion to the northward.

While we were visiting honest Humphry in Clerkenwell prison, my uncle received a much more extraordinary visit at his own lodgings. Mr. Martin, of whom I have made such honourable mention, desired permission to pay him his respects, and was admitted accordingly. He told him, that having observed him, at Mr. Buzzard's, a good deal disturbed by what had happened to his servant, he had come to assure him he had nothing to apprehend for Clinker's life; for, if it was possible that any jury could find him guilty upon such evidence, he, Martin himself, would produce in court a person, whose deposition would bring him off clear as the sun at noon.—Sure, the fellow would not be so romantic as to take the robbery upon himself!—He said, the postilion was an infamous fellow, who had been a dabbler in the same profession, and saved his life at the Old Bailey[6] by impeaching his companions; that being now reduced to great poverty, he had made this desperate push, to swear away the life of an innocent man, in hopes of having the reward upon his conviction; but that he would find himself miserably disappointed, for the justice and his myrmidons were determined to admit of no interloper in this branch of business; and that he did not at all doubt but that they would find matter enough to shop the evidence himself before the next gaol-delivery. He affirmed, that all these circumstances were well known to the justice; and that his severity to Clinker was no other than a hint to his master to make him a present in private, as an acknowledgement of his candour and humanity.

This hint, however, was so unpalatable to Mr. Bramble, that he declared, with great warmth, he would rather confine himself for life to London, which he detested, than be at liberty to leave it to-morrow, in consequence of encouraging corruption in a magistrate. Hearing, however, how favorable Mr. Mead's report had been for the prisoner, he is resolved to take the advice of counsel in what manner to proceed for his immediate enlargement. I make no doubt, but that in a day or two this troublesome business may be discussed; and in this hope we are prepar-

---

6. The main criminal court.

ing for our journey. If our endeavours do not miscarry, we shall have taken the field before you hear again from

Yours,

London, June 11.   J. MELFORD.

To Dr. LEWIS.

Thank Heaven! dear Lewis, the clouds are dispersed, and I have now the clearest prospect of my summer campaign, which, I hope, I shall be able to begin to-morrow. I took the advice of counsel, with respect to the case of Clinker, in whose favour a lucky incident has intervened. The fellow who accused him, has had his own battery turned upon himself. —Two days ago, he was apprehended for a robbery on the highway, and committed, on the evidence of an accomplice. Clinker, having moved for a writ of *habeas corpus*, was brought before the lord chief justice, who, in consequence of an affidavit of the gentleman who had been robbed, importing that the said Clinker was not the person who stopped him on the highway, as well as in consideration of the postilion's character and present circumstances, was pleased to order, that my servant should be admitted to bail, and he has been discharged accordingly, to the unspeakable satisfaction of our whole family, to which he has recommended himself in an extraordinary manner, not only by his obliging deportment, but by his talents of preaching, praying, and singing psalms, which he has exercised with such effect, that even Tabby respects him as a chosen vessel. If there was any thing like affectation or hypocrisy in this excess of religion, I would not keep him in my service; but, so far as I can observe, the fellow's character is downright simplicity, warmed with a kind of enthusiasm, which renders him very susceptible of gratitude and attachment to his benefactors.

As he is an excellent horseman, and understands farriery, I have bought a stout gelding for his use, that he may attend us on the road, and have an eye to our cattle, in case the coachman should not mind his business. My nephew, who is to ride his own saddle-horse, has taken, upon trial, a servant just come from abroad with his former master, sir William Strollop, who vouches for his honesty. The fellow, whose name is Dutton, seems to be a petit-maitre.—He has got a smattering of French, bows, and grins, and shrugs, and takes snuff *a la mode de France*, but values himself chiefly upon his skill and dexterity in hair-dressing. —If I am not much deceived by appearance, he is, in all respects, the very contrast of Humphry Clinker.

My sister has made up matters with lady Griskin; though, I must own, I should not have been sorry to see that connexion entirely destroyed: but Tabby is not of a disposition to forgive Barton, who, I understand, is gone to his seat in Berkshire for the summer season. I cannot help suspecting, that in the treaty of peace, which has been lately ratified betwixt those two females, it is stipulated, that her ladyship shall use her best endeavours to provide an agreeable help-mate for our sister Tabitha, who seems to be quite desperate in her matrimonial designs. Perhaps, the match-maker is to have a valuable consideration in the way of brokerage, which she will most certainly deserve, if she can find any man in his senses, who will yoke with Mrs. Bramble from motives of affection or interest.

I find my spirits and my health affect each other reciprocally—that is to say, every thing that discomposes my mind, produces a correspondent disorder in my body; and my bodily complaints are remarkably mitigated by those considerations that dissipate the clouds of mental chagrin. —The imprisonment of Clinker brought on those symptoms which I mentioned in my last, and now they are vanished at his discharge.—It must be owned, indeed, I took some of the tincture of ginseng, prepared according to your prescription, and found it exceedingly grateful to the stomach; but the pain and sickness continued to return, after short intervals, till the anxiety of my mind was entirely removed, and then I found myself perfectly at ease. We have had fair weather these ten days, to the astonishment of the Londoners, who think it portentous. If you enjoy the same indulgence in Wales, I hope Barns has got my hay made, and safe cocked, by this time. As we shall be in motion for some weeks, I cannot expect to hear from you as usual; but I shall continue to write from every place at which we make any halt, that you may know our track, in case it should be necessary to communicate any thing to

Your assured friend,
London, June 14.   MATT. BRAMBLE.

To Mrs. MARY JONES, at Brambleton-hall, &c.

DEAR MARY,

Having the occasion of my cousin Jenkins of Aberga'ny, I send you, as a token, a turkey-shell comb, a kiple of yards of green ribbon, and a sarment upon the nothingness of good works, which was preached in the Tabernacle;[7] and you will also recieve a horn buck for Saul, whereby she may learn her letters; for I'm much consarned about the state of her poor sole—and what are all the pursuits of this life to the consarns of that immortal part?—What is life but a veil of affliction? O Mary! the whole family have been in such a constipation!—Mr. Clinker has been in trouble, but the gates of hell have not been able to prevail again him. ——His virtue is like poor gould, seven times tried in the fire. He was

7. Whitefield was the principal preacher in the Tabernacle and a leader in the Calvinist wing of the Methodist movement, which elevated faith over good works as a means of salvation.

tuck up for a rubbery, and had before gustass Busshard, who made his mittamouse; and the pore youth was sent to prison upon the false oaf of a willian, that wanted to sware his life away for the looker of cain.

The 'squire did all in his power, but could not prevent his being put in chains, and confined among common manufactors, where he stud like an innocent sheep in the midst of wolves and tygers.—Lord knows, what mought have happened to this pyehouse young man, if master had not applied to Apias Korkus, who lives with the ould bailiff, and is, they say, five hundred years ould, (God bless us!) and a congeror: but, if he be, sure I am he don't deal with the devil, otherwise he wouldn't have sought out Mr. Clinker, as he did, in spite of stone walls, iron bolts, and double locks, that flew open at his command; for Ould Scratch [8] has not a greater enemy upon hearth than Mr. Clinker, who is, indeed, a very powerfull labourer in the Lord's vineyard. I do no more than yuse the words of my good lady, who has got the infectual calling; and, I trust, that even myself, though unworthy, shall find grease to be excepted.——Miss Liddy has been touch'd to the quick, but is a little timorsome: howsomever, I make no doubt, but she, and all of us, will be brought, by the endeavours of Mr. Clinker, to produce blessed fruit of generation and repentance.——As for master and the young 'squire, they have as yet had narro glimpse of the new light.——I doubt as how their harts are hardened by worldly wisdom, which, as the pyebill faith, is foolishness in the sight of God.

O Mary Jones, pray without seizing for grease to prepare you for the operations of this wonderful instrument, which, I hope, will be exorcised this winter upon you and others at Brambleton-hall.——To-morrow, we are to set out in a cox and four for Yorkshire; and, I believe, we shall travel that way far, and far, and farther than I can tell; but I shan't go so far as to forget my friends; and Mary Jones will always be remembred as one of them by her

humble sarvant,

London, June 14. WIN. JENKINS.

To Mrs. GWYLLIM, house-keeper at Brambleton-hall.

MRS. GWILLIM,

I can't help thinking it very strange, that I never had an answer to the letter I wrote you some weeks ago from Bath, concerning the sour bear, the gander, and the maids eating butter, which I won't allow to be wasted.——We are now going upon a long gurney to the north, whereby I desire you will redouble your care and circumflexion, that the family may be well manged in our absence; for, you know, you must render

8. The Devil.

accunt, not only to your earthly master, but also to him that is above; and if you are found a good and faithfull sarvant, great will be your reward in haven. I hope there will be twenty stun of cheese ready for market by the time I get huom, and as much owl spun, as will make half a dozen pair of blankets; and that the savings of the butter-milk fetch me a good penny before Martinmass, as the two pigs are to be fed for baking with bitchmast and acrons.[9]

I wrote to doctor Lews for the same porpuss, but he never had the good manners to take the least notice of my letter; for which reason, I shall never favour him with another, though he beshits me on his bended knees. You will do well to keep a watchfull eye over the hind Villiams, who is one of his amissories, and, I believe, no better than he should be at bottom. God forbid that I should lack christian charity; but charity begins at huom, and sure nothing can be a more charitable work than to rid the family of such vermine. I do suppose, that the brindled cow has been had to the parson's bull, that old Moll has had another litter of pigs, and that Dick is become a mighty mouser. Pray order every thing for the best, and be frugal, and keep the maids to their labour.—If I had a private opportunity, I would send them some hymns to sing instead of profane ballads; but, as I can't, they and you must be contented with the prayers of

                                          Your assured friend,

London, June 14.   T. BRAMBLE.

To Sir WATKIN PHILLIPS, Bar[t]. of Jesus college, Oxon.

DEAR PHILLIPS,

The very day after I wrote my last, Clinker was set at liberty—As Martin had foretold, the accuser was himself committed for a robbery, upon unquestionable evidence. He had been for some time in the snares of the thief-taking society; who, resenting his presumption in attempting to incroach upon their monopoly of impeachment, had him taken up and committed to Newgate, on the deposition of an accomplice, who has been admitted as evidence for the king. The postilion being upon record as an old offender, the chief justice made no scruple of admitting Clinker to bail, when he perused the affidavit of Mr. Mead, importing that the said Clinker was not the person that robbed him on Blackheath; and honest Humphry was discharged—When he came home, he expressed great eagerness to pay his respects to his master, and here his elocution failed him, but his silence was pathetic; he fell down at his feet, and embraced his knees, sheding a flood of tears, which my uncle did not see

---

9. The fruit of the beech tree, called mast, and acorns from the oak were used as feed for pigs.

without emotion—He took snuff in some confusion; and, putting his hand in his pocket, gave him his blessing in something more substantial than words—"Clinker, (said he) I am so well convinced, both of your honesty and courage, that I am resolved to make you my life-guard-man on the highway."

He was accordingly provided with a case of pistols, and a carbine to be slung a-cross his shoulders; and every other preparation being made, we set out last Thursday, at seven in the morning; my uncle, with the three women in the coach; Humphry, well mounted on a black gelding bought for his use; myself a-horseback, attended by my new valet, Mr. Dutton, an exceeding coxcomb, fresh from his travels, whom I have taken upon trial—The fellow wears a solitaire,[1] uses paint,[2] and takes rappee[3] with all the grimace of a French marquis. At present, however, he is in a riding-dress, jack-boots, leather breeches, a scarlet waistcoat, with gold binding, a laced hat, a hanger,[4] a French posting-whip in his hand, and his hair en queue.[5]

Before we had gone nine miles, my horse lost one of his shoes; so that I was obliged to stop at Barnet to have another, while the coach proceeded at an easy pace over the common. About a mile short of Hatfield, the postilions, stopping the carriage, gave notice to Clinker that there were two suspicious fellows a-horse-back, at the end of a lane, who seemed waiting to attack the coach. Humphry forthwith apprised my uncle, declaring he would stand by him to the last drop of his blood; and, unslinging his carbine, prepared for action. The 'squire had pistols in the pockets of the coach, and resolved to make use of them directly; but he was effectually prevented by his female companions, who flung themselves about his neck, and screamed in concert—At that instant, who should come up at a hand-gallop, but Martin, the highway-man, who, advancing to the coach, begged the ladies would compose themselves for a moment; then, desiring Clinker to follow him to the charge, he pulled a pistol out of his bosom, and they rode up together to give battle to the rogues, who, having fired at a great distance, fled a-cross the common. They were in pursuit of the fugitives when I came up, not a little alarmed at the shreiks in the coach, where I found my uncle in a violent rage, without his periwig, struggling to disentangle himself from Tabby and the other two, and swearing with great vociferation. Before I had time to interpose, Martin and Clinker returned from the pursuit, and the former payed his compliments with great politeness, giving us to understand, that the fellows had scampered off, and that he believed they were a couple of raw 'prentices from London. He commended Clinker for his

1. A loose necktie in the French fashion.
2. Makeup.
3. Strong, dark-brown snuff.
4. A light sword, still in fashion in England among

the upper classes, but passing out of fashion.
5. In a tail or braid. Jery's use of the French phrase indicates that Dutton believes it to be in the French fashion.

courage, and said, if we would give him leave, he would have the honour to accompany us as far as Stevenage, where he had some business.

The 'squire, having recollected and adjusted himself, was the first to laugh at his own situation; but it was not without difficulty, that Tabby's arms could be untwisted from his neck, Liddy's teeth chattered, and Jenkins was threatened with a fit as usual. I had communicated to my uncle the character of Martin, as it was described by the constable, and he was much struck with its singularity—He could not suppose the fellow had any design on our company, which was so numerous and well armed; he therefore thanked him, for the service he had just done them, said he would be glad of his company, and asked him to dine with us at Hatfield. This invitation might not have been agreeable to the ladies, had they known the real profession of our guest, but this was a secret to all, except my uncle and myself—Mrs. Tabitha, however, would by no means consent to proceed with a case of loaded pistols in the coach, and they were forthwith discharged in complaisance to her and the rest of the women.

Being gratified in this particular, she became remarkably good-humoured, and at dinner behaved in the most affable manner to Mr. Martin, with whose polite address and agreeable conversation she seemed to be much taken. After dinner, the landlord accosting me in the yard, asked, with a significant look, if the gentleman that rode the sorrel belonged to our company?—I understood his meaning, but answered, *no*; that he had come up with us on the common, and helped us to drive away two fellows, that looked like highwaymen—He nodded three times distinctly, as much as to say, he knows his cue. Then he inquired, if one of those men was mounted on a bay mare, and the other on a chesnut gelding with a white streak down his forehead? and being answered in the affirmative, he assured me they had robbed three post-chaises this very morning—I inquired, in my turn, if Mr. Martin was of his acquaintance; and, nodding thrice again, he answered, that *he had seen the gentleman.*

Before we left Hatfield, my uncle, fixing his eyes on Martin with such expression as is more easily conceived than described, asked, if he often travelled that road? and he replied with a look which denoted his understanding the question, that he very seldom did business in that part of the country. In a word, this adventurer favoured us with his company to the neighbourhood of Stevenage, where he took his leave of the coach and me, in very polite terms, and turned off upon a cross-road, that led to a village on the left—At supper, Mrs. Tabby was very full in the praise of Mr. Martin's good-sense and good-breeding, and seemed to regret that she had not a further opportunity to make some experiment upon his affection. In the morning, my uncle was not a little surprised to receive, from the waiter, a billet couched in these words—

"Sir,

"I could easily perceive from your looks, when I had the honour to converse with you at Hatfield, that my character is not unknown to you; and, I dare say, you won't think it strange, that I should be glad to change my present way of life, for any other honest occupation, let it be ever so humble, that will afford me bread in moderation, and sleep in safety—Perhaps you may think I flatter, when I say, that from the moment I was witness to your generous concern in the cause of your servant, I conceived a particular esteem and veneration for your person; and yet what I say is true. I should think myself happy, if I could be admitted into your protection and service, as house-steward, clerk, butler, or bailiff, for either of which places I think myself tolerably well qualified; and, sure I am, I should not be found deficient in gratitude and fidelity—At the same time, I am very sensible how much you must deviate from the common maxims of discretion, even in putting my professions to the trial; but I don't look upon you as a person that thinks in the ordinary stile; and the delicacy of my situation, will, I know, justify this address to a heart warmed with beneficence and compassion—Understanding you are going pretty far north, I shall take an opportunity to throw myself in your way again, before you reach the borders of Scotland; and, I hope, by that time, you will have taken into consideration, the truly distressful case of,

> honoured sir,
>
> your very humble,
>
> and devoted servant,
>
> EDWARD MARTIN.

The 'squire, having perused this letter, put it into my hand, without saying a syllable; and when I had read it, we looked at each other in silence. From a certain sparkling in his eyes, I discovered there was more in his heart, than he cared to express with his tongue, in favour of poor Martin; and this was precisely my own feeling, which he did not fail to discern, by the same means of communication—"What shall we do (said he) to save this poor sinner from the gallows, and make him a useful member of the commonwealth? and yet the proverb says, Save a thief from the gallows, and he'll cut your throat." I told him, I really believed Martin was capable of giving the proverb the lie; and that I should heartily concur in any step he might take in favour of his sollicitation. We mutually resolved to deliberate upon the subject, and, in the mean time, proceeded on our journey. The roads, having been broke up by the heavy rains in the spring, were so rough, that although we travelled very slowly, the jolting occasioned such pain to my uncle, that he was become exceedingly peevish when we arrived at this place, which lies about eight miles from the post-road, between Wetherby and Boroughbridge.

Harrigate-water, so celebrated for its efficacy in the scurvy and other distempers, is supplied from a copious spring, in the hollow of a wild common, round which, a good many houses have been built for the convenience of the drinkers, though few of them are inhabited. Most of the company lodge at some distance, in five separate inns, situated in different parts of the common, from whence they go every morning to the well, in their own carriages. The lodgers of each inn form a distinct society, that eat together; and there is a commodious public room, where they breakfast in dishabille, at separate tables, from eight o'clock till eleven, as they chance or chuse to come in—Here also they drink tea in the afternoon, and play at cards or dance in the evening. One custom, however, prevails, which I look upon as a solecism in politeness—The ladies treat with tea in their turns; and even girls of sixteen are not exempted from this shameful imposition——There is a public ball by subscription every night at one of the houses, to which all the company from the others are admitted by tickets; and, indeed, Harrigate treads upon the heels of Bath, in the articles of gaiety and dissipation—with this difference, however, that here we are more sociable and familiar. One of the inns is already full up to the very garrets, having no less than fifty lodgers, and as many servants. Our family does not exceed thirty-six; and I should be sorry to see the number augmented, as our accommodations won't admit of much increase.

At present, the company is more agreeable than one could expect from an accidental assemblage of persons, who are utter strangers to one another—There seems to be a general disposition among us to maintain good-fellowship, and promote the purposes of humanity, in favour of those who come hither on the score of health. I see several faces which we left at Bath, although the majority are of the Northern counties, and many come from Scotland for the benefit of these waters—In such a variety, there must be some originals, among whom Mrs. Tabitha Bramble is not the most inconsiderable—No place where there is such an intercourse between the sexes, can be disagreeable to a lady of her views and temperament—She has had some warm disputes at table, with a lame parson from Northumberland, on the new birth,[6] and the insignificance of moral virtue; and her arguments have been reinforced by an old Scotch lawyer, in a tye periwig, who, though he has lost his teeth, and the use of his limbs, can still wag his tongue with great volubility. He has paid her such fulsome compliments, upon her piety and learning, as seem to have won her heart; and she, in her turn, treats him with such attention as indicates a design upon his person; but, by all accounts, he is too much a fox to be inveigled into any snare that she can lay for his affection.

We do not propose to stay long at Harrigate, though, at present, it is our headquarters, from whence we shall make some excursions, to visit

6. The religious experience of being born again.

two or three of our rich relations, who are settled in this county.——Pray, remember me to all our friends of Jesus, and allow me to be still

yours affectionately,

Harrigate, June 23.   J. MELFORD.

To Dr. LEWIS.

DEAR DOCTOR,

Considering the tax we pay for turnpikes, the roads of this country constitute a most intolerable grievance. Between Newark and Weatherby, I have suffered more from jolting and swinging than ever I felt in the whole course of my life, although the carriage is remarkably commodious and well hung, and the postilions were very careful in driving. I am now safely housed at the New Inn, at Harrigate, whither I came to satisfy my curiosity, rather than with any view of advantage to my health; and, truly, after having considered all the parts and particulars of the place, I cannot account for the concourse of people one finds here, upon any other principle but that of caprice, which seems to be the character of our nation.

Harrigate is a wild common, bare and bleak, without tree or shrub, or the least signs of cultivation; and the people who come to drink the water, are crowded together in paltry inns, where the few tolerable rooms are monopolized by the friends and favourites of the house, and all the rest of the lodgers are obliged to put up with dirty holes, where there is neither space, air, nor convenience. My apartment is about ten feet square; and when the folding bed is down, there is just room sufficient to pass between it and the fire. One might expect, indeed, that there would be no occasion for a fire at Midsummer; but here the climate is so backward, that an ash tree, which our landlord has planted before my window, is just beginning to put forth its leaves; and I am fain to have my bed warmed every night.

As for the water, which is said to have effected so many surprising cures, I have drank it once, and the first draught has cured me of all desire to repeat the medicine.——Some people say it smells of rotten eggs, and others compare it to the scourings of a foul gun.——It is generally supposed to be strongly impregnated with sulphur; and Dr. Shaw,[7] in his book upon mineral waters, says, he has seen flakes of sulphur floating in the well.—*Pace tanti viri;*[8] I, for my part, have never observed any thing like sulphur, either in or about the well, neither do I find that any brimstone has ever been extracted from the water. As for the smell, if I may be

7. Dr. Peter Shaw (1694–1763) was physician to George II and George III. He wrote several books, but the one probably alluded to here is *New Exper-* *iments and Observations upon Mineral Waters* (1746).
8. With all due deference to such a great man.

allowed to judge from my own organs, it is exactly that of bilge-water; and the saline taste of it seems to declare that it is nothing else than salt water putrified in the bowels of the earth. I was obliged to hold my nose with one hand, while I advanced the glass to my mouth with the other; and after I had made shift to swallow it, my stomach could hardly retain what it had received.—The only effects it produced were sickness, griping, and insurmountable disgust.——I can hardly mention it without puking. ——The world is strangely misled by the affectation of singularity. I cannot help suspecting, that this water owes its reputation in a great measure to its being so strikingly offensive.—On the same kind of analogy, a German doctor[9] has introduced hemlock and other poisons, as specifics,[1] into the *materia medica*.[2]——I am persuaded, that all the cures ascribed to the Harrigate water, would have been as efficaciously, and infinitely more agreeably performed, by the internal and external use of sea-water. Sure I am, this last is much less nauseous to the taste and smell, and much more gentle in its operation as a purge, as well as more extensive in its medical qualities.

Two days ago, we went across the country to visit 'squire Burdock, who married a first cousin of my father, an heiress, who brought him an estate of a thousand a year. This gentleman is a declared opponent of the ministry in parliament; and having an opulent fortune, piques himself upon living in the country, and maintaining *old English hospitality*. ——By the bye, this is a phrase very much used by the English themselves, both in words and writing; but I never heard of it out of the island, except by way of irony and sarcasm. What the hospitality of our fore-fathers has been I should be glad to see recorded, rather in the memoirs of strangers who have visited our country, and were the proper objects and judges of such hospitality, than in the discourse and lucubrations of the modern English, who seem to describe it from theory and conjecture. Certain it is, we are generally looked upon by foreigners, as a people totally destitute of this virtue; and I never was in any country abroad, where I did not meet with persons of distinction, who complained of having been inhospitably used in Great Britain. A gentleman of France, Italy, or Germany, who has entertained and lodged an Englishman at his house, when he afterwards meets with his guest at London, is asked to dinner at the Saracen's-head, the Turk's-head, the Boar's-head, or the Bear,[3] eats raw beef and butter, drinks execrable port, and is allowed to pay his share of the reckoning.

But to return from this digression, which my feeling for the honour of my country obliged me to make——our Yorkshire cousin has been a mighty fox-hunter *before the Lord*;[4] but now he is too fat and unwieldy to

---

9. Byron W. Gassman suggests that this refers to Anton von Stoerck.
1. A substance used in treating a specific disease.
2. List of substances used in treating diseases.

3. These are pubs and coaching inns in various parts of London.
4. From the Book of Genesis I. 9, where it describes Nimrod, a mighty hunter.

leap ditches and five-bar gates; nevertheless, he still keeps a pack of hounds, which are well exercised; and his huntsman every night entertains him with the adventures of the day's chace, which he recites in a tone and terms that are extremely curious and significant. In the mean time, his broad brawn is scratched by one of his grooms.——This fellow, it seems, having no inclination to curry any beast out of the stable, was at great pains to scollop his nails in such a manner that the blood followed at every stroke.——He was in hopes that he would be dismissed from this disagreeable office, but the event turned out contrary to his expectation. ——His master declared he was the best scratcher in the family; and now he will not suffer any other servant to draw a nail upon his carcase.

The 'squire's lady is very proud, without being stiff or inaccessible. ——She receives even her inferiors in point of fortune with a kind of arrogant civility; but then she thinks she has a right to treat them with the most ungracious freedoms of speech, and never fails to let them know she is sensible of her own superior affluence.——In a word, she speaks well of no living soul, and has not one single friend in the world. Her husband hates her mortally; but, although the brute is sometimes so very powerful in him that he will have his own way, he generally truckles to her dominion, and dreads, like a school-boy, the lash of her tongue. On the other hand, she is afraid of provoking him too far, lest he should make some desperate effort to shake off her yoke.——She, therefore, acquiesces in the proofs he daily gives of his attachment to the liberty of an English freeholder, by saying and doing, at his own table, whatever gratifies the brutality of his disposition, or contributes to the ease of his person. The house, though large, is neither elegant nor comfortable.—It looks like a great inn, crowded with travellers, who dine at the landlord's ordinary, where there is a great profusion of victuals and drink, but mine host seems to be misplaced; and I would rather dine upon filberts with a hermit, than feed upon venison with a hog. The footmen might be aptly compared to the waiters of a tavern, if they were more serviceable and less rapacious; but they are generally insolent and inattentive, and so greedy, that, I think, I can dine better, and for less expence, at the Star and Garter in Pall mall,[5] than at our cousin's castle in Yorkshire. The 'squire is not only accommodated with a wife, but he is also blessed with an only son, about two and twenty, just returned from Italy, a complete fidler and *dillettante*; and he slips no opportunity of manifesting the most perfect contempt for his own father.

When we arrived, there was a family of foreigners at the house, on a visit to this virtuoso, with whom they had been acquainted at the Spa: it was the count de Melville, with his lady, on their way to Scotland. Mr. Burdock had met with an accident, in consequence of which both the

---

5. A fashionable and expensive tavern noted for its wine.

count and I would have retired, but the young gentleman and his mother insisted upon our staying dinner; and their serenity seemed to be so little ruffled by what had happened, that we complied with their invitation. The 'squire had been brought home over night in his post-chaise, so terribly belaboured about the pate, that he seemed to be in a state of stupefaction, and had ever since remained speechless. A country apothecary, called Grieve, who lived in a neighbouring village, having been called to his assistance, had let him blood, and applied a poultice to his head, declaring, that he had no fever, nor any other bad symptom but the loss of speech, if he really had lost that faculty. But the young 'squire said this practitioner was an *ignorantaccio*, that there was a fracture in the *cranium*, and that there was a necessity for having him trepanned[6] without loss of time. His mother, espousing this opinion, had sent an express to York for a surgeon to perform the operation, and he was already come with his 'prentice and instruments. Having examined the patient's head, he began to prepare his dressings; though Grieve still retained his first opinion that there was no fracture, and was the more confirmed in it as the 'squire had passed the night in profound sleep, uninterrupted by any catching or convulsion. The York surgeon said he could not tell whether there was a fracture, until he should take off the scalp; but, at any rate, the operation might be of service in giving vent to any blood that might be extravasated, either above or below the *dura mater*. The lady and her son were clear for trying the experiment; and Grieve was dismissed with some marks of contempt, which, perhaps, he owed to the plainness of his appearance. He seemed to be about the middle age, wore his own black hair without any sort of dressing; by his garb, one would have taken him for a quaker, but he had none of the stiffness of that sect, on the contrary, he was very submissive, respectful, and remarkably taciturn.

Leaving the ladies in an apartment by themselves, we adjourned to the patient's chamber, where the dressings and instruments were displayed in order upon a pewter dish. The operator, laying aside his coat and periwig, equipped himself with a night-cap, apron, and sleeves, while his 'prentice and footman, seizing the 'squire's head, began to place it in a proper posture.——But mark what followed.—The patient, bolting upright in the bed, collared each of these assistants with the grasp of Hercules, exclaiming, in a bellowing tone, "I ha'n't lived so long in Yorkshire to be trepanned by such vermin as you;" and leaping on the floor, put on his breeches quietly, to the astonishment of us all. The surgeon still insisted upon the operation, alledging it was now plain that the brain was injured, and desiring the servants to put him into bed again; but no body would venture to execute his orders, or even to interpose:

---

6. The word means both "to be operated on with a trepan" (a bone saw for the skull) and to be tricked.

when the 'squire turned him and his assistants out of doors, and threw his apparatus out at the window. Having thus asserted his prerogative, and put on his cloaths with the help of a valet, the count, with my nephew and me, were introduced by his son, and received with his usual stile of rustic civility; then turning to signor Macaroni, with a sarcastic grin, "I tell thee what, Dick, (said he) a man's scull is not to be bored every time his head is broken; and I'll convince thee and thy mother, that I know as many tricks as e'er an old fox in the West Riding."[7]

We afterwards understood he had quarrelled at a public house with an exciseman, whom he challenged to a bout at single stick, in which he had been worsted; and that the shame of this defeat had tied up his tongue. As for madam, she had shewn no concern for his disaster, and now heard of his recovery without emotion.—She had taken some little notice of my sister and niece, though rather with a view to indulge her own petulance, than out of any sentiment of regard to our family.—She said Liddy was a fright, and ordered her woman to adjust her head before dinner; but she would not meddle with Tabby, whose spirit, she soon perceived, was not to be irritated with impunity. At table, she acknowledged me so far as to say she had heard of my father; though she hinted, that he had disobliged her family by making a poor match in Wales. She was disagreeably familiar in her enquiries about our circumstances; and asked, if I intended to bring up my nephew to the law. I told her, that, as he had an independent fortune, he should follow no profession but that of a country gentleman; and that I was not without hopes of procuring for him a seat in parliament.——"Pray, cousin, (said she) what may his fortune be?" When I answered, that, with what I should be able to give him, he would have better than two thousand a year, she replied, with a disdainful toss of her head, that it would be impossible for him to preserve his independence on such a paltry provision.

Not a little nettled at this arrogant remark, I told her, I had the honour to sit in parliament with her father, when he had little more than half that income; and I believed there was not a more independent and incorruptible member in the house. "Ay; but times are changed, (cried the 'squire) —Country gentlemen now-a-days live after another fashion.—My table alone stands me in a cool thousand a quarter, though I raise my own stock, import my own liquors, and have every thing at the first hand.—True it is, I keep open house, and receive all comers, for the honour of Old England." "If that be the case, (said I) 'tis a wonder you can maintain it at so small an expence; but every private gentleman is not expected to keep a *caravansera* for the accommodation of travellers: indeed, if every individual lived in the same stile, you would not have such a number of

---

7. Yorkshire was broken into three administrative districts, the West Riding (from "thriding," the old word for the third part), the East Riding, and the North Riding.

guests at your table, of consequence your hospitality would not shine so bright for the glory of the West Riding." The young 'squire, tickled by this ironical observation, exclaimed, "*O che burla!*"[8]—his mother eyed me in silence with a supercilious air; and the father of the feast, taking a bumper of October,[9] "My service to you, cousin Bramble, (said he) I have always heard there was something keen and biting in the air of the Welch mountains."

I was much pleased with the count de Melville, who is sensible, easy, and polite; and the countess is the most amiable woman I ever beheld. In the afternoon they took leave of their entertainers, and the young gentleman, mounting his horse, undertook to conduct their coach through the park, while one of their servants rode round to give notice to the rest, whom they had left at a public house on the road. The moment their backs were turned, the censorious dæmon took possession of our Yorkshire landlady and our sister Tabitha.—The former observed, that the countess was a good sort of a body, but totally ignorant of good breeding, consequently aukward in her address. The 'squire said he did not pretend to the breeding of any thing but colts; but that the jade would be very handsome, if she was a little more in flesh. "Handsome! (cried Tabby) she has indeed a pair of black eyes without any meaning; but then there is not a good feature in her face." "I know not what you call good features in Wales; (replied our landlord) but they'll pass in Yorkshire." Then turning to Liddy, he added, "What say you, my pretty Redstreak?[1] —what is your opinion of the countess?" "I think, (cried Liddy, with great emotion) she's an angel." Tabby chid her for talking with such freedom in company; and the lady of the house said, in a contemptuous tone, she supposed miss had been brought up at some country boarding-school.

Our conversation was suddenly interrupted by the young gentleman, who galloped into the yard all aghast, exclaiming, that the coach was attacked by a great number of highwaymen. My nephew and I rushing out, found his own and his servant's horse ready saddled in the stable, with pistols in the caps.—We mounted instantly, ordering Clinker and Dutton to follow with all possible expedition; but notwithstanding all the speed we could make, the action was over before we arrived, and the count with his lady, safe lodged at the house of Grieve, who had signalized himself in a very remarkable manner on this occasion. At the turning of a lane, that led to the village where the count's servants remained, a couple of robbers a-horseback suddenly appeared, with their pistols advanced: one kept the coachman in awe, and the other demanded the count's money, while the young 'squire went off at full speed, without

---

8. Oh, what a joke!
9. A brimming glass of the strong ale traditionally brewed in October.

1. A common apple used for cider, and here a comment on the high color of Liddy's cheeks.

ever casting a look behind. The count desiring the thief to withdraw his pistol, as the lady was in great terror, delivered his purse without making the least resistance; but not satisfied with this booty, which was pretty considerable, the rascal insisted upon rifling her of her ear-rings and necklace, and the countess screamed with affright. Her husband, exasperated at the violence with which she was threatened, wrested the pistol out of the fellow's hand, and turning it upon him, snapped it in his face; but the robber knowing there was no charge in it, drew another from his bosom, and in all probability would have killed him on the spot, had not his life been saved by a wonderful interposition. Grieve, the apothecary, chancing to pass that very instant, ran up to the coach, and with a crab-stick, which was all the weapon he had, brought the fellow to the ground with the first blow; then seizing his pistol, presented it to his colleague, who fired his piece at random, and fled without further opposition. The other was secured by the assistance of the count and the coachman; and his legs being tied under the belly of his own horse, Grieve conducted him to the village, whither also the carriage proceeded. It was with great difficulty the countess could be kept from swooning; but at last she was happily conveyed to the house of the apothecary, who went into the shop to prepare some drops for her, while his wife and daughter administered to her in another apartment.

I found the count standing in the kitchen with the parson of the parish, and expressing much impatience to see his protector, whom as yet he had scarce found time to thank for the essential service he had done him and the countess.—The daughter passing at the same time with a glass of water, monsieur de Melville could not help taking notice of her figure, which was strikingly engaging.—"Ay, (said the parson) she is the prettiest girl, and the best girl in all my parish; and if I could give my son an estate of ten thousand a year, he should have my consent to lay it at her feet. If Mr. Grieve had been as sollicitous about getting money, as he has been in performing all the duties of a primitive Christian, Fy would not have hung so long upon his hands." "What is her name?" said I. "Sixteen years ago (answered the vicar) I christened her by the names of Seraphina Melvilia." "Ha! what! how! (cried the count eagerly) sure, you said Seraphina Melvilia." "I did; (said he) Mr. Grieve told me those were the names of two noble persons abroad, to whom he had been obliged for more than life."

The count, without speaking another syllable, rushed into the parlour, crying, "This is your god-daughter, my dear." Mrs. Grieve, then seizing the countess by the hand, exclaimed with great agitation, "O madam! —O sir!—I am—I am your poor Elinor.——This is my Seraphina Melvilia.——O child! these are the count and countess of Melville, the generous—the glorious benefactors of thy once unhappy parents."

The countess rising from her seat, threw her arms about the neck of the amiable Seraphina, and clasped her to her breast with great tenderness, while she herself was embraced by the weeping mother. This moving scene was completed by the entrance of Grieve himself, who falling on his knees before the count, "Behold (said he) a penitent, who at length can look upon his patron without shrinking." "Ah, Ferdinand! (cried he, raising and folding him in his arms) the play-fellow of my infancy—the companion of my youth!—Is it to you then I am indebted for my life?" "Heaven has heard my prayer, (said the other) and given me an opportunity to prove myself not altogether unworthy of your clemency and protection." He then kissed the hand of the countess, while monsieur de Melville saluted his wife and lovely daughter, and all of us were greatly affected by this pathetic recognition.

In a word, Grieve was no other than Ferdinand count Fathom, whose adventures were printed many years ago.[2] Being a sincere convert to virtue, he had changed his name, that he might elude the enquiries of the count, whose generous allowance he determined to forego, that he might have no dependence but upon his own industry and moderation. He had accordingly settled in this village as a practitioner in surgery and physic, and for some years wrestled with all the miseries of indigence, which, however, he and his wife had borne with the most exemplary resignation. At length, by dint of unwearied attention to the duties of his profession, which he exercised with equal humanity and success, he had acquired a tolerable share of business among the farmers and common people, which enabled him to live in a decent manner. He had been scarce ever seen to smile; was unaffectedly pious; and all the time he could spare from the avocations of his employment he spent in educating his daughter, and in studying for his own improvement.—In short, the adventurer Fathom was, under the name of Grieve, universally respected among the commonalty of this district, as a prodigy of learning and virtue. These particulars I learned from the vicar, when we quitted the room, that they might be under no restraint in their mutual effusions. I make no doubt that Grieve will be pressed to leave off business, and re-unite himself to the count's family; and as the countess seemed extremely fond of his daughter, she will, in all probability, insist upon Seraphina's accompanying her to Scotland.

Having paid our compliments to these noble persons, we returned to the 'squire's, where we expected an invitation to pass the night, which was wet and raw; but, it seems, 'squire Burdock's hospitality reached not so far for the honour of Yorkshire: we therefore departed in the evening, and lay at an inn, where I caught cold.

In hope of riding it down before it could take fast hold on my constitution, I resolved to visit another relation, one Mr. Pimpernel, who

2. Smollett here takes the liberty of re-introducing characters from his earlier work *The Adventures of Ferdinand, Count Fathom* (1753).

lived about a dozen miles from the place where we lodged. Pimpernel being the youngest of four sons, was bred an attorney at Furnival's-inn;[3] but all his elder brothers dying, he got himself called to the bar for the honour of his family, and soon after this preferment, succeeded to his father's estate, which was very considerable. He carried home with him all the knavish chicanery of the lowest pettifogger, together with a wife whom he had purchased of a drayman for twenty pounds; and he soon found means to obtain a *Dedimus*[4] as an acting justice of peace. He is not only a sordid miser in his disposition, but his avarice is mingled with a spirit of despotism, which is truly diabolical.—He is a brutal husband, an unnatural parent, a harsh master, an oppressive landlord, a litigious neighbour, and a partial magistrate.——Friends he has none; and in point of hospitality and good breeding, our cousin Burdock is a prince in comparison of this ungracious miscreant, whose house is the lively representation of a gaol. Our reception was suitable to the character I have sketched. Had it depended upon the wife, we should have been kindly treated.—She is really a good sort of a woman, in spite of her low original, and well respected in the county; but she has not interest enough in her own house to command a draught of table-beer, far less to bestow any kind of education on her children, who run about, like ragged colts, in a state of nature.—Pox on him! he is such a dirty fellow, that I have not patience to prosecute the subject.

By that time we reached Harrigate, I began to be visited by certain rheumatic symptoms. The Scotch lawyer, Mr. Micklewhimmen, recommended a hot bath of these waters so earnestly, that I was over-persuaded to try the experiment.—He had used it often with success, and always stayed an hour in the bath, which was a tub filled with Harrigate water, heated for the purpose. If I could hardly bear the smell of a single tumbler when cold, you may guess how my nose was regaled by the steams arising from a hot bath of the same fluid. At night, I was conducted into a dark hole on the ground floor, where the tub smoaked and stunk like the pot of Acheron,[5] in one corner, and in another stood a dirty bed provided with thick blankets, in which I was to sweat after coming out of the bath. My heart seemed to die within me when I entered this dismal bagnio, and found my brain assaulted by such insufferable effluvia.—I cursed Micklewhimmen for not considering that my organs were formed on this side of the Tweed;[6] but being ashamed to recoil upon the threshold, I submitted to the process.

3. An inn of the Court of Chancery where attorneys had their offices and often their homes, and where young men "read the law" in a kind of apprentice program.
4. The usual short form for a writ of *dedimus potestatum* (we have given the power), which allowed a person not a judge to act in place of one.

5. The river of woe in Hades, one of the two great rivers of the classical underworld.
6. The River Tweed was the border between Scotland and England, and here Matt claims that his delicate olfactory sense is because of his not being a Scot.

After having endured all but real suffocation for above a quarter of an hour in the tub, I was moved to the bed and wrapped in blankets.—There I lay a full hour panting with intolerable heat; but not the least moisture appearing on my skin, I was carried to my own chamber, and passed the night without closing an eye, in such a flutter of spirits as rendered me the most miserable wretch in being. I should certainly have run distracted, if the rarefaction of my blood, occasioned by that Stygian bath, had not burst the vessels, and produced a violent hæmorrhage, which, though dreadful and alarming, removed the horrible disquiet.—I lost two pounds of blood, and more, on this occasion; and find myself still weak and languid; but, I believe, a little exercise will forward my recovery; and therefore I am resolved to set out to-morrow for York, in my way to Scarborough, where I propose to brace up my fibres by sea-bathing, which, I know, is one of your favourite specifics. There is, however, one disease, for which you have found as yet no specific, and that is old age, of which this tedious unconnected epistle is an infallible symptom:—what, therefore, *cannot be cured, must be endured,*[7] by you, as well as by

Yours,

Harrigate, June 26.   MATT. BRAMBLE.

To Sir WATKIN PHILLIPS, Bart. of Jesus college, Oxon.

DEAR KNIGHT,

The manner of living at Harrigate was so agreeable to my disposition, that I left the place with some regret—Our aunt Tabby would have probably made some objection to our departing so soon, had not an accident embroiled her with Mr. Micklewhimmen, the Scotch advocate, on whose heart she had been practising, from the second day after our arrival—That original, though seemingly precluded from the use of his limbs, had turned his genius to good account—In short, by dint of groaning, and whining, he had excited the compassion of the company so effectually, that an old lady, who occupied the very best apartment in the house, gave it up for his ease and convenience. When his man led him into the Long Room, all the females were immediately in commotion —One set an elbow-chair; another shook up the cushion; a third brought a stool; and a fourth a pillow, for the accommodation of his feet—Two ladies (of whom Tabby was always one) supported him into the dining-room, and placed him properly at the table; and his taste was indulged with a succession of delicacies, culled by their fair hands. All this attention he repaid with a profusion of compliments and benedictions, which were not the less agreeable for being delivered in the Scottish

---

7. Lewis Knapp has pointed out that this proverbial phrase appears in William Langland's *Piers Plowman.*

dialect. As for Mrs. Tabitha, his respects were particularly addressed to her, and he did not fail to mingle them with religious reflections, touching free grace, knowing her biass to methodism, which he also professed upon a calvinistical model.

For my part, I could not help thinking this lawyer was not such an invalid as he pretended to be. I observed he ate very heartily three times a-day; and though his bottle was marked *stomachic tincture*, he had recourse to it so often, and seemed to swallow it with such peculiar relish, that I suspected it was not compounded in the apothecary's shop, or the chemist's laboratory. One day, while he was earnest in discourse with Mrs. Tabitha, and his servant had gone out on some occasion or other, I dexterously exchanged the labels, and situation of his bottle and mine; and having tasted his tincture, found it was excellent claret. I forthwith handed it about to some of my neighbours, and it was quite emptied before Mr. Micklewhimmen had occasion to repeat his draught. At length, turning about, he took hold of my bottle, instead of his own, and, filling a large glass, drank to the health of Mrs. Tabitha——It had scarce touched his lips, when he perceived the change which had been put upon him, and was at first a little out of countenance——He seemed to retire within himself, in order to deliberate, and in half a minute his resolution was taken; addressing himself to our quarter, "I give the gentleman cradit for his wit (said he); it was a gude practical joke; but sometimes *hi joci in seria ducunt mala* [8]——I hope for his own sake he has na drank all the liccor; for it was a vara poorful infusion of jallap [9] in Bourdeaux wine; and its possable he may ha ta'en sic a dose as will produce a terrible catastrophe in his ain booels——"

By far the greater part of the contents had fallen to the share of a young clothier from Leeds, who had come to make a figure at Harrigate, and was, in effect a great coxcomb in his way. It was with a view to laugh at his fellow-guests, as well as to mortify the lawyer, that he had emptied the bottle, when it came to his turn, and he had laughed accordingly: but now his mirth gave way to his apprehension——He began to spit, to make wry faces, and writhe himself into various contorsions——"Damn the stuff! (cried he) I thought it had a villanous twang——pah! He that would cozen a Scot, mun get oop betimes, and take Old Scratch for his counsellor——" "In troth mester what d'ye ca'um, (replied the lawyer) your wit has run you into a filthy puddle——I'm truly consarned for your waeful case——The best advice I can give you, in sic a delemma, is to send an express to Rippon for doctor Waugh, without delay, and, in the mean time, swallow all the oil and butter you can find in the hoose, to defend your poor stomach and intastins from the villication of the particles of the jallap, which is vara violent, even when taken in moderation."

8. These jokes will lead to serious problems: misquoted from Horace's *Ars Poetica* ll. 451–52.   9. A purgative drug, usually spelled "jalap."

The poor clothier's torments had already begun: he retired, roaring with pain, to his own chamber; the oil was swallowed, and the doctor sent for; but before he arrived, the miserable patient had made such discharges upwards and downwards, that nothing remained to give him further offence; and this double evacuation, was produced by imagination alone; for what he had drank was genuine wine of Bourdeaux, which the lawyer had brought from Scotland for his own private use. The clothier, finding the joke turn out so expensive and disagreeable, quitted the house next morning, leaving the triumph to Micklewhimmen, who enjoyed it internally, without any outward signs of exultation—on the contrary, he affected to pity the young man for what he had suffered; and acquired fresh credit from this shew of moderation.

It was about the middle of the night, which succeeded this adventure, that the vent of the kitchen chimney being foul, the soot took fire, and the alarm was given in a dreadful manner—Every body leaped naked out of bed, and in a minute the whole house was filled with cries and confusion—There were two stairs in the house, and to these we naturally ran; but they were both so blocked up, by the people pressing one upon another, that it seemed impossible to pass, without throwing down and trampling upon the women. In the midst of this anarchy, Mr. Micklewhimmen, with a leathern portmanteau on his back, came running as nimble as a buck along the passage; and Tabby, in her under-petticoat, endeavouring to hook him under the arm, that she might escape through his protection, he very fairly pushed her down, crying, "Na, na, gude faith, charity begins at hame!" Without paying the least respect to the shrieks and intreaties of his female friends, he charged through the midst of the crowd, overturning every thing that opposed him; and actually fought his way to the bottom of the stair-case—By this time Clinker had found a ladder, by which he entered the window of my uncle's chamber, where our family was assembled, and proposed that we should make our exit successively by that conveyance. The 'squire exhorted his sister to begin the descent; but, before she could resolve, her woman, Mrs. Winifred Jenkins, in a transport of terror, threw herself out at the window upon the ladder, while Humphry dropped upon the ground, that he might receive her in her descent——This maiden was just as she had started out of bed, the moon shone very bright, and a fresh breeze of wind blowing, none of Mrs. Winifred's beauties could possibly escape the view of the fortunate Clinker, whose heart was not able to withstand the united force of so many charms; at least, I am much mistaken, if he has not been her humble slave from that moment—He received her in his arms, and, giving her his coat to protect her from the weather, ascended again with admirable dexterity.

At that instant, the landlord of the house called out with an audible voice, that the fire was extinguished, and the ladies had nothing further to fear: this was a welcome note to the audience, and produced an

immediate effect; the shrieking ceased, and a confused sound of expostulation ensued. I conducted Mrs. Tabitha and my sister to their own
chamber, where Liddy fainted away; but was soon brought to herself.
Then I went to offer my services to the other ladies, who might want
assistance—They were all scudding through the passage to their several
apartments; and as the thoroughfair was lighted by two lamps, I had a
pretty good observation of them in their transit; but as most of them were
naked to the smock, and all their heads shrouded in huge night-caps, I
could not distinguish one face from another, though I recognized some of
their voices—These were generally plaintive; some wept, some scolded,
and some prayed—I lifted up one poor old gentlewoman, who had been
overturned and sore bruised by a multitude of feet; and this was also the
case with the lame parson from Northumberland, whom Micklewhimmen had in his passage overthrown, though not with impunity, for the
cripple, in falling, gave him such a good pelt on the head with his crutch,
that the blood followed.

As for this lawyer, he waited below till the hurly burly was over, and
then stole softly to his own chamber, from whence he did not venture to
make a second sally till eleven in the forenoon, when he was led into the
Public Room by his own servant and another assistant, groaning most
woefully, with a bloody napkin round his head. But things were greatly
altered—The selfish brutality of his behaviour on the stairs had steeled
their hearts against all his arts and address——Not a soul offered to
accommodate him with chair, cushion, or footstool; so that he was
obliged to sit down on a hard wooden bench—In that position, he looked
around with a rueful aspect, and, bowing very low, said in a whining tone,
"Your most humble servant, ladies—Fire is a dreadful calamity—" "Fire
purifies gold, and it tries friendship," cried Mrs. Tabitha, bridling. "Yea,
madam (replied Micklewhimmen); and it trieth discretion also—" "If
discretion consists in forsaking a friend in adversity, you are eminently
possessed of that virtue," resumed our aunt—"Na, madam, (rejoined the
advocate) well I wot, I cannot claim any merit from the mode of my
retreat—Ye'll please to observe ladies, there are twa independent
principles that actuate our nature—One is instinct, which we have in
common with the brute creation, and the other is reason—Noo, in
certain great emergencies, when the faculty of reason is suspended,
instinct taks the lead, and when this predominates, having no affinity
with reason, it pays no sort of regard to its connections; it only operates
for the preservation of the individual, and that by the most expeditious
and effectual means; therefore, begging your pardon, ladies, I'm no
accountable in *foro conscientiæ*,[1] for what I did, while under the influence
of this irresistible pooer."

1. In conscience's forum.

Here my uncle interposing, "I should be glad to know, (said he) whether it was instinct that prompted you to retreat with bag and baggage; for, I think, you had a portmanteau on your shoulder—" The lawyer answered, without hesitation, "Gif I might tell my mind freely, withoot incuring the suspicion of presumption, I should think it was something superior to either reason or instinct which suggested that measure, and this on a twafald accoont: in the first place, the portmanteau contained the writings of a worthy nobleman's estate; and their being burnt would have occasioned a loss that could not be repaired; secondly, my good angel seems to have laid the portmantle on my shoulders, by way of defence, to sustain the violence of a most inhuman blow, from the crutch of a reverend clergyman; which, even in spite of that medium, hath wounded me sorely, even unto the pericranium." "By your own doctrine, (cried the parson, who chanced to be present) I am not accountable for the blow, which was the effect of instinct." "I crave your pardon, reverend sir, (said the other) instinct never acts but for the preservation of the individual; but your preservation was out of the case ——you had already received the damage, and therefore the blow must be imputed to revenge, which is a sinful passion, that ill becomes any Christian, especially a protestant divine; and let me tell you, most reverend doctor, gin I had a mind to plea, the law would hauld my libel relevant." "Why, the damage is pretty equal on both sides (cried the parson); your head is broke, and my crutch is snapt in the middle—Now, if you will repair the one, I will be at the expence of curing the other."

This sally raised the laugh against Micklewhimmen, who began to look grave; when my uncle, in order to change the discouse, observed, that instinct had been very kind to him in another respect; for it had restored to him the use of his limbs, which, in his exit, he had moved with surprising agility.——He replied, that it was the nature of fear to brace up the nerves;[2] and mentioned some surprising feats of strength and activity performed by persons under the impulse of terror; but he complained, that in his own particular, the effects had ceased when the cause was taken away—The 'squire said, he would lay a tea-drinking on his head, that he should dance a Scotch measure, without making a false step; and the advocate grinning, called for the piper—A fiddler being at hand, this original started up, with his bloody napkin over his black tye-periwig, and acquitted himself in such a manner as exerted the mirth of the whole company; but he could not regain the good graces of Mrs. Tabby, who did not understand the principle of instinct; and the lawyer did not think it worth his while to proceed to further demonstration.

---

2. Not in the contemporary restricted sense, but more nearly those elements which constitute the main strength of a man, though it can be used for either "sinews" or "muscles" in the usage of the period.

From Harrigate, we came hither, by the way of York, and here we shall tarry some days, as my uncle and Tabitha are both resolved to make use of the waters. Scarborough, though a paltry town, is romantic from its situation along a cliff that over-hangs the sea. The harbour is formed by a small elbow of land that runs out as a natural mole, directly opposite to the town; and on that side is the castle, which stands very high, of considerable extent, and, before the invention of gun-powder, was counted impregnable. At the other end of Scarborough are two public rooms for the use of the company, who resort to this place in the summer, to drink the waters and bathe in the sea; and the diversions are pretty much on the same footing here as at Bath. The Spa is a little way beyond the town, on this side, under a cliff, within a few paces of the sea, and thither the drinkers go every morning in dishabille; but the descent is by a great number of steps, which invalids find very inconvenient. Betwixt the well and the harbour, the bathing machines are ranged along the beach, with all their proper utensils and attendants——You have never seen one of these machines——Image to yourself a small, snug, wooden chamber, fixed upon a wheel-carriage, having a door at each end, and on each side a little window above, a bench below——The bather, ascending into this apartment by wooden steps, shuts himself in, and begins to undress, while the attendant yokes a horse to the end next the sea, and draws the carriage forwards, till the surface of the water is on a level with the floor of the dressing-room, then he moves and fixes the horse to the other end——The person within, being stripped, opens the door to the sea-ward, where he finds the guide ready, and plunges headlong into the water——After having bathed, he re-ascends into the apartment, by the steps which had been shifted for that purpose, and puts on his clothes at his leisure, while the carriage is drawn back again upon the dry land; so that he has nothing further to do, but to open the door, and come down as he went up——Should he be so weak or ill as to require a servant to put off and on his clothes, there is room enough in the apartment for half a dozen people. The guides who attend the ladies in the water, are of their own sex, and they and the female bathers have a dress of flannel for the sea; nay, they are provided with other conveniences for the support of decorum. A certain number of the machines are fitted with tilts, that project from the sea-ward ends of them, so as to screen the bathers from the view of all persons whatsoever——The beach is admirably adapted for this practice, the descent being gently gradual, and the sand soft as velvet; but then the machines can be used only at a certain time of the tide, which varies every day; so that sometimes the bathers are obliged to rise very early in the morning——For my part, I love swimming as an exercise, and can enjoy it at all times of the tide, without the formality of an apparatus——You and I have often plunged together into the Isis; but the sea is a much more noble bath, for health as well as pleasure. You cannot conceive what a flow of spirits it gives, and how it braces every sinew of the human frame. Were I to enumerate half the diseases which are every day cured by sea-bathing, you might justly say you had received a treatise, instead of a letter, from

your affectionate friend

and servant,

Scarborough, July 1.   J. MELFORD.

To Dr. LEWIS.

I have not found all the benefit I expected at Scarborough, where I have been these eight days—From Harrigate we came hither by the way of York, where we stayed only one day to visit the Castle, the Minster, and the Assembly-room. The first, which was heretofore a fortress, is now converted to a prison, and is the best, in all respects, I ever saw at home or abroad—It stands in a high situation, extremely well ventilated; and has a spacious area within the walls, for the health and convenience of all the prisoners, except those whom it is necessary to secure in close confinement——Even these last have all the comforts that the nature of their situation can admit. Here the assizes are held, in a range of buildings erected for that purpose.

As for the Minster, I know not how to distinguish it, except by its great size and the height of its spire, from those other antient churches in different parts of the kingdom, which used to be called monuments of Gothic architecture; but it is now agreed, that this stile is Saracen rather than Gothic;[3] and, I suppose, it was first imported into England from Spain, great part of which was under the dominion of the Moors. Those British architects, who adopted this stile, don't seem to have considered the propriety of their adoption. The climate of the country, possessed by the Moors or Saracens, both in Africa and Spain, was so exceedingly hot and dry, that those who built places of worship for the multitude, employed their talents in contriving edifices that should be cool; and, for this purpose, nothing could be better adopted than those buildings; vast, narrow, dark, and lofty, impervious to the sun-beams, and having little communication with the scorched external atmosphere; but ever affording a refreshing coolness, like subterranean cellars in the heats of summer, or natural caverns in the bowels of huge mountains. But nothing could be more preposterous, than to imitate such a mode of architecture in a country like England, where the climate is cold, and the air eternally loaded with vapours; and where, of consequence, the builder's intention should be to keep the people dry and warm—For my part, I never entered the Abbey church at Bath but once, and the moment I stept over

3. Bramble is here echoing Sir Christopher Wren in his use of "saracen" to describe the gothic York Minster.

the threshold, I found myself chilled to the very marrow of my bones
—When we consider, that in our churches, in general, we breathe a gross
stagnated air, surcharged with damps from vaults, tombs, and charnel-
houses, may we not term them so many magazines of rheums, created for
the benefit of the medical faculty? and safely aver, that more bodies are
lost, than souls saved, by going to church, in the winter especially, which
may be said to engross eight months in the year. I should be glad to know,
what offence it would give to tender consciences, if the house of God was
made more comfortable, or less dangerous to the health of valetudinarians; and whether it would not be an encouragement to piety, as well as
the salvation of many lives, if the place of worship was well floored,
wainscotted, warmed, and ventilated, and its area kept sacred from the
pollution of the dead. The practice of burying in churches was the effect
of ignorant superstition, influenced by knavish priests, who pretended
that the devil could have no power over the defunct, if he was interred in
holy ground; and this, indeed, is the only reason that can be given for
consecrating all cemeteries, even at this day.

The external appearance of an old cathedral cannot be but displeasing
to the eye of every man, who has any idea of propriety and proportion,
even though he may be ignorant of architecture as a science; and the long
slender spire puts one in mind of a criminal impaled, with a sharp stake
rising up through his shoulder—These towers, or steeples, were likewise
borrowed from the Mahometans; who, having no bells, used such
minarets for the purpose of calling the people to prayers—They may be
of further use, however, for making observations and signals; but I would
vote for their being distinct from the body of the church, because they
serve only to make the pile more barbarous, or Saracencial.

There is nothing of this Arabic architecture in the Assembly Room,[4]
which seems to me to have been built upon a design of Palladio,[5] and
might be converted into an elegant place of worship; but it is indifferently contrived for that sort of idolatry which is performed in it at
present: the grandeur of the fane gives a diminutive effect to the little
painted divinities that are adored in it, and the company, on a ball-night,
must look like an assembly of fantastic fairies, revelling by moon-light
among the columns of a Grecian temple.

Scarborough seems to be falling off, in point of reputation——All
these places (Bath excepted) have their vogue, and then the fashion
changes—I am persuaded, there are fifty spaws in England as efficacious
and salutary as that of Scarborough, though they have not yet risen to
fame; and, perhaps, never will, unless some medical encomiast should
find an interest in displaying their virtues to the public view——Be that

4. The Assembly Rooms at York were designed by
the Earl of Burlington in 1730.
5. Andrea Palladio (1518–80) was an Italian architect, particularly of country retreats. His work was
very influential in the eighteenth century in England.

as it may, recourse will always be had to this place for the convenience of sea-beathing, while this practice prevails; but it were to be wished, they would make the beach more accessible to invalids.

I have here met with my old acquaintance, H——t,[6] whom you have often heard me mention as one of the most original characters upon earth ——I first knew him at Venice, and afterwards saw him in different parts of Italy, where he was well known by the nick-name of Cavallo Bianco, from his appearing always mounted on a pale horse, like Death in the Revelations. You must remember the account I once gave you of a curious dispute he had at Constantinople, with a couple of Turks, in defence of the Christian religion; a dispute from which he acquired the epithet of Demonstrator[7]—The truth is, H—— owns no religion but that of nature; but, on this occasion, he was stimulated to shew his parts, for the honour of his country—Some years ago, being in the Campidog-lio[8] at Rome, he made up to the bust of Jupiter, and, bowing very low, exclaimed in the Italian language, "I hope, sir, if ever you get your head above water again, you will remember that I paid my respects to you in your adversity." This sally was reported to the cardinal Camerlengo, and by him laid before pope Benedict XIV. who could not help laughing at the extravagance of the address, and said to the cardinal, "Those English heretics think they have a right to go to the devil in their own way."

Indeed H—— was the only Englishman I ever knew, who had resolution enough to live in his own way, in the midst of foreigners; for, neither in dress, diet, customs, or conversation, did he deviate one tittle from the manner in which he had been brought up. About twelve years ago, he began a Giro or circuit, which he thus performed—At Naples, where he fixed his head-quarters, he embarked for Marseilles, from whence he travelled with a Voiturin[9] to Antibes—There he took his passage to Genoa and Lerici; from which last place he proceeded, by the way of Cambratina, to Pisa and Florence—After having halted some time in this metropolis, he set out with a Vetturino[1] for Rome, where he reposed himself a few weeks, and then continued his route for Naples, in order to wait for the next opportunity of embarkation—After having twelve times described this circle, he lately flew off at a tangent to visit some trees at his country-house in England, which he had planted above twenty years ago, after the plan of the double colonnade in the piazza of St. Peter's at Rome——He came hither to Scarborough, to pay his respects to his noble friend and former pupil, the M— of G——,[2] and,

6. Colonel William Hewett (1693–1766) was a well-known traveler and eccentric.
7. This is a delicate allusion to an indelicate story. Samuel Pegge in *Anonymiana* (2nd ed., London, 1818, p. 196) suppresses the story while essentially revealing it. Hewett's argument with the Turks concerned the Paradise of Mahomet, which was said to provide faithful Muslim men with beautiful women called houris, and Hewett argued that Christians were better qualified to enjoy them than either Jews or Turks. Apparently he then demonstrated the superiority in the form of an uncircumcised penis.
8. One of the classical hills of Rome and a popular stop for visitors.
9. French coach driver.
1. Driver of an Italian carriage.
2. The Marquis of Granby, John Manners (1721–

forgetting that he is now turned of seventy, sacrificed so liberally to Bacchus, that next day he was seized with a fit of the apoplexy, which has a little impaired his memory; but he retains all the oddity of his character in perfection, and is going back to Italy, by the way of Geneva, that he may have a conference with his friend Voltaire,[3] about giving the last blow to the Christian superstition—He intends to take shipping here for Holland or Hamburgh; for it is a matter of great indifference to him at what part of the continent he first lands.

When he was going abroad the last time, he took his passage in a ship bound for Leghorn, and his baggage was actually embarked. In going down the river by water, he was by mistake put on board of another vessel under sail; and, upon inquiry, understood she was bound to Petersburgh——"Petersburgh, —Petersburgh[4]—(said he) I don't care if I go along with you." He forthwith struck a bargain with the captain; bought a couple of shirts of the mate, and was safe conveyed to the court of Muscovy, from whence he travelled by land to receive his baggage at Leghorn——He is now more likely than ever to execute a whim of the same nature; and I will hold any wager, that as he cannot be supposed to live much longer, according to the course of nature, his exit will be as odd as his life has been extravagant.[5]

But, to return from one humorist to another; you must know I have received benefit, both from the chalybeate[6] and the sea, and would have used them longer, had not a most ridiculous adventure, by making me the town-talk, obliged me to leave the place; for I can't bear the thoughts of affording a spectacle to the multitude——Yesterday morning, at six o'clock, I went down to the bathing-place, attended by my servant Clinker, who waited on the beach as usual—The wind blowing from the north, and the weather being hazy, the water proved so chill, that when I rose from my first plunge, I could not help sobbing and bawling out, from the effects of the cold. Clinker, who heard me cry, and saw me indistinctly a good way without the guide, buffeting the waves, took it for granted I was drowning, and rushing into the sea, clothes and all, overturned the guide in his hurry to save his master. I had swam out a few strokes, when hearing a noise, I turned about and saw Clinker, already up to his neck, advancing towards me, with all the wildness of terror in his

70).
3. François Marie Arouet (1694–1778), known as Voltaire, was a famous French philosopher and writer.
4. Saint Petersburg, the former name of Leningrad.
5. This gentleman crossed the sea to France, visited and conferred with Mr. de Voltaire at Fernay, resumed his old circuit at Genoa, and died in 1767 [actually 1766], at the house of Vanini in Florence. Being taken with a suppression of urine, he resolved, in imitation of Pomponius Atticus, to take himself off by abstinence; and this resolution he executed like an ancient Roman. He saw company to the last, cracked his jokes, conversed freely, and entertained his guests with music. On the third day of his fast, he found himself entirely freed of his complaint; but refused taking sustenance. He said the most disagreeable part of the voyage was past, and he should be a cursed fool indeed, to put about ship, when he was just entering the harbour. In these sentiments he persisted, without any marks of affectation, and thus finished his course with such ease and serenity, as would have done honour to the firmest Stoic of antiquity. [Smollett's note.]
6. A spring which yielded mineral water impregnated with iron.

aspect—Afraid he would get out of his depth, I made haste to meet him, when, all of a sudden, he seized me by one ear, and dragged me bellowing with pain upon the dry beach, to the astonishment of all the people, men, women, and children there assembled.

I was so exasperated by the pain of my ear, and the disgrace of being exposed in such an attitude, that, in the first transport, I struck him down; then, running back into the sea, took shelter in the machine where my clothes had been deposited. I soon recollected myself so far as to do justice to the poor fellow, who, in great simplicity of heart, had acted from motives of fidelity and affection—Opening the door of the machine, which was immediately drawn on shore, I saw him standing by the wheel, dropping like a water-work, and trembling from head to foot; partly from cold, and partly from the dread of having offended his master—I made my acknowledgments for the blow he had received, assured him I was not angry, and insisted upon his going home immediately, to shift his clothes; a command which he could hardly find in his heart to execute, so well disposed was he to furnish the mob with further entertainment at my expence. Clinker's intention was laudable without all doubt, but, nevertheless, I am a sufferer by his simplicity—I have had a burning-heat, and a strange buzzing noise in that ear, ever since it was so roughly treated; and I cannot walk the street without being pointed at, as the monster that was hauled naked a-shore upon the beach—Well, I affirm that folly is often more provoking than knavery, aye and more mischievous too; and whether a man had not better choose a sensible rogue, than an honest simpleton for his servant, is no matter of doubt with

yours,

Scarborough, July 4.   MATT. BRAMBLE.

To Sir WATKIN PHILLIPS, Bar^t. of Jesus college, Oxon.

DEAR WATT,

We made a precipitate retreat from Scarborough, owing to the excessive delicacy of our 'squire, who cannot bear the thoughts of being *prætereuntium digito monstratus*.[7]

One morning, while he was bathing in the sea, his man Clinker took it in his head that his master was in danger of drowning; and, in this conceit, plunging into the water, he lugged him out naked on the beach, and almost pulled off his ear in the operation. You may guess how this atchievement was relished by Mr. Bramble, who is impatient, irascible, and has the most extravagant ideas of decency and decorum in the œconomy of his own person—In the first ebullition of his choler, he

---

7. Pointed out by the fingers of passers-by: adapted from Horace's *Carmina* IV. iii. 22.

knocked Clinker down with his fist; but he afterwards made him amends for this outrage, and, in order to avoid the further notice of the people, among whom this incident had made him remarkable, he resolved to leave Scarborough next day.

We set out accordingly over the moors, by the way of Whitby, and began our journey betimes, in hopes of reaching Stockton that night; but in this hope we were disappointed—In the afternoon, crossing a deep gutter, made by a torrent, the coach was so hard strained, that one of the irons, which connect the frame, snapt, and the leather sling on the same side, cracked in the middle—The shock was so great, that my sister Liddy struck her head against Mrs. Tabitha's nose with such violence that the blood flowed; and Win Jenkins was darted through a small window, in that part of the carriage next the horses, where she stuck like a bawd in the pillory, till she was released by the hand of Mr. Bramble. We were eight miles distant from any place where we could be supplied with chaises, and it was impossible to proceed with the coach, until the damage should be repaired—In this dilemma, we discovered a black-smith's forge on the edge of a small common, about half a mile from the scene of our disaster, and thither the postilions made shift to draw the carriage slowly, while the company walked a-foot; but we found the black-smith had been dead some days; and his wife, who had been lately delivered, was deprived of her senses, under the care of a nurse, hired by the parish. We were exceedingly mortified at this disappointment, which, however, was surmounted by the help of Humphry Clinker, who is a surprising compound of genius and simplicity. Finding the tools of the defunct, together with some coals in the smithy, he unscrewed the damaged iron in a twinkling, and, kindling a fire, united the broken pieces with equal dexterity and dispatch—While he was at work upon this operation, the poor woman in the straw,[8] struck with the well-known sound of the hammer and anvil, started up, and, notwithstanding all the nurse's efforts, came running into the smithy, where, throwing her arms about Clinker's neck, "Ah, Jacob! (cried she) how could you leave me in such a condition?"

This incident was too pathetic to occasion mirth——it brought tears into the eyes of all present. The poor widow was put to bed again; and we did not leave the village without doing something for her benefit—Even Tabitha's charity was awakened on this occasion. As for the tender-hearted Humphry Clinker, he hammered the iron and wept at the same time—But his ingenuity was not confined to his own province of farrier and black-smith—it was necessary to join the leather sling, which had been broke; and this service he likewise performed, by means of a broken

8. I.e., the woman who had just given birth to a child. The phrase probably comes from the associ- ation with the straw which is placed in the stalls of livestock when they are giving birth.

awl, which he new-pointed and ground, a little hemp, which he spun into lingels,[9] and a few tacks which he made for the purpose—Upon the whole, we were in a condition to proceed in little more than one hour; but even this delay obliged us to pass the night at Gisborough—Next day we crossed the Tees at Stockton, which is a neat agreeable town; and there we resolved to dine, with purpose to lie at Durham.

Whom should we meet in the yard, when we alighted, but Martin the adventurer? Having handed out the ladies, and conducted them into an apartment, where he payed his compliments to Mrs. Tabby, with his usual address, he begged leave to speak to my uncle in another room; and there, in some confusion, he made an apology for having taken the liberty to trouble him with a letter at Stevenage. He expressed his hope, that Mr. Bramble had bestowed some consideration on his unhappy case, and repeated his desire of being taken into his service.

My uncle, calling me into the room, told him, that we were both very well inclined to rescue him from a way of life that was equally dangerous and dishonourable; and that he should have no scruples in trusting to his gratitude and fidelity, if he had any employment for him, which he thought would suit his qualifications and his circumstances; but that all the departments he had mentioned in his letter, were filled up by persons of whose conduct he had no reason to complain; of consequence he could not, without injustice, deprive any one of them of his bread—Nevertheless, he declared himself ready to assist him in any feasible project, either with his purse or credit.

Martin seemed deeply touched at this declaration—The tear started in his eye, while he said, in a faultering accent—"Worthy sir—your generosity oppresses me—I never dreamed of troubling you for any pecuniary assistance—indeed I have no occasion—I have been so lucky at billiards and betting in different places, at Buxton, Harrigate, Scarborough, and Newcastle races, that my stock in ready-money amounts to three hundred pounds, which I would willingly employ, in prosecuting some honest scheme of life; but my friend, justice Buzzard, has set so many springs for my life, that I am under the necessity of either retiring immediately to a remote part of the country, where I can enjoy the protection of some generous patron, or of quitting the kingdom altogether——It is upon this alternative that I now beg leave to ask your advice—I have had information of all your route, since I had the honour to see you at Stevenage; and, supposing you would come this way from Scarborough, I came hither last night from Darlington, to pay you my respects."

"It would be no difficult matter to provide you with an asylum in the country (replied my uncle); but a life of indolence and obscurity would not suit with your active and enterprizing disposition—I would therefore

9. The waxed threads used by shoemakers and harnessmakers.

advise you to try your fortune in the East Indies—I will give you a letter to a friend in London, who will recommend you to the direction, for a commission in the company's service; and if that cannot be obtained, you will at least be received as a volunteer—in which case, you may pay for your passage, and I shall undertake to procure you such credentials, that you will not be long without a commission."

Martin embraced the proposal with great eagerness; it was therefore resolved, that he should sell his horse, and take a passage by sea for London, to execute the project without delay—In the mean time he accompanied us to Durham, where we took up our quarters for the night —Here, being furnished with letters from my uncle, he took his leave of us, with strong symptoms of gratitude and attachment, and set out for Sunderland, in order to embark in the first collier, bound for the river Thames. He had not been gone half an hour, when we were joined by another character, which promised something extraordinary—A tall, meagre figure, answering, with his horse, the description of Don Quixote mounted on Rozinante, appeared in the twilight at the inn door, while my aunt and Liddy stood at a window in the dining-room—He wore a coat, the cloth of which had once been scarlet, trimmed with Brandenburgs,[1] now totally deprived of their metal, and he had holster-caps and housing of the same stuff and same antiquity. Perceiving ladies at the window above, he endeavoured to dismount with the most graceful air he could assume; but the ostler neglecting to hold the stirrup when he wheeled off his right foot, and stood with his whole weight on the other, the girth unfortunately gave way, the saddle turned, down came the cavalier to the ground, and his hat and periwig falling off, displayed a head-piece of various colours, patched and plaistered in a woeful condition—The ladies, at the window above, shrieked with affright, on the supposition that the stranger had received some notable damage in his fall; but the greatest injury he had sustained arose from the dishonour of his descent, aggravated by the disgrace of exposing the condition of his cranium; for certain plebeians that were about the door, laughed aloud, in the belief that the captain had got either a scald head, or a broken head, both equally opprobrious.[2]

He forthwith leaped up in a fury, and snatching one of his pistols, threatened to put the ostler to death, when another squall from the women checked his resentment. He then bowed to the window, while he kissed the butt-end of his pistol, which he replaced; adjusted his wig in great confusion, and led his horse into the stable—By this time I had come to the door, and could not help gazing at the strange figure that

1. Ornamental facings on the breast of officers' coats, usually brightly colored and embroidered with silver or gold thread.
2. The low-class observers believe Lismahago's scalp to be suffering from a skin disease, perhaps venereal in origin or because of uncleanliness, or from having the skin broken in a fight, probably by a cudgel; in either case, they find him an object of condescending humor.

First appearance of the gallant Lismahago.

presented itself to my view—He would have measured above six feet in height, had he stood upright; but he stooped very much; was very narrow in the shoulders, and very thick in the calves of his legs, which were cased in black spatterdashes—As for his thighs, they were long and slender, like those of a grasshopper; his face was, at least, half a yard in length, brown and shrivelled, with projecting cheek-bones, little grey eyes on the greenish hue, a large hook-nose, a pointed chin, a mouth from ear to ear, very ill furnished with teeth, and a high, narrow fore-head, well furrowed with wrinkles. His horse was exactly in the stile of its rider; a resurrection of dry bones, which (as we afterwards learned) he valued exceedingly, as the only present he had ever received in his life.

Having seen this favourite steed properly accommodated in the stable, he sent up his compliments to the ladies, begging permission to thank them in person for the marks of concern they had shewn at his disaster in the court-yard—As the 'squire said they could not decently decline his visit, he was shewn up stairs, and paid his respects in the Scotch dialect, with much formality—"Laddies, (said he) perhaps ye may be scandaleezed at the appearance my heed made, when it was uncovered by accident; but I can assure you, the condition you saw it in, is neither the effects of disease, nor of drunkenness; but an honest scar received in the service of my country." He then gave us to understand, that having been wounded at Ticonderoga, in America, a party of Indians rifled him, scalped him, broke his scull with the blow of a tomahawk, and left him for dead on the field of battle; but that being afterwards found with signs of life, he had been cured in the French hospital, though the loss of substance could not be repaired; so that the scull was left naked in several places, and these he covered with patches.

There is no hold by which an Englishman is sooner taken than that of compassion—We were immediately interested in behalf of this veteran—Even Tabby's heart was melted; but our pity was warmed with indignation, when we learned, that in the course of two sanguinary wars, he had been wounded, maimed, mutilated, taken, and enslaved, without ever having attained a higher rank than that of lieutenant——My uncle's eyes gleamed, and his nether lip quivered, while he exclaimed, "I vow to God, sir, your case is a reproach to the service—The injustice you have met with is so flagrant——" "I must crave your pardon, sir, (cried the other, interrupting him) I complain of no injustice—I purchased an ensigncy thirty years ago; and, in the course of service, rose to be a lieutenant, according to my seniority—" "But in such a length of time, (resumed the 'squire) you must have seen a great many young officers put over your head—" "Nevertheless, (said he) I have no cause to murmur—They bought their preferment with their money—I had no money to carry to market—that was my misfortune; but no body was to blame—" "What! no friend to advance a sum of money?" (said Mr. Bramble) "Perhaps, I might have borrowed money for the purchase of a company (answered the other); but that loan must have been refunded; and I did not chuse to incumber myself with a debt of a thousand pounds, to be payed from an income of ten shillings a-day." "So you have spent the best part of your life, (cried Mr. Bramble) your youth, your blood, and your constitution, amidst the dangers, the difficulties, the horrors and hardships of war, for the consideration of three or four shillings a-day—a consideration—" "Sir, (replied the Scot, with great warmth) you are the man that does me injustice, if you say or think I have been actuated by any such paultry consideration——I am a gentleman; and entered the service as other gentlemen do, with such hopes and sentiments as honourable ambition inspires—If I have not been lucky in the lottery of life, so neither do I think myself unfortunate—I owe no man a farthing; I can always command a clean shirt, a mutton-chop, and a truss of straw; and when I die, I shall leave effects sufficient to defray the expence of my burial."

My uncle assured him, he had no intention to give him the least offence, by the observations he had made; but, on the contrary, spoke from a sentiment of friendly regard to his interest—The lieutenant thanked him with a stiffness of civility, which nettled our old gentleman, who perceived that his moderation was all affected; for, whatsoever his tongue might declare, his whole appearance denoted dissatisfaction —In short, without pretending to judge of his military merit, I think I may affirm, that this Caledonian is a self-conceited pedant, aukward, rude, and disputacious—He has had the benefit of a school-education, seems to have read a good number of books, his memory is tenacious, and he pretends to speak several different languages; but he is so addicted to wrangling, that he will cavil at the clearest truths, and, in the pride of argumentation, attempt to reconcile contradictions——Whether his address and qualifications are really of that stamp which is agreeable to the taste of our aunt, Mrs. Tabitha, or that indefatigable maiden is determined to shoot at every sort of game, certain it is she has begun to practise upon the heart of the lieutenant, who favoured us with his company to supper.

I have many other things to say of this man of war, which I shall communicate in a post or two; mean while, it is but reasonable that you should be indulged with some respite from those weary lucubrations of

yours,

Newcastle upon Tyne, July 10.   J. MELFORD.

To Sir WATKIN PHILLIPS, Bar^t. of Jesus college, Oxon.

DEAR PHILLIPS,

In my last I treated you with a high flavoured dish, in the character of the Scotch lieutenant, and I must present him once more for your entertainment. It was our fortune to feed upon him the best part of three days; and I do not doubt that he will start again in our way before we shall have finished our northern excursion. The day after our meeting with him at Durham proved so tempestuous that we did not choose to proceed on our journey; and my uncle persuaded him to stay till the weather should clear up, giving him, at the same time, a general invitation to our mess. The man has certainly gathered a whole budget of shrewd observations, but he brings them forth in such an ungracious manner as would be extremely disgusting, if it was not marked by that characteristic oddity which never fails to attract the attention.—He and Mr. Bramble discoursed, and even disputed, on different subjects in war, policy, the belles lettres, law, and metaphysics; and sometimes they were warmed into such altercation as seemed to threaten an abrupt dissolution of their society; but Mr. Bramble set a guard over his own irascibilty, the more vigilantly as the officer was his guest; and when, in spite of all his efforts, he began to wax warm, the other prudently cooled in the same proportion.

Mrs. Tabitha chancing to accost her brother by the familiar diminutive of Matt, "Pray, sir, (said the lieutenant) is your name Matthias?" You must know, it is one of our uncle's foibles to be ashamed of his name Matthew, because it is puritanical; and this question chagrined him so much, that he answered, "No, by G—d!" in a very abrupt tone of displeasure.—The Scot took umbrage at the manner of his reply, and bristling up, "If I had known (said he) that you did not care to tell your name, I should not have asked the question—The leddy called you Matt, and I naturally thought it was Matthias:———perhaps, it may be Methuselah, or Metrodorus, or Metellus, or Mathurinus, or Malthinnus, or Matamoros, or———" "No, (cried my uncle laughing) it is neither of those, captain:—my name is Matthew Bramble, at your service.—The truth is, I have a foolish pique at the name of Matthew, because it savours of those canting hypocrites, who, in Cromwell's time, christened all their children by names taken from the scripture."———"A foolish pique indeed, (cried Mrs. Tabby) and even sinful, to fall out with your name because it is taken from holy writ.—I would have you to know, you was called after great-uncle Matthew ap Madoc ap Meredith, esquire, of Llanwysthin, in Montgomeryshire, justice of the *quorum*, and *crusty ruttleorum*,[3] a

3. Originally, only the justices of the peace who served on the term courts were termed "of the quorum," but the phrase later was applied to all justices. The custo rotulorum was the senior justice in a county and had charge of the rolls.

gentleman of great worth and property, descended in a strait line, by the female side, from Llewellyn, prince of Wales."[4]

This genealogical anecdote seemed to make some impression upon the North-Briton, who bowed very low to the descendants of Llewellyn, and observed that he himself had the honour of a scriptural nomination. The lady expressing a desire of knowing his address, he said, he designed himself Lieutenant Obadiah Lismahago;[5] and, in order to assist her memory, he presented her with a slip of paper inscribed with these three words, which she repeated with great emphasis, declaring, it was one of the most noble and sonorous names she had ever heard. He observed, that Obadiah was an adventitious appellation, derived from his great-grandfather, who had been one of the original covenanters;[6] but Lismahago was the family surname, taken from a place in Scotland so called.[7] He likewise dropped some hints about the antiquity of his pedigree, adding, with a smile of self-denial, *Sed genus et proavos, et quæ non fecimus ipsi, vix ea nostra voco*,[8] which quotation he explained in deference to the ladies; and Mrs. Tabitha did not fail to compliment him on his modesty in waving the merit of his ancestry, adding, that it was the less necessary to him, as he had such a considerable fund of his own. She now began to glew herself to his favour with the grossest adulation.—She expatiated upon the antiquity and virtues of the Scottish nation, upon their valour, probity, learning, and politeness.—She even descended to encomiums on his own personal address, his gallantry, good sense, and erudition.—She appealed to her brother, whether the captain was not the very image of our cousin governor Griffith.—She discovered a surprising eagerness to know the particulars of his life, and asked a thousand questions concerning his atchievements in war; all which Mr. Lismahago answered with a sort of jesuitical reserve, affecting a reluctance to satisfy her curiosity on a subject that concerned his own exploits.

By dint of her interrogations, however, we learned, that he and ensign Murphy had made their escape from the French hospital at Montreal, and taken to the woods, in hope of reaching some English settlement; but mistaking their route, they fell in with a party of Miamis, who carried them away in captivity. The intention of these Indians was to give one of them as an adopted son to a venerable sachem, who had lost his own in the course of the war, and to sacrifice the other according to the custom of

---

4. Llewellyn ap Iorwerth (died 1240), known as the Great, was the most prominent ruler of Wales during the Middle Ages.

5. Several scholars have noted that some of the experiences ascribed to this character resemble events in the life of Capt. Robert Stobo (1727–70), a Scottish soldier who took part in several American campaigns.

6. The original covenanters were those who signed the covenant in 1638 to uphold the presbyterian form of worship and church organization in Scotland despite the strong attempts by English authorities to impose an episcopal form on both organization and worship. This was an important event in both church history and Scottish national history, and Lismahago's claim for the name ties him to Scotland's heroes. Many of the original covenanters took names from the *Bible*.

7. Lesmahago is a village about twenty miles southeast of Glasgow.

8. But as to race, ancestors, and those things which we did not do ourselves, I can hardly call those our own: from Ovid's *Metamorphoses* XIII. 140.

the country. Murphy, as being the younger and handsomer of the two, was designed to fill the place of the deceased, not only as the son of the sachem, but as the spouse of a beautiful squaw, to whom his predecessor had been betrothed; but in passing through the different whigwhams or villages of the Miamis, poor Murphy was so mangled by the women and children, who have the privilege of torturing all prisoners in their passage, that, by the time they arrived at the place of the sachem's residence, he was rendered altogether unfit for the purposes of marriage: it was determined therefore, in the assembly of the warriors, that ensign Murphy should be brought to the stake, and that the lady should be given to lieutenant Lismahago, who had likewise received his share of torments, though they had not produced emasculation.—A joint of one finger had been cut, or rather sawed off with a rusty knife; one of his great toes was crushed into a mash betwixt two stones; some of his teeth were drawn, or dug out with a crooked nail; splintered reeds had been thrust up his nostrils and other tender parts; and the calves of his legs had been blown up with mines of gunpowder dug in the flesh with the sharp point of the tomahawk.

The Indians themselves allowed that Murphy died with great heroism, singing, as his death song, the *Drimmendoo*,[9] in concert with Mr. Lismahago, who was present at the solemnity. After the warriors and the matrons had made a hearty meal upon the muscular flesh which they pared from the victim, and had applied a great variety of tortures, which he bore without flinching, an old lady, with a sharp knife, scooped out one of his eyes, and put a burning coal in the socket. The pain of this operation was so exquisite that he could not help bellowing, upon which the audience raised a shout of exultation, and one of the warriors stealing behind him, gave him the *coup de grace* with a hatchet.

Lismahago's bride, the squaw Squinkinacoosta, distinguished herself on this occasion.——She shewed a great superiority of genius in the tortures which she contrived and executed with her own hands.—She vied with the stoutest warrior in eating the flesh of the sacrifice; and after all the other females were fuddled with dram-drinking, she was not so intoxicated but that she was able to play the game of the platter with the conjuring sachem, and afterwards go through the ceremony of her own wedding, which was consummated that same evening. The captain had lived very happily with this accomplished squaw for two years, during which she bore him a son, who is now the representative of his mother's tribe; but, at length, to his unspeakable grief, she had died of a fever, occasioned by eating too much raw bear, which they had killed in a hunting excursion.

---

9. James Wright helped the editor discover that this Irish song was popular among the supporters of the Pretender during the Jacobite wars. Its title is an English approximation of the original *Drom-* *fionn Dubh*, which signifies a white-backed black cow. The title is allegorical. The choral rendition of the song makes Lismahago appear to be a sympathizer with the Jacobite cause.

By this time, Mr. Lismahago was elected sachem, acknowledged first warrior of the Badger tribe, and dignified with the name or epithet of Occacanastaogarora, which signifies *nimble as a weasel*; but all these advantages and honours he was obliged to resign, in consequence of being exchanged for the orator of the community, who had been taken prisoner by the Indians that were in alliance with the English. At the peace, he had sold out upon half-pay, and was returned to Britain, with a view to pass the rest of his life in his own country, where he hoped to find some retreat where his slender finances would afford him a decent subsistence. Such are the out-lines of Mr. Lismahago's history, to which Tabitha *did seriously incline her ear*;—indeed, she seemed to be taken with the same charms that captivated the heart of Desdemona, who loved the Moor *for the dangers he had past*.[1]

The description of poor Murphy's sufferings, which threw my sister Liddy into a swoon, extracted some sighs from the breast of Mrs. Tabby: when she understood he had been rendered unfit for marriage, she began to spit, and ejaculated, "Jesus, what cruel barbarians!" and she made wry faces at the lady's nuptial repast; but she was eagerly curious to know the particulars of her marriage-dress; whether she wore high-breasted stays or boddice, a robe of silk or velvet, and laces of Mechlin or minionette[2] —she supposed, as they were connected with the French, she used *rouge*, and had her hair dressed in the Parisian fashion. The captain would have declined giving a categorical explanation of all these particulars, observing, in general, that the Indians were too tenacious of their own customs to adopt the modes of any nation whatsoever: he said, moreover, that neither the simplicity of their manners, nor the commerce of their country, would admit of those articles of luxury which are deemed magnificence in Europe; and that they were too virtuous and sensible to encourage the introduction of any fashion which might help to render them corrupt and effeminate.

These observations served only to inflame her desire of knowing the particulars about which she had enquired; and, with all his evasion, he could not help discovering the following circumstances—that his princess had neither shoes, stockings, shift, nor any kind of linen—that her bridal dress consisted of a petticoat of red bays,[3] and a fringed blanket, fastened about her shoulders with a copper skewer; but of ornaments she had great plenty.—Her hair was curiously plaited, and interwoven with bobbins of human bone—one eye-lid was painted green, and the other yellow; the cheeks were blue, the lips white, the teeth red, and there was a black list drawn down the middle of the forehead as far as the tip of the nose—a couple of gaudy parrot's feathers were stuck through the division

---

1. An adaptation from Shakespeare's *Othello* I. iii. 146, 167.
2. Mechlin is a place in Belgium known for fine

lace, and hence the name refers to the fine lace itself; minionette is another type of lace.
3. A soft woolen material, usually spelled "baize."

of the nostrils—there was a blue stone set in the chin—her ear-rings consisted of two pieces of hickery, of the size and shape of drumsticks —her arms and legs were adorned with bracelets of wampum—her breast glittered with numerous strings of glass beads—she wore a curious pouch, or pocket, of woven grass, elegantly painted with various colours —about her neck was hung the fresh scalp of a Mohawk warrior, whom her deceased lover had lately slain in battle—and, finally, she was anointed from head to foot with bear's grease, which sent forth a most agreeable odour.

One would imagine that these paraphernalia would not have been much admired by a modern fine lady; but Mrs. Tabitha was resolved to approve of all the captain's connexions.—She wished, indeed, the squaw had been better provided with linen; but she owned there was much taste and fancy in her ornaments; she made no doubt, therefore, that madam Squinkinacoosta was a young lady of good sense and rare accomplishments, and a good christian at bottom. Then she asked whether his consort had been high-church or low-church, presbyterian or anabaptist, or had been favoured with any glimmering of the new light of the gospel? When he confessed that she and her whole nation were utter strangers to the christian faith, she gazed at him with signs of astonishment, and Humphry Clinker, who chanced to be in the room, uttered a hollow groan.

After some pause, "In the name of God, captain Lismahago, (cried she) what religion do they profess?" "As to religion, madam, (answered the lieutenant) it is among those Indians a matter of great simplicity—they never heard of any *Alliance between Church and State.*—They, in general, worship two contending principles; one the Fountain of all Good, the other the source of evil.—The common people there, as in other countries, run into the absurdities of superstition; but sensible men pay adoration to a Supreme Being, who created and sustains the universe." "O! what pity, (exclaimed the pious Tabby) that some holy man has not been inspired to go and convert these poor heathens!"

The lieutenant told her, that while he resided among them, two French missionaries arrived, in order to convert them to the catholic religion; but when they talked of mysteries and revelations, which they could neither explain nor authenticate, and called in the evidence of miracles which they believed upon hearsay; when they taught, that the Supreme Creator of Heaven and Earth had allowed his only Son, his own equal in power and glory, to enter the bowels of a woman, to be born as a human creature, to be insulted, flagellated, and even executed as a malefactor; when they pretended to create God himself, to swallow, digest, revive, and multiply him *ad infinitum*, by the help of a little flour and water, the Indians were shocked at the impiety of their presumption. —They were examined by the assembly of the sachems, who desired them to prove the divinity of their mission by some miracle.—They answered, that it was not in their power.——"If you were really sent by Heaven for our conversion, (said one of the sachems) you would certainly have some supernatural endowments, at least you would have the gift of tongues, in order to explain your doctrine to the different nations among which you are employed; but you are so ignorant of our language, that you cannot express yourselves even on the most trifling subjects."

In a word, the assembly were convinced of their being cheats, and even suspected them of being spies:——they ordered them a bag of Indian corn a-piece, and appointed a guide to conduct them to the frontiers; but the missionaries having more zeal than discretion, refused to quit the vineyard.——They persisted in saying mass, in preaching, baptizing, and squabbling with the conjurers, or priests of the country, till they had thrown the whole community into confusion.——Then the assembly proceeded to try them as impious impostors, who represented the Almighty as a trifling, weak, capricious being, and pretended to make, unmake, and reproduce him at pleasure: they were, therefore, convicted of blasphemy and sedition, and condemned to the stake, where they died singing *Salve regina*,[4] in a rapture of joy, for the crown of martyrdom which they had thus obtained.

In the course of this conversation, lieutenant Lismahago dropt some hints by which it appeared he himself was a free-thinker. Our aunt seemed to be startled at certain sarcasms he threw out against the creed of saint Athanasius.[5]——He dwelt much upon the words, *reason, philosophy*, and *contradiction in terms*——he bid defiance to the eternity of hell-fire; and even threw such squibs at the immortality of the soul, as singed a little the whiskers of Mrs. Tabitha's faith; for, by this time, she began to look upon Lismahago as a prodigy of learning and sagacity.——In short, he could be no longer insensible to the advances she made towards his affection; and although there was something repulsive in his nature, he overcame it so far as to make some return to her civilities.——Perhaps, he thought it would be no bad scheme, in a superannuated lieutenant on half-pay, to effect a conjunction with an old maid, who, in all probability, had fortune enough to keep him easy and comfortable in the fag-end of his days.——An ogling correspondence forthwith commenced between this amiable pair of originals.——He began to sweeten the natural acidity of his discourse with the treacle of compliment and commendation. ——He from time to time offered her snuff, of which he himself took great quantities, and even made her a present of a purse of silk grass, woven by the hands of the amiable Squinkinacoosta, who had used it as a shot-pouch in her hunting-expeditions.

<hr>

4. These are the opening words of a sung prayer, hailing the Queen of Heaven, Mary, and asking her to intercede with Christ for their salvation.
5. This creed was long attributed to Saint Athana-sius (c. 296–373) but it is now known to be of much later composition. It affirms the divinity of Christ and is thus the object of "freethinking" sarcasm.

From Doncaster northwards, all the windows of all the inns are scrawled with doggrel rhimes,[6] in abuse of the Scotch nation; and what surprised me very much, I did not perceive one line written in the way of recrimination—Curious to hear what Lismahago would say on this subject, I pointed out to him a very scurrilous epigram against his countrymen, which was engraved on one of the windows of the parlour where we sat.——He read it with the most starched composure; and when I asked his opinion of the poetry, "It is vara terse and vara poignant; (said he) but with the help of a wat dish-clout, it might be rendered more clear and parspicous.—I marvel much that some modern wit has not published a collection of these essays under the title of the *Glazier's Triumph over Sawney the Scot*——I'm persuaded it would be a vara agreable offering to the patriots of London and Westminster." When I expressed some surprize that the natives of Scotland, who travel this way, had not broke all the windows upon the road, "With submission, (replied the lieutenant) that were but shallow policy—it would only serve to make the satire more cutting and severe; and, I think, it is much better to let it stand in the window, than have it presented in the reckoning."

My uncle's jaws began to quiver with indignation.——He said, the scribblers of such infamous stuff deserved to be scourged at the cart's tail for disgracing their country with such monuments of malice and stupidity.—"These vermin (said he) do not consider, that they are affording their fellow-subjects, whom they abuse, continual matter of self-gratulation, as well as the means of executing the most manly vengeance that can be taken for such low, illiberal attacks. For my part, I admire the philosophic forbearance of the Scots, as much as I despise the insolence of those wretched libellers, which is akin to the arrogance of the village cock, who never crows but upon his own dunghill." The captain, with an affectation of candour, observed, that men of illiberal minds were produced in every soil; that in supposing those were the sentiments of the English in general, he should pay too great a compliment to his own country, which was not of consequence enough to attract the envy of such a flourishing and powerful people.

Mrs. Tabby broke forth again in praise of his moderation, and declared that Scotland was the soil which produced every virtue under heaven. —When Lismahago took his leave for the night, she asked her brother if the captain was not the prettiest gentleman he had ever seen; and whether there was not something wonderfully engaging in his aspect? —Mr. Bramble having eyed her some time in silence, "Sister, (said he) the lieutenant is, for aught I know, an honest man, and a good officer—he has a considerable share of understanding, and a title to more encourage-

6. The tradition of inscribing verse on windows with a diamond was apparently widespread. For more on the subject, see Mary Claire Randolph, "Diamond-Satires in the Eighteenth Century," *Notes and Queries*, 185 (1943): 62–65.

ment than he seems to have met with in life; but I cannot, with a safe conscience, affirm, that he is the prettiest gentleman I ever saw; neither can I discern any engaging charm in his countenance, which, I vow to Gad, is, on the contrary, very hard-favoured and forbidding."

I have endeavoured to ingratiate myself with this North-Briton, who is really a curiosity; but he has been very shy of my conversation ever since I laughed at his asserting that the English tongue was spoke with more propriety at Edinburgh that at London. Looking at me with a double squeeze of souring in his aspect, "If the old definition be true, (said he) that risibility is the distinguishing characteristic of a rational creature, the English are the most distinguished for rationality of any people I ever knew." I owned, that the English were easily struck with any thing that appeared ludicrous, and apt to laugh accordingly; but it did not follow, that, because they were more given to laughter, they had more rationality than their neighbours: I said, such an inference would be an injury to the Scots, who were by no means defective in rationality, though generally supposed little subject to the impressions of humour.

The captain answered, that this supposition must have been deduced either from their conversation or their compositions, of which the English could not possibly judge with precision, as they did not understand the dialect used by the Scots in common discourse, as well as in their works of humour. When I desired to know what those works of humour were, he mentioned a considerable number of pieces, which he insisted were equal in point of humour to any thing extant in any language dead or living.———He, in particular, recommended a collection of detached poems, in two small volumes, intituled, The Ever-green, [7] and the works of Allan Ramsay, which I intend to provide myself with at Edinburgh.—He observed, that a North-Briton is seen to a disadvantage in an English company, because he speaks in a dialect that they can't relish, and in a phraseology which they don't understand.—He therefore finds himself under a restraint, which is a great enemy to wit and humour. —These are faculties which never appear in full lustre, but when the mind is perfectly at ease, and, as an excellent writer says, enjoys her elbow-room. [8]

He proceeded to explain his assertion that the English language was spoken with greater propriety at Edinburgh than in London.—He said, what we generally called the Scottish dialect was, in fact, true, genuine old English, with a mixture of some French terms and idioms, adopted in a long intercourse betwixt the French and Scotch nations; that the modern English, from affectation and false refinement, had weakened, and even corrupted their language, by throwing out the guttural sounds,

7. The Ever Green, Being a Collection of Scots Poems, Wrote... before 1600 was assembled and published by the poet Allan Ramsay in Edinburgh in 1724 and again in 1761.

8. The phrase appears in "A Day" (1761), a poem by Dr. John Armstrong (1707–79), author, physician, and long-time friend of Smollett's.

altering the pronunciation and the quantity, and disusing many words and terms of great significance. In consequence of these innovations, the works of our best poets, such as Chaucer, Spenser, and even Shakespeare, were become, in many parts, unintelligible to the natives of South-Britain, whereas the Scots, who retain the antient language, understand them without the help of a glossary. "For instance, (said he) how have your commentators been puzzled by the following expression in the *Tempest*—*He's gentle, and not fearful;*[9] as if it was a paralogism to say, that being *gentle,* he must of course be *courageous:* but the truth is, one of the original meanings, if not the sole meaning, of that word was, *noble, high-minded*; and to this day, a Scotch woman, in the situation of the young lady in the *Tempest,* would express herself nearly in the same terms—Don't provoke him; for being gentle, that is, *high spirited,* he won't tamely bear an insult. Spenser, in the very first stanza of his *Fairy Queen,* says,

'A *gentle* knight was pricking on the plain;'

which knight, far from being *tame* and fearful, was so stout that

'Nothing did he dread, but ever was ydrad.'

To prove that we had impaired the energy of our language by false refinement, he mentioned the following words, which, though widely different in signification, are pronounced exactly in the same manner —*wright, write, right, rite*; but among the Scots, these words are as different in pronunciation, as they are in meaning and orthography; and this is the case with many others which he mentioned by way of illustration.——He, moreover, took notice, that we had (for what reason he could never learn) altered the sound of our vowels from that which is retained by all the nations in Europe; an alteration which rendered the language extremely difficult to foreigners, and made it almost impracticable to lay down general rules for orthography and pronunciation. Besides, the vowels were no longer simple sounds in the mouth of an Englishman, who pronounced both *i* and *u* as diphthongs. Finally, he affirmed, that we mumbled our speech with our lips and teeth, and ran the words together without pause or distinction, in such a manner, that a foreigner, though he understood English tolerably well, was often obliged to have recourse to a Scotchman to explain what a native of England had said in his own language.

The truth of this remark was confirmed by Mr. Bramble from his own experience; but he accounted for it on another principle.—He said, the same observation would hold in all languages; that a Swiss talking French was more easily understood than a Parisian, by a foreigner who had not made himself master of the language; because every language had its

9. *The Tempest* I. ii. 468.

peculiar recitative, and it would always require more pains, attention, and practice, to acquire both the words and the music, than to learn the words only; and yet no body would deny, that the one was imperfect without the other: he therefore apprehended, that the Scotchman and the Swiss were better understood by learners, because they spoke the words only, without the music, which they could not rehearse. One would imagine this check might have damped the North-Briton; but it served only to agitate his humour for disputation.——He said, if every nation had its own recitative or music, the Scots had theirs, and the Scotchman who had not yet acquired the cadence of the English, would naturally use his own in speaking their language; therefore, if he was better understood than the native, his recitative must be more intelligible than that of the English; of consequence, the dialect of the Scots had an advantage over that of their fellow-subjects, and this was another strong presumption that the modern English had corrupted their language in the article of pronunciation.

The lieutenant was, by this time, become so polemical, that every time he opened his mouth out flew a paradox, which he maintained with all the enthusiasm of altercation; but all his paradoxes savoured strong of a partiality for his own country. He undertook to prove that poverty was a blessing to a nation; that *oatmeal* was preferable to *wheat-flour*; and that the worship of Cloacina,[1] in temples which admitted both sexes, and every rank of votaries promiscuously, was a filthy species of idolatry that outraged every idea of delicacy and decorum. I did not so much wonder at his broaching these doctrines, as at the arguments, equally whimsical and ingenious, which he adduced in support of them.

In fine, lieutenant Lismahago is a curiosity which I have not yet sufficiently perused; and therefore I shall be sorry when we lose his company, though, God knows, there is nothing very amiable in his manner or disposition.——As he goes directly to the south-west division of Scotland, and we proceed in the road to Berwick, we shall part to-morrow at a place called Felton-bridge; and, I dare say, this separation will be very grievous to our aunt Mrs. Tabitha, unless she has received some flattering assurance of his meeting her again. If I fail in my purpose of entertaining you with these unimportant occurrences, they will at least serve as exercises of patience, for which you are indebted to

Yours always,

Morpeth, July 13.   J. MELFORD.

---

1. A mock member of the classical pantheon, the goddess of the cloaca, or common sewer.

To Dr. LEWIS.

DEAR DOCTOR,

I have now reached the northern extremity of England, and see, close to my chamber-window, the Tweed gliding through the arches of that bridge which connects this suburb to the town of Berwick.—Yorkshire you have seen, and therefore I shall say nothing of that opulent province. The city of Durham appears like a confused heap of stones and brick, accumulated so as to cover a mountain, round which a river winds its brawling course. The streets are generally narrow, dark, and unpleasant, and many of them almost impassible in consequence of their declivity. The cathedral is a huge gloomy pile; but the clergy are well lodged. ———The bishop lives in a princely manner—the golden prebends keep plentiful tables—and, I am told, there is some good sociable company in the place; but the country, when viewed from the top of Gateshead Fell, which extends to Newcastle, exhibits the highest scene of cultivation that ever I beheld. As for Newcastle, it lies mostly in a bottom, on the banks of the Tyne, and makes an appearance still more disagreeable than that of Durham; but it is rendered populous and rich by industry and commerce; and the country lying on both sides the river, above the town, yields a delightful prospect of agriculture and plantation. Morpeth and Alnwick are neat, pretty towns, and this last is famous for the castle which has belonged so many ages to the noble house of Piercy, earls of Northumberland.—It is, doubtless, a large edifice, containing a great number of apartments, and stands in a commanding situation; but the strength of it seems to have consisted not so much in its site, or the manner in which it is fortified, as in the valour of its defendants.

Our adventures since we left Scarborough, are scarce worth reciting; and yet I must make you acquainted with my sister Tabby's progress in husband-hunting, after her disappointments at Bath and London. She had actually begun to practise upon a certain adventurer, who was in fact a highwayman by profession; but he had been used to snares much more dangerous than any she could lay, and escaped accordingly.—Then she opened her batteries upon an old weather-beaten Scotch lieutenant, called Lismahago, who joined us at Durham, and is, I think, one of the most singular personages I ever encountered.—His manner is as harsh as his countenance; but his peculiar turn of thinking, and his pack of knowledge made up of the remnants of rarities, rendered his conversation desirable, in spite of his pedantry and ungracious address.—I have often met with a crab-apple in a hedge, which I have been tempted to eat for its flavour, even while I was disgusted by its austerity. The spirit of contradiction is naturally so strong in Lismahago, that I believe in my conscience he has rummaged, and read, and studied with indefatigable attention, in order to qualify himself to refute established maxims, and thus raise trophies for the gratification of polemical pride.—Such is the asperity of his self-conceit, that he will not even acquiesce in a transient compliment made to his own individual in particular, or to his country in general.

When I observed, that he must have read a vast number of books to be able to discourse on such a variety of subjects, he declared he had read little or nothing, and asked how he should find books among the woods of America, where he had spent the greatest part of his life. My nephew remarking that the Scots in general were famous for their learning, he denied the imputation, and defied him to prove it from their works. —"The Scots (said he) have a slight tincture of letters, with which they make a parade among people who are more illiterate than themselves; but they may be said to float on the surface of science, and they have made very small advances in the useful arts." "At least, (cried Tabby) all the world allows that the Scots behaved gloriously in fighting and conquering the savages of America." "I can assure you, madam, you have been misinformed; (replied the lieutenant) in that continent the Scots did nothing more than their duty, nor was there one corps in his majesty's service that distinguished itself more than another.—Those who affected to extol the Scots for superior merit, were no friends to that nation."

Though he himself made free with his countrymen, he would not suffer any other person to glance a sarcasm at them with impunity. One of the company chancing to mention lord B——'s inglorious peace,[2] the lieutenant immediately took up the cudgels in his lordship's favour, and argued very strenuously to prove that it was the most honourable and advantageous peace that England had ever made since the foundation of the monarchy.—Nay, between friends, he offered such reasons on this subject, that I was really confounded, if not convinced.—He would not allow that the Scots abounded above their proportion in the army and navy of Great-Britain, or that the English had any reason to say his countrymen had met with extraordinary encouragement in the service. —"When a South and North-Briton (said he) are competitors for a place or commission, which is in the disposal of an English minister or an English general, it would be absurd to suppose that the preference will not be given to the native of England, who has so many advantages over his rival.—First and foremost, he has in his favour that laudable partiality, which, Mr. Addison[3] says, never fails to cleave to the heart of an Englishman; secondly, he has more powerful connexions, and a greater share of parliamentary interest, by which those contests are generally decided; and lastly, he has a greater command of money to smooth the way to his success. For my own part, (said he) I know no Scotch officer,

2. The treaty of Paris, agreed to in 1762 and proclaimed in 1763, ended hostilities between England on one side and France and Spain on the other. Though England gained both Canada and Florida in the peace negotiations, the treaty was controversial, at least in part because Lord Bute, who helped to reach it, was himself controversial.
3. In *The Spectator*, no. 38.

who has risen in the army above the rank of a subaltern, without purchasing every degree of preferment either with money or recruits; but I know many gentlemen of that country, who, for want of money and interest, have grown grey in the rank of lieutenants; whereas very few instances of this ill fortune are to be found among the natives of South-Britain.—Not that I would insinuate that my countrymen have the least reason to complain.—Preferment in the service, like success in any other branch of traffic, will naturally favour those who have the greatest stock of cash and credit, merit and capacity being supposed equal on all sides."

But the most hardy of all this original's positions were these:—That commerce would, sooner or later, prove the ruin of every nation, where it flourishes to any extent—that the parliament was the rotten part of the British constitution—that the liberty of the press was a national evil —and that the boasted institution of juries, as managed in England, was productive of shameful perjury and flagrant injustice. He observed, that traffick was an enemy to all the liberal passions of the soul, founded on the thirst of lucre, a sordid disposition to take advantage of the necessities of our fellow-creatures.——He affirmed, the nature of commerce was such, that it could not be fixed or perpetuated, but, having flowed to a certain height, would immediately begin to ebb, and so continue till the channels should be left almost dry; but there was no instance of the tide's rising a second time to any considerable influx in the same nation. Mean while the sudden affluence occasioned by trade, forced open all the sluices of luxury and overflowed the land with every species of profligacy and corruption; a total pravity of manners would ensue, and this must be attended with bankruptcy and ruin. He observed of the parliament, that the practice of buying boroughs, and canvassing for votes, was an avowed system of venality, already established on the ruins of principle, integrity, faith, and good order, in consequence of which the elected and the elector, and, in short, the whole body of the people, were equally and universally contaminated and corrupted. He affirmed, that of a parliament thus constituted, the crown would always have influence enough to secure a great majority in its dependence, from the great number of posts, places, and pensions it had to bestow; that such a parliament would (as it had already done) lengthen the term of its sitting and authority, whenever the prince should think it for his interest to continue the representatives; for, without doubt, they had the same right to protract their authority *ad infinitum*, as they had to extend it from three to seven years. —With a parliament, therefore, dependent upon the crown, devoted to the prince, and supported by a standing army, garbled and modelled for the purpose, any king of England may, and probably some ambitious sovereign will, totally overthrow all the bulwarks of the constitution; for it is not to be supposed that a prince of a high spirit will tamely submit to be thwarted in all his measures, abused and insulted by a populace of unbridled ferocity, when he has it in his power to crush all opposition

192 • *Humphry Clinker*

under his feet with the concurrence of the legislature. He said, he should always consider the liberty of the press as a national evil, while it enabled the vilest reptile to soil the lustre of the most shining merit, and furnished the most infamous incendiary with the means of disturbing the peace and destroying the good order of the community. He owned, however, that, under due restrictions, it would be a valuable privilege; but affirmed, that at present there was no law in England sufficient to restrain it within proper bounds.

With respect to juries, he expressed himself to this effect:——Juries are generally composed of illiterate plebeians, apt to be mistaken, easily misled, and open to sinister influence; for if either of the parties to be tried, can gain over one of the twelve jurors, he has secured the verdict in his favour; the juryman thus brought over will, in despight of all evidence and conviction, generally hold out till his fellows are fatigued, and harrassed, and starved into concurrence; in which case the verdict is unjust, and the jurors are all perjured: but cases will often occur, when the jurors are really divided in opinion, and each side is convinced in opposition to the other; but no verdict will be received, unless they are unanimous, and they are all bound, not only in conscience, but by oath, to judge and declare according to their conviction.—What then will be the consequence?—They must either starve in company, or one side must sacrifice their conscience to their convenience, and join in a verdict which they believe to be false. This absurdity is avoided in Sweden, where a bare majority is sufficient; and in Scotland, where two thirds of the jury are required to concur in the verdict.

You must not imagine that all these deductions were made on his part, without contradiction on mine.—No—the truth is, I found myself piqued in point of honour, at his pretending to be so much wiser than his neighbours.—I questioned all his assertions, started innumerable objections, argued and wrangled with uncommon perseverance, and grew very warm, and even violent, in the debate.—Sometimes he was puzzled, and once or twice, I think, fairly refuted; but from those falls he rose again, like Antæus,[4] with redoubled vigour, till at length I was tired, exhausted, and really did not know how to proceed, when luckily he dropped a hint, by which he discovered he had been bred to the law; a confession which enabled me to retire from the dispute with a good grace, as it could not be supposed that a man like me, who had been bred to nothing, should be able to cope with a veteran in his own profession. I believe, however, that I shall for some time continue to chew the cud of reflection upon many observations which this original discharged.

---

4. Antæus was a Giant who was invincible as long as he could touch the earth and when thrown to the ground would arise with renewed vigor. Hercules finally killed him by holding him in the air and crushing him.

Whether our sister Tabby was really struck with his conversation, or is resolved to throw at every thing she meets in the shape of a man, till she can fasten the matrimonial noose, certain it is, she has taken desperate strides towards the affection of Lismahago, who cannot be said to have met her half way, tho' he does not seem altogether insensible to her civilities.—She insinuated more than once how happy we should be to have his company through that part of Scotland which we proposed to visit, till at length he plainly told us, that his road was totally different from that which we intended to take; that, for his part, his company would be of very little service to us in our progress, as he was utterly unacquainted with the country, which he had left in his early youth; consequently, he could neither direct us in our inquiries, nor introduce us to any family of distinction. He said, he was stimulated by an irresistible impulse to revisit the *paternus lar*, or *patria domus*,[5] though he expected little satisfaction, inasmuch as he understood that his nephew, the present possessor, was but ill qualified to support the honour of the family.—He assured us, however, as we design to return by the west road, that he will watch our motions, and endeavour to pay his respects to us at Dumfries.———Accordingly he took his leave of us at a place half way betwixt Morpeth and Alnwick, and pranced away in great state, mounted on a tall, meagre, raw-boned, shambling grey gelding, without e'er a tooth in his head, the very counter-part of the rider; and, indeed, the appearance of the two was so picturesque, that I would give twenty guineas to have them tolerably represented on canvas.

Northumberland is a fine county, extending to the Tweed, which is a pleasant pastoral stream; but you will be surprised when I tell you that the English side of that river is neither so well cultivated nor so populous as the other.—The farms are thinly scattered, the lands uninclosed, and scarce a gentleman's seat is to be seen in some miles from the Tweed; whereas the Scots are advanced in crowds to the very brink of the river, so that you may reckon above thirty good houses, in the compass of a few miles, belonging to proprietors whose ancestors had fortified castles in the same situations, a circumstance that shews what dangerous neighbours the Scots must have formerly been to the northern counties of England.

Our domestic oeconomy continues on the old footing.—My sister Tabby still adheres to methodism, and had the benefit of a sermon at Wesley's meeting in Newcastle;[6] but I believe the passion of love has in some measure abated the fervour of devotion both in her and her woman, Mrs. Jenkins, about whose good graces there has been a violent contest betwixt my nephew's valet, Mr. Dutton, and my man, Humphry Clinker.

5. Paternal hearth or paternal home.
6. John Wesley (1703–91) and his brother Samuel (1707–88) were prominent evangelists. John was the founder of Methodism and preached in Newcastle in May of 1766, when Smollett may have heard him.

—Jery has been obliged to interpose his authority to keep the peace; and to him I have left the discussion of that important affair, which had like to have kindled the flames of discord in the family of

Yours always,

Tweedmouth, July 15.   MATT. BRAMBLE.

To Sir WATKIN PHILLIPS, Bar[t]. at Oxon.

DEAR WAT,

In my two last you had so much of Lismahago, that I suppose you are glad he is gone off the stage for the present.—I must now descend to domestic occurrences.—Love, it seems, is resolved to assert his dominion over all the females of our family.—After having practised upon poor Liddy's heart, and played strange vagaries with our aunt Mrs. Tabitha, he began to run riot in the affections of her woman Mrs. Winifred Jenkins, whom I have had occasion to mention more than once in the course of our memoirs. Nature intended Jenkins for something very different from the character of her mistress; yet custom and habit have effected a wonderful resemblance betwixt them in many particulars. Win, to be sure, is much younger and more agreeable in her person; she is likewise tender-hearted and benevolent, qualities for which her mistress is by no means remarkable, no more than she is for being of a timorous disposition, and much subject to fits of the mother, which are the infirmities of Win's constitution: but then she seems to have adopted Mrs. Tabby's manner with her cast cloaths.—She dresses and endeavours to look like her mistress, although her own looks are much more engaging.——She enters into her scheme of oeconomy, learns her phrases, repeats her remarks, imitates her stile in scolding the inferior servants, and, finally, subscribes implicitly to her system of devotion —This, indeed, she found the more agreeable, as it was in a great measure introduced and confirmed by the ministry of Clinker, with whose personal merit she seems to have been struck ever since he exhibited the pattern of his naked skin at Marlborough.

Nevertheless, though Humphry had this double hank[7] upon her inclinations, and exerted all his power to maintain the conquest he had made, he found it impossible to guard it on the side of vanity, where poor Win was as frail as any female in the kingdom. In short, my rascal Dutton professed himself her admirer, and, by dint of his outlandish qualifications, threw his rival Clinker out of the saddle of her heart. Humphry may be compared to an English pudding, composed of good wholesome flour and suet, and Dutton to a syllabub or iced froth, which, though

7. Shackle.

agreeable to the taste, has nothing solid or substantial. The traitor not only dazzled her with his second-hand finery, but he fawned, and flattered, and cringed—he taught her to take rappee, and presented her with a snuff-box of *papier maché*—he supplied her with a powder for her teeth—he mended her complexion, and he dressed her hair in the Paris fashion—he undertook to be her French master and her dancing-master, as well as friseur, and thus imperceptibly wound himself into her good graces. Clinker perceived the progress he had made, and repined in secret.—He attempted to open her eyes in the way of exhortation, and finding it produced no effect had recourse to prayer. At Newcastle, while he attended Mrs. Tabby to the methodist meeting, his rival accompanied Mrs. Jenkins to the play. He was dressed in a silk coat, made at Paris for his former master, with a tawdry waistcoat of tarnished brocade; he wore his hair in a great bag with a huge solitaire, and a long sword dangled from his thigh. The lady was all of a flutter with faded lutestring, washed gauze, and ribbons three times refreshed; but she was most remarkable for the frisure of her head, which rose, like a pyramid, seven inches above the scalp, and her face was primed and patched from the chin up to the eyes; nay, the gallant himself had spared neither red nor white in improving the nature of his own complexion. In this attire, they walked together through the high street to the theatre, and as they passed for players ready dressed for acting, they reached it unmolested; but as it was still light when they returned, and by that time the people had got information of their real character and condition, they hissed and hooted all the way, and Mrs. Jenkins was all bespattered with dirt, as well as insulted with the opprobrious name of *painted Jezabel*, so that her fright and mortification threw her into an hysteric fit the moment she came home.

Clinker was so incensed at Dutton, whom he considered as the cause of her disgrace, that he upbraided him severely for having turned the poor young woman's brain. The other affected to treat him with contempt, and mistaking his forbearance for want of courage, threatened to horse-whip him into good manners. Humphry then came to me, humbly beging I would give him leave to chastise my servant for his insolence—"He has challenged me to fight him at sword's point; (said he) but I might as well challenge him to make a horse-shoe, or a plough-iron; for I know no more of the one than he does of the other.—Besides, it doth not become servants to use those weapons, or to claim the privilege of gentlemen to kill one another when they fall out; moreover, I would not have his blood upon my conscience for ten thousand times the profit or satisfaction I should get by his death; but if your honour won't be angry, I'll engage to gee en a good drubbing, that, may hap, will do 'en service, and I'll take care it shall do 'en no harm." I said, I had no objection to what he proposed, provided he could manage matters so as not to be found the aggressor, in case Dutton should prosecute him for an assault and battery.

Thus licensed, he retired; and that same evening easily provoked his rival to strike the first blow, which Clinker returned with such interest that he was obliged to call for quarter, declaring, at the same time, that he would exact severe and bloody satisfaction the moment we should pass the border, when he could run him through the body without fear of the consequence.——This scene passed in presence of lieutenant Lismahago, who encouraged Clinker to hazard a thrust of cold iron with his antagonist. "Cold iron (cried Humphry) I shall never use against the life of any human creature; but I am so far from being afraid of his cold iron, that I shall use nothing in my defence but a good cudgel, which shall always be at his service." In the mean time, the fair cause of this contest, Mrs. Winifred Jenkins, seemed overwhelmed with affliction, and Mr. Clinker acted much on the reserve, though he did not presume to find fault with her conduct.

The dispute between the two rivals was soon brought to a very unexpected issue. Among our fellow-lodgers at Berwick, was a couple from London, bound to Edinburgh, on the voyage of matrimony. The female was the daughter and heiress of a pawn-broker deceased, who had given her guardians the slip, and put herself under the tuition of a tall Hibernian, who had conducted her thus far in quest of a clergyman to unite them in marriage, without the formalities required by the law of England.[8] I know not how the lover had behaved on the road, so as to decline in the favour of his innamorata; but, in all probability, Dutton perceived a coldness on her side, which encouraged him to whisper, it was a pity she should have cast her affections upon a taylor, which he affirmed the Irishman to be. This discovery completed her disgust, of which my man taking the advantage, began to recommend himself to her good graces, and the smooth-tongued rascal found no difficulty to insinuate himself into the place of her heart, from which the other had been discarded—Their resolution was immediately taken. In the morning, before day, while poor Teague lay snoring a-bed, his indefatigable rival ordered a post-chaise, and set out with the lady for Coldstream, a few miles up the Tweed, where there was a parson who dealt in this branch of commerce, and there they were noosed, before the Irishman ever dreamt of the matter. But when he got up at six o'clock, and found the bird was flown, he made such a noise as alarmed the whole house. One of the first persons he encountered, was the postilion returned from Coldstream, where he had been witness to the marriage, and over and above an handsome gratuity, had received a bride's favour,[9] which he now wore in his cap—When the forsaken lover understood they were

8. The Hardwicke Act of 1753 required that banns be asked three times on successive Sundays for all who wished to be married, excepting only Quakers, Jews, and royalty, or those with a license from a bishop. There were severe penalties for violating the act, but the requirements could be avoided by going to Scotland, where they did not apply.
9. A decorative piece of lace or ribbon, often in the form of a bow, which was designed to be removed from the bride's costume and presented to well-wishers at the wedding.

actually married, and set out for London; and that Dutton had discovered to the lady, that he (the Hibernian) was a taylor, he had like to have run distracted. He tore the ribbon from the fellow's cap, and beat it about his ears. He swore he would pursue him to the gates of hell, and ordered a post-chaise and four to be got ready as soon as possible; but, recollecting that his finances would not admit of this way of travelling, he was obliged to countermand this order.

For my part, I knew nothing at all of what had happened, till the postilion brought me the keys of my trunk and portmanteau, which he had received from Dutton, who sent me his respects, hoping I would excuse him for his abrupt departure, as it was a step upon which his fortune depended—Before I had time to make my uncle acquainted with this event, the Irishman burst into my chamber, without any introduction, exclaiming,—"By my soul, your sarvant has robbed me of five thousand pounds, and I'll have satisfaction, if I should be hanged to-morrow.—" When I asked him who he was, "My name (said he) is Master Macloughlin—but it should be Leighlin Oneale, for I am come from Ter-Owen the Great;[1] and so I am as good a gentleman as any in Ireland; and that rogue, your sarvant, said I was a taylor, which was as big a lie as if he had called me the pope—I'm a man of fortune, and have spent all I had; and so being in distress, Mr. Coshgrave, the fashioner in Shuffolk-street, tuck me out, and made me his own private shecretary: by the same token, I was the last he bailed; for his friends obliged him to tie himself up, that he would bail no more above ten pounds; for why, becaase as how, he could not refuse any body that asked, and therefore in time would have robbed himself of his whole fortune, and, if he had lived long at that rate, must have died bankrupt very soon—and so I made my addresses to Miss Skinner, a young lady of five thousand pounds fortune, who agreed to take me for better nor worse; and, to be sure, this day would have put me in possession, if it had not been for that rogue, your sarvant, who came like a tief, and stole away my property, and made her believe I was a taylor; and that she was going to marry the ninth part of a man: but the devil burn my soul, if ever I catch him on the mountains of Tulloghobegly, if I don't shew him that I'm nine times as good a man as he, or e'er a bug of his country."

When he had rung out his first alarm, I told him I was sorry he had allowed himself to be so jockied; but it was no business of mine; and that the fellow who robbed him of his bride, had likewise robbed me of my servant—"Didn't I tell you then, (cried he,) that Rogue was his true Christian name.—Oh if I had but one fair trust with him upon the sod, I'd give him lave to brag all the rest of his life."

---

1. This Irishman is claiming a noble ancestry from the fifth-century king of Ireland, Niall, who had a son named Eoghan (Owen) from whom the O'Neills were descended, including Hugh O'Neill, Lord of Ter-Owen, or Tyrone, in the twelfth century. Tulloghobegly, below, is a mountainous area in County Clare, in the west of Ireland.

My uncle hearing the noise, came in, and being informed of this adventure, began to comfort Mr. Oneale for the lady's elopement; observing that he seemed to have had a lucky escape, that it was better she should elope before, than after marriage—The Hibernian was of a very different opinion. He said, "If he had been once married, she might have eloped as soon as she pleased; he would have taken care that she should not have carried her fortune along with her—Ah (said he) she's a Judas Iscariot, and has betrayed me with a kiss; and, like Judas, she carried the bag, and has not left me money enough to bear my expences back to London; and so as I'm come to this pass, and the rogue that was the occasion of it has left you without a sarvant, you may put me in his place; and by Jasus, it is the best thing you can do.—" I begged to be excused, declaring I could put up with any inconvenience, rather than treat as a footman the descendant of Tir-Owen the Great. I advised him to return to his friend, Mr. Cosgrave, and take his passage from Newcastle by sea, towards which I made him a small present, and he retired, seemingly resigned to his evil fortune. I have taken upon trial a Scotchman, called Archy M'Alpin, an old soldier, whose last master, a colonel, lately died at Berwick. The fellow is old and withered; but he has been recommended to me for his fidelity, by Mrs. Humphreys, a very good sort of a woman, who keeps the inn at Tweedmouth, and is much respected by all the travellers on this road.

Clinker, without doubt, thinks himself happy in the removal of a dangerous rival, and he is too good a Christian, to repine at Dutton's success. Even Mrs. Jenkins will have reason to congratulate herself upon this event, when she cooly reflects upon the matter; for, howsoever she was forced from her poise for a season, by snares laid for her vanity, Humphrey is certainly the north-star to which the needle of her affection would have pointed at the long run. At present, the same vanity is exceedingly mortified, upon finding herself abandoned by her new admirer, in favour of another innamorata. She received the news with a violent burst of laughter, which soon brought on a fit of crying; and this gave the finishing blow to the patience of her mistress, which had held out beyond all expectation. She now opened all those floodgates of reprehension, which had been shut so long. She not only reproached her with her levity and indiscretion, but attacked her on the score of religion, declaring roundly that she was in a state of apostacy and reprobation; and finally, threatened to send her a-packing at this extremity of the kingdom. All the family interceded for poor Winifrid, not even excepting her slighted swain, Mr. Clinker, who, on his knees, implored and obtained her pardon.

There was, however, another consideration that gave Mrs. Tabitha some disturbance. At Newcastle, the servants had been informed by some wag, that there was nothing to eat in Scotland, but *oat-meal* and *sheep's-heads*; and Lieutenant Lismahago being consulted, what he said served rather to confirm than to refute the report. Our aunt being apprised of this circumstance, very gravely advised her brother to provide a sumpter horse with store of hams, tongues, bread, biscuit, and other articles for our subsistence, in the course of our peregrination, and Mr. Bramble as gravely replied, that he would take the hint into consideration: but, finding no such provision was made, she now revived the proposal, observing that there was a tolerable market at Berwick, where we might be supplied; and that my man's horse would serve as a beast of burthen—The 'squire, shrugging up his shoulders, eyed her askance with a look of ineffable contempt; and, after some pause, "Sister, (said he) I can hardly persuade myself you are serious." She was so little acquainted with the geography of the island, that she imagined we could not go to Scotland but by sea; and, after we had passed through the town of Berwick, when he told her we were upon Scottish ground, she could hardly believe the assertion—If the truth must be told, the South Britons in general are woefully ignorant in this particular. What, between want of curiosity, and traditional sarcasms, the effect of ancient animosity, the people at the other end of the island know as little of Scotland as of Japan.

If I had never been in Wales, I should have been more struck with the manifest difference in appearance betwixt the peasants and commonalty on different sides of the Tweed. The boors of Northumberland are lusty fellows, fresh complexioned, cleanly, and well cloathed; but the labourers in Scotland are generally lank, lean, hard-featured, sallow, soiled, and shabby, and their little pinched blue caps have a beggarly effect. The cattle are much in the same stile with their drivers, meagre, stunted, and ill equipt. When I talked to my uncle on this subject, he said, "Though all the Scottish hinds would not bear to be compared with those of the rich counties of South Britain, they would stand very well in competition with the peasants of France, Italy, and Savoy—not to mention the mountaineers of Wales, and the redshanks of Ireland."

We entered Scotland by a frightful moor of sixteen miles, which promises very little for the interior parts of the kingdom; but the prospect mended as we advanced. Passing through Dunbar, which is a neat little town, situated on the sea-side, we lay at a country inn, where our entertainment far exceeded our expectation; but for this we cannot give the Scots credit, as the landlord is a native of England. Yesterday we dined at Haddington, which has been a place of some consideration, but is now gone to decay; and in the evening arrived at this metropolis, of which I can say very little. It is very romantic, from its situation on the declivity of a hill, having a fortified castle at the top, and a royal palace at the bottom. The first thing that strikes the nose of a stranger, shall be nameless;[2] but what first strikes the eye, is the unconscionable height of

2. The smell of raw sewage, which was dumped into the streets (see below, p. 205), and the coal smoke combined to give Edinburgh its nickname of "Old Reeky."

the houses, which generally rise to five, six, seven, and eight stories, and, in some places, (as I am assured) to twelve. This manner of building, attended with numberless inconveniences, must have been originally owing to want of room. Certain it is, the town seems to be full of people: but their looks, their language, and their customs, are so different from ours, that I can hardly believe myself in Great-Britain.

The inn at which we put up, (if it may be so called) was so filthy and disagreeable in all respects, that my uncle began to fret, and his gouty symptoms to recur—Recollecting, however, that he had a letter of recommendation to one Mr. Mitchelson, a lawyer,[3] he sent it by his servant, with a compliment, importing that he would wait upon him next day in person; but that gentleman visited us immediately, and insisted upon our going to his own house, until he could provide lodgings for our accommodation. We gladly accepted of his invitation, and repaired to his house, where we were treated with equal elegance and hospitality, to the utter confusion of our aunt, whose prejudices, though beginning to give way, were not yet entirely removed. Today, by the assistance of our friend, we are settled in convenient lodgings, up four pair of stairs, in the High-street, the fourth story being, in this city, reckoned more genteel than the first. The air is, in all probability, the better; but it requires good lungs to breathe it at this distance above the surface of the earth.—While I do remain above it, whether higher or lower, provided I breathe at all,

I shall ever be,

dear Phillips, yours,

July 18.   J. MELFORD.

To Dr. LEWIS.

DEAR LEWIS,

That part of Scotland contiguous to Berwick, nature seems to have intended as a barrier between two hostile nations. It is a brown desert of considerable extent, that produces nothing but heath and fern; and what rendered it the more dreary when we passed, there was a thick fog that hindered us from seeing above twenty yards from the carriage—My sister began to make wry faces, and use her smelling-bottle; Liddy looked blank, and Mrs. Jenkins dejected; but in a few hours these clouds were dissipated; the sea appeared upon our right, and on the left the mountains retired a little, leaving an agreeable plain betwixt them and the beach; but, what surprised us all, this plain, to the extent of several miles, was covered with as fine wheat as ever I saw in the most fertile parts of South

3. Samuel Mitchelson (d. 1788) was an attorney and an acquaintance of Smollett's. He was a writer to the Signet, which allowed him to prepare royal writs and charters.

Britain——This plentiful crop is raised in the open field, without any inclosure, or other manure than the *alga marina*, or sea-weed, which abounds on this coast; a circumstance which shews that the soil and climate are favourable; but that agriculture in this country is not yet brought to that perfection which it has attained in England. Inclosures would not only keep the grounds warm, and the several fields distinct, but would also protect the crop from the high winds, which are so frequent in this part of the island.

Dunbar is well situated for trade, and has a curious bason, where ships of small burthen may be perfectly secure; but there is little appearance of business in the place——From thence, all the way to Edinburgh, there is a continual succession of fine seats, belonging to noblemen and gentlemen; and as each is surrounded by its own parks and plantation, they produce a very pleasing effect in a country which lies otherwise open and exposed. At Dunbar there is a noble park, with a lodge, belonging to the Duke of Roxburgh,[4] where Oliver Cromwell had his head-quarters, when Lesley, at the head of a Scotch army, took possession of the mountains in the neighbourhood, and hampered him in such a manner, that he would have been obliged to embark and get away by sea, had not the fanaticism of the enemy forfeited the advantage which they had obtained by their general's conduct——Their ministers, by exhortation, prayer, assurance, and prophecy, instigated them to go down and slay the Philistines in Gilgal,[5] and they quitted their ground accordingly, notwithstanding all that Lesley could do to restrain the madness of their enthusiasm——When Oliver saw them in motion, he exclaimed, "Praised be the Lord, he hath delivered them into the hands of his servant!" and ordered his troops to sing a psalm of thanksgiving, while they advanced in order to the plain, where the Scots were routed with great slaughter.

In the neighbourhood of Haddington, there is a gentleman's house,[6] in the building of which, and the improvements about it, he is said to have expended forty thousand pounds: but I cannot say I was much pleased with either the architecture or the situation; though it has in front a pastoral stream, the banks of which are laid out in a very agreeable manner. I intended to pay my respects to lord Elibank,[7] whom I had the honour to know at London many years ago. He lives in this part of Lothian; but was gone to the North, on a visit——You have often heard me

4. The Duke of Roxburgh, John Ker (1740–1804), whose seat was called both *Fleurs* and Broxmouth.
5. In Joshua 4–6, the story is told of the parting of the River Jordan to allow the Jews to pass, and their setting up camp at Gilgal, a place on the lowlands near Jericho, where the walls fell before the victorious Jews. Apparently, the fanatic preachers found some parallel between the lowlands from which the successful attack was launched and their own position, for they recommended giving up the high position with disastrous results. The Philistines were not the enemy at the battle of Jericho, but the term was and is used about an unlearned and uncultured opposition.
6. This house has been identified as Amisfield, which had formerly been the seat of Col. Francis Charteris (1675–1732), a notorious profligate.
7. Baron Elibank, Patrick Murray (1703–78), was a friend of Smollett's and an intelligent patron of the arts.

mention this nobleman, whom I have long revered for his humanity and universal intelligence, over and above the entertainment arising from the originality of his character—At Musselburgh, however, I had the good-fortune to drink tea with my old friend Mr. Cardonel;[8] and at his house I met with Dr. C——,[9] the parson of the parish, whose humour and conversation inflamed me with a desire of being better acquainted with his person—I am not at all surprised that these Scots make their way in every quarter of the globe.

This place is but four miles from Edinburgh, towards which we proceeded along the sea-shore, upon a firm bottom of smooth sand, which the tide had left uncovered in its retreat——Edinburgh, from this avenue, is not seen to much advantage—We had only an imperfect view of the Castle and upper parts of the town, which varied incessantly according to the inflexions of the road, and exhibited the appearance of detached spires and turrets, belonging to some magnificent edifice in ruins. The palace of Holyrood house stands on the left, as you enter the Canongate—This is a street continued from hence to the gate called Nether Bow, which is now taken away; so that there is no interruption for a long mile, from the bottom to the top of the hill on which the Castle stands in a most imperial situation——Considering its fine pavement, its width, and the lofty houses on each side, this would be undoubtedly one of the noblest streets in Europe, if an ugly mass of mean buildings, called the Lucken-Booths,[1] had not thrust itself, by what accident I know not, into the middle of the way, like Middle-Row in Holborn.[2] The city stands upon two hills, and the bottom between them; and, with all its defects, may very well pass for the capital of a moderate kingdom—It is full of people, and continually resounds with the noise of coaches and other carriages, for luxury as well as commerce. As far as I can perceive, here is no want of provisions—The beef and mutton are as delicate here as in Wales; the sea affords plenty of good fish; the bread is remarkably fine; and the water is excellent, though I'm afraid not in sufficient quantity to answer all the purposes of cleanliness and convenience; articles in which, it must be allowed, our fellow-subjects are a little defective—The water is brought in leaden pipes from a mountain in the neighbourhood, to a cistern on the Castle-hill, from whence it is distributed to public conduits in different parts of the city—From these it is carried in barrels, on the backs of male and female porters, up two, three, four, five, six, seven, and eight pair of stairs, for the use of particular families—Every story is a complete house, occupied by a

8. Mansfelt Cardonnel was an illegitimate great-grandson of Charles II and a customs commissioner for Scotland. He lived in a suburb of Edinburgh named Musselburgh.
9. Alexander Carlyle (1722–1805), known as "Jupiter" because of his good looks, also lived in Musselburgh, where he was a clergyman. He was a

good friend and correspondent of Smollett.
1. A row of buildings in the High Street, near St. Giles's Cathedral. They were finally removed in 1817.
2. A block of houses which protruded into Holborn Street, in London, until they were removed in 1868.

separate family; and the stair being common to them all, is generally left in a very filthy condition; a man must tread with great circumspection to get safe housed with unpolluted shoes—Nothing can form a stronger contrast, than the difference betwixt the outside and inside of the door; for the good-women of this metropolis are remarkably nice in the ornaments and propriety of their apartments, as if they were resolved to transfer the imputation from the individual to the public. You are no stranger to their method of discharging all their impurities from their windows, at a certain hour of the night, as the custom is in Spain, Portugal, and some parts of France and Italy—A practice to which I can by no means be reconciled; for notwithstanding all the care that is taken by their scavengers to remove this nuisance every morning by break of day, enough still remains to offend the eyes, as well as other organs of those whom use has not hardened against all delicacy of sensation.

The inhabitants seem insensible to these impressions, and are apt to imagine the disgust that we avow is little better than affectation; but they ought to have some compassion for strangers, who have not been used to this kind of sufferance; and consider, whether it may not be worth while to take some pains to vindicate themselves from the reproach that, on this account, they bear among their neighbours. As to the surprising height of their houses, it is absurd in many respects; but in one particular light I cannot view it without horror; that is, the dreadful situation of all the families above, in case the common stair-case should be rendered impassable by a fire in the lower stories—In order to prevent the shocking consequences that must attend such an accident, it would be a right measure to open doors of communication from one house to another, on every story, by which the people might fly from such a terrible visitation. In all parts of the world, we see the force of habit prevailing over all the dictates of convenience and sagacity—All the people of business at Edinburgh, and even the genteel company, may be seen standing in crowds every day, from one to two in the afternoon, in the open street, at a place where formerly stood a market-cross, which (by the bye) was a curious piece of Gothic architecture, still to be seen in lord Sommerville's[3] garden in this neighbourhood—I say, the people stand in the open street from the force of custom, rather than move a few yards to an Exchange that stands empty on one side, or to the Parliament-close on the other, which is a noble square, adorned with a fine equestrian statue of king Charles II.—The company thus assembled, are entertained with a variety of tunes, played upon a set of bells, fixed in a steeple hard by—As these bells are well-toned, and the musician, who has a salary from the city, for playing upon them with keys, is no bad performer, the entertainment is really agreeable, and very striking to the ears of a stranger.

3. Lord Somerville, James Somerville (1727–96).

The public inns of Edinburgh, are still worse than those of London; but by means of a worthy gentleman, to whom I was recommended, we have got decent lodgings in the house of a widow gentlewoman, of the name of Lockhart; and here I shall stay until I have seen every thing that is remarkable in and about this capital. I now begin to feel the good effects of exercise——I eat like a farmer, sleep from mid-night till eight in the morning without interruption, and enjoy a constant tide of spirits, equally distant from inanition and excess; but whatever ebbs or flows my constitution may undergo, my heart will still declare that I am,

Dear Lewis,

Your affectionate friend and servant,

Edr. July 18.   MATT. BRAMBLE.

To Mrs. MARY JONES, at Brambleton-hall.

DEAR MARY,

The 'squire has been so kind as to rap my bit of nonsense under the kiver of his own sheet—O, Mary Jones! Mary Jones! I have had trials and trembulation. God help me! I have been a vixen and a griffin these many days—Sattin has had power to temp me in the shape of van Ditton, the young 'squire's wally de shamble;[4] but by God's grease he did not purvail —I thoft as how, there was no arm in going to a play at Newcastle, with my hair dressed in the Parish fashion; and as for the trifle of paint, he said as how my complexion wanted rouch, and so I let him put it on with a little Spanish owl;[5] but a mischievous mob of colliers, and such promiscous ribble rabble, that could bare no smut but their own, attacked us in the street, and called me *hoar* and *painted Issabel*, and splashed my close, and spoiled me a complete set of blond lace triple ruffles, not a pin the worse for the ware—They cost me seven good sillings, to lady Griskin's woman at London.

When I axed Mr. Clinker what they meant by calling me Issabel, he put the byebill into my hand, and I read of van Issabel a painted harlot, that vas thrown out of a vindore, and the dogs came and licked her blood —But I am no harlot; and, with God's blessing, no dog shall have my poor blood to lick: marry, Heaven forbid, amen! As for Ditton, after all his courting, and his compliment, he stole away an Irishman's bride, and took a French leave of me and his master; but I vally not his going a farting; but I have had hanger on his account—Mistriss scoulded like mad; thof I have the comfit that all the family took my part, and even Mr. Clinker pleaded for me on his bended knee; thof, God he knows, he had raisins enuff to

---

4. Valet de chambre or personal servant.
5. Spanish wool was wool impregnated with a red dye which was used as rouge.

complain; but he's a good sole, abounding with Christian meekness, and one day will meet with his reward.

And now, dear Mary, we have got to Haddingborrough, among the Scots, who are civil enuff for our money, thof I don't speak their lingo —But they should not go for to impose upon foreigners; for the bills in their houses say, they have different *easements* to let; and behold there is nurro geaks[6] in the whole kingdom, nor any thing for poor sarvants, but a barrel with a pair of tongs thrown a-cross; and all the chairs in the family are emptied into this here barrel once a-day; and at ten o'clock at night the whole cargo is flung out of a back windore that looks into some street or lane, and the maid calls *gardy loo*[7] to the passengers, which signifies *Lord have mercy upon you!* and this is done every night in every house in Haddingborrough; so you may guess, Mary Jones, what a sweet savour comes from such a number of profuming pans; but they say it is wholsome, and, truly, I believe it is; for being in the vapours, and thinking of Issabel and Mr. Clinker, I was going into a fit of astericks, when this fiff,[8] saving your presence, took me by the nose so powerfully that I sneezed three times, and found myself wonderfully refreshed; and this to be sure is the raisin why there are no fits in Haddingborrough.

I was likewise made believe, that there was nothing to be had but *oat-meal* and *seeps-heads*; but if I hadn't been a fool, I mought have known there could be no *heads* without kerkasses——This very blessed day I dined upon a delicate leg of Velsh mutton and cully-flower; and as for the oat-meal, I leave that to the sarvants of the country, which are pore drudges, many of them without shoes or stockings—Mr. Clinker tells me here is a great call of the gospel; but I wish, I wish some of our family be not fallen off from the rite way—O, if I was given to tail-baring, I have my own secrets to discover——There has been a deal of huggling and flurtation betwixt mistress and an ould Scots officer, called Kismycago. He looks for all the orld like the scarecrow that our gardener set up to frite away the sparrows; and what will come of it, the Lord nows; but come what will, it shall never be said that I menchioned a syllabub of the matter—Remember me kindly to Saul and the kitten——I hope they got the horn-buck, and will put it to a good yuse, which is the constant prayer of,

Dear Molly,

your loving friend,

Addingborough, July 18.   WIN. JENKINS.

6. Not a single jakes, the ordinary word for "outhouse" at the time.

7. From the French *gardez l'eau*, "Look out for the water!"
8. Whiff.

To Sir WATKIN PHILLIPS, Bar[t]. of Jesus college, Oxon.

DEAR PHILLIPS,

If I stay much longer at Edinburgh, I shall be changed into a down-right Caledonian—My uncle observes, that I have already acquired something of the country accent. The people here are so social and attentive in their civilities to strangers, that I am insensibly sucked into the channel of their manners and customs, although they are in fact much more different from ours than you can imagine—That difference, how-ever, which struck me very much at my first arrival, I now hardly perceive, and my ear is perfectly reconciled to the Scotch accent, which I find even agreeable in the mouth of a pretty woman—It is a sort of Doric dialect, which gives an idea of amiable simplicity——You cannot imag-ine how we have been caressed and feasted in the *good town of Edinburgh*, of which we are become free denizens and guild brothers, by the special favour of the magistracy.

I had a whimsical commission from Bath, to a citizen of this metropolis —Quin, understanding our intention to visit Edinburgh, pulled out a guinea, and desired the favour I would drink it at a tavern, with a particular friend and bottle-companion of his, one Mr. R—C—,[9] a lawyer of this city—I charged myself with the commission, and, taking the guinea, "You see (said I) I have pocketed your bounty." "Yes (replied Quin, laughing); and a head-ake into the bargain, if you drink fair." I made use of this introduction to Mr. C——, who received me with open arms, and gave me the rendezvous, according to the cartel. He had provided a company of jolly fellows, among whom I found myself extremely happy; and did Mr. C——and Quin all the justice in my power; but, alas, I was no more than a tiro among a troop of veterans, who had compassion upon my youth, and conveyed me home in the morning, by what means I know not—Quin was mistaken, however, as to the head-ake; the claret was too good to treat me so roughly.

While Mr. Bramble holds conferences with the graver literati of the place, and our females are entertained at visits by the Scotch ladies, who are the best and kindest creatures upon earth, I pass my time among the bucks of Edinburgh; who, with a great share of spirit and vivacity, have a certain shrewdness and self-command that is not often found among their neighbours, in the high-day of youth and exultation——Not a hint escapes a Scotchman that can be interpreted into offence by any individual in the company; and national reflections are never heard—In this particular, I must own, we are both unjust and ungrateful to the Scots; for, as far as I am able to judge, they have a real esteem for the

9. Robert Cullen (d. 1810) was an attorney and later a judge. He was noted as a mimic and pleasant companion.

natives of South-Britain; and never mention our country, but with expressions of regard—Nevertheless, they are far from being servile imitators of our modes and fashionable vices. All their customs and regulations of public and private œconomy, of business and diversion, are in their own stile. This remarkably predominates in their looks, their dress, and manner, their music, and even their cookery. Our 'squire declares, that he knows not another people upon earth, so strongly marked with a national character—Now we are upon the article of cookery, I must own, some of their dishes are savoury, and even delicate; but I am not yet Scotchman enough to relish their singed sheep's-head and haggice, which were provided at our request, one day at Mr. Mitchelson's, where we dined—The first put me in mind of the history of Congo, in which I had read of negros' heads sold publickly in the markets; the last, being a mess of minced lights, livers, suet, oat-meal, onions, and pepper, inclosed in a sheep's stomach, had a very sudden effect upon mine, and the delicate Mrs. Tabby changed colour; when the cause of our disgust was instantaneously removed at the nod of our entertainer. The Scots, in general, are attached to this composition, with a sort of national fondness, as well as to their oat-meal bread; which is presented at every table, in thin triangular cakes, baked upon a plate of iron, called a girdle; and these, many of the natives, even in the higher ranks of life, prefer to wheaten-bread, which they have here in perfection—You know we used to vex poor Murray of Baliol-college,[1] by asking, if there was really no fruit but turnips in Scotland?——Sure enough, I have seen turnips make their appearance, not as a desert, but by way of *hors d'oeuvres*, or whets, as radishes are served up betwixt more substantial dishes in France and Italy; but it must be observed, that the turnips of this country are as much superior in sweetness, delicacy, and flavour, to those of England, as a musk-melon is to the stock of a common cabbage. They are small and conical, of a yellowish colour, with a very thin skin; and, over and above their agreeable taste, are valuable for their antiscorbutic quality—As to the fruit now in season, such as cherries, gooseberries, and currants, there is no want of them at Edinburgh; and in the gardens of some gentlemen, who live in this neighbourhood, there is now a very favourable appearance of apricots, peaches, nectarines, and even grapes: nay, I have seen a very fine shew of pine-apples within a few miles of this metropolis. Indeed, we have no reason to be surprised at these particulars, when we consider how little difference there is, in fact, betwixt this climate and that of London.

All the remarkable places in the city and its avenues, for ten miles around, we have visited, much to our satisfaction. In the Castle are some

---

1. Perhaps Gideon Murray, the younger brother of Lord Elibank. The younger Murray was a student at Balliol College, Oxford, from 1729 to 1736, which would be before Jery's birth, but Smollett may be alluding to him nevertheless.

royal apartments, where the sovereign occasionally resided; and here are
carefully preserved the regalia of the kingdom, consisting of a crown, said
to be of great value, a sceptre, and a sword of state, adorned with jewels
—Of these symbols of sovereignty, the people are exceedingly jealous
—A report being spread, during the sitting of the union-parliament,[2]
that they were removed to London, such a tumult arose, that the lord
commissioner would have been torn in pieces, if he had not produced
them for the satisfaction of the populace.

The palace of Holyrood-house is an elegant piece of architecture, but
sunk in an obscure, and, as I take it, unwholesome bottom, where one
would imagine it had been placed on purpose to be concealed. The
apartments are lofty, but unfurnished; and as for the pictures of the
Scottish kings, from Fergus I. to king William, they are paultry daubings,
mostly by the same hand, painted either from the imagination, or porters
hired to sit for the purpose. All the diversions of London we enjoy at
Edinburgh, in a small compass. Here is a well-conducted concert,[3] in
which several gentlemen perform on different instruments—The Scots
are all musicians—Every man you meet plays on the flute, the violin, or
violoncello; and there is one nobleman,[4] whose compositions are universally admired—Our company of actors is very tolerable; and a subscription is now on foot for building a new theatre;[5] but their assemblies
please me above all other public exhibitions.

We have been at the hunters ball, where I was really astonished to see
such a number of fine women—The English, who have never crossed the
Tweed, imagine erroneously, that the Scotch ladies are not remarkable
for personal attractions; but, I can declare with a safe conscience, I never
saw so many handsome females together, as were assembled on this
occasion. At the Leith races, the best company comes hither from the
remoter provinces; so that, I suppose, we had all the beauty of the
kingdom concentrated as it were into one focus; which was, indeed, so
vehement, that my heart could hardly resist its power—Between friends,
it has sustained some damage from the bright eyes of the charming miss
R——n,[6] whom I had the honour to dance with at the ball—The
countess of Melvile attracted all eyes, and the admiration of all present
—She was accompanied by the agreeable miss Grieve, who made many
conquests; nor did my sister Liddy pass unnoticed in the assembly—She
is become a toast at Edinburgh, by the name of the Fair Cambrian, and

2. Apparently the Scottish Parliament which met
in 1706–7 to pass the Act of Union between
England and Scotland. There was considerable
popular unrest during the period.
3. Weekly concerts began in Edinburgh in 1728.
4. The Earl of Kellie, Thomas Alexander Erskine
(1732–81) was an accomplished violinist and
composer.

5. The Theatre Royal was formally opened at the
end of 1769.
6. Lewis Knapp suggests that this is probably Miss
Cecilia Renton, but could possibly be her sister
Eleanora. The former young woman married Alexander Telfer, Smollett's nephew, who later took
the name of Smollett.

has already been the occasion of much wine-shed; but the poor girl met with an accident at the ball, which has given us great disturbance.

A young gentleman, the express image of that rascal Wilson, went up to ask her to dance a minuet; and his sudden appearance shocked her so much, that she fainted away—I call Wilson a rascal, because, if he had been really a gentleman, with honourable intentions, he would have, ere now, appeared in his own character—I must own, my blood boils with indignation when I think of that fellow's presumption; and Heaven confound me if I don't—But I won't be so womanish as to rail—Time will, perhaps, furnish occasion—Thank God, the cause of Liddy's disorder remains a secret. The lady directress of the ball, thinking she was overcome by the heat of the place, had her conveyed to another room, where she soon recovered so well, as to return and join in the country-dances, in which the Scotch lasses acquit themselves with such spirit and agility, as put their partners to the height of their mettle—I believe our aunt, Mrs. Tabitha, had entertained hopes of being able to do some execution among the cavaliers at this assembly———She had been several days in consultation with milliners and mantua-makers, preparing for the occasion, at which she made her appearance in a full suit of damask, so thick and heavy, that the sight of it alone, at this season of the year, was sufficient to draw drops of sweat from any man of ordinary imagination—She danced one minuet with our friend, Mr. Mitchelson, who favoured her so far, in the spirit of hospitality and politeness; and she was called out a second time by the young laird of Ballymawhawple,[7] who, coming in by accident, could not readily find any other partner; but as the first was a married man, and the second payed no particular homage to her charms, which were also over-looked by the rest of the company, she became dissatisfied and censorious—At supper, she observed that the Scotch gentlemen made a very good figure, when they were a little improved by travelling; and therefore it was pity they did not all take the benefit of going abroad—She said the women were aukward, masculine creatures; that, in dancing, they lifted their legs like so many colts; that they had no idea of graceful motion, and put on their clothes in a frightful manner; but if the truth must be told, Tabby herself was the most ridiculous figure, and the worst dressed of the whole assembly —The neglect of the male sex rendered her malcontent and peevish; she now found fault with every thing at Edinburgh, and teized her brother to leave the place, when she was suddenly reconciled to it on a religious consideration———There is a sect of fanaticks, who have separated themselves from the established kirk, under the name of Seceders[8] —They acknowledge no earthly head of the church, reject lay-patronage,

7. There is a Laird of Balmarwhopple in *Waverley, or 'Tis Sixty Years Since* (1814) by Sir Walter Scott, but this gentleman remains unidentified. A laird was a landed proprietor, and should not be confused with a lord, a member of the peerage.
8. A sect which left the Kirk of Scotland (presbyterian) in the 1730's.

and maintain the methodist doctrines of the new birth, the new light, the efficacy of grace, the insufficiency of works, and the operations of the spirit. Mrs. Tabitha, attended by Humphry Clinker, was introduced to one of their conventicles, where they both received much edification; and she has had the good fortune to come acquainted with a pious Christian, called Mr. Moffat, who is very powerful in prayer, and often assists her in private exercises of devotion.

I never saw such a concourse of genteel company at any races in England, as appeared on the course of Leith—Hard by, in the fields called the Links, the citizens of Edinburgh divert themselves at a game called golf, in which they use a curious kind of bats, tipt with horn, and small elastic balls of leather, stuffed with feathers, rather less than tennis balls, but of a much harder consistence—This they strike with such force and dexterity from one hole to another, that they will fly to an incredible distance. Of this diversion the Scots are so fond, that when the weather will permit, you may see a multitude of all ranks, from the senator of justice to the lowest tradesmen, mingled together in their shirts, and following the balls with the utmost eagerness—Among others, I was shewn one particular set of golfers, the youngest of whom was turned of fourscore——They were all gentlemen of independent fortunes, who had amused themselves with this pastime for the best part of a century, without having ever felt the least alarm from sickness or disgust; and they never went to bed, without having each the best part of a gallon of claret in his belly. Such uninterrupted exercise, cooperating with the keen air from the sea, must, without all doubt, keep the appetite always on edge, and steel the constitution against all the common attacks of distemper.

The Leith races gave occasion to another entertainment of a very singular nature—There is at Edinburgh a society or corporation of errand-boys, called cawdies, who ply in the streets at night with paper lanthorns, and are very serviceable in carrying messages—These fellows, though shabby in their appearance, and rudely familiar in their address, are wonderfully acute, and so noted for fidelity, that there is no instance of a cawdy's having betrayed his trust—Such is their intelligence, that they know, not only every individual of the place, but also every stranger, by that time he has been four and twenty hours in Edinburgh; and no transaction, even the most private, can escape their notice—They are particularly famous for their dexterity in executing one of the functions of Mercury;[9] though, for my own part, I never employed them in this department of business—Had I occasion for any service of this nature, my own man Archy M'Alpine, is as well qualified as e'er a cawdie in Edinburgh; and I am much mistaken, if he has not been heretofore of their fraternity. Be that as it may, they resolved to give a dinner and a ball

9. The classical god Mercury was occasionally called upon to act as a procurer.

at Leith, to which they formally invited all the young noblemen and gentlemen that were at the races; and this invitation was reinforced by an assurance that all the celebrated ladies of pleasure would grace the entertainment with their company.—I received a card on this occasion, and went thither with half a dozen of my acquaintance.—In a large hall the cloth was laid on a long range of tables joined together, and here the company seated themselves, to the number of about fourscore, lords, and lairds, and other gentlemen, courtezans and cawdies mingled together, as the slaves and their masters were in the time of the Saturnalia in ancient Rome.—The toastmaster, who sat at the upper end, was one Cawdie Fraser, a veteran pimp, distinguished for his humour and sagacity, well known and much respected in his profession by all the guests, male and female, that were here assembled.—He had bespoke the dinner and the wine: he had taken care that all his brethren should appear in decent apparel and clean linen; and he himself wore a periwig with three tails, in honour of the festival—I assure you the banquet was both elegant and plentiful, and seasoned with a thousand sallies, that promoted a general spirit of mirth and good humour.—After the desert, Mr. Fraser proposed the following toasts, which I don't pretend to explain.—"The best in Christendom."—"Gibb's contract."—"The beggar's bennison."[1] —"King and kirk."—"Great-Britain and Ireland."———Then, filling a bumper, and turning to me, "Mester Malford, (said he) may a' unkind-ness cease betwixt John Bull and his sister Moggy."—The next person he singled out, was a nobleman who had been long abroad.—"Ma lord, (cried Fraser) here is a bumper to a' those noblemen who have virtue enough to spend their rents in their ain countray."—He afterwards addressed himself to a member of parliament in these words:—"Mester —I'm sure ye'll ha' nae objection to my drinking, Disgrace and dule to ilka Scot, that sells his conscience and his vote."—He discharged a third sarcasm at a person very gaily dressed, who had risen from small beginnings, and made a considerable fortune at play.—Filling his glass, and calling him by name, "Lang life (said he) to the wylie loon that gangs a-field with a toom poke at his lunzie,[2] and comes hame with a sackful of siller."———All these toasts being received with loud bursts of applause, Mr. Fraser called for pint glasses, and filled his own to the brim: then standing up, and all his brethren following his example, "Ma lords and gentlemen (cried he), here is a cup of thanks for the great and undeserved honour you have done your poor errand-boys this day."—So saying, he and they drank off their glasses in a trice, and, quitting their seats, took their station each behind one of the other guests;—exclaiming, "Noo we're your honours cawdies again."

1. The first of these three toasts is "To the best cunt in Christendom," the second may refer to the court fool of James V of Scotland, and the third is "May your prick and your purse never fail you."

Jery probably expects his correspondent to recall the bawdy parts.
2. Empty purse at his side.

The nobleman who had bore the first brunt of Mr. Fraser's satire, objected to his abdication. He said, as the company was assembled by invitation from the cawdies, he expected they were to be entertained at their expence. "By no means, my lord, (cried Fraser) I wad na be guilty of sic presumption for the wide warld—I never affronted a gentleman since I was born; and sure at this age, I wonnot offer an indignity to sic an honourable convention." "Well, (said his Lordship) as you have expended some wit, you have a right to save your money. You have given me good counsel, and I take it in good part. As you have voluntarily quitted your seat, I will take your place with the leave of the good company, and think myself happy to be hailed, *Father of the Feast*." He was forthwith elected into the chair, and complimented in a bumper in his new character.

The claret continued to circulate without interruption, till the glasses seemed to dance upon the table, and this, perhaps, was a hint to the ladies to call for music—At eight in the evening the ball began in another apartment: at midnight we went to supper; but it was broad day before I found the way to my lodgings; and, no doubt, his Lordship had a swinging bill to discharge.

In short, I have lived so riotously for some weeks, that my uncle begins to be alarmed on the score of my constitution, and very seriously observes, that all his own infirmities are owing to such excesses indulged in his youth—Mrs. Tabitha says it would be more for the advantage of my soul as well as body, if, instead of frequenting these scenes of debauchery, I would accompany Mr. Moffat and her to hear a sermon of the reverend Mr. M'Corkindale.—Clinker often exhorts me, with a groan, to take care of my precious health; and even Archy M'Alpine, when he happens to be overtaken,[3] (which is oftener the case than I could wish) reads me a long lecture upon temperance and sobriety; and is so very wise and sententious, that, if I could provide him with a professor's chair, I would willingly give up the benefit of his admonitions and service together; for I was tutor-sick at alma mater.

I am not, however, so much engrossed by the gaieties of Edinburgh, but that I find time to make parties in the family way.—We have not only seen all the villas and villages within ten miles of the capital, but we have also crossed the Firth, which is an arm of the sea seven miles broad, that divides Lothian from the shire, or, as the Scots call it, the *kingdom of Fife*. There is a number of large open sea-boats that ply on this passage from Leith to Kinghorn, which is a borough on the other side. In one of these our whole family embarked three days ago, excepting my sister, who, being exceedingly fearful of the water, was left to the care of Mrs. Mitchelson. We had an easy and quick passage into Fife, where we visited a number of poor towns on the sea-side, including St. Andrew's,

3. Drunk.

which is the skeleton of a venerable city; but we were much better pleased with some noble and elegant seats and castles, of which there is a great number in that part of Scotland. Yesterday we took boat again on our return to Leith, with fair wind and agreeable weather; but we had not advanced half-way when the sky was suddenly overcast, and the wind changing, blew directly in our teeth; so that we were obliged to turn, or tack the rest of the way. In a word, the gale increased to a storm of wind and rain, attended with such a fog, that we could not see the town of Leith, to which we were bound, nor even the castle of Edinburgh, notwithstanding its high situation. It is not to be doubted but that we were all alarmed on this occasion. And at the same time, most of the passengers were seized with a nausea that produced violent retchings. My aunt desired her brother to order the boatmen to put back to Kinghorn, and this expedient he actually proposed; but they assured him there was no danger. Mrs. Tabitha finding them obstinate, began to scold, and insisted upon my uncle's exerting his authority as a justice of the peace. Sick and peevish as he was, he could not help laughing at this wise proposal, telling her, that his commission did not extend so far, and, if it did, he should let the people take their own way; for he thought it would be great presumption in him to direct them in the exercise of their own profession. Mrs. Winifred Jenkins made a general clearance with the assistance of Mr. Humphrey Clinker, who joined her both in prayer and ejaculation.—As he took it for granted that we should not be long in this world, he offered some spiritual consolation to Mrs. Tabitha, who rejected it with great disgust, bidding him keep his sermons for those who had leisure to hear such nonsense.—My uncle sat, recollected in himself, without speaking; my man Archy had recourse to a brandy-bottle, with which he made so free, that I imagined he had sworn to die of drinking any thing rather than sea-water: but the brandy had no more effect upon him in the way of intoxication, than if it had been sea water in good earnest.—As for myself, I was too much engrossed by the sickness at my stomach, to think of any thing else.—Meanwhile the sea swelled mountains high, the boat pitched with such violence, as if it had been going to pieces; the cordage rattled, the wind roared; the lightning flashed, the thunder bellowed, and the rain descended in a deluge —Every time the vessel was put about, we ship'd a sea that drenched us all to the skin.—When, by dint of turning, we thought to have cleared the pier head, we were driven to leeward, and then the boatmen themselves began to fear that the tide would fail before we should fetch up our lee-way: the next trip, however, brought us into smooth water, and we were safely landed on the quay, about one o'clock in the afternoon.—"To be sure (cried Tabby, when she found herself on *terra firma*,) we must all have perished, if we had not been the particular care of Providence."—"Yes, (replied my uncle) but I am much of the honest highlander's mind—after he had made such a passage as this: his friend told him he was much indebted to Providence;—"Certainly, (said Donald) but, by my saul, mon, I'se ne'er trouble Providence again, so long as the brig of Stirling stands."——You must know the brig, or bridge of Stirling, stands above twenty miles up the river Forth, of which this is the outlet—I don't find that our 'squire has suffered in his health from this adventure; but poor Liddy is in a peaking way—I'm afraid this unfortunate girl is uneasy in her mind; and this apprehension distracts me, for she is really an amiable creature.

We shall set out to-morrow or next day for Stirling and Glasgow; and we propose to penetrate a little way into the Highlands, before we turn our course to the southward—In the mean time, commend me to all our friends round Carfax, and believe me to be, ever yours,

Edinburgh, Aug. 8.   J. MELFORD.

END OF THE SECOND VOLUME.

Volume III

To Dr. Lewis.

I should be very ungrateful, dear Lewis, if I did not find myself disposed to think and speak favourably of this people, among whom I have met with more kindness, hospitality, and rational entertainment, in a few weeks, than ever I received in any other country during the whole course of my life.—Perhaps, the gratitude excited by these benefits may interfere with the impartiality of my remarks; for a man is as apt to be prepossessed by particular favours as to be prejudiced by private motives of disgust. If I am partial, there is, at least, some merit in my conversion from illiberal prejudices which had grown up with my constitution.

The first impressions which an Englishman receives in this country, will not contribute to the removal of his prejudices; because he refers every thing he sees to a comparison with the same articles in his own country; and this comparison is unfavourable to Scotland in all its exteriors, such as the face of the country in respect to cultivation, the appearance of the bulk of the people, and the language of conversation in general.—I am not so far convinced by Mr. Lismahago's arguments, but that I think the Scots would do well, for their own sakes, to adopt the English idioms and pronunciation; those of them especially, who are resolved to push their fortunes in South-Britain.——I know, by experience, how easily an Englishman is influenced by the ear, and how apt he is to laugh, when he hears his own language spoken with a foreign or provincial accent.—I have known a member of the house of commons speak with great energy and precision, without being able to engage attention, because his observations were made in the Scotch dialect, which (no offence to lieutenant Lismahago) certainly gives a clownish air even to sentiments of the greatest dignity and decorum.—I have declared my opinion on this head to some of the most sensible men of this country, observing, at the same time, that if they would employ a few natives of England to teach the pronunciation of our vernacular tongue, in twenty years there would be no difference, in point of dialect, between the youth of Edinburgh and of London.

The civil regulations of this kingdom and metropolis are taken from very different models from those of England, except in a few particular establishments, the necessary consequences of the union.—Their college of justice is a bench of great dignity, filled with judges of character and ability.—I have heard some causes tried before this venerable tribunal; and was very much pleased with the pleadings of their advocates, who are by no means deficient either in argument or elocution. The Scottish legislation is founded, in a great measure, on the civil law; consequently, their proceedings vary from those of the English tribunals; but, I think, they have the advantage of us in their method of examining witnesses apart, and in the constitution of their jury, by which they certainly avoid the evil which I mentioned in my last from Lismahago's observation.

The university of Edinburgh is supplied with excellent professors in all the sciences; and the medical school, in particular, is famous all over Europe.—The students of this art have the best opportunity of learning it to perfection, in all its branches, as there are different courses for the *theory of medicine*, and the *practice of medicine*; for *anatomy*, *chemistry*, *botany*, and the *materia medica*, over and above those of *mathematics* and *experimental philosophy*; and all these are given by men of distinguished talents. What renders this part of education still more complete, is the advantage of attending the infirmary, which is the best instituted charitable foundation that I ever knew. Now we are talking of charities, here are several hospitals, exceedingly well endowed, and maintained under admirable regulations; and these are not only useful, but ornamental to the city. Among these, I shall only mention the general work-house, in which all the poor, not otherwise provided for, are employed, according to their different abilities, with such judgment and effect, that they nearly maintain themselves by their labour, and there is not a beggar to be seen within the precincts of this metropolis. It was Glasgow that set the example of this establishment, about thirty years ago.—Even the kirk of Scotland, so long reproached with fanatacism and canting, abounds at present with ministers celebrated for their learning, and respectable for their moderation.—I have heard their sermons with equal astonishment and pleasure.—The good people of Edinburgh no longer think dirt and cobwebs essential to the house of God.—Some of their churches have admitted such ornaments as would have excited sedition, even in England, a little more than a century ago; and psalmody is here practised and taught by a professor from the cathedral of Durham:[4]—I should not be surprised, in a few years, to hear it accompanied with an organ.

Edinburgh is a hot bed of genius.——I have had the good fortune to be made acquainted with many authors of the first distinction; such as the two Humes, Robertson, Smith, Wallace, Blair, Ferguson, Wilkie,[5] &c. and I have found them all as agreeable in conversation as they are

4. Cornforth Gilson, a professional singer, arrived in Edinburgh about 1753.

5. The two Humes are David Hume (1711–76), philosopher, critic, and historian, and John Home (pronounced "Hume") (1722–1808), who wrote the controversial tragedy *Douglas* in 1756. Dr. William Robertson (1721–93) was a historian, educator, and churchman who published a *History of Scotland* in 1759. Adam Smith (1723–90) was to prove his genius as an economist with *The Wealth of Nations* (1776). Dr. Robert Wallace (1697–1771) was a churchman and author. Hugh Blair (1718–1800) was a churchman, critic, and professor of rhetoric and belles lettres at Edinburgh University. Adam Ferguson (1723–1816), a philosopher, was professor of what we now call science at Edinburgh University. William Wilkie (1721–72) was called by some "the Scottish Homer." He wrote a long poem based on Homer called *The Epigoniad*, and was also a professor of science at St. Andrews University.

instructive and entertaining in their writings. These acquaintances I owe to the friendship of Dr. Carlyle,[6] who wants nothing but inclination to figure with the rest upon paper. The magistracy of Edinburgh is changed every year by election, and seems to be very well adapted both for state and authority.—The *lord provost* is equal in dignity to the *lord mayor of London*; and the *four bailies* are equivalent to the rank of aldermen. —There is a *dean of guild*, who takes cognizance of mercantile affairs; a treasurer; a town-clerk; and the council is composed of deacons, one of whom is returned every year, in rotation, as representative of every company of artificers or handicraftsmen. Though this city, from the nature of its situation, can never be made either very convenient or very cleanly, it has, nevertheless, an air of magnificence that commands respect.—The castle is an instance of the sublime in scite and architecture.—Its fortifications are kept in good order, and there is always in it a garrison of regular soldiers, which is relieved every year; but it is incapable of sustaining a siege carried on according to the modern operations of war.——The castle hill, which extends from the outward gate to the upper end of the high-street, is used as a public walk for the citizens, and commands a prospect, equally extensive and delightful, over the county of Fife, on the other side of the Frith, and all along the sea-coast, which is covered with a succession of towns that would seem to indicate a considerable share of commerce; but, if the truth must be told, these towns have been falling to decay ever since the union, by which the Scots were in a great measure deprived of their trade with France.—The palace of Holyrood-house is a jewel in architecture, thrust into a hollow where it cannot be seen; a situation which was certainly not chosen by the ingenious architect, who must have been confined to the scite of the old palace, which was a convent. Edinburgh is considerably extended on the south side, where there are divers little elegant squares built in the English manner; and the citizens have planned some improvements on the north, which, when put in execution, will add greatly to the beauty and convenience of this capital.

The sea-port is Leith, a flourishing town, about a mile from the city, in the harbour of which I have seen above one hundred ships lying all together. You must know, I had the curiosity to cross the Frith in a passage-boat, and stayed two days in Fife, which is remarkably fruitful in corn, and exhibits a surprising number of fine seats, elegantly built, and magnificently furnished. There is an incredible number of noble houses in every part of Scotland that I have seen.—Dalkeith, Pinkie, Yester, and lord Hopton's,[7] all of them within four or five miles of Edinburgh, are princely palaces, in every one of which a sovereign might reside at his

6. Dr. Alexander Carlyle (1722–1805) published little during his lifetime.
7. Dalkeith Palace was the seat of the Duke of Buccleugh. Pinkie and Yester were country homes of the Marquis of Tweeddale. Lord Hopton (or Hopetown) built a house designed by Sir William Bruce.

ease.—I suppose the Scots affect these monuments of grandeur.—If I may be allowed to mingle censure with my remarks upon a people I revere, I must observe, that their weak side seems to be vanity.—I am afraid that even their hospitality is not quite free of ostentation.—I think I have discovered among them uncommon pains taken to display their fine linen, of which, indeed, they have great plenty, their furniture, plate, house-keeping, and variety of wines, in which article, it must be owned, they are profuse, if not prodigal.—A burgher of Edinburgh, not content to vie with a citizen of London, who has ten times his fortune, must excel him in the expence as well as elegance of his entertainments.

Though the villas of the Scotch nobility and gentry have generally an air of grandeur and state, I think their gardens and parks are not comparable to those of England; a circumstance the more remarkable, as I was told by the ingenious Mr. Philip Miller of Chelsea,[8] that almost all the gardeners of South-Britain were natives of Scotland. The verdure of this country is not equal to that of England.—The pleasure-grounds are, in my opinion, not so well laid out according to the *genius loci*; nor are the lawns, and walks, and hedges kept in such delicate order.—The trees are planted in prudish rows, which have not such an agreeable natural effect, as when they are thrown into irregular groupes, with intervening glades; and the firs, which they generally raise around their houses, look dull and funereal in the summer season.——I must confess, indeed, that they yield serviceable timber, and good shelter against the northern blasts; that they grow and thrive in the most barren soil, and continually perspire a fine balsam of turpentine, which must render the air very salutary and sanative to lungs of a tender texture.

Tabby and I have been both frightened in our return by sea from the coast of Fife.——She was afraid of drowning, and I of catching cold, in consequence of being drenched with sea-water; but my fears, as well as her's, have been happily disappointed.——She is now in perfect health; I wish I could say the same of Liddy.——Something uncommon is the matter with that poor child; her colour fades, her appetite fails, and her spirits flag.——She is become moping and melancholy, and is often found in tears.——Her brother suspects internal uneasiness on account of Wilson, and denounces vengeance against that adventurer.——She was, it seems, strongly affected at the ball by the sudden appearance of one Mr. Gordon, who strongly resembles the said Wilson; but I am rather suspicious that she caught cold by being overheated with dancing. —I have consulted Dr. Gregory,[9] an eminent physician of an amiable character, who advises the highland air, and the use of goat-milk whey, which, surely, cannot have a bad effect upon a patient who was born and

8. Philip Miller (1691–1771) was a botanist and superintendent of the Royal Botanical Gardens at Chelsea from 1722 until 1767. Smollett probably knew him while he resided in Chelsea.

9. John Gregory (1724–73) was professor of medicine at Edinburgh University.

bred among the mountains of Wales.—The doctor's opinion is the more agreeable, as we shall find those remedies in the very place which I proposed as the utmost extent of our expedition—I mean the borders of Argyle.

Mr. Smollett,[1] one of the judges of the commissary court, which is now sitting, has very kindly insisted upon our lodging at his country-house, on the banks of Lough-Lomond, about fourteen miles beyond Glasgow. For this last city we shall set out in two days, and take Stirling in our way, well provided with recommendations from our friends at Edinburgh, whom, I protest, I shall leave with much regret. I am so far from thinking it any hardship to live in this country, that, if I was obliged to lead a town life, Edinburgh would certainly be the headquarters of

Yours always,

Edr. August 8.   MATT. BRAMBLE.

To Sir WATKIN PHILLIPS, Bar[t]. of Jesus college, Oxon.

DEAR KNIGHT,

I am now little short of the *Ultima Thule*, if this appellation properly belongs to the Orkneys or Hebrides. These last are now lying before me, to the amount of some hundreds, scattered up and down the Deucalidonian sea,[2] affording the most picturesque and romantic prospect I ever beheld——I write this letter in a gentleman's house, near the town of Inverary, which may be deemed the capital of the West Highlands, famous for nothing so much as for the stately castle begun, and actually covered in by the late duke of Argyle, at a prodigious expence—Whether it will ever be completely finished is a question——

But, to take things in order.——We left Edinburgh ten days ago; and the further North we proceed, we find Mrs. Tabitha the less manageable; so that her inclinations are not of the nature of the loadstone; they point not towards the pole. What made her leave Edinburgh with reluctance at last, if we may believe her own assertions, was a dispute which she left unfinished with Mr. Moffat, touching the eternity of hell torments. That gentleman, as he advanced in years, began to be sceptical on this head, till, at length, he declared open war against the common acceptation of the word *eternal*. He is now persuaded, that *eternal* signifies no more than an indefinite number of years; and that the most enormous sinner may be

1. James Smollett was a cousin of Tobias and was known by the title of "Commissary" from his seat on that court, which dealt largely with inheritances. He erected a monument to his cousin in 1773.
2. Andre Parreaux has pointed out that this word is a pun which depends on "Caledonian" and "Deucalion's flood." "Caledonian" means Scottish, and Deucalion, a mythical king of Thessaly, saw the entire world inundated by a flood during his reign. A map of 1631 labels the area northwest of Scotland "Oceanus Deucalidonius," however, so the pun may be accidental.

quit for *nine millions, nine hundred thousand, nine hundred and ninety-nine years of hell-fire;* which term or period, as he very well observes, forms but an inconsiderable drop, as it were, in the ocean of eternity —For this mitigation he contends, as a system agreeable to the ideas of goodness and mercy, which we annex to the supreme Being—Our aunt seemed willing to adopt this doctrine in favour of the wicked; but he hinted, that no person whatever was so righteous as to be exempted entirely from punishment in a future state; and that the most pious Christian upon earth might think himself very happy to get off for a fast of seven or eight thousand years in the midst of fire and brimstone. Mrs. Tabitha revolted at this dogma, which filled her at once with horror and indignation—She had recourse to the opinion of Humphry Clinker, who roundly declared it was the popish doctrine of purgatory, and quoted scripture in defence of the *fire everlasting, prepared for the devil and his angels*—The reverend mester Mackcorkendale, and all the theologists and saints of that persuasion were consulted, and some of them had doubts about the matter; which doubts and scruples had begun to infect our aunt, when we took our departure from Edinburgh.

We passed through Linlithgow, where there was an elegant royal palace, which is now gone to decay, as well as the town itself—This too is pretty much the case with Stirling, though it still boasts of a fine old castle, in which the kings of Scotland were wont to reside in their minority—But Glasgow is the pride of Scotland, and, indeed, it might very well pass for an elegant and flourishing city in any part of Christendom. There we had the good fortune to be received into the house of Mr. Moore,[3] an eminent surgeon, to whom we were recommended by one of our friends at Edinburgh; and, truly, he could not have done us more essential service—Mr. Moore is a merry facetious companion, sensible and shrewd, with a considerable fund of humour; and his wife an agreeable woman, well bred, kind, and obliging—Kindness, which I take to be the essence of good-nature and humanity, is the distinguishing characteristic of the Scotch ladies in their own country —Our landlord shewed us every thing, and introduced us to all the world at Glasgow; where, through his recommendation, we were complimented with the freedom of the town. Considering the trade and opulence of this place, it cannot but abound with gaiety and diversions ——Here is a great number of young fellows that rival the youth of the capital in spirit and expence; and I was soon convinced, that all the female beauties of Scotland were not assembled at the hunters ball in Edinburgh—The town of Glasgow flourishes in learning, as well as in commerce—Here is an university, with professors in all the different

---

3. Dr. John Moore (1729–1802) was apprenticed to the same surgeon as Smollett, and they remained friends and correspondents until Smollett's death in 1771. Some time after this event, Moore was able to give up the practice of medicine and became a traveler and writer. He also edited Smollett's *Works* (1797) to which he contributed a biography of the author.

branches of science, liberally endowed, and judiciously chosen—It was vacation time when I passed, so that I could not entirely satisfy my curiosity; but their mode of education is certainly preferable to ours in some respects—The students are not left to the private instruction of tutors; but taught in public schools or classes, each science by its particular professor or regent.

My uncle is in raptures with Glasgow—He not only visited all the manufactures of the place, but made excursions all round, to Hamilton, Paisley, Renfrew, and every other place within a dozen miles, where there was any thing remarkable to be seen in art or nature. I believe the exercise, occasioned by these jaunts, was of service to my sister Liddy, whose appetite and spirits begin to revive—Mrs. Tabitha displayed her attractions as usual, and actually believed she had entangled one Mr. Maclellan, a rich inkle-manufacturer,[4] in her snares; but when matters came to an explanation, it appeared that his attachment was altogether spiritual, founded upon an intercourse of devotion, at the meeting of Mr. John Wesley;[5] who, in the course of his evangelical mission, had come hither in person—At length, we set out for the banks of Lough-Lomond, passing through the little borough of Dumbarton, or (as my uncle will have it) Dunbritton, where there is a castle, more curious than any thing of the kind I had ever seen—It is honoured with a particular description by the elegant Buchannan,[6] as an *arx inexpugnabilis*,[7] and, indeed, it must have been impregnable by the antient manner of besieging. It is a rock of considerable extent, rising with a double top, in an angle formed by the confluence of two rivers, the Clyde and the Leven; perpendicular and inaccessible on all sides, except in one place where the entrance is fortified; and there is no rising-ground in the neighbourhood from whence it could be damaged by any kind of battery.

From Dumbarton, the West Highlands appear in the form of huge, dusky mountains, piled one over another; but this prospect is not at all surprising to a native of Glamorgan—We have fixed our head-quarters at Cameron, a very neat country-house belonging to commissary Smollett, where we found every sort of accommodation we could desire—It is situated like a Druid's temple, in a grove of oak, close by the side of Lough-Lomond, which is a surprising body of pure transparent water, unfathomably deep in many places, six or seven miles broad, four and twenty miles in length, displaying above twenty green islands, covered with wood; some of them cultivated for corn, and many of them stocked with red deer—They belong to different gentlemen, whose seats are scattered along the banks of the lake, which are agreeably romantic beyond all conception. My uncle and I have left the women at Cameron,

4. A maker of linen tape.
5. Wesley visited Glasgow a number of times and may have met Smollett there in 1766.
6. George Buchanan (1506–82) published a popu-
lar study of Scottish places in Latin in the sixteenth century which was still available in the 1760's. He was an accomplished Latinist.
7. An impregnable fortress.

222 • Humphry Clinker

as Mrs. Tabitha would by no means trust herself again upon the water, and to come hither it was necessary to cross a small inlet of the sea, in an open ferryboat——This country appears more and more wild and savage the further we advance; and the people are as different from the Lowland Scots, in their looks, garb, and language, as the mountaineers of Brecknock are from the inhabitants of Herefordshire.

When the Lowlanders want to drink a chearupping-cup, they go to the public house, called the Change-house, and call for a chopine[8] of twopenny, which is a thin, yeasty beverage, made of malt; not quite so strong as the table-beer of England—This is brought in a pewter stoop, shaped like a skittle, from whence it is emptied into a quaff; that is, a curious cup made of different pieces of wood, such as box and ebony, cut into little staves, joined alternately, and secured with delicate hoops, having two ears or handles—It holds about a gill, is sometimes tipt round the mouth with silver, and has a plate of the same metal at bottom, with the landlord's cypher engraved—The Highlanders, on the contrary, despise this liquor, and regale themselves with whisky; a malt spirit, as strong as geneva,[9] which they swallow in great quantities, without any signs of inebriation. They are used to it from the cradle, and find it an excellent preservative against the winter cold, which must be extreme on these mountains—I am told that it is given with great success to infants, as a cordial in the confluent smallpox, when the erruption seems to flag, and the symptoms grow unfavourable—The Highlanders are used to eat much more animal food than falls to the share of their neighbours in the Low-country—They delight in hunting; have plenty of deer and other game, with a great number of sheep, goats, and black-cattle running wild, which they scruple not to kill as venison, without being at much pains to ascertain the property.

Inverary is but a poor town, though it stands immediately under the protection of the duke of Argyle, who is a mighty prince in this part of Scotland. The peasants live in wretched cabins, and seem very poor; but the gentlemen are tolerably well lodged, and so loving to strangers, that a man runs some risque of his life from their hospitality—It must be observed that the poor Highlanders are now seen to disadvantage—They have been not only disarmed by act of parliament; but also deprived of their antient garb,[1] which was both graceful and convenient; and what is a greater hardship still, they are compelled to wear breeches; a restraint which they cannot bear with any degree of patience: indeed, the majority wear them, not in the proper place, but on poles or long staves over their shoulders——They are even debared the use of their striped stuff, called Tartane, which was their own manufacture, prized by them above all the

8. A half-pint measure used in Scotland.
9. Gin.
1. After the defeat of the Scottish Jacobite troops at Culloden in 1746, Parliament passed a Disarming Act which prohibited the wearing of the kilt and forced the Highlanders to disarm.

velvets, brocards, and tissues of Europe and Asia. They now lounge along in loose great coats, of coarse russet, equally mean and cumbersome, and betray manifest marks of dejection—Certain it is, the government could not have taken a more effectual method to break their national spirit.

We have had princely sport in hunting the stag on these mountains —These are the lonely hills of Morven, where Fingal[2] and his heroes enjoyed the same pastime: I feel an enthusiastic pleasure when I survey the brown heath that Ossian wont to tread; and hear the wind whistle through the bending grass——When I enter our landlord's hall, I look for the suspended harp of that divine bard, and listen in hopes of hearing the aerial sound of his respected spirit—The Poems of Ossian are in every mouth—A famous antiquarian of this country, the laird of Mackfarlane,[3] at whose house we dined a few days ago, can repeat them all in the original Gaelick, which has a great affinity to the Welch, not only in the general sound, but also in a great number of radical words; and I make no doubt but that they are both sprung from the same origin. I was not a little surprised, when asking a Highlander one day, if he knew where we should find any game? he replied, "hu niel Sassenagh," which signifies No English: the very same answer I should have received from a Welchman, and almost in the same words. The Highlanders have no other name for the people of the Low-country, but Sassenagh, or Saxons; a strong presumption, that the Lowland Scots and the English are derived from the same stock——The peasants of these hills strongly resemble those of Wales in their looks, their manners, and habitations; every thing I see, and hear, and feel, seems Welch——The mountains, vales, and streams; the air and climate; the beef, mutton, and game, are all Welch—It must be owned, however, that this people are better provided than we in some articles—They have plenty of red deer and roebuck, which are fat and delicious at this season of the year—Their sea teems with amazing quantities of the finest fish in the world; and they find means to procure very good claret at a very small expence.

Our landlord is a man of consequence in this part of the country; a cadet from the family of Argyle, and hereditary captain of one of his castles[4]—His name, in plain English, is Dougal Campbell; but as there is a great number of the same appellation, they are distinguished (like the Welch) by patronimics; and as I have known an antient Briton called Madoc ap-Morgan, ap-Jenkin, ap-Jones, our Highland chief designs himself Dou'l Mac-amish mac-'oul ich-ian, signifying Dougal, the son of James, the son of Dougal, the son of John—He has traveled in the course

2. James Macpherson (1736–96) published a body of poetry known collectively as *The Poems of Ossian* in the 1760's. They were said to be ancient Scottish epic poetry about a hero named Fingal, and to have been written by Ossian. They caused a considerable controversy, particularly about their authenticity, but the poetry was extremely popular in Scotland and on the Continent. They are now deemed to be largely Macpherson's own work.
3. Walter Macfarlane (d. 1767) was a Scottish antiquary.
4. Lewis Knapp has suggested that this is the castle of Dunstaffnage, also known as St. Stephen's Mountain.

of his education, and is disposed to make certain alterations in his domestic œconomy; but he finds it impossible to abolish the antient customs of the family; some of which are ludicrous enough—His piper, for example, who is an hereditary officer of the household, will not part with the least particle of his privileges——He has a right to wear the kilt, or antient Highland dress, with the purse, pistol, and durk—a broad yellow ribbon, fixed to the chanter-pipe, is thrown over his shoulder, and trails along the ground, while he performs the function of his minstrelsy; and this, I suppose, is analogous to the pennon or flag which was formerly carried before every knight in battle——He plays before the laird every Sunday in his way to the kirk, which he circles three times, performing the family march, which implies defiance to all the enemies of the clan; and every morning he plays a full hour by the clock, in the great hall, marching backwards and forwards all the time, with a solemn pace, attended by the laird's kinsmen, who seem much delighted with the music—In this exercise, he indulges them with a variety of pibrachs or airs, suited to the different passions, which he would either excite or assuage.

Mr. Campbell himself, who performs very well on the violin, has an invincible antipathy to the sound of the Highland bag-pipe, which sings in the nose with a most alarming twang, and, indeed, is quite intolerable to ears of common sensibility, when aggravated by the echo of a vaulted hall—He therefore begged the piper would have some mercy upon him, and dispense with this part of the morning service——A consultation of the clan being held on this occasion, it was unanimously agreed, that the laird's request could not be granted without a dangerous encroachment upon the customs of the family—The piper declared, he could not give up for a moment the privilege he derived from his ancestors; nor would the laird's relations forego an entertainment which they valued above all others—There was no remedy; Mr. Campbell, being obliged to acquiesce, is fain to stop his ears with cotton; to fortify his head with three or four night-caps, and every morning retire into the penetralia of his habitation, in order to avoid this diurnal annoyance. When the music ceases, he produces himself at an open window that looks into the court-yard, which is by this time filled with a crowd of his vassals and dependents, who worship his first appearance, by uncovering their heads, and bowing to the earth with the most humble prostration. As all these people have something to communicate in the way of proposal, complaint, or petition, they wait patiently till the laird comes forth, and, following him in his walks, are favoured each with a short audience in his turn. Two days ago, he dispatched above an hundred different sollicitors, in walking with us to the house of a neighbouring gentleman, where we dined by invitation. Our landlord's house-keeping is equally rough and hospitable, and savours much of the simplicity of ancient times: the great hall, paved with flat stones, is about forty-five feet by twenty-two, and serves not only for a dining-room, but also for a bed-chamber to gentlemen-dependents and hangers-on of the family. At night, half a dozen occasional beds are ranged on each side along the wall. These are made of fresh heath, pulled up by the roots, and disposed in such a manner as to make a very agreeable couch, where they lie, without any other covering than the plaid—My uncle and I were indulged with separate chambers and down beds, which we begged to exchange for a layer of heath; and indeed I never slept so much to my satisfaction. It was not only soft and elastic, but the plant, being in flower, diffused an agreeable fragrance, which is wonderfully refreshing and restorative.

Yesterday we were invited to the funeral of an old lady, the grand-mother of a gentleman in this neighbourhood, and found ourselves in the midst of fifty people, who were regaled with a sumptuous feast, accompanied by the music of a dozen pipers. In short, this meeting had all the air of a grand festival; and the guests did such honour to the entertainment, that many of them could not stand when we were reminded of the business on which we had met. The company forthwith taking horse, rode in a very irregular cavalcade to the place of interment, a church, at the distance of two long miles from the castle. On our arrival, however, we found we had committed a small oversight, in leaving the corpse behind;[5] so that we were obliged to wheel about, and met the old gentlewoman half way, carried upon poles by the nearest relations of her family, and attended by the *coronach*, composed of a multitude of old hags, who tore their hair, beat their breasts, and howled most hideously. At the grave, the orator, or *senachie*, pronounced the panegyric of the defunct, every period being confirmed by a yell of the *coronach*. The body was committed to the earth, the pipers playing a pibroch all the time; and all the company standing uncovered. The ceremony was closed with the discharge of pistols; then we returned to the castle, resumed the bottle, and by midnight there was not a sober person in the family, the females excepted. The 'squire and I were, with some difficulty, permitted to retire with our landlord in the evening; but our entertainer was a little chagrined at our retreat; and afterwards seemed to think it a disparagement to his family, that not above a hundred gallons of whisky had been drank upon such a solemn occasion. This morning we got up by four, to hunt the roebuck, and, in an half an hour, found breakfast ready served in the hall. The hunters consisted of Sir George Colquhoun[6] and me, as strangers, (my uncle not chusing to be of the party) of the *laird in person, the laird's brother, the laird's brother's son, the laird's sister's son, the laird's father's brother's son*, and all their *foster brothers*, who are counted parcel

5. This was an oft-repeated anecdote of Scottish funerals.
6. Sir James Colquhoun (1714–86) actually had a seat near Cameron House, where the party is putatively staying. While it has been suggested that there is also a real Sir George Colquhoun, a military officer from Tiliquahoun, little can be learned of him, and it is safe to presume that Sir George is an imaginary relative of Sir James.

of the family: but we were attended by an infinite number of *Gaellys*, or ragged Highlanders, without shoes or stockings.

The following articles formed our morning's repast: one kit of boiled eggs; a second, full of butter; a third, full of cream; an entire cheese, made of goat's milk; a large earthen pot full of honey; the best part of a ham; a cold venison pasty; a bushel of oat meal, made in thin cakes and bannocks, with a small wheaten loaf in the middle for the strangers; a large stone bottle full of whisky, another of brandy, and a kilderkin of ale. There was a laddle chained to the cream kit, with curious wooden bickers to be filled from this reservoir. The spirits were drank out of a silver quaff, and the ale out of horns: great justice was done to the collation by the guests in general; one of them in particular ate above two dozen of hard eggs, with a proportionable quantity of bread, butter, and honey; nor was one drop of liquor left upon the board. Finally, a large roll of tobacco was presented by way of desert, and every individual took a comfortable quid, to prevent the bad effects of the morning air. We had a fine chace over the mountains, after a roebuck, which we killed, and I got home time enough to drink tea with Mrs. Campbell and our 'squire. To-morrow we shall set out on our return for Cameron. We propose to cross the Frith of Clyde, and take the towns of Greenock and Port-Glasgow in our way. This circuit being finished, we shall turn our faces to the south, and follow the sun with augmented velocity, in order to enjoy the rest of the autumn in England, where Boreas is not quite so biting as he begins already to be on the tops of these northern hills. But our progress from place to place shall continue to be specified in these detached journals of,

yours always,

Argyleshire, Septr. 3.   J. MELFORD.

To Dr. LEWIS.

DEAR DICK,

About a fortnight is now elapsed, since we left the capital of Scotland, directing our course towards Stirling, where we lay—The castle of this place is such another as that of Edinburgh, and affords a surprising prospect of the windings of the river Forth, which are so extraordinary, that the distance from hence to Alloa by land, is but four miles, and by water it is twenty-four. Alloa is a neat thriving town, that depends in a great measure on the commerce of Glasgow, the merchants of which send hither tobacco and other articles, to be deposited in warehouses for exportation from the Frith of Forth. In our way hither we visited a flourishing iron-work, where, instead of burning wood, they use coal, which they have the art of clearing in such a manner as frees it from the sulphur, that would otherwise render the metal too brittle for working. Excellent coal is found in almost every part of Scotland.

The soil of this district produces scarce any other grain but oats and barley; perhaps because it is poorly cultivated, and almost altogether uninclosed. The few inclosures they have consist of paultry walls of loose stones gathered from the fields, which indeed they cover, as if they had been scattered on purpose. When I expressed my surprize that the peasants did not disencumber their grounds of these stones; a gentleman, well aquainted with the theory as well as practice of farming, assured me that the stones, far from being prejudicial, were serviceable to the crop. This philosopher had ordered a field of his own to be cleared, manured and sown with barley, and the produce was more scanty than before. He caused the stones to be replaced, and next year the crop was as good as ever. The stones were removed a second time, and the harvest failed; they were again brought back, and the ground retrieved its fertility. The same experiment has been tried in different parts of Scotland with the same success—Astonished at this information, I desired to know in what manner he accounted for this strange phenomenon; and he said there were three ways in which the stones might be serviceable. They might possibly restrain an excess in the perspiration of the earth, analogous to colliquative sweats,[7] by which the human body is sometimes wasted and consumed. They might act as so many fences to protect the tender blade from the piercing winds of the spring; or, by multiplying the reflexion of the sun, they might increase the warmth, so as to mitigate the natural chilness of the soil and climate—But, surely this excessive perspiration might be more effectually checked by different kinds of manure, such as ashes, lime, chalk, or marl, of which last it seems there are many pits in this kingdom: as for the warmth, it would be much more equally obtained by inclosures; one half of the ground which is now covered, would be retrieved; the cultivation would require less labour; and the ploughs, harrows, and horses, would not suffer half the damage which they now sustain.

These north-western parts are by no means fertile in corn. The ground is naturally barren and moorish. The peasants are poorly lodged, meagre in their looks, mean in their apparel, and remarkably dirty. This last reproach they might easily wash off, by means of those lakes, rivers, and rivulets of pure water, with which they are so liberally supplied by nature. Agriculture cannot be expected to flourish where the farms are small, the leases short, and the husbandman begins upon a rack rent, without a sufficient stock to answer the purposes of improvement. The granaries of Scotland are the banks of the Tweed, the counties of East and Mid-Lothian, the Carse of Gowrie,[8] in Perthshire, equal in fertility

---

7. A sweat so profuse that it causes the body to waste away.

8. The low, alluvial land along the north side of the Tay between Perth and Dundee.

to any part of England, and some tracts in Aberdeenshire and Murray, where I am told the harvest is more early than in Northumberland, although they lie above two degrees farther north. I have a strong curiosity to visit many places beyond the Forth and the Tay, such as Perth, Dundee, Montrose, and Aberdeen, which are towns equally elegant and thriving; but the season is too far advanced, to admit of this addition to my original plan.

I am so far happy as to have seen Glasgow, which, to the best of my recollection and judgment, is one of the prettiest towns in Europe; and, without all doubt, it is one of the most flourishing in Great Britain. In short, it is a perfect bee-hive in point of industry. It stands partly on a gentle declivity; but the greatest part of it is in a plain, watered by the river Clyde. The streets are straight, open, airy, and well paved; and the houses lofty and well built of hewn stone. At the upper end of the town, there is a venerable cathedral, that may be compared with York minster or Westminster; and, about the middle of the descent from this to the Cross, is the college, a respectable pile of building, with all manner of accommodation for the professors and students, including an elegant library, and an observatory well provided with astronomical instruments. The number of inhabitants is said to amount to thirty thousand; and marks of opulence and independency appear in every quarter of this commercial city, which, however, is not without its inconveniences and defects. The water of their public pumps is generally hard and brackish, an imperfection the less excusable, as the river Clyde runs by their doors, in the lower part of the town; and there are rivulets and springs above the cathedral, sufficient to fill a large reservoir with excellent water, which might be thence distributed to all the different parts of the city. It is of more consequence to consult the health of the inhabitants in this article, than to employ so much attention in beautifying their town with new streets, squares, and churches. Another defect, not so easily remedied, is the shallowness of the river, which will not float vessels of any burthen within ten or twelve miles of the city; so that the merchants are obliged to load and unload their ships at Greenock and Port-Glasgow, situated about fourteen miles nearer the mouth of the Frith, where it is about two miles broad.

The people of Glasgow have a noble spirit of enterprise—Mr. Moore, a surgeon, to whom I was recommended from Edinburgh, introduced me to all the principal merchants of the place. Here I became acquainted with Mr. Cochran,[9] who may be stiled one of the sages of this kingdom. He was first magistrate at the time of the last rebellion. I sat as member when he was examined in the house of commons; upon which occasion

9. Andrew Cochran (c. 1692–1777) was provost (mayor) of Glasgow, and successfully sought funds from Parliament in reparation for the damages suffered by the city during the Rebellion of 1745–46.

Mr. P——[1] observed he had never heard such a sensible evidence given at that bar—I was also introduced to Dr. John Gordon,[2] patriot of a truly Roman spirit, who is the father of the linen manufacture in this place, and was the great promoter of the city workhouse, infirmary, and other works of public utility. Had he lived in ancient Rome, he would have been honoured with a statue at the public expence. I moreover conversed with one Mr. G—ssf—d,[3] whom I take to be one of the greatest merchants in Europe. In the last war, he is said to have had at one time five and twenty ships, with their cargoes, his own property, and to have traded for above half a million sterling a year. The last war was a fortunate period for the commerce of Glasgow—The merchants, considering that their ships bound for America, launching out at once into the Atlantic by the north of Ireland, pursued a track very little frequented by privateers, resolved to insure one another, and saved a very considerable sum by this resolution, as few or none of their ships were taken——You must know I have a sort of national attachment to this part of Scotland —The great church dedicated to St. Mongah, the river Clyde, and other particulars that smack of our Welch language and customs, contribute to flatter me with the notion, that these people are the descendants of the Britons, who once possessed this country. Without all question, this was a Cumbrian kingdom: its capital was Dumbarton (a corruption of Dumbritton) which still exists as a royal borough, at the influx of the Clyde and Leven, ten miles below Glasgow. The same neighbourhood gave birth to St. Patrick, the apostle of Ireland, at a place where there is still a church and village, which retain his name. Hard by are some vestiges of the famous Roman wall, built in the reign of Antonine, from the Clyde to the Forth, and fortified with castles, to restrain the incursions of the Scots or Caledonians, who inhabited the West-Highlands. In a line parallel to this wall, the merchants of Glasgow have determined to make a navigable canal betwixt the two Friths, which will be of incredible advantage to their commerce, in transporting merchandize from one side of the island to the other.[4]

From Glasgow we travelled along the Clyde, which is a delightful stream, adorned on both sides with villas, towns, and villages. Here is no want of groves, and meadows, and corn-fields interspersed; but on this side of Glasgow, there is little other grain than oats and barley; the first are much better, the last much worse, than those of the same species in England. I wonder, there is so little rye, which is a grain that will thrive in almost any soil; and it is still more surprising, that the cultivation of potatoes should be so much neglected in the Highlands, where the poor

1. Either William Pitt (1708–78) or Henry Pelham (1695?–1754), both of whom were prominent politicians during the period of the hearing on Glasgow's losses.
2. The surgeon to whom Smollett was apprenticed in the 1730's.
3. John Glassford (1715–83), a prominent tobacco merchant.
4. The Forth-Clyde canal was probably being discussed in Scotland when Smollett visited in 1766. It was begun in 1768 and completed in 1791.

people have not meal enough to supply them with bread through the winter. On the other side of the river are the towns of Paisley and Renfrew. The first, from an inconsiderable village, is become one of the most flourishing places of the kingdom, enriched by the linen, cambrick, flowered lawn, and silk manufactures. It was formerly noted for a rich monastery of the monks of Clugny, who wrote the famous *Scoti-Chronicon,* called *The Black Book of Paisley.*[5] The old abbey still remains, converted into a dwelling-house, belonging to the earl of Dundonald.[6] Renfrew is a pretty town, on the banks of Clyde, capital of the shire, which was heretofore the patrimony of the Stuart family, and gave the title of baron to the king's eldest son, which is still assumed by the prince of Wales.

The Clyde we left a little on our left-hand at Dunbritton, where it widens into an æstuary or frith, being augmented by the influx of the Leven. On this spot stands the castle formerly called Alcluyd, washed by these two rivers on all sides, except a narrow isthmus, which at every spring-tide is overflowed. The whole is a great curiosity, from the quality and form of the rock, as well as from the nature of its situation—We now crossed the water of Leven, which, though nothing near so considerable as the Clyde, is much more transparent, pastoral, and delightful. This charming stream is the outlet of Lough-Lomond, and through a tract of four miles pursues its winding course, murmuring over a bed of pebbles, till it joins the Frith at Dunbritton. A very little above its source, on the lake, stands the house of Cameron, belonging to Mr. Smollett, so embosomed in an oak wood, that we did not see it till we were within fifty yards of the door. I have seen the Lago di Garda, Albano, De Vico, Bolsena, and Geneva, and, upon my honour, I prefer Lough-Lomond to them all; a preference which is certainly owing to the verdant islands that seem to float upon its surface, affording the most inchanting objects of repose to the excursive view. Nor are the banks destitute of beauties, which even partake of the sublime. On this side they display a sweet variety of woodland, corn-field, and pasture, with several agreeable villas emerging as it were out of the lake, till, at some distance, the prospect terminates in huge mountains covered with heath, which being in the bloom, affords a very rich covering of purple. Every thing here is romantic beyond imagination. This country is justly stiled the Arcadia of Scotland; and I don't doubt but it may vie with Arcadia in every thing but climate.—I am sure it excels it in verdure, wood, and water.—What say you to a natural bason of pure water, near thirty miles long, and in some places seven miles broad, and in many above a hundred fathom deep, having four and twenty habitable islands, some of them stocked with

5. This earliest attempt at a chronicle of Scottish history was actually written by John of Fordun (d. 1384) and brought up to the year 1437 by Walter Bower (fl. 1450).
6. Earl of Dundonald, Thomas Cochrane (1691–1778).

deer, and all of them covered with wood; containing immense quantities of delicious fish, salmon, pike, trout, perch, flounders, eels, and powans, the last a delicate kind of fresh-water herring peculiar to this lake; and finally communicating with the sea, by sending off the Leven, through which all those species (except the powan) make their exit and entrance occasionally?

Inclosed I send you the copy of a little ode to this river, by Dr. Smollett,[7] who was born on the banks of it, within two miles of the place where I am now writing.—It is at least picturesque and accurately descriptive, if it has no other merit.—There is an idea of truth in an agreeable landscape taken from nature, which pleases me more than the gayest fiction which the most luxuriant fancy can display.

I have other remarks to make; but as my paper is full, I must reserve them till the next occasion. I shall only observe at present, that I am determined to penetrate at least forty miles into the Highlands, which now appear like a vast fantastic vision in the clouds, inviting the approach of

Yours always,

Cameron, Aug. 28.   MATT. BRAMBLE.

ODE to LEVEN-WATER.

On Leven's banks, while free to rove,
And tune the rural pipe to love;
I envied not the happiest swain
That ever trod th' Arcadian plain.

Pure stream! in whose transparent wave
My youthful limbs I wont to lave;
No torrents stain thy limpid source;
No rocks impede thy dimpling course,
That sweetly warbles oe'r its bed,
With white, round, polish'd pebbles spread;
While, lightly pois'd, the scaly brood
In myriads cleave thy crystal flood;
The springing trout in speckled pride;
The salmon, monarch of the tide;
The ruthless pike, intent on war;
The silver eel, and motled par.[8]

7. Smollett here takes the opportunity to present his poem about his birthplace under his own name. The monument later erected by his cousin is near the banks of the Leven.

8. The par is a small fish, not unlike the smelt, which it rivals in delicacy and flavour. [Smollett's note.]

Devolving from thy parent lake,
A charming maze thy waters make,
By bow'rs of birch, and groves of pine,
And hedges flow'r'd with eglantine.

Still on thy banks so gayly green,
May num'rous herds and flocks be seen,
And lasses chanting o'er the pail,
And shepherd's piping in the dale,
And ancient faith that knows no guile,
And industry imbrown'd with toil,
And hearts resolv'd, and hands prepar'd,
The blessings they enjoy to guard.

To Dr. LEWIS.

DEAR DOCTOR,

If I was disposed to be critical, I should say this house of Cameron is too near the lake, which approaches, on one side, to within six or seven yards of the window. It might have been placed in a higher site, which would have afforded a more extensive prospect and a drier atmosphere; but this imperfection is not chargeable on the present proprietor, who purchased it ready built, rather than be at the trouble of repairing his own family-house of Bonhill, which stands two miles from hence on the Leven, so surrounded with plantation, that it used to be known by the name of the Mavis (or thrush) Nest. Above that house is a romantic glen or clift of a mountain, covered with hanging woods, having at bottom a stream of fine water that forms a number of cascades in its descent to join the Leven; so that the scene is quite enchanting. A captain of a man of war, who had made the circuit of the globe with Mr. Anson, being conducted to this glen, exclaimed, "Juan Fernandez, by God!"[9]

Indeed, this country would be a perfect paradise, if it was not, like Wales, cursed with a weeping climate, owing to the same causes in both, the neighbourhood of high mountains, and a westerly situation, exposed to the vapours of the Atlantic ocean. This air, however, notwithstanding its humidity, is so healthy, that the natives are scarce ever visited by any other disease than the small-pox, and certain cutaneous evils, which are the effects of dirty living, the great and general reproach of the commonalty of this kingdom. Here are a great many living monuments of longævity; and among the rest a person, whom I treat with singular

9. Juan Fernandez is a small group of islands in the South Pacific off the coast of Chile. Capt. George Anson (1697–1762) refitted his ships there in 1741 during his trip around the world. Capt. Robert Mann (d. 1762) was a member of the expedition and later became a friend of Smollett's. Smollett's *British Magazine* reprinted a selection from Anson's *Voyage round the World* (1748) which described Juan Fernandez.

respect, as a venerable druid, who has lived near ninety years, without pain or sickness, among oaks of his own planting.—He was once proprietor of these lands; but being of a projecting spirit, some of his schemes miscarried, and he was obliged to part with his possession, which hath shifted hands two or three times since that period; but every succeeding proprietor hath done every thing in his power, to make his old age easy and comfortable. He has a sufficiency to procure the necessaries of life; and he and his old woman resided in a small convenient farm-house, having a little garden which he cultivates with his own hands. This ancient couple live in great health, peace, and harmony, and, knowing no wants, enjoy the perfection of content. Mr. Smollet calls him the admiral,[1] because he insists upon steering his pleasure-boat upon the lake; and he spends most of his time in ranging through the woods, which he declares he enjoys as much as if they were still his own property—I asked him the other day, if he was never sick, and he answered, Yes; he had a slight fever the year before the union. If he was not deaf, I should take much pleasure in his conversation; for he is very intelligent, and his memory is surprisingly retentive—These are the happy effects of temperance, exercise, and good nature—Notwithstanding all his innocence, however, he was the cause of great perturbation to my man Clinker, whose natural superstition has been much injured, by the histories of witches, fairies, ghosts, and goblins, which he has heard in this country —On the evening after our arrival, Humphrey strolled into the wood, in the course of his meditation, and all at once the admiral stood before him, under the shadow of a spreading oak. Though the fellow is far from being timorous in cases that are not supposed preternatural, he could not stand the sight of this apparition, but ran into the kitchen, with his hair standing on end, staring wildly, and deprived of utterance. Mrs. Jenkins, seeing him in this condition, screamed aloud, "Lord have mercy upon us, he has seen something!" Mrs. Tabitha was alarmed, and the whole house in confusion. When he was recruited with a dram, I desired him to explain the meaning of all this agitation; and, with some reluctance, he owned he had seen a spirit, in the shape of an old man with a white beard, a black cap, and a plaid night gown. He was undeceived by the admiral in person, who, coming in at this juncture, appeared to be a creature of real flesh and blood.

Do you know how we fare in this Scottish paradise? We make free with our landlord's mutton, which is excellent, his poultry-yard, his garden, his dairy, and his cellar, which are all well stored. We have delicious salmon, pike, trout, perch, par, &c. at the door, for the taking. The Frith of Clyde, on the other side of the hill, supplies us with mullet, red and

---

1. Donald Govan once owned Cameron House, where James "Commissary" Smollett lived and the travelers are staying. Govan was called the "Old Admiral" by the author's cousin. "The union" mentioned below was the union between Scotland and England, and it took place in 1706, some sixty years before the events in the novel.

grey, cod, mackarel, whiting, and a variety of sea-fish, including the finest fresh herrings I ever tasted. We have sweet, juicy beef, and tolerable veal, with delicate bread from the little town of Dunbritton; and plenty of partridge, growse, heath-cock, and other game in presents.

We have been visited by all the gentlemen in the neighbourhood, and they have entertained us at their houses, not barely with hospitality, but with such marks of cordial affection, as one would wish to find among near relations, after an absence of many years.

I told you, in my last, I had projected an excursion to the Highlands, which project I have now happily executed, under the auspices of Sir George Colquhoun, a colonel in the Dutch service, who offered himself as our conductor on this occasion. Leaving our women at Cameron, to the care and inspection of Lady H———C———,[2] we set out on horseback for Inverary, the county town of Argyle, and dined on the road with the Laird of Macfarlane, the greatest genealogist I ever knew in any country, and perfectly acquainted with all the antiquities of Scotland.

The Duke of Argyle has an old castle at Inverary, where he resides when he is in Scotland; and hard by is the shell of a noble Gothic palace, built by the last duke, which, when finished, will be a great ornament to this part of the Highlands. As for Inverary, it is a place of very little importance.

This country is amazingly wild, especially towards the mountains, which are heaped upon the backs of one another, making a most stupendous appearance of savage nature, with hardly any signs of cultivation, or even of population. All is sublimity, silence, and solitude. The people live together in glens or bottoms, where they are sheltered from the cold and storms of winter: but there is a margin of plain ground spread along the sea side, which is well inhabited and improved by the arts of husbandry; and this I take to be one of the most agreeable tracts of the whole island; the sea not only keeps it warm, and supplies it with fish, but affords one of the most ravishing prospects in the whole world; I mean the appearance of the Hebrides, or Western Islands, to the number of three hundred, scattered as far as the eye can reach, in the most agreeable confusion. As the soil and climate of the Highlands are but ill adapted to the cultivation of corn, the people apply themselves chiefly to the breeding and feeding of black cattle, which turn to good account. Those animals run wild all the winter, without any shelter or subsistence, but what they can find among the heath. When the snow lies so deep and hard, that they cannot penetrate to the roots of the grass, they make a diurnal progress, guided by a sure instinct, to the sea-side at low water, where they feed on the *alga marina*, and other plants that grow upon the beach.

2. Lady Helen Colquhoun (1717–91) was the wife of Sir James Colquhoun.

Perhaps this branch of husbandry, which requires very little attendance and labour, is one of the principal causes of that idleness and want of industry, which distinguishes these mountaineers in their own country —When they come forth into the world, they become as diligent and alert as any people upon earth. They are undoubtedly a very distinct species from their fellow-subjects of the Lowlands, against whom they indulge an ancient spirit of animosity; and this difference is very discernible even among persons of family and education. The Lowlanders are generally cool and circumspect, the Highlanders fiery and ferocious: but this violence of their passions serves only to inflame the zeal of their devotion to strangers, which is truly enthusiastic.

We proceeded about twenty miles beyond Inverary, to the house of a gentleman, a friend of our conductor, where we stayed a few days, and were feasted in such a manner, that I began to dread the consequence to my constitution.

Notwithstanding the solitude that prevails among these mountains, there is no want of people in the Highlands. I am credibly informed that the duke of Argyle can assemble five thousand men in arms, of his own clan and surname, which is Campbell; and there is besides a tribe of the same appellation, whose chief is the Earl of Breadalbine. The Macdonalds are as numerous, and remarkably warlike: the Camerons, M'Leods, Frasers, Grants, M'Kenzies, M'Kays, M'Phersons, M'Intoshes, are powerful clans; so that if all the Highlanders, including the inhabitants of the Isles, were united, they could bring into the field an army of forty thousand fighting men, capabable of undertaking the most dangerous enterprize. We have lived to see four thousand of them, without discipline, throw the whole kingdom of Great Britain into confusion. They attacked and defeated two armies of regular troops, accustomed to service. They penetrated into the centre of England; and afterwards marched back with deliberation, in the face of two other armies, through an enemy's country, where every precaution was taken to cut off their retreat.[3] I know not any other people in Europe, who, without the use or knowledge of arms, will attack regular forces sword in hand, if their chief will head them in battle. When disciplined, they cannot fail of being excellent soldiers. They do not walk like the generality of mankind, but trot and bounce like deer, as if they moved upon springs. They greatly excel the Lowlanders in all the exercises that require agility; they are incredibly abstemious, and patient of hunger and fatigue; so steeled against the weather, that in travelling, even when the ground is covered with snow, they never look for a house, or any other shelter but their

3. This is an essentially accurate narration of Scottish involvement in the Jacobite rebellion which began in June 1745 and ended with the battle of Culloden in April 1746. The Scottish troops, who actually numbered about 5,500, penetrated England as far as Derby before retreating. *Divide et impera*, below, means divide and rule or conquer, and is an ancient political maxim cited by Machiavelli.

plaid, in which they wrap themselves up, and go to sleep under the cope of heaven. Such people, in quality of soldiers, must be invincible, when the business is to perform quick marches in a difficult country, to strike sudden strokes, beat up the enemy's quarters, harrass their cavalry, and perform expeditions without the formality of magazines, baggage, forage, and artillery. The chieftainship of the Highlanders is a very dangerous influence operating at the extremity of the island, where the eyes and hands of government cannot be supposed to see and act with precision and vigour. In order to break the force of clanship, administration has always practised the political maxim, *Divide et impera*. The legislature hath not only disarmed these mountaineers, but also deprived them of their ancient garb, which contributed in a great measure to keep up their military spirit; and their slavish tenures are all dissolved by act of parliament; so that they are at present as free and independent of their chiefs, as the law can make them: but the original attachment still remains, and is founded on something prior to the *feudal system*, about which the writers of this age have made such a pother, as if it was a new discovery, like the *Copernican system*.[4] Every peculiarity of policy, custom, and even temperament, is affectedly traced to this origin, as if the feudal constitution had not been common to almost all the natives of Europe. For my part, I expect to see the use of trunk-hose and buttered ale ascribed to the influence of the *feudal system*. The connection between the clans and their chiefs is, without all doubt, *patriarchal*. It is founded on hereditary regard and affection, cherished through a long succession of ages. The clan consider the chief as their father, they bear his name, they believe themselves descended from his family, and they obey him as their lord, with all the ardour of filial love and veneration; while he, on his part, exerts a paternal authority, commanding, chastising, rewarding, protecting, and maintaining them as his own children. If the legislature would entirely destroy this connection, it must compel the Highlanders to change their habitation and their names. Even this experiment has been formerly tried without success—In the reign of James VI. a battle was fought within a few short miles of this place, between two clans, the M'Gregors and the Colquhouns, in which the latter were defeated: the Laird of M'Gregor made such a barbarous use of his victory, that he was forfeited and outlawed by act of parliament: his lands were given to the family of Montrose, and his clan were obliged to change their name. They obeyed so far, as to call themselves severally Campbell, Graham, or Drummond, the surnames of the families of Argyle, Montrose, and Perth, that they might enjoy the protection of those houses; but they still added M'Gregor to their new appellation; and

4. This refers to the rising interest in Medievalism which was represented, for instance, by Bishop Richard Hurd's *Letters on Chivalry and Romance* (1762).

as their chief was deprived of his estate, they robbed and plundered for his subsistence.—Mr. Cameron of Lochiel,[5] the chief of that clan, whose father was attainted for having been concerned in the last rebellion, returning from France in obedience to a proclamation and act of parliament, passed at the beginning of the late war, payed a visit to his own country, and hired a farm in the neighbourhood of his father's house, which had been burnt to the ground. The clan, though ruined and scattered, no sooner heard of his arrival than they flocked to him from all quarters, to welcome his return, and in a few days stocked his farm with seven hundred black cattle, which they had saved in the general wreck of their affairs: but their beloved chief, who was a promising youth, did not live to enjoy the fruits of their fidelity and attachment.

The most effectual method I know to weaken, and at length destroy this influence, is to employ the commonalty in such a manner as to give them a taste of property and independence—In vain the government grants them advantageous leases on the forfeited estates, if they have no property to prosecute the means of improvement—The sea is an inexhaustible fund of riches; but the fishery cannot be carried on without vessels, casks, salt, lines, nets, and other tackle. I conversed with a sensible man of this country, who, from a real spirit of patriotism, had set up a fishery on the coast, and a manufacture of coarse linen, for the employment of the poor Highlanders. Cod is here in such plenty, that he told me he had seen seven hundred taken on one line, at one hawl—It must be observed, however, that the line was of immense length, and had two thousand hooks, baited with muscles; but the fish was so superior to the cod caught on the banks of New-foundland, that his correspondent at Lisbon sold them immediately at his own price, although Lent was just over when they arrived, and the people might be supposed quite cloyed with this kind of diet—His linen manufacture was likewise in a prosperous way, when the late war intervening, all his best hands were pressed into the service.

It cannot be expected, that the gentlemen of this country should execute commercial schemes to render their vassals independent; nor, indeed, are such schemes suited to their way of life and inclination; but a company of merchants might, with proper management, turn to good account a fishery established in this part of Scotland——Our people have a strange itch to colonize America, when the uncultivated parts of our own island might be settled to greater advantage.

After having rambled through the mountains and glens of Argyle, we visited the adjacent islands of Ila, Jura, Mull, and Icolmkill. In the first, we saw the remains of a castle, built in a lake, where Macdonald, lord or king

---

5. Probably Charles, the third son of Donald Cameron. The elder Cameron took a leading role in fighting for the Pretender in 1745–6, and died in exile.

of the isles, formerly resided. Jura is famous for having given birth to one Mackcrain,[6] who lived one hundred and eighty years in one house, and died in the reign of Charles the Second. Mull affords several bays, where there is safe anchorage; in one of which, the Florida, a ship of the Spanish armada, was blown up by one of Mr. Smollett's ancestors—About forty years ago, John duke of Argyle is said to have consulted the Spanish registers, by which it appeared, that this ship had the military chest on board—He employed experienced divers to examine the wreck; and they found the hull of the vessel still entire, but so covered with sand, that they could not make their way between decks; however, they picked up several pieces of plate, that were scattered about in the bay, and a couple of fine brass cannon.

Icolmkill, or Iona, is a small island which St. Columba chose for his habitation—It was respected for its sanctity, and college or seminary of ecclesiastics—Part of its church is still standing, with the tombs of several Scottish, Irish, and Danish sovereigns, who were here interred —These islanders are very bold and dexterous watermen, consequently the better adapted to the fishery: in their manners they are less savage and impetuous than their countrymen on the continent; and they speak the Erse or Gaelick[7] in its greatest purity. Having sent round our horses by land, we embarked in the district of Cowal, for Greenock, which is a neat little town, on the other side of the Frith, with a curious harbour, formed by three stone jetties, carried out a good way into the sea ——Newport-Glasgow is such another place, about two miles higher up —Both have a face of business and plenty, and are supported entirely by the shipping of Glasgow, of which I counted sixty large vessels in these harbours—Taking boat again at Newport, we were in less than an hour landed on the other side, within two short miles of our head-quarters, where we found our women in good health and spirits—They had been two days before joined by Mr. Smollett and his lady, to whom we have such obligations as I cannot mention, even to you, without blushing.

To-morrow we shall bid adieu to the Scotch Arcadia, and begin our progress to the southward, taking our way by Lanerk and Nithsdale, to the west borders of England. I have received so much advantage and satisfaction from this tour, that if my health suffers no revolution in the winter, I believe I shall be tempted to undertake another expedition to the Northern extremity of Caithness,[8] unencumbered by those impediments which now clog the heels of,

yours,

Cameron, Sept. 6.   MATT. BRAMBLE.

6. Gillour Mack-Crain, of whom Smollett had written earlier.
7. The ancient language of Scotland; a Celtic language.

8. Caithness is the county at the extreme northeast corner of Scotland, overlooking the Orkney Islands.

To Miss LÆTITIA WILLIS, at Gloucester.

MY DEAREST LETTY,

Never did poor prisoner long for deliverance, more than I have longed for an opportunity to disburthen my cares into your friendly bosom; and the occasion which now presents itself, is little less than miraculous —Honest Saunders Macawly, the travelling Scotchman, who goes every year to Wales, is now at Glasgow, buying goods, and coming to pay his respects to our family, has undertaken to deliver this letter into your own hand—We have been six weeks in Scotland, and seen the principal towns of the kingdom, where we have been treated with great civility —The people are very courteous; and the country being exceedingly romantic, suits my turn and inclinations—I contracted some friendships at Edinburgh, which is a large and lofty city, full of gay company; and, in particular, commenced an intimate correspondence with one miss R—t —n,[9] an amiable young lady of my own age, whose charms seemed to soften, and even to subdue the stubborn heart of my brother Jery; but he no sooner left the place than he relapsed into his former insensibility ——I feel, however, that this indifference is not the family-constitution —I never admitted but one idea of love, and that has taken such root in my heart, as to be equally proof against all the pulls of discretion, and the frosts of neglect.

Dear Letty! I had an alarming adventure at the hunters ball in Edinburgh—While I sat discoursing with a friend in a corner, all at once the very image of Wilson stood before me, dressed exactly as he was in the character of Aimwell![1] It was one Mr. Gordon, whom I had not seen before—Shocked at the sudden apparition, I fainted away, and threw the whole assembly in confusion——However, the cause of my disorder remained a secret to every body but my brother, who was likewise struck with the resemblance, and scolded after we came home—I am very sensible of Jery's affection, and know he spoke as well with a view to my own interest and happiness, as in regard to the honour of the family; but I cannot bear to have my wounds probed severely—I was not so much affected by the censure he passed upon my own indiscretion, as with the reflection he made on the conduct of Wilson—He observed, that if he was really the gentleman he pretended to be, and harboured nothing but honourable designs, he would have vindicated his pretensions in the face of day—This remark made a deep impression upon my mind——I endeavoured to conceal my thoughts; and this endeavour had a bad effect upon my health and spirits; so it was thought necessary that I should go to the Highlands, and drink the goat-milk-whey.

9. See note 6, p. 208, above.
1. One of the romantic heroes of George Far-
quahar's *The Beaux' Stratagem* (1707), the play presented at Gloucester.

We went accordingly to Lough-Lomond, one of the most enchanting spots in the whole world; and what with this remedy, which I had every morning fresh from the mountains, and the pure air, and chearful company, I have recovered my flesh and appetite; though there is something still at bottom, which it is not in the power of air, exercise, company, or medicine to remove———These incidents would not touch me so nearly, if I had a sensible confidant to sympathize with my affliction, and comfort me with wholesome advice—I have nothing of this kind, except Win Jenkins, who is really a good body in the main, but very ill qualified for such an office—The poor creature is weak in her nerves, as well as in her understanding; otherwise I might have known the true name and character of that unfortunate youth—But why do I call him *unfortunate?* perhaps the epithet is more applicable to me for having listened to the false professions of———But, hold! I have as yet no right, and sure I have no inclination to believe any thing to the prejudice of his honour—In that reflection I shall still exert my patience—As for Mrs. Jenkins, she herself is really an object of compassion—Between vanity, methodism, and love, her head is almost turned. I should have more regard for her, however, if she had been more constant in the object of her affection; but, truly, she aimed at conquest, and flirted at the same time with my uncle's footman, Humphry Clinker, who is really a deserving young man, and one Dutton, my brother's valet de chambre, a debauched fellow; who, leaving Win in the lurch, ran away with another man's bride at Berwick.

My dear Willis, I am truly ashamed of my own sex———We complain of advantages which the men take of our youth, inexperience, sensibility, and all that; but I have seen enough to believe, that our sex in general make it their business to ensnare the other; and for this purpose, employ arts which are by no means to be justified———In point of constancy, they certainly have nothing to reproach the male part of the creation—My poor aunt, without any regard to her years and imperfections, has gone to market with her charms in every place where she thought she had the least chance to dispose of her person, which, however, hangs still heavy on her hands—I am afraid she has used even religion as a decoy, though it has not answered her expectation—She has been praying, preaching, and catechising among the methodists, with whom this country abounds; and pretends to have such manifestations and revelations, as even Clinker himself can hardly believe, though the poor fellow is half crazy with enthusiasm. As for Jenkins, she affects to take all her mistress's reveries for gospel—She has also her heart-heavings and motions of the spirit; and God forgive me if I think uncharitably, but all this seems to me to be downright hypocrisy and deceit—Perhaps, indeed, the poor girl imposes on herself—She is generally in a flutter, and is much subject to vapours —Since we came to Scotland, she has seen apparitions, and pretends to prophesy———If I could put faith in all these supernatural visitations, I should think myself abandoned of grace; for I have neither seen, heard, nor felt any thing of this nature, although I endeavour to discharge the duties of religion with all the sincerity, zeal, and devotion, that is in the power of,

Dear Letty,

your ever affectionate,

Glasgow, Sept. 7.   LYDIA MELFORD.

We are so far on our return to Brambleton-hall; and I would fain hope we shall take Gloucester in our way, in which case I shall have the inexpressible pleasure of embracing my dear Willis—Pray remember me to my worthy governess.

To Mrs. MARY JONES, at Brambleton-hall.

DEAR MARY,

Sunders Macully, the Scotchman, who pushes directly for Vails, has promised to give it you into your own hand, and therefore I would not miss the oportunity to let you now as I am still in the land of the living; and yet I have been on the brink of the other world since I sent you my last letter.—We went by sea to another kingdom called Fife, and coming back, had like to have gone to pot in a storm.—What between the frite and sickness, I thought I should have brought my heart up; even Mr. Clinker was not his own man for eight and forty hours after we got ashore.—It was well for some folks that we scaped drownding; for mistress was very frexious, and seemed but indifferently prepared for a change; but, thank God, she was soon put in a better frame by the private exaltations of the reverend Mr. Macrocodile.—We afterwards churned to Starling and Grascow, which are a kiple of handsome towns; and then we went to a gentleman's house at Loff-Loming, which is a wonderful sea of fresh water, with a power of hylands in the midst on't.—They say as how it has got n'er a bottom, and was made by a musician; and, truly, I believe it; for it is not in the coarse of nature.—It has got *waves without wind, fish without fins, and a floating hyland;* [2] and one of them is a crutch-yard, where the dead are buried; and always before the person dies, a bell rings of itself to give warning.

O Mary! this is the land of congyration—The bell knolled when we were there—I saw lights, and heard lamentations.—The gentleman, our landlord, has got another house, which he was fain to quit, on account of a mischievious ghost, that would not suffer people to lie in their beds. —The fairies dwell in a hole of Kairmann, a mounting hard by; and they

2. An ancient legend about Loch Lomond.

steal away the good women that are in the straw, [3] if so be as how there a'n't a horshoe nailed to the door: and I was shewn an ould vitch, called Elspath Ringavey, with a red petticoat, bleared eyes, and a mould of grey bristles on her sin.—That she mought do me no harm, I crossed her hand with a taster, [4] and bid her tell my fortune; and she told me such things —descriving Mr. Clinker to a hair—but it shall ne'er be said, that I minchioned a word of the matter.—As I was troubled with fits, she advised me to bathe in the loff, which was holy water; and so I went in the morning to a private place along with the house-maid, and we bathed in our birth-day soot, [5] after the fashion of the country; and behold, whilst we dabbled in the loff, sir Gorge Coon started up with a gun; but we clapt our hands to our faces, and passed by him to the place where we had left our smocks—A civil gentleman would have turned his head another way. —My comfit is, he new not which was which; and, as the saying is, *all cats in the dark are grey*. [6]——Whilst we stayed at Loff-Loming, he and our two squires went three or four days churning among the wild men of the mountings; a parcel of selvidges that lie in caves among the rocks, devour young children, speak Velch, but the vords are different. Our ladies would not part with Mr. Clinker, because he is so stout, and so pyehouse, that he fears neither man nor devils, if so be as they don't take him by surprise.—Indeed, he was once so flurried by an operition, that he had like to have sounded.—He made believe as if it had been the ould edmiral; but the ould edmiral could not have made his air to stand on end, and his teeth to shatter; but he said so in prudence, that the ladies mought not be affear'd. Miss Liddy has been puny, and like to go into a decline—I doubt her pore art is too tinder—but the got's-fey [7] has sat her on her legs again.—You nows got's-fey is mother's milk to a Velchvoman. As for mistress, blessed be God, she ails nothing.—Her stomick is good, and she improves in grease and godliness; but, for all that, she may have infections like other people, and I believe, she wouldn't be sorry to be called *your ladyship*, whenever sir George thinks proper to ax the question.—But, for my part, whatever I may see or hear, not a praticle shall ever pass the lips of,

Dear Molly,

Your loving friend,

Grasco, Sept. 7.

WIN. JENKINS.

3. See note 8, p. 173, above. Folk beliefs about the supernatural were still prevalent in Scotland.
4. Tester is a colloquial term for a sixpenny coin, worth half a shilling.
5. This is a very early recorded usage of the modern meaning of this phrase, which is "to be completely nude." In the seventeenth and eighteenth centuries it more often referred to the ex-

travagant costumes worn by courtiers to celebrate the sovereign's birthday.
6. A bawdy proverb which means that women may not be distinguished by their private parts, though its primary meaning refers to intercourse rather than to sighting.
7. The whey, or watery liquid, of goat's milk after it has curdled.

Remember me, as usual, to Sall.—We are now coming home, though not the nearest road.——I do suppose, I shall find the kitten a fine boar at my return.

To Sir WATKIN PHILLIPS, Bar^t. at Oxon.

DEAR KNIGHT,

Once more I tread upon English ground, which I like not the worse for the six weeks' ramble I have made among the woods and mountains of Caledonia; no offence to the *land of cakes, where bannocks grow upon straw*.[8] I never saw my uncle in such health and spirits as he now enjoys. Liddy is perfectly recovered; and Mrs. Tabitha has no reason to complain. Nevertheless, I believe, she was, till yesterday, inclined to give the whole Scotch nation to the devil, as a pack of insensible brutes, upon whom her accomplishments had been displayed in vain.—At every place where we halted, did she mount the stage, and flourished her rusty arms, without being able to make one conquest. One of her last essays was against the heart of sir George Colquhoun, with whom she fought all the weapons more than twice over.—She was grave and gay by turns—she moralized and methodized—she laughed, and romped, and danced, and sung, and sighed, and ogled, and lisped, and fluttered, and flattered—but all was preaching to the desart—The baronet, being a well-bred man, carried his civilities as far as she could in conscience expect, and, if evil tongues are to be believed, some degrees farther; but he was too much a veteran in gallantry, as well as in war, to fall into any ambuscade that she could lay for his affection.—While we were absent in the Highlands, she practised also upon the laird of Ladrishmore, and even gave him the rendezvous in the wood of Drumscailloch; but the laird had such a reverend care of his own reputation, that he came attended with the parson of the parish, and nothing passed but spiritual communication.
——After all these miscarriages, our aunt suddenly recollected lieutenant Lismahago, whom, ever since our first arrival at Edinburgh, she seemed to have utterly forgot, but now she expressed her hopes of seeing him at Dumfries, according to his promise.

We set out from Glasgow by the way of Lanerk, the county-town of Clydesdale, in the neighbourhood of which, the whole river Clyde, rushing down a steep rock, forms a very noble and stupendous cascade. Next day we were obliged to halt in a small borough, until the carriage, which had received some damage, should be repaired; and here we met with an incident which warmly interested the benevolent spirit of Mr. Bramble.—As we stood at the window of an inn that fronted the public prison, a person arrived on horseback, genteelly, tho' plainly, dressed in a

8. Scotland was widely known for its form of oat-bread, which was called cake, and for bannocks, which were larger cakes made of barley.

blue frock, with his own hair cut short, and a gold-laced hat upon his head.—Alighting, and giving his horse to the landlord, he advanced to an old man who was at work in paving the street, and accosted him in these words: "This is hard work for such an old man as you."—So saying, he took the instrument out of his hand, and began to thump the pavement. —After a few strokes, "Have you never a son (said he) to ease you of this labour?" "Yes, an please your honour, (replied the senior) I have three hopeful lads, but, at present, they are out of the way." "Honour not me (cried the stranger); it more becomes me to honour your grey hairs. —Where are those sons you talk of?" The ancient paviour said, his eldest son was a captain in the East-Indies; and the youngest had lately inlisted as a soldier, in hopes of prospering like his brother. The gentleman desiring to know what was become of the second, he wiped his eyes, and owned, he had taken upon him his old father's debts, for which he was now in the prison hard by.

The traveller made three quick steps towards the jail, then turning short, "Tell me, (said he) has that unnatural captain sent you nothing to relieve your distresses?" "Call him not unnatural (replied the other); God's blessing be upon him! he sent me a great deal of money; but I made a bad use of it; I lost it by being security for a gentleman that was my landlord, and was stript of all I had in the world besides." At that instant a young man, thrusting out his head and neck between two iron bars in the prison-window, exclaimed, "Father! father! if my brother William is in life, that's he!" "I am!—I am!—(cried the stranger, clasping the old man in his arms, and shedding a flood of tears)—I am your son Willy, sure enough!" Before the father, who was quite confounded, could make any return to this tenderness, a decent old woman bolting out from the door of a poor habitation, cried, "Where is my bairn? where is my dear Willy?"—The captain no sooner beheld her, than he quitted his father, and ran into her embrace.[9]

I can assure you, my uncle, who saw and heard every thing that passed, was as much moved as any one of the parties concerned in this pathetic recognition—He sobbed, and wept, and clapped his hands, and hollowed, and finally ran down into the street. By this time, the captain had retired with his parents, and all the inhabitants of the place were assembled at the door.—Mr. Bramble, nevertheless, pressed thro' the crowd, and entering the house, "Captain, (said he) I beg the favour of your acquaintance—I would have travelled a hundred miles to see this affecting scene; and I shall think myself happy, if you and your parents will dine with me at the public house." The captain thanked him for his kind invitation, which, he said, he would accept with pleasure; but, in the mean time, he could not think of eating or drinking, while his poor brother was in

---

9. This unlikely story of Captain Brown is based on the actual experiences of Martin White of Milton, a village near Lanark.

trouble.—He forthwith deposited a sum equal to the debt in the hands of the magistrate, who ventured to set his brother at liberty without farther process; and then the whole family repaired to the inn with my uncle, attended by the crowd, the individuals of which shook their townsman by the hand, while he returned their caresses without the least sign of pride or affectation.

This honest favourite of fortune, whose name was Brown, told my uncle, that he had been bred a weaver, and, about eighteen years ago, had, from a spirit of idleness and dissipation, enlisted as a soldier in the service of the East-India company; that, in the course of duty, he had the good fortune to attract the notice and approbation of lord Clive,[1] who preferred him from one step to another, till he attained the rank of captain and pay-master to the regiment, in which capacities he had honestly amassed above twelve thousand pounds, and, at the peace, resigned his commission.—He had sent several remittances to his father, who received the first only, consisting of one hundred pounds; the second had fallen into the hands of a bankrupt; and the third had been consigned to a gentleman of Scotland, who died before it arrived; so that it still remained to be accounted for by his executors. He now presented the old man with fifty pounds for his present occasions, over and above bank notes for one hundred, which he had deposited for his brother's release. —He brought along with him a deed ready executed, by which he settled a perpetuity of fourscore pounds upon his parents, to be inherited by their other two sons after their decease.—He promised to purchase a commission for his youngest brother; to take the other as his own partner in a manufacture which he intended to set up, to give employment and bread to the industrious; and to give five hundred pounds, by way of dower, to his sister, who had married a farmer in low circumstances. —Finally, he gave fifty pounds to the poor of the town where he was born, and feasted all the inhabitants without exception.

My uncle was so charmed with the character of captain Brown, that he drank his health three times successively at dinner.—He said, he was proud of his acquaintance; that he was an honour to his country, and had in some measure redeemed human nature from the reproach of pride, selfishness, and ingratitude.—For my part, I was as much pleased with the modesty as with the filial virtue of this honest soldier, who assumed no merit from his success, and said very little of his own transactions, though the answers he made to our inquiries were equally sensible and laconic. Mrs. Tabitha behaved very graciously to him until she understood that he was going to make a tender of his hand to a person of low estate, who had been his sweet-heart while he worked as a journeyman weaver.—Our aunt was no sooner made acquainted with this design, than she starched up her behaviour with a double proportion of reserve;

1. Baron Clive, Robert Clive (1725–74) was viceroy of India.

and when the company broke up, she observed, with a toss of her nose, that Brown was a civil fellow enough, considering the lowness of his origin; but that Fortune, though she had mended his circumstances, was incapable to raise his ideas, which were still humble and plebeian.

On the day that succeeded this adventure, we went some miles out of our road to see Drumlanrig, a seat belonging to the duke of Queensberry,[2] which appears like a magnificent palace erected by magic, in the midst of a wilderness.—It is indeed a princely mansion, with suitable parks and plantations, rendered still more striking by the nakedness of the surrounding country, which is one of the wildest tracts in all Scotland. —This wildness, however, is different from that of the Highlands; for here the mountains, instead of heath, are covered with a fine green swarth, affording pasture to innumerable flocks of sheep. But the fleeces of this country, called Nithsdale, are not comparable to the wool of Galloway, which is said to equal that of Salisbury plain. Having passed the night at the castle of Drumlanrig, by invitation from the duke himself, who is one of the best men that ever breathed, we prosecuted our journey to Dumfries, a very elegant trading town near the borders of England, where we found plenty of good provision and excellent wine, at very reasonable prices, and the accommodation as good in all respects as in any part of South-Britain.—If I was confined to Scotland for life, I would chuse Dumfries as the place of my residence. Here we made enquiries about captain Lismahago, of whom hearing no tidings, we proceeded, by the Solway Frith, to Carlisle. You must know, that the Solway sands, upon which travellers pass at low water, are exceedingly dangerous, because, as the tide makes, they become quick in different places, and the flood rushes in so impetuously, that passengers are often overtaken by the sea, and perish.

In crossing these treacherous Syrtes[3] with a guide, we perceived a drowned horse, which Humphry Clinker, after due inspection, declared to be the very identical beast which Mr. Lismahago rode when he parted with us at Felton-bridge in Northumberland. This information, which seemed to intimate that our friend the lieutenant had shared the fate of his horse, affected us all, and above all our aunt Tabitha, who shed salt tears, and obliged Clinker to pull a few hairs out of the dead horse's tail, to be worn in a ring as a remembrance of his master: but her grief and ours was not of long duration; for one of the first persons we saw in Carlisle, was the lieutenant in propria persona,[4] bargaining with a horse-dealer for another steed, in the yard of the inn where we alighted.—Mrs. Bramble was the first that perceived him, and screamed as if she had seen a ghost; and, truly, at a proper time and place, he might very well have

2. Drumlanrig, the seat of the Duke of Queensberry, Charles Douglas (1698–1778), was built in the late seventeenth century.

3. The proper name of two quicksands off the north coast of Africa, and hence any quicksands.
4. In his own person.

passed for an inhabitant of another world; for he was more meagre and grim than before—We received him the more cordially for having supposed he had been drowned; and he was not deficient in expressions of satisfaction at this meeting.—He told us, he had enquired for us at Dumfries, and been informed by a travelling merchant from Glasgow, that we had resolved to return by the way of Coldstream.—He said, that in passing the sands without a guide, his horse had knocked up; and he himself must have perished, if he had not been providentially relieved by a return post-chaise.—He moreover gave us to understand, that his scheme of settling in his own country having miscarried, he was so far on his way to London, with a view to embark for North-America, where he intended to pass the rest of his days among his old friends the Miamis, and amuse himself in finishing the education of the son he had by his beloved Squinkinacoosta.

This project was by no means agreeable to our good aunt, who expatiated upon the fatigues and dangers that would attend such a long voyage by sea, and afterwards such a tedious journey by land—She enlarged particularly on the risque he would run, with respect to the concerns of his precious soul, among savages who had not yet received the glad tidings of salvation; and she hinted that his abandoning Great-Britain might, perhaps, prove fatal to the inclinations of some deserving person, whom he was qualified to make happy for life. My uncle, who is really a Don Quixote in generosity, understanding that Lismahago's real reason for leaving Scotland was the impossibility of subsisting in it with any decency upon the wretched provision of a subaltern's half-pay, began to be warmly interested on the side of compassion.—He thought it very hard, that a gentleman who had served his country with honour, should be driven by necessity to spend his old age, among the refuse of mankind, in such a remote part of the world.—He discoursed with me upon the subject; observing, that he would willingly offer the lieutenant an asylum at Brambleton-hall, if he did not foresee that his singularities and humour of contradiction would render him an intolerable house-mate, though his conversation at some times might be both instructive and entertaining: but, as there seemed to be something particular in his attention to Mrs. Tabitha, he and I agreed in opinion, that this intercourse should be encouraged, and improved, if possible, into a matrimonial union; in which case there would be a comfortable provision for both; and they might be settled in a house of their own, so that Mr. Bramble should have no more of their company than he desired.

In pursuance of this design, Lismahago has been invited to pass the winter at Brambleton-hall, as it will be time enough to execute his American project in the spring.—He has taken time to consider of this proposal; mean while, he will keep us company as far as we travel in the road to Bristol, where he has hopes of getting a passage for America. I make no doubt but that he will postpone his voyage, and prosecute his addresses to a happy consummation; and sure, if it produces any fruit, it must be of a very peculiar flavour. As the weather continues favourable, I believe, we shall take the Peak of Derbyshire and Buxton Wells in our way.—At any rate, from the first place where we make any stay, you shall hear again from

Yours always,

Carlisle, Sept. 12.   J. MELFORD.

To Dr. LEWIS.

DEAR DOCTOR,

   The peasantry of Scotland are certainly on a poor footing all over the kingdom; and yet they look better, and are better cloathed than those of the same rank in Burgundy, and many other places of France and Italy; nay, I will venture to say they are better fed, notwithstanding the boasted wine of these foreign countries. The country people of North-Britain live chiefly on oat-meal, and milk, cheese, butter, and some garden-stuff, with now and then a pickled-herring, by way of delicacy; but flesh-meat they seldom or never taste; nor any kind of strong liquor, except two-penny,[5] at times of uncommon festivity—Their breakfast is a kind of hasty pudding, of oat-meal or pease-meal, eaten with milk. They have commonly pottage to dinner, composed of cale or cole, leeks, barley or big,[6] and butter; and this is reinforced with bread and cheese, made of skimmed-milk—At night they sup on sowens or flummery of oat-meal —In a scarcity of oats, they use the meal of barley and pease, which is both nourishing and palatable. Some of them have potatoes; and you find parsnips in every peasant's garden—They are cloathed with a coarse kind of russet of their own making, which is both decent and warm —They dwell in poor huts, built of loose stones and turf, without any mortar, having a fire-place or hearth in the middle, generally made of an old mill-stone, and a hole at top to let out the smoke.

   These people, however, are content, and wonderfully sagacious—All of them read the Bible, and are even qualified to dispute upon the articles of their faith; which, in those parts I have seen, is entirely Presbyterian. I am told, that the inhabitants of Aberdeenshire are still more acute. I once knew a Scotch gentleman at London, who had declared war against this part of his countrymen; and swore that the impudence and knavery of the Scots, in that quarter, had brought a reproach upon the whole nation.

5. A kind of ale sold in Scotland for two pence per Scots pint, which is equal to three imperial pints.

6. Big, more usually bigg, is a hardier but inferior variety of barley.

The river Clyde, above Glasgow, is quite pastoral; and the banks of it are every where adorned with fine villas. From the sea to its source, we may reckon the seats of many families of the first rank, such as the duke of Argyle at Roseneath, the earl of Bute in the isle of that name, the earl of Glencairn at Finlayston, lord Blantyre at Areskine, the dutchess of Douglas at Bothwell, duke Hamilton at Hamilton, the duke of Douglas at Douglas, and the earl of Hyndford at Carmichael. Hamilton is a noble palace, magnificently furnished; and hard by is the village of that name, one of the neatest little towns I have seen in any country. The old castle of Douglas being burned to the ground by accident, the late duke[7] resolved, as head of the first family in Scotland, to have the largest house in the kingdom, and ordered a plan for this purpose; but there was only one wing of it finished when he died. It is to be hoped that his nephew, who is now in possession of his great fortune,[8] will complete the design of his predecessor—Clydesdale is in general populous and rich, containing a great number of gentlemen, who are independent in their fortune; but it produces more cattle than corn—This is also the case with Tweedale, through part of which we passed, and Nidsdale, which is generally rough, wild, and mountainous—These hills are covered with sheep; and this is the small delicious mutton, so much preferable to that of the London-market. As their feeding costs so little, the sheep are not killed till five years old, when their flesh, juices, and flavour, are in perfection; but their fleeces are much damaged by the tar, with which they are smeared to preserve them from the rot in winter, during which they run wild night and day, and thousands are lost under huge wreaths of snow——'Tis pity the farmers cannot contrive some means to shelter this useful animal from the inclemencies of a rigorous climate, especially from the perpetual rains, which are more prejudicial than the greatest extremity of cold weather.

On the little river Nid, is situated the castle of Drumlanrig, one of the noblest seats in Great-Britain, belonging to the duke of Queensberry; one of those few noblemen whose goodness of heart does honour to human-nature—I shall not pretend to enter into a description of this palace, which is really an instance of the sublime in magnificence, as well as in situation, and puts one in mind of the beautiful city of Palmyra,[9] rising like a vision in the midst of the wilderness. His grace keeps open house, and lives with great splendour—He did us the honour to receive us with great courtesy, and detain us all night, together with above twenty other guests, with all their servants and horses, to a very considerable number—The dutchess was equally gracious, and took our

7. The Duke of Douglas, Archibald Douglas (1694–1761).
8. A long court case followed the death of the duke, who died without children. The Duke of Hamilton claimed the estate, as did Archibald Douglas, the nephew of the deceased duke. The nephew was awarded the fortune in 1769.
9. A city in ancient Syria, purportedly built by Solomon and famed for its beauty.

ladies under her immediate protection. The longer I live, I see more reason to believe that prejudices of education are never wholly eradicated, even when they are discovered to be erroneous and absurd. Such habits of thinking as interest the grand passions, cleave to the human heart in such a manner, that though an effort of reason may force them from their hold for a moment, this violence no sooner ceases, than they resume their grasp with an encreased elasticity and adhesion.

I am led into this reflection, by what passed at the duke's table after supper. The conversation turned upon the vulgar notions of spirits and omens, that prevail among the commonalty of North-Britain, and all the company agreed, that nothing could be more ridiculous. One gentleman, however, told a remarkable story of himself, by way of speculation —"Being on a party of hunting in the North, (said he) I resolved to visit an old friend, whom I had not seen for twenty years—So long he had been retired and sequestered from all his acquaintance, and lived in a moping melancholy way, much afflicted with lowness of spirits, occasioned by the death of his wife, whom he had loved with uncommon affection. As he resided in a remote part of the country, and we were five gentlemen with as many servants, we carried some provision with us from the next market town, lest we should find him unprepared for our reception. The roads being bad, we did not arrive at the house till two o'clock in the afternoon; and were agreeably surprised to find a very good dinner ready in the kitchen, and the cloth laid with six covers. My friend himself appeared in his best apparel at the gate, and received us with open arms, telling me he had been expecting us these two hours—Astonished at this declaration, I asked who had given him intelligence of our coming? and he smiled without making any other reply—However, presuming upon our former intimacy, I afterwards insisted upon knowing; and he told me, very gravely, he had seen me in a vision of the second sight—Nay, he called in the evidence of his steward, who solemnly declared, that his master had the day before apprised him of my coming, with four other strangers, and ordered him to provide accordingly; in consequence of which intimation, he had prepared the dinner which we were now eating; and laid the covers according to the number foretold." The incident we all owned to be remarkable, and I endeavoured to account for it by natural means. I observed, that as the gentleman was of a visionary turn, the casual idea, or remembrance of his old friend, might suggest those circumstances, which accident had for once realized; but that in all probability he had seen many visions of the same kind, which were never verified. None of the company directly dissented from my opinion; but from the objections that were hinted, I could plainly perceive, that the majority were persuaded there was something more extraordinary in the case.

Another gentleman of the company, addressing himself to me, "Without all doubt, (said he) a diseased imagination is very apt to produce visions; but we must find some other method to account for something of this kind, that happened within these eight days in my neighbourhood ——A gentleman of a good family, who cannot be deemed a visionary in any sense of the word, was near his own gate, in the twilight, visited by his grandfather, who has been dead these fifteen years—The spectre was mounted seemingly on the very horse he used to ride, with an angry and terrible countenance, and said something, which his grandson, in the confusion of his fear, could not understand. But this was not all—He lifted up a huge horse-whip, and applied it with great violence to his back and shoulders, on which I saw the impression with my own eyes. The apparition was afterwards seen by the sexton of the parish, hovering about the tomb where his body lies interred; as the man declared to several persons in the village, before he knew what had happened to the gentleman—Nay, he actually came to me as a justice of the peace, in order to make oath of these particulars, which, however, I declined administering. As for the grandson of the defunct, he is a sober, sensible, worldly-minded fellow, too intent upon schemes of interest to give into reveries. He would have willingly concealed the affair; but he bawled out in the first transport of his fear, and, running into the house, exposed his back and his sconce to the whole family; so that there was no denying it in the sequel. It is now the common discourse of the country, that this appearance and behaviour of the old man's spirit, portends some great calamity to the family, and the good woman has actually taken to her bed in this apprehension."

Though I did not pretend to explain this mystery, I said, I did not at all doubt, but it would one day appear to be a deception; and, in all probability, a scheme executed by some enemy of the person who had sustained the assault; but still the gentleman insisted upon the clearness of the evidence, and the concurrence of testimony, by which two creditable witnesses, without any communication one with another, affirmed the appearance of the same man, with whose person they were both well acquainted—From Drumlanrig we pursued the course of the Nid to Dumfries, which stands several miles above the place where the river falls into the sea; and is, after Glasgow, the handsomest town I have seen in Scotland—The inhabitants, indeed, seem to have proposed that city as their model; not only in beautifying their town and regulating its police, but also in prosecuting their schemes of commerce and manufacture, by which they are grown rich and opulent.

We re-entered England, by the way of Carlisle, where we accidentally met with our friend Lismahago, whom we had in vain inquired after at Dumfries and other places—It would seem that the captain, like the prophets of old, is but little honoured in his own country, which he has now renounced for ever—He gave me the following particulars of his visit to his native soil—In his way to the place of his nativity, he learned that his nephew had married the daughter of a burgeois, who directed a weaving manufacture, and had gone into partnership with his father-in-law: chagrined with this information, he had arrived at the gate in the twilight, where he heard the sound of treddles in the great hall, which had exasperated him to such a degree, that he had like to have lost his senses: while he was thus transported with indignation, his nephew chanced to come forth, when, being no longer master of his passion, he cried, "Degenerate rascal! you have made my father's house a den of thieves;" and at the same time chastised him with his horse-whip; then, riding round the adjoining village, he had visited the burying-ground of his ancestors by moon-light; and, having paid his respects to their *manes*, travelled all night to another part of the country——Finding the head of his family in such a disgraceful situation, all his own friends dead or removed from the places of their former residence, and the expence of living encreased to double of what it had been, when he first left his native country, he had bid it an eternal adieu, and was determined to seek for repose among the forests of America.

I was no longer at a loss to account for the apparition, which had been described at Drumlanrig; and when I repeated the story to the lieutenant, he was much pleased to think his resentment had been so much more effectual than he intended; and he owned, he might at such an hour, and in such an equipage, very well pass for the ghost of his father, whom he was said greatly to resemble——Between friends, I fancy Lismahago will find a retreat without going so far as the wigwams of the Miamis. My sister Tabby is making continual advances to him, in the way of affection; and, if I may trust to appearances, the captain is disposed to take opportunity by the forelock. For my part, I intend to encourage this correspondence, and shall be glad to see them united——In that case, we shall find a way to settle them comfortably in our own neighbourhood. I, and my servants, will get rid of a very troublesome and tyrannic gouvernante;[1] and I shall have the benefit of Lismahago's conversation, without being obliged to take more of his company than I desire; for though an olla[2] is a high-flavoured dish, I could not bear to dine upon it every day of my life.

I am much pleased with Manchester, which is one of the most agreeable and flourishing towns in Great-Britain; and I perceive that this is the place which hath animated the spirit, and suggested the chief manufactures of Glasgow. We propose to visit Chatsworth,[3] the Peak,[4] and Buxton,[5] from which last place we shall proceed directly homewards, though by easy journies. If the season has been as favourable in Wales as

---

1. Female chaperone.
2. A dish of Spanish origin made of a wide variety of ingredients which are cooked together in an earthenware pot, or olla, and highly seasoned.
3. Chatsworth House was the famous Palladian seat of the Dukes of Devonshire. In addition to a fine art collection, it had recently had its gardens improved by the well-known landscape gardener Capability Brown. It is located near Rowsley, in Derbyshire.
4. A hilly district in Derbyshire which is popular among hikers and seekers of picturesque scenery.
5. Another of the well-attended spas of the period.

in the North, your harvest is happily finished; and we have nothing left to think of but our October, of which let Barns be properly reminded. You will find me much better in flesh than I was at our parting; and this short separation has given a new edge to those sentiments of friendship with which I always have been, and ever shall be,

yours,

Manchester, Sept. 15.   MATT. BRAMBLE.

To Mrs. GWYLLIM, house-keeper at Brambleton-hall.

MRS. GWILLIM,

It has pleased Providence to bring us safe back to England, and partake us in many pearls by land and water, in particular the *Devil's Harse a pike*,[6] and *Hoyden's Hole*,[7] which hath got no bottom; and, as we are drawing huomwards, it may be proper to uprise you, that Brambleton-hall may be in a condition to receive us, after this long gurney to the islands of Scotland. By the first of next month you may begin to make constant fires in my brother's chamber and mine; and burn a fagget every day in the yellow damask room: have the tester and curtains dusted, and the fatherbed and matrosses well haired, because, perhaps, with the blissing of haven, they may be yoosed on some occasion. Let the ould hogsheads be well skewred and seasoned for bear, as Mat is resolved to have his seller choak fool.

If the house was mine, I would turn over a new leaf——I don't see why the sarvants of Wales should'n't drink fair water, and eat hot cakes and barley cale, as they do in Scotland, without troubling the botcher above once a quarter——I hope you keep accunt of Roger's purseeding in reverence to the butter-milk. I expect my dew when I come huom, without baiting an ass, I'll assure you.—As you must have layed a great many more eggs than would be eaten, I do suppose there is a power of turks, chickings, and guzzling about the house; and a brave kergo of cheese ready for market; and that the owl has been sent to Crickhowel, saving what the maids spun in the family.

Pray let the whole house and furniture have a thorough cleaning from top to bottom, for the honour of Wales; and let Roger search into, and make a general clearance of the slit holes which the maids have in secret;[8] for I know they are much given to sloth and uncleanness. I hope you have worked a reformation among them, as I exhorted you in my last, and set

6. The Devil's Arse or Peak's Arse was a cavern near Castleton, in the Peak district.
7. This feature has not been identified but may derive from Howden or Heyden Moor, actual features in the area. A hoyden is, of course, a boisterous, ill-bred girl.
8. The editor is forced to conjecture that Tabitha is asking that Roger examine the mattresses of the servant girls, where they might have slit holes in the cover in order to secrete things within.

their hearts upon better things than they can find in junkitting and caterwauling with the fellows of the country.

As for Win Jenkins, she has undergone a perfect metamurphysis, and is become a new creeter from the ammunition of Humphrey Clinker, our new footman, a pious young man, who has laboured exceedingly, that she may bring forth fruits of repentance. I make no doubt but he will take the same pains with that pert hussey Mary Jones, and all of you; and that he may have power given to penetrate and instill his goodness, even into your most inward parts, is the fervent prayer of

your friend in the spirit,

Septr. 18.   TAB. BRAMBLE.

To Dr. LEWIS.

DEAR LEWIS,

Lismahago is more paradoxical than ever.—The late gulp he had of his native air, seems to have blown fresh spirit into all his polemical faculties. I congratulated him the other day on the present flourishing state of his country, observing that the Scots were now in a fair way to wipe off the national reproach of poverty, and expressing my satisfaction at the happy effects of the union, so conspicuous in the improvement of their agriculture, commerce, manufactures, and manners—The lieutenant, screwing up his features into a look of dissent and disgust, commented on my remarks to this effect—"Those who reproach a nation for its poverty, when it is not owing to the profligacy or vice of the people, deserve no answer. The Lacedæmonians[9] were poorer than the Scots, when they took the lead among all the free states of Greece, and were esteemed above them all for their valour and their virtue. The most respectable heroes of ancient Rome, such as Fabricius, Cincinnatus, and Regulus, were poorer than the poorest freeholder in Scotland; and there are at this day individuals in North-Britain, one of whom can produce more gold and silver than the whole republic of Rome could raise at those times when her public virtue shone with unrivalled lustre; and poverty was so far from being a reproach, that it added fresh laurels to her fame, because it indicated a noble contempt of wealth, which was proof against all the arts of corruption—If poverty be a subject for reproach, it follows that wealth is the object of esteem and veneration—In that case, there are Jews and others in Amsterdam and London, enriched by usury, peculation, and different species of fraud and extortion, who are more estimable than the most virtuous and illustrious members of the community. An absurdity which no man in his senses will offer to maintain.—Riches are

9. Spartans.

certainly no proof of merit: nay they are often (if not most commonly) acquired by persons of sordid minds and mean talents: nor do they give any intrinsic worth to the possessor; but, on the contrary, tend to pervert his understanding, and render his morals more depraved. But, granting that poverty were really matter of reproach, it cannot be justly imputed to Scotland. No country is poor that can supply its inhabitants with the necessaries of life, and even afford articles for exportation. Scotland is rich in natural advantages: it produces every species of provision in abundance, vast herds of cattle and flocks of sheep, with a great number of horses; prodigious quantities of wool and flax, with plenty of copse wood, and in some parts large forests of timber. The earth is still more rich below than above the surface. It yields inexhaustible stores of coal, free-stone, marble, lead, iron, copper, and silver, with some gold. The sea abounds with excellent fish, and salt to cure them for exportation; and there are creeks and harbours round the whole kingdom, for the convenience and security of navigation. The face of the country displays a surprising number of cities, towns, villas, and villages, swarming with people; and there seems to be no want of art, industry, government, and police: such a kingdom can never be called poor, in any sense of the word, though there may be many others more powerful and opulent. But the proper use of those advantages, and the present prosperity of the Scots, you seem to derive from the union of the two kingdoms!"

I said, I supposed he would not deny that the appearance of the country was much mended; that the people lived better, had more trade, and a greater quantity of money circulating since the union, than before. "I may safely admit these premises, (answered the lieutenant) without subscribing to your inference. The difference you mention, I should take to be the natural progress of improvement—Since that period, other nations, such as the Swedes, the Danes, and in particular the French, have greatly increased in commerce, without any such cause assigned. Before the union, there was a remarkable spirit of trade among the Scots, as appeared in the case of their Darien company,[1] in which they had embarked no less than four hundred thousand pounds sterling; and in the flourishing state of the maritime towns in Fife, and on the eastern coast, enriched by their trade with France, which failed in consequence of the union. The only solid commercial advantage reaped from that measure, was the privilege of trading to the English plantations; yet, excepting Glasgow and Dumfries, I don't know any other Scotch towns concerned in that traffick. In other respects, I conceive the Scots were losers by the union.—They lost the independency of their state, the greatest prop of national spirit; they lost their parliament, and their courts of justice were subjected to the revision and supremacy of an English tribunal."

1. This company was founded in 1695 to control trade with the East Indies. It established a short-lived colony on the Isthmus of Panama which had to be abandoned because of disease and famine.

"Softly, captain, (cried I) you cannot be said to have lost your own parliament, while you are represented in that of Great-Britain." "True, (said he, with a sarcastic grin) in debates of national competition, the sixteen peers and forty-five commoners of Scotland, must make a formidable figure in the scale, against the whole English legislature." "Be that as it may, (I observed) while I had the honour to sit in the lower house, the Scotch members had always the majority on their side." "I understand you, Sir, (said he) they generally side with the majority; so much the worse for their constituents. But even this evil is not the worst they have sustained by the union. Their trade has been saddled with grievous impositions, and every article of living severely taxed, to pay the interest of enormous debts, contracted by the English, in support of measures and connections in which the Scots had no interest nor concern." I begged he would at least allow, that by the union the Scots were admitted to all the privileges and immunities of English subjects; by which means multitudes of them were provided for in the army and navy, and got fortunes in different parts of England, and its dominions. "All these, (said he) become English subjects to all intents and purposes, and are in a great measure lost to their mother-country. The spirit of rambling and adventure has been always peculiar to the natives of Scotland. If they had not met with encouragement in England, they would have served and settled, as formerly, in other countries, such as Muscovy, Sweden, Denmark, Poland, Germany, France, Piedmont, and Italy, in all which nations their descendents continue to flourish even at this day."

By this time my patience began to fail, and I exclaimed, "For God's sake, what has England got by this union which, you say, has been so productive of misfortune to the Scots." "Great and manifold are the advantages which England derives from the union (said Lismahago, in a solemn tone.) First and foremost, the settlement of the protestant succession, a point which the English ministry drove with such eagerness, that no stone was left unturned, to cajole and bribe a few leading men, to cram the union down the throats of the Scottish nation, who were surprisingly reverse to the expedient. They gained by it a considerable addition of territory, extending their dominion to the sea on all sides of the island, thereby shutting up all back-doors against the enterprizes of their enemies. They got an accession of above a million of useful subjects, constituting a never-failing nursery of seamen, soldiers, labourers, and mechanics; a most valuable acquisition to a trading country, exposed to foreign wars, and obliged to maintain a number of settlements in all the four quarters of the globe. In the course of seven years, during the last war, Scotland furnished the English army and navy with seventy thousand men, over and above those who migrated to their colonies, or mingled with them at home in the civil departments of life. This was a very considerable and seasonable supply to a nation, whose people had been for many years decreasing in number, and whose lands and manufactures were actually suffering for want of hands. I need not remind you of the hackneyed maxim, that, to a nation in such circumstances, a supply of industrious people is a supply of wealth; nor repeat an observation, which is now received as an eternal truth, even among the English themselves, that the Scots who settle in South Britain are remarkably sober, orderly, and industrious."

I allowed the truth of this remark, adding, that by their industry, oeconomy, and circumspection, many of them in England, as well as in her colonies, amassed large fortunes, with which they returned to their own country, and this was so much lost to South-Britain.——"Give me leave, sir, (said he) to assure you, that in your fact you are mistaken, and in your deduction, erroneous.—Not one in two hundred that leave Scotland ever returns to settle in his own country; and the few that do return, carry thither nothing that can possibly diminish the stock of South-Britain; for none of their treasure stagnates in Scotland—There is a continual circulation, like that of the blood in the human body, and England is the heart, to which all the streams which it distributes are refunded and returned: nay, in consequence of that luxury which our connexion with England hath greatly encouraged, if not introduced, all the produce of our lands, and all the profits of our trade, are engrossed by the natives of South-Britain; for you will find that the exchange between the two kingdoms is always against Scotland; and that she retains neither gold nor silver sufficient for her own circulation.—The Scots, not content with their own manufactures and produce, which would very well answer all necessary occasions, seem to vie with each other in purchasing superfluities from England; such as broad-cloth, velvets, stuffs, silks, lace, furs, jewels, furniture of all sorts, sugar, rum, tea, chocolate, and coffee; in a word, not only every mode of the most extravagant luxury, but even many articles of convenience, which they might find as good, and much cheaper in their own country. For all these particulars, I conceive, England may touch about one million sterling a-year.—I don't pretend to make an exact calculation; perhaps, it may be something less, and, perhaps, a great deal more.—The annual revenue arising from all the private estates of Scotland cannot fall short of a million sterling; and, I should imagine, their trade will amount to as much more.—I know, the linen manufacture alone returns near half a million, exclusive of the home-consumption of that article.—If, therefore, North-Britain pays a balance of a million annually to England, I insist upon it, that country is more valuable to her in the way of commerce, than any colony in her possession, over and above the other advantages which I have specified: therefore, they are no friends, either to England or to truth, who affect to depreciate the northern part of the united kingdom."

I must own, I was at first a little nettled to find myself schooled in so many particulars.——Though I did not receive all his assertions as gospel, I was not prepared to refute them; and I cannot help now acquiescing in his remarks so far as to think, that the contempt for Scotland, which prevails too much on this side the Tweed, is founded on prejudice and error.——After some recollection, "Well, captain, (said I) you have argued stoutly for the importance of your own country: for my part, I have such a regard for our fellow-subjects of North-Britain, that I shall be glad to see the day, when your peasants can afford to give all their oats to their cattle, hogs, and poultry, and indulge themselves with good wheaten loaves, instead of such poor, unpalatable, and inflammatory diet." Here again I brought myself into a premunire[2] with the disputaceous Caledonian. He said, he hoped he should never see the common people lifted out of that sphere for which they were intended by nature and the course of things; that they might have some reason to complain of their bread, if it were mixed, like that of Norway, with sawdust and fish-bones; but that oatmeal was, he apprehended, as nourishing and salutary as wheat-flour, and the Scots in general thought it at least as savoury.——He affirmed, that a mouse, which, in the article of self-preservation, might be supposed to act from infallible instinct, would always prefer oats to wheat, as appeared from experience; for, in a place where there was a parcel of each, that animal had never begun to feed upon the latter till all the oats were consumed: for their nutritive quality, he appealed to the hale, robust constitutions of the people who lived chiefly upon oatmeal; and, instead of being inflammatory, he asserted, that it was a cooling sub-acid, balsamic and mucilaginous; insomuch, that in all inflammatory distempers, recourse was had to water-gruel, and flummery made of oatmeal.

"At least, (said I) give me leave to wish them such a degree of commerce as may enable them to follow their own inclinations."——"Heaven forbid! (cried this philosopher) Woe be to that nation, where the multitude is at liberty to follow their own inclinations! Commerce is undoubtedly a blessing, while restrained within its proper channels; but a glut of wealth brings along with it a glut of evils: it brings false taste, false appetite, false wants, profusion, venality, contempt of order, engendering a spirit of licentiousness, insolence, and faction, that keeps the community in continual ferment, and in time destroys all the distinctions of civil society; so that universal anarchy and uproar must ensue. Will any sensible man affirm, that the national advantages of opulence are to be sought on these terms?" "No, sure; but I am one of those who think, that, by proper regulations, commerce may produce every national benefit, without the allay of such concomitant evils."

So much for the dogmata of my friend Lismahago, whom I describe the more circumstantially, as I firmly believe he will set up his rest in Monmouthshire. Yesterday, while I was alone with him, he asked, in

---

2. Originally a particular kind of legal writ, but generalized to mean an argumentative difficulty.

some confusion, if I should have any objection to the success of a gentleman and a soldier, provided he should be so fortunate as to engage my sister's affection. I answered, without hesitation, that my sister was old enough to judge for herself; and that I should be very far from disapproving any resolution she might take in his favour.—His eyes sparkled at this declaration. He declared, he should think himself the happiest man on earth to be connected with my family; and that he should never be weary of giving me proofs of his gratitude and attachment. I suppose Tabby and he are already agreed; in which case, we shall have a wedding at Brambleton-hall, and you shall give away the bride. —It is the least thing you can do, by way of atonement for your former cruelty to that poor love-sick maiden, who has been so long a thorn in the side of

Yours,

Sept. 20. MATT. BRAMBLE.

We have been at Buxton; but, as I did not much relish either the company or the accommodations, and had no occasion for the water, we stayed but two nights in the place.

TO Sir WATKIN PHILLIPS, Bar^t. at Oxon.

DEAR WAT,

Adventures begin to thicken as we advance to the southward.—Lismahago has now professed himself the admirer of our aunt, and carries on his addresses under the sanction of her brother's approbation; so that we shall certainly have a wedding by Christmas. I should be glad you was present at the nuptials, to help me to throw the stocking,[3] and perform other ceremonies peculiar to that occasion——I am sure it will be productive of some diversion; and, truly, it would be worth your while to come across the country on purpose to see two such original figures in bed together, with their laced night-caps; he, the emblem of good chear, and she, the picture of good nature. All this agreeable prospect was clouded, and had well nigh vanished entirely, in consequence of a late misunderstanding between the future brothers-in-law, which, however, is now happily removed.

A few days ago, my uncle and I, going to visit a relation, met with lord Oxmington at his house, who asked us to dine with him next day, and we accepted the invitation.—Accordingly, leaving our women under the

3. Until the mid-nineteenth century, the brides-maids and groomsmen publicly assisted the bride and groom to bed with much hilarity and ribaldry. The attendents sat on either side of the bed and threw the stockings of the bride and groom over their shoulders. The tradition held that if a girl hit the groom or a boy hit the bride, the thrower would soon marry. The modern custom of the bride's throwing her bouquet derived from this ancient custom.

care of captain Lismahago, at the inn where we had lodged the preceding night, in a little town, about a mile from his lordship's dwelling, we went at the hour appointed, and had a fashionable meal served up with much ostentation to a company of about a dozen persons, none of whom we had ever seen before.—His lordship is much more remarkable for his pride and caprice, than for his hospitality and understanding; and, indeed, it appeared, that he considered his guests merely as objects to shine upon, so as to reflect the lustre of his own magnificence.—There was much state, but no courtesy; and a great deal of compliment without any conversation.—Before the desert was removed, our noble entertainer proposed three general toasts; then calling for a glass of wine, and bowing all round, wished us a good afternoon. This was the signal for the company to break up, and they obeyed it immediately, all except our 'squire, who was greatly shocked at the manner of this dismission.—He changed countenance, bit his lip in silence, but still kept his seat, so that his lordship found himself obliged to give us another hint, by saying, he should be glad to see us another time. "There is no time like the present time (cried Mr. Bramble); your lordship has not yet drank a bumper to *the best in Christendom.*" "I'll drink no more bumpers to-day (answered our landlord); and I am sorry to see you have drank too many.—Order the gentleman's carriage to the gate."—So saying, he rose and retired abruptly; our 'squire starting up at the same time, laying his hand upon his sword, and eying him with a most ferocious aspect. The master having vanished in this manner, our uncle bad one of the servants to see what was to pay; and the fellow answering, "This is no inn," "I cry you mercy, (cried the other) I perceive it is not; if it were, the landlord would be more civil.—There's a guinea, however; take it, and tell your lord, that I shall not leave the country till I have had an opportunity to thank him in person for his politeness and hospitality."

We then walked down stairs through a double range of lacqueys, and getting into the chaise, proceeded homewards. Perceiving the 'squire much ruffled, I ventured to disapprove of his resentment, observing, that as lord Oxmington was well known to have his brain very ill timbered, a sensible man should rather laugh, than be angry at his ridiculous want of breeding.—Mr. Bramble took umbrage at my presuming to be wiser than he upon this occasion; and told me, that as he had always thought for himself in every occurrence in life, he would still use the same privilege, with my good leave.

When we returned to our inn, he closeted Lismahago; and having explained his grievance, desired that gentleman to go and demand satisfaction of lord Oxmington in his name.—The lieutenant charged himself with this commission, and immediately set out a horseback for his lordship's house, attended, at his own request, by my man Archy Macalpine, who had been used to military service; and truly, if Macalpine had been mounted upon an ass, this couple might have passed for the knight of La Mancha[4] and his 'squire Panza. It was not till after some demur that Lismahago obtained a private audience, at which he formally defied his lordship to single combat, in the name of Mr. Bramble, and desired him to appoint the time and place. Lord Oxmington was so confounded at this unexpected message, that he could not, for some time, make any articulate reply; but stood staring at the lieutenant with manifest marks of perturbation. At length, ringing a bell with great vehemence, he exclaimed, "What! a commoner send a challenge to a peer of the realm!—Privilege! privilege!—Here's a person brings me a challenge from the Welshman that dined at my table—An impudent fellow!—My wine is not yet out of his head."

The whole house was immediately in commotion.—Macalpine made a soldierly retreat with the two horses; but the captain was suddenly surrounded and disarmed by the footmen, whom a French valet de chambre headed in this exploit; his sword was passed through a close-stool,[5] and his person through the horse-pond.—In this plight he returned to the inn, half mad with his disgrace.—So violent was the rage of his indignation, that he mistook its object.—He wanted to quarrel with Mr. Bramble; he said, he had been dishonoured on his account, and he looked for reparation at his hands.—My uncle's back was up in a moment; and he desired him to explain his pretensions.—"Either compel lord Oxmington to give me satisfaction, (cried he) or give it me in your own person." "The latter part of the alternative is the most easy and expeditious (replied the 'squire, starting up): if you are disposed for a walk, I'll attend you this moment."

Here they were interrupted by Mrs. Tabby, who had overheard all that passed.——She now burst into the room, and running betwixt them, in great agitation, "Is this your regard for me, (said she to the lieutenant) to seek the life of my brother?" Lismahago, who seemed to grow cool as my uncle grew hot, assured her he had a very great respect for Mr. Bramble, but he had still more for his own honour, which had suffered pollution; but if that could be once purified, he should have no further cause of dissatisfaction.——The 'squire said, he should have thought it incumbent upon him to vindicate the lieutenant's honour; but, as he had now carved for himself, he might swallow and digest it as well as he could ——In a word, what betwixt the mediation of Mrs. Tabitha, the recollection of the captain, who perceived he had gone too far, and the remonstrances of your humble servant, who joined them at this juncture, those two originals were perfectly reconciled; and then we proceeded to deliberate upon the means of taking vengeance for the insults they had received from the petulant peer; for, until that aim should be accomplished, Mr. Bramble swore, with great emphasis, that he would not

---

4. Don Quixote.
5. The sword was considered to be the symbol of a man's honor, and passing it through a close-stool, or chamber-pot, would be a gross insult.

Lieut. Lismahago carries a Challenge to Lord Oxmington.

leave the inn where we now lodged, even if he should pass his Christmas on the spot.

In consequence of our deliberations, we next day, in the forenoon, proceeded in a body to his lordship's house, all of us, with our servants, including the coachman, mounted a-horseback, with our pistols loaded and ready primed.—Thus prepared for action, we paraded solemnly and slowly before his lordship's gate, which we passed three times in such a manner, that he could not but see us, and suspect the cause of our appearance.—After dinner we returned, and performed the same cavalcade, which was again repeated the morning following; but we had no occasion to persist in these manœuvres.——About noon, we were visited by the gentleman, at whose house we had first seen lord Oxmington. —He now came to make apologies in the name of his lordship, who declared he had no intention to give offence to my uncle, in practising what had been always the custom of his house; and that as for the indignities which had been put upon the officer, they were offered without his lordship's knowledge, at the instigation of his valet de chambre.—"If that be the case, (said my uncle, in a peremptory tone) I shall be contented with lord Oxmington's personal excuses; and I hope my friend will be satisfied with his lordship's turning that insolent rascal out of his service."—"Sir, (cried Lismahago) I must insist upon taking personal vengeance for the personal injuries I have sustained."

After some debate, the affair was adjusted in this manner.——His lordship, meeting us at our friend's house, declared he was sorry for what had happened; and that he had no intention to give umbrage.—The valet de chambre asked pardon of the lieutenant upon his knees, when Lismahago, to the astonishment of all present, gave him a violent kick on the face, which laid him on his back, exclaiming in a furious tone, "*Oui je te pardonne, gens foutre.*"[6]

Such was the fortunate issue of this perilous adventure, which threatened abundance of vexation to our family; for the 'squire is one of those who will sacrifice both life and fortune, rather than leave what they conceive to be the least speck or blemish upon their honour and reputation. His lordship had no sooner pronounced his apology, with a very bad grace, than he went away in some disorder, and, I dare say, he will never invite another Welchman to his table.

We forthwith quitted the field of this atchievement, in order to prosecute our journey; but we follow no determinate course.——We make small deviations, to see the remarkable towns, villas, and curiosities on each side of our route; so that we advance by slow steps towards the

6. The first part of this sentence is French for "Yes, I pardon thee," but the last two words are not clear. *Gens* can mean a certain category of persons, and *foutre* is the infinitive of a vulgar verb meaning "to have sexual intercourse with," but the combination does not make grammatical sense. Andre Parreaux, Lewis Knapp, and Denise Sanlaville have speculated that the two words may be a phonetic mistake for *jean-foutre*, "blockhead."

borders of Monmouthshire: but in the midst of these irregular motions, there is no abberration nor eccentricity in that affection with which I am, dear Wat,

Yours always,

Sept. 28.   J. MELFORD.

To Dr. LEWIS.

DEAR DICK,

At what time of life may a man think himself exempted from the necessity of sacrificing his repose to the punctilios of a contemptible world? I have been engaged in a ridiculous adventure, which I shall recount at meeting; and this, I hope, will not be much longer delayed, as we have now performed almost all our visits, and seen every thing that I think has any right to retard us in our journey homewards——A few days ago, understanding by accident, that my old friend Baynard was in the country, I would not pass so near his habitation without paying him a visit, though our correspondence had been interrupted for a long course of years.

I felt myself very sensibly affected by the ideas of our past intimacy, as we approached the place where we had spent so many happy days together; but when we arrived at the house, I could not recognize any one of those objects, which had been so deeply impressed upon my remembrance——The tall oaks that shaded the avenue, had been cut down, and the iron gates at the end of it removed, together with the high wall that surrounded the court yard. The house itself, which was formerly a convent of Cistercian monks, had a venerable appearance; and along the front that looked into the garden, was a stone gallery, which afforded me many an agreeable walk, when I was disposed to be contemplative——Now the old front is covered with a screen of modern architecture; so that all without is Grecian, and all within Gothic——As for the garden, which was well stocked with the best fruit which England could produce, there is not now the least vestage remaining of trees, walls, or hedges——Nothing appears but a naked circus of loose sand, with a dry bason and a leaden triton in the middle.

You must know, that Baynard, at his father's death, had a clear estate of fifteen hundred pounds a-year, and was in other respects extremely well qualified to make a respectable figure in the commonwealth; but, what with some excesses of youth, and the expence of a contested election, he in a few years found himself encumbered with a debt of ten thousand pounds, which he resolved to discharge by means of a prudent marriage —He accordingly married a miss Thomson, whose fortune amounted to double the sum that he owed—She was the daughter of a citizen, who had failed in trade; but her fortune came by an uncle, who died in the East-Indies—Her own parents being dead, she lived with a maiden aunt, who had superintended her education; and, in all appearance, was well enough qualified for the usual purposes of the married state—Her virtues, however, stood rather upon a negative, than a positive foundation—She was neither proud, insolent, nor capricious, nor given to scandal, nor addicted to gaming, nor inclined to gallantry—She could read, and write, and dance, and sing, and play upon the harpsichord, and smatter French, and take a hand at whist and ombre; but even these accomplishments she possessed by halves—She excelled in nothing. Her conversation was flat, her stile mean, and her expression embarrassed —In a word, her character was totally insipid. Her person was not disagreeable; but there was nothing graceful in her address, nor engaging in her manners; and she was so ill qualified to do the honours of the house, that when she sat at the head of the table, one was always looking for the mistress of the family in some other place.

Baynard had flattered himself, that it would be no difficult matter to mould such a subject after his own fashion, and that she would chearfully enter into his views, which were wholly turned to domestic happiness. He proposed to reside always in the country, of which he was fond to a degree of enthusiasm, to cultivate his estate, which was very improvable; to enjoy the exercise of rural diversions; to maintain an intimacy of correspondence with some friends that were settled in his neighbourhood; to keep a comfortable house, without suffering his expence to exceed the limits of his income; and to find pleasure and employment for his wife in the management and avocations of her own family——This, however, was a visionary scheme, which he never was able to realize. His wife was as ignorant as a new-born babe of every thing that related to the conduct of a family; and she had no idea of a country life—Her understanding did not reach so far as to comprehend the first principles of discretion; and, indeed, if her capacity had been better than it was, her natural indolence would not have permitted her to abandon a certain routine, to which she had been habituated. She had not taste enough to relish any rational enjoyment; but her ruling passion was vanity, not that species which arises from self-conceit of superior accomplishments, but that which is of a bastard and idiot nature, excited by shew and ostentation, which implies not even the least consciousness of any personal merit.

The nuptial peal of noise and nonsense being rung out in all the usual changes, Mr. Baynard thought it high time to make her acquainted with the particulars of the plan which he had projected——He told her that his fortune, though sufficient to afford all the comforts of life, was not ample enough to command all the superfluities of pomp and pageantry, which, indeed, were equally absurd and intolerable—He therefore hoped she would have no objection to their leaving London in the spring, when he would take the opportunity to dismiss some unnecessary domestics, whom he had hired for the occasion of their marriage—She heard him in silence, and after some pause, "So, (said she) I am to be buried in the country!" He was so confounded at this reply, that he could not speak for some minutes: at length he told her, he was much mortified to find he had proposed any thing that was disagreeable to her ideas—"I am sure (added he) I meant nothing more than to lay down a comfortable plan of living within the bounds of our fortune, which is but moderate." "Sir, (said she) you are the best judge of your own affairs—My fortune, I know, does not exceed twenty thousand pounds——Yet, even with that pittance, I might have had a husband who would not have begrudged me a house in London—" "Good God! my dear, (cried poor Baynard, in the utmost agitation) you don't think me so sordid—I only hinted what I thought —But, I don't pretend to impose—" "Yes, sir, (resumed the lady) it is your prerogative to command, and my duty to obey—"

So saying, she burst into tears and retired to her chamber, where she was joined by her aunt—He endeavoured to recollect himself, and act with vigour of mind on this occasion; but was betrayed by the tenderness of his nature, which was the greatest defect of his constitution. He found the aunt in tears, and the niece in a fit, which held her the best part of eight hours, at the expiration of which, she began to talk incoherently about *death* and her *dear busband,* who had sat by her all this time, and now pressed her hand to his lips, in a transport of grief and penitence for the offence he had given—From thence forward, he carefully avoided mentioning the country; and they continued to be sucked deeper and deeper into the vortex of extravagance and dissipation, leading what is called a fashionable life in town—About the latter end of July, however, Mrs. Baynard, in order to exhibit a proof of conjugal obedience, desired of her own accord, that they might pay a visit to his country house, as there was no company left in London. He would have excused himself from this excursion, which was no part of the œconomical plan he had proposed; but she insisted upon making this sacrifice to his taste and prejudices, and away they went with such an equipage as astonished the whole country—All that remained of the season was engrossed by receiving and returning visits in the neighbourhood; and, in this inter-course, it was discovered that sir John Chickwell had a house-steward and one footman in livery more than the complement of Mr. Baynard's household. This remark was made by the aunt at table, and assented to by the husband, who observed that sir John Chickwell might very well afford to keep more servants than were found in the family of a man who had not half his fortune. Mrs. Baynard ate no supper that evening; but was seized with a violent fit, which completed her triumph over the spirit of her consort. The two supernumerary servants were added—The family plate was sold for old silver, and a new service procured;

fashionable furniture was provided, and the whole house turned topsy turvy.

At their return to London, in the beginning of winter, he, with a heavy heart, communicated these particulars to me in confidence. Before his marriage, he had introduced me to the lady as his particular friend; and I now offered in that character, to lay before her the necessity of reforming her œconomy, if she had any regard to the interest of her own family, or complaisance for the inclinations of her husband—But Baynard declined my offer, on the supposition that his wife's nerves were too delicate to bear expostulation; and that it would only serve to overwhelm her with such distress as would make himself miserable.

Baynard is a man of spirit, and had she proved a termagant, he would have known how to deal with her; but, either by accident or instinct, she fastened upon the weak side of his soul, and held it so fast, that he has been in subjection ever since—I afterwards advised him to carry her abroad to France or Italy, where he might gratify her vanity for half the expence it cost him in England; and this advice he followed accordingly —She was agreeably flattered with the idea of seeing and knowing foreign parts, and foreign fashions; of being presented to sovereigns, and living familiarly with princes. She forthwith seized the hint which I had thrown out on purpose, and even pressed Mr. Baynard to hasten his departure; so that in a few weeks they crossed the sea to France, with a moderate train, still including the aunt; who was her bosom counsellor, and abetted her in all her opposition to her husband's will——Since that period, I have had little or no opportunity to renew our former correspondence—All that I knew of his transactions, amounted to no more than that after an absence of two years, they returned so little improved in œconomy, that they launched out into new oceans of extravagance, which, at length, obliged him to mortgage his estate—By this time she had bore him three children, of which the last only survives, a puny boy of twelve or thirteen, who will be ruined in his education by the indulgence of his mother.

As for Baynard, neither his own good sense, nor the dread of indigence, nor the consideration of his children, has been of force sufficient to stimulate him into the resolution of breaking at once the shameful spell by which he seems enchanted——With a taste capable of the most refined enjoyment, a heart glowing with all the warmth of friendship and humanity, and a disposition strongly turned to the more rational pleasures of a retired and country life, he is hurried about in a perpetual tumult, amidst a mob of beings pleased with rattles, baubles, and gew-gaws, so void of sense and distinction, that even the most acute philosophy would find it a very hard task to discover for what wise purpose of providence they were created—Friendship is not to be found; nor can the amusements for which he sighs be enjoyed within the rotation of absurdity, to which he is doomed for life. He has long resigned all views of improving his fortune by management and attention to the exercise of husbandry, in which he delighted; and as to domestic happiness, not the least glimpse of hope remains to amuse his imagination. Thus blasted in all his prospects, he could not fail to be overwhelmed with melancholy and chagrin, which have preyed upon his health and spirits in such a manner, that he is now threatened with a consumption.

I have given you a sketch of the man, whom the other day I went to visit—At the gate we found a great number of powdered lacquies, but no civility—After we had sat a considerable time in the coach, we were told, that Mr. Baynard had rode out, and that his lady was dressing; but we were introduced to a parlour, so very fine and delicate, that in all appearance it was designed to be seen only, not inhabited. The chairs and couches were carved, gilt, and covered with rich damask, so smooth and slick, that they looked as if they had never been sat upon. There was no carpet on the floor; but the boards were rubbed and waxed in such a manner, that we could not walk, but were obliged to slide along them; and as for the stove, it was too bright and polished to be polluted with sea-coal, or stained by the smoke of any gross material fire—When we had remained above half an hour sacrificing to the inhospitable powers in this *temple of cold reception*, my friend Baynard arrived, and understanding we were in the house, made his appearance, so meagre, yellow, and dejected, that I really should not have known him, had I met with him in any other place——Running up to me, with great eagerness, he strained me in his embrace, and his heart was so full, that for some minutes he could not speak—Having saluted us all round, he perceived our uncomfortable situation, and conducting us into another apartment, which had fire in the chimney, called for chocolate——Then, withdrawing, he returned with a compliment from his wife, and, in the mean time, presented his son Harry, a shambling, blear-eyed boy, in the habit of a hussar; very rude, forward, and impertinent—His father would have sent him to a boarding-school, but his mamma and aunt would not hear of his lying out of the house; so that there was a clergyman engaged as his tutor in the family.

As it was but just turned of twelve, and the whole house was in commotion to prepare a formal entertainment, I foresaw it would be late before we dined, and proposed a walk to Mr. Baynard, that we might converse together freely. In the course of this perambulation, when I expressed some surprise that he had returned so soon from Italy, he gave me to understand, that his going abroad had not at all answered the purpose, for which he left England; that although the expence of living was not so great in Italy as at home, respect being had to the same rank of life in both countries, it had been found necessary for him to lift himself above his usual stile, that he might be on some footing with the counts, marquises, and cavalieres, with whom he kept company——He was obliged to hire a great number of servants, to take off a great variety of rich cloaths, and to keep a sumptuous table for the fashionable scorocconi[7] of the country; who, without a consideration of this kind, would not have payed any attention to an untitled foreigner, let his family or fortune be ever so respectable—Besides, Mrs. Baynard was continually surrounded by a train of expensive loungers, under the denominations of language-masters, musicians, painters, and ciceroni;[8] and had actually fallen into the disease of buying pictures and antiques upon her own judgment, which was far from being infallible—At length she met with an affront, which gave her a disgust to Italy, and drove her back to England with some precipitation. By means of frequenting the dutchess of B——'s[9] conversazione,[1] while her grace was at Rome, Mrs. Baynard became acquainted with all the fashionable people of that city, and was admitted to their assemblies without scruple—Thus favoured, she conceived too great an idea of her own importance, and when the duchess left Rome, resolved to have a conversazione that should leave the Romans no room to regret her grace's departure. She provided hands for a musical entertainment, and sent biglietti[2] of invitation to every person of distinction; but not one Roman of the female sex appeared at her assembly—She was that night seized with a violent fit, and kept her bed three days, at the expiration of which she declared that the air of Italy would be the ruin of her constitution. In order to prevent this catastrophe, she was speedily removed to Geneva, from whence they returned to England by the way of Lyons and Paris. By the time they arrived at Calais, she had purchased such a quantity of silks, stuffs, and laces, that it was necessary to hire a vessel to smuggle them over, and this vessel was taken by a custom-house cutter; so that they lost the whole cargo, which had cost them above eight hundred pounds.

It now appeared, that her travels had produced no effect upon her, but that of making her more expensive and fantastic than ever:—She affected to lead the fashion, not only in point of female dress, but in every article of taste and connoisseurship. She made a drawing of the new facade to the house in the country; she pulled up the trees, and pulled down the walls of the garden, so as to let in the easterly wind, which Mr. Baynard's ancestors had been at great pains to exclude. To shew her taste in laying out ground; she seized into her own hand a farm of two hundred acres, about a mile from the house, which she parcelled out into walks and shrubberies, having a great bason in the middle, into which she poured a whole stream that turned two mills, and afforded the best trout in the country. The bottom of the bason, however, was so ill secured, that it

---

7. A misspelling of the Italian *scrocconi*, "spongers" or "parasites."
8. Guides to the antiquities.
9. David Herbert has speculated that this could be the Duchess of Bedford, Gertrude Russell, but there is little evidence to support any identification.
1. Reception or assembly.
2. Tickets or notes.

would not hold the water which strained through the earth, and made a bog of the whole plantation: in a word, the ground which formerly payed him one hundred and fifty pounds a year, now cost him two hundred pounds a year to keep it in tolerable order, over and above the first expence of trees, shrubs, flowers, turf, and gravel. There was not an inch of garden ground left about the house, nor a tree that produced fruit of any kind; nor did he raise a truss of hay, or a bushel of oats for his horses, nor had he a single cow to afford milk for his tea; far less did he ever dream of feeding his own mutton, pigs, and poultry: every article of house-keeping, even the most inconsiderable, was brought from the next market town, at the distance of five miles, and thither they sent a courier every morning to fetch hot rolls for breakfast. In short, Baynard fairly owned that he spent double his income, and that in a few years he should be obliged to sell his estate for the payment of his creditors. He said his wife had such delicate nerves, and such imbecillity of spirit, that she could neither bear remonstrance, be it ever so gentle, nor practise any scheme of retrenchment, even if she perceived the necessity of such a measure. He had therefore ceased struggling against the stream, and endeavoured to reconcile himself to ruin, by reflecting that his child at least, would inherit his mother's fortune, which was secured to him by the contract of marriage.

The detail which he gave me of his affairs, filled me at once with grief and indignation. I inveighed bitterly against the indiscretion of his wife, and reproached him with his unmanly acquiescence under the absurd tyranny which she exerted. I exhorted him to recollect his resolution, and make one effectual effort to disengage himself from a thraldom, equally shameful and pernicious. I offered him all the assistance in my power. I undertook to regulate his affairs, and even to bring about a reformation in his family, if he would only authorise me to execute the plan I should form for his advantage. I was so affected by the subject, that I could not help mingling tears with my remonstrances, and Baynard was so penetrated with these marks of my affection, that he lost all power of utterance. He pressed me to his breast with great emotion, and wept in silence. At length he exclaimed, "Friendship is undoubtedly the most precious balm of life! Your words, dear Bramble, have in a great measure recalled me from an abyss of despondence, in which I have been long overwhelmed—I will, upon honour, make you acquainted with a distinct state of my affairs, and, as far as I am able to go, will follow the course you prescribe. But there are certain lengths which my nature——The truth is, there are tender connexions, of which a bachelor has no idea—Shall I own my weakness? I cannot bear the thoughts of making that woman uneasy—" "And yet, (cried I) she has seen you unhappy for a series of years—unhappy from her misconduct, without ever shewing the least inclination to alleviate your distress—" "Nevertheless (said he) I am persuaded she loves me with the most warm affection; but these are incongruities in the composition of the human mind which I hold to be inexplicable."

I was shocked at his infatuation, and changed the subject, after we had agreed to maintain a close correspondence for the future—He then gave me to understand, that he had two neighbours, who, like himself, were driven by their wives at full speed, in the high road to bankruptcy and ruin. All the three husbands were of dispositions very different from each other, and, according to this variation, their consorts were admirably suited to the purpose of keeping them all three in subjection. The views of the ladies were exactly the same. They vied in grandeur, that is, in ostentation, with the wife of Sir Charles Chickwell,[3] who had four times their fortune; and she again piqued herself upon making an equal figure with a neighbouring peeress, whose revenue trebled her own. Here then was the fable of the frog and the ox, realized in four different instances within the same county: one large fortune, and three moderate estates, in a fair way of being burst by the inflation of female vanity; and in three of these instances, three different forms of female tyranny were exercised. Mr. Baynard was subjugated by practising upon the tenderness of his nature. Mr. Milksan, being of a timorous disposition, truckled to the insolence of a termagant. Mr. Sowerby, who was of a temper neither to be moved by fits, nor driven by menaces, had the fortune to be fitted with a helpmate, who assailed him with the weapons of irony and satire; sometimes sneering in the way of compliment; sometimes throwing out sarcastic comparisons, implying reproaches upon his want of taste, spirit, and generosity: by which means she stimulated his passions from one act of extravagance to another, just as the circumstances of her vanity required.

All these three ladies have at this time the same number of horses, carriages, and servants in and out of livery; the same variety of dress; the same quantity of plate and china; the like ornaments in furniture; and in their entertainments they endeavour to exceed one another in the variety, delicacy, and expence of their dishes. I believe it will be found upon enquiry, that nineteen out of twenty, who are ruined by extravagance, fall a sacrifice to the ridiculous pride and vanity of silly women, whose parts are held in contempt by the very men whom they pillage and enslave. Thank heaven, Dick, that among all the follies and weaknesses of human nature, I have not yet fallen into that of matrimony.

After Baynard and I had discussed all these matters at leisure, we returned towards the house, and met Jery with our two women, who had come forth to take the air, as the lady of the mansion had not yet made her appearance. In short, Mrs. Baynard did not produce herself, till about a quarter of an hour before dinner was upon the table. Then her husband

---

3. Just above, p. 266, Smollett has Matt refer to this fictional knight as "sir John Chickwell," so one or the other reference is a slip.

brought her into the parlour, accompanied by her aunt and son, and she received us with a coldness of reserve sufficient to freeze the very soul of hospitality. Though she knew I had been the intimate friend of her husband, and had often seen me with him in London, she shewed no marks of recognition or regard, when I addressed myself to her in the most friendly terms of salutation. She did not even express the common complement of, *I am glad to see you*; or, *I hope you have enjoyed your health since we had the pleasure of seeing you*; or some such words of course: nor did she once open her mouth in the way of welcome to my sister and my niece: but sat in silence like a statue, with an aspect of insensibility. Her aunt, the model upon which she had been formed, was indeed the very essence of insipid formality: but the boy was very pert and impudent, and prated without ceasing.

At dinner, the lady maintained the same ungracious indifference, never speaking but in whispers to her aunt; and as to the repast, it was made up of a parcel of kickshaws,[4] contrived by a French cook, without one substantial article adapted to the satisfaction of an English appetite. The pottage[5] was little better than bread soaked in dishwashings, lukewarm. The ragouts looked as if they had been once eaten and half digested: the fricassees[6] were involved in a nasty yellow poultice;[7] and the rotis[8] were scorched and stinking, for the honour of the fumet.[9] The desert consisted of faded fruit and iced froth, a good emblem of our landlady's character; the table-beer was sour, the water foul, and the wine vapid; but there was a parade of plate and china, and a powdered lacquey stood behind every chair, except those of the master and mistress of the house, who were served by two valets dressed like gentlemen. We dined in a large old Gothic parlour, which was formerly the hall. It was now paved with marble, and, notwithstanding the fire, which had been kindled about an hour, struck me with such a chill sensation, that when I entered it the teeth chattered in my jaws—In short, every thing was cold, comfortless, and disgusting, except the looks of my friend Baynard, which declared the warmth of his affection and humanity.

After dinner we withdrew into another apartment, where the boy began to be impertinently troublesome to my niece Liddy. He wanted a play-fellow, forsooth; and would have romped with her, had she encouraged his advances—He was even so impudent as to snatch a kiss, at which she changed countenance, and seemed uneasy; and though his father checked him for the rudeness of his behaviour, he became so

---

4. This English word derives from the French *quelque chose*, "something," and is used in this context to indicate contempt for a fancy but insubstantial dish.
5. A soup, especially a thick one, but used sarcastically here, with perhaps an allusion to Esau's sale of his birthright to Jacob for a "mess of pottage" (Genesis 25).
6. Ragouts and fricassees are dishes of meat or

fowl cut into small pieces and prepared with spices or sauces.
7. A soft mass of material pressed to part of the body as a treatment for injury or infection. Matt uses the term metaphorically.
8. Roast meat; another borrowed French word.
9. The term used to describe the smell of game or other meat when it is "high" or well-aged.

outrageous as to thrust his hand in her bosom: an insult to which she did not tamely submit, though one of the mildest creatures upon earth. Her eyes sparkling with resentment, she started up, and lent him such a box in the ear, as sent him staggering to the other side of the room.

"Miss Melford, (cried his father) you have treated him with the utmost propriety—I am only sorry that the impertinence of any child of mine should have occasioned this exertion of your spirit, which I cannot but applaud and admire." His wife was so far from assenting to the candour of his apology, that she rose from table, and, taking her son by the hand, "Come, child, (said she) your father cannot abide you." So saying, she retired with this hopeful youth, and was followed by her gouvernante: but neither the one nor the other deigned to take the least notice of the company.

Baynard was exceedingly disconcerted; but I perceived his uneasiness was tinctured with resentment, and derived a good omen from this discovery. I ordered the horses to be put to the carriage, and, though he made some efforts to detain us all night, I insisted upon leaving the house immediately; but, before I went away, I took an opportunity of speaking to him again in private. I said every thing I could recollect, to animate his endeavours in shaking off those shameful trammels. I made no scruple to declare, that his wife was unworthy of that tender complaisance which he had shewn for her foibles: that she was dead to all the genuine sentiments of conjugal affection; insensible of her own honour and interest, and seemingly destitute of common sense and reflection. I conjured him to remember what he owed to his father's house, to his own reputation, and to his family, including even this unreasonable woman herself, who was driving on blindly to her own destruction. I advised him to form a plan for retrenching superfluous expence, and try to convince the aunt of the necessity for such a reformation, that she might gradually prepare her niece for its execution; and I exhorted him to turn that disagreeable piece of formality out of the house, if he should find her averse to his proposal.

Here he interrupted me with a sigh, observing that such a step would undoubtedly be fatal to Mrs. Baynard—"I shall lose all patience, (cried I), to hear you talk so weakly—Mrs. Baynard's fits will never hurt her constitution. I believe in my conscience they are all affected: I am sure she has no feeling for your distresses; and, when you are ruined, she will appear to have no feeling for her own." Finally, I took his word and honour, that he would make an effort, such as I had advised; that he would form a plan of œconomy, and, if he found it impracticable without my assistance, he would come to Bath in the winter, where I promised to give him the meeting, and contribute all in my power to the retrieval of his affairs—With this mutual engagement we parted; and I shall think myself supremely happy, if, by my means, a worthy man, whom I love and esteem, can be saved from misery, disgrace, and despair.

I have only one friend more to visit in this part of the country, but he is of a complexion very different from that of Baynard. You have heard me mention Sir Thomas Bullford,[1] whom I knew in Italy. He is now become a country gentleman; but, being disabled by the gout from enjoying any amusement abroad, he entertains himself within doors, by keeping open house for all comers, and playing upon the oddities and humours of his company: but he himself is generally the greatest original at his table. He is very good-humoured, talks much, and laughs without ceasing. I am told that all the use he makes of his understanding at present, is to excite mirth, by exhibiting his guests in ludicrous attitudes. I know not how far we may furnish him with entertainment of this kind, but I am resolved to beat up his quarters, partly with a view to laugh with the knight himself, and partly to pay my respects to his lady, a good-natured sensible woman, with whom he lives upon very easy terms, although she has not had the good fortune to bring him an heir to his estate.

And now, dear Dick, I must tell you for your comfort, that you are the only man upon earth to whom I would presume to send such a long-winded epistle, which I could not find in my heart to curtail, because the subject interested the warmest passions of my heart; neither will I make any other apology to a correspondent who has been so long accustomed to the impertinence of

Sept. 30.   MATT. BRAMBLE.

To Sir WATKIN PHILLIPS, Bar[t]. at Oxon.

DEAR KNIGHT,

I believe, there is something mischievious in my disposition, for nothing diverts me so much as to see certain characters tormented with false terrors.——We last night lodged at the house of sir Thomas Bullford, an old friend of my uncle, a jolly fellow, of moderate intellects, who, in spite of the gout, which hath lamed him, is resolved to be merry to the last; and mirth he has a particular knack in extracting from his guests, let their humour be never so caustic or refractory.——Besides our company, there was in the house a fat-headed justice of the peace, called Frogmore, and a country practitioner in surgery, who seemed to be our landlord's chief companion and confidant.——We found the knight sitting on a couch, with his crutches by his side, and his feet supported on cushions; but he received us with a hearty welcome, and seemed greatly rejoiced at our arrival.——After tea, we were entertained with a sonata on the harpsichord by lady Bullford, who sung and played to admiration; but

---

1. It has been suggested that this character was based on Thomas Gatehouse, son-in-law to William Huggins, but there is little evidence to support the assertion.

sir Thomas seemed to be a little asinine in the article of ears, though he affected to be in raptures, and begged his wife to favour us with an *arietta*[2] of her own composing.—This *arietta*, however, she no sooner began to perform, than he and the justice fell asleep; but the moment she ceased playing, the knight waked snorting, and exclaimed, "O *cara*! what d'ye think, gentlemen? Will you talk any more of your Pargolesi[3] and your Corelli?"[4]—At the same time, he thrust his tongue in one cheek, and leered with one eye at the doctor and me, who sat on his left hand. —He concluded the pantomime with a loud laugh, which he could command at all times extempore.—Notwithstanding his disorder, he did not do penance at supper, nor did he ever refuse his glass when the toast went round, but rather encouraged a quick circulation, both by precept and example.

I soon perceived the doctor had made himself very necessary to the baronet.—He was the whetstone of his wit, the butt of his satire, and his operator in certain experiments of humour, which were occasionally tried upon strangers.—Justice Frogmore was an excellent subject for this species of philosophy; sleek and corpulent, solemn and shallow, he had studied Burn[5] with uncommon application, but he studied nothing so much as the art of living (that is, eating) well.—This fat buck had often afforded good sport to our landlord; and he was frequently started with tolerable success, in the course of this evening; but the baronet's appetite for ridicule seemed to be chiefly excited by the appearance, address, and conversation of Lismahago, whom he attempted in all the different modes of exposition; but he put me in mind of a contest that I once saw betwixt a young hound and an old hedge-hog—The dog turned him over and over, and bounced, and barked, and mumbled; but as often as he attempted to bite, he felt a prickle in his jaws, and recoiled in manifest confusion:—The captain, when left to himself, will not fail to turn his ludicrous side to the company, but if any man attempts to force him into that attitude, he becomes stubborn as a mule, and unmanageable as an elephant unbroke.

Divers tolerable jokes were cracked upon the justice, who ate a most unconscionable supper, and, among other things, a large plate of broiled mushrooms, which he had no sooner swallowed than the doctor observed, with great gravity, that they were of the kind called *champignons*, which in some constitutions had a poisonous effect.—Mr. Frogmore, startled at this remark, asked, in some confusion, why he had not been so kind as to give him that notice sooner.—He answered, that he took it for granted, by his eating them so heartily, that he was used to the dish; but

2. A little aria, or melody for accompanied voice.
3. Giovanni Battista Pergolesi (1710–36), an Italian composer.
4. Arcangelo Corelli (1653–1713), an Italian composer and musician.

5. The standard work of reference for country magistrates, *The Justice of the Peace and Parish Officer* (1755), was written by Richard Burn (1709–85).

as he seemed to be under some apprehension, he prescribed a bumper of plague water,[6] which the justice drank off immediately, and retired to rest, not without marks of terror and disquiet.

At midnight we were shewn to our different chambers, and in half an hour, I was fast asleep in bed; but about three o'clock in the morning I was waked with a dismal cry of *Fire!* and starting up, ran to the window in my shirt.—The night was dark and stormy; and a number of people half-dressed ran backwards and forwards thro' the court-yard, with links and lanthorns, seemingly in the utmost hurry and trepidation.—Slipping on my cloaths in a twinkling, I ran down stairs, and, upon inquiry, found the fire was confined to a back-stair, which led to a detached apartment where Lismahago lay.——By this time, the lieutenant was alarmed by bawling at his window, which was in the second story, but he could not find his cloaths in the dark, and his room-door was locked on the outside.——The servants called to him, that the house had been robbed; that, without all doubt, the villains had taken away his cloaths, fastened the door, and set the house on fire, for the stair-case was in flames.—In this dilemma the poor lieutenant ran about the room naked like a squirrel in a cage, popping out his head at the window between whiles, and imploring assistance.—At length, the knight in person was brought out in his chair, attended by my uncle and all the family, including our aunt Tabitha, who screamed, and cried, and tore her hair, as if she had been distracted.—Sir Thomas had already ordered his people to bring a long ladder, which was applied to the captain's window, and now he exorted him earnestly to descend.—There was no need of much rhetoric to persuade Lismahago, who forthwith made his exit by the window, roaring all the time to the people below to hold fast the ladder.

Notwithstanding the gravity of the occasion, it was impossible to behold this scene without being seized with an inclination to laugh. The rueful aspect of the lieutenant in his shirt, with a quilted night-cap fastened under his chin, and his long lank limbs and posteriors exposed to the wind, made a very picturesque appearance, when illumined by the links and torches which the servants held up to light him in his descent. —All the company stood round the ladder, except the knight, who sat in his chair, exclaiming from time to time, "Lord have mercy upon us! —save the gentleman's life!—mind your footing, dear captain!—softly! —stand fast!—clasp the ladder with both hands!—there!—well done, my dear boy!—O bravo!—an old soldier for ever!—bring a blanket——bring a warm blanket to comfort his poor carcase——warm the bed in the green room——give me your hand, dear captain—I'm rejoiced to see thee safe and sound with all my heart." Lismahago was received at the foot of the ladder by his innamorata, who snatching a blanket from one of the maids, wrapped it about his body; two men-servants took him under

6. Usually an infusion of herbs and roots in wine to ward off the plague.

the arms, and a female conducted him to the green room, still accompanied by Mrs. Tabitha, who saw him fairly put to bed.—During this whole transaction, he spoke not a syllable, but looked exceeding grim, sometimes at one, sometimes at another of the spectators, who now adjourned in a body to the parlour where we had supped, every one surveying another with marks of astonishment and curiosity.

The knight being seated in an easy chair, seized my uncle by the hand, and bursting into a long and loud laugh, "Matt, (cried he) crown me with oak, or ivy, or laurel, or parsley, or what you will, and acknowledge this to be a *coup de maitre*[7] in the way of waggery—ha, ha, ha!—Such a *camisicata, scagliata, beffata!*—O, *che roba!*[8]—O, what a subject!——O, what *caricatura!*—O, for a Rosa,[9] a Rembrandt,[1] a Schalken![2]—Zooks, I'll give a hundred guineas to have it painted!——what a fine descent from the cross, or ascent to the gallows!—what lights and shadows! —what a groupe below!—what expression above!—what an aspect!—did you mind the aspect?—ha, ha, ha!—and the limbs, and the muscles —every toe denoted terror!—ha, ha, ha!——then the blanket!—O, what *costume!* St. Andrew! St. Lazarus! St. Barrabas!—ha, ha, ha!" "After all then, (cried Mr. Bramble very gravely) this was no more than a false alarm.—We have been frightened out of our beds, and almost out of our senses, for the joke's sake." "Ay, and such a joke! (cried our landlord) such a farce! such a *denouement!*[3] such a *catastrophe!*"[4]

"Have a little patience (replied our 'squire); we are not yet come to the *catastrophe*; and pray God it may not turn out a tragedy instead of a farce. ——The captain is one of those saturnine subjects, who have no idea of humour.—He never laughs in his own person; nor can he bear that other people should laugh at his expence—Besides, if the subject had been properly chosen, the joke was too severe in all conscience." " 'Sdeath! (cried the knight) I could not have bated him an ace had he been my own father; and as for the subject, such another does not present itself once in half a century." Here Mrs. Tabitha interposing, and bridling up, declared, she did not see that Mr. Lismahago was a fitter subject for ridicule than the knight himself; and that she was very much afraid, he would very soon find he had mistaken his man.——The baronet was a good deal disconcerted by this intimation, saying, that he must be a Goth and a barbarian, if he did not enter into the spirit of such a happy and humorous contrivance.—He begged, however, that Mr. Bramble and his sister would bring him to reason; and this request was reinforced by lady

7. Master-stroke.
8. Sir Thomas's Italian is confused but probably means something like: "Such a night sally, what a scaling operation, what a practical joke! Oh, what a thing!"
9. Salvator Rosa (c. 1615–73) was an artist whose works were much in vogue in England in the eighteenth century.
1. Rembrandt van Rijn (1606–69), the great Dutch artist.
2. Godfried Schalken (1643–1706), another Dutch artist.
3. This word has been naturalized into English from French and means the part of the drama in which the plot is resolved.
4. Another word for denouement, but of Greek origin and also carrying the modern meaning of disaster.

Bullford, who did not fail to read the baronet a lecture upon his indiscretion, which lecture he received with submission on one side of his face, and a leer upon the other.

We now went to bed for the second time; and before I got up, my uncle had visited Lismahago in the green room, and used such arguments with him, that when we met in the parlour he seemed to be quite appeased. —He received the knight's apology with a good grace, and even professed himself pleased at finding he had contributed to the diversion of the company.——Sir Thomas shook him by the hand, laughing heartily; and then desired a pinch of snuff, in token of perfect reconciliation—The lieutenant, putting his hand in his waistcoat pocket, pulled out, instead of his own Scotch mull,[5] a very fine gold snuff box, which he no sooner perceived than he said, "Here is a small mistake." "No mistake at all (cried the baronet): a fair exchange is no robbery.—Oblige me so far, captain, as to let me keep your mull as a memorial." "Sir, (said the lieutenant) the mull is much at your service; but this machine I can by no means retain.—It looks like compounding a sort of felony in the code of honour.—Besides, I don't know but there may be another joke in this conveyance; and I don't find myself disposed to be brought upon the stage again.——I won't presume to make free with your pockets, but I beg you will put it up again with your own hand."——So saying, with a certain austerity of aspect, he presented the snuff-box to the knight, who received it in some confusion, and restored the mull, which he would by no means keep, except on the terms of exchange.

This transaction was like to give a grave cast to the conversation, when my uncle took notice that Mr. Justice Frogmore had not made his appearance either at the night-alarm, or now at the general rendezvous. The baronet hearing Frogmore mentioned, "Odso! (cried he) I had forgot the justice.—Pr'ythee, doctor, go and bring him out of his kennel." —Then laughing till his sides were well shaken, he said he would shew the captain, that he was not the only person of the drama exhibited for the entertainment of the company. As to the night-scene, it could not affect the justice, who had been purposely lodged in the farther end of the house, remote from the noise, and lulled with a dose of opium into the bargain. In a few minutes, Mr. Justice was led into the parlour in his night-cap and loose morning gown, rolling his head from side to side, and groaning piteously all the way.—"Jesu! neighbour Frogmore, (exclaimed the baronet) what is the matter?—you look as if you was not a man for this world.——Set him down softly on the couch——poor gentleman!—Lord have mercy upon us!—What makes him so pale, and yellow, and bloated?" "Oh, sir Thomas! (cried the justice) I doubt 'tis all over with me ——Those mushrooms I eat at your table have done my business——ah!

---

5. Snuff-box in Scottish usage.

oh! hey!" "Now the Lord forbid! (said the other)—what! man, have a good heart.—How does thy stomach feel?—hah?"

To this interrogation he made no reply, but throwing aside his night gown, discovered that his waistcoat would not meet upon his belly by five good inches at least. "Heaven protect us all! (cried sir Thomas)—what a melancholy spectacle!—never did I see a man so suddenly swelled, but when he was either just dead, or just dying.——Doctor, can'st thou do nothing for this poor object?" "I don't think the case is quite desperate (said the surgeon), but I would advise Mr. Frogmore to settle his affairs with all expedition; the parson may come and pray by him, while I prepare a glyster⁶ and an emetic draught."⁷ The justice, rolling his languid eyes, ejaculated with great fervency, "Lord, have mercy upon us! Christ, have mercy upon us!"——Then he begged the surgeon, in the name of God, to dispatch—"As for my worldly affairs, (said he) they are all settled but one mortgage, which must be left to my heirs—but my poor soul! my poor soul! what will become of my poor soul?—miserable sinner that I am!" "Nay, pr'ythee, my dear boy, compose thyself (resumed the knight); consider the mercy of heaven is infinite; thou can'st not have any sins of a very deep dye on thy conscience, or the devil's in't." "Name not the devil (exclaimed the terrified Frogmore), I have more sins to answer for than the world dreams of.—Ah! friend, I have been sly—sly—damn'd sly!——Send for the parson without loss of time, and put me to bed, for I am posting to eternity."—He was accordingly raised from the couch, and supported by two servants, who led him back to his room; but before he quitted the parlour, he intreated the good company to assist him with their prayers.—He added, "Take warning by me, who am suddenly cut off in my prime, like a flower of the field; and God forgive you, sir Thomas, for suffering such poisonous trash to be eaten at your table."

He was no sooner removed out of hearing, than the baronet abandoned himself to a violent fit of laughing, in which he was joined by the greatest part of the company; but we could hardly prevent the good lady from going to undeceive the patient, by discovering, that while he slept his waistcoat had been straitened by the contrivance of the surgeon; and that the disorder in his stomach and bowels was occasioned by some antimonial wine,⁸ which he had taken over night, under the denomination of plague-water.——She seemed to think that his apprehension might put an end to his life: the knight swore he was no such chicken, but a tough old rogue, that would live long enough to plague all his neighbours. —Upon enquiry, we found his character did not intitle him to much compassion or respect, and therefore we let our landlord's humour take

6. An enema.
7. A drink to induce vomiting.

8. Wine treated with a compound of antimony to make it produce emetic effects.

its course.—A glyster was actually administered by an old woman of the family, who had been sir Thomas's nurse, and the patient took a draught made with oxymel of squills[9] to forward the operation of the antimonial wine, which had been retarded by the opiate of the preceding night. He was visited by the vicar, who read prayers, and began to take an account of the state of his soul, when those medicines produced their effect; so that the parson was obliged to hold his nose while he poured forth spiritual consolation from his mouth. The same expedient was used by the knight and me, who, with the doctor, entered the chamber at this juncture, and found Frogmore enthroned on an easing-chair, under the pressure of a double evacuation. The short intervals betwixt every heave he employed in crying for mercy, confessing his sins, or asking the vicar's opinion of his case; and the vicar answered, in a solemn snuffling tone, that heightened the ridicule of the scene. The emetic having done its office, the doctor interfered, and ordered the patient to be put in bed again. When he examined the *egista*,[1] and felt his pulse, he declared that much of the *virus* was discharged, and, giving him a composing draught, assured him he had good hopes of his recovery.—This welcome hint he received with the tears of joy in his eyes, protesting, that if he should recover, he would always think himself indebted for his life to the great skill and tenderness of his doctor, whose hand he squeezed with great fervor; and thus he was left to his repose.

We were pressed to stay dinner, that we might be witnesses of his resuscitation; but my uncle insisted upon our departing before noon, that we might reach this town before it should be dark.—In the mean time, lady Bullford conducted us into the garden to see a fish-pond just finished, which Mr. Bramble censured as being too near the parlour, where the knight now sat by himself, dozing in an elbow-chair after the fatigues of his morning atchievement.——In this situation he reclind, with his feet wrapped in flannel, and supported in a line with his body, when the door flying open with a violent shock, lieutenant Lismahago rushed into the room with horror in his looks, exclaiming, "A mad dog! a mad dog!" and throwing up the window sash, leaped into the garden.—Sir Thomas, waked by this tremendous exclamation, started up, and forgetting his gout, followed the lieutenant's example by a kind of instinctive impulse. —He not only bolted thro' the window like an arrow from a bow, but ran up to his middle in the pond before he gave the least sign of recollection. Then the captain began to bawl, "Lord, have mercy upon us!—pray, take care of the gentleman!—for God's sake, mind your footing, my dear boy! —get warm blankets—comfort his poor carcase—warm the bed in the green room."

9. A medicinal syrup of vinegar, honey, and a variety of onion.

1. The excreted matter.

Lady Bullford was thunder-struck at this phænomenon, and the rest of the company gazed in silent astonishment, while the servants hastened to assist their master, who suffered himself to be carried back into the parlour without speaking a word.——Being instantly accommodated with dry clothes and flannels, comforted with a cordial, and replaced *in statu quo,* one of the maids was ordered to chafe his lower extremities, an operation in consequence of which his senses seemed to return and his good humour to revive.——As we had followed him into the room, he looked at every individual in his turn, with a certain ludicrous expression in his countenance, but fixed his eye in particular upon Lismahago, who presented him with a pinch of snuff, and when he took it in silence, "Sir Thomas Bullford, (said he) I am much obliged to you for all your favours, and some of them I have endeavoured to repay in your own coin." "Give me thy hand (cried the baronet); thou hast indeed payed me *Scot and lot;* [2] and even left a balance in my hands, for which, in presence of this company, I promise to be accountable."——So saying, he laughed very heartily, and even seemed to enjoy the retaliation which had been exacted at his own expence; but lady Bullford looked very grave; and in all probability thought the lieutenant had carried his resentment too far, considering that her husband was valetudinary—but, according to the proverb, *he that will play at bowls must expect to meet with rubbers.* [3]

I have seen a tame bear, very diverting when properly managed, become a very dangerous wild beast when teized for the entertainment of the spectators.——As for Lismahago, he seemed to think the fright and the cold bath would have a good effect upon his patient's constitution; but the doctor hinted some apprehension that the gouty matter might, by such a sudden shock, be repelled from the extremities and thrown upon some of the more vital parts of the machine.——I should be very sorry to see this prognostic verified upon our facetious landlord, who told Mrs. Tabitha at parting, that he hoped she would remember him in the distribution of the bride's favours, as he had taken so much pains to put the captain's parts and mettle to the proof.——After all, I am afraid our 'squire will appear to be the greatest sufferer by the baronet's wit; for his constitution is by no means calculated for night-alarms.——He has yawned and shivered all day, and gone to bed without supper; so that, as we have got into good quarters, I imagine we shall make a halt to-morrow; in which case, you will have at least one day's respite from the persecution of

Oct. 3.   J. MELFORD.

---

2. Originally a municipal tax, but used to mean "to pay off thoroughly."
3. Rubbers are the odd, and hence decisive, games at bowls, so this proverbial saying, which Smollett used in at least two other contexts, means something like: "If you play the game, you must take your chances."

To Mrs. MARY JONES, at Brambleton-hall.

DEAR MARY JONES,

Miss Liddy is so good as to unclose me in a kiver as fur as Gloster, and the carrier will bring it to hand—God send us all safe to Monmouthshire, for I'm quite jaded with rambling—'Tis a true saying, *live and learn*—O woman, what chuckling and changing have I seen!—Well, there's nothing sartain in this world——Who would have thought that mistriss, after all the pains taken for the good of her prusias sole, would go for to throw away her poor body? that she would cast the heys of infection upon such a carryingcrow as Lashmihago! as old as Matthewsullin, as dry as a red herring, and as pore as a starved veezel—O, Molly! hadst thou seen him come down the ladder, in a shurt so scanty, that it could not kiver his nakedness!—The young 'squire called him Dunquickset; but he looked for all the world like Cradoc-ap Morgan, the ould tinker, that suffered at Abergany for steeling of kettle—Then he's a profane scuffle, and, as Mr. Clinker says, no better than an impfiddle, continually playing upon the pyebill and the newburth—I doubt he has as little manners as money; for he can't say a civil word, much more make me a present of a pair of gloves for good-will; but he looks as if he wanted to be very forewood and familiar—O! that ever a gentlewoman of years and discretion should tare her air, and cry and disporridge herself for such a nubjack! as the song goes—

> "I vow she would fain have a burd
> That bids such a price for an owl."[4]

but, for sartain, he must have dealt with some Scotch musician to bring her to this pass——As for me, I put my trust in the Lord; and I have got a slice of witch elm sowed in the gathers of my under petticoat;[5] and Mr. Clinker assures me, that by the new light of grease, I may deify the devil and all his works—But I nose what I nose—If mistriss should take up with Lashmyhago, this is no sarvice for me—Thank God, there's no want of places; and if it wan't for wan thing, I would——but, no matter—Madam Baynar's woman has twenty good pounds a-year and parquisites; and dresses like a parson of distinkson——I dined with her and the valley de shambles, with bags and golden jackets; but there was nothing kimfittable to eat, being as how they live upon board, and having nothing but a piss of could cuddling tart and some blamangey,[6] I was tuck with the

4. Byron Gassman discovered a similar pair of lines in *The Roxburghe Ballads* (1883) IV, 72:

> They say, they have need of a Bird,
> that will give a Groat for an Owl.

5. In Wales, witch hazel or witch elm twigs were woven into a wishing cap which would grant the wearer's desire, which may apply here; or it may be that the slice is an amulet to keep the devil away.

6. Blancmange, a sweet, white pudding. The cold tart just above is probably a pie made with coddle, an Irish stew of bacon, sausage, and vegetables, but it may be an apple pie made with coddlings, which are cooking apples.

cullick, and a murcy it was that mistriss had her viol of assings in the cox. But, as I was saying, I think for sartain this match will go forewood; for things are come to a creesus; and I have seen with my own hays, such smuggling——But I scorn for to exclose the secrets of the family; and if it wance comes to marrying, who nose but the frolick may go round——I believes as how, Miss Liddy would have no reversion if her swan would appear; and you would be surprised, Molly, to receive a bride's fever from your humble sarvant——but this is all suppository, dear girl; and I have sullenly promised to Mr. Clinker, that neither man, woman, nor child, shall no that arrow said a civil thing to me in the way of infection——I hopes to drink your health at Brambleton-hall, in a horn of October, before the month be out——Pray let my bed be turned once a-day, and the windore opened, while the weather is dry; and burn a few billets with some brush in the footman's garret, and see their mattrash be dry as a bone; for both our gentlemen have got a sad could by lying in damp shits at sir Tummas Ballfart's. No more at present, but my sarvice to Saul and the rest of our fellow-sarvents, being,

> Dear Mary Jones,
>
> always yours,

Oct. 4.   WIN. JENKINS.

To Miss LÆTITIA WILLIS, at Gloucester.

MY DEAR LETTY,

   This method of writing to you from time to time, without any hopes of an answer, affords me, I own, some ease and satisfaction in the midst of my disquiet, as it in some degree lightens the burthen of affliction; but it is at best a very imperfect enjoyment of friendship, because it admits of no return of confidence and good counsel——I would give the whole world to have your company for a single day——I am heartily tired of this itinerant way of life——I am quite dizzy with a perpetual succession of objects——Besides it is impossible to travel such a length of way, without being exposed to inconveniences, dangers, and disagreeable accidents, which prove very grievous to a poor creature of weak nerves like me, and make me pay very dear for the gratification of my curiosity.

   Nature never intended me for the busy world——I long for repose and solitude, where I can enjoy that disinterested friendship which is not to be found among crouds, and indulge those pleasing reveries that shun the hurry and tumult of fashionable society——Unexperienced as I am in the commerce of life, I have seen enough to give me a disgust to the generality of those who carry it on——There is such malice, treachery, and dissimulation, even among professed friends and intimate companions, as cannot fail to strike a virtuous mind with horror; and when Vice quits the stage for a moment, her place is immediately occupied by Folly, which is often too serious to excite any thing but compassion—Perhaps I ought to be silent on the foibles of my poor aunt; but with you, my dear Willis, I have no secrets; and, truly, her weaknesses are such as cannot be concealed. Since the first moment we arrived at Bath, she has been employed constantly in spreading nets for the other sex; and, at length, she has caught a superannuated lieutenant, who is in a fair way to make her change her name—My uncle and my brother seem to have no objection to this extraordinary match, which, I make no doubt, will afford abundance of matter of conversation and mirth; for my part, I am too sensible of my own weaknesses, to be diverted with those of other people ——At present, I have something at heart that employs my whole attention, and keeps my mind in the utmost terror and suspence.

Yesterday in the forenoon, as I stood with my brother at the parlour window of an inn, where we had lodged, a person passed a-horseback, whom (gracious Heaven!) I instantly discovered to be Wilson! He wore a white riding-coat, with the cape buttoned up to his chin; looked remarkably pale, and passed at a round trot, without seeming to observe us——Indeed, he could not see us; for there was a blind that concealed us from the view. You may guess how I was affected at this apparition—The light forsook my eyes; and I was seized with such a palpitation and trembling, that I could not stand. I sat down upon a couch, and strove to compose myself, that my brother might not perceive my agitation; but it was impossible to escape his prying eyes—He had observed the object that alarmed me; and, doubtless, knew him at the first glance—He now looked at me with a stern countenance; then he ran out into the street, to see what road the unfortunate horseman had taken—He afterwards dispatched his man for further intelligence, and seemed to meditate some violent design. My uncle, being out of order, we remained another night at the inn; and all day long Jery acted the part of an indefatigable spy upon my conduct—He watched my very looks with such eagerness of attention, as if he would have penetrated into the utmost recesses of my heart—This may be owing to his regard for my honour, if it is not the effect of his own pride; but he is so hot, and violent, and unrelenting, that the sight of him alone throws me into a flutter; and really it will not be in my power to afford him any share of my affection, if he persists in persecuting me at this rate. I am afraid he has formed some scheme of vengeance, which will make me completely wretched! I am afraid he suspects some collusion from this appearance of Wilson.——Good God! did he really appear? or was it only a phantom, a pale spectre to apprise me of his death?

O Letty, what shall I do?—where shall I turn for advice and consola- tion?—shall I implore the protection of my uncle, who has been always kind and compassionate.—This must be my last resource.—I dread the thoughts of making him uneasy; and would rather suffer a thouland deaths than live the cause of dissension in the family.—I cannot perceive the meaning of Wilson's coming hither:—perhaps, he was in quest of us, in order to disclose his real name and situation:—but wherefore pass without staying to make the least inquiry?—My dear Willis, I am lost in conjecture.—I have not closed an eye since I saw him.—All night long have I been tossed about from one imagination to another.—The reflection finds no resting place.—I have prayed, and sighed, and wept plentifully.——If this terrible suspence continues much longer, I shall have another fit of illness, and then the whole family will be in confusion. —If it was consistent with the wise purposes of Providence, would I were in my grave.—But it is my duty to be resigned.—My dearest Letty, excuse my weakness—excuse these blots—my tears fall so fast that I cannot keep the paper dry—yet I ought to consider that I have as yet no cause to despair——but I am such a faint-hearted timorous creature!

Thank God, my uncle is much better than he was yesterday.—He is resolved to pursue our journey strait to Wales.—I hope we shall take Gloucester in our way—that hope chears my poor heart—I shall once more embrace my best beloved Willis, and pour all my griefs into her friendly bosom.——O heaven! is it possible that such happiness is reserved for

The dejected and forlorn

Oct. 4.   LYDIA MELFORD.

To Sir WATKIN PHILLIPS, Bar[t]. of Jesus college, Oxon.

DEAR WATKIN,

I yesterday met with an incident which I believe you will own to be very surprising—As I stood with Liddy at the window of the inn where we had lodged, who should pass by but Wilson a-horse-back!—I could not be mistaken in the person, for I had a full view of him as he advanced; I plainly perceived by my sister's confusion that she recognized him at the same time. I was equally astonished and incensed at his appearance, which I could not but interpret into an insult, or something worse. I ran out at the gate, and, seeing him turn the corner of the street, I dispatched my servant to observe his motions, but the fellow was too late to bring me that satisfaction. He told me, however, that there was an inn, called the Red Lion, at that end of the town, where he supposed the horseman had alighted, but that he would not enquire without further orders. I sent him back immediately to know what strangers were in the house, and he returned with a report that there was one Mr. Wilson lately arrived. In consequence of this information I charged him with a note directed to that gentleman, desiring him to meet me in half an hour in a certain field at the town's end, with a case of pistols, in order to decide the difference which could not be determined at our last rencounter: but I did not think proper to subscribe the billet.[7] My man assured me he had delivered it into his own hand; and, that having read it, he declared he would wait upon the gentleman at the place and time appointed.

M'Alpine being an old soldier, and luckily sober at the time, I entrusted him with my secret. I ordered him to be within call, and, having given him a letter to be delivered to my uncle in case of accident, I repaired to the rendezvous, which was an inclosed field at a little distance from the highway. I found my antagonist had already taken his ground, wrapped in a dark horseman's coat, with a laced hat flapped over his eyes; but what was my astonishment, when, throwing off this wrapper, he appeared to be a person whom I had never seen before! He had one pistol stuck in a leather belt, and another in his hand ready for action, and, advancing a few steps, called to know if I was ready—I answered, "No," and desired a parley; upon which he turned the muzzle of his piece towards the earth; then replaced it in his belt, and met me half way —When I assured him he was not the man I expected to meet, he said, *it might be so:* that he had received a slip of paper directed to Mr. Wilson, requesting him to come hither; and that as there was no other in the place of that name, he naturally concluded the note was intended for him, and him only—I then gave him to understand, that I had been injured by a person who assumed that name, which person I had actually seen within the hour, passing through the street on horseback; that hearing there was a Mr. Wilson at the Red Lion, I took it for granted he was the man, and in that belief had writ the billet; and I expressed my surprize, that he, who was a stranger to me and my concerns, should give me such a rendezvous, without taking the trouble to demand a previous explanation—He replied, that there was no other of his name in the whole county; that no such horseman had alighted at the Red Lion since nine o'clock, when he arrived—that having had the honour to serve his majesty, he thought he could not decently decline any invitation of this kind, from what quarter soever it might come; and that if any explanation was necessary, it did not belong to him to demand it, but to the gentleman who summoned him into the field—Vexed as I was at this adventure, I could not help admiring the coolness of this officer, whose open countenance prepossessed me in his favour.—He seemed to be turned of forty; wore his own short black hair, which curled naturally about his ears, and was very plain in his apparel—When I begged pardon for the trouble I had given him, he received my apology with great good humour.—He told me that he lived about ten miles off, at a small farm-house, which would afford me tolerable lodging, if I would come and take the diversion of hunting with him for a few weeks; in which case we might, perhaps, find out the man who had given me offence—I thanked him very sincerely for his

7. Sign the letter.

courteous offer, which, I told him, I was not at liberty to accept at present, on account of my being engaged in a family partie; and so we parted, with mutual professions of good will and esteem.

Now tell me, dear knight, what am I to make of this singular adventure?—Am I to suppose that the horseman I saw was really a thing of flesh and blood, or a bubble that vanished into air?—or must I imagine Liddy knows more of the matter than she chuses to disclose?—If I thought her capable of carrying on any clandestine correspondence with such a fellow, I should at once discard all tenderness, and forget that she was connected with me by the ties of blood—But how is it possible that a girl of her simplicity and inexperience, should maintain such an intercourse, surrounded, as she is with so many eyes, destitute of all opportunity, and shifting quarters every day of her life!—Besides, she has solemnly promised—No—I can't think the girl so base—so insensible to the honour of her family.—What disturbs me chiefly, is the impression which these occurrences seem to make upon her spirits—These are the symptoms from which I conclude that the rascal has still a hold on her affection—surely I have a right to call him a rascal, and to conclude that his designs are infamous—But it shall be my fault if he does not one day repent his presumption——I confess I cannot think, much less write on this subject, with any degree of temper or patience; I shall therefore conclude with telling you, that we hope to be in Wales by the latter end of the month: but before that period you will probably hear again from

your affectionate

Oct. 4.   J. MELFORD.

To Sir WATKIN PHILLIPS, Bar^t. at Oxon.

DEAR PHILLIPS,

When I wrote you by last post, I did not imagine I should be tempted to trouble you again so soon: but I now sit down with a heart so full that it cannot contain itself; though I am under such agitation of spirits, that you are to expect either method or connexion in this address—We have been this day within a hair's breadth of losing honest Matthew Bramble, in consequence of a cursed accident, which I will endeavour to explain.—In crossing the country to get into the post road, it was necessary to ford a river, and we that were a-horseback passed without any danger or difficulty; but a great quantity of rain having fallen last night and this morning, there was such an accumulation of water, that a mill-head gave way, just as the coach was passing under it, and the flood rushed down with such impetuosity, as first floated, and then fairly overturned the carriage in the middle of the stream—Lismahago and I, and the two servants, alighting instantaneously, ran into the river to give all the assistance in our power.—Our aunt, Mrs. Tabitha, who had the good fortune to be uppermost, was already half way out of the coach window, when her lover approaching, disengaged her entirely; but, whether his foot slipt, or the burthen was too great, they fell over head and ears in each other's arms. He endeavoured more than once to get up, and even to disentangle himself from her embrace, but she hung about his neck like a mill-stone (no bad emblem of matrimony,) and if my man had not proved a staunch auxiliary, those two lovers would in all probability have gone hand in hand to the shades below—For my part, I was too much engaged to take any cognizance of their distress.—I snatched out my sister by the hair of the head, and, dragging her to the bank, recollected that my uncle had not yet appeared—Rushing again into the stream, I met Clinker hauling ashore Mrs. Jenkins, who looked like a mermaid with her hair dishevelled about her ears; but, when I asked if his master was safe, he forthwith shook her from him, and she must have gone to pot, if a miller had not seasonably come to her relief.—As for Humphrey, he flew like lightning to the coach, that was by this time filled with water, and, diving into it, brought up the poor 'squire, to all appearance, deprived of life—It is not in my power to describe what I felt at this melancholy spectacle—it was such an agony as baffles all description! The faithful Clinker, taking him up in his arms, as if he had been an infant of six months, carried him ashore, howling most piteously all the way, and I followed him in a transport of grief and consternation—When he was laid upon the grass, and turned from side to side, a great quantity of water ran out at his mouth, then he opened his eyes, and fetched a deep sigh—Clinker perceiving these signs of life, immediately tied up his arm with a garter, and, pulling out a horse-fleam,[8] let him blood in the farrier stile.—At first a few drops only issued from the orifice; but the limb being chafed, in a little time the blood began to flow in a continued stream, and he uttered some incoherent words, which were the most welcome sounds that ever saluted my ear. There was a country inn hard by, the landlord of which had by this time come with his people to give their assistance.—Thither my uncle being carried, was undressed and put to bed, wrapped in warm blankets; but having been moved too soon, he fainted away, and once more lay without sense or motion, notwithstanding all the efforts of Clinker and the landlord, who bathed his temples with Hungary water,[9] and held a smelling-bottle to his nose. As I had heard of the efficacy of salt in such cases, I ordered all that was in the house to be laid under his head and body; and whether this application had the desired effect, or nature of herself prevailed, he, in less than a quarter of an hour, began to breathe regularly, and soon retrieved his recollection, to the unspeakable joy of all

---

8. A lancet for opening the veins of a horse for bleeding, a common treatment for all sorts of ailments of horses and men during the period.

9. A liquid, much like cologne, made of spirits of wine infused with rosemary flowers.

the by-standers. As for Clinker, his brain seemed to be affected.—He laughed, and wept, and danced about in such a distracted manner, that the landlord very judiciously conveyed him out of the room. My uncle, seeing me dropping wet, comprehended the whole of what had happened, and asked if all the company was safe?—Being answered in the affirmative, he insisted upon my putting on dry clothes; and, having swallowed a little warm wine, desired he might be left to his repose. Before I went to shift myself, I inquired about the rest of the family—I found Mrs. Tabitha still delirious from her fright, discharging very copiously the water she had swallowed. She was supported by the captain, distilling drops from his uncurled periwig, so lank and so dank, that he looked like father Thame without his sedges, embracing Isis, while she cascaded in his urn.[1] Mrs. Jenkins was present also, in a loose bed-gown, without either cap or handkerchief; but she seemed to be as little *compos mentis* as her mistress, and acted so many cross purposes in the course of her attendance, that, between the two, Lismahago had occasion for all his philosophy. As for Liddy, I thought the poor girl would have actually lost her senses. The good-woman of the house had shifted her linen, and put her into bed; but she was seized with the idea that her uncle had perished, and in this persuasion made a dismal out-cry; nor did she pay the least regard to what I said, when I solemnly assured her he was safe. Mr. Bramble hearing the noise, and being informed of her apprehension, desired she might be brought into his chamber; and she no sooner received this intimation, than she ran thither half naked, with the wildest expression of eagerness in her countenance—Seeing the 'squire sitting up in the bed, she sprung forwards, and, throwing her arms about his neck, exclaimed in a most pathetic tone, "Are you—Are you indeed my uncle—My dear uncle!—My best friend! My father!—Are you really living? or is it an illusion of my poor brain!" Honest Matthew was so much affected, that he could not help shedding tears, while he kissed her forehead, saying, "My dear Liddy, I hope I shall live long enough to shew how sensible I am of your affection—But your spirits are fluttered, child—You want rest—Go to bed and compose yourself—" "Well, I will (she replied)—but still methinks this cannot be real—The coach was full of water—My uncle was under us all—Gracious God! —You was under water—How did you get out?—tell me that? or I shall think this is all a deception—" "In what manner I was brought out, I know as little as you do, my dear (said the 'squire); and, truly, that is a circumstance of which I want to be informed." I would have given him a detail of the whole adventure, but he would not hear me until I should change my clothes; so that I had only time to tell him, that he owed his

---

1. The editor has not located a particular work of art which fits this passage, but it seems to refer to a painting, a statue, or even a fountain, of the personified Father Thames embracing the River Isis, as it does at Oxford. Such allegorical works of art were common during the period.

life to the courage and fidelity of Clinker; and having given him this hint, I conducted my sister to her own chamber.

This accident happened about three o'clock in the afternoon, and in little more than an hour the hurricane was all over; but as the carriage was found to be so much damaged, that it could not proceed without considerable repairs, a blacksmith and wheelwright were immediately sent for to the next market-town, and we congratulated ourselves upon being housed at an inn, which, though remote from the post-road, afforded exceeding good lodging. The women being pretty well composed, and the men all a-foot, my uncle sent for his servant, and, in the presence of Lismahago and me, accosted him in these words—"So, Clinker, I find you are resolved I shan't die by water—As you have fished me up from the bottom at your own risque, you are at least entitled to all the money that was in my pocket, and there it is—" So saying, he presented him with a purse containing thirty guineas, and a ring nearly of the same value—"God forbid! (cried Clinker) your honour shall excuse me—I am a poor fellow; but I have a heart—O! if your honour did but know how I rejoice to see—Blessed be his holy name, that made me the humble instrument—But as for the lucre of gain, I renounce it—I have done no more than my duty—No more than I would have done for the most worthless of my fellow-creatures—No more than I would have done for captain Lismahago, or Archy Macalpine, or any sinner upon earth —But for your worship, I would go through fire as well as water——" "I do believe it, Humphry (said the 'squire); but as you think it was your duty to save my life at the hazard of your own, I think it is mine to express the sense I have of your extraordinary fidelity and attachment—I insist upon your receiving this small token of my gratitude; but don't imagine that I look upon this as an adequate recompence for the service you have done me—I have determined to settle thirty pounds a-year upon you for life; and I desire these gentlemen will bear witness to this my intention, of which I have a memorandum in my pocket-book." "Lord make me thankful for all these mercies! (cried Clinker, sobbing) I have been a poor bankrupt from the beginning—your honour's goodness found me, when I was—naked—when I was—sick and forlorn——I understand your honour's looks—I would not give offence—but my heart is very full—and if your worship won't give me leave to speak,—I must vent it in prayers to heaven for my benefactor." When he quitted the room, Lismahago said, he should have a much better opinion of his honesty, if he did not whine and cant so abominably; but that he had always observed those weeping and praying fellows were hypocrites at bottom. Mr. Bramble made no reply to this sarcastic remark, proceeding from the lieutenant's resentment of Clinker's having, in pure simplicity of heart, ranked him with M'Alpine and the sinners of the earth.——The landlord being called to receive some orders about the beds, told the 'squire that his house was very much at his service, but he was sure he should not have the honour to lodge him and his company. He gave us to understand that his master, who lived hard by, would not suffer us to be at a public house, when there was accommodation for us at his own; and that, if he had not dined abroad in the neighbourhood he would have undoubtedly come to offer his services at our first arrival. He then launched out in praise of that gentleman, whom he had served as butler, representing him as a perfect miracle of goodness and generosity. He said he was a person of great learning, and allowed to be the best farmer in the country:—that he had a lady who was as much beloved as himself, and an only son, a very hopeful young gentleman, just recovered from a dangerous fever, which had like to have proved fatal to the whole family; for, if the son had died, he was sure the parents would not have survived their loss—He had not yet finished the encomium of Mr. Dennison, when this gentleman arrived in a post-chaise, and his appearance seemed to justify all that had been said in his favour. He is pretty well advanced in years, but hale, robust, and florid, with an ingenuous countenance, expressive of good sense and humanity. Having condoled with us on the accident which had happened, he said he was come to conduct us to his habitation, where we should be less incommoded than at such a paultry inn, and expressed his hope that the ladies would not be the worse for going thither in his carriage, as the distance was not above a quarter of a mile. My uncle having made a proper return to this courteous exhibition, eyed him attentively, and then asked if he had not been at Oxford, a commoner of Queen's college? When Mr. Dennison answered, "Yes," with some marks of surprise—"Look at me then (said our 'squire) and let us see if you can recollect the features of an old friend, whom you have not seen these forty years."——The gentleman, taking him by the hand, and gazing at him earnestly,—"I protest, (cried he,) I do think I recal the idea of Matthew Loyd of Glamorganshire, who was student of Jesus." "Well remembered, my dear friend, Charles Dennison, (exclaimed my uncle, pressing him to his breast), I am that very identical Matthew Loyd of Glamorgan." Clinker, who had just entered the room with some coals for the fire, no sooner heard these words, than, throwing down the scuttle on the toes of Lismahago, he began to caper as if he was mad, crying —"Matthew Loyd of Glamorgan!—O Providence!—Matthew Loyd of Glamorgan!"——Then, clasping my uncle's knees, he went on in this manner——"Your worship must forgive me—Matthew Loyd of Glamorgan!—O Lord, Sir!—I can't contain myself!—I shall lose my senses —" "Nay, thou hast lost them already, I believe, (said the 'squire, peevishly) prithee Clinker be quiet——What is the matter?" ——Humphrey, fumbling in his bosom, pulled out an old wooden snuff-box, which he presented in great trepidation to his master, who, opening it immediately, perceived a small cornelian [2] seal, and two scraps of paper

2. A red or reddish mineral which can be worked to provide a design for a seal to be impressed on wax.

—At sight of these articles he started, and changed colour, and, casting his eye upon the inscriptions—"Ha!—how!—what!—where (cried he) is the person here named?" Clinker, knocking his own breast, could hardly pronounce these words—"Here—here—here is Matthew Loyd, as the certificate sheweth—Humphrey Clinker was the name of the farrier that took me 'prentice"—"And who gave you these tokens,"—said my uncle, hastily—"My poor mother on her death-bed"—replied the other—"And who was your mother?" "Dorothy Twyford, an please your honour, heretofore barkeeper at the Angel at Chippenham."[3]—"And why were not these tokens produced before?" "My mother told me she had wrote to Glamorganshire, at the time of my birth, but had no answer; and that afterwards, when she made enquiry, there was no such person in that county." "And so in consequence of my changing my name and going abroad at that very time, thy poor mother and thou have been left to want and misery—I am really shocked at the consequence of my own folly." —Then, laying his hand on Clinker's head, he added, "Stand forth, Matthew Loyd—You see, gentlemen, how the sins of my youth rise up in judgment against me—Here is my direction written with my own hand, and a seal which I left at the woman's request; and this is a certificate of the child's baptism, signed by the curate of the parish." The company were not a little surprised at this discovery, upon which Mr. Dennison facetiously congratulated both the father and the son: for my part, I shook my new-found cousin heartily by the hand, and Lismahago complimented him with the tears in his eyes, for he had been hopping about the room, swearing in broad Scotch, and bellowing with the pain occasioned by the fall of the coal-scuttle upon his foot. He had even vowed to drive the saul out of the body of that mad rascal: but, perceiving the unexpected turn which things had taken, he wished him joy of his good fortune, observing that it went very near his heart, as he was like to be a great toe out of pocket by the discovery—Mr. Dennison now desired to know for what reason my uncle had changed the name by which he knew him at Oxford, and our 'squire satisfied him, by answering to this effect. —"I took my mother's name, which was Loyd, as heir to her lands in Glamorganshire; but, when I came of age, I sold that property, in order to clear my paternal estate, and resumed my real name; so that I am now Matthew Bramble of Brambleton-hall in Monmouthshire, at your service; and this is my nephew, Jeremy Melford of Belfield, in the county of Glamorgan." At that instant the ladies entering the room, he presented Mrs. Tabitha as his sister, and Liddy as his niece. The old gentleman saluted them very cordially, and seemed struck with the appearance of my sister, whom he could not help surveying with a mixture of complacency and surprize——"Sister, (said my uncle) there is a poor relation

3. The Angel Hotel was a prominent landmark in Chippenham.

that recommends himself to your good graces—The quondam Humphrey Clinker is metamorphosed into Matthew Loyd; and claims the honour of being your carnal kinsman—in short, the rogue proves to be a crab of my own planting in the days of hot blood and unrestrained libertinism." Clinker had by this time dropt upon one knee, by the side of Mrs. Tabitha, who, eyeing him askance, and flirting her fan with marks of agitation, thought proper, after some conflict, to hold out her hand for him to kiss, saying, with a demure aspect, "Brother, you have been very wicked: but I hope you'll live to see the folly of your ways—I am very sorry to say the young man, whom you have this day acknowledged, has more grace and religion, by the gift of God, than you with all our profane learning, and repeated opportunity—I do think he has got the trick of the eye, and the tip of the nose of my uncle Loyd of Flluydwellyn; and as for the long chin, it is the very moral of the governor's—Brother, as you have changed his name pray change his dress also; that livery doth not become any person that hath got our blood in his veins."—Liddy seemed much pleased with this acquisition to the family.—She took him by the hand, declaring she should always be proud to own her connexion with a virtuous young man, who had given so many proofs of his gratitude and affection to her uncle.—Mrs. Winifred Jenkins, extremely fluttered between her surprize at this discovery, and the apprehension of losing her sweet-heart, exclaimed in a giggling tone,—"I wish you joy, Mr. Clinker—Floyd—I would say—hi, hi, hi!—you' ll be so proud you won't look at your poor fellow servants, oh, oh, oh!" Honest Clinker owned, he was overjoyed at his good fortune, which was greater than he deserved —"But wherefore should I be proud? (said he) a poor object conceived in sin, and brought forth in iniquity, nursed in a parish work-house, and bred in a smithy—Whenever I seem proud, Mrs. Jenkins, I beg of you to put me in mind of the condition I was in, when I first saw you between Chippenham and Marlborough."

When this momentous affair was discussed to the satisfaction of all parties concerned, the weather being dry, the ladies declined the carriage; so that we walked all together to Mr. Dennison's house, where we found the tea ready prepared by his lady, an amiable matron, who received us with all the benevolence of hospitality.—The house is old fashioned and irregular, but lodgeable and commodious. To the south it has the river in front, at the distance of a hundred paces; and on the north, there is a rising ground, covered with an agreeable plantation; the greens and walks are kept in the nicest order, and all is rural and romantic. I have not yet seen the young gentleman, who is on a visit to a friend in the neighbourhood, from whose house he is not expected 'till to-morrow.

In the mean time, as there is a man going to the next market-town with letters for the post, I take this opportunity to send you the history of this day, which has been remarkably full of adventures; and you will own I give you them like a beef-steak at Dolly's,[4] *hot* and *hot*, without ceremony and parade, just as they come from the recollection of

Yours,

J. MELFORD.

To Dr. LEWIS.

DEAR DICK,

Since the last trouble I gave you, I have met with a variety of incidents, some of them of a singular nature, which I reserve as a fund for conversation; but there are others so interesting, that they will not keep in *petto* till meeting.

Know then, it was a thousand pounds to a sixpence, that you should now be executing my will, instead of perusing my letter! Two days ago, our coach was overturned in the midst of a rapid river, where my life was saved with the utmost difficulty, by the courage, activity, and presence of mind of my servant Humphry Clinker—But this is not the most surprising circumstance of the adventure—The said Humphry Clinker proves to be Matthew Loyd, natural son of one Matthew Loyd of Glamorgan, if you know any such person—You see, Doctor, that notwithstanding all your philosophy, it is not without some reason that we Welchmen ascribe such energy to the force of blood—But we shall discuss this point on some future occasion.

This is not the only discovery which I made in consequence of our disaster—We happened to be wrecked upon a friendly shore—The lord of the manor is no other than Charles Dennison, our fellow-rake at Oxford—We are now happily housed with that gentleman, who has really attained to that pitch of rural felicity, at which I have been aspiring these twenty years in vain. He is blessed with a consort, whose disposition is suited to his own in all respects; tender, generous, and benevolent —She, moreover, possesses an uncommon share of understanding, fortitude, and discretion, and is admirably qualified to be his companion, confidant, counsellor, and coadjutrix. These excellent persons have an only son, about nineteen years of age, just such a youth as they could have wished that Heaven would bestow to fill up the measure of their enjoyment—In a word, they know no other allay to their happines, but their apprehension and anxiety about the life and concerns of this beloved object.

Our old friend, who had the misfortune to be a second brother, was bred to the law, and even called to the bar; but he did not find himself qualified to shine in that province, and had very little inclination for his

4. Dolly's tavern in London was named for its cook, who had her portrait painted by Gainsborough.

profession—He disobliged his father, by marrying for love, without any consideration of fortune; so that he had little or nothing to depend upon for some years but his practice, which afforded him a bare subsistence; and the prospect of an increasing family, began to give him disturbance and disquiet. In the mean time, his father dying, was succeeded by his elder brother, a fox-hunter and a sot, who neglected his affairs, insulted and oppressed his servants, and in a few years had well nigh ruined the estate, when he was happily carried off by a fever, the immediate consequence of a debauch. Charles, with the approbation of his wife, immediately determined to quit business, and retire into the country, although this resolution was strenuously and zealously opposed by every individual, whom he consulted on the subject. Those who had tried the experiment, assured him that he could not pretend to breathe in the country for less than the double of what his estate produced; that, in order to be upon the footing of a gentleman, he would be obliged to keep horses, hounds, carriages, with a suitable number of servants, and maintain an elegant table for the entertainment of his neighbours; that farming was a mystery, known only to those who had been bred up to it from the cradle, the success of it depending not only upon skill and industry, but also upon such attention and œconomy as no gentleman could be supposed to give or practise; accordingly, every attempt made by gentlemen miscarried, and not a few had been ruined by their prosecution of agriculture—Nay, they affirmed that he would find it cheaper to buy hay and oats for bis cattle, and to go to market for poultry, eggs, kitchen herbs, and roots, and every the most inconsiderable article of house-keeping, than to have those articles produced on his own ground.

These objections did not deter Mr. Dennison, because they were chiefly founded on the supposition, that he would be obliged to lead a life of extravagance and dissipation, which he and his consort equally detested, despised, and determined to avoid—The objects he had in view, were health of body, peace of mind, and the private satisfaction of domestic quiet, unallayed by actual want, and uninterrupted by the fears of indigence—He was very moderate in his estimate of the necessaries, and even of the comforts of life—He required nothing but wholesome air, pure water, agreeable exercise, plain diet, convenient lodging, and decent apparel. He reflected, that if a peasant without education, or any great share of natural sagacity, could maintain a large family, and even become opulent upon a farm, for which he payed an annual rent of two or three hundred pounds to the landlord, surely he himself might hope for some success from his industry, having no rent to pay, but, on the contrary, three or four hundred pounds a-year to receive—He considered, that the earth was an indulgent mother, that yielded her fruits to all her children without distinction. He had studied the theory of agriculture with a degree of eagerness and delight; and he could not conceive there was any mystery in the practice, but what he should be able to disclose by dint of care and application. With respect to houshold expence, he entered into a minute detail and investigation, by which he perceived the assertions of his friends were altogether erroneous—He found he should save sixty pounds a-year in the single article of house-rent, and as much more in pocket-money and contingencies; that even butcher's-meat was twenty per cent. cheaper in the country than in London; but that poultry, and almost every other circumstance of house-keeping, might be had for less than one half of what they cost in town; besides, a considerable saving on the side of dress, in being delivered from the oppressive imposition of ridiculous modes, invented by ignorance, and adopted by folly.

As to the danger of vying with the rich in pomp and equipage, it never gave him the least distrubance. He was now turned of forty, and, having lived half that time in the busy scenes of life, was well skilled in the science of mankind. There cannot be in nature a more contemptible figure than that of a man, who with five hundred a year presumes to rival in expence a neighbour who possesses five times that income—His ostentation, far from concealing, serves only to discover his indigence, and render his vanity the more shocking; for it attracts the eyes of censure, and excites the spirit of inquiry. There is not a family in the county, nor a servant in his own house, nor a farmer in the parish, but what knows the utmost farthing that his lands produce, and all these behold him with scorn or compassion. I am surprised that these reflections do not occur to persons in this unhappy dilemma, and produce a salutary effect; but the truth is, of all the passions incident to human nature, vanity is that which most effectually perverts the faculties of the understanding; nay, it sometimes becomes so incredibly depraved, as to aspire at infamy, and find pleasure in bearing the stigmas of reproach.

I have now given you a sketch of the character and situation of Mr. Dennison, when he came down to take possession of this estate; but as the messenger, who carries the letters to the next town is just setting off, I shall reserve what further I have to say on this subject, till the next post, when you shall certainly hear from

Yours always,

Oct. 8.   MATT. BRAMBLE.

To Dr. LEWIS.

Once more, dear doctor, I resume the pen for your amusement.—It was on the morning after our arrival that, walking out with my friend, Mr. Dennison, I could not help breaking forth into the warmest expressions of applause at the beauty of the scene, which is really inchanting; and I signified, in particular, how much I was pleased with the disposition of some detached groves, that afforded at once shelter and ornament to his habitation.

"When I took possession of these lands, about two and twenty years ago, (said he) there was not a tree standing within a mile of the house, except those of an old neglected orchard, which produced nothing but leaves and moss.—It was in the gloomy month of November, when I arrived, and found the house in such a condition, that it might have been justly stiled the *tower of desolation*.—The court-yard was covered with nettles and docks, and the garden exhibited such a rank plantation of weeds as I had never seen before;—the window-shutters were falling in pieces;——the sashes broken;——and owls and jack-daws had taken possession of the chimneys.—The prospect within was still more dreary. —All was dark, and damp, and dirty beyond description;—the rain penetrated in several parts of the roof;—in some apartments the very floors had given way;—the hangings were parted from the walls, and shaking in mouldy remnants;—the glasses were dropping out of their frames;—the family-pictures were covered with dust;—and all the chairs and tables worm-eaten and crazy.——There was not a bed in the house that could be used, except one old-fashioned machine, with a high gilt tester, and fringed curtains of yellow mohair, which had been, for aught I know, two centuries in the family.—In short, there was no furniture but the utensils of the kitchen; and the cellar afforded nothing but a few empty butts and barrels, that stunk so abominably, that I would not suffer any body to enter it until I had flashed a considerable quantity of gunpowder to qualify the foul air within.

"An old cottager and his wife, who were hired to lie in the house, had left it with precipitation, alledging, among other causes of retreat, that they could not sleep for frightful noises, and that my poor brother certainly walked after his death.—In a word, the house appeared uninhabitable; the barn, stable, and out-houses were in ruins; all the fences broken down, and the fields lying waste.

"The farmer who kept the key never dreamed I had any intention to live upon the spot.—He rented a farm of sixty pounds, and his lease was just expiring.—He had formed a scheme of being appointed bailiff to the estate, and of converting the house and the adjacent grounds to his own use.—A hint of his intention I received from the curate at my first arrival; I therefore did not pay much regard to what he said by way of discouraging me from coming to settle in the country; but I was a little startled when he gave me warning that he should quit the farm at the expiration of his lease, unless I would abate considerably in the rent.

"At this period I accidentally became acquainted with a person, whose friendship laid the foundation of all my prosperity. In the next market-town, I chanced to dine at an inn with a Mr. Wilson, who was lately come to settle in the neighbourhood.—He had been lieutenant of a man of war: but quitted the sea in some disgust, and married the only daughter of farmer Bland, who lives in this parish, and has acquired a good fortune in the way of husbandry.—Wilson is one of the best natured men I ever knew; brave, frank, obliging, and ingenuous.—He liked my conversation, I was charmed with his liberal manner; an acquaintance immediately commenced, and this was soon improved into a friendship without reserve.—There are characters which, like similar particles of matter, strongly attract each other.—He forthwith introduced me to his father-in-law, farmer Bland, who was well acquainted with every acre of my estate, of consequence well qualified to advise me on this occasion. —Finding I was inclined to embrace a country life, and even to amuse myself with the occupations of farming, he approved of my design—He gave me to understand that all my farms were under-lett; that the estate was capable of great improvement; that there was plenty of chalk in the neighbourhood; and that my own ground produced excellent marle for manure.—With respect to the farm, which was like to fall into my hands, he said he would willingly take it at the present rent; but at the same time owned, that if I would expend two hundred pounds in enclosure, it would be worth more than double the sum.

"Thus encouraged, I began the execution of my scheme without further delay, and plunged into a sea of expence, though I had no fund in reserve, and the whole produce of the estate did not exceed three hundred pounds a year.—In one week, my house was made weather tight, and thoroughly cleansed from top to bottom; then it was well ventilated by throwing all the doors and windows open, and making blazing fires of wood in every chimney from the kitchen to the garrets.—The floors were repaired, the sashes new glazed, and out of the old furniture of the whole house, I made shift to fit up a parlour and three chambers in a plain yet decent manner.—The court-yard was cleared of weeds and rubbish, and my friend Wilson charged himself with the dressing of the garden; bricklayers were set at work upon the barn and stable; and labourers engaged to restore the fences, and begin the work of hedging and ditching, under the direction of farmer Bland, at whose recommendation I hired a careful hind to lie in the house, and keep constant fires in the apartments.

"Having taken these measures, I returned to London, where I forthwith sold off my houshold-furniture, and, in three weeks from my first visit, brought my wife hither to keep her Christmas.————Considering the gloomy season of the year, the dreariness of the place, and the decayed aspect of our habitation, I was afraid that her resolution would sink under the sudden transition from a town-life to such a melancholy state of rustication; but I was agreeably disappointed.————She found the reality less uncomfortable than the picture I had drawn.————By this time, indeed, things were mended in appearance.—The out-houses had risen out of their ruins; the pigeon-house was rebuilt, and replenished by Wilson, who also put my garden in decent order, and provided a good stock of poultry, which made an agreeable figure in my yard; and the house, on the whole, looked like the habitation of human creatures. —Farmer Bland spared me a milch-cow for my family, and an ordinary saddle-horse for my servant to go to market at the next town.—I hired a country lad for a footman; the hind's daughter was my house-maid, and my wife had brought a cook-maid from London.

"Such was my family when I began house-keeping in this place, with three hundred pounds in my pocket, raised from the sale of my superfluous furniture—I knew we should find occupation enough through the day to employ our time; but I dreaded the long winter evenings; yet for these too we found a remedy.——The curate, who was a single man, soon became so naturalized to the family, that he generally lay in the house; and his company was equally agreeable and useful.—He was a modest man, a good scholar, and perfectly well qualified to instruct me in such country matters as I wanted to know.—Mr. Wilson brought his wife to see us, and she became so fond of Mrs. Dennison, that she said she was never so happy as when she enjoyed the benefit of her conversation. —She was then a fine buxom country lass, exceedingly docile, and as good-natured as her husband Jack Wilson; so that a friendship ensued among the women, which hath continued to this day.

"As for Jack, he hath been my constant companion, counsellor, and commissary.——I would not for a hundred pounds you should leave my house without seeing him.——Jack is an universal genius—his talents are really astonishing—He is an excellent carpenter, joiner, and turner, and a cunning artist in iron and brass.—He not only superintended my œconomy, but also presided over my pastimes.—He taught me to brew beer, to make cyder, perry, mead, usquebaugh,[5] and plague-water; to cook several outlandish delicacies, such as *ollas, pepper-pots, pillaws, corys, chabobs*, and *stufatas*.[6]—He understands all manner of games from chess down to chuck-farthing,[7] sings a good song, plays upon the violin, and dances a hornpipe with surprising agility.—He and I walked, and rode, and hunted, and fished together, without minding the vicissitudes of the weather; and I am persuaded, that in a raw, moist climate, like this of England, continual exercise is as necessary as food to the preservation

5. This word usually denotes whiskey, but it has been suggested that here it means a drink composed of brandy, licorice, dried fruits, and spices. Since whiskey requires distillation, which the other drinks on this list do not, the suggestion may be accurate.
6. All of these terms signify more or less sophisticated dishes. An olla is a dish of Spanish origin made of a wide variety of ingredients which are cooked together in an earthenware pot, or olla, and highly seasoned. Pepper-pot is of West Indian invention and includes red peppers and other spices cooked with meat and fish. A pillaw is an oriental dish consisting of rice cooked with spices

and meat. "Corys" is probably an unusual form for "curries," highly spiced East Indian dishes of rice with various meats or seafood and condiments served over it. "Chabobs" have been interpreted as various varieties of fish, but the editor suggests that the word is an early form of "kabob," which was admitted into English just a little later. A kabob consists of meat or meat and vegetables broiled on skewers of metal or wood. "Stufata" is probably a kind of Italian stew, as the word is Italian for stewed meat or stew.
7. A game, the object of which is to toss a small coin closest to a mark.

of the individual.—In the course of two and twenty years, there has not been one hour's interruption or abatement in the friendship subsisting between Wilson's family and mine; and, what is a rare instance of good fortune, that friendship is continued to our children.—His son and mine are nearly of the same age and the same disposition; they have been bred up together at the same school and college, and love each other with the warmest affection.

"By Wilson's means, I likewise formed an acquaintance with a sensible physician, who lives in the next market-town; and his sister, an agreeable old maiden, passed the Christmas holidays at our house. —Mean while I began my farming with great eagerness, and that very winter planted these groves that please you so much.—As for the neighbouring gentry, I had no trouble from that quarter during my first campaign; they were all gone to town before I settled in the country; and by the summer I had taken measures to defend myself from their attacks. —When a gay equipage came to my gates, I was never at home; those who visited me in a modest way, I received; and according to the remarks I made on their characters and conversation, either rejected their advances, or returned their civility.—I was in general despised among the fashionable company, as a low fellow, both in breeding and circumstances; nevertheless, I found a few individuals of moderate fortune, who gladly adopted my stile of living; and many others would have acceded to our society, had they not been prevented by the pride, envy, and ambition of their wives and daughters.—Those, in times of luxury and dissipation, are the rocks upon which all the small estates in the country are wrecked.

"I reserved in my own hands, some acres of ground adjacent to the house, for making experiments in agriculture, according to the directions of Lyle, Tull, Hart, Duhamel,[8] and others who have written on this subject; and qualified their theory with the practical observations of farmer Bland, who was my great master in the art of husbandry.——In short, I became enamoured of a country life; and my success greatly exceeded my expectation.——I drained bogs, burned heath, grubbed up furze and fern; I planted copse and willows where nothing else would grow; I gradually inclosed all my farms, and made such improvements, that my estate now yields me clear twelve hundred pounds a year.—All this time my wife and I have enjoyed uninterrupted health, and a regular flow of spirits, except on a very few occasions, when our chearfulness was invaded by such accidents as are inseparable from the condition of life. —I lost two children in their infancy, by the small-pox, so that I have one

8. Well-known writers on agriculture. Edward Lyle, or Lisle (c. 1677–1722) was the author of *Observations in Husbandry* (1757) which was edited by his son Thomas. Jethro Tull (1674–1741) was a pioneer in the modernization of farming, invented several agricultural machines, and wrote *Horse-hoing Husbandry* (1731). Walter Harte (1709–74) wrote *Essays on Husbandry* (1764). Henri Louis Duhamel de Monceau (1700–81) was a French writer on agriculture whose work was translated into English as *The Elements of Agriculture* (1764).

son only, in whom all our hopes are centred.—He went yesterday to visit a friend, with whom he has stayed all night, but he will be here to dinner. —I shall this day have the pleasure of presenting him to you and your family; and I flatter myself you will find him not altogether unworthy of our affection.

"The truth is, either I am blinded by the partiality of a parent, or he is a boy of a very amiable character; and yet his conduct has given us unspeakable disquiet.—You must know, we had projected a match between him and a gentleman's daughter in the next county, who will in all probability be heiress of a considerable fortune; but, it seems, he had a personal disgust to the alliance.—He was then at Cambridge, and tried to gain time on various pretences; but being pressed in letters by his mother and me to give a definitive answer, he fairly gave his tutor the slip, and disappeared about eight months ago.—Before he took this rash step, he wrote me a letter, explaining his objections to the match, and declaring, that he would keep himself concealed until he should understand that his parents would dispense with his contracting an engagement that must make him miserable for life, and he prescribed the form of advertising in a certain newspaper, by which he might be apprized of our sentiments on this subject.

"You may easily conceive how much we were alarmed and afflicted by this elopement, which he had made without dropping the least hint to his companion Charles Wilson, who belonged to the same college.—We resolved to punish him with the appearance of neglect, in hopes that he would return of his own accord; but he maintained his purpose till the young lady chose a partner for herself; then he produced himself, and made his peace by the mediation of Wilson.—Suppose we should unite our families by joining him with your niece, who is one of the most lovely creatures I ever beheld.—My wife is already as fond of her as if she were her own child, and I have a presentiment that my son will be captivated by her at first sight." "Nothing could be more agreeable to all our family (said I) than such an alliance; but, my dear friend, candour obliges me to tell you, that I am afraid Liddy's heart is not wholly disengaged——there is a cursed obstacle——" "You mean the young stroller at Gloucester (said he)—You are surprised that I should know this circumstance; but you will be more surprised when I tell you that stroller is no other than my son George Dennison—That was the character he assumed in his eclipse." "I am, indeed, astonished and overjoyed, (cried I) and shall be happy beyond expression to see your proposal take effect."

He then gave me to understand that the young gentleman, at his emerging from concealment, had disclosed his passion for Miss Melford, the niece of Mr. Bramble of Monmouthshire. Though Mr. Dennison little dreamed that this was his old friend Matthew Loyd, he nevertheless furnished his son with proper credentials, and he had been at Bath, London, and many other places in quest of us, to make himself and his pretensions known.—The bad success of his enquiry had such an effect upon his spirits, that immediately at his return he was seized with a dangerous fever, which overwhelmed his parents with terror and affliction; but he was now happily recovered, though still weak and disconsolate. My nephew joining us in our walk, I informed him of these circumstances, with which he was wonderfully pleased. He declared he would promote the match to the utmost of his power, and that he longed to embrace young Mr. Dennison as his friend and brother.—Mean while, the father went to desire his wife to communicate this discovery gradually to Liddy, that her delicate nerves might not suffer too sudden a shock; and I imparted the particulars to my sister Tabby, who expressed some surprize, not altogether unmixed, I believe, with an emotion of envy; for, though she could have no objection to an alliance at once so honourable and advantageous, she hesitated in giving her consent, on pretence of the youth and inexperience of the parties: at length, however, she acquiesced, in consequence of having consulted with captain Lismahago.

Mr. Dennison took care to be in the way when his son arrived at the gate, and, without giving him time or opportunity to make any enquiry about the strangers, brought him up stairs to be presented to Mr. Loyd and his family—The first person he saw, when he entered the room, was Liddy, who, notwithstanding all her preparation, stood trembling in the utmost confusion—At sight of this object he was fixed motionless to the floor, and, gazing at her with the utmost eagerness of astonishment, exclaimed, "Sacred heaven! what is this!—ha! wherefore—." Here his speech failing, he stood straining his eyes, in the most emphatic silence —"George (said his father) this is my friend Mr. Loyd." Roused at this intimation, he turned and received my salute, when I said, "Young gentleman, if you had trusted me with your secret at our last meeting, we should have parted upon better terms." Before he could make any answer, Jery came round and stood before him with open arms.—At first, he started and changed colour; but after a short pause, he rushed into his embrace, and they hugged one another as if they had been intimate friends from their infancy: then he payed his respects to Mrs. Tabitha, and advancing to Liddy, "Is it possible, (cried he) that my senses do not play me false!—that I see Miss Melford under my father's roof—that I am permitted to speak to her without giving offence—and that her relations have honoured me with their countenance and protection." Liddy blushed, and trembled, and faultered—"To be sure, sir, (said she) it is a very surprising circumstance——a great—a providential——I really know not what I say—but I beg you will think I have said what's agreeable."

Mrs. Dennison interposing said, "Compose yourselves, my dear children.—Your mutual happiness shall be our peculiar care." The son going up to his mother, kissed one hand; my niece bathed the other with her tears; and the good old lady pressed them both in their turns to her breast.—The lovers were too much affected to get rid of their embarrassment for one day; but the scene was much enlivened by the arrival of Jack Wilson, who brought, as usual, some game of his own killing——His honest countenance was a good letter of recommendation.—I received him like a dear friend after a long separation; and I could not help wondering to see him shake Jery by the hand as an old acquaintance. ——They had, indeed, been acquainted some days, in consequence of a diverting incident, which I shall explain at meeting.—That same night a consultation was held upon the concerns of the lovers, when the match was formally agreed to, and all the marriage-articles were settled without the least dispute.—My nephew and I promised to make Liddy's fortune five thousand pounds. Mr. Dennison declared, he would make over one half of his estate immediately to his son, and that his daughter-in-law should be secured in a jointure of four hundred.—Tabby proposed, that, considering their youth, they should undergo one year at least of probation before the indissoluble knot should be tied; but the young gentleman being very impatient and importunate, and the scheme implying that the young couple should live in the house, under the wings of his parents, we resolved to make them happy without further delay.

As the law requires that the parties should be some weeks resident in the parish, we shall stay here till the ceremony is performed.——Mr. Lismahago requests that he may take the benefit of the same occasion; so that next Sunday the banns will be published for all four together.—I doubt, I shall not be able to pass my Christmas with you at Brambleton-hall. —Indeed, I am so agreeably situated in this place, that I have no desire to shift my quarters; and I foresee, that when the day of separation comes, there will be abundance of sorrow on all sides.—In the mean time, we must make the most of those blessings which Heaven bestows. —Considering how you are tethered by your profession, I cannot hope to see you so far from home; yet the distance does not exceed a summer-day's journey, and Charles Dennison, who desires to be remembered to you, would be rejoiced to see his old compotator;[9] but as I am now stationary, I expect regular answers to the epistles of

Yours invariably,

Oct. 11.   MATT BRAMBLE.

9. Drinking companion.

To Sir WATKIN PHILLIPS, Bar.ᵗ at Oxon.

DEAR WAT,

Every day is now big with incident and discovery——Young Mr. Dennison proves to be no other than that identical person whom I have execrated so long, under the name of Wilson—He had eloped from college at Cambridge, to avoid a match that he detested, and acted in different parts of the country as a stroller, until the lady in question made choice of a husband for herself; then he returned to his father, and disclosed his passion for Liddy, which met with the approbation of his parents, though the father little imagined that Mr. Bramble was his old companion Matthew Loyd. The young gentleman, being impowered to make honourable proposals to my uncle and me, had been in search of us all over England, without effect; and he it was whom I had seen pass on horseback by the window of the inn, where I stood with my sister, but he little dreamed that we were in the house—As for the real Mr. Wilson, whom I called forth to combat, by mistake, he is the neighbour and intimate friend of old Mr. Dennison, and this connexion had suggested to the son the idea of taking that name while he remained in obscurity.

You may easily conceive what pleasure I must have felt on discovering that the honour of our family was in no danger from the conduct of a sister, whom I love with uncommon affection; that, instead of debasing her sentiments and views to a wretched stroller, she had really captivated the heart of a gentleman, her equal in rank and superior in fortune; and that, as his parents approved of his attachment, I was on the eve of acquiring a brother-in-law so worthy of my friendship and esteem. George Dennison is, without all question, one of the most accomplished young fellows in England. His person is at once elegant and manly, and his understanding highly cultivated. Tho' his spirit is lofty, his heart is kind; and his manner so engaging, as to command veneration and love, even from malice and indifference. When I weigh my own character with his, I am ashamed to find myself so light in the balance; but the comparison excites no envy—I propose him as a model for imitation—I have endeavoured to recommend myself to his friendship, and hope I have already found a place in his affection. I am, however, mortified to reflect what flagrant injustice we every day commit, and what absurd judgment we form, in viewing objects through the falsifying medium of prejudice and passion. Had you asked me a few days ago, the picture of Wilson the player, I should have drawn a portrait very unlike the real person and character of George Dennison—Without all doubt, the greatest advantage acquired in travelling and perusing mankind in the original, is that of dispelling those shameful clouds that darken the faculties of the mind, preventing it from judging with candour and precision.

The real Wilson is a great original, and the best tempered, companion-able man I ever knew—I question if ever he was angry or low-spirited in his life. He makes no pretensions to letters; but he is an adept in every thing else that can be either useful or entertaining. Among other qualifications, he is a complete sportsman, and counted the best shot in the county. He and Dennison, and Lismahago and I, attended by Clinker, went a-shooting yesterday, and made great havock among the partridges —To-morrow we shall take the field against the wood-cocks and snipes. In the evening we dance and sing, or play at commerce, loo, and quadrille. [1]

Mr. Dennison is an elegant poet, and has written some detached pieces on the subject of his passion for Liddy, which must be very flattering to the vanity of a young woman—Perhaps he is one of the greatest theatrical geniuses that ever appeared. He sometimes entertains us with reciting favourite speeches from our best plays. We are resolved to convert the great hall into a theatre, and get up the *Beaux Stratagem* [2] without delay—I think I shall make no contemptible figure in the character of *Scrub*; and Lismahago will be very great in *Captain Gibbet* —Wilson undertakes to entertain the country people with *Harlequin Skeleton*, [3] for which he has got a jacket ready painted with his own hand.

Our society is really enchanting. Even the severity of Lismahago relaxes, and the vinegar of Mrs. Tabby is remarkably dulcified, ever since it was agreed that she should take precedence of her niece in being first noosed: for, you must know, the day is fixed for Liddy's marriage; and the banns for both couples have been already once published in the parish church. The Captain earnestly begged that one trouble might serve for all, and Tabitha assented with a vile affectation of reluctance. Her inamorato, who came hither very slenderly equipt, has sent for his baggage to London, which, in all probability, will not arrive in time for the wedding; but it is of no great consequence, as every thing is to be transacted with the utmost privacy—Meanwhile, directions are given for making out the contracts of marriage, which are very favourable for both females; Liddy will be secured in a good jointure; and her aunt will remain mistress of her own fortune, except one half of the interest, which her husband shall have a right to enjoy for his natural life: I think this is as little in conscience as can be done for a man who yokes with such a partner for life.

These expectants seem to be so happy, that if Mr. Dennison had an agreeable daughter, I believe I should be for making the third couple in this country dance. The humour seems to be infectious; for Clinker, alias Loyd, has a month's mind to play the fool, in the same fashion, with Mrs.

---

1. Card games which were popular earlier in the century.
2. The comedy by Farquahar which was presented at Gloucester. Scrub is a servant and Captain Gibbet a highwayman in the play.
3. This title probably refers to a largely extemporaneous performance focusing on the antics of the featured Harlequin.

Winifred Jenkins. He has even sounded me on the subject; but I have given him no encouragement to prosecute this scheme—I told him I thought he might do better, as there was no engagement nor promise subsisting; that I did not know what designs my uncle might have formed for his advantage; but I was of opinion, that he should not, at present, run the risque of disobliging him by any premature application of this nature ——Honest Humphry protested he would suffer death sooner than do or say any thing that should give offence to the 'squire: but he owned he had a kindness for the young woman, and had reason to think she looked upon him with a favourable eye; that he considered this mutual manifestation of good will, as an engagement understood, which ought to be binding to the conscience of an honest man; and he hoped the 'squire and I would be of the same opinion, when we should be at leisure to bestow any thought about the matter—I believe he is in the right; and we shall find time to take his case into consideration—You see we are fixed for some weeks at least, and as you have had a long respite, I hope you will begin immediately to discharge the arrears due to

Your affectionate,

Oct. 14.   J. MELFORD.

To Miss LÆTITIA WILLIS, at Gloucester.

MY DEAR, DEAR LETTY,

Never did I sit down to write in such agitation as I now feel—In the course of a few days, we have met with a number of incidents so wonderful and interesting, that all my ideas are thrown into confusion and perplexity—You must not expect either method or coherence in what I am going to relate—my dearest Willis. Since my last, the aspect of affairs is totally changed!—and so changed!—but, I would fain give you a regular detail—In passing a river, about eight days ago, our coach was overturned, and some of us narrowly escaped with life—My uncle had well nigh perished—O Heaven, I cannot reflect upon that circumstance without horror—I should have lost my best friend, my father and protector, but for the resolution and activity of his servant Humphry Clinker, whom Providence really seems to have placed near him for the necessity of this occasion.—I would not be thought superstitious; but surely he acted from a stronger impulse than common fidelity—Was it not the voice of nature that loudly called upon him to save the life of his own father? for, O Letty, it was discovered that Humphry Clinker was my uncle's natural son.

Almost at the same instant, a gentleman, who came to offer us his assistance, and invite us to his house, turned out to be a very old friend of Mr. Bramble—His name is Mr. Dennison, one of the worthiest men

living; and his lady is a perfect saint upon earth. They have an only son
—who do you think is this only son?—O Letty!—O gracious heaven! how
my heart palpitates, when I tell you that this only son of Mr. Dennison, is
that very identical youth who, under the name of Wilson, has made such
ravage in my heart!—Yes, my dear friend! Wilson and I are now lodged in
the same house, and converse together freely—His father approves of his
sentiments in my favour; his mother loves me with all the tenderness of a
parent; my uncle, my aunt, and my brother, no longer oppose my
inclinations—On the contrary, they have agreed to make us happy
without delay; and in three weeks or a month, if no unforeseen accident
intervenes, your friend Lydia Melford, will have changed her name and
condition—I say, if *no accident intervenes*, because such a torrent of
success makes me tremble!—I wish there may not be something treacherous in this sudden reconciliation of fortune—I have no merit—I have no
title to such felicity? Far from enjoying the prospect that lies before me,
my mind is harrassed with a continued tumult, made up of hopes and
wishes, doubts and apprehensions—I can neither eat nor sleep, and my
spirits are in perpetual flutter.—I more than ever feel that vacancy in my
heart, which your presence alone can fill.—The mind, in every disquiet,
seeks to repose itself on the bosom of a friend; and this is such a trial as I
really know not how to support without your company and counsel—I
must therefore, dear Letty, put your friendship to the test—I must beg
you will come and do the last offices of maidenhood to your companion
Lydia Melford.

This letter goes inclosed in one to our worthy governess, from Mrs.
Dennison, entreating her to interpose with your mamma, that you may
be allowed to favour us with your company on this occasion; and I flatter
myself that no material objection can be made to our request—The
distance from hence to Gloucester, does not exceed one hundred miles,
and the roads are good.—Mr. Clinker, alias Loyd, shall be sent over to
attend your motions—If you step into the post-chaise, with your maid
Betty Barker, at seven in the morning, you will arrive by four in the
afternoon at the half-way house, where there is good accommodation.
There you shall be met by my brother and myself, who will next day
conduct you to this place, where, I am sure, you will find yourself
perfectly at your ease in the midst of an agreeable society.—Dear Letty, I
will take no refusal—if you have any friendship—any humanity—you
will come.—I desire that immediate application may be made to your
mamma; and that the moment her permission is obtained, you will
apprise

Your ever faithful,

LYDIA MELFORD.

Oct. 14.

To Mrs. JERMYN, at her house in Gloucester.

DEAR MADAM,

Though I was not so fortunate as to be favoured with an answer to the letter with which I troubled you in the spring, I still flatter myself that you retain some regard for me and my concerns. I am sure the care and tenderness with which I was treated, under your roof and tuition, demand the warmest returns of gratitude and affection on my part, and these sentiments, I hope, I shall cherish to my dying day—At present, I think it my duty to make you acquainted with the happy issue of that indiscretion by which I incurred your displeasure.—Ah! madam, the slighted Wilson is metamorphosed into George Dennison, only son and heir of a gentleman, whose character is second to none in England, as you may understand upon inquiry. My guardians, my brother and I, are now in his house; and an immediate union of the two families is to take place in the persons of the young gentleman and your poor Lydia Melford.—You will easily conceive how embarrassing this situation must be to a young inexperienced creature like me, of weak nerves and strong apprehensions; and how much the presence of a friend and confidante would encourage and support me on this occasion. You know, that of all the young ladies, Miss Willis was she that possessed the greatest share of my confidence and affection; and, therefore, I fervently wish to have the happiness of her company at this interesting crisis.

Mrs. Dennison, who is the object of universal love and esteem, has, at my request, written to you on this subject, and I now beg leave to reinforce her sollicitation.—My dear Mrs. Jermyn! my ever honoured governess! let me conjure you by that fondness which once distinguished your favourite Liddy! by that benevolence of heart which disposes you to promote the happiness of your fellow-creatures in general! lend a favourable ear to my petition, and use your influence with Letty's mamma, that my most earnest desire may be gratified. Should I be indulged in this particular, I will engage to return her safe, and even to accompany her to Glocester, where, if you will give me leave, I will present to you, under another name,

Dear madam,

Your most affectionate

humble servant,

and penitent,

LYDIA MELFORD.

Oct. 14.

To Mrs. MARY JONES, at Brambleton-hall.

O MARY JONES! MARY JONES!

I have met with so many axidents, suprisals, and terrifications, that I am in a parfeck fantigo, and believe I shall never be my own self again. Last week I was dragged out of a river like a drowned rat, and lost a bran-new night-cap, with a sulfur stay-hook, that cost me a good half-a-crown, and an odd shoe of green gallow monkey; besides wetting my cloaths and taring my smuck, and an ugly gash made in the back part of my thy, by the stump of a tree—To be sure Mr. Clinker tuck me out of the cox; but he left me on my back in the water, to go to the 'squire; and I mought have had a watry grave, if a millar had not brought me to the dry land —But, O! what choppings and changes girl—The player man that came after miss Liddy, and frightened me with a beard at Bristol Well, is now matthewmurphy'd into a fine young gentleman, son and hare of 'squire Dollison—We are all together in the same house, and all parties have agreed to the match, and in a fortnite the surrymony will be preformed.

But this is not the only wedding we are to have—Mistriss is resolved to have the same frolick, in the naam of God! Last Sunday in the parish crutch, if my own ars may be trusted, the clerk called the banes of marridge betwixt Opaniah Lashmeheygo, and Tapitha Brample, spinster; he mought as well have called her inkle-weaver, for she never spun and hank of yarn in her life—Young 'squire Dollison and miss Liddy make the second kipple; and there might have been a turd, but times are changed with Mr. Clinker—O, Molly! what do'st think? Mr. Clinker is found to be a pye-blow of our own 'squire, and his rite naam is Mr. Mattew Loyd (thof God he nose how that can be); and he is now out of livery, and wares ruffles—but I new him when he was out at elbows, and had not a rag to kiver his pistereroes; so he need not hold his head so high —He is for sartain very umble and compleasant, and purtests as how he has the same regard as before; but that he is no longer his own master, and cannot portend to marry without the 'squire's consent—He says we must wait with patience, and trust to Providence, and such nonsense—But if so be as how his regard be the same, why stand shilly shally? Why not strike while the iron is hot, and speak to the 'squire without loss of time? —What subjection can the 'squire make to our coming together?—Thof my father wan't a gentleman, my mother was an honest woman—I did'n't come on the wrong side of the blanket, girl—My parents were marred according to the rights of holy mother crutch, in the face of men and angles—Mark that, Mary Jones.

Mr. Clinker (Loyd I would say) had best look to his tackle—There be other chaps in the market, as the saying is——What would he say if I should except the soot and sarvice of the young 'squire's valley? Mr. Machappy is a gentleman born, and has been abroad in the wars—He has a world of buck larning, and speaks French, and Ditch, and Scotch, and all manner of outlandish lingos; to be sure he's a little the worse for the ware, and is much given to drink; but then he's good-tempered in his liquor, and a prudent woman mought wind him about her finger—But I have no thoughts of him, I'll assure you——I scorn for to do, or to say, or to think any thing that mought give unbreech to Mr. Loyd, without furder occasion—But then I have such vapours, Molly—I sit and cry by myself, and take ass of etida,[4] and smill to burnt fathers, and kindal-snuffs; and I pray constantly for grease, that I may have a glimpse of the new-light, to shew me the way through this wretched veil of tares—And yet, I want for nothing in this family of love, where every sole is so kind and so courteous, that wan would think they are so many saints in haven. Dear Molly, I recommend myself to your prayers, being, with my sarvice to Saul,

> your ever loving,
>
> and discounselled friend,

Octr. 14.   WIN. JENKINS.

To Dr. LEWIS.

DEAR DICK,

You cannot imagine what pleasure I have in seeing your hand-writing, after such a long cessation on your side of our correspondence—Yet, Heaven knows, I have often seen your hand-writing with disgust—I mean, when it appeared in abbreviations of apothecary's Latin—I like your hint of making interest for the reversion of the collector's place, for Mr. Lismahago, who is much pleased with the scheme, and presents you with his compliments and best thanks for thinking so kind of his concerns —The man seems to mend, upon further acquaintance. That harsh reserve, which formed a disagreeable husk about his character, begins to peel off in the course of our communication——I have great hopes that he and Tabby will be as happily paired as any two draught animals in the kingdom; and I make no doubt but that he will prove a valuable acquisition to our little society, in the article of conversation, by the fire-side in winter.

Your objection to my passing this season of the year at such a distance from home, would have more weight if I did not find myself perfectly at my ease where I am; and my health so much improved, that I am disposed to bid defiance to gout and rheumatism.—I begin to think I have put

4. As noted above (p. 17), this smelly resin, called assafetida, was used for medicinal purposes, including, as here, as a cure for the "vapors," minor fits of depression. Smelling burnt feathers and the snuffing of candles was also believed to have a salutary effect in raising one's spirits.

myself on the superannuated list too soon, and absurdly sought for health in the retreats of laziness—I am persuaded that all valetudinarians are too sedentary, too regular, and too cautious——We should sometimes increase the motion of the machine, to *unclog the wheels of life;*[5] and now and then take a plunge amidst the waves of excess, in order to case-harden the constitution. I have even found a change of company as necessary as a change of air, to promote a vigorous circulation of the spirits, which is the very essence and criterion of good health.

Since my last, I have been performing the duties of friendship, that required a great deal of exercise, from which I hope to derive some benefit—Understanding, by the greatest accident in the world, that Mr. Baynard's wife was dangerously ill of a pleuritic fever, I borrowed Dennison's post-chaise, and went a-cross the country to his habitation, attended only by Loyd (quondam Clinker) on horseback.—As the distance is not above thirty miles, I arrived about four in the afternoon, and meeting the physician at the door, was informed that his patient had just expired.—I was instantly seized with a violent emotion, but it was not grief.—The family being in confusion, I ran up stairs into the chamber, where, indeed, they were all assembled—The aunt stood wringing her hands in a kind of stupefaction of sorrow, but my friend acted all the extravagancies of affliction——He held the body in his arms, and poured forth such a lamentation, that one would have thought he had lost the most amiable consort and valuable companion upon earth.

Affection may certainly exist independent of esteem; nay, the same object may be lovely in one respect, and detestable in another—The mind has a surprising faculty of accommodating, and even attaching itself, in such a manner, by dint of use, to things that are in their own nature disagreeable, and even pernicious, that it cannot bear to be delivered from them without reluctance and regret. Baynard was so absorbed in his delirium, that he did not perceive me when I entered, and desired one of the women to conduct the aunt into her own chamber. —At the same time I begged the tutor to withdraw the boy, who stood gaping in a corner, very little affected with the distress of the scene. —These steps being taken, I waited till the first violence of my friend's transport was abated, then disengaged him gently from the melancholy object, and led him by the hand into another apartment; though he struggled so hard, that I was obliged to have recourse to the assistance of his valet de chambre.——In a few minutes, however, he recollected himself, and folding me in his arms, "This (cried he) is a friendly office, indeed!——I know not how you came hither; but, I think, Heaven sent you to prevent my going distracted.—O Matthew! I have lost my dear Harriet!—my poor, gentle, tender creature, that loved me with such

5. Probably an allusion to or misquotation of a poem by Smollett's friend John Armstrong, called *The Art of Preserving Health* (1744), where the line is "unloads the wheels of life."

warmth and purity of affection—my constant companion of twenty years!—She's gone—she's gone for ever!—Heaven and earth! where is she?——Death shall not part us!"

So saying, he started up, and could hardly be with-held from returning to the scene we had quitted—You will perceive it would have been very absurd for me to argue with a man that talked so madly.—On all such occasions, the first torrent of passion must be allowed to subside gradually.—I endeavoured to beguile his attention by starting little hints and insinuating other objects of discourse imperceptibly; and being exceedingly pleased in my own mind at this event, I exerted myself with such an extraordinary flow of spirits as was attended with success.——In a few hours, he was calm enough to hear reason, and even to own that Heaven could not have interposed more effectually to rescue him from disgrace and ruin.—That he might not, however, relapse into weaknesses for want of company, I passed the night in his chamber, in a little tent bed brought thither on purpose; and well it was I took this precaution, for he started up in bed several times, and would have played the fool, if I had not been present.

Next day he was in a condition to talk of business, and vested me with full authority over his household, which I began to exercise without loss of time, tho' not before he knew and approved of the scheme I had projected for his advantage.—He would have quitted the house immediately; but this retreat I opposed.——Far from encouraging a temporary disgust, which might degenerate into an habitual aversion, I resolved, if possible, to attach him more than ever to his Household Gods.—I gave directions for the funeral to be as private as was consistent with decency; I wrote to London, that an inventory and estimate might be made of the furniture and effects in his town-house, and gave notice to the landlord, that Mr. Baynard should quit the premises at Lady-day; I set a person at work to take account of every thing in the country-house, including horses, carriages, and harness; I settled the young gentleman at a boarding-school, kept by a clergyman in the neighbourhood, and thither he went without reluctance, as soon as he knew that he was to be troubled no more with his tutor, whom we dismissed.—The aunt continued very sullen, and never appeared at table, though Mr. Baynard payed his respects to her every day in her own chamber; there also she held conferences with the waiting-women and other servants of the family: but, the moment her niece was interred, she went away in a post-chaise prepared for that purpose: she did not leave the house, however, without giving Mr. Baynard to understand, that the wardrobe of her niece was the perquisite of her woman; accordingly that worthless drab received all the clothes, laces, and linen of her deceased mistress, to the value of five hundred pounds, at a moderate computation.

The next step I took was to disband that legion of supernumerary domestics, who had preyed so long upon the vitals of my friend: a parcel of idle drones, so intolerably insolent, that they even treated their own master with the most contemptuous neglect. They had been generally hired by his wife, according to the recommendation of her woman, and these were the only patrons to whom they payed the least deference. I had therefore uncommon satisfaction in clearing the house of those vermin. The woman of the deceased, and a chambermaid, a valet de chambre, a butler, a French cook, a master gardener, two footmen, and a coachman, I payed off, and turned out of the house immediately, paying to each a month's wages in lieu of warning. Those whom I retained, consisted of a female cook, who had been assistant to the Frenchman, a house maid, an old lacquey, a postilion, and under-gardener. Thus I removed at once a huge mountain of expence and care from the shoulders of my friend, who could hardly believe the evidence of his own senses, when he found himself so suddenly and so effectually relieved. His heart, however, was still subject to vibrations of tenderness, which returned at certain intervals, extorting sighs, and tears, and exclamations of grief and impatience: but these fits grew every day less violent and less frequent, 'till at length his reason obtained a complete victory over the infirmities of his nature.

Upon an accurate inquiry into the state of his affairs, I find his debts amount to twenty thousand pounds, for eighteen thousand pounds of which sum his estate is mortgaged; and as he pays five per cent. interest, and some of his farms are unoccupied, he does not receive above two hundred pounds a year clear from his lands, over and above the interest of his wife's fortune, which produced eight hundred pounds annually. For lightening this heavy burthen, I devised the following expedient.—His wife's jewels, together with his superfluous plate and furniture in both houses, his horses and carriages, which are already advertised to be sold by auction, will, according to the estimate, produce two thousand five hundred pounds in ready money, with which the debt will be immediately reduced to eighteen thousand pounds—I have undertaken to find him ten thousand pounds at four per cent. by which means he will save one hundred a-year in the article of interest, and perhaps we shall be able to borrow the other eight thousand on the same terms. According to his own scheme of a country life, he says he can live comfortably for three hundred pounds a year; but, as he has a son to educate, we will allow him five hundred; then there will be an accumulating fund of seven hundred a-year, principal and interest, to pay off the incumbrance; and, I think, we may modestly add three hundred, on the presumption of new-leasing and improving the vacant farms: so that, in a couple of years, I suppose there will be above a thousand a-year appropriated to liquidate a debt of sixteen thousand.

We forthwith began to class and set apart the articles designed for sale, under the direction of an upholder from London; and, that nobody in the house might be idle, commenced our reformation without doors, as well as within. With Baynard's good leave, I ordered the gardner to turn the rivulet into its old channel, to refresh the fainting Naiads, who had so long languished among mouldring roots, withered leaves, and dry pebbles.—The shrubbery is condemned to extirpation; and the pleasure-ground will be restored to its original use of corn-field and pasture. —Orders are given for rebuilding the walls of the garden at the back of the house, and for planting clumps of firs, intermingled with beech and chesnut, at the east end, which is now quite exposed to the surly blasts that come from that quarter. All these works being actually begun, and the house and auction left to the care and management of a reputable attorney, I brought Baynard along with me in the chaise, and made him acquainted with Dennison, whose goodness of heart would not fail to engage his esteem and affection.—He is indeed charmed with our society in general, and declares that he never saw the theory of true pleasure reduced to practice before.—I really believe it would not be an easy task to find such a number of individuals assembled under one roof, more happy than we are at present.

I must tell you, however, in confidence, I suspect Tabby of tergiversation.—I have been so long accustomed to that original, that I know all the caprices of her heart, and can often perceive her designs while they are yet in embrio—She attached herself to Lismahago for no other reason but that she despaired of making a more agreeable conquest.—At present, if I am not much mistaken in my observation, she would gladly convert the widowhood of Baynard to her own advantage.—Since he arrived, she has behaved very coldly to the captain, and strove to fasten on the other's heart, with the hooks of over-strained civility.—These must be the instinctive efforts of her constitution, rather than the effects of any deliberate design; for matters are carried to such a length with the lieutenant, that she could not retract with any regard to conscience or reputation. Besides, she will meet with nothing but indifference or aversion on the side of Baynard, who has too much sense to think of such a partner at any time, and too much delicacy to admit a thought of any such connexion at the present juncture—Meanwhile, I have prevailed upon her to let him have four thousand pounds at four per cent. towards paying off his mortgage. Young Dennison has agreed that Liddy's fortune shall be appropriated to the same purpose, on the same terms.—His father will sell out three thousand pounds stock for his accommodation. —Farmer Bland has, at the desire of Wilson, undertaken for two thousand; and I must make an effort to advance what further will be required to take my friend out of the hands of the Philistines. He is so pleased with the improvements made on this estate, which is all cultivated like a garden, that he has entered himself as a pupil in farming to Mr. Dennison, and resolved to attach himself wholly to the practice of husbandry.

Every thing is now prepared for our double wedding. The marriage-articles for both couples are drawn and executed; and the ceremony only waits until the parties shall have been resident in the parish the term prescribed by law. Young Dennison betrays some symptoms of impatience; but, Lismahago bears this necessary delay with the temper of a philosopher.—You must know, the captain does not stand altogether on the foundation of personal merit. Besides his half-pay, amounting to two and forty pounds a year, this indefatigable œconomist has amassed eight hundred pounds, which he has secured in the funds. This sum arises partly from his pay's running up while he remained among the Indians; partly from what he received as a consideration for the difference between his full appointment and the half-pay, to which he is now restricted; and partly from the profits of a little traffic he drove in peltry, during his sachemship among the Miamis.

Liddy's fears and perplexities have been much assuaged by the company of one Miss Willis, who had been her intimate companion at the boarding-school. Her parents had been earnestly sollicited to allow her making this friendly visit on such an extraordinary occasion; and two days ago she arrived with her mother, who did not chuse that she should come without a proper gouvernante. The young lady is very sprightly, handsome, and agreeable, and the mother a mighty good sort of a woman; so that their coming adds considerably to our enjoyment. But we shall have a third couple yoked in the matrimonial chain. Mr. Clinker Loyd has made humble remonstrance, through the canal of my nephew, setting forth the sincere love and affection mutually subsisting between him and Mrs. Winifred Jenkins, and praying my consent to their coming together for life. I would have wished that Mr. Clinker had kept out of this scrape; but as the nymph's happiness is at stake, and she has had already some fits in the way of despondence, I, in order to prevent any tragical catastrophe, have given him leave to play the fool, in imitation of his betters; and I suppose we shall in time have a whole litter of his progeny at Brambleton-hall. The fellow is stout and lusty, very sober and conscientious; and the wench seems to be as great an enthusiast in love as in religion.

I wish you would think of employing him some other way, that the parish may not be overstocked—you know he has been bred a farrier, consequently belongs to the faculty; and as he is very docile, I make no doubt but, with your good instruction, he may be, in a little time, qualified to act as a Welsh apothecary. Tabby, who never did a favour with a good grace, has consented, with great reluctance, to this match. Perhaps it hurts her pride, as she now considers Clinker in the light of a relation; but, I believe, her objections are of a more selfish nature. She declares she cannot think of retaining the wife of Matthew Loyd in the character of a servant; and she foresees, that on such an occasion the woman will expect some gratification for her past services. As for Clinker, exclusive of other considerations, he is so trusty, brave, affectionate, and alert, and I owe him such personal obligations, that he merits more than all the indulgence that can possibly be shewn him, by

yours,

Oct. 26.[6]   MATT. BRAMBLE.

To Sir WATKIN PHILLIPS, Bar[t]. at Oxon.

DEAR KNIGHT,

The fatal knots are now tied. The comedy is near a close; and the curtain is ready to drop: but, the latter scenes of this act I shall recapitulate in order.—About a fortnight ago, my uncle made an excursion across the country, and brought hither a particular friend, one Mr. Baynard, who has just lost his wife, and was for some time disconsolate, though by all accounts he had much more cause for joy than for sorrow at this event.—His countenance, however, clears up apace; and he appears to be a person of rare accomplishments.—But, we have received another still more agreeable reinforcement to our company, by the arrival of Miss Willis from Glocester. She was Liddy's bosom friend at boarding-school, and being earnestly sollicited to assist at the nuptials, her mother was so obliging as to grant my sister's request, and even to come with her in person. Liddy, accompanied by George Dennison and me, gave them the meeting half-way, and next day conducted them hither in safety. Miss Willis is a charming girl, and, in point of disposition, an agreeable contrast to my sister, who is rather too grave and sentimental for my turn of mind.—The other is gay, frank, a little giddy, and always good-humoured. She has, moreover, a genteel fortune, is well born, and remarkably handsome.—Ah Phillips! if these qualities were permanent —if her humour would never change, nor her beauties decay, what efforts would I not make—But these are idle reflections—my destiny must one day be fulfilled.

At present we pass the time as agreeably as we can.—We have got up several farces, which afforded unspeakable entertainment by the effects they produced among the country people, who are admitted to all our exhibitions.—Two nights ago, Jack Wilson acquired great applause in Harlequin Skeleton, and Lismahago surprized us all in the character of Pierot.—His long lank sides, and strong marked features, were all peculiarly adapted to his part.——He appeared with a ludicrous stare, from which he had discharged all meaning: he adopted the impressions of

6. Franklin B. Newman has argued that the dating of this letter should follow the second edition, which changes this date to October 25 and the letter of Jery just below from November 8 to November 14. This would bring the chronology of the latter stages of the novel into conformity with the marriage laws of the period. While the argument is appealing, there is little evidence that Smollett was concerned with precise chronology in the novel or that he had a hand in preparing the second edition, so the editor has retained the dates of the first edition.

fear and amazement so naturally, that many of the audience were infected by his looks; but when the skeleton held him in chace his horror became most divertingly picturesque, and seemed to endow him with such præternatural agility as confounded all the spectators. It was a lively representation of Death in pursuit of Consumption, and had such an effect upon the commonalty, that some of them shrieked aloud, and others ran out of the hall in the utmost consternation.

This is not the only instance in which the lieutenant has lately excited our wonder. His temper, which had been soured and shrivelled by disappointment and chagrin, is now swelled out, and smoothed like a raisin in plum-porridge. From being reserved and punctilious, he is become easy and obliging. He cracks jokes, laughs and banters, with the most facetious familiarity; and, in a word, enters into all our schemes of merriment and pastime—The other day his baggage arrived in the waggon from London, contained in two large trunks and a long deal box not unlike a coffin. The trunks were filled with his wardrobe, which he displayed for the entertainment of the company, and he freely owned, that it consisted chiefly of the *opima spolia*[7] taken in battle. What he selected for his wedding suit, was a tarnished white cloth faced with blue velvet, embroidered with silver; but, he valued himself most upon a tye-periwig, in which he had made his first appearance as a lawyer above thirty years ago. This machine had been in buckle[8] ever since, and now all the servants in the family were employed to frizz it out for the occasion, which was yesterday celebrated at the parish church. George Dennison and his bride were distinguished by nothing extraordinary in their apparel. His eyes lightened with eagerness and joy, and she trembled with coyness and confusion. My uncle gave her away, and her friend Willis supported her during the ceremony.

But my aunt and her paramour took the pas,[9] and formed, indeed, such a pair of originals, as, I believe, all England could not parallel. She was dressed in the stile of 1739; and the day being cold, put on a manteel of green velvet laced with gold: but this was taken off by the bridegroom, who threw over her shoulders a fur cloak of American sables, valued at fourscore guineas, a present equally agreeable and unexpected. Thus accoutred, she was led up to the altar by Mr. Dennison, who did the office of her father: Lismahago advanced in the military step with his French coat reaching no farther than the middle of his thigh, his campaign wig that surpasses all description, and a languishing leer upon his countenance, in which there seemed to be something arch and ironical. The ring, which he put upon her finger, he had concealed till the moment it was used. He now produced it with an air of self-complacency. It was a

---

7. A reversal of a Latin tag from Virgil, *spolia opima*, which means the spoils taken from the enemy's general when slain by the commander of the army himself.
8. Kept in the same curled state.
9. Step.

curious antique, set with rose diamonds: he told us afterwards, it had been in his family two hundred years, and was a present from his grand-mother. These circumstances agreeably flattered the pride of our aunt Tabitha, which had already found uncommon gratification in the cap-tain's generosity; for he had, in the morning, presented my uncle with a fine bear's skin, and a Spanish fowling-piece, and me with a case of pistols curiously mounted with silver. At the same time he gave Mrs. Jenkins an Indian purse, made of silk grass, containing twenty crown pieces. You must know, this young lady, with the assistance of Mr. Loyd, formed the third couple who yesterday sacrificed to Hymen. I wrote to you in my last, that he had recourse to my mediation, which I employed successfully with my uncle; but Mrs. Tabitha held out 'till the love-sick Jenkins had two fits of the mother; then she relented, and those two cooing turtles were caged for life—Our aunt made an effort of generosity in furnishing the bride with her superfluities of clothes and linen, and her example was followed by my sister; nor did Mr. Bramble and I neglect her on this occasion. It was, indeed, a day of peace offering—Mr. Dennison insisted upon Liddy's accepting two bank notes of one hundred pounds each, as pocket-money; and his lady gave her a diamond necklace of double that value. There was, besides, a mutual exchange of tokens among the individuals of the two families thus happily united.

As George Dennison and his partner were judged improper objects of mirth, Jack Wilson had resolved to execute some jokes on Lismahago, and after supper began to ply him with bumpers, when the ladies had retired; but the captain perceiving his drift, begged for quarter, alledging that the adventure, in which he had engaged, was a very serious matter; and that it would be more the part of a good Christian to pray that he might be strengthened, than to impede his endeavours to finish the adventure.—He was spared accordingly, and permitted to ascend the nuptial couch with all his senses about him.—There he and his consort sat in state, like Saturn and Cybele, while the benediction-posset was drank; and a cake being broken over the head of Mrs. Tabitha Lis-mahago, the fragments were distributed among the bystanders, accord-ing to the custom of the antient Britons, on the supposition that every person who ate of this hallowed cake, should that night have a vision of the man or woman whom Heaven designed should be his or her wedded mate.

The weight of Wilson's waggery fell upon honest Humphry and his spouse, who were bedded in an upper room, with the usual ceremony of throwing the stocking.—This being performed, and the company with-drawn, a sort of catter-wauling ensued, when Jack found means to introduce a real cat shod with walnut-shells, which galloping along the boards, made such a dreadful noise as effectually discomposed our lovers.
——Winifred screamed aloud, and shrunk under the bed-cloaths.—Mr. Loyd, believing that Satan was come to buffet him *in propria persona*, laid

The Marriage of Lieut. Lismahago and Mrs Tabitha &^c.

aside all carnal thoughts, and began to pray aloud with great fervency.
—At length, the poor animal, being more afraid than either, leaped into
the bed, and meauled with the most piteous exclamation.—Loyd, thus
informed of the nature of the annoyance, rose and set the door wide
open, so that this troublesome visitant retreated with great expedition;
then securing himself, by means of a double bolt, from a second intrusion,
he was left to enjoy his good fortune without further disturbance.

If one may judge from the looks of the parties, they are all very well
satisfied with what has passed.—George Dennison and his wife are too
delicate to exhibit any strong-marked signs of their mutual satisfaction,
but their eyes are sufficiently expressive.—Mrs. Tabitha Lismahago is
rather fulsome in signifying her approbation of the captain's love; while
his deportment is the very pink of gallantry.—He sighs, and ogles, and
languishes at this amiable object; he kisses her hand, mutters ejaculations
of rapture, and sings tender airs; and, no doubt, laughs internally at her
folly in believing him sincere.—In order to shew how little his vigour was
impaired by the fatigues of the preceding day, he this morning danced a
Highland sarabrand over a naked back-sword, and leaped so high, that I
believe he would make no contemptible figure as a vaulter at Sadler's
Wells.—Mr. Matthew Loyd, when asked how he relishes his bargain,
throws up his eyes, crying, "For what we have received, Lord make us
thankful: amen."——His helpmate giggles, and holds her hand before
her eyes, affecting to be ashamed of having been in bed with a man.
—Thus all these widgeons[1] enjoy the novelty of their situation; but,
perhaps their note will be changed, when they are better acquainted with
the nature of the decoy.

As Mrs. Willis cannot be persuaded to stay, and Liddy is engaged by
promise to accompany her daughter back to Gloucester, I fancy there
will be a general migration from hence, and that most of us will spend the
Christmas holidays at Bath; in which case, I shall certainly find an
opportunity to beat up your quarters.—By this time, I suppose, you are
sick of *alma mater*, and even ready to execute that scheme of peregrination, which was last year concerted between you and

Your affectionate

Nov. 8.   J. MELFORD.

1. Simpletons; literally, a kind of duck.

To Dr. LEWIS.

DEAR DOCTOR,

My niece Liddy is now happily settled for life; and captain Lismahago has taken Tabby off my hands; so that I have nothing further to do, but to comfort my friend Baynard, and provide for my son Loyd, who is also fairly joined to Mrs. Winifred Jenkins.—You are an excellent genius at hints.—Dr. Arbuthnot[2] was but a type[3] of Dr. Lewis in that respect. ——What you observe of the vestry-clerk deserves consideration.—I make no doubt but Matthew Loyd is well enough qualified for the office; but, at present, you must find room for him in the house.——His incorruptible honesty and indefatigable care will be serviceable in superintending the œconomy of my farm; tho' I don't mean that he shall interfere with Barns, of whom I have no cause to complain.—I am just returned with Baynard, from a second trip to his house, where every thing is regulated to his satisfaction.—He could not, however, review the apartments without tears and lamentation, so that he is not yet in a condition to be left alone; therefore I will not part with him till the spring, when he intends to plunge into the avocations of husbandry, which will at once employ and amuse his attention.—Charles Dennison has promised to stay with him a fortnight, to set him fairly afloat in his improvements; and Jack Wilson will see him from time to time; besides, he has a few friends in the country, whom his new plan of life will not exclude from his society.—In less than a year, I make no doubt, but he will find himself perfectly at ease both in his mind and body, for the one had dangerously affected the other; and I shall enjoy the exquisite pleasure of seeing my friend rescued from misery and contempt.

Mrs. Willis being determined to return with her daughter, in a few days, to Gloucester, our plan has undergone some alteration.—Jery has persuaded his brother-in-law to carry his wife to Bath; and I believe his parents will accompany him thither.—For my part, I have no intention to take that route.—It must be something very extraordinary that will induce me to revisit either Bath or London.——My sister and her husband, Baynard and I, will take leave of them at Gloucester, and make the best of our way to Brambleton-hall, where I desire you will prepare a good chine and turkey for our Christmas dinner.——You must also employ your medical skill in defending me from the attacks of the gout, that I may be in good case to receive the rest of our company, who promise to visit us in their return from the Bath.——As I have laid in a considerable stock of health, it is to be hoped you will not have much trouble with me in the way of physic, but I intend to work you on the side

2. Dr. John Arbuthnot (1667–1735) was a physician to Queen Anne, and close friend to Alexander Pope, Jonathan Swift, and John Gay. He reportedly gave many authors hints for their works.
3. A forerunner, as John the Baptist was a type of Christ.

of exercise.—I have got an excellent fowling-piece from Mr. Lismahago, who is a keen sportsman, and we shall take the heath in all weathers. —That this scheme of life may be prosecuted the more effectually, I intend to renounce all sedentary amusements, particularly that of writing long letters; a resolution, which, had I taken it sooner, might have saved you the trouble which you have lately taken in reading the tedious epistles of

Nov. 20.   MATT. BRAMBLE.

To Mrs. GWYLLIM, at Brambleton-hall.

GOOD MRS. GWILLIM,

Heaven, for wise porpuses, hath ordained that I should change my name and citation in life, so that I am not to be considered any more as manger of my brother's family; but as I cannot surrender up my stewardship till I have settled with you and Williams, I desire you will get your accunts ready for inspection, as we are coming home without further delay.——My spouse, the captain, being subject to rummaticks, I beg you will take great care to have the blew chamber, up two pair of stairs, well warmed for his reception.—Let the sashes be secured, the crevices stopt, the carpets laid, and the beds well tousled.—Mrs. Loyd, late Jenkins, being married to a relation of the family, cannot remain in the capacity of a sarvant; therefore, I wish you would cast about for some creditable body to be with me in her room—If she can spin, and is mistress of plain-work, so much the better—but she must not expect extravagant wages—having a family of my own, I must be more occumenical than ever. No more at present, but rests

Your loving friend,

Nov. 20.   TAB. LISMAHAGO.

To Mrs. MARY JONES, at Brambleton-hall.

MRS. JONES,

Providinch hath bin pleased to make great halteration in the pasture of our affairs.——We were yesterday three kiple chined, by the grease of God, in the holy bands of mattermoney, and I now subscrive myself Loyd at your sarvice.—All the parish allowed that young 'squire Dallison and his bride was a comely pear for to see.—As for madam Lashmiheygo, you nose her picklearities—her head, to be sure, was fintastical; and her spouse had rapt her with a long marokin furze cloak from the land of the selvidges, thof they say it is of immense bally.—The captain himself had a huge hassock of air, with three tails, and a tumtawdry coat, boddered with sulfur.—Wan said he was a monkey-bank; and the ould bottler swore he was the born imich of Titidall. [4]——For my part, I says nothing, being as how the captain has done the handsome thing by me.—Mr. Loyd was dressed in a lite frog, and checket with gould binding; and thof he don't enter in caparison with great folks of quality, yet he has got as good blood in his veins as arrow privet 'squire in the county; and then his pursing is far from contentible.—Your humble sarvant had on a plain pea-green tabby sack, with my Runnela cap, [5] ruff toupee, and side curls. —They said, I was the very moral of lady Rickmanstone, but not so pale —that may well be, for her layship is my elder by seven good years and more.—Now, Mrs. Mary, our satiety is to suppurate—Mr. Millfart goes to Bath along with the Dallisons, and the rest of us push home to Wales, to pass our Chrishmarsh at Brampleton hall.—As our apartment is to be the yellow pepper, in the thurd story, pray carry my things thither. ——Present my cumpliments to Mrs. Gwyllim, and I hope she and I will live upon dissent terms of civility.—Being, by God's blessing, removed to a higher spear, you'll excuse my being familiar with the lower sarvents of the family; but, as I trust you'll behave respectful, and keep a proper distance, you may always depend upon the good will and purtection of

Yours,

Nov. 20.   W. LOYD.

FINIS.

4. Probably the devil Titivil, who was a character in the mystery plays, and whose name came to mean reprobate. Monkey bank, just above, is Win's approximation of mountebank, a patent medicine showman who worked from a raised stage.
5. A Ranelagh cap, which was named after the fashionable park in London.

Contemporary
Responses

The Critical Review†

Though novels have long since been divested of that extravagance which characterised the earlier productions in Romance, they have, nevertheless, continued, in the hands of meaner writers, to be distinguished by a similarity of fable, which, notwithstanding it is of a different cast, and less unnatural than the former, is still no less unfit for affording agreeable entertainment. From the wild excursions of fancy, invention is brought home to range through the probable occurrences of life; but, however, it may have improved in point of credibility, it is certainly too often deficient with regard to variety of adventure. With many, an adherence to simplicity has produced the effects of dulness; and, with most, too close an imitation of their predecessors has excluded the pleasure of novelty.

The celebrated author of this production is one of those few writers who have discovered an original genius. His novels are not more distinguished for the natural management of the fable, and a fertility of interesting incidents, than for a strong, lively, and picturesque description of characters. The same vigour of imagination that animates his other works, is conspicuous in the present, where we are entertained with a variety of scenes and characters almost unanticipated. Those, in particular, of Mr. Bramble, Mrs. Tabitha Bramble, and lieutenant Lismahago, are painted with the highest touches of discriminating humour and expression. As to Humphry Clinker, he is only to be considered as the nominal hero of the work.

The inimitable descriptions of life, which we have already observed to be so remarkable in our author's works, receive, if possible, an additional force from the epistolary manner, in which this novel is written; which is farther enhanced by the contrast that arises from the general alternate insertion of the letters of the several correspondents.[1]

* * *

The letters from Mr. Bramble, and Mr. Melford, his nephew, upon their expedition to North Britain, contain so many interesting observations, that they must not only gratify every reader of curiosity, but also tend to correct many wrong notions concerning that part of the island. We would willingly give an account of many of the particulars related of Edinburgh and its inhabitants, but as our readers are probably less acquainted with the manners of the people farther North, we shall extract the representation which is given of the oeconomy in the house of a Highland gentleman.

---

† From *The Critical Review* 32 (August 1771): 81–88.
1. At this point the reviewer inserts a selection from Jery's letter describing Matt's conduct with the widow.

* * *

We should deprive our readers of a prospect of, perhaps, one of the most beautiful rural scenes that exists in nature, did we not produce the account of the water of Leven, with Dr. Smollett's description of it, in an highly poetical ode. We find, from another passage in the work, that Lough Lomond, from whence the river Leven issues, is a body of pure transparent water, unfathomably deep in many places, six or seven miles broad, and four and twenty miles in length, displaying above twenty green islands, covered with wood; some of them cultivated for corn, and many of them stocked with red deer.

* * *

Instead of visionary scenes and persons, the usual subjects of romance, we are frequently presented with many uncommon anecdotes, and curious exhibitions of real life, described in such a manner as to afford a pleasure even superior to what arises from the portraits of fancy. We are every where entertained with the narration or description of something interesting and extraordinary, calculated at once to amuse the imagination, and release the understanding from prejudice. Upon the whole, the various merit of this production might raise to eminence a writer of inferior reputation to that of its celebrated author; and we should have indulged ourselves in extracting more copiously from it, were we not certain that the original must come into the hands of all such as are readers of taste, by whom we may venture to affirm it will be ranked among the most entertaining performances of the kind.

Hibernian Magazine†

The singular merit of the Expedition of Humphry Clinker just published in Dublin, (by the author of Roderick Random) hath induced us to present our Readers with the following extracts, being satirical Descriptions of London and Bath, which, we doubt not, will be agreeable and entertaining.

Court and City Magazine‡

The characters are strongly marked in point of spirit and humour, and supported with great propriety. Old Bramble is a curious original, and does honour even to the pen of Dr. Smollett.

† From the *Hibernian Magazine* (Dublin), 1 (1771): 324. This Dublin journal did not usually print extracts from novels but made an exception in the case of *Humphry Clinker*.

‡ From the *Court and City Magazine* 2 (1771): 324. This London periodical also printed excerpts from the novel, contrary to its usual practice.

Town and Country Magazine†

We seldom make Extracts from printed Books, as our Intention is to furnish our Readers with original Matter, a Plan never before attempted; but the singular Merit of *Humphry Clinker*, (by the author of *Roderick Random*) has made us so far deviate from our general Plan, as to present our Readers with the following satirical Descriptions of London and Bath, which we doubt not will to them be agreeable and entertaining.[2]

* * *

The author of [*Humphry Clinker*] has so completely established his reputation as a novel writer, that to say this performance is not inferior to any of his former pieces, will be a sufficient recommendation of the work.

Gentleman's Magazine‡

This work is by no means a novel or romance, of which Humphry Clinker is the hero; Humphry makes almost as inconsiderable a figure in this work as the dog does in the history of Tobit: nor is it indeed principally a narrative of events, but rather a miscellany containing dissertations on various subjects, exhibitions of character, and descriptions of places. Many of the characters are drawn with a free but a masterly hand; in some particulars perhaps they are exaggerated, but are not therefore the less entertaining or instructive: Some appear to be pictures of particular persons, but others of human nature, represented indeed in individuals peculiarly distinguished, but drawn rather from imagination than life. Some, however, are as extravagant as the fancies of Calot, but though they do not less deviate from nature, their irregularities discover the same vivacity and spirit.

In this part of the work consists its principal excellence, and its principal defect is the want of events. The whole story might be told in a few pages, and the author has been so parsimonious of his invention, that he has twice overturned a coach, and twice introduced a fire, to exhibit a scene of ridiculous distress, by setting women on their heads, and making some of his dramatic characters descend from a window by a ladder, as they rose out of bed.

It is by no means deficient in sentiment, and it abounds with satire that is equally sprightly and just. It has, however, blemishes, which would be less regretted where there was less to commend. In the celebrated treatise on the art of sinking in poetry, under the article stile, the incomparable author[3] considers one, which on account of the source

† From the *Town and Country Magazine* 3 (1771): 317, 323.

2. The *Town and Country Magazine* introduced its excerpts from the novel with the preceding paragraph, and in the same issue, in the section devoted to accounts of new books and pamphlets, the editors added a further mention.

‡ From the *Gentleman's Magazine* 41 (July 1771): 317.

3. Alexander Pope (1688–1744) published *Peri Bathous or The Art of Sinking in Poetry* in 1728. It was a mock criticism.

whence it is derived, he calls the *prurient*; there is another stile, which, with respect to its source, may justly be termed the *stercoraceous*.[4] The stercoraceous stile would certainly have found a place in the art of sinking, if had been then to be found in any author not wholly contemptible. But it was not then in being; its original author was Swift,[5] the only writer who had ever made nastiness the vehicle of wit: since his time they have frequently been confounded, and by those who could not distinguish better, the nastiness has been mistaken for the wit: Swift therefore has been imitated in this particular by those who could imitate him in nothing else; and others have, under the sanction of Swift, taken the liberty to be filthy, who were under no necessity to seek occasions for wit in an hospital or a jakes.

-The stile of this work is frequently *stercoraceous*, and sometimes it is also *prurient*. The *prurient* however is as harmless as the *stercoraceous*, as it tends much more to chill than to inflame every imagination, except perhaps those of the thieves and bunters in Broad St. Giles's, to whom the coarsest terms being familiar, they convey sensual ideas without the antidote of disgust.

Among other parts of this work which might have been spared, is the description of several places both in England and Scotland that are well known; but among the pictures of life, which may serve as monitors to the supine and thoughtless, the extravagant and the vain, is the following, which is inserted at once as a specimen and recommendation of the work.

The Universal Magazine †

Critical Remarks upon Humphry Clinker.

The Captain finding Mr. Crab in the library reading, according to custom, asked him if he had got any thing new. Yes, says Mr. Crab, it is The Expedition of Humphry Clinker. And how do you like it, says the Captain? I am sorry to say, replied Mr. Crab, that I am greatly disappointed—I expected something better from the author of Roderick Random. It seems to me to be exceptionable in every thing but the style and language—Humphry Clinker is a lusus naturae a kind of human animal that never existed but in the brain of the author. Indeed he figures so seldom in the business of the drama, and furnishes so little entertainment to his guest the reader, that the book might as well have been intitled The Feast of Duke Humphry.[6] Mr. Bramble, who, it must be confessed, has some originality about him, is represented as a man of

4. Made up of dung or feces.
5. Jonathan Swift (1667–1745) was sometimes criticized for his inclusion of bodily functions in his works.

† From *The Universal Magazine* 49 (November 1771): 256–57.
6. A proverbial phrase meaning "to go hungry."

sense and erudition; and, he is the principle conduit-pipe, through which our author conveys his own real sentiments of men and things.

He makes a tour from Gloucester to Bristol—Bath and London. In these three great cities, so renowned, so celebrated all over Europe for their trade, riches, magnificence, &c. Mr. Bramble can find nothing to commend, but much to blame and condemn. Bristol-wells is a stinking dog-hole—A miserable hospital for wretched incurables. The new buildings at Bath are tasteless, inconvenient, and crouded upon one another, like the houses of cards built by children. Their amusements are irrational—The ill-breeding of such a motly mixture of people insufferable—And the noise, non-sense and knavery, not to be borne by any man of common sense. London, forasmuch as it exceeds the other two cities in size and circumference, excels them in every thing that is eminently pernicious both to body and mind. The air is not fit to breathe, the water to drink, nor the bread to eat. The first becomes noxious by being frequently respired through putrid lungs, or contaminated with the infectious effluvia of old venereal ulcers, &c. The second is an infusion of dead carcasses, human excrement, and the poisonous sweepings of mechanics shops and warehouses. The third is a mixture of chalk, allum, and bone ashes. The butter is manufactured with candle-grease and kitchen-stuff. But his analysis of London milk comprehends such an assemblage of filth and nastiness, as nothing but the stream down Snow-hill, in Swift's Description of a City Shower, can equal. The provisions in general are sophisticated, and rendered so destructive to health, that a foreigner (from this account) would think it impossible for a human being to survive six months within the bills of mortality.

This most unfaithful portrait of poor Old England does mend a little upon us, when Mr. Bramble quits London to travel north-wards, though we find matters queer enough in Northumberland, and even amongst his own relations. For he says, that hospitality, which is constantly in the mouth of every Englishman, is no where so little practiced as in England; and, that if a Frenchman, German, or Italian, should come over to visit a Gentleman in London, whom he had entertained at his house abroad in the genteelest manner, the Islander would carry him to the Saracen's-head or Blue-Boar, and make him pay his share of the reckoning.

I was at a loss to guess at the author's drift and design, till Mr. Bramble had crossed the Tweed; and then I found that England was sacrificed, and, as it were, thrown into shadow, in order to bring the mother-country forwards, and shew her in a more brilliant light. Every thing between the Tweed and the Orkneys is enchanting—The houses magnificent—The people polite, and their entertainments elegant. When he calls Edinburgh a hot bed of genius, I was inclined to think he meant some sarcasm, alluding to the rich manure that is nightly ejected from every window into the streets of that famous city. But when I saw the respectable names of the two Humes, Robertson, Wilkie, &c. I dropped the thought and adopted the metaphor. However, it must be acknowledged, that great ingenuity and a most pregnant imagination were necessary, to draw so many beautiful pictures from the contemplation of so barren a subject.

I am the more displeased with this flagrant partiality to Scotland, as I fear it will tend rather to widen than heal the breach that at present subsists betwixt the South and North Britons, whom every lover of his country would wish to see united without distinction or difference.

Setting aside this objection, I think the book abounds in many masterly strokes, and has a great deal of merit; though I hate that Hottentot, Captain Lismahago; and the ridiculous letters of Mrs. Tabitha Bramble, and her maid Jenkins, are too childish to amuse the meanest capacity.

London Magazine †

Dr. Smollet's reputation is so justly established, particularly in the walk of novel-writing, that very little need be said to recommend the present performance to the public. Yet, though we have read it with much satisfaction, we cannot pretend to say it is wholly without imperfections: the title is certainly an improper one, because Humphrey Clinker is one of the least considerable in the whole catalogue of persons; there is besides, no great contrivance in the plan, nor any thing extremely interesting in the incidents. The characters, however, are marked with all that strength of colouring, for which Smollet's pencil is deservedly celebrated; and the reader is either continually entertained with some whimsical relation, or what is still better, instructed with some original remarks upon men and things, that do honour to the good-sense and humanity of the author.

The chief characters of this novel are, Mr. Bramble, a Welch batchellor of great benevolence and extensive understanding: He has a sister, an old maid, the very reverse of himself in the amiable particulars we have mentioned, together with a niece and a nephew both under age, to whom he is guardian. Having a desire for a journey into Scotland, he goes from Bath to London, and thence northwards accompanied by this family and their domestics. Previous to the tour, Miss Melford, his niece, discovers a prepossession for a strolling player, which nearly involves her brother in a duel, and excites the displeasure of her uncle and aunt; but promising never more to hold the smallest intercourse with Mr. Wilson, the actor, she is forgiven, and our travellers proceed in as much harmony as the irascibility of Mrs. Tabitha Bramble will admit, who is generally miserable herself, or endeavoring to make others miserable. On the road, this virago quarrelling with one of the servants, Humphrey Clinker, a poor country fellow, pickt up in a stable-yard, is engaged through necessity in his room; and though at first strongly disliked by the old maid, becomes a remarkable favourite in consequence of being a very warm methodist. The description of Scarborough, Harrowgate, and the various places through which the family pass in their way to Scotland, as well as in their return constitutes from this period the chief part of the expedition, and the whole is concluded by a marriage between Miss Melford and Mr. Wilson, who turns out a gentleman of fortune; with another marriage between Mr. Tabitha and one Lismahago, a Scotch lieutenant on half pay, a very extraordinary personage; and a third between Tabitha's woman, Winifred Jenkins, and Humphrey Clinker, who proves in the catastrophe a natural son to Mr. Bramble.

From these materials the reader will see, that much of the dreadful dangers, the surprizing escapes, the deep distresses, and the romantic passions which characterize our modern novel-writers, is not to be expected in this performance; in fact, it is something greatly preferable to a novel; it is a pleasing, yet an important lesson on life; and that part of it which describes the Scotch nation, is at once calculated to entertain the most gay, and to give the most serious a very useful fund of information.

Monthly Review †

Some modern wits appear to have entertained a notion that there is but one kind of *indecency* in writing; and that, provided they exhibit nothing of a lascivious nature, they may freely paint, with their pencils dipt in the most odious materials that can possibly be raked together for the most filthy and disgusting colouring.—These nasty geniuses seem to follow their great leader, Swift, only in his obscene and dirty walks. The present Writer, Nevertheless, has humour and wit, as well as grossness and ill nature.—But we need not enlarge on his literary character, which is well known to the public. Roderick Random and Peregrine Pickle have long been numbered with the best of our English romances. His present work, however, is not equal to these; but it is superior to his Ferdinand Fathom, and perhaps equal to the Adventures of an Atom.

Letter from John Gray to Tobias Smollett ‡

London, July 8, 1771

* * *

I have read the Adventures of Humphry Clinker with great delight, and think it calculated to give a very great run, and to add to the reputation of the author, who has, by the magic of his pen, turned the banks of Loch Lomond into classic ground. If I had seen the MS. I should like to have struck out the episode of Mr Pouncefort. The strictures upon

† From *Monthly Review* 45 (1771): 152.
‡ Reprinted from *The Miscellaneous Works of Tobias Smollett, M. D. With Memoirs of His Life* and *Writings by Robert Anderson, M. D.*, the Sixth Edition (Edinburgh: Stirling & Slade et al., 1820) I, 196–97.

Aristarchus are but too just; shallow judges, I find, are not so well satisfied with the performance as the best judges, who are lavish in its praises. Your half-animated sots say they don't see the humour. Cleland[7] gives it the stamp of excellence, with the enthusiastic emphasis of voice and fist; and puts it before any thing you ever wrote. With many, I find, it has the effect of exciting inquiries about your other works, which they had not heard of before. I expected to have seen an account of it in both Reviews, but it is reserved for next month.

7. Probably John Cleland (1708–89), the author of *Fanny Hill* (1749).

Criticism

SIR WALTER SCOTT†

[Tobias Smollett]

Shortly after the publication of *The Adventures of an Atom*, [1769]
Disease again assailed Smollett with redoubled violence. Attempts being
vainly made to obtain for him the office of Consul, in some port of the
Mediteranean, he was compelled to seek a warmer climate, without
better means of provision than his own precarious finances could afford.
The kindness of his distinguished friend and countryman, Dr Armstrong,
(then abroad) procured for Dr and Mrs. Smollett a house at Monte Novo,
a village situated on the side of a mountain overlooking the sea, in the
neighborhood of Leghorn, a romantic and salutary abode, where he
prepared for the press the last, and, like music, "sweetest in the close,"
the most pleasing of his compositions, *The Expedition of Humphry
Clinker*. This delightful work was published in 1771, in three volumes,
12mo, and very favourably received by the public.

The very ingenious scheme of describing the various effects produced
upon different members of the same family by the same objects, was not
original, though it has been supposed to be so. Anstey, the facetious
author of the *New Bath Guide*, had employed it six or seven years before
Humphry Clinker appeared. But Anstey's diverting satire was but a light
sketch, compared to the finished and elaborate manner in which Smollett
has, in the first place, identified his characters, and then fitted them with
language, sentiments, and powers of observation, in exact correspondence with their talents, temper, condition, and disposition. The portrait
of Matthew Bramble, in which Smollett described his own peculiarities,
using towards himself the same rigid anatomy which he exercised upon
others, is unequalled in the line of fictitious composition. It is peculiarly
striking to observe, how often, in admiring the shrewd and sound sense,
active benevolence, and honourable sentiments combined in Matthew,
we lose sight of the humorous peculiarities of his character, and with
what effect they are suddenly recalled to our remembrance, just at the
time and in the manner when we least expect them. All shrewish old
maids, and simple waiting-women, which shall hereafter be drawn, must
be contented with the praise of approaching in merit to Mrs Tabitha
Bramble, and Winifred Jenkins. The peculiarities of the hot-headed

† Reprinted from Sir Walter Scott, "Prefatory
Memoir" to Tobias Smollett, *The Expedition of*   *Humphry Clinker* (London: Ballantyne, 1821), pp.
xxix–xlii.

young Oxonian, and the girlish romance of his sister, are admirably contrasted with the sense, and pettish half-playful misanthropy of their uncle; and Humphry Clinker (who by the way resembles Strap, supposing that excellent person to have a turn towards methodism) is, as far as he goes, equally delightful. Captain Lismahago was probably no violent caricature, allowing for the manners of the time. We can remember a good and gallant officer who was said to have been his prototype, but believe the opinion was only entertained from the striking resemblance which he bore in externals to the doughty captain.

When *Humphry Clinker* appeared in London, the popular odium against the Scotch nation, which Wilkes and Churchill had excited, was not yet appeased, and Smollet had enemies amongst the periodical critics, who failed not to charge him with undue partiality to his own country. They observed, maliciously, but not untruly, that the cynicism of Matthew Bramble becomes gradually softened as he journies northward, and that he who equally detested Bath and London, becomes wonderfully reconciled to walled cities and the hum of men, when he finds himself an inhabitant of the northern metropolis. It is not worth defending so excellent a work against so weak an objection. The author was a dying man, and his thoughts were turned towards the scenes of youthful gaiety and the abode of early friends, with a fond partiality, which, had they been even less deserving of his attachment, would have been not only pardonable, but praiseworthy.

Moritur, et moriens dulces reminiscitur Argos. [1]

Smollett failed not, as he usually did, to introduce himself, with the various causes which he had to complain of the world, into the pages of this delightful romance. He appears as Mr Serle, and more boldly under his own name, and in describing his own mode of living, he satirizes without mercy the book-makers of the day, who had experienced his kindness without repaying him by gratitude. It does not, however, seem perfectly fair to make them atone for their ungracious return to his hospitality by serving up their characters as a banquet to the public; and, in fact, it too much resembles the design of which Pallet accuses the Physician, of converting his guests into patients, in order to make him amends for the expence of the entertainment. [2]

* * *

In leaving Smollett's personal for his literary character, it is impossible not to consider the latter as contrasted with that of his eminent contemporary, Fielding. It is true, that such comparisons, though recom-

1. "He dies, and dying, his thoughts return to his well-loved Argos." *Aeneid*, X, 782. Antores, one of the warriors of Argos who has settled in Italy, is mortally wounded by a lance, and his dying thoughts return to his homeland. [*Editor*]
2. Pallet is a painter in *Peregrine Pickle* (1758) by Smollett, where he says what is here ascribed to him. [*Editor*]

mended by the example of Plutarch, are not in general the best mode of estimating individual merit. But in the present case, the history, accomplishments, talents, pursuits, and, unfortunately, the fates of these two great authors, are so closely allied, that it is scarce possible to name the one without exciting recollections of the other. Fielding and Smollett were both born in the highest rank of society, both educated to learned professions, yet both obliged to follow miscellaneous literature as the means of subsistence. Both were confined, during their lives, by the narrowness of their circumstances,—both united a humorous cynicism with generosity and good nature,—both died of the diseases incident to a sedentary life, and to literary labour,—and both drew their last breath in a foreign land, to which they retreated under the adverse circumstances of a decayed constitution, and an exhausted fortune.

Their studies were no less similar than their lives. They both wrote for the stage, and neither of them successfully. They both meddled in politics; they both wrote travels, in which they shewed that their good humour was wasted under the sufferings of their disease; and, to conclude, they were both so eminently successful as novelists, that no other English author of that class has a right to be mentioned in the same breath with Fielding and Smollett.

* * *

In the comic part of their writings, we have already said, Fielding is pre-eminent in grave irony, a Cervantic species of pleasantry, in which Smollett is not equally successful. On the other hand, the Scotchman, (notwithstanding the general opinion denies that quality to his countrymen,) excels in broad and ludicrous humour. His fancy seems to run riot in accumulating ridiculous circumstances one upon another, to the utter destruction of all power of gravity; and perhaps no books ever written have excited such peals of inextinguishable laughter as those of Smollett. The descriptions which affect us thus powerfully, border sometimes upon what is called farce or caricature; but if it be the highest praise of pathetic composition that it draws forth tears, why should it not be esteemed the greatest excellence of the ludicrous that it compels laughter? The one tribute is at least as genuine an expression of natural feeling as the other; and he who can read the calamities of Trunnion and Hatchway,[3] when run away with by their mettled steeds, or the inimitable absurdities of the feast of the ancients, without a good hearty burst of honest laughter, must be well qualified to look sad and gentleman-like with Lord Chesterfield or Master Stephen.[4]

3. Commodore Hawser Trunnion and Lieutenant Hatchway are comic characters in *Peregrine Pickle*. [*Editor*]
4. Philip Dormer Stanhope, fourth Earl of Chesterfield (1694–1773), author of *Letters to His Son*, was known for his gentlemanly qualities, which he recommended to his son. The editor has not been able to identify Master Stephen. [*Editor*]

Upon the whole, the genius of Smollett may be said to resemble that of Rubens.[5] His pictures are often deficient in grace; sometimes coarse, and even vulgar in conception; deficient too in keeping, and in the due subordination of parts to each other; and intimating too much carelessness on the part of the artist. But these faults are redeemed by such richness and brilliancy of colours; such a profusion of imagination—now bodying forth the grand and terrible—now the natural, the easy, and the ludicrous; there is so much of life, action, and bustle, in every groupe he has painted; so much force and individuality of character, that we readily grant to Smollett an equal rank with his great rival Fielding, while we place both far above any of their successors in the same line of fictitious composition.

LEWIS M. KNAPP

Smollett's Self-Portrait in *The Expedition of Humphry Clinker*†

The impressive merit of *Humphry Clinker* is largely due to the fact that it embodies the breath and finer spirit of its remarkable author. Properly to understand Smollett is to realize that interlocked within him were two distinct trends. One comprised his capacity for reason, his ability to create literary satire not always dripping with anger, and his concern over being a sensible and decorous gentleman rather than a "singular" author tinged with grubstreet eccentricities. The other trend included his ebullient emotionalism, expressed in some of his personal correspondence, in his fiercest satire, in his best verse, and in his miniature self-portraits, found, for example, in the preface to *Count Fathom*, and in *Humphry Clinker*. Smollett's notorious temper resulted in the ruthless personal satire in his early verse and fiction. Of this unfortunate lack of rational control Smollett was keenly aware. In his youth, in particular, he was not always a canny or a closemouthed Scot: he confessed the "Weakness and Leakiness [loquaciousness]" of his disposition to his friend Carlyle in 1749. Moreover, Smollett was subjected to bitter conflicts and frustrations. Add to all this the fact that no writer of his time disciplined himself by such an exhausting schedule of professional composition, and it is obvious that there developed within him powerful psychological tensions, for which some type of release was sorely needed.

5. Peter Paul Rubens (1577–1640) was a Flemish artist whose works were noted for richness, vitality, and robustness. [*Editor*]

† From *The Age of Johnson*, ed. Frederick W. Hilles (New Haven: Yale University Press, 1949), pp. 149–58.

How Smollett vented his rages no biographer can wholly say. It is clear that he did not forfeit the affection of his wife, or the devotion of Tolloush, his servant. And it is safe to say that he released many of his tensions in the more splenetic outbursts of his correspondence, reviews, and occasional literary libels.

There is, however, in the extensive body of Smollett's creative work vastly more than the element of angry satire. There are many pages of comical farce, and there is a large amount of dispassionately objective realism. Most of this realism is rooted, I believe, in his personal observations and experiences. Thackeray's suggestion, offered nearly a century ago, that Smollett "did not invent much . . . but had the keenest perceptive faculty, and described what he saw with wonderful relish," has been confirmed repeatedly, and appears to be especially applicable to the brilliant panorama of persons and places etched in the pages of his last novel written in his final years.

Unfortunately, there is no way of ascertaining precisely when Smollett wrote *Humphry Clinker*. During the spring and summer of 1766, while on his travels in Scotland, he may have kept a journal, from which he later drew details for its Scottish scenes and characters. While he was at Bath and at London from 1766 to 1768 it is probable that he recorded some of the material contained in the epistles written by Bramble and his entourage in those same centers. There is undeniable proof, to which I shall allude later, that he could not have prepared his satire on Paunceford (found in the latter half of the first volume) until the spring of 1768. It is possible that he worked upon some parts of *Humphry Clinker* before leaving for Italy in the autumn of 1768. Yet there is no certainty that he had progressed very far with it because of the fact that before he left England he supposedly completed *The Atom*, which, according to newspaper publicity, was in the press by December, 1768. If this very violent and unpleasant political allegory, traditionally attributed to Smollett (there is no sign that he ever acknowledged it), was motivated by his failure, about July, 1767, to obtain a consulship at Nice, then it must be assumed that he concentrated upon *The Atom* during his final year in England, having laid aside, perhaps, whatever fragments of *Humphry Clinker* he had previously prepared. Consequently, good grounds exist for accepting the Italian tradition that he completed *Humphry Clinker* at his mountain villa near Leghorn. In other words, it is fairly certain that from 1768 to 1770 Smollett labored intermittently on his best novel.

Humphry Clinker contains a kaleidoscopic variety of localities, characters, and social criticism. Because its plot is as stereotyped and fragile as a sprig of dry heather, its outline is easy to follow. The style, even when distorted by comic malapropisms, is somewhat varied to suit the several letter writers, and is usually admirable whether in achieving humor, farce, pathos, irony, or slashing satire. Permeating and vitalizing the entire opus is the *élan vital* of Smollett, who found in his final work a pliant medium through which to project his personal experience, temperamental traits, and characteristic ideas, during the days of his physical decline. Significant it is that about 40 per cent of this novel consists of letters written by Bramble, who, in the essential traits of his character, is Smollettian; it is also significant that some 50 per cent of the book is made up of letters composed by Jerry, Bramble's nephew, and one given to amusing but sympathetic comment on his uncle. Consequently Smollett provided for himself two media (and the lips of Lismahago as well) for his varied self-revelation.

After introducing Bramble and his traveling group, Smollett held them at Bath during the April and May of their expedition. Smollett, of course, had resided at fashionable Bath in Gay Street from 1766 to 1768. The critical Bramble described this street as "so steep, and slippery, that, in wet weather, it must be exceedingly dangerous, both for those that ride in carriages, and those that walk afoot; and," he added, "when the street is covered with snow, as it was for fifteen days successively this very winter, I don't see how any individual could go either up or down, without the most imminent hazard of broken bones." This comment is a neat example of Smollett's recollection of actual conditions because the allusion to snow "this very winter" referred to the extraordinary snowdrifts in Bath in January, 1767. (See *The Whitehall Evening Post: Or London Intelligencer* for January 15, 1767.) Furthermore, through the amusing associations of Bramble and Tabitha with the diminutive Derrick, Master of Ceremonies at Bath, Smollett recalled, surely, his own observation of Samuel Derrick from 1765 to 1768. There is good reason to assume that Smollett knew Derrick fairly well: he subscribed for his *Original Poems* in 1755, and seems to have hired him as a minor contributor to *The Critical Review*. In the delectable scenes, depicted by Jerry, of the most cordial reunion between Bramble and the great actor, Quin, there is every indication that Smollett was again utilizing personal experience: this time he recalled, as Professor Buck showed, his joyful reconciliation with Quin in Bath shortly before the latter's death in January, 1766. Young Jerry averred with emotion that he "would give an hundred guineas to see Mr. Quin act the part of Falstaff," whereupon Quin responded, "And I would give a thousand . . . that I could gratify your longing." And many would give guineas today to peruse an authentic account of anecdotes exchanged by Quin and Smollett at The Three Tuns over the claret and a John Dory. Equally enjoyable would it be to learn more about Bramble's ecstatic meeting with those crippled army and navy eccentrics, Rear Admiral Balderick and Colonel Cockril, whose real identities and histories remain obscure.

To such pleasant associations at Bath there was one notable exception recorded by Smollett, namely, his observation of a considerable ingrate disguised in *Humphry Clinker* under the connotative title of Paunceford.

By a roundabout device in Jerry's letter of May 10, Smollett, under the pseudonym of Mr. Serle, wrote a bitterly satirical account of Paunceford's callous ingratitude. Smollett declared that he had been most generous to Paunceford in the old days but that the latter, though he had recently returned with his pockets full of gold from India, made not the slightest gesture to repay him. At long last the identification of Paunceford is complete: he was one Alexander Campbell, who returned from India to Bath with a fortune in the spring of 1768. Further details about him are available in my recent biography of Smollett.

Having completed the episodes set in Bath, Smollett transferred Bramble and his party to London for a stay of some two months. For this rich section of the novel he again dipped into his own memories of London and of Chelsea. He pictured such celebrities as Chatham, "the grand pensionary," and the Duke of Newcastle as in association with the Duke of Cumberland, who died in 1765, thus implying that in his satire of them he relied on what he had seen or heard of them before going to France in 1763. From a still earlier period he reconstructed certain events in his own life in Jerry's memorable description of Mr. S——'s Sunday dinners at Chelsea, where Mr. S——(Smollett himself, of course) regaled his hack writers for *The Critical Review* and for other projects with "beef, pudding, and potatoes, port, punch, and Calvert's entire butt-beer," and was amused by their many eccentricities. This scene, the humorous episodes embedded in it, and Smollett's concluding self-vindication (see the end of Jerry's epistle from London, June 10) are all essentially autobiographical: they certainly display the author himself about 1760 as painted by his own hand some eight or ten years later, when as a chronic invalid he dreamed of his days of boundless vitality.

Similarly, Smollett must have enjoyed the recollection of personal experience embodied in the mellow chapters describing Bramble's expedition to Edinburgh and Glasgow and his tour of the Highlands. The varied social joys of Bramble during this trip were essentially those of Smollett, the seasoned continental traveler, now returning for a last breath of Scottish air and for a happy view of his circle of friends and relatives, some of whom he had visited in 1753 and in 1760. I do not imply that Smollett had the strength to participate in every activity experienced by Bramble. Nor do I infer that Smollett later composed all the letters from Scotland with aids to his memory, such as manuscript journals or printed accounts of that Arcadian land north of the Tweed. Nevertheless, indelible memories of that summer he surely cherished: the hours with his mother and his sister, not alluded to in the novel; his visit with his cousin, the Commissary, at Cameron House on Loch Lomond, so glowingly painted; his farewell sessions with old friends like Dr. Moore, "Jupiter" Carlyle, and others; and at least a glimpse of the Highlands, where, to quote Bramble, all was "sublimity, silence, and solitude."

Such, in general, are the peaks of Smollett's experience and recollection in *Humphry Clinker*. I have still to suggest how this work expresses his character and his social criticism.

One of several reasons why Smollett was fortunate in taking a few hints from Anstey's *New Bath Guide* was that he hit upon the plan of featuring as his central character a valetudinarian in search of health. Thus, through Bramble, Smollett could easily project consciously and subconsciously and with piquant humor certain prevailing moods which he "felt in the blood and felt along the heart." He conveyed through Bramble his own physical distress, his peevish, fretful, and crusty humor, or, to quote Bramble, his "soreness of mind," his excessive sensibility. Smollett never lost his *vis comica*, his capacity to laugh at himself as well as at the follies of mankind. Consider Jerry's diagnosis of Bramble:

> He is as tender as a man without a skin, who cannot bear the slightest touch without flinching. What tickles another would give him torment; and yet he has what we may call lucid intervals, when he is remarkably facetious. Indeed, I never knew a hypochondriac so apt to be infected with good humour. He is the most risible misanthrope I ever met with. A lucky joke, or any ludicrous incident, will set him a-laughing immoderately even in one of his most gloomy paroxysms; and when the laugh is over, he will curse his own imbecility.

Read superficially, this appears as a cleverly concocted and exaggerated compound of laughable incongruities, but Jerry's description is, I suspect, very true to the psychology of the novelist in his declining years. Smollett has been called misanthropic; *quasi misantropo* wrote his Italian doctor, Gentili, who observed him in his last illness; and certain critics have labeled him a complete misanthropist. The latter judgment is very dubious; nearer the truth is Jerry's view of Bramble: "He affects misanthropy, in order to conceal the sensibility of a heart which is tender even to a degree of weakness." Indoctrinated in the Augustan age of rationalism, Smollett felt that it was more decorous to appear misanthropic than to succumb to a Shandean emotionalism.

In still other ways Bramble is Smollett's exact portrait. Like his creator, he was compassionate to his relatives and notably generous to the poor. Like Smollett he could enjoy the tender, melting, and humanitarian mood. Like Smollett he was outraged by the noisome filth in the bathing pools of Bath or by the nocturnal stench drifting along the streets of Edinburgh. Identical with Smollett's was Bramble's disillusionment and stoicism as well as his pronounced enthusiasm for the pleasures of a clean country life. Of all these similarities there is abundant proof written large in the pages of *Humphry Clinker*.

In complete harmony with Smollett's oft-expressed views is Bramble's criticism of British and Scottish personalities and manners. Some of the author's criticism was also projected through the comments of Jerry, but the reactions of Lydia, Tabitha, and Winifred are largely irrelevant, although they are an effective foil to the central criticism, which, in turn, is both satirical and complimentary. Among the individuals whom Bramble praised was John Taylor, a young painter at Bath. He also complimented his landlady, one Mrs. Norton, in whose house by Golden Square the Smolletts resided for an indefinite period from 1765 to 1768. Bramble also acclaimed the new Blackfriars Bridge, and the British Museum, for the improvement of which he proffered suggestions. In Scotland there was much to admire: the universities of Edinburgh and of Glasgow; at the former center a group of distinguished authors (John Home, David Hume, William Robertson, Adam Smith, and others); the flourishing city of Glasgow; charming Cameron House, the country seat of Smollett's cousin; and the romantic beauties of the Highlands. Such favorable impressions, plus the rich and extravagant comedy of *Humphry Clinker* arising from incongruities within the characters, as well as from external caricature, fantastic malapropisms, and highly seasoned anecdotes, give the book a predominant spirit of mellowness and good nature. And yet this novel contains samples of Smollett's well-known violence; a louring rack remains in the sunset sky of his art; the thunder of wrath is often audible; the lightning bolts of satire and invective still flash and strike home, although not always with their former power.

It is unnecessary to enumerate all the smaller targets. A pompous one, Dr. Diederick Wessel Linden, sometime authority on Hyde-Spaw-Water in Gloucestershire and on the etymology of stench and of various racial attitudes toward this topic, suffered humiliating treatment from Jerry and from Bramble. Paunceford, Pitt, Newcastle, and Townshend were larger objects of satire. Harder hit, however, were two weedlike and boorish Yorkshire squires named Burdock and Pimpernel.

Smollett, in *Humphry Clinker*, launched his heaviest bolts not against individuals but against groups of people and against sundry social institutions. He attacked the tumult and rush of life at Bath and at London. Like Goldsmith, he warned against the dangers of unregulated commerce and the great evils of luxury and widespread corruption. He inveighed against the exorbitant cost of living at Bath, and against the adulterated food and drink of London. He struck out at the evils of an unrestricted press and of politically biased juries. Against the vulgarity of Ranelagh and Vauxhall he fulminated repeatedly. He declared that the British public, with no social distinction or subordination left, was rapidly losing its wits. Conservative in politics and fastidious in his tastes, Smollett, like Swift, detested any kind of a mob. Bramble raged against it at Bath:

[The] mob is a monster I never could abide, either in its head, tail, midriff, or members: I detest the whole of it, as a mass of ignorance, presumption, malice, and brutality; and in this term of reprobation, I include, without respect of rank, station, or quality, all those of both sexes who affect its manners, and court its society.

Any mob was repulsive to Bramble, but the worst of all mobs was that composed in large part of the *nouveaux riches*, as it contaminated the streets of Bath:

> Every upstart of fortune, harnessed in the trappings of the mode, presents himself at Bath, as in the very focus of observation. Clerks and factors from the East Indies, loaded with the spoil of plundered provinces; planters, negro-drivers, and hucksters, from our American plantations, enriched they know not how; agents, commissaries, and contractors, who have fattened, in two successive wars, on the blood of the nation; usurers, brokers, and jobbers of every kind; men of low birth, and no breeding, have found themselves suddenly translated into a state of affluence, unknown to former ages; and no wonder that their brains should be intoxicated with pride, vanity, and presumption. Knowing no other criterion of greatness, but the ostentation of wealth, they discharge their affluence without taste or conduct, through every channel of the most absurd extravagance; ... Even the wives and daughters of low tradesmen, who, like shovel-nosed sharks, prey upon the blubber of those uncouth whales of fortune, are infected with the same rage of displaying their importance. ... Such is the composition of what is called the fashionable company at Bath; where a very inconsiderable proportion of genteel people are lost in a mob of impudent plebeians, who have neither understanding nor judgment, nor the least idea of propriety and decorum; and seem to enjoy nothing so much as an opportunity of insulting their betters.

To this brilliant exposé of the evils of the urban Vanity Fair in eighteenth-century England must be added a cluster of other satirical scenes in other novels by Smollett. Modern social historians now admit that he was not guilty of exaggeration.

In contrast to the folly and depravity of urban life is Smollett's idealized picture of country life in several letters in *Humphry Clinker* dealing with the unfortunate Mr. Baynard and the very fortunate Mr. Dennison. Of course it was "in character" for Bramble, the Welsh country squire, to idealize the country, but there is no doubt but that Smollett enjoyed the rural air of his Chelsea garden and hoped at one time to end his days by the shores of Loch Lomond.

To appreciate his concluding outlook on life it should be recalled that the death of his daughter (his only child), in 1763, had been a heavy affliction. Added to this was his cruel illness, a combination of asthma, rheumatism, and tuberculosis, which first affected him about 1759. How ill he was has not always been recognized. Upon his return in 1765 from his sojourn at Nice he wrote to Dr. Moore that he had "brought back no more than the skeleton" of what he had been. Gone forever were long stretches of Herculean labor in his study at Monmouth House. In the irrecoverable past lay the hours in which he had entertained the tavern table with repartee and salty anecdotes preserved by no Boswell. At Bath in 1766 he was dangerously ill, and in Scotland that same year he was benumbed by a kind of stupor or *coma vigil*, as, with probable exaggeration, he described it. During the spring of 1767 he improved temporarily. In the brilliant Italian sunshine (at Pisa, Florence, Lucca Baths, and Leghorn), thanks to his indomitable will, he clung to life, his vitality apparently improving until he was struck down by an intestinal infection in September, 1771.

Despite his physical weakness and suffering, and despite the fact that as a doctor he must have realized keenly enough after 1766 that his years were limited, Smollett appears not always to have been psychologically depressed, at least not unduly so when he set pen to paper to create what Thackeray called "the most laughable story . . . written since the goodly art of novel-writing began." Inevitably, however, the sheer physical labor of composing *Humphry Clinker* was an ordeal. It "Galls me to the Soul," declared his widow in 1773, "when I think how much that poor Dear Man Suffered while he wrote that novel." Yet it seems certain that Smollett enjoyed his final writing. It enabled him to recapture in imagination many exciting scenes and moods now recollected in relative tranquillity; it heightened for him what Bramble called "the humor in the farce of life," which he was determined to enjoy as long as he could; and it allowed him to express a considered appraisal of British and Scottish society so well known to him not only through books but also from his extremely keen observation as a traveler. In part, at least, *Humphry Clinker* was a happy escape from a painful and frustrating existence. Remembering Quin, at Bath, Smollett had Jerry write, "My uncle [Bramble] and he [Quin] are perfectly agreed in their estimate of life, which Quin says, would stink in his nostrils, if he did not steep it in claret." In similar fashion, Smollett sweetened the stench of political and social corruption and mitigated his own physical distress by the rich vintage of his creative imagination.

BYRON GASSMAN

The Economy of *Humphry Clinker*†

Ever since Henry James mastered the art of fiction, one of the most popular ways to assert a novel's excellence has been to demonstrate how every element of it relates to a pervasive purpose or vision and how all

† From *Tobias Smollett: Bicentennial Essays Presented to Lewis M. Knapp*, ed. G. S. Rousseau and P.-G. Boucé (New York: Oxford University Press, 1971), pp. 155–168.

elements are molded into significant form by a controlling point of view. Perhaps one of the reasons Smollett has remained in a somewhat lower firmament than Fielding, Richardson, and Sterne is the difficulty of submitting a novel such as Humphry Clinker to the kind of analysis that produces scholarly articles entitled "The Unity of Such and Such" or "Meaning and Point of View in So and So." Written at the end of one of the most diversified careers in English literary history, Humphry Clinker was used by Smollett to resurvey many of the subjects he had interested himself in during the nearly twenty-year period when he was one of the busiest writers on the literary scene of London. With material ranging from crude practical jokes to sentimental reunions, from an analysis of the British constitution to a merry account of Scottish funeral customs, from well-limned character sketches to animadversions on unhealthful sanitary conditions, the novel has almost always struck readers and critics as a veritable grab-bag of British life in the mid-1700's, filled with gusto when analyzed piecemeal, but unyielding to any attempt to define a synthesizing principle.

In a remark typical of many earlier comments on Humphry Clinker, George Saintsbury hit exactly this note in his introduction to the novel. After commenting on Smollett's lack of method, he observed that "the distinguishing excellence of Humphry Clinker is the excellence of the particulars" and went on to speak of its "cheerful divagation from pillar to post."[1] Most scholarship and criticism of the twentieth century has implicitly endorsed Saintsbury's observations by undertaking to illuminate or explicate particular elements of the novel,[2] although there have been recent attempts to provide holistic views of it.[3] Persuasive and useful as these latter have often been, when they are examined alongside the complete work, it is clear that there is much material from the grab-bag that no system-oriented view of the novel can fully account for.

Not only are the materials of Humphry Clinker manifold, but the purposes to which Smollett puts them may easily be viewed as at least threefold. In the first place, as announced by the prefatory correspondence, Humphry Clinker shares with the collections of travel letters so popular during the eighteenth century the purpose of disseminating

1. The Works of Tobias Smollett, ed. George Saintsbury (New York, n.d.), VI, pp. xi, xvii–xviii.
2. Characteristic and very well known are Knapp's discussion of the autobiographical elements, Martz's of certain descriptive passages, and Kahrl's of travelogue materials: Lewis M. Knapp, "Smollett's Self-Portrait in The Expedition of Humphry Clinker" in The Age of Johnson (New Haven, 1949); Louis L. Martz, The Later Career of Tobias Smollett (New Haven, 1942); George M. Kahrl, Tobias Smollett: Traveler-Novelist (Chicago, 1945).
3. Probably the most striking of these is M. A. Goldberg's discussion of Humphry Clinker as "A Study in Primitivism and Progress" in Smollett and the Scottish School (Albuquerque, 1959). Along similar lines are David L. Evans, "Humphry Clinker: Smollett's Tempered Augustanism," Criticism 9 (1967): 257–74; and B. L. Reid, "Smollett's Healing Journey," Virginia Quarterly Review 41 (1965): 549–70. All of these suggest a reading of Humphry Clinker as a journey of reconciliation. The notion of the action of Humphry Clinker as a kind of archetypal pilgrimage may perhaps be traced to Robert Gorham Davis's introduction to the Rinehart edition (New York, 1950).

information on geography, history, customs, and manners. But *Humphry Clinker* is obviously more than a perceptive journalist's account of travels through England and Scotland, more than a companion volume to Smollett's own *Travels* and the other works referred to in the prefatory correspondence. It finds its way into the novel section of our literary history because, simultaneously with his reporting, Smollett effects the creation of a company of characters to delight the reader by their actions and reactions. The creation of entertaining characters and incident, and the interaction of the two, is a second very evident purpose of the work. Moreover, the novel goes beyond the scope of the usual travel book of the mid-eighteenth century by adding a marked note of criticism and didactic commentary on the English milieu of the 1760's, and the reader can identify this didactic purpose as a third basic strand in the variegated fabric of the novel.

Since *Humphry Clinker* is so clearly a multi-purpose work, incorporating a wide variety of heterogeneous materials, one always runs the risk of appearing overingenious in trying to lay out some formal principle which gives significance to the work as a whole or in trying to identify some controlling idea which functions as a basis for structural unity. Nevertheless I believe it possible to show that Smollett, in writing *Humphry Clinker*, did handle disparate material and diverse aims in such a way as to achieve, if not a unified work, at least a fairly economical one, one in which his purposes of reporting, characterizing, and moralizing are neatly interfused and his diverse materials tellingly exploited.

In choosing to describe the "economy" of *Humphry Clinker*, I desire to label as conveniently and precisely as words allow two related qualities of the novel. In one respect, I am trying to suggest something not so tightly handled as the term *unity* would suggest, something with more loose ends, with more variety—one can hardly think of Henry James taking time out of *The Ambassadors* to discourse on French marriage customs —but nonetheless suggesting some sense of perceptible structure and, even more, an effective manipulation of function.[4] And still more precisely, I should like the term to suggest that quality we designate when we use *economy* to describe thrifty management, the husbanding of resources to make every expenditure produce the best possible return.[5]

The achievement of *Humphry Clinker* in these senses may well be approached by briefly noting some of the problems Smollett had in the structure and handling of material in the earlier novels. The single purpose, "to represent modest merit struggling with every difficulty to which a friendless orphan is exposed,"[6] and single career of *Roderick*

4. Cf. *OED* definition 8: "The organization, internal constitution, apportionment of functions, of any complex unity."
5. Cf. *OED* definition 4: "Careful management of resources, so as to make them go as far as possible."
6. "The Preface" to *Roderick Random*.

348 • *Byron Gassman*

Random, for example, seem to have encouraged Smollett into a spendthrift extravagance of incident and attitude, a proliferation of episodic discontinuity that makes difficult any serious attempt at structural or thematic synthesis. Alan McKillop pinpointed a similar problem of economy in point of view with his comment on *Roderick Random* that "the story is not controlled throughout by an effective commentator, a voice of reason."[7] Indeed *Roderick Random* seems liable to most of the difficulties of control to which first-person fictional memoirs are prone: the difficulty of distinguishing between the thoughts and reactions of the moment (as an incident occurs) and the reflections upon it as the incident is supposedly written down years afterwards, and the difficulty of the actual author in validating or commenting on the values and attitudes of his narrator. In *Roderick Random* the reader is often confused by the shifting moral awareness of Roderick—and the same confusion is equally troublesome in *Peregrine Pickle* even when Smollett turns to a third-person narrative and produces a more perceptible plan. At one moment the hero may strike the reader as a young man of keen ethical sensitivity, a straightforward spokesman for his creator, and at the next moment as a crude barbarian, delighting in the pain of his fellow creatures and quite insensitive to any niceties in the demands of justice or mercy, a person for whom neither the author nor the reader could be expected to have much sympathy.

As Tuvia Bloch recently pointed out, a continuing problem for Smollett, even after he gave up the first-person point of view of *Roderick Random*, was that of maintaining a consistent and thus, for the reader, an interpretable stance toward his narrative and his characters. Unlike Fielding, Smollett found it difficult to distance his characters by ironic style.[8] He often moves from a distancing rhetoric to an unmediated reaction that leaves the reader in uncertain territory. Thus the implied economy that may arise from the steady view of an informing creative intelligence frequently fails to develop in Smollett's first four novels. Such a wavering point of view becomes a considerable hindrance to the creation of any coherent moral underpinning to a novel. If one has trouble in sustaining a single point of view or in giving one's putative narrator consistency, then some additional or substitute device is needed for straightening out perspective.

Paradoxically it was Smollett's decision to turn from the basically single point of view used in his earlier novels and to let his last novel take shape as the work of several letter-writers that provided the device on which the economy of *Humphry Clinker* depends. At first glance, one might expect that, having had trouble with a single point of view, Smollett might find a multiple point of view entailing an even greater

---

7. Alan Dugald McKillop, *The Early Masters of English Fiction* (Lawrence, Kans., 1956), p. 152.

8. Tuvia Bloch, "Smollett's Quest for Form," *Modern Philology* 65 (1967): 109–10.

expenditure of unassimilated effort and posing the danger of a *Clarissa*-like prolixity. But in the event, it enabled Smollett to evolve a consistent, interpretable stance toward his characters, their actions, and their society, and to achieve his purposes with an economy that would do full credit to the proverbial thriftiness of his homeland. The author of *Roderick Random* and *Peregrine Pickle* is like a juggler with only one ball to handle: he can be fairly extravagant and even uncoordinated in his motions and still engage his audience's attention by keeping the ball moving. The author of *Humphry Clinker* is like the juggler with numerous paraphernalia: he must be much more economical in his movements, not only trying to avoid uncoordinated movements but often making the same motion simultaneously serve the purposes of balancing, catching, and throwing.

The most obvious feature of Smollett's multiple point of view is the manner in which each letter-writer characterizes himself through his reaction to the sights and scenes encountered on the expedition. At the same time that the reader is being given typical data about the social customs of Bath or the mushrooming growth of London, he is being intimately introduced to the personality of the observer. A characteristic instance is Win Jenkins's letter describing her impressions of London. Here the reader finds some good first-hand reporting about the tumult of London streets, the sights of the Tower of London, and the entertainment at Sadler's Wells, data about the London of the 1760's that is good primary material for the modern historian.[9] But all is described in a delightfully malapropian prose that effectively delineates Win's character. When she remarks, "I have seen the Park, and the paleass of Saint Gimses, and the king's and the queen's magisterial pursing, and the sweet young princes, and the hillyfents, and pye-bald ass, and all the rest of the royal family" (WJ—June 3), the reader has actually been given an accurate account of what the traveler might have seen in Saint James's Park, but the ludicrous confusion with which it is told is also a piece of superb characterization. In the letters of Matthew Bramble the physical layout and the social routines of Bath are as fully reported as in most of the travel journals of the time. But the descriptions are strained through the imagined writer's sensibility in such a way as to acquaint us equally and simultaneously with Bath and Matthew Bramble. Of the famous Bath balls, Bramble grumbles that he "could not help wondering that so many hundreds of those that rank as rational creatures, could find entertainment in seeing a succession of insipid animals, describing the same dull figure for a whole evening, on an area, not much bigger than a taylor's shop-board" (MB—May 8). Highly individualized in its expres-

9. The usefulness of the letters of the Bramble party to modern historians is well illustrated by consulting the entry *Smollett* in such works as Sir Walter Besant, *London in the Eighteenth Century* (London, 1903); and Rosamond Bayne-Powell, *Eighteenth-Century London Life* (New York, 1938).

sion, such a statement nonetheless is substantially accurate as a report of Bath assemblies.[1]

The effect of characterization by means of personalized reporting is particularly noticeable when two letter-writers, most often Bramble and Lydia Melford, react to the same sight or event. In the early portions of the novel, Lydia's point of view is often used by Smollett to neutralize somewhat Bramble's crabbed observations. Bramble's "pretty baubles" (MB—Apr. 23) at Bath become "sumptuous palaces" (LM—Apr. 26) in Lydia's eyes. Bramble characteristically complains of "the dirt, the stench, the chilling blasts, and perpetual rains" (MB—Apr. 20) at the Hot Well. The next day the impressionable Lydia rapturously writes, "The air is so pure; the Downs are so agreeable . . . the weather so soft . . . the prospect so amusing" (LM—Apr. 21). For Bramble, Vauxhall is "a composition of baubles, overcharged with paltry ornaments, ill conceived, and poorly executed" (MB—May 29). For Lydia, in the very next letter, it is "a spacious garden, part laid out in delightful walks . . . part exhibiting a wonderful assemblage of the most picturesque and striking objects" (LM—May 31). In setting Bramble's and Lydia's accounts of Vauxhall and Ranelagh together, one hardly knows whether more praise should go to the masterful job of reporting the temper and tempo of these haunts of pleasure or to the creative skill that brings to life the characters through whose words the report is made. In the last analysis the praise goes to Smollett's genius which makes his method at once serve both purposes.

Thus while managing a clear account of topographical and historical data, habits, customs, manners, travel anecdotes—the type of material to be found in any travel-book of the day—Smollett is also creating a small gallery of individualized letter-writers who command interest in their own right. At least this is true with Matthew Bramble, Tabitha Bramble, Lydia Melford, and Winifred Jenkins. It is not so true in the case of the fifth letter-writer, Jeremy Melford, who remains considerably less individualized, keeping free of the situations that embarrass and distress the others. He is tolerant and amused, but seldom carried away into excesses of pleasure or displeasure, excitement or disgust, as are his fellow-writers. He is, in brief, a good reporter, narrating events without the embroidery of personal animus or affectation, describing scenes with affable objectivity, and, in direct contrast with the others, keeping his own personality and opinions fairly well in the background.

Smollett makes efficient use of the objective point of view provided by Jery Melford in working out the economy of *Humphry Clinker*. The reader's appraisal of the characters of his fellow-travelers is validated as

1. Cf. Oliver Goldsmith's account of Bath balls in *The Life of Richard Nash* in *Collected Works*, ed. Arthur Friedman (Oxford, 1966), III, p. 304. Goldsmith's account follows closely an earlier one by John Wood.

they are seen, not through their own sensibility or the idiosyncratic accounts of others, but through a point of view not grossly individualized. Jery's letters are highly useful in letting the reader see his traveling companions in action. It is perhaps oversimplified but nevertheless generally accurate to say that the letters of Bramble, Lydia, Tabitha, and Win are letters of reaction, those of Jery, letters of action. Jery himself does suffer some loss of vitality thereby. Bramble's early characterization of him as "a pert jackanapes, full of college-petulance and self-conceit" (MB—Apr. 17) and the early episodes of the challenge to Wilson and the affair with Miss Blackerby offer hints from which a new Peregrine Pickle might have developed, but nothing much materializes from these hints. However, the loss of another *Peregrine Pickle*—arguably Smollett's most verbose performance—and a certain pallidness in Jery's character are compensated for by the narrative efficiency achieved through the straightforward and well-paced reporting of events in Jery's letters. Without violating his conception of an epistolary novel, Smollett gains Richardson's effect of letting his work form itself from the interplay of his characters' reactions while also, through Jery's letters of action, providing a means for effective propulsion of the narrative. Unimpeded by the generous indignation, the gross resentment, or the humane sentiments that seemed at times in the earlier novels to work at cross purposes with the Smollettian vivacity, Jery becomes Smollett's most efficient and effective narrator. Availability of the other four letter-writers relieves him of some of the tasks that created awkwardness and uncertainty in Smollett's earlier narrative voices. In addition, a resource is provided for a well-handled playing back and forth between narrative action and character reaction and comment that makes *Humphry Clinker* a model of how to manage a grab-bag of material and purpose in fictional form.

One way in which Smollett characteristically employs this resource to good advantage may be demonstrated by an early episode in the book. Bramble ends his first few letters with requests to Dr. Lewis to relieve the misfortunes of various dependents, thus revealing an apparently charitable disposition. Tabitha, in her first letter, is totally concerned with her own comforts and her own profits on the Bramble estate, thus exposing an apparently selfish character. The impressions gained by the reader from these self-revealing letters are confirmed by events when Jery reports the little scene in which his uncle tries secretly to relieve the distress of an ensign's widow with a twenty-pound note, only to have Tabitha pounce on the pair, snatch the note, and accuse her brother of concupiscence. Later Bramble voices a complaint about the noise and tumult of Bath, while Jery actually narrates the confused and noisy reception they meet upon their arrival. Bramble is dismayed by the mean state of the literary world of London; Jery relates his experiences with a motley group of literary hacks who have Sunday dinner with Smollett. It is Jery who keeps the narrative moving, who gets the travelers from place to place. It is he who narrates most of the memorable and typically Smollettian adventures: the evening spent with Quin, Ulic Mackilligut's encounter with Tabitha's dog, the meeting with Humphry on the road between Bath and London and the exposure of his bare posteriors, the fire in the inn at Harrowgate, the cawdie festival in Edinburgh, the practical jokes of Sir Thomas Bullford. Most of those events in which the interest lies more in the event itself than in the narrator's reaction are customarily given to Jery Melford.

The usefulness of the difference between the highly individualized, subjective point of view of Bramble and the objective point of view of Jery in weaving diverse material into the fabric of *Humphry Clinker* is equally noticeable when we direct our attention to the didactic purposes of the work. To any reader of the novel it soon becomes obvious that Matthew Bramble has assumed for himself the role of moralist and social critic among the travelers, but it is perhaps not so immediately obvious how seriously Smollett intended his readers to respond to Bramble's criticisms of English society. It is at least possible for the reader to consider Bramble's querulous denunciations as merely another characterizing device, emphasizing again his peevish and eccentric disposition. But even assuming that the reader is more convinced by the humors of Bramble's character than by the soundness of his moral judgments, and that the reader concludes his pronouncements to be mere eccentricities to be smiled at rather than pondered over, there is another source of didactic effect that acts as a corroboration of Bramble's pronouncements. This source is Jery's objective reporting of events and situations which carry with them an implicit moral or comment on society. A very obvious example occurs while the travelers are at Bath. Bramble is constantly complaining about the heterogeneous society at Bath and asserting that the mixture of all classes can only lead to the vulgarization of them all. His nephew, in conversation with him, opines that it tends to polish the inferior ones. The question is resolved the next day when a general tea-drinking is turned into a near riot; the guests charge the dining tables at the sound of a bell, and both the aristocracy and the mob debase themselves. Regardless of how little convinced the reader may have been by Bramble's fears, the event itself, as reported by Jery, resolves the difference of opinion. Later Bramble's frequently voiced suspicions of the *nouveaux riches* are confirmed when Jery reports how the newly affluent Paunceford ungenerously neglects his old benefactor Serle. Again when the travelers arrive in London, Bramble reprehends the political system of the day and complains about self-serving factions, venal office holders, and prostitute ministers. His complaints are dramatized when Jery encounters some of the "great men of the kingdom" at a high festival at court, particularly the bumbling Duke of Newcastle, whose ridiculous and fulsome behavior, as reported by Jery, bears out most of Bramble's criticisms.

A further didactic emphasis wrought through alternating points of view is provided occasionally by the coincidence of Lydia's opinion with Bramble's. As indicated above, Lydia is used, especially in the early parts of the novel, to soften Bramble's harsh pronouncements and leave a more neutral impresssion of sights and events viewed by the travelers. But occasionally her viewpoint is used to reinforce some pronouncement by Bramble, and when this occurs the reader becomes even more conscious of the importance of the pronouncement to the didactic contours of the book. When Humphry is discovered preaching Methodism, Bramble takes him to task in a typical outburst: "Heark-ye, Clinker, you are either an hypocritical knave, or a wrong-headed enthusiast" (JM—June 10). Later in the book, Lydia comments on her aunt's Methodist activities: "She has been praying, preaching, and catechising among the method-ists, . . . and pretends to have such manifestations and revelations, as even Clinker himself can hardly believe. . . . God forgive me if I think uncharitably, but all this seems to me to be downright hypocrisy and deceit" (LM—Sept. 7). The reader of course expects a harsh verdict from the mouth of Bramble, but he is not quite prepared for so severe a judgment as Lydia delivers, and, as a result, the indictment of Methodism from the usually uncritical young girl comes with even more persuasive force. Similarly Bramble's frequent reiteration of the evils of life in the city as compared with the felicities of rural life at Brambleton-hall may not strike the reader with full force because of Bramble's propensity to complain. But Bramble's complaints are given increased emphasis in enforcing the didactic aims of the novel when Lydia, who is charmed and delighted by almost all that she encounters, nevertheless expresses herself thus: "I wish my weak head may not grow giddy in the midst of all this gallantry and dissipation; though, as yet, I can safely declare, I could gladly give up all these tumultuous pleasures, for country solitude, and a happy retreat with those we love" (LM—May 31). Thus Bramble's moralizing and his criticism of the social values of Bath and London are given additional validity by the comments of the person in the letter-writing group who is usually most different from him in her reactions and impressions. When a crotchety but charitable old man and an impres-sionable but good-hearted young girl agree in their judgment, as Lydia and Bramble do on several issues, they may still both be wrong, but the agreement multiplies the chances that their judgment is sound.

The value of multiple point of view in establishing the validity and economy of both the reporting and the moralizing of *Humphry Clinker* may be further emphasized by considering what might have been the result had Smollett restricted his work to one letter writer, say Matthew Bramble. In such a case, *Humphry Clinker* might well have turned out to be another *Travels through France and Italy*, the idiosyncratic impres-sions of a hypersensitive and hypochondriacal traveler, interesting and readable no doubt, but without the telling and structurally consolidating force that contrasting and corroborating points of view provide. And the reader, after a certain amount of exposure to the crabbed remarks of Bramble, unrelieved by the malapropian versions of Tabitha and Win, unmodified by the impressions of Lydia, unconfirmed by the objective accounts of Jery, might well react as Sterne did to the learned Smelfungus of the *Travels*: "I'll tell it, cried Smelfungus, to the world. You had better tell it, said I, to your physician."[2]

The preceding comments on the economy engendered by Smollett's use of multiple point of view are in general much more applicable to the English section of the novel than they are to the Scottish section. In fact the value it had for Smollett can be pointed up by contrasting the English letters with the Scottish ones. Tabitha writes no letters at all from Scotland, and Lydia writes only one at the conclusion of the tour through the northern kingdom; in this she pays only the briefest of compliments to the politeness of the Scots and the beauties of Loch Lomond. Only from two letters written by Win Jenkins does the reader get any of the interplay between new sights and the female personality that blended the reporting and characterizing functions in the English letters. The dissevering of these functions becomes even more obvious in the Scottish letters of Matthew Bramble. The mellowing effect of Scotland on Bramble has often been remarked; the crabbed critic of Bath and London suddenly becomes the admirer of Edinburgh, Glasgow, and Loch Lomond.

But the apparent change in Bramble occurs partly because in the Scottish letters Smollett does not characterize him by individual tone and diction to the extent that he did in the English letters. Bramble characteristically complains briefly about sanitary conditions in Edinburgh, and the reader can detect the Bramble acid punctuating many of his remarks. But there are numerous descriptive paragraphs and even pages in which Bramble goes on merely retailing typical travel data in an unindividualized tone of approval, unmodified by any subjective reaction that would distinguish his report from the accounts of Scotland written by Defoe or Pennant or Smollett himself as editor of *The Present State of All Nations*.[3] Especially after leaving Edinburgh, Bramble often seems merely a convenient peg for Smollett on which to hang facts and observations, and the idiosyncrasies of his point of view are not so neatly exploited as in the earlier parts of the journey. The economy of the novel weakens, and it becomes for many pages little more than the compilation of pedestrian travel letters it was originally announced to be.

In Scotland Jery Melford continues to write his genial reports of events such as the cawdie dinner, the rough voyage on the return from

2. Laurence Sterne, *A Sentimental Journey Through France and Italy*, World's Classics ed. (London, 1928), p. 51.
3. Martz, Chaps. V–VI, points out the extent to which Smollett derived his description of Scotland in *Humphry Clinker* from materials in *Present State*, which in turn were often derived from other published accounts.

the excursion into Fife, and the festive Highland funeral at which the corpse is left behind, but even in his letters we get long factual passages which are little different from the conventional travel report. In brief, because in the Scottish section of the novel there is less emphasis on self-characterization as well as on the type of characterization that was so brilliantly developed in the early letters by multiple reflection from one point of view to another, and because Smollett apparently weakens in his ability to interlock reporting and moralizing from letter-writer to letter-writer, most readers, finishing the Scottish letters, are apt to feel that there has been some loss of creative control over material and purpose, a control that was exercised in the earlier part of the book by imaginative handling of several points of view.

When the travelers return to England, their interest in sights and scenes, an interest which has been strong throughout the novel and especially dominant in Scotland, begins to fade, and they turn their attention to their own affairs. What little conventional plot the novel has is wound up with the revelation of Humphry's parentage and the triple wedding. One additional element in the final pages of the novel is, however, worthy of comment because it demonstrates again how Smollett uses objective reporting to reinforce subjective reaction and didactic purpose. In his letter of June 8, about one-third of the way through the novel, Bramble pours forth his accumulated dislike for urban living with a point-by-point contrast between his "town grievances, and . . . country comforts." At Brambleton-hall, the air is pure, the food and drink wholesome, the amusements innocent, and friends and dependents honest and trusty. In London, the air is putrid, food and drink contaminated, amusements insipid or corrupting, and "your tradesmen are without conscience, your friends without affection, and your dependents without fidelity." In the final section of the novel, the Bramble party meets two of Matthew's old friends, Baynard and Dennison. Baynard is on the verge of ruin because of a wife who has forced him into the vortex of fashionable living centered in the ostentatious city. Dennison, on the other hand, is in a prosperous and happy situation because he has refused to be enticed by the luxury and show of the city and has been content to husband judiciously his rural resources. The situations of Baynard and Dennison, reported in the last series of letters, are clearly objective confirmations of the many strictures on English society made by Bramble during his stays in Bath and London. A certain symmetry thus emerges from the rambles of *Humphry Clinker* by using the objective reports of the careers of Baynard and Dennison in the last part of the novel to verify the criticism of English society which threaded its insistent way through the subjective reactions of Bramble in the first part.

It seems likely that Smollett, aware of his rapidly deteriorating health, sensed that *Humphry Clinker* was to be his last opportunity to get into print a multitude of ideas and experiences that he had accumulated over the years and that were energizing still his imagination. The reader can speculate, but he cannot actually know in what terms Smollett viewed the problem of giving fictional form to this multitude of material demanding expression. Quite possibly he was not particularly conscious of any formal problem and was quite content to work up his material in such a way as to suggest Hazlitt's fine phrase, "the most pleasant gossiping novel that ever was written."[4] Hazlitt's response has been that of many readers, both casual and scholarly, and it suggests a perspective useful to keep in mind in any study of the novel: Humphry Clinker is too much of a "gossiping novel," too much of a pleasant potpourri of events, persons, data, observations, criticism, satire, and moralizing ever to submit to the kind of analysis that discovers a single unifying principle dictating form and content to a work of fiction. But in spite of this amorphous quality, the case can be made that Smollett effectively blended his variegated materials and diverse aims by his use of multiple point of view. Never a master of form, Smollett was a master of material, and by his fortunate discovery or adoption of a multiple point of view, he brilliantly and effectively assembled the materials and ideas of a lifetime into Humphry Clinker to produce one of the enduring delights of English fiction.

MARY WAGONER

On the Satire in Humphry Clinker†

If Tobias Smollett's literary ancestry has been traced more often to the continental picaresque romancers Cervantes, LeSage, and the author of Lazarillo de Tormes than to British satirists, an obvious explanation lies in the critical prefaces to Smollett's own novels.[1] He praises the Europeans and largely ignores the Britons except in the peevish first chapter of Ferdinand Count Fathom where he complains of readers "who, when Swift or Pope represents a coxcomb in the act of swearing, scruple not to laugh at the ridiculous execrations; but, in a less reputed author, condemn the use of such profane expletives."[2]

In the structure of his novels, Smollett does generally follow picaresque models. His novels are episodic travelogues that examine representatives of various social levels. Yet the raison d'être of his novels, as he regularly pointed out, is the reformation of manners through satire,[3] and

4. William Hazlitt, Lectures on the English Comic Writers, in Complete Works, ed. P. P. Howe (London, 1931), VI, p. 117.
† From Papers on Language and Literature 2 (1966): 109–116.
1. See the Preface to Roderick Random, Vols. I–II

in The Works of Tobias Smollett. 6 vols. (New York, [n.d.]), I, xlviii, or the Dedication of Ferdinand Count Fathom, Vol. V of Works, I, 3–4.
2. Fathom, I, 9–10.
3. Note the objection that Gil Blas "prevents that generous indignation which ought to animate the

as a satirist he seldom achieves the picaresque mood. The laughter of the picaresques, in Chandler's apt phrase, arises from "hungry comedy."[4] It arises from the picaro outsider's cynically puncturing the value scheme of his society. Living by his wits in a social order that has no place for him, he subverts that order by surviving at all, and the punitive satire he generates is directed against himself rather than society only when he suffers lapses in judgment and allows himself to be caught at his roguery.

This sort of justification for roguery is to be found in none of Smollett's novels, not even *Ferdinand Count Fathom*. His novels are aligned with the social order, not against it. His complaints against the larger license of Swift and Pope notwithstanding, the scheme of values of their satire rather than that of the picaresque romancers controls his laughter, most markedly in his last and best novel, *Humphry Clinker*.

To examine the nature of this control, let us consider the characters Smollett subjects to satire, noting particularly the vehemence with which they are handled, for his comic methods develop a kind of yardstick of shortcomings. By observing the degree to which the character's personality is treated satirically, we may gauge his need for reform. In the effects of such reformation we may find the code of behavior Smollett urges.

The prime target in *Humphry Clinker* for both situational satire and unsympathetic mirth from other characters is Mrs. Tabitha Bramble. Described by her brother as a "wild cat" and "a domestic demon," by her nephew as "an implacable virago" and "of all antiquated maidens the most diabolically capricious," Tabby combines the vices of intemperate egoism, avarice, arrogance, and ignorance. Her ignorance and penury are firmly established in her scolding letters to her housekeeper and to Dr. Lewis, but Smollett fills the novel with rowdy farcical proofs of her shortcomings, from her prattle to James Quin about the "Ghost of Gimlet" to her egregious mistakes about the intentions of her niece's suitor, her brazen appearances at public functions, and her scolding harassment of the whole family.[5]

The point of the farce, significantly, is never the falsity of society's standards but the antisocial quality of Tabby's. Her peculiarities do not victimize society; she is inevitably foiled by her own unthinking, unabashed self-interest.

The vignette of Tabby and the ailing Scottish lawyer Micklewhimmen, though less laughable than most of her scenes, is sufficiently

reader against the sordid and vicious disposition of the world" in the Preface to *Roderick Random*, I, xlviii, or the comment on efforts "to subject folly to ridicule, and vice to indignation" in the Dedication to *Fathom*, I, 4.

4. Frank Wadleigh Chandler, *The Literature of Roguery* (Boston and New York, 1907), I, 1–6.
5. Tabby explains to Quin: "I was once vastly entertained with your playing the Ghost of Gimlet, at Drury Lane, when you rose up through the stage, with a white face and red eyes, and spoke of *quails upon the frightful porcupine*. Do, pray, spout a little of the Ghost of Gimlet." For the account of her announcing her engagement of Lydia's Mr. Barton, see Jerry's letters of June 10 and June 11 and Bramble's letter of June 12. Tabby's notable public appearances are in the baths at Bath, in the Bath dining room, at Vauxhall, at the Edinburgh ball, and at her wedding.

condensed to illustrate the nature of the satire against her. Her nephew Jerry offers a grotesque picture of Tabby's courting the lawyer by assisting him to the table and of the conversations in which his respects to her are mingled with "religious reflections, touching free grace, knowing her bias toward Methodism, which he also professed upon a Calvinistical model." Flaunting decorous restraint and using her religiosity to man-hunt, Tabby is thus ready for the trap Smollett springs in a fire alarm: "In the midst of this anarchy, Mr. Micklewhimmen, with a leathern portmanteau on his back, came running as nimbly as a buck along the passage, and Tabby, in her under petticoat, endeavoring to hook him under her arm, that she might escape through his protection, he fairly pushed her down, crying, 'Na, na, gude faith, charity begins at hame!'"

The episode focuses at once on Tabby's interested false judgment of the man, on her verbal piety, and on her officiousness, and these motives are interrelated. She is left stripped, figuratively and physically, while her prey escapes crying the very phrase Tabby consistently uses to avoid benevolence. The affair dissolves in farcical violence, in total suspension of sympathy for Tabby. Her unchecked, forcible, selfish intentions have been stymied in raucous uproar.

The other character subjected to this level of violent reversal shares, interestingly, Tabby's arational judgments and shallow pretensions, even though she is, on the whole, far more engaging since her naïvete is genuine. The maid Win Jenkins is also a creature of strong physical appetite as well as vanity. Her flaws are expressed in silliness more often than in real perversity, but as her shortcomings are broadly exhibited, so is she broadly caught short. In one letter, for instance, she can offer the following advice:

O Molly! let not your poor heart be puffed up with vanity.
I had almost forgot to tell you, that I have had my hair cut and pippered, and singed, and bolstered, and buckled in the newest fashion, by a French freezer. *Parley vow Francey—Vee Madmansell.* ... Last night coming huom from the meeting, I was taken by lampsight for an imminent poulterer's daughter, a great beauty. But as I was saying, this is all vanity and vexation of spirit. The pleasures of London are no better than sower whey and stale cyder, when compared to the joys of the New Gerusalem.

And she goes on to suggest, "and I pray of all love, you will mind your vriting and your spelling; for, craving your pardon, Molly, it made me suet to disseyffer your last scrabble. ..." Predictably Win's major reverses result from her playing the grand lady, and these reverses are signalized by her losing her petticoat at Bath, her being attacked and called *hoar* and painted *Issabel* in the streets of Edinburgh when she allows "van Ditton, the young squire's wally-de-shamble" to dress her up, or her being jilted by the valet for an heiress.

In short, these characters, whose self-esteem depends most heavily on physical vanity and presumption, the cardinal sins of the neoclassical satirists, are treated with particularly vehement laughter that explodes their presumption by demolishing their claims to dignity.

The third roughly handled character, Obadiah Lismahago, is satirized less for physical than for intellectual vanity, another standard neoclassical sin. The laughter he arouses centers on his polemical arrogance and his stiff military decorum, and where he does not bend with these qualities, Smollett breaks him in farce. The returned warrior, attempting stiff formality, is, for instance, sprawled from his saddle or maneuvered into descending a ladder in the nude. But in his case Smollett does not rely solely on violent disorder. The satire of Lismahago develops over longer spans and with more subtlety. The Lieutenant is never so thoroughly flayed as Tabby or Win. He is always left with the dignity of an honorable career even when his remarkable arguments, which fill five of Matthew Bramble's lengthiest letters, are comically dogmatic. He stuns his hearers instead of convincing them, and he reasons himself into positions blatantly contrary to his own interest, defending the system of military preferment, though he has suffered from it, or arguing against great merit in Scots despite his glowering nationalism. As Bramble remarks, "The man has certainly gathered a whole budget of shrewd observations, but he brings them forth in such an ungracious manner as would be extremely disgusting, if it was not marked by that characteristic oddity which never fails to attract the attention." Moreover, Lismahago, in effect, argues his way into the Bramble family, and there is satiric point in his having survived the American Indians to seek peace in his old age as Tabby's husband.

The satire emerging from the portrait of simple, pious Humphry Clinker turns similarly on the effects of one misdirected intelligence on others, and it similarly keeps Humphry from being totally laughable. The key issue with Humphry is his Methodism and the absurdities he generates through his enthusiastic good will. He will not declare himself innocent when falsely accused of robbery, he strands his master naked on the beach under the erroneous assumption that he is calling for help, and more particularly, he engages in street sermons and disrupts the prison system by converting the inmates. Humphry's training for his role of ghostly conductor is, after all, that

> I can read and write, and do the business of the stable indifferent well. I can dress a horse and shoe him, and bleed and rowl him; and, as for the practice of sow-gelding, I won't turn my back on e'er a he in the county of Wilts. Then I can make hogs puddings and hob-nails, mend kettles, and tin saucepans.... I know something of a single stick and psalmody. ... I can play upon the Jew's harp, sing Black-eyed Susan, Arthur

O'Bradley, and divers other songs. I can dance a Welsh jig and Nancy Dawson; wrestle a fall with any lad of my inches, when I'm in heart, and, under correction, I can find a hare when your honor wants a bit of game.

Humphry's comedy is double-edged. There is a pointed contrast between his primitive goodness and Tabby's sanctimony, for example. Tabby objects fiercely when, shirtless, he has "the impudence to shock her sight by showing his posteriors," but she eagerly embraces his religious guidance when it serves her turn.[6] Notably Bramble respects and protects Humphry for his simple, natural virtues. Nonetheless Bramble acknowledges dangers in uninformed good feeling: "Well, I affirm that folly is often more provoking than knavery, ay, and more mischievous too; and whether a man had not better choose a sensible rogue, than an honest simpleton, for his servant, is no matter of doubt with yours. . . ."

As religious enthusiasm, genuine and faked, is examined through Humphry Clinker, romanticizing on various levels is considered with the young people, Jerry and Lydia Melford. As satiric targets neither is given much attention and both function largely in providing narrative threads —Lydia with her love affair, Jerry with his self-consciously comic reporting. Lydia amuses primarily in her indiscriminate ecstacies, Jerry in the miscarriage of his playing the blasé young man of affairs whose projected duel is easily averted.

The key figure in the novel is crusty old Matthew Bramble, the experienced, rational man who sees through his family with painful clarity, recognizing Tabby as "a precious commodity," Jerry as "a pert young jackanapes," Lydia as "soft as butter," Humphry as a simpleton, Lismahago as an austere but strong-flavored crab-apple.

In both his actions and his views Bramble represents a satiric norm. His benevolence, for example, is quiet but effective, and it enables us to measure Tabby's babbling against his performance with Humphry, with his tenants, with the reformed highwayman. Bramble's manners are forthright and easy even when those about him are engaged in elaborate ceremony. He always measures from a human scale, rejecting architectural pretension in the Scarborough church or in Bath's Crescent or in Mrs. Baynard's remodeling of her husband's estate. He rejects party enthusiasm in London as he rejects religious enthusiasm in Clinker and the females of his family. He is appalled at the idiosyncratic lord who dismisses his dinner guests. He is antagonized by affectation and failure to observe decorum in the crowds at Bath. He is doubtful about medical

6. Milton A. Goldberg, *Smollett and the Scottish School* (Albuquerque, N.M., 1959), pp. 170–73. Goldberg sees the shift in Tabby's reactions as a major point in support of his thesis that *Clinker*'s theme is related to the century's interest in primitivism and progress.

experimentation in the doctor at Bath. He is troubled by the growth of corrupting luxury in London.

Indeed, in attitude and tastes and even in literary style (for his letters are notably lucid and witty) Bramble is an urbane, "civilized" eighteenth-century British gentleman.

His scheme of values is most tellingly offered in his comparison of his serene country life with life in London. He praises Brambleton Hall for its "elbow-room indoors," its "clear, elastic salutary air," its wholesome food, modest entertainment—identified as conversation with sensible, select friends, and fruitful cultivation of land. The whole catalog curiously parallels the good life of the Houyhnhnms, i.e., spaciousness, freshness, wholesomeness, preservation of "decency and civility in the highest degrees," and adherence to a code in which "friendship and benevolence are the two principle virtues."[7] London, in contrast, is a sink of Yahoodom to Bramble, who condemns it on both rational and aesthetic grounds for its filth, unclean food, brawling noise, lack of sanitation, and people motivated by schemes of interest or ambition until "you are preyed upon by idle mendicants, who beg in the phrase of borrowing, and live upon the spoils of the stranger," or "your tradesmen are without conscience, your friends without affection, and your dependents without fidelity."

Bramble is never subjected to satiric laughter because of this scheme of values. In fact the adventures of his family are, in effect, proofs of the rightness of his judgment. He does become a target when, having set off on the journey, having come "plague-hunting in London with a leash of females in my train," he, like Gulliver, tries too hard to resist identification with the Yahoos. His irritable efforts at aloofness are made into comedy with his spluttering that "I have done with the science of men and must now endeavor to amuse myself with the novelty of things." Yet Bramble is obsessed with men, and his experiences are a series of farcical demonstrations to remind him of that fact. He is reduced by horseplay only as his outbursts become intemperate, as when, for example, his outrage at indecorous behavior rises to periodic heights. Whenever it does and he indulges an outburst, he is abruptly reminded of his identity with other men. He faints in public, his carriages are overturned, he is hauled naked on a beach. Smollett, in fact, climaxes the satire of Bramble's peculiar excess, his Gulliverlike rejection of flaw-ridden mankind, with a plot resolution that links him, the man of reason, with the nonreasonable, artless Humphry Clinker, the natural son who is evidence of his father's passion.

The end of the novel, significantly, finds Bramble still rational, still civilized, still benevolent, but in far better control of his irritable sensitivity which, after all, is the flaw subjecting him to laughter.

7. Jonathan Swift, *Gulliver's Travels*, ed. William A. Eddy (New York, 1933), p. 319.

The resolution also suggests a toning down of the other characters' comic excesses. Tabby's self-interest is, for instance, rechanneled toward her husband, the Lieutenant whom she promotes to "my spouse, the captain." She unbends enough to sign herself, "Your loving friend," in her last letter to her housekeeper. Win Jenkins becomes somewhat less silly and more generally restrained. The token of her restraint comes in the letter announcing her marriage to Humphry: "Present my compliments to Mrs. Guillim, and I hope she and I will live upon dissent terms of civility," since she has "by God's blessing, removed to a higher spear." Lismahago begins to argue less and relaxes enough to clown: "He sighs and ogles and languishes at this amiable object [Tabby]; he kisses her hand, mutters ejaculations of rapture, and sings tender airs; and, no doubt, laughs internally at her folly in believing him sincere." Humphry Clinker, now Lloyd, finds enough pride to be a member of the family rather than a servant, and Lydia writes surprisingly mature letters of invitation to her wedding. Even Jerry drops his man-of-the-world pose long enough to consider, briefly, marrying himself.

As resolutions of plot these developments are, perhaps, none too convincing. Causal connections between events have not made them necessary. Rather, Smollett ends *Humphry Clinker* when, apparently, the laughter has gone on long enough to make his satiric points, when he is ready to stop by announcing that the shortcomings which produced the various levels of farce have been ameliorated.

The amelioration has, with each character, been a movement toward the norm of easier, more tolerant, more reasonable behavior, a movement away from idiosyncrasy and peculiarity. No character has been able to escape reforming satire; none has hoodwinked the group. There have, in short, been no successful picaros in *Humphry Clinker*.

WILLIAM PARK

Fathers and Sons: *Humphry Clinker*†

In *Humphry Clinker* Smollett employed a comic plot similar to the one used by Shakespeare in his romantic comedies. A group of travellers, some diseased in mind and body, others sexually frustrated, set out in search of health and happiness, and after passing through the wasteland of Bath, London, and England itself, move on to the Arcadia represented in this novel by Scotland. Here instead of polluted waters, discord, political corruption, intellectual sterility, and social anarchy, they discover the crystal waters of the Leven, country dances, hospitality,

† From *Literature and Psychology* 16 (1966): 166–174.

intellectual brilliance, social order, and progress. From thence they can with new vigor return to England, discover their true identities, find their lovers, and celebrate a triple marriage.

That Smollett consciously had Shakespeare or any archetypal plot in mind when he composed his last novel seems highly improbable. As Northrop Frye has said, "no one will suspect Smollett of deliberate mythopoeia." [1] Yet toward the end of the story, the characters approach a "point of ritual death" in which they "are nearly drowned in an accident with an upset carriage; they are then taken to a nearby house to dry off, and a *cognito* takes place, in the course of which their family relationships are regrouped, secrets of birth brought to light, and names changed." In mythic terms then, the overturning of the coach in a swollen mill stream serves as a ritual drowning or baptism from which the family, like the voyagers in *The Tempest*, are reborn into a better life. And as in that play the journey to an enchanted land makes possible a new life in the familiar world.

Not only does *Humphry Clinker* partake of an archetypal plot in which the protagonists journey from a "mad world" of folly and knavery into a "green" one of fertility and joy, but also its particular matter consists of overt and latent quests which both unify and shape the story. Consciously Bramble has set out to regain his health; consciously Taby, Lydia, and Win look for husbands and in turn are sought after. But latent in this novel is still a third quest—that of son for father and father for son. Though to be sure, neither Bramble nor Clinker are looking for relatives, their discovery of one another immediately precedes the union of Lydia and Dennison, and as it turns out, the health which Bramble yearns for and, indeed, his life itself depends upon Clinker. By the climax of the novel then, this unconscious or latent quest has humorously and sentimentally been brought to the surface and inextricably bound up with the fulfillment of all the desires of the family.

If as Joseph Campbell claims, the search for a mystical marriage and the journey toward atonement with the father comprise two essential parts of quest literature and are often combined in the same story, [2] we should not be surprised to find them juxtaposed and interrelated as they are in *Humphry Clinker*. Though Smollett has submerged these archetypal desires and discoveries, or, as Frye would say, has "displaced" them into a world of realistic travel reporting, and though he has treated them humorously and sentimentally, nevertheless they are present in the novel. In this paper I wish to demonstrate how one of these quests, the mutual discovery of a father and son and the psychological complications attendant upon such an event pervade *Humphry Clinker* from the very outset, forming a pattern of images and motifs which more than amply

---

1. *Anatomy of Criticism* (Princeton, 1957), p. 179.
2. *The Hero with a Thousand Faces* (New York, 1956), pp. 109–149.

364 • William Park

prepares the reader for the comical, surprising, and satisfying revelation that Clinker is Bramble's love-begotten child.

Curiously enough, Smollett begins by reversing the usual order of quest literature, for instead of the son's search for the father in order to gain strength and power, it seems to be the father who stands more in need of the son for health, peace of mind, and perhaps maturity itself. Clinker, the son, appears to the family in the disguise often taken by fathers when they first meet their sons—that of a beggar dressed in rags. Like Telemachos, Bramble passes this "test" successfully by clothing Clinker, giving him money, and reprimanding the landlord for treating the fellow so poorly. Though Clinker has only been hired to act as postillion as far as Marlborough, he pleads to be taken into service, saying he is so grateful to Bramble that he has not the "heart to part with him" and will "follow him to the world's end, and serve all the days of his life without fee or reward." Again Bramble passes the test, hires Clinker, and is immediately rewarded by being able for the first time to stand up to his termagant sister. Outraged at Clinker's being hired, because he had offended her by innocently showing his bare posteriors, she insists that Bramble choose between her and "a beggarly foundling, taken from the dunghill." Bramble replies that she can instead choose between staying with the family or getting rid or Chowder, her irritating and troublesome dog. The energy and seriousness with which he issues this proposal cause Taby to back down. From this point on she ceases to plague him as before, and shortly thereafter gives away the pesty Chowder.

Psychologically the need of a son for a father is usually related to his need to get away from his mother's domination. He must discover his father in order to discover his own manhood and the means to virility and power. As Campbell points out, he must, in a sense, become his own father.[3] Though one need not deny the mother in this process, some change in the relationship between mother and son is necessary, and in literature and life this change is often symbolized by some ritual rejection of a strong or tempting woman, as when Jesus for instance denies Mary. In *Humphry Clinker* this motif begins with Bramble's triumph over his sister, but takes its most intense form in Bramble's pleading with his friend Baynard to throw off the yoke of his wife's thraldom, a wife who characteristically keeps her own son from his father, saying to him, "Come, child . . . your father cannot abide you." Even in the climactic scene, when the coach overturns in the stream, we find this motif, for Clinker, just after saving Win from the floor, drops her back into the water in order to save his father. Of course, once he is recognized by Bramble, he can consummate his love for Win. Shortly after this incident, as in a dream or fantasy, Mrs. Baynard unexpectedly dies, whereupon Bramble can act the friend and mentor (or father figure) and

3. Campbell, p. 145.

help Baynard to recover his ruined estate and manhood. In keeping with this reestablishment of order and the new reign of sexual harmony, Jery, at the end of the novel, compares Taby and Lismahago to Cybele and Saturn. Instead of the earth mother's being potentially a devouring woman, reigning with her doomed son-lover Adonis, she is now properly coupled to the father of the gods, here represented by the doughty and competent veteran Lismahago.

The failure of any man to become his own father results in impotence and psychological castration.[4] This motif appears not only in the plight of the dominated Baynard, but also more vividly in Lismahago's adventures. After escaping from the French hospital at Montreal, Lismahago and an ensign Murphy are captured by a party of Miamis:

> The intention of these Indians was to give one of them as an adopted son to a venerable sachem, who had lost his own in the course of the war, and to sacrifice the other according to the custom of the country. Murphy, as being the younger and handsomer of the two, was designed to fill the place of the deceased, not only as the son of the sachem, but as the spouse of a beautiful squaw, to whom his predecessor had been betrothed; but in passing through the different whigwhams or villages of the Miamis, poor Murphy was so mangled by the women and children who have the privilege of torturing all prisoners in their passage, that, by the time they arrived at the place of the sachem's residence, he was rendered altogether unfit for the purposes of marriage: it was determined, therefore, in the assembly of the warriors, that ensign Murphy should be brought to the stake, and that the lady should be given to lieutenant Lismahago, who had likewise received his share of torments, though they had not produced emasculation.

Before he dies Murphy himself is further tortured in a manner reminiscent of Oedipus, for "an old lady, with a sharp knife, scooped out one of his eyes, and put a burning coal in the socket."

Chief among the celebrants at this festival is Lismahago's bride-to-be, the squaw Squinkacoosta.

> She shewed a great superiority of genius in the tortures which she contrived and executed with her own hands. She vied with the stoutest warrior in eating the flesh of the sacrifice; and after all the other females were fuddled with dram-drinking, she was not so intoxicated but that she was able to play the game of the platter with the conjuring sachem and afterward go through the ceremony of her own wedding, which was consummated that same evening.

Though all this appears to be only a grotesque anecdote, it contains many of the themes of the book—the search of a father for a son, the castration by women and children, Lismahago's successful overcoming of an ordeal, and his domination of a torturing and flesh-eating female. It

4. Campbell, p. 137.

would almost seem that Lismahago's being already scalped served as some kind of ritual castration which immunized him against the sad fate suffered by Murphy.

Later in the story, Lismahago several times proves himself to be a proper son; first by leaving Taby in order to follow an "irresistible impulse" to revisit the "*paternus lar*, or patria domus," then by chastizing his nephew for turning his father's house into a factory, or as he calls it "a den of thieves." After paying his respects to the "manes" of his ancestors, he can then rejoin the Bramble family and actively and successfully court Taby. In being such a stalwart son and lover, Lismahago parallels Clinker. But in his age, misanthropy, and in relieving Bramble of the incestuous burden of Taby's often misdirected affection, he acts as a substitute for Bramble himself. Thus while being a magnificent "original" in his own right, he also serves as an analogue who comically links the qualities of Clinker and Bramble.

Once Bramble stands up to Taby, Smollett turns more of his attention to the ordeal of Humphry Clinker. In London this young man suffers a terrible injury from his father, one which could possibly serve as some kind of ritual castration for him. This occurs when Bramble calls him down from the pulpit and severely rebukes him for his setting up as a preacher. Here Bramble plays the role of the ogre father, the holdfast who wants to keep all power and sexuality to himself. Typically for this type of figure, Bramble appears to be particularly infuriated because he finds "all the females of the family among the audience." Again it is Taby who urged Clinker to stand up to Bramble and quit his service, but Clinker wisely, at least for the purposes of myth, declines and on his knees begs to be allowed to continue in the squire's service. Thus he acts the part of the good son who successfully passes the test—here the extremely severe one of renouncing his preaching and suspecting his "inner light" for the sake of his master, a master who at this point shows the son only the horrifying and ogre-like qualities of the father.

Bramble, however, seems to be immediately punished for his severity. His next letter opens with complaints about his stomach and bowels and immediately afterward Clinker is taken from him and thrown into jail as a highwayman, an event which increases Bramble's anxiety and sickness. Only when he recognizes the good effect Clinker has on the felons and realizes that this simple good man has not a grain of affectation or hypocrisy in him, and only after Clinker returns, can Bramble regain his health. As Bramble puts it, "The imprisonment of Clinker brought on those symptoms which I mentioned in my last, and now they are vanished at his discharge." Because loyalty and obedience of the son requires recognition, reward, trust, and perhaps even dependence on the part of the father, Bramble now designates Clinker as his "life-guard-man on the highway."

In this capacity Clinker saves the naked Win Jenkins from a fire at an inn. Then at Scarborough, hearing his master gasp at the coldness of the sea, Clinker, thinking that Bramble is drowning, races into the water, grasps Bramble by the ear, and drags him up naked on the beach, much to the amusement of a crowd of spectators. For this indignity Bramble strikes Clinker down, but then forgives him, knowing full well that Clinker cannot bear to be in his bad graces. Though here Clinker's enthusiasm for Bramble turns to the folly of the clumsy apprentice and nearly causes his dismissal, the incident obviously serves as a comic prelude to the actual rescue of Bramble.

As a "life-guard-man" Clinker immediately redeems himself when on the next day the coach breaks down. Making use of a nearby forge, whose owner has recently died, Clinker shows his talents as both smithy and farrier and soon has the coach in proper working order. While he repairs the coach, however, the smith's widow, who has lately been delivered of a child, mistakes Clinker for her deceased husband, throws her arms about his neck, and blames him for leaving her "in such a condition." All this serves to evoke the tears and benevolence of the Bramble family and produces a touching, sentimental incident. In retrospect however, it turns out that this mother's plight is strikingly similar to that of Clinker's mother, who was abandoned in her distress by Bramble himself. Therefore, by dream logic, Clinker, in being mistaken for the absent father and husband, actually plays the role of his own father, who left Clinker's mother "in such a condition."

By the time the family reaches Scotland, both Bramble and Clinker have survived a number of tests and ordeals, have become dependent upon one another, and are almost ready for the final revelation. From the point of view of dream and fantasy life, however, to take a father's place, to become a man, or to find one's identity, can be terrifying events. Like Hamlet on the verge of manhood one is likely to see ghosts and to become confused or frightened by the very power within one's self striving to be realized. From an external point of view of course, such fears appear to be nonsense. The world expects Hamlet and the rest of us to grow up and get about our business. But growing up seems to be finally a psychological or spiritual event, one which can occur only when we overcome the subjective terrors we have placed in our own paths. In literature and myth this final obstacle often takes the form of some spiritual testing or supernatural visitation which comes to the hero on the eve of a great discovery at a time when he has been isolated from his companions, as for instance, when Jacob wrestles with the angel.

It is characteristic of both Smollett and mid-eighteenth-century novelists in general to debunk such material, known to them as the "marvellous," and to reduce it to comedy, mock-heroics, or some form of enlightened attack on ignorance and superstition. Yet curiously enough the matter remains, though in a negative form, and serves its time-honored psychological function. Such a scene occurs in Humphry Clinker when Humphry, strolling in the woods at night, comes upon the old admiral, the "venerable druid" as Bramble calls him, and nearly frightened out of his wits, his hair standing on end, he returns to the group to say that he has seen a "spirit in the shape of an old man." All this of course produces much mirth for the sophisticated. In her next letter Win continues the joke. She describes the incident, calls Scotland a "land of congyration" and tells how she bathed in "loff" Lomond, which she says is "holy water," in order to overcome her fears.

Had this incident occurred at any other point in the novel I would hesitate to discuss it as part of the quest in Humphry Clinker, but Smollett has placed it exactly at that moment when the Bramble family has reached the very summit of the green world. They have arrived at Smollett's own birthplace. Bramble introduces Smollett's "Ode to Leven-Water" into his letters, and he exclaims immediately prior to his anecdote of the apparition, "indeed, this country would be a perfect paradise, if it was not, like Wales, cursed with a weeping climate." In the common sense spirit of the mid-eighteenth-century novel this is as close as one can get to a heavenly vision. According to Joseph Campbell's terminology then, Loch Lomond and Smollett's birth place serve in this novel as the "world navel," or in orthodox terms as a new Eden, a spiritual place in this world where an eighteenth-century traveller can, like Bramble, lay up "a considerable stock of health" before returning to his accustomed life.

Because of the crucial importance of this locale and because the next action in which Clinker figures is that one where he discovers his actual father, I cannot help thinking that however ridiculous this scene is meant to be, it prefigures the ultimate revelation and serves as a psychological preparation for it. In fact, the other incident concerning ghosts seems to parallel this one.

In his next letter Bramble reports on tales of the second sight and of how a gentleman of the neighborhood was actually whipped by the ghost of his grandfather. The ghost turns out to be none other than Lismahago appearing in the night to chastize his commercial nephew. But since he is taken to be the ghost of his father, and since we are led to believe that he is acting as his father would wish him to do, again by dream logic, he has become his father, and the ridiculous ghost story contains a psychological truth. Only after his dutiful behavior can Lismahago rejoin the Brambles and successfully court his spiritual bride.

Aside from these central actions and incidents concerning fathers and sons, others appear throughout the novel. The most telling occurs at the moment when the family touches English ground once more. Shortly after crossing the Clyde, Jery reports "we met with an incident which warmly interested the benevolent spirit of Mr. Bramble," namely that in which a genteel young man on horseback seeing an old man at work paving a street says, "Have you never a son . . . to ease you of this labor?" The old man replies that he has three—the eldest in the East Indies, the younger gone a-soldiering, and the second hard by in prison for having taken upon himself his father's debts. Then the genteel young man asks why the eldest has not sent money, whereupon the old man says that he has, but that he lost it when he acted as security for his landlord. At this moment the second son shouts from the jailhouse window, "Father, father! if my brother William is in life, that's he," and the gentleman says, "(. . . clasping the old man in his arms, and shedding a flood of tears) —I am your son Willy, sure enough!" Bramble was so affected by this scene, says Jery, that he "sobbed, and wept, and clasped his hands, and hollowed, and finally ran down into the street." Bramble himself says to the elder son, "I would have travelled a hundred miles to see this affecting scene." Of course his whole journey will soon culminate when he, like the other old man, will be saved by a redeeming son.

As opposed to these good sons, the novel provides several examples of less than successful young men. Paunceford, for instance, has made a fortune in the East, but refuses to share any of it with the elderly gentleman who helped him on the path to riches. Another example occurs at Smollett's house where that author, despite his "paternal authority over this irritable tribe" is reviled and abused by the very hacks he supports. Baynard, of course, as Bramble states, has forgotten what he "owed to his father's house."

Smollett also provides variations on this theme of undutiful children, first with Martin the highwayman and then with Dennison senior. Martin, having privately married his employer's daughter, is discharged and turned out of doors with his wife, who dies soon afterwards. Since then he has earned his living on the highway, though he appears to be a Templar in Justice Buzzard's court. It was for his crime that Humphry Clinker was apprehended. Martin, who has only experienced ogre-like elders is impressed by Bramble's benevolence and his concern for his servant, and asks for a position in the family. Though his request is denied, he is given money and the opportunity to begin a new life. Dennison, the father of Lydia's beloved, also "disobliged his father by marrying for love." After suffering many privations, however, he returns to the family estate with the approval of his wife (who thus contrasts with Mrs. Baynard), and by dint of much work and common sense, restores it to a seat of felicity and prosperity.

It may even be that some submerged hostility to this motif of actual or expected filial obedience occurs in the curious episode where Jery for the second time challenges Wilson to a duel. Instead of young Dennison's appearing as he expected, the true Wilson, a middle-aged man of great assurance and coolness, shows up ready for the duel. The misunderstanding is quickly cleared up. It turns out that this Wilson had helped the Dennisons reestablish their estate and that young Dennison took Wilson's name because he admired the man greatly. Amidst scenes of good-hearted fathers and saving sons, Smollett includes one in which a high-spirited young man almost blows out the brains of an established elder or is himself almost slain.

The main course of the novel however is the positive and comical one in which father and son are united. What differentiates *Humphry Clinker* from the main body of myth, but perhaps not from the main body of Christian literature, is that here the son must not only find his father but the father is perhaps even more dependent on his son and must assume responsibility for him. As part of Bramble's initial complaint about his constipation and distress of mind and body, he exclaims, "As if I had not plagues enough of my own those children of my sister are left for me a perpetual source of vexation; what business have people to get children to plague their neighbors?" In his next letter he adds, "I am conscious of no sins that ought to entail such family plagues upon me. Why the devil should not I shake off these torments at once? I an't married to Taby, thank Heaven! nor did I beget the other two ...." This notion of paternity and responsibility is then jokingly alluded to by Jery Melford who, suspected of getting a Miss Blackerby with child, is told by Bramble "with great good humour" that between the ages of twenty and forty he was "obliged to provide for nine bastards, sworn to him by women who he never saw." Though all this seems good fun, Bramble says at the moment of Clinker's discovery: "'I am really shocked at the consequences of my own folly.' Then, laying his hand on Clinker's head, he added, 'Stand forth, Matthew Loyd. You see gentlemen, how the sins of my youth rise up in judgment against me.'" Only by acknowledging Clinker, laying his hand upon his son's head and owning up to the consequences of his own actions, does Bramble finally answer his original questions and once and for all overcome his peevishness. Only after this confession does a healthy Bramble, who will no longer need physic, restore the Baynard estate and preside over the triple wedding in his family.

In conclusion, I would like to suggest a few other associations which join this motif of father and son to other patterns of imagery in the novel. Perhaps the most dominant of these images is water. In his pursuit of health, Bramble travels to various spas, which in England are found to be sinks of filth and corruption, but in Scotland and particularly at the banks of the Leven, are discovered to be the fountains of health for which he searches. Clinker of course twice rescues Bramble from the water, and the novel abounds with splashings, dunkings, and dissertations on the nature of the water at the resorts. Such imagery is of course entirely appropriate and conventional for a story which tells of discovery, bliss, and rejuvenation. In this watery context I cannot help thinking that the name of Clinker's mother, Dorothy Twyford, takes its place in the general pattern. The two fords would appear to be the waters which the family, and especially Bramble, cross first in order to enter the magical world and then to return with their treasures to the normal one. Scotland is separated from England by rivers, and neatly, Bramble drowns just before entering and just after leaving it. Or the two fords may be related to the fact that as the family ends where it began, so must Bramble journey not only away from the deeds of his youth but must also come home again by recognizing his son, the bastard who proceeded out of Mrs. Twyford.

Another important image, as Sheridan Baker has pointed out, is that of stench and excrement.[5] In his initial complaint Bramble mentions his constipation even before his wards, and not until the family has passed through the archetypal filthy stream, which actually leads to the waters of health, does he feel easy. Crossing this threshold takes place not at Bristol or Bath whose healthy waters contaminate, but in Edinburgh whose stale waters restore. At least Win Jenkins, in one of her best letters, comes to this conclusion, one that is not only comically satisfying but psychologically profound, for only by accepting one's excrement can one be free of constipation and life destroying fastidiousness. By verbal association and images of anality it would seem that Humphry Clinker himself is the excrement which Bramble must acknowledge as his own. At his first appearance in the novel, Clinker makes a stunning impression on the ladies by virtue of his bare posteriors. His name "Clinker" has as one of its meanings "dung," and Taby reprimands her brother for preferring this foundling "taken from a dunghill." Then Bramble himself states that his internal disorders vanish at Clinker's "discharge" from prison. There may even be some further unconscious excremental associations involved in the name of the woman thought to be with child by Jery, Miss *Black*erby, a word which then seems to be played upon in London where the senile Duke mistakes Bramble for a relation of Bishop Blackberry, to which Bramble replies, "'Very likely, my Lord . . . the Blackberry is the fruit of the Bramble.'"

In his acceptance of Blackberries and Clinkers, Bramble not only comes to terms with his own filth and the sins of his youth, but perhaps as a consequence of these personal gains, he also can feel more at ease in the world at large. Throughout the course of the novel, as toleration and love grow, more of society is accepted or becomes included in the Bramble circle. Whereas each member begins by being isolated through interest and temperament from the others—all seemingly working to vex one another—by the end of the novel they become, as Win puts it, "a family of love." Bramble's and Jery's rigid notions of class are entirely upset and modified by with the discovery that a superstitious beggar is a near relation and a strolling player a young gentleman. Scotland turns out to

5. "*Humphry Clinker* as Comic Romance," *Papers of the Michigan Academy of Science, Arts, and Letters* 56 (Ann Arbor, 1961): 651–54.

be the fairest region of Great Britain; Ferdinand Count Fathom, formerly a villain, has changed into a worthy country doctor; Smollett's old enemy, the actor Quin, viciously attacked in both *Roderick Random* and *Peregrine Pickle*, appears as a great wit and jolly good fellow; old friends reappear; and all the eligible ladies find worthy husbands. By the time the expedition of Humphry Clinker has been successfully completed, the gentry and the low, the past and the present, the regions of Britain, friends and lovers, the mind and the body, all have been joined in a vision of harmony and joy. Once more does Saturn, father of the Gods, reign peacefully with his bride, Cybele, mother of all the earth.

WOLFGANG ISER

The Generic Control of the Aesthetic Response: An Examination of Smollett's *Humphry Clinker*† [1]

Ford Madox Ford once said, "You must have your eyes forever on your Reader. That alone constitutes . . . Technique!" In the light of this principle, a text would have to be studied according to the influence it exercises over the reader. Such an approach to the text would concern itself less with the actual subjects portrayed than with the means of communication by which the reader is brought into contact with the reality represented by the author. In other words, this observation is concerned primarily with the form of a work, insofar as one defines form basically as a means of communication or as a negotiation of insight. Kenneth Burke has introduced into the critical discussion of form the terms 'semantic' and 'poetic meaning'. He defines 'semantic meaning' with the statement that "the semantic ideal would attempt to get at a description by the elimination of attitude." 'Poetic meaning', on the other hand, is intended to awaken specific attitudes in the reader by what Burke calls the "strategy of communication." It is worth noting that he equates the term 'poetic' with the effect a text has upon the reader.

It is certainly not easy to define this poetic meaning, but one might perhaps suggest that it lies in the communication of new experiences hitherto unknown to the reader. In support of this contention, we could quote Henry James, who wrote in 1882: "The success of a work of art may be measured by the degree to which it produces a certain illusion; that

† From *The Southern Humanities Review* 3 (1969): 243–257.
1. This paper was delivered as a lecture and its form has been retained. Much of the material was drawn from a more extensive German version originally published under the following title: 'Wirklichkeit und Form in Smolletts *Humphry Clinker'. Europäische Aufklärung. Herbert Dieckmann zum 60. Geburtstag.* Herausgegeben von Hugo Friedrich und Fritz Schalk, München 1967, pp. 87–115. Some new points have been added, others elaborated. Many of the references are to be found in the German version.

illusion makes it appear to us for the time that we have lived another life —that we have had a miraculous enlargement of experience." If one examines a text from the standpoint of what reactions it might arouse in the reader, it must be admitted that there are as yet very few reliable criteria for such a study. One could of course analyse the rhetoric contained in a text, since the interplay of rhetorical devices has the function of persuading, and so manipulating the reader. In his book *The Rhetoric of Fiction*, Wayne Booth developed certain classifications for the rhetoric of prose. They show that the reader can be influenced by applying various devices: disclosure, partial disclosure, concealment, direction of intention, evocation of suspense, introduction of the unexpected—these are all means of stimulating a specific reaction in the reader. If one follows that line, works of art should be analysed less from the point of view of representation than from that of suggestion. The text should be understood as a combination of forms and signs designed to guide the imagination of the reader.

The effectiveness of a text does not depend solely on rhetoric, however. The critic must also take into consideration the reader's expectations. Through his past experience, the educated reader expects specific things from prose and poetry; but many works of art play about with those expectations formed by particular periods of literature in the past. The expectations can be shattered, altered, surpassed or deceived, so that the reader is confronted with something unexpected which necessitates a re-adjustment. If this does happen, the reader gains what Henry James called an "enlargement of experience." However, texts do not necessarily have to be based on expectations formed by the literature of the past. They can themselves awaken false expectations, alternately bringing about surprise and frustration, and this in turn gives rise to an aesthetic experience consisting of a continuous interplay between 'deductive' and 'inductive' operations which the reader must carry out for himself. In this way, the experience communicated through the work of art becomes real to the reader. For whenever his expectations are not fulfilled, the reader's mental faculties are at once directed towards an attempt to comprehend the new situation with which he is confronted. Furthermore, it is common literary experience that a text has different effects at different times. Certainly the inconstancy of our own ideas may be largely responsible for this change, but at the same time the text itself must contain the conditions by which it can take on a different appearance at different times. The various effects produced by the great works of art from Homer down to the present age are sufficient evidence for this. An analysis of expectations thus also enables the critic to appreciate the many-sidedness of meaning contained in a text. Finally, the study of the effectiveness of a text also sheds light on the problem of mixed "genres," for the overlapping of different forms makes it possible to communicate the unknown through the known which brings about the expansion of our experience. As a result of this, an analysis of effects is bound to take into consideration the historical dimension of literature, which has been at times unduly neglected by those who tried to direct our intentions to a thorough analysis of literary form.

Now let us look at *Humphry Clinker* from this point of view. The following examination of Smollett's last novel is just an attempt at studying the aesthetic response brought about by a new combination of significant forms which had been developed in eighteenth-century prose fiction. Smollett's *Humphry Clinker* indicates a conspicuous transition in the eighteenth century to that form of narrative prose which had found its first visible outlines a good fifty years before in Defoe's *Robinson Crusoe*, written in 1719. But the passing of this tradition of the novel, created by Defoe and culminating in Richardson and Fielding, should not be misconstrued as an exhaustion of all its possibilities; in fact the traditional forms of the novel, developed during the eighteenth century, undergo a definite transformation in Smollett's last work, in which we can find both an adherence to tradition and a departure in new directions. A few years before the publication of *Humphry Clinker*, the first Gothic novel, Walpole's *The Castle of Otranto*, had appeared in 1764. With his introduction of the miraculous, Walpole intended to surpass the traditional novel. In his preface to the second edition he says: "It was an attempt to blend the two kinds of Romance, the ancient and the modern. In the former, all was imagination and improbability; in the latter, nature is always intended to be, and sometimes has been, copied with success." In view of this statement, *Humphry Clinker* is well worth our attention; for, like Walpole, Smollett attempted a blend of his own by using the forms of the epistolary novel, the book of travels, and the picaresque novel—all of which were greatly favoured in the eighteenth century. Thus we can say that *Humphry Clinker* marks the point of intersection in the development of narrative prose. The interplay of the traditional forms in this novel is an indication that Smollett was concerned with meeting the most diverse expectations of his public. Yet the various novel forms, combined in *Humphry Clinker*, do begin to influence one another, thereby changing the traditional expectations of the eighteenth century reader.

In discussing these various forms, first of all we should perhaps examine them separately. *Humphry Clinker* consists of eighty-two letters, divided up among five correspondents. Two thirds of the letters are written by Matthew Bramble, head of a Welsh family, and his nephew Jerry Melford, who has just come down from Oxford. Eleven letters are from Jerry's sister Lydia, six from Bramble's sister Tabitha, and ten from the maid Winifred Jenkins. The letters are addressed to various people, but the replies are not included in the novel. This one-sided correspondence sets *Humphry Clinker* apart from those novels based on an exchange of letters, as exemplified, most strikingly, in Richardson's *Clarissa Harlowe*. The Bramble family is on tour, and their letters give an account of their impressions of the various events that occur during their journey from Wales to Bath, London and Scotland. In this way the epistolary novel and the travel book are combined in a single form so that Maynadier, in his introduction to *Humphry Clinker*, could assert that: "There is no doubt, then, that *Humphry Clinker* is a novel in the shape of a book of travels, or travels in the shape of a novel, whichever way you choose to put it."

Humphry Clinker is different not only from this kind of travel book, but also from the epistolary novel developed by Richardson. Richardson's novels grew out of a background of puritanical literature, and dealt with the spiritual life of the characters. The letter-form offered itself as a means whereby Richardson could capture the introspection he sought to portray. In the preface to *Clarissa Harlowe* he wrote the following about his characters: ". . . it will be found, in the progress of the Work, that they very often make such reflections upon each other, and each upon himself and his own actions, as reasonable beings must make, who disbelieve not a Future State of Rewards and Punishments, and who one day propose to reform. . . ." The letter-form facilitates this self-examination insofar as it externalizes inner emotions. Richardson continues in his preface to *Clarissa Harlowe*: "All the Letters are written while the hearts of the writers must be supposed to be wholly engaged in their subjects (The events at the time generally dubious): So that they abound not only with critical Situations, but with what may be called instantaneous Descriptions and Reflections (proper to be brought home to the breast of the youthful Reader). . . ." This writing "to the Moment," as Richardson put it in his preface to *Sir Charles Grandison*, brings about an extraordinary close relationship between the events and the characters' reactions. The letter-writer never manages to stand away from the events or from himself, thus lending a personal immediacy to the situations he is in, a fact which is moreover indicated by the use of the present tense. In this way, the self-examination is presented as if it were a real event. Richardson claimed that his form of presentation was not only a "novelty" but also "a Story designed to represent real Life." The intention of this story was to point out to Richardson's reader the principle of self-knowledge on which he was to base his life. This self-examination inevitably calls for an increasing variety of every-day situations, as can be seen from the ever broadening scope of Richardson's novels after *Pamela*, but there always remains a moral code as the fixed yard-stick by which the growing multiplicity of human actions is to be measured.

If *Humphry Clinker* is considered against this background, only the form of observation that we find in the different correspondents can be equated with that developed by Richardson. The individual personality of the letter-writer is present in everything he records. However, in Smollett the observations are no longer concerned with self-analysis, but with the changing situations that occur during the journey through town and country. For Richardson, the letter-form was a means of self-revelation to be achieved through a variety of situations, and it was on this central theme of self-discovery that the events of the epistolary novel were hinged. For Smollett, this central theme loses its importance. Richardson attached importance to the individual situation of his heroines only insofar as it led them to self-analysis and all the consequences resulting from it, but Smollett takes the situation itself as a theme. Richardson's presentation of reality served mainly to portray the moral attitude of his heroines, while Smollett's is not concerned with this function, and precisely on this account his presentation becomes all the more complex and subtle, since it is seen through the filter, as it were, of individual observation. Consequently, Bramble's and Melford's letters are no longer characterized by a certain motivation, as Richardson demanded with his presentation of "the fair Writer's most secret Thoughts" and "undisguised Inclinations." Bramble and Melford often jump from one subject or observation to another, for neither of them is concerned with pondering over his moral situation—they both want to reproduce the world around them.

This even applies to those sections where the letter-writers speak of their own emotions. Bramble tells Dr. Lewis—the addressee of his letters—how, quite unexpectedly, he met a number of old friends whom he had not seen for forty years or more. He revels in the possibilities of friendship and draws a vivid picture of the jolly company of his friends. But he does not forget to include the concrete details of this unexpected reunion. When he introduces himself to one of his friends, he tells us: "The moment I told him who I was, he exclaimed, 'Ha! Matt, my old fellow-cruiser, still afloat!' and, starting up, hugged me in his arms. His transport, however, boded me no good; for, in saluting me, he thrust the spring of his spectacles into my eye, and at the same time, set his wooden stump upon my gouty toe; an attack that made me shed tears in sad earnest." The overflow of feelings is suffused with the prosaic description of the unexpected pain in eye and toe; then suddenly the pain again turns to laughter, and finally the initial joy of the reunion passes and they each recall the trials and tribulations of the years gone by. Bramble only reports what happened, and there is no moralizing stylization in this account of a potentially very emotional situation. Pain and joy, sadness and sorrow are the elements he combines in this single situation, and the frequent changes of emotion show that, even when the letter is dealing with the personal feelings of the writer, it is still meant to be nothing but a transcription of his observations. The writer is concerned with what is happening around him, and he depicts the events as they appear to him.

The difference, then, between the letter-form developed by Richardson and that used by Smollett is plain to see. In *Humphry Clinker*, introspection with subsequent moral examination is no longer the focal point of events. Instead, the letter-form becomes the medium for an intensified observation of the outside world, as the complexity of changing situations is no longer visualized from the standpoint of a single interpretation. The very fact that Smollett's characters do not look at the outside world from the single vantage point of a moral standard, makes the reality of that world all the richer. This may well be at the expense of the co-ordination Richardson achieved through the moral orientation of his work, but, as we shall see later, Smollett accomplished this in another form. And so we can say that Smollett took over the letter-form which had been perfected in *Clarissa Harlowe*, removed its moral significance and made it into a perspective for the observation of man and his environment.

This observation is extended by the travel book form, which unfolds a detailed picture of all the different localities visited by the Bramble family. The full title of the novel is *The Expedition of Humphry Clinker*; the travel book and the epistolary forms are its component parts, and their superimposition one on the other results in each of them undergoing a certain change. The description of the journey in *Humphry Clinker* is markedly different from that which Smollett himself had given in his voluminous *Compendium of Voyages*, at which we shall look for a moment. This compendium makes use of all the travel literature available at the time to impart the most detailed information on *Customs, Manners, Religion, Government, Commerce, and Natural History of most Nations in the Known World*—as we learn from the sub-title of the work. Martz characterizes this *Compendium* as an attempt at a massive synthesis: "To meet the trend of the times, with its increasing insistence on classification and synthesis, these scattered facts must now be marshalled into order. . . . Thus in the segregation of narrative and descriptive details the process of systematization takes another step forward."

In *Humphry Clinker*, this form of travel book is not retained. There is a good deal of information about individual localities, but the communication of such information is no longer an end in itself. This fact becomes obvious when the same place is presented to us from two or even more than two separate points of view. A clear illustration of this is provided by the different impressions of Ranelagh, the famous London pleasure resort, conveyed by Bramble and Lydia in their letters. Bramble writes: "The diversions of the times are not ill suited to the genius of this incongruous monster, called the public. Give it noise, confusion, glare, and glitter, it has no idea of elegance and propriety. What are the amusements at Ranelagh? One half of the company are following one another's tails, in an eternal circle, like so many blind asses in an olive mill, where they can neither discourse, distinguish, nor be distinguished;

while the other half are drinking hot water, under the denomination of tea, till nine or ten o'clock at night, to keep them awake for the rest of the evening. As for the orchestra, the vocal music especially, it is well for the performers that they cannot be heard distinctly." Lydia describes the same place as follows: "Ranelagh looks like the enchanted palace of a genius, adorned with the most exquisite performances of painting, carving, and gilding, enlightened with a thousand golden lamps, that emulate the noonday sun; crowded with the great, the rich, the gay, the happy, and the fair; glittering with cloth of gold and silver, lace, embroidery, and precious stones. While these exulting sons and daughters of felicity tread this round of pleasure, or regale in different parties, and separate lodges, with fine imperial tea and other delicious refreshments, their ears are entertained with the most ravishing delights of music, both instrumental and vocal. There I heard the famous Tenducci, a thing from Italy—it looks for all the world like a man, though they say it is not. The voice, to be sure, is neither man's nor woman's; but it is more melodious than either; and it warbled so divinely, that, while I listened I really thought myself in paradise."

The breaking-up of identical realities according to different points of view forms a basic element of the whole novel and brings about a substantial change in the motivation that lay behind the travel book. Even where the epistolary form had been imposed on the travel book form—as in Smollett's *Travels through France and Italy*—the accounts had remained authoritative because they were given by one traveller only. The possibility of differing impressions, however, is contrary to the purpose of the travel book: namely, to convey information about unknown places. In the two examples we quoted above there is no longer any question of conveying information about the famous London pleasure resort; the divergent impressions simply draw attention to the extent to which the same thing can look different to different people. And so Smollett's presentation of the journey is not concerned with the things that are experienced, but with the way in which they are experienced. Thus the events reported take on a double meaning: first, they reveal the subjectivity that colours the perception of the individual, as we see in the reactions of Bramble and Lydia to Ranelagh; and second, they rouse a greater interest in the various possibilities of perception that are opened up to the reader's imagination. What one person sees, another will miss; yet both seem to experience something that is characteristic of the situation. Here the revelation is no longer one of factual information, but is concerned with the abundance of viewpoints contained even in the most trivial of situations, which will still have as many sides as there are observers. In the traditional travel book, the description of a locality helped to build up a complete factual picture of the relevant place or region, but in Smollett's novel the accounts of towns and scenes are relieved of this function. If they are to be presented for their own sakes, they must be sufficiently interesting in their own right; and so they have to be considered from all angles; this in turn means that the reader must use his own imagination to bring about a coordination of the different aspects of reality. By dispensing with the compilation of knowledge as the central theme of the travel book, Smollett facilitates a more vivid presentation of the towns and regions included in the journey. At the same time the individual episodes contribute greatly towards the delineation of the characters, whose own personalities condition their vision and so effect the splitting up of individual realities and events into their various aspects.

In addition to the forms we have been discussing, *Humphry Clinker* also shows at least the rudiments of a third form—the picaresque novel. Critics are generally agreed that there are few traces of the picaresque in Smollett's later work, but we should not ignore those traces which are to be found. Smollett's early novels are largely under the influence of Le Sage. In his preface to *Roderick Random*, he describes the intention of his satire: "The same method has been practised by other Spanish and French authors, and by none more successfully than by Monsieur Le Sage, who in his Adventures of Gil Blas, has described the knavery and foibles of life, with infinite humor and sagacity. The following sheets I have modelled on his plan, taking the liberty, however, to differ from him in the execution, where I thought his particular situations were uncommon, extravagant, or peculiar to the country in which the scene is laid." Shortly after the publication of *Roderick Random* in 1748, Smollett translated *Gil Blas*. Although the chief forms of presentation used in *Humphry Clinker* are the travel book and the epistolary novel, neither the hero nor some of the adventures of the Bramble family can come under the heading of these genres. The picaro is still the hero of the title, but he is a mere shadow of himself: he does not write a single letter and is presented only in the subjective visions of different people; he is a ragamuffin picked up on the way, employed as a servant, and exposed to the whims and fancies of the Bramble family. His introduction into the story may be seen as an indication of his function: before Melford actually names the hero in a letter, Humphry Clinker is portrayed in a situation that is scarcely happy for him in the eyes of Bramble and Tabitha who are, respectively, amazed and deeply shocked by his somewhat scanty attire. This double perspective, occasionally supplemented by further points of view, is maintained almost to the end of the novel. Moreover, the relations between individual members of the family and Clinker are characterized by strange inconsistencies, and the family is never quite unanimous in its judgment of Clinker; when eventually we do find unanimity, the end of the novel is in sight.

Smollett did not call his novel 'The Expedition of Matthew Bramble' —which would have corresponded to the actual course of events in the book; neither does his titular hero fulfill the functions of a picaro. Clinker does resemble the picaro in his behaviour, but he is in no way the cunning rascal that looks at the world from the standpoint of the outsider and joins all the merry tales together in his account. In the traditional picaresque novel, the picaro had the function of drawing a satirical picture of the world through the story of his life, but in Smollett this function is replaced by another. Instead of presenting his hero as looking back over his life, Clinker becomes real to us only insofar as he is seen by the other characters in the novel. Thus he inevitably loses that superiority which the cunning picaro always kept in the face of all adversity; in Smollett's novel he is not even given the chance to express his own point of view, as he appears only in the views given of him by other people. Since Clinker never speaks for himself, he seems more helpless than all the others, but this only throws into relief the manner in which they behave towards him. Thus we see how inconsistent human relationships really are, and how strongly they are influenced by chance occurrences and trivialities. Until *Humphry Clinker*, the literature of the eighteenth century has always presented human relationships as being based on good-nature and mutual benevolence, but now this presentation no longer applies. The picaro Clinker mirrors the world insofar as he always appears a little different in the various letters about him. His mere presence has the effect of splitting up into a spectrum of possibilities the human relationship which the eighteenth century had always regarded as unambiguous. The reader cannot help being struck by the differently motivated views through which Clinker is seen, and the passiveness of the hero will arouse his sympathy: the inconsistency of human relationships will draw his attention to the fact that here one of the basic principles of eighteenth century literature is split up into all its empirical possibilities.

Now that we have examined the picaresque traits in *Humphry Clinker*, we can perhaps formulate a provisional conclusion from the remarks so far. In its structure, *Humphry Clinker* contains three forms of novel, which are interwoven almost without a visible join. Only if one examines the historical conditions and the subject matter of *Humphry Clinker* does the combination become apparent. It is this interweaving of the three forms—if one may include the travel book as a form of novel—and the discarding of their original basic functions which constitutes the originality of *Humphry Clinker*. Smollett takes over from Richardson the complex letter-form with several correspondents, but leaves out the self-examination leading to moral analysis which had been the central theme of the epistolary novel in the first half of the eighteenth century. He also takes over the travel book form as giving a panoramic view of a number of localities, but he no longer interprets this as a compendium of topographical information. Finally, he joins on the picaresque novel, but removes the satirical intention of the picaro's adventures. All three forms on their own are characterized by the fact that they each give empirical reality a certain meaning. The epistolary novel of the Richardson school is only concerned with the everyday world insofar as it provides a means of testing the moral strength of the characters. The travel book demands an abundance of empirical details because they alone can bring about the necessary information. The picaresque novel has need of the empirical world so that it can set it up for satirical examination. In all these forms empirical reality is limited by each specific intention. But Smollett brings them all together in his novel, removes the basic intention of each form, and so releases reality from its former restrictions. As a result, the reality presented by Smollett does not appear without order, but at the same time it does not serve to establish a preconceived meaning. The combination of the three forms transforms them into channels of perception through which reality is to be seen. Observation of the empirical world is only possible if this world can be classified, and the forms of letter, travel book and picaresque novel perform precisely this function when their task is reduced to that of describing and classifying.

At the same time this combination of forms leads to an increased breadth and vividness: the letter presents reality through intimate observation, the travel book displays a panorama of ever-changing pictures, and the traces remaining of the picaresque novel reflect the complexity of human relationships through contrasts and varying viewpoints. This combination, however, is not meant merely to do away with the basic principle in each form, but it is to exploit to the utmost the possibilities of vivid, concrete presentation inherent in those forms. This redirection is necessary if empirical reality is no longer to serve as a guide to a preconceived truth, but is to be examined in its own right. Indeed, we can say that the more forms of observation are combined in the study of empirical reality, the greater will seem its variety of aspects. The nineteenth century novel was developed along these lines. In any case, Smollett's technique shows that there is no short cut to the presentation of reality. If one wishes to get as accurate a vision of empirical reality as possible, the methods of perception must be freed from all preconceptions. In this respect, Smollett's novel shows the spirit of Scottish Empiricism.

The arrangement of the three forms co-ordinates empirical reality for the reader's imagination, since it is only through them that the varieties of perception can be made concrete. Through the letter-form, the reader is confronted directly with the characters, and since none of the addressees writes in return, the reader must take their place. The events are not co-ordinated for him; he himself must combine the pieces of information he finds in the various letters. This relationship is in accordance with the three-fold purpose of the novel: the over-all structure of the novel gives a shape to empirical reality, then this reality is split up among the varying viewpoints of the characters, and, finally, the multiplicity of concrete —but limited—aspects must 'coalesce' in the reader's imagination, to use a term from eighteenth-century associative psychology. The variety of addressees, and the fact that Smollett does not print their attitude to the Bramble family's letters, helps to stimulate the reader's imagination. If the recipients of the letters were to reply, as in Richardson's *Clarissa Harlowe*, they would surely express their own views on the events, and the reader's reaction would be limited to judging them. Here, however, the reader must take the place of the recipients, and in the novel these are construed as people varying in temperament, so that a large number of different attitudes towards the whole correspondence are suggested to the reader. His knowledge surpasses that of the individual characters, and since the author has, to a large extent, withdrawn himself from the action, and no longer comments on it, the reader himself becomes the agent that must combine all the different elements. He can put himself in the place of each addressee, and simply because of his greater knowledge he can understand the letters of each correspondent not only as a source of information but also as a revelation of character. In several of the letters this device is stated explicitly. When Melford has drawn, as he often does, a character sketch of one of the people in his uncle's circle, he ends by saying: "Having given you this sketch of Squire Paunceford, I need not make any comment on his character, but leave it at the mercy of your own reflection." In order not only to promote but also to direct the reflection on the part of the reader, the individual characters had to be composed in such a manner as to bring the blending of three forms of novel to full fruition.

Smollett's characters are humours. It is characteristic of the humour that he only sees things in relation to his oddity, which grows in proportion to the uniqueness in which individual observations are combined. In this way, the singularity of a humour establishes most individual, though perfectly understandable, connections within the outside world, and this fact shows us that reality can be perceived only if it is divided up among an indefinite number of idiosyncratic dispositions. We might say that the humour, through his extreme reactions, increases the possibilities of perception; it paves new ways of seeing things, while others are completely ignored. In nearly every letter, some situation is depicted at one particular moment, which entails its reduction to one single viewpoint. Generally, the following letters correct this viewpoint inasmuch as they supplement or question it—at the price of other one-sided and eccentric viewpoints, as must be added. For the reader, the succession of letters brings about a telescoping of situations in which —paradoxically enough—the characters reveal themselves and their surroundings through the very fact that they see everything from their own limited point of view. Consequently, the task of co-ordination is handed over to the reader, for he alone has all the information at his disposal. The one-sidedness of these viewpoints gives a sharp outline to the world that is described, whereas their blending results in its modification. It is this interrelation that forms lively images in the mind of the reader and enables him to be transported into the individual character and his experience of reality. In this respect, the ideas developed by Lord Kames just ten years before the publication of Smollett's novel, in an important section entitled 'Narration and Description' in his *Elements of Criticism,* sound almost like a commentary on *Humphry Clinker:* "In narration as well as in description, objects ought to be painted so accurately as to form in the mind of the reader distinct and lively images. . . . The force of language consists in raising complete images; which have the effect to transport the reader as by magic into the very place of the important action, and to convert him as it were into a spectator, beholding everything that passes. . . . Writers of genius, sensible that the eye is the best avenue to the heart, represent every thing as passing in our sight; and, from readers or hearers, transform us as it were into spectators: a skilful writer conceals himself, and presents his personages: in a word, every thing becomes dramatic as much as possible." This transformation of the reader into a spectator—which Lord Kames designates as the prime quality of narrative literature—is achieved in *Humphry Clinker* by the interaction of different forms; with its combination of three kinds of novel, its interplay between character and world, and its telescoping of different perspectives of observation in each of the letters, *Humphry Clinker* presents "distinct and lively images" of man and his surroundings. It suggests various possibilities of combination without giving them a final shape, so that this task is left to the reader's imagination. It is only natural that the forms and elements combined here—i.e., letter, travel book, picaresque novel, humour—should undergo a reduction in the meaning attributed to them in the traditional eighteenth-century novel, for only thus could they be used for new possibilities. This transition from representing reality to suggesting it shows that the world in *Humphry Clinker* is no longer meant to depict a set principle, but that through the interplay of forms and elements, the possibilities of human experience are to be suggested to the reader. The complex technique of the novel serves this purpose, and it is certainly no coincidence that *Humphry Clinker* and *Tristram Shandy,* which mark the end of the traditional eighteenth-century novel, should both induce the reader, through the form of composition, to take a fuller part in the co-ordination of events.

This very process is described by Dugald Stewart in his analysis of the imagination in *Elements of the Philosophy of the Human Mind.* This work, published in 1792, forms the culminating point of the traditional theory of the imagination in the eighteenth century. Stewart belonged to the Scottish Common Sense School, of which there are many traces in Smollett's work. In the *Elements* we read:

> When the history or the landscape Painter indulges his genius, in forming new combinations of his own, he vies with the Poet in the noblest exertion of the poetical art: and he avails himself of his professional skill, as the Poet avails himself of language, only to convey the ideas in his mind. To deceive the eye by accurate representations of particular forms, is no longer his aim, but, by the touches of an expressive pencil, to speak to the imaginations of others. Imitation, therefore, is not the end which he proposes to himself, but the means which he employs in order to accomplish it: nay, if the imitation be carried so far as to preclude all exercise of the spectator's imagination, it will disappoint, in a great measure, the purpose of the artist. In Poetry, and in every other species of composition, in which one person attempts, by means of language, to present to the mind of another, the objects of his own imagination; this power is necessary, though not in the same degree, to the author and to the reader. When we peruse a description, we naturally feel a disposition to form, in our own minds, a distinct picture of what is described; and in proportion to the attention and interest which the subject excites, the picture becomes steady and determinate. It is scarcely possible for us to hear much of a particular town without forming some notion of its figure and size and situation; and in reading history and poetry, I believe it seldom happens, that we do not annex imaginary appearances to the names of our favourite characters. It is, at the same time, almost certain, that the imaginations of no two men coincide upon such occasions; and, therefore, though both may be pleased, the agreeable impressions which they feel, may be widely different from each other, according as the pictures by which they are produced are more or less happily imagined.

The "new combinations" which Stewart stressed promote the reader's participation, which is true of Smollett's novel in the sense that the various forms anticipate specific expectations on the part of the reader. Letter, travel book, picaresque novel and humours are the elements of the eighteenth-century novel which form the link with what the reader is accustomed to. Their interplay makes him see these familiar forms in a new combination, thus opening his eyes to new possibilities of human experience. In this respect, *Humphry Clinker* preconditions the pattern of communication brought to perfection in the nineteenth-century realistic novel, with the difference, however, that the forms combined by Smollett imply more of their original contents than we find in the nineteenth-century novel, which, instead, develops a more elaborate technique of narration. This development can be exemplified by the increasing refinement of technique as a means of influencing the reader's imagination. The actual differences, however, between Smollett and the nineteenth-century realistic novel do not affect their relation: The pattern of communication in *Humphry Clinker*, with its anticipation of the reader's expectations through the use of certain forms for the purpose of creating—by their interplay—a multiple perspective of reality, is to be found again in the realistic novel of the nineteenth century.

This fact reveals an important aesthetic implication, which is contained but not actually brought to the fore in the pattern we have described. In concluding, we shall cast a brief glance at this implication. We have seen that for various reasons the forms are combined more or less without a join; a flaw in this join therefore indicates a failure in the attempt at combination rather than any deliberate intention. One can, however, imagine a case in which the forms are deliberately made to clash with one another. In this case there will be a radical change in the intention underlying the conception of the novel, for the clash of forms must destroy one of the prime intentions of the realistic novel: the illusion of reality. Instead of evoking a manifold picture of reality, this clash of forms will create a semantic reality of its own, which can be tackled by the reader only through interpretation. This, however, is a problem that concerns the modern novel, and is, so to speak, another story.

JOHN SEKORA

The Politics of *Humphry Clinker*†

We are not what we were; patriotism is not the growth of these days; luxury has taken root too deeply for sudden eradication.—Critical Review, *1756*

... the wise patriots of London have taken it into their heads, that all regulation is inconsistent with liberty; and that every man ought to live in his own way, without restraint—Nay, as there is not sense enough left among them, to be discomposed ... they may, for aught I care, wallow in the mire of their own pollution.—Matthew Bramble, June 8

Thus far it has been necessary to consider luxury in its material aspect—its presence and influence in European history, in eighteenth-century controversy, and in Smollett. It is now possible to make the inevitable transition to its formal features. For three millennia the attack upon luxury conveyed the dominant values and attitudes of Western society, and moralists pursued their condemnations with certain impunity, for no one would seriously defend immorality. Well before the birth of Christ the attack had acquired a distinctive form. It had become so common as to be conventional, so familiar as to take on a definite shape. Individual writers would retain this general shape—as preachers would keep the overarching form of the homily—while contributing their own specific

† From *Luxury: The Concept in Western Thought, Eden to Smollett* (Baltimore: Johns Hopkins University Press, 1977), pp. 215–38.

details. Theirs would be variations upon a traditional theme, contemporary manifestations of a universal malaise.

The attack upon luxury may be regarded as a relatively distinct literary mode, with its own characteristic devices and methods of persuasion. It can more usefully be considered a mode rather than a genre, for it has been expressed in many genres. Because it seeks to reveal the (often hidden) dimension of causes, relations, and devolutions, it is primarily a heuristic, narrative mode, usually found in those forms which express developing awareness or expanding experience: quest, journey, psychomachia, imaginary voyage, retrospective elegy, nostalgic pastoral, panoramic survey, or moral history. It is the mode of Cato and Seneca, the Republic and the City of God, Paradise Lost and Aureng-Zebe, Joseph Andrews and the Deserted Village; of Swift and Bolingbroke, Davenant and John Brown. When that awareness is directed toward the historical past—as in Samuel and Kings, Sallust, Plutarch, and Gibbon—it nonetheless culminates in lessons drawn to redeem the present. And even in those rare instances where the attack has been shown to be successful —as in Prudentius and the Christian theologians—that victory over luxury must be guarded by constant vigilance and discipline.

From the Deuteronomic writers through Brown, Fawconer, and Goldsmith, the attack upon luxury normally represented an explanation and a warning, a portrait of a nation in rapid decline, perhaps in final devolution. The lesson is stated, then demonstrated in a series of marked contrasts: obedience–rebellion; old glory–new misery; political unity–competition and insubordination; social harmony–crime and ambition and confusion; the proud men of the ancient order–the debased representatives of the present; places of past greatness–sites of new debauchery; rural felicity–urban corruption; disciplined youth–depraved youth; a society guided by divinity and masculinity–one ruled by effeminate passion. So terrible and so persistent was the idea of luxury that it made an indelible imprint upon the European sensibility, and the list could be extended almost indefinitely. What had been a theological lesson became a theological pattern, forecasting God's punishment onto the present and future. It then yielded a logical pattern, a historical one, and a literary one. One sign of the vitality of the literary pattern is its early refinement. By the time of Herodotus the story is told by someone who is (or claims to be) relatively objective—a sage, historian, or foreign visitor. And within a generation, by the time of Aristophanes, the technique is developed further, with the superaddition for contrast of the views of various kinds of victims—the young, the naive, the gullible, and the unscrupulous.

Preceding chapters have sought to demonstrate that Smollett used this familiar mode in his major nonfiction after 1756. Is there reason to believe it is present also in his final work, the novel that is considered his masterpiece? On the prima facie level of direct textual evidence, the answer is clear. Twice in the first quarter of *Humphry Clinker*, Bramble delivers long and memorable tirades against the social customs of his time, first in Bath, then in London. He concludes his diatribe against Bath with the generalization: "All these absurdities arise from the general tide of luxury, which hath overspread the nation,and swept away all, even the very dregs of the people" (MB, April 23). In London he again sees a "tide of luxury" inundating the capital in social evils he has taken pains to specify: "they may be all resolved into the grand source of luxury and corruption" (MB, May 29). As Bramble turns his mind, briefly, to more pleasant matters during the journey northward, the theme—and the metaphor—is taken up by Lismahago: "Mean while the sudden affluence occasioned by trade, forced open all the sluices of luxury and overflowed the land with every species of profligacy and corruption; a total pravity of manners would ensue, and this must be attended with bankruptcy and ruin" (MB, July 15). Such open, direct denunciation is voiced by five different characters—Bramble, Jery, Lismahago, Dennison, and Baynard-and elaborated in eighteen different letters, letters that as a rule are the longest in the novel.

Such evidence establishes that the attack upon luxury is materially present, but it does not establish its necessity to a work of fiction. For this latter task only close analysis of forms will suffice. I shall argue in this [essay] that *Humphry Clinker* does indeed deserve to be read in the light of the Western tradition, eighteenth-century controversy, and Smollett's own two decades of attack—in their light and as their epitome. While this contention is in no way iconoclastic, so far as I can discover no major work of English or Continental literature has been the subject of such a reading. The argument follows from the earlier portion of this study and from two truistic assumptions. First, the novel is inexhaustible and merits reading in as many ways as possible. The attack upon luxury is not the single golden key that will unlock its treasures. There is no such unique key, for Smollett is patently engaged in tasks (like the celebration of Scotland) other than the exposure of luxury. Yet it is the only approach not yet pursued by modern criticism, and it does provide access to much that can be gotten at in no other way: Smollett's method of combining general and particular satire, his cultivation of a mixed response for a bittersweet portrait of contemporary Britain, and the tradition in which it was written and read. The value of further access is clear if one accepts the argument of E. D. Hirsch that readers usually approach a new work through mode or type. [1] Retrospectively, we today tend to view eighteenth-century fiction under the all-absorbing rubric of *novel*. Contemporary readers, however, could not and did not. For what we know as the early novel was a fluid and hybrid form, the major writers incorporating much that was old into the "new species of writing." One has but to recall

1. E. D. Hirsch, *Validity in Interpretation* (New Haven, 1967), p. 74.

the influence of spiritual autobiography upon Defoe, model letters upon
Richardson, the epic upon Fielding, and Rabelaisian satire upon Sterne
to realize how comfortable Smollett would have been expressing his
loathing of luxury in the new form.

Second, an idea like luxury can easily enter into the formal constituent
part of a literary work. To admit that the attack upon luxury can be a
literary mode is to acknowledge that ideas can be embedded in the
narrative structure itself. An accomplished novelist like Smollett requires us to absorb the experience of his fictional characters, to assume it,
to comprehend it, to regard it as natural. To present a luxurious world in
action is by definition to make a series of metaphysical statements, for
luxury is precisely that concept which for Smollett and others encloses all
vital issues of human value. Novel-writing could be akin to cultural
criticism. Moreover, the attack upon luxury may be metaphysical in still
another sense. In an early essay Lionel Trilling writes of "the real basis of
the novel" in England and on the Continent as "the tension between a
middle class and an aristocracy which brings manners into observable
relief as the living representation of ideals and the living comment on
ideas."[2] Trilling's observation is not self-evidently valid for all great
novels, but to the extent that it holds for many it elevates the importance
of luxury. A traditionalist like Smollett would explain the tension
Trilling finds in terms of the cultured few upholding a standard, a
national way of life, a sanctified truth, "an England," against the
subversive luxury of the barbarian horde. Extending Trilling, one could
say that the attack upon luxury is "the real basis" of "the real basis of the
novel."

To read *Humphry Clinker* as formally an attack upon luxury is to alter
several modern critical emphases, including those that see Smollett as
essentially simple (or if that is too harsh, then *transparent*), separate the
man from his work, dismiss the social and political commentary, regard
all main characters as coequal, reduce Bramble and Lismahago to
decorative eccentrics, and see the organization of the novel as random
and purposeless. To cite but one example, Alan Dugald McKillop
considers the milieu of the novel a region of endless absurdity but little
indignation: "While the great world may rage without, the obliquities of
these originals are harmless, and manifest themselves in a well-grounded
order of things."[3] This is a plausible modern reading. But contemporary

2. The essay is Trilling's "Art and Fortune" in *The Liberal Imagination* (1950; reprinted New York, 1953), pp. 247–71. The approach suggested here could be used with several early fictional narratives. In *Tom Jones*, for example, Fielding uses luxury as concept and as characteristic in the middle and latter portions of the novel. When Tom enters the inn at Hambrook or Upton, he is beholding a world of perfervid pretense as repellent as that Bramble found in the Pump Room at

Bath, and the degeneracy he finds in London has the same roots as that Bramble found.
3. A comparable but more recent reading of the novel is John M. Warner's "Smollett's Development as a Novelist," *Novel* 5 (Winter 1972): 148–61. Warner's essay is a well-written and (in its own terms) closely argued exposition of what he considers to be Smollett's movement away from satire and toward irony. It contains direct or tacit evaluations of all the important elements of *Humphry*

readers were aware that the great world indeed roars within the pages of the novel as the genesis of the endless absurdities McKillop notes; and if the obliquities of Bramble and Lismahago now strike us as harmless the reason is far different from the one he finds. The well-grounded order of things Smollett cherished has in fact been much eroded, and the imprecations of his characters are delivered against a changing order they regard as disturbing and inferior. A Bramble and a Lismahago possess the confidence of buoyant assertation and do indeed embody values which are clear and self-confident, but they stand together as adversaries, not representatives, of the development of English society. So deeply and so carefully is the attack upon luxury embedded in the novel that the task of criticism is almost one of excavation. This [essay] will seek to uncover the primary elements of Smollett's attack in the political configurations * * * of the novel. The remainder of this chapter attempts to demonstrate, in plain but ample fashion, that *Humphry Clinker* is a highly political novel, one of the most politically charged of the century.

To call *Humphry Clinker* a political novel might strike a modern reader (to put it charitably) as mildly paradoxical. Although many political figures are introduced, few are worthy, most contemptible; at best we meet men like the monarch who keep aloof from the routine duplicity of factions and parties. Political action, insofar as it is shown, is enveloped by chaos—sometimes hilarious, sometimes mortifying; political policy, we learn, is deceit practiced upon ignorance. Yet there is a familiar resonance to the scene. It had been predicted by Plato, Seneca, Bolingbroke, and Smollett—the time when the public graces have been swallowed up by the voracious maw of luxury. It is moreover the scene explained and described by Bramble in his first letter from London, May 29. Luxury has been as acid upon the nation he once revered, dissolving all into corruption, rebellion, and political frenzy. Moving from the general to the particular, Bramble personalizes the dissolution in several ways, most poignantly by reference to past friendships: "I have seen some old friends ... but they are so changed in manners and disposition, that we hardly know or care for one another." The sentiment returns, he finds, throughout his tour of England, for merit and reward no longer travel together. Most of his old friends have changed for the worse: those who have retained their integrity have lost income and standing; those who have kept social position have squandered their morality. The

Clinker, but without a single reference to the literary history of its own time. From his own perspective Warner can discover Smollett to be much closer as a novelist to Henry James and Lawrence Durrell than to Henry Fielding.

In what might become a similar situation, readers a century or so from now may wonder at the sudden and ambiguous appearance in the later 1960's of black characters in novels by white American authors who had previously left untouched all aspects of black life—for example, John Updike's *Rabbit Redux*, Bernard Malamud's *The Tenants*, Walker Percy's *Love in the Ruins*, and especially Saul Bellow's *Mr. Sammler's Planet*.

traveler's sense of loss is indicative of the political tone of the novel, a withdrawal approaching despair. The madness luxury has released has driven out all hope for major, public reform; English politics is exhausted in vain self-interest. Only private hope, personal dreams remain. This fact marks a certain diminution in Smollett's ambitions, literary as well as political, and may explain part of the vitality and attraction of the novel. In contrast to his other projects, *Humphry Clinker* is a work of limits, restraint, proportion. Relatively, it is a work of modest ambition, the kind appropriate to an age of rancor and excess. Certainly not mellow, it is simply measured—a political novel for a time when legitimate politics is dead.

On the one hand, Smollett sought to give the novel an appearance of political involvement but impartiality. This was the role he has assumed for himself as early as the *Complete History*, writing in it, the *Continuation*, the *Critical Review*, and the *Briton* that he was of no party. (In the last he also wrote that neither Bute nor any member of his ministry was politically partisan. Like contemporary opponents, however, later historians have tried in vain to discover a genuine Whig within the administration.) In the novel his chief male characters are close observers of contemporary politics, Bramble as a former Member of Parliament, Jery as an aspirant to its chambers, and Lismahago as a student of the law. Yet they are explicitly noted to be nonpartisan. Introducing Barton, a friend and fellow Oxonian, Jery remarks:

> He has not gall enough in his constitution to be enflamed with the rancour of party, so as to deal in scurrilous invectives; but, since he obtained a place, he is become a warm partizan of the ministry, and sees every thing through such an exaggerating medium, as *to me, who am happily of no party*, is altogether incomprehensible—Without all doubt, the fumes of faction not only disturb the faculty of reason, but also pervert the organs of sense; and I would lay a hundred guineas to ten, that if Barton on one side, and the most conscientious patriot in the opposition on the other, were to draw, upon honour, the picture of the k——or m——, *you and I, who are still uninfected, and unbiassed*, would find both painters equally distant from the truth. [JM, June 2, italics added]

In the same letter Bramble mentions his own political independence: "Whilst I sat in parliament, I never voted with the ministry but three times, when my conscience told me they were in the right." In Namier's terms, Bramble was therefore of the independent country party during the ministries, presumably, of Newcastle and Pitt, and hence a proper commentator upon those two politicians. As a freeholder and country gentleman, he is placed in a relatively disinterested political position, untainted by the selfish motives of professional politicians, courtiers, merchants, and financiers.[4] The third major character, Lismahago, is represented as equally free from partisan spirit. Himself a victim of much political chicanery, he calls for a plague upon both parties. The specific political commentary, wide-ranging though it is, is largely confined to five of the more than eighty letters of the novel: JM, June 2; MB, June 2; JM, June 5; MB, July 15; and MB, September 20. Even in these, Smollett feels compelled to defend its inclusion. In Bramble's letter of September 20, for instance, Lismahago's political opinions—identical to Bramble's —are reported in detail, and the novelist has Bramble conclude: "So much for the dogmata of my friend Lismahago, whom I describe the more circumstantially, as I firmly believe he will set up his rest in Monmouthshire." Bramble seeks to limit the influence of that "daemon of party" not only in his own life, but also in the life of literature and the arts; hence his alarm that "the daemon of party seems to have usurped every department of life. Even the world of literature and taste is divided into the most virulent factions, which revile, decry, and traduce the works of one another" (MB, June 2). For Smollett, who wrote or edited nearly seventy volumes of historical and political commentary between *Count Fathom* and *Humphry Clinker* and was increasingly associated with partisan causes, such isolation and restraint are quite striking. They may be interpreted as either the self-restraint demanded by the novel or the reduction to proper size of the role of partisan issues in everyday life; I would argue that they are both, the transcendence of false politics by the true. What is certain is that Smollett endured a series of bitter disappointments after 1763; vicious personal attack, the failure of the *Briton,* Bute's ingratitude and later fall from power, repeated acute illness joined to chronic ill-health, failure to receive a government post abroad, continued worry over money, and most important, the death of his only child, the fifteen-year-old Elizabeth. Political and paternal grief are intermingled in his summary of recent years for the opening letter of the *Travels* 1766):

> You knew, and pitied my situation, traduced by malice, persecuted by faction, abandoned by false patrons, and overwhelmed by the sense of a domestic calamity, which it was not in the power of fortune to repair.
> You knew with what eagerness I fled from my country as a scene of illiberal dispute, and incredible infatuation, where a few worthless

---

4. In his preface to the opening volume of the *Continuation* (1760), Smollett professes that,

he will carefully avoid the imputation of enthusiasm. In the midst of his transports he hopes to remember his duty, and check the exuberance of zeal with the rigid severity of historical truth.
    This is the guiding star by which he hath hitherto steered his dangerous course; the star whose chearing radiance has conducted him safe through the rocks of prejudice and the tides of faction. Guiltless of all connexions that might be supposed to affect his candour, and endanger his integrity, he is determined to proceed with that fearless spirit of independence by which he flatters himself the former part of the work hath been remarkably distinguished.[1:v]

incendiaries had, by dint of perfidious calumnies and atrocious abuse, kindled up a flame which threatened all the horrors of civil dissention.

On the other hand, he fashioned in *Humphry Clinker* a highly political design: the counterpointing of England and Scotland, city and country, change and tradition; the major characters' Welsh background; Bramble's flight from moral squalor to moral virtue, the equation in his person of physical sensitivity and moral sensibility; the journey of education of Jery and Lydia; the presence of a distressed veteran of the colonial wars; the alternation in the letters of frivolous and mature points of view. Each of these circumstances underlines Smollett's intention to provide serious comment upon familiar, public topics. Moreover, the novel is at its most vigorous as a tract against the times. Giving colorful illustration of what it condemns, *Humphry Clinker* proceeds with the logic of discourse. The irritations of Hot Well are succeeded by the provocations of Bath and the enormities of the capital. At Bath we are introduced to the nature and manifestations of luxury, at London to its agents and brutal consequences. Similarly, in discussing London Smollett first gives us the venal politicians who pander to false tastes (June 2, June 5), and then their handiwork in the near ruin of everyday living (June 8). Famous personages appear together in the three London letters, where they are introduced as if on permanent exhibit in a great hall of statuary. Thus Bramble asks, in the midst of the tour, "'Well, Mr. Barton, what figure do you call next?' The next person he pointed out, was the favorite *yearl*; who stood solitary by one of the windows" (JM, June 2). Barton makes his judgment, Bramble sustains or denies, and Jery finds for his uncle. Commenting upon issues, the London letters reinforce one another closely, with an opinion broached in the first letter repeated in the second and again in the third. To a lesser extent Smollett uses the same method with personalities, such as Newcastle, who is *said* to be an ass in the first and *shown* to be one in the third. The two later letters from Scotland, representing Lismahago's political disquisitions, serve to recall and further reinforce those of the English half. Smollett insured that his considered thoughts on luxury and politics would appear in each of the original three volumes of *Humphry Clinker*.

Certain opinions, such as that of the licentiousness of the press, are sustained throughout the five letters. Jery asserts the evil of the press in the first. In the second Bramble affirms the charge and Barton reaffirms, then illustrates it. In the third Bramble repeats himself; in the fourth and fifth Lismahago echoes and reechoes Bramble. On many occasions in the Scottish half of the novel, it will be remembered, Bramble is allowed to forget his earlier positions in order to stand as temporary adversary to Lismahago, thereby softening a little the lieutenant's didactic voice. Yet Lismahago does have his own particular function as political spokesman for Smollett, as he describes the methods of English exploitation of

Scotland. And it is he, proud Scotsman and veteran soldier, who is called upon to defend the Treaty of Paris. Two-thirds of the way through the novel—hundreds of miles away, that is, from the king, Bute, Pitt, and the City—Smollett inserts a brief reference to the cause linked so intimately with his name: "One of the company chancing to mention lord B——'s inglorious peace, the lieutenant immediately took up the cudgels in his lordship's favour, and argued very strenuously to prove that it was the most honourable and advantageous peace that England had ever made since the foundation of the monarchy" (MB, July 15). Bramble, acting here in the uncommon role of disinterested narrator, immediately closes the episode for Dr. Lewis by noting: "Nay, between friends, he offered such reasons on this subject, that I was really confounded, if not convinced."

Smollett's powers of dramatic presentation are at full stretch not with the glories of Edinburgh, but with the horrors of London. Even within the Scottish half, the pattern recurs. Whereas we are told of the hospitality of Commissary Smollett, we are shown the household of Lord Oxmington, and Jery's comments come not as summary but as introduction: "His lordship is much more remarkable for his pride and caprice, than for his hospitality and understanding; and indeed, it appeared, that he considered his guests merely as objects to shine upon, so as to reflect the lustre of his own magnificence.—There was much state, but no courtesy; and a great deal of compliment without any conversation" (JM, September 28). In addition, Smollett seems to be offering solutions to quasi-political problems. More often than not, the resolution of temporary grievance is not through persuasion and agreement, but through the direct use of force. To obtain quiet in his lodgings at Bath, Bramble must cudgel the offending musicians. He and Lismahago both recommended the severe beating of libelous printers. The travelers can gain Oxmington's respect only by a massive show of arms and strength, and Lismahago's kick is shown to be the proper response to the nobleman's lackey. Baynard cannot salvage his estate merely by following wise counsel: he and his affairs must be placed totally in the hands of Bramble and Dennison.

Seldom varied, the pattern of Smollett's political tour of England is renewed each time the party travels to a new place. Upon arrival, one of the males—usually Bramble and usually in the manner of the *Present State*—provides a synoptic view of the ills pervading the town. Against later letters from the same place, this introduction is taut and concise, vivid and impassioned: it is so relentless a portrait of human folly that we at first assume it must be eccentric to a novel of comic intentions, so extreme that it must be qualified, if not erased. As the party moves about the town, however, subsequent letters reveal the incarnation of those very ills in the men and women who dominate social affairs. The later letters, penned mostly by Jery, are more numerous, tentative, disinterested, and tolerant; yet their ultimate effect is to affirm the keenness and truth of the opening survey.[5]

Humphry Clinker includes many of Smollett's old crotchets, and the overarching issues are the most familiar, what we have come to know through his own work as the syndrome of luxury. In the wake of the vice flows an unholy emphasis upon trade and commerce. Hence Bramble follows his attack upon the luxury of Bath with a tirade against merchants and their morality of profit (MB, April 23), Lismahago asserts that "a glut of wealth . . . destroys all the distinctions of civil society; so that universal anarchy and uproar must ensue" (MB, September 20), and the Scotsman exposes, in the long passage already cited, the effects of English luxury in the depletion of the Scottish economy. Explaining why commerce must be tightly supervised, Lismahago also voices in a metaphor the novelist's rather feudal view of fluctuations in trade: "the nature of commerce was such, that it could not be fixed or perpetuated, but, having flowed to a certain height, would immediately begin to ebb, and so continue till the channels should be left almost dry; but there was no instance of the tide's rising a second time to any considerable influx in the same nation" (MB, July 15). He observes further:

> That commerce would, sooner or later, prove the ruin of every nation, where it flourishes to any extent. . . . He observed, that traffick was an enemy to all the liberal passions of the soul, founded on the thirst of lucre, a sordid disposition to take advantage of the necessities of our fellow-creatures. . . . Mean while the sudden affluence occasioned by trade, forced open all the sluices of luxury and overflowed the land with every species of profligacy and corruption; a total pravity of manners would ensue, and this must be attended with bankruptcy and ruin. [MB, July 15]

As Smollett had done in his histories, Lismahago in a later letter conjoins the effects of commerce and the behavior of the multitude.

> "Woe be to that nation, where the multitude is at liberty to follow their own inclinations! Commerce is undoubtedly a blessing, while restrained within its proper channels; but a glut of wealth brings along with it a glut of evils: it brings false taste, false appetite, false wants, profusion, venality, contempt of order, engendering a spirit of licentiousness, insolence, and faction, that keeps the community in continual ferment, and in time destroys all the distinctions of civil society; so that universal anarchy and uproar must ensue."[MB, September 20][6]

Bramble and Lismahago likewise express by implication what Smollett elsewhere states directly: commerce is the efficient cause of English

5. I have not tried to demonstrate further the working of this pattern, for it will be taken up in following chapters. Nor have I attempted to encompass all the political issues touched upon in the novel, but have restricted myself here to the most prominent.
6. Compare the nobleman's lecture to Harrison on the effects of luxury upon a nation in book 11, chapter 2 ("Matters Political") of *Amelia*.

degeneracy. It is associated in the novel with virtually all the horrors of London life and most of the ills of the rest of Britain—inflation, highway crime, depopulation of the country, ruin of the small landowner, eradication of frugality and simplicity, the decline of education and the arts.

Corruption of government is the most despicable of the many horrors of the capital, and among its many contemporary manifestations Bramble continually remarks a nearly universal currying of favor. Instead of doing the work of the kingdom, English politicians are absorbed in endless rounds of otiose flattery and bribery, the ugliest of which is cultivation of the mob. In an oblique reference to Pitt, Bramble exclaims:

> Notwithstanding my contempt for those who flatter a minister, I think there is something still more despicable in flattering a mob. When I see a man of birth, education, and fortune, put himself on a level with the dregs of the people, mingle with low mechanics, feed with them at the same board, and drink with them in the same cup, flatter their prejudices, harangue in praise of their virtues, expose themselves to the belchings of their beer, the fumes of their tobacco, the grossness of their familiarity, and the impertinence of their conversation, I cannot help despising him, as a man guilty of the vilest prostitution, in order to effect a purpose equally selfish and illiberal. [MB, June 2]

A sure sign that Smollett's polemical flame was still lambent, this passage covers three-quarters of the population under the slurs "mob" and "dregs of the people." It recalls the criticism of Antony by a cold Octavius that Antony would "keep the turn of tippling with a slave" and then "stand the buffet / with knaves that smell of sweat." A figure like Pitt would certainly come into physical closeness with the middle-class voters of the City. But "dregs," "low mechanics," "prejudices," "belchings," "beer," "grossness," and "impertinence"—these terms identify the mass of workers and unemployed who, whatever their fearsome habits, had no voting rights and no direct political influence. Smollett would have his readers dismiss such distinctions.

With Lismahago the indictment becomes broader, as the old soldier argues that elections are themselves a species of bribery and that even the English form of limited representative democracy is evil. Calling Parliament "the rotten part of the British constitution," Lismahago traces present corruption to Walpole's putative habit of buying a legislature to suit him. Elections, at least those under George II, therefore amount to no more than than "an avowed system of venality, already established on the ruins of principle, integrity, faith, and good order, in consequence of which the elected and the elector, and, in short, the whole body of the people, were equally and universally contaminated and corrupted." As if to anticipate all ripostes, Lismahago pursues his logic to a fatal stop:

He affirmed, that of a parliament thus constituted, the crown would always have influence enough to secure a great majority in its dependence, from the great number of posts, places, and pensions it had to bestow; that such a parliament would (as it had already done) lengthen the term of its sitting and authority, whenever the prince should think it for his interest to continue the representatives. . . . With a parliament, therefore, dependent upon the crown, devoted to the prince, and supported by a standing army, garbled and modelled for the purpose, any king of England may, and probably some ambitious sovereign will, totally overthrow all the bulwarks of the constitution; for it is not to be supposed that a prince of a high spirit will tamely submit to be thwarted in all his measures, abused and insulted by a populace of unbridled ferocity, when he has it in his power to crush all opposition under his feet with the concurrence of the legislature. [MB, July 15][7]

This passage reflects two aspects of Smollett's polemical writing. He strives to produce a bold and vivid assertion and then argues aggressively within the terms of the original assertion. More a habit than a conscious technique, this aspect of the novelist's style gives his argument an air of confidence while also avoiding the disquieting problems of definition, qualification, and evaluation. It also leads on occasion to a clash of conflicting assertions. If, as Lismahago holds, the crown has the power to create a Parliament of its own design and thereafter to retain it, then that Parliament is the impotent, not the rotten, part of the British constitution. The passage further shows the novelist's penchant for repeating with small changes of phrase his cherished statements from earlier works. To his familiar warnings of a manipulated Parliament, he here adds a reference to the political controversies of the earlier 1760s—"a prince of high spirit . . . abused and insulted by a populace of unbridled ferocity" —which would recall the alleged libels of the *North Briton*.

If Lismahago is anxious over the possibility of a tyranny imposed from above, Bramble is yet more exercised over signs of a revolution from below. Like thousands of moralists before him, the Welshman is convinced that insubordination represents the death fever, the final madness of a nation infected by luxury. In almost every English city he visits, he perceives its symptoms, particularly in social leveling, factions, freedom of the press, and the operation of the jury system. Since he believes that the various ranks of a society are immiscible, he finds frequent occasion to deplore such places as Vauxhall where classes and sexes mix more

7. This passage has troubled several crities, who have wondered why on this issue alone Smollett should be challenging the government of George III. But as discussion of the *Complete History* has shown, Lismahago is here recalling the practices of Walpole under George II. The review of *An Additional Dialogue of the Dead* in the *Critical Review* for June 1760, cited in chapter 5, calls elections the chance politicians have for "soothing, cajoling, corrupting and destroying the morals of their constituents" (9:466). Its conclusion merits repeating: "Consult history, consult your own mind . . . there can [never] be a dependence on the integrity of the people, where luxury and interest contribute in rendering corrupt, those on whom they have devolved their rights, and constituted their representatives" (9:467).

readily than elsewhere. On the one hand, the respectable persons found there are guilty of degrading themselves: "When I see a number of well-dressed people, of both sexes, sitting on the covered benches, exposed to the eyes of the mob . . . I can't help compassionating their temerity; while I despise their want of taste and decorum" (MB, May 29). On the other, the common people are guilty of criminal failure to conform to class distinctions in dress: "Every clerk, apprentice, and even waiter of tavern or coffee-house . . . assumes the air and apparel of a petit maitre—The gayest places of public entertainment are filled with fashionable figures; which, upon inquiry, will be found to be journeymen taylors, serving-men, and abigails, disguised like their betters." Even small examples of social mixing, like Win's comically ill-fated visit to the theater, can be interpreted as political rebellion if one assumes that every inch of new freedom granted to an apprentice removes that amount from the prerogatives of a lord. Hence Bramble's conclusion follows from his premise: "In short, there is no distinction or subordination left—The different departments of life are jumbled together—The hod-carrier, the low mechanic, the tapster, the publican, the shop-keeper, the pettifogger, the citizen, and the courtier, all tread upon the kibes of one another: actuated by the demons of profligacy and licentiousness . . . and crashing in one vile ferment of stupidity and corruption" (MB, May 29). Repeating Smollett's earlier contentions from the *Complete History*, moreover, he finds that the insubordination of the poor inevitably leads not only to sedition but also to crime.

> The tide of luxury has swept all the inhabitants from the open country —The poorest 'squire, as well as the richest peer, must have his house in town, and make a figure with an extraordinary number of domestics. The plough-boys, cow-herds, and lower hinds, are debauched and seduced by the appearance and discourse of those coxcombs in livery, when they make their summer excursions. They desert their dirt and drudgery, and swarm up to London, in hopes of getting into service, where they can live luxuriously and wear fine clothes, without being obliged to work; for idleness is natural to man—Great numbers of these, being disappointed in their expectation, become thieves and sharpers; and London being an immense wilderness, in which there is neither watch nor ward of any signification, nor any order or police, affords them lurking-places as well as prey. [MB, May 29]

In a nation beset by luxury, spurious political divisions are encouraged, while genuine authority and legitimate order go ignored. Various groups are permitted to compete for the leadership that can never rightfully be theirs. They rival one another with false claims, false reports, false promises. As Bramble's above letter has raised the central issues, Jery's next, of June 2, begins the process of illustrating the stinks given off by the vice, noting, "Without all doubt, the fumes of faction not only disturb the faculty of reason, but also pervert the organs of sense." In the same letter Bramble is quoted as saying that while in power Newcastle was rightly ridiculed, but when he lost power and "unfurled the banners of faction" he was hailed as "a wise, experienced statesman; chief pillar of the Protestant succession." Barton explains this contradiction by identifying faction with mob mentality: "I don't pretend to justify the extravagations of the multitude; who, I suppose, were as wild in their former censure, as in their present praise." In his letter of the same date, Bramble repeats and extends these themes. Explaining to Dr. Lewis why needed improvements of the British Museum "will never be reduced to practice," he says, "Considering the temper of the times, it is a wonder to see any institution whatsoever established, for the benefit of the public. The spirit of party is risen to a kind of phrenzy, unknown to former ages, or rather degenerated to a total extinction of honesty and candour" (MB, June 2). He then promptly moves to the most egregious public example of faction. "You know I have observed, for some time, that the public papers are become the infamous vehicles of the most cruel and perfidious defamation: every rancorous knave—every desperate incendiary, that can afford to spend half a crown or three shillings, may skulk behind the press of a news-monger, and have a stab at the first character in the kingdom, without running the least hazard of detection or punishment" (MB, June 2).

Barton is then introduced in order to confirm Bramble's opinion. Referring to his penchant for eulogizing the current ministry, Bramble notes that he had seen one of Barton's favorites so stigmatized in the press, "that if one half of what was said of him was true, he must be not only unfit to rule, but even unfit to live." He tells Barton that at first he could not credit the charges, but when the favorite failed to vindicate himself he began to entertain suspicions. Smollett's manipulation of his main character is obvious: in the space of two sentences Bramble is transformed from a cynic to an innocent. Barton's considered response is thus elicited, and echoing the conversation in *Macbeth* between Malcolm and Macduff, it turns upon the depraved tastes and perverted loyalties of the mob:

> "And pray, sir, (said Mr. Barton) what steps would you have him take? —Suppose he should prosecute the publisher, who screens the anonymous accuser, and bring him to the pillory for a libel; this is so far from being counted a punishment, *in terrorem*, that it will probably make his fortune. The multitude immediately take him into their protection, as a martyr to the cause of defamation, which they have always espoused —They pay his fine, they contribute to the increase of his stock, his shop is crowded with customers, and the sale of his paper rises in proportion to the scandal it contains. All this time the prosecutor is inveighed against as a tyrant and oppressor, for having chosen to proceed by the way of information, which is deemed a grievance; but if he lays an action for damages, he must prove the damage, and I leave

you to judge, whether a gentleman's character may not be brought into contempt, and all his views in life blasted by calumny, without his being able to specify the particulars of the damage he has sustained." [MB, June 2]

This belief in the delicacy of a gentleman's honor, something not to be entrusted to the judgment of such gross plebeians as usually make up a jury, is part of Smollett's contention that the freedom of the press and the composition of juries are parallel instances of rank insubordination, which if permitted to continue will produce not only scandal but sedition: "This spirit of defamation is a kind of heresy, that thrives under persecution. *The liberty of the press* is a term of great efficacy; and, like that of *the Protestant religion,* has often served the purposes of sedition." When Bramble interrupts Barton's harangue to comment further upon juries, neither the tone nor the substance of the passage is altered in the least: "Certain it is, a gentleman's honour is a very delicate subject to be handled by a jury, composed of men, who cannot be supposed remarkable either for sentiment or impartiality—In such a case, indeed, the defendant is tried, not only by his peers, but also by his party; and I really think, that of all patriots, he is the most resolute who exposes himself to such detraction, for the sake of his country" (MB, June 2). Lismahago's later attack upon the "illiterate plebeians" who generally make up a jury seeks to expose the injustice of the jury system.

> Juries are generally composed of illiterate plebeians, apt to be mistaken, easily misled, and open to sinister influence; for if either of the parties to be tried, can gain over one of the twelve jurors, he has secured the verdict in his favour; the juryman thus brought over will, in despite of all evidence and conviction, generally hold out till his fellows are fatigued, and harrassed, and starved into concurrence; in which case the verdict is unjust, and the jurors are all perjured. [MB, July 15]

Bramble, however, is aware of a likelier means of redress than "the ignorance and partiality of juries." To a gentleman traduced in the press, he recommends recourse to "the publishers bones" and "the ribs of an author." Should the gentleman himself be reluctant to try such measures he may employ "certain useful instruments, such as may be found in all countries, to give [an offender] the bastinado." Thus Smollett does find some occasional value in the violence of the mob. Although he has found an effective solution, Bramble is not able to relinquish the problem.

> As for the liberty of the press, like every other privilege, it must be restrained within certain bounds; for if it is carried to a breach of law, religion, and charity, it becomes one of the greatest evils that ever annoyed the community. If the lowest ruffian may stab your good-name with impunity in England, will you be so uncandid as to exclaim against Italy for the practice of common assassination? To what

purpose is our property secured, if our moral character is left defenceless? People thus baited, grow desperate; and the despair of being able
to preserve one's character, untainted by such vermin, produces a total
neglect of fame; so that one of the chief incitements to the practice of
virtue is effectually destroyed. [MB, June 2]

And in the second half of the novel Lismahago is once more called upon
to return attention to the seriousness of the problem: "He said, he should
always consider the liberty of the press as a national evil, while it enabled
the vilest reptile to soil the lustre of the most shining merit, and furnished
the most infamous incendiary with the means of disturbing the peace and
destroying the good order of the community. He owned, however, that,
under due restrictions, it would be a valuable privilege; but affirmed, that
at present there was no law in England sufficient to restrain it within
proper bounds" (MB, July 15).

The viciousness of the press was thus to Smollett another consequence
of a climate of luxury and insubordination. It seemed to him that the
masses wished to erase the distinctions that by nature existed between
themselves and men of rank, to drag men of character down to their own
level. (Bramble's letter of June 2, it should be noted, applies the epithet of
mob to men able to pay the fines of popular publishers as well as to read
their papers, and castigates as the *lowest* ruffian not only a man able to
read and write but one who also can afford to buy the full apparatus of
publishing.) The press became a vehicle of such infamous craving when
it pandered to the tastes of the mob, a monster Bramble never could
abide. The contemporary political condition of England was doubly
perilous, moreover, because certain politicians as well as the press
appeared to be pandering to the masses. Hence in his letter of June 2
Bramble moves quickly and effortlessly from a denunciation of the press
to an attack on the complementary evil, the gentleman who flatters the
mob. This theme is of course repeated by Bramble and Lismahago
throughout the novel. In an earlier letter Bramble had said: "Indeed, I
know nothing so abject as the behavior of a man canvassing for a seat in
parliament—This mean prostration, (to borough-electors, especially)
has, I imagine, contributed in great measure to raise that spirit of
insolence among the vulgar; which, like the devil, will be found very
difficult to lay" (MB, May 19). The fundamental assumption is that the
traditional exclusion of the great majority of Englishmen from the
political process must be maintained; the primary condition of good
order is stated plainly by Lismahago: "He said, he hoped he should never
see the common people lifted out of that sphere for which they were
intended by nature and the course of things" (MB, September 20).

Being the folly of the mindless and tasteless, insubordination is
represented in *Humphry Clinker* by men and women who are largely
faceless. Some are named, but most are merely neutered members of one
or another organ of the mob—the City, the Methodists, the Legion. One

could say that for Smollett they are not human personalities to be described, but problems to be solved, at best groups to be controlled. This is certainly not to say that the novelist could exclude his adversaries among the Old Whig Gang; about certain heads he could be as driven as any Mr. Dick. The founder of the gang, Walpole, is ushered in briefly by Bramble as "a first-mover, who was justly stiled and stigmatized as the father of corruption" (JM, June 2). Pitt, the present leader, appears as "the great political bully" and "that overbearing Hector" (JM, June 5), and directly in Jery's letter of June 2: "Ha, there's the other great phaenomenon, the grand pensionary, that weathercock of patriotism that veers about in every point of the political compass, and still feels the wind of popularity in his tail. He too, like a portentous comet, has risen again above the court-horizon; but how long he will continue to ascend, it is not easy to foretel, considering his great eccentricity." Newcastle is presented as the clown prince of the gang in two of the most comically acid scenes of the novel. In the one Bramble calls him "an ape in politics" for thirty years, and Jery describes him as hopelessly senile (JM, June 2). In the other he moves from one absurdity to another at his own levee, scandalizing visitors like the ambassador from Algiers: "he scarce ever opened his mouth without making some blunder, in relation to the person or business of the party with whom he conversed; so that he really looked like a comedian, hired to burlesque the character of a minister" (JM, June 5). The gang is rounded off with Townshend, who is in constant fear of Pitt (JM, June 5), and the pseudonymous factota, Pitt's "two satellites." The first is probably Wilkes: "without a drop of red blood in his veins . . . a cold intoxicating vapour in his head; and rancour enough in his heart to inoculate and affect a whole nation." The second, Temple: "Without principle, talent, or intelligence, he is ungracious as a hog, greedy as a vulture, and thievish as a jackdaw" (JM, June 2).[8]

Relatively, these individualized sketches are few, enveloped by the collective presence of the mob. Seemingly omnipotent and omnipresent in England, the mob befouls everything it touches, from the spas to the churches, the courts to the papers, Ranelagh to Parliament. Put politically, the Whig oligarchs require no strength of numbers, for they possess such willing tools in the City, the Methodist chapels, and the gin shops. Smollett felt obliged to expose the folly and ignorance of the men of the City. That lesson is certainly part of the intention of *Humphry Clinker*. The original title page carried lines from the *Sermones* of Horace: *Quorsum haec tam putida tendunt, / Furcifer? ad te, inquam.* (To what object are these disagreeable facts directed, you rogue? To you, I said.) The most disagreeable collective portrait in the novel is of the men

---

8. These identifications are explained, and several others for pseudonymous characters attempted, in a forthcoming note in *Notes & Queries* (1977).

of the middle orders who come down from London and in their barbarity despoil the graces of Bath.

> Clerks and factors from the East Indies, loaded with the spoil of plundered provinces; planters, negro-drivers, and hucksters, from our American plantations, enriched they know not how; agents, commissaries, and contractors, who have fattened, in two successive wars, on the blood of the nation; usurers, brokers, and jobbers of every kind; men of low birth, and no breeding, have found themselves suddenly translated into a state of affluence, unknown to former ages; and no wonder that their brains should be intoxicated with pride, vanity, and presumption. Knowing no other criterion of greatness, but the ostentation of wealth, they discharge their affluence without taste or conduct, through every channel of the most absurd extravagance; and all of them hurry to Bath, because here, without any further qualification, they can mingle with the princes and nobles of the land. Even the wives and daughters of low tradesmen, who, like shovel-nosed sharks, prey upon the blubber of those uncouth whales of fortune, are infected with the same rage of displaying their importance; and the slightest indisposition serves them for a pretext to insist upon being conveyed to Bath, where they may hobble country-dances and cotillons among lordlings, 'squires, counsellors, and clergy. These delicate creatures from Bedfordbury, Butcher-row, Crutched-Friers, and Botolph-lane, cannot breathe in the gross air of the Lower Town, or conform to the vulgar rules of a common lodging-house; the husband, therefore, must provide an entire house, or elegant apartments in the new buildings. Such is the composition of what is called the fashionable company at Bath; where a very inconsiderable proportion of genteel people are lost in a *mob of impudent plebeians, who have neither understanding nor judgment, nor the least idea of propriety and decorum; and seem to enjoy nothing so much as an opportunity of insulting their betters.* [MB, April 23; italics added]

Once again the City Whigs represent the confluence of Smollett's national, political, and social antipathies, the intersection of large issues and small personalities. Bramble finds luxury and insubordination indigenous to London, whence they are carried outward, most notably to Bath, but also at times to the northern countryside (by persons like Mrs. Baynard and her aunt). The evils of the time encounter little resistance in England but much in Scotland, where they are fated to languish and die. Lismahago's two tirades (MB, July 15; and MB, September 20), though delivered on the road north, are directed against English influences. In Scotland neither commerce nor the men engaged in it are in any way subversive of the social and political order. On at least three occasions (MB, August 28; JM, September 12; and MB, September 20), Smollett gives praise to the effects of Scottish commerce and to the men who have brought it to such a productive state. In Scotland the pursuit of wealth is restrained by reason and virtue, as Lismahago asserts when he refutes the typical English notion of his country's deprivation:

> "Those who reproach a nation for its poverty, when it is not owing to the profligacy or vice of the people, deserve no answer. . . . The most respectable heroes of ancient Rome, such as Fabricius, Cincinnatus, and Regulus, were poorer than the poorest freeholder in Scotland; and there are at this day individuals in North-Britain, one of whom can produce more gold and silver than the whole republic of Rome could raise at those times when her public virtue shone with unrivalled lustre; and poverty was so far from being a reproach, that it added fresh laurels to her fame, because it indicated a noble contempt of wealth, which was proof against all the arts of corruption—If poverty be a subject for reproach, it follows that wealth is the object of esteem and veneration. . . . An absurdity which no man in his senses will offer to maintain.—Riches are certainly no proof of merit: nay they are often (if not most commonly) acquired by persons of sordid minds and mean talents: nor do they give any intrinsic worth to the possessor; but, on the contrary, tend to pervert his understanding, and render his morals more depraved." [MB, September 20]

Scots merchants, it can be assumed, are thus to their English counterparts as Captain Brown is to Paunceford. (Just as Smollett nowhere attacks an individual or group of Scottish merchants, nowhere does he rebuke any contemporary Scottish political figure.) Furthermore, because of his inherent abilities, a Scotsman's true merit cannot be known from his outward appearance. Lismahago seems an impoverished veteran, but in fact he is a cultivated man of the world, trained in the law. In the same fashion, Bramble calls his apothecary "a proud Scotchman, very thin skinned, and, for aught I know, may have his degree in his pocket —A right Scotchman has always two strings to his bow, and is *in utrumque paratus*" (MB, June 8).

This dispensation applies with especial force to young Humphry Clinker. As Bramble's long-lost son, he shares in his father's strength of character and hence cannot be the "poor Wiltshire lad" he at first appears. On that initial appearance (JM, May 24), Tabby calls him "a beggarly rascal" and "a filthy tatterdemalion," and Jery finds his condition "equally queer and pathetic."

> He seemed to be about twenty years of age, of a middling size, with bandy legs, stooping shoulders, high forehead, sandy locks, pinking eyes, flat nose, and long chin—but his complexion was of a sickly yellow: his looks denoted famine; and the rags that he wore, could hardly conceal what decency requires to be covered—[JM, May 24]

Like native-born Scots, however, the sons of Welsh gentlemen cannot be known by their first appearance, as Jery reports.

In the afternoon, as our aunt stept into the coach, she observed, with some marks of satisfaction, that the postilion, who rode next to her, was not a shabby wretch like the ragamuffin who had drove them into Marlborough. Indeed, the difference was very conspicious: this was a smart fellow, with a narrow-brimmed hat, with gold cording, a cut bob, a decent blue jacket, leather breeches, and a clean linen shirt, puffed above the waist-band. When we arrived at the castle on Spin-hill, where we lay, this new postilion was remarkably assiduous, in bringing in the loose parcels; and, at length, displayed the individual counte-nance of Humphry Clinker, who had metamorphosed himself in this manner, by receiving from pawn part of his own clothes, with the money he had received from Mr. Bramble. [JM, May 24]

The revelation is made complete when, under Bramble's questioning, Humphry discloses that he too is *in utrumque paratus*.

"Suppose I was inclined to take you into my service, (said he) what are your qualifications? what are you good for?" "An please your honour, (answered this original) I can read and write, and do the business of the stable indifferent well—I can dress a horse, and shoe him, and bleed and rowel him; and, as for the practice of sow-gelding, I won't turn my back on e'er a he in the county of Wilts—Then I can make hog's-puddings and hob-nails, mend kettles, and tin saucepans—" Here uncle burst out a-laughing; and enquired, what other accomplishments he was master of—"I know something of single-stick, and psalmody, (proceeded Clinker) I can play upon the Jew's-harp, sing Black-ey'd Susan, Arthur-o'Bradley, and divers other songs; I can dance a Welsh jig, and Nancy Dawson; wrestle a fall with any lad of my inches, when I'm in heart; and, under correction, I can find a hare when your honour wants a bit of game." "Foregad! thou art a complete fellow, (cried my uncle, still laughing) I have a good mind to take thee into my family—" [JM, May 24]

If the Scots and Welsh are invulnerable to luxury by reason of national virtue, the English upper orders are similarly protected by reason of superior birth. In his periodicals as in *Humphry Clinker*, Smollett attacks opponents among the higher classes not for their luxury, but for their politics, or more specifically, for their political characters. Unlike Boling-broke thirty years before, he could not merely dismiss them as upstarts. Newcastle is a dolt, Pitt a despot, Townshend a knave. Lord Oxmington, likewise, is mean of spirit, but not luxurious (JM, September 28). Even Walpole is portrayed in the *Complete History* as not himself luxurious, but as the manipulator for his own corrupt ends of the luxury of others. Yet even this class-bound view of luxury is open to modification by politics. One English merchant, "G. H———," George Heathcote (1700–68), does receive Smollett's praise in *Humphry Clinker* as "really an enthusiast in patriotism." Although a lord mayor of London in 1742, Heathcote is not to be regarded as a Popular Whig. A nephew of one of the founders of the East India Company, he was usually allied with the oligarchic wing of Newcastle's coalition and considered the leader of the Jacobite party in London in the 1740's. In the 1750's he was denounced as "a great Jacobite" by members of the Common Council, and later Horace Walpole wrote of him as "a paltry, worthless Jacobite." A pamphlet Heathcote published in 1749 deplores the depravity of the times in tones reminiscent of Bolingbroke. While sharing many of Smollett's political attitudes, he is also an insider, and thus an effective critic of the "citizens of London," telling Bramble, "with the tears in his eyes, that he had lived above thirty years in the city of London, and dealt in the way of commerce with all the citizens of note in their turns; but that, as he should answer to God, he had never, in the whole course of his life, found above three or four whom he could call thoroughly honest" (MB, May 19).[9]

The narrator-atom of the *Adventures of an Atom* claimed that nineteen-twentieths of the inhabitants of London were followers of the devil, and Smollett had not reduced that proportion by *Humphry Clinker.* While the City Whigs increase their sedition against authority, the Methodists openly promote sedition against reason. Walking through the city, Jery and his uncle discover Humphry haranguing a crowd in a lane behind Longacre. When Bramble berates him for presumption, Humphry pleads that he was moved by the new light of God's grace. To which his employer responds: "What you imagine to be the new light of grace . . . I take to be a deceitful vapour, glimmering through a crack in your upper story—In a word, Mr. Clinker, I will have no light in my family but what pays the king's taxes, unless it be the light of reason, which you don't pretend to follow" (JM, June 10). Bramble then continues:

> "Heark-ye, Clinker, you are either an hypocritical knave, or a wrong-headed enthusiast; and, in either case, unfit for my service—If you are a quack in sanctity and devotion, you will find it an easy matter to impose upon silly women, and others of crazed understanding, who will contribute lavishly to your support—if you are really seduced by the reveries of a disturbed imagination, the sooner you lose your sense entirely, the better for yourself and the community." [JM, June 10]

Bramble's suspicions are soon proved correct. What Humphry had felt as "such strong impulsions, as made him believe he was certainly moved by

---

9. In the *Continuation*, Smollett interrupts his narrative to praise Heathcote and to apologize for an "injury done him in an earlier volume [*Complete History*, 4:575]in classing him with partisans of the ministry."

We think it our duty to declare, upon better information, that alderman Heathcote, far from being a partisan of any ministry, always distinguished himself in parliament by a constant and uniform opposition to all ministerial measures, which tended to the prejudice or dishonour of the nation; and ever approved himself an honest, resolute, and zealous assertor of the rights and liberties of the people. [3:442]

Further information on Heathcote is contained in the *DNB*; Sutherland, *The East India Company in Eighteenth-Century Politics*; and Namier and Brooke, *History of Parliament.*

the spirit," Bramble discovers to have been the machinations of Lady Griskin, who sought out the Methodist meeting as part of a scheme to marry Tabby off to Barton and to that end prompted Clinker to mount the rostrum, "to the true secret of which he was an utter stranger" (JM, June 10). Humphry is shown to be free of fanaticism (MB, June 14), and after London his Methodism is hardly perceptible.

Meanwhile, however, Tabby has attached herself with zeal to the sect; she is of course both a silly woman and a person of crazed understanding, thus always vulnerable to the deceit and enthusiasm of the Methodists. Bramble is unable to admonish his sister as he did Clinker, but does guess that her religious devotion is no more than a convenient cloak for a less spiritual quest. We are thus permitted a knowledgeable smile upon learning that Tabby "has had the good fortune to come acquainted with a pious Christian, called Mr. Moffat, who is very powerful in prayer, and often assists her in private exercises of devotion" (JM, August 8). Later we appreciate the irony involved when Jery reports that, "Mrs. Tabitha displayed her attractions as usual, and actually believed she had entangled one Mr. Maclellan, a rich inkle-manufacturer, in her snares; but when matters came to an explanation, it appeared that his attachment was altogether spiritual, founded upon an intercourse of devotion, at the meeting of Mr. John Wesley" (JM, September 3). Resolution of Tabby's search, in the shape of Lismahago, serves to confirm Bramble's early observation, when the passion of love does indeed abate the fervor of her devotion (MB, July 15). This view is tinged with brotherly tolerance, and we have reason to surmise that in this instance Smollett has transposed the usual roles of Bramble and Lydia. Usually mild and romantic, Liddy is frank and harsh in her appraisal of her aunt's behavior:

> My poor aunt, without any regard to her years and imperfections, has gone to market with her charms in every place where she thought she had the least chance to dispose of her person, which, however, hangs still heavy on her hands—I am afraid she has used even religion as a decoy, though it has not answered her expectation—She has been praying, preaching, and catechising among the methodists, with whom this country abounds; and pretends to have such manifestations and revelations, as even Clinker himself can hardly believe, though the poor fellow is half crazy with enthusiasm. . . . God forgive me if I think uncharitably, but all this seems to me to be downright hypocrisy and deceit—[LM, September 7]

In the activities of the Methodists, Smollett certainly saw insubordination: the pretensions of the lower orders to some measure of religious authority and illumination, and the leveling of class distinctions in ecclesiastical practices. In the activities of the City, he saw a complementary kind of political rebellion. He has Humphry Clinker assume the repudiation of both. Humphry easily proves himself a stranger to luxury, but remains suspect in Bramble's eyes until he can answer charges of fanaticism. After catechizing him over his preaching to the mob, Bramble affirms, "If there was anything like affectation or hypocrisy in this excess of religion, I would not keep him in my service; but, so far as I can observe, the fellow's character is downright simplicity, warmed with a kind of enthusiasm, which renders him very susceptible of gratitude and attachment to his benefactors" (MB, June 14). In keeping with his habits of association, Smollett here suggests that as simplicity with obedience is proof against luxury, so simplicity with humility is proof against fanaticism.[1]

Discovery of Humphry brings Bramble much personal comfort during the expedition, but it does nothing to allay his anxieties over the state of England. He finds a companion and later a son, but his search for honest politics and decent politicians is futile; there are no worthy men of influence to be found in England. Against the venality of the times stands only one public figure, George III, whom Bramble calls "A very honest kind-hearted gentleman . . . he's too good for the times" (JM, June 2).[2] Yet the monarch cannot administer the kingdom alone and must make do with the caliber of politician elected to Parliament. The contrast is stark between honest, kindhearted king and dishonest, heartless ministers and sycophants. No *public* response to the ills introduced by luxury appears possible. The process of degeneration has gone too far. The people, their representatives, and their institutions have all been corrupted. What is left is a humbler, smaller opportunity. Private men of good will can maintain their privacy against the infiltration of the times; they can renounce public haunts and public squalor. When national values have been twisted, personal choices alone remain, and these cannot represent the ideal but merely the inevitable. Hence *Humphry Clinker* ends, for Bramble and Lismahago, with retreat and self-exile in Monmouthshire.

---

1. Byron Gassman takes a different approach to Methodism in the novel in his "Religious Values in the World of *Humphry Clinker*," *Brigham Young University Studies* 6 (Winter 1965): 65–72. A valuable study of attacks on the sect is Albert M. Lyles, *Methodism Mocked* (London, 1961). In a letter to John Chute, 10 October 1766, Horace Walpole describes a Methodist chapel he visited at Bath and concludes that luxury can be found even here.
2. Repeatedly through the 1760's Smollett identified himself as a sturdy warrior on behalf of the king's causes. The recurring praise of the young monarch in the *Briton* had been preceded by the encomiums of the *Critical* and was followed by yet stronger advocacy in the *Continuation* and the *Atom*. In the *Continuation* he wrote:

[The people's] love was heightened to rapture and admiration . . . when they were made acquainted with the transcendent virtues of his heart, and the uncommon extent of his understanding; when they knew he was mild, affable, social, and sympathizing; susceptible of all the emotions which private friendship inspires; kind and generous to his dependents, liberal to merit . . . when they knew his heart was intirely British; warmed with the most cordial love of his native country, and animated with plans of the most genuine patriotism; when they learned . . . that he possessed almost every accomplishment that art could communicate, or application acquire. [4:151–52]

JOHN F. SENA

Ancient Designs and Modern Folly: Architecture in *The Expedition of Humphry Clinker*†

Few eighteenth-century fictional characters exhibit the extensive interests of Matthew Bramble. Medicine, politics, religion, social change, to name but a few; are topics on which he discourses freely during his journey, most often for the purpose of setting forth the opinions and sentiments of his real-life creator. While Bramble's involvement with these topics and their significance in the novel have been frequently discussed, one of his most absorbing interests—his preoccupation with architecture—and its function in the work have been virtually ignored.

It is readily apparent from the length, frequency, and quality of Bramble's architectural observations that the subject is important to him. Major portions of his epistles from Bath and London, for instance, consist of detailed descriptions of local structures; in fact, architecture is so prominent a subject in those letters that our impressions of Bath and London are probably as much a result of his depiction of their buildings as they are of his description of their entertainments, social institutions, smells, and sounds. Bramble's architectural observations are not, of course, confined to those two cities, nor are they restricted exclusively to buildings. His remarks, rather, extend throughout his entire journey and include a full range of architectural concerns: the design of pleasure gardens, the pattern and construction of streets, the relationship of architectural style to climate, and the general arrangement of physical structures within a city. It is also evident that his analyses are not superficial or cursory, but reflect, instead, an extensive knowledge of the field. He generally employs, for instance, technical terms in his descriptions with accuracy and precision, and virtually always bases his judgments, not on subjective norms, but on the criteria enunciated by classical or humanist architects. In brief, Bramble's letters suggest that he is as interested in the state of contemporary architecture as he is in any topic that he discusses, and that he has a knowledge of the subject commensurate with his interest.

To be sure, one would expect a novel that may be included in the genre of travel literature to contain observations on buildings, streets, and town planning. Yet the prominence of architecture in the novel and the importance associated with it by the age suggest that Bramble's comments are not simply decorative ornaments intended solely or even primarily to supply the reader with local color. Architecture, it should be

† From the *Harvard Library Bulletin* 27 (1979): 86–113.

remembered, from the time of the ancients through the eighteenth century had a moral as well as a physical function; buildings were conceived of as not only providing man with shelter from the elements, but also embodying the moral strength and virtue, the order and harmony, of the society that created them. Contemporary writers were not unmindful of the moral implications of architecture; in fact, Paul Fussell reminds us that for eighteenth-century humanist writers "architectural imagery and moral imperatives seem never very far separated." [1] With this relationship in mind, we shall see that Bramble's architectural remarks are not merely superfluous comments intended to lend a degree of realism to the novel, but have instead a vital moral function. Through Bramble's architectural analyses, Smollett is able to present a general indictment of English society—a society which he saw as vain and proud, as cut off from tradition, as tearing down all hierarchical distinctions —while asserting the essential virtue and integrity of Scotland. [2]

In evaluating the architecture of England and Scotland, Bramble employs, as I have suggested, the precepts of a type of architecture that began with the ancients and is generally referred to as "classical" or "humanist." [3] The architectural principles of the Greeks and Romans were first codified by Vitruvius in his *De Architectura*, a work which became for subsequent ages the most influential single source for classical architectural practices. When a complete copy of the *De Architectura*, which was only available in fragmented form in the Middle Ages, was discovered in a monastery in the fifteenth century, it inspired the architects of Renaissance Italy, most notably Leon Battista Alberti and Andrea Palladio. The designs of Alberti and Palladio were, in turn, popularized in England in the seventeenth and eighteenth centuries by Inigo Jones and Lord Burlington. Stimulated by the buildings of antiquity and Renaissance Italy and guided by the works of Vitruvius, Alberti, and Palladio, a substantial number of eighteenth-century English archi-

1. *The Rhetorical World of Augustan Humanism* (Oxford: Clarendon Press, 1965), p. 172. For an excellent discussion of the use of architecture for moral instruction, as well as the widespread contemporary interest in architecture, see chap. 8. I wish to thank my colleague, Professor Dan Barnes, for the guidance he provided at all stages of this essay.
2. Bramble may be assumed to be Smollett's architectural spokesman. His observations, notwithstanding two fleeting dissenting remarks by Lydia, stand without challenge or balance by the other four letter-writers, while the moral and social values—the essentially conservative position —that one may infer from his analyses may be found in Smollett's historical and fictional works. For a discussion of the similarity between the conservative attitudes expressed by Bramble and Smollett's personal views enunciated in *The Critical Review* (1756–63), *A Complete History of England* (1757–58), *Continuation of the Complete*

History of England (1760–65), and *The Present State of All Nations* (1768), see John Sekora, "Smollett and Social Controversy: Luxury, Politics, and *Humphry Clinker*" (Dissertation, Princeton University, 1972). For an excellent overview of the conservative nature of Smollett's philosophy and its embodiment in his satires, see Michael Rosenblum, "Smollett as Conservative Satirist," *ELH*, XLII (1975), 556–579.
3. For an examination of the principles of "classical" or "humanist" architecture, see Geoffrey Scott, *The Architecture of Humanism* (Boston: Houghton Mifflin, 1914); John Summerson, *The Classical Language of Architecture* (Cambridge: M.I.T. Press, 1963); Rudolf Wittkower, *Architectural Principles in the Age of Humanism* (New York: Random House, 1965). I shall follow the practice of architectural historians and use the terms "classical" and "humanist" interchangeably.

tects—Robert Morris, John Gwynn, Colin Campbell, Henry Wotton, Isaac Ware, to name only a few—endorsed in theory and practice the principles of classical architecture. The precepts, then, upon which Bramble bases his evaluation of contemporary architecture are not peculiar to him, nor are they reflections of his eccentricity, but have a genealogy that is approximately 1800 years old.[4]

* * *

The first object of Bramble's architectural attention is the Circus at Bath. It is significant that he should begin with the Circus, for it was regarded by many as the most notable and famous structure in that city. Begun in 1754 by John Wood from the unfinished designs left by his father, and completed in 1764, the Circus was a three-story, semicircular building which contained thirty-three contiguous residences. In its houses, which shared a common façade, were lodged the rich and powerful who came to Bath, not primarily to benefit from the waters, but for the opulent balls, the gaming tables, and the midnight fêtes. At a time when the city was experiencing a rapid building program, with structures such as the Royal Crescent and the buildings on Queen Square arising, the Circus was often considered to be the most elaborate and impressive building in Bath, a paragon of architectural splendor that could serve as a model for countless other modern buildings. By beginning his analyses with the Circus, then, Bramble was doing more than simply depicting a building that he happened to see on his tour. He was, rather, describing a symbol of the spirit and achievement of Bath, a building that embodied the temper and pride—the Zeitgeist—of the city and the people who gathered there.

Bramble begins his description of the Circus by criticizing its appearance in terms of the two concepts that humanist architects asserted were essential constituents of beauty or magnificence—proportion and unity of design: "If we consider it in point of magnificence, the great number of small doors belonging to the separate houses, the inconsiderable height of the different orders, the affected ornaments of the architrave, which are both childish and misplaced, and the areas projecting into the street, surrounded with iron rails, destroy a good part of its effect upon the eye. ..." To the humanist architect, for a structure to be beautiful, its elements—the columns, doors, windows—had to be in precise proportion to one another and to the building as a whole. Furthermore, the various parts of the building had to be integrated into the whole so that

<hr>

4. Given the popular interest in architecture and the reverence for classical architectural ideals, it is likely that Smollett's audience would have readily understood the criteria employed by Bramble: "One reason why the eighteenth-century imagination is so full of architectural images is that everybody who was anybody was either 'building' or had friends who were. Just as a minimum techni-cal knowledge of fortification was assumed in any civilized person, so anyone of the middle or upper class was expected to possess some technical architectural learning. ... During all this activity, Rome never diminished as a focus of architectural interest and imitation ..." (Fussell [note 1, above], P. 173).

nothing could be added, removed, or altered without destroying the sense of oneness or completeness of the entire structure. Anything that detracted from the impression of coherence and unity—elaborate ornaments or excessive decorations, for instance—was anathema. Palladio, who wrote at length on the nature of beauty in architecture, epitomized the humanist view when he described beauty in terms of proportion and wholeness. "BEAUTY," he wrote in *Four Books of Architecture,* "will result from the form and correspondence of the whole, with respect to the several parts, of the parts with regard to each other, and of these again to the whole; that the structure may appear an entire and compleat body, wherein each member agrees with the other."[5]

It is evident that Bramble is displeased with the appearance of the Circus precisely because it lacks proportion and unity. In his judgment the "several parts" of the building—the doors and the columns—are out of proportion "to the whole," for the doors should be larger and the columns higher in order to be in proportion to the façade of the Circus. In addition, the "misplaced" ornaments and the patios in front destroy the unity and coherence of the design.[6] The failure of the Circus to have a good "effect upon the eye" of Bramble, then, results from the rejection by its architect of nature as an aesthetic norm in favor of subjective standards for beauty. Although Wood has paid lip service to classical forms, perhaps in an effort to capture the grandeur of the past through the pseudo-classical façade of the Circus, he has succeeded only in creating a fatuous imitation of ancient architecture. Ultimately, the architectural failure of the Circus stands as a testimonial, not only to the egotism of its creator and the lack of taste of its admirers, but to the failure of contemporary English society to re-create the heroism and virtue of the ancients.

If the Circus, when judged by the humanist criteria for beauty, is found deficient, it is "still more defective," according to Bramble, "if we view it in the light of convenience." There was no architectural principle more important to the humanist architect than convenience. The concept meant, in simple terms, that a building must be useful and practical; it

5. Palladio, *Four Books of Architecture,* trans. Isaac Ware (London: 1783), Bk. I, chap. I. Alberti, *Ten Books on Architecture,* trans. James Leoni (1726), ed. Joseph Rykwert (London: Alec Tiranti, 1955) offered a similar definition of beauty: "I shall define Beauty to be a Harmony of all the Parts ... fitted together with such Proportion and Connection, that nothing could be added, diminished or altered, but for the Worse" (Bk. 6, chap. 2). See also Robert Morris, *Lectures on Architecture. Consisting of Rules Founded Upon Harmonick and Arithmetical Proportions in Building* (London, 1759): "BEAUTY and *Proportion* are inseparable, for which Reason Beauty is always center'd in Proportion, and Proportion is ever beautiful ..." (p. 120). In his *Defence* he printed an engraving of a modern "irregular" building so that the reader could judge its unattractiveness compared to the "geometrical" and proportional beauty of a classically designed building.
6. "Redundancy of Members, Ornaments, and Dress," averred Morris, "are the Productions of unthinking Geniuses. Undecorated Plainness ... in a well proportioned Building will ever please" (Robert Morris, *Rural Architecture* [London, 1750], p. vi). Isaac Ware, in *A Complete Body of Architecture* (London, 1756), divided architects into "the superficial and the judicious," and asserted that the former are "always influenced by the ornament, the other by the proportion ..." (p. 128).

must serve the function for which it was designed. In its broadest sense, the concept included, in addition to the design of a building, its relationship with its physical location as well. Convenience demanded, for instance, that a building be constructed on a site (or situation) that would promote the health of its inhabitants. Since moist and noxious air was generally considered to be inimical to health, it became a commonplace among humanist architects that locations exposed to impure or vaporish air must be avoided at all costs. Alberti, for example, echoing the remarks of his master, Vitruvius, declared anathema sites "where there is a continued Collection of thick Clouds and stinking Vapours," or areas exposed to "gross Winds" which carry "pestiferous" vapors, or "Neighbourhoods from which any noxious Particles may be brought." He even went so far as to theorize that people who breathe pure, dry air will not only be healthy but will have "better Understandings than those who breathe a heavy moist one." In a vaporish climate, "the Understanding can never be clear, the spirits being dampt and stupified ... their Minds will never be free from Vexation and Uneasiness."[7] Writing under the influence of Vitruvius and Alberti, Palladio also condemned building sites surrounded by damp air. Especially dangerous, he argued, was the practice of building too close to mountains, for such a situation is "entirely contrary to health; because the earth being impregnated by the rains that settle there, sends forth pestiferous vapours, infecting both the body and mind; the spirits being by them weaken'd, the joints and nerves emasculated...."[8]

Bramble's description of the situation of the Circus suggests the extent to which modern builders have ignored this vital concept. Instead of constructing it, for instance, where it would be free from moist and noxious air, it was placed in a location permeated with "humid and unwholesome" air. Instead of selecting a site where air would circulate freely, it was built—in defiance of Palladio's injunction—too close to a hill, with the result that "clouds, formed by the constant evaporation from the baths and rivers in the bottom, will, in their ascent this way, be first attracted and detained by the hill that rises close behind the Circus, and load the air with a perpetual succession of vapours...." Furthermore, when the wind blows, smoke is "forced down the chimneys, by the gusts of wind reverberated from the hill behind...."

7. *Ten Books on Architecture* (note 5 above), Bk. I, chaps. 3, 4. In Book I (chaps. 4, 6) of his *De Architectura* (trans. and ed. Frank Granger, Loeb Classical Library [Cambridge: Harvard University Press], 1931) Vitruvius enjoins architects to select healthy sites, free from moist air, excessive rain, and strong winds, when constructing an individual building or an entire city. Similar notions may be found throughout the works of English humanists: see, for instance, Henry Wotton's recommendation at the beginning of his popular *The Elements of Architecture* (London, 1624) to build near salubrious air and to avoid "foggy noysomnesse" (p. 3), as well as Ware's statement that "Pleasure can never be where there is not health; therefore such a situation is to be chosen as is not infected with damp or other unwholesome vapours..." (*A Complete Body* [note 6 above], p. 95).

8. *Four Books of Architecture* (note 5 above), Bk. 2, chap. 12. Ware expresses a similar idea in Bk. 2, part 1, chap. 2 ("Of the Air") in his *A Complete Body* (note 6 above), pp. 97–99.

The concept of convenience was also ignored in designing the access routes to the Circus. Classical architects stressed that the roads, streets, and paths that lead to a building should be broad, straight, and safe. Slippery or precipitous walks or thoroughfares should be avoided, as well as building sites which are, in the words of Sir Henry Wotton, author of the widely read *The Elements of Architecture* (1624), "of too steepie and incommodious *Accesse* to the trouble both of friends and *familie*."[9] Furthermore, climatic peculiarities, according to Palladio, must also be taken into consideration when designing walks or streets. Porticos, he asserted, should be constructed in inclement areas so that "the citizens might, under cover, go and do their business, without being molested by the sun, by the rains and snow. . . ."[1] The access routes leading to the Circus defy, according to Bramble, these injunctions. "The only entrance to it," he tells us, ". . . is so difficult, steep, and slippery, that, in wet weather, it must be exceedingly dangerous, both for those that ride in carriages, and those that walk a-foot. . . ." In the winter walking to the Circus is especially perilous, for when the precipitous entrance to the building is covered with snow, "I don't see how any individual could go either up or down, without the most imminent hazard of broken bones." In addition to the possibility of causing broken bones, the unprotected streets will aggravate more serious disorders, for carriages and chairs are forced to remain from morning to night in the rain, "till they become so many boxes of wet leather, for the benefit of the gouty and rheumatic. . . ." Bramble's remedy is not unlike Palladio's suggestion for the use of porticos. The iron rails in front of the Circus ("which seem to be of very little use") should, he avers, be replaced by arcades which would provide pedestrians with a "covered walk" and shelter "the poor chairmen and their carriages from the rain, which is here almost perpetual."

Ignoring the concept of convenience in selecting a site for and in building access routes to the Circus suggests more than simply a deviation from a specific principle of classical architecture. For the concept of convenience acknowledged that, in the most fundamental sense, the purpose of a building is to contribute to man's health and comfort by providing him with shelter from the inclemencies of his environment. The Circus, as we have seen, makes no such contribution; in fact, it imperils rather than preserves health. Its deviation from this architectural principle, then, calls into question the very purpose of building. It is a deviation not simply from tradition, but from reason itself. In its rejection of convenience, the Circus stands as Smollett's indictment of Wood and modern architects in general, as well as the vain and supercilious society which allows them to flourish, a society which

---

9. P. 4. For a general discussion—which greatly influenced seventeenth- and eighteenth-century British architects—of the classical criteria for roads, see Palladio's *Four Books of Architecture* (note 5 above), Bk 3, chap. I ("Of Roads"). 1. *Ibid.*, Bk. 3, chap. 2.

values appearance and pretension more than the health and well-being of its people.

In addition to employing classical architectural principles in his analysis, Bramble draws a direct comparison between the Bath Circus and one of the most famous buildings of classical antiquity, the Coliseum: "The Circus is a pretty bauble; contrived for shew, and looks like Vespasian's amphitheatre turned outside in." The reference to Vespasian's amphitheatre provides us with a specific structure—not simply abstract precepts—for judging the Circus and the society that produced it. Whereas, for instance, the Coliseum was a massive and majestic edifice, suggestive of the strength of the Romans, the Circus is a mere "bauble" which reflects the superficiality and ostentation of contemporary Englishmen. Whereas the Coliseum was an arena where physically powerful men engaged in life-and-death struggles, the Circus, its modern equivalent, is the home of fops and coquettes who spend their time absorbed in petty squabbles and vicious gossip. In a larger sense, if the Coliseum, along with the other surviving structures of Rome, is a physical reflection of the virtue and grandeur of the entire Roman culture, a "virtue and grandeur, which" (in the words of Palladio) "perhaps had not otherwise been believed,"[2] then the Circus may be seen as a reflection of the failure of Hanoverian England to re-create the spirit and achievement of ancient Rome. The vision of an Augustan England, cherished by Smollett, that would resemble and rival the reign of Caesar Augustus has been shattered by fifty-five years of Hanoverian and Whiggish rule.[3] The hope epitomized by Barton's remarks when, upon seeing George III, he described him as "Augustus, in patronizing merit; Titus Vespasian in generosity; Trajan in beneficence; and Marcus Aurelius, in philosophy" has turned to cynicism. Contemporary England, like the Circus, bears only an inverted relationship to its model; instead of being a new Rome, eighteenth-century England is a Rome "turned outside in."

Immediately after his account of the Circus, Bramble moves on to a general description of Bath. Applying the same criteria that he did to the Circus, he condemns the "want of beauty and proportion" and the inconvenience of the entire city:

... but the rage of building has laid hold on such a number of adventurers, that one sees new houses starting up in every out-let and every corner of Bath; contrived without judgment, executed without solidity, and stuck together, with so little regard to plan and propriety, that the different lines of the new rows and buildings interfere with, and intersect one another in every different angle of conjunction. They look like the wreck of streets and squares disjointed by an earthquake,

2. *Ibid.*, Bk. 3, "Preface."
3. For a discussion of what Byron Gassman calls Smollett's "dual vision of George III's England," see his article, "'Humphry Clinker' and the Two Kingdoms of George III," *Criticism*, XVI (1974), 95–108.

which hath broken the ground into a variety of holes and hillocks; or, as if some Gothic devil had stuffed them altogether in a bag, and left them to stand higgledy piggledy, just as chance directed. What sort of a monster Bath will become in a few years, with those growing excrescences, may be easily conceived; but the want of beauty and proportion is not the worst effect of these new mansions; they are built so slight, with the soft crumbling stone found in this neighbourhood, that I should never sleep quietly in one of them . . . and, I am persuaded, that my hind, Roger Williams, or any man of equal strength, would be able to push his foot through the strongest part of their walls. . . .

Bramble's description of the streets of Bath in particular—chaotic, without plan or regularity—recalls the importance humanist architects gave to properly designed thoroughfares. The greatness of Rome, according to Palladio, could be seen not only in her buildings but in her roads and streets which were so designed "that also in them might be known the grandeur and the magnificence of their minds."[4] Palladio's standards for a properly designed street were similar to his standards for a properly designed building: it should be beautiful and convenient. For a street to be beautiful, it must be straight and commodious and afford the traveler delightful views of beautiful houses; for it to be useful it must be safe, clean, broad, and airy.[5] The streets of Bath—unlike the streets of the Romans—obviously will never convince future generations of the grandeur and magnificence of the minds of the city's inhabitants.

The importance Renaissance architects ascribed to designing streets that were beautiful and useful was reflected as well by Smollett's contemporaries. John Gwynn, for instance, who is perhaps best known to literary students as the man whose plans for the Blackfriars Bridge were adamantly defended by Samuel Johnson, made an impassioned plea in 1766 for town planners to lay out streets in an orderly and regular fashion. Reiterating the sentiments of Wren and Evelyn, who wanted London's streets redesigned in a more logical fashion after the great fire of 1666, Gwynn contended that for a city to be "magnificent" and "convenient" it is essential that the "ground-plan" be "composed of right lines, and that the streets intersected each other at right angles. . . ." Acute angles should be avoided at all costs, for "they are not only disagreeable to the sight, but constantly waste the ground and spoil the buildings. . . ."[6] In his opinion, there should be at least three major thoroughfares running across London with other major arteries intersecting them "at right angles." London, however, because of "tasteless builders" and selfish property owners, has grown, like Bath, without plan or regularity until it is now, in a passage that resembles Bramble's description of the streets

4. *Four Books* (note 5 above), Bk. 3, "Preface."
5. *Ibid.*, Bk. 3, chaps. I, 2.

6. John Gwynn, *London and Westminster Improved*(London, 1766), p. 6.

and houses of Bath, "nothing more than a confused heap, an irregular, slovenly, ill-digested composition, of all that is absurd and ungraceful; that its principal avenues are narrow and crooked, that the greatest part of the crawl is composed of blind alleys and narrow unconnected passages, equally inconvenient and unwholsome, that some of its houses are suffered to project before the others. . . ."[7] Resolute action, according to Gwynn, must be taken immediately, for architecture, he avers, is the cornerstone of all the arts and an index to the refinement and taste of the public.[8] In the context, then, of Gwynn's and Palladio's work, it is likely that Smollett's readers would have seen the bizarre design of the streets of Bath as a rejection of classical architectural principles as well as symptomatic of the moral and aesthetic decline of contemporary society.

Immediately after describing the buildings and streets of Bath, Bramble provides us with an explanation of the causes for the city's architectural blight:

All these absurdities arise from the general tide of luxury, which hath overspread the nation, and swept away all, even the very dregs of the people. Every upstart of fortune, harnessed in the trappings of the mode, presents himself at Bath, as in the very focus of observation —Clerks and factors from the East Indies, loaded with the spoil of plundered provinces; planters, negro-drivers, and hucksters, from our American plantations, enriched they know not how; agents, commissaries, and contractors, who have fattened . . . usurers, brokers, and jobbers of every kind; men of low birth, and no breeding, have found themselves suddenly translated into a state of affluence unknown to former ages . . . all of them hurry to Bath, because here, without any further qualification, they can mingle with the princes and nobles of the land.

The lack of order and regularity in the plan of the city, the disarray of the buildings, the absence of intersecting streets at clearly defined intervals may be seen, then, not simply as examples of local color, but as metaphors for a chaotic and confused society, one without social stratification, class distinction, or a sense of hierarchy, a society which, like its buildings and streets, is "higgledy piggledy." The general sense of architectural grotesqueness may be seen as a physical representation of the moral and spiritual grotesqueness that permeates the city, while the weakness and impermanence of the buildings suggest, as they do in Hogarth's *Gin Lane*, a society that has no future, a society that stands on the brink of apocalyptic doom. Bath has become a worshipper of the "Gothic devil" instead of the Divine Architect.

7. *Ibid.*, pp. 5, 7. Gwynn's explanations for London's rapid expansion in population also bear a similarity to Bramble's: the "migration of foreigners" (p. 16); the influx of the *nouveau riche* (p. 17); and people deserting "their native homes and quitting their innocent country retreats for the sake of tasting the pleasures of this great city . . ." (p. 16).
8. *Ibid.*, pp. 1, 11–12.

Bramble intersperses his letters from London, as he did from Bath, with frequent architectural references, some of them at least partially complimentary. He applauds, for instance, the Bridge at Blackfriars, judging it—in terms of humanist architecture—to be a work of "magnificence and utility." Immediately, however, he undercuts his tribute to the people of the city by expressing his surprise and "wonder" at "how they stumbled upon" such a structure, implying that the bridge was the result of a fortuitous accident rather than conscious planning. He also finds the streets of London—judged according to Palladio's criteria—"spacious, regular, and airy"; but this too is subverted by his description of the city in general as overcrowded and unplanned, "an overgrown monster" with a "dropsical head."

Less ambivalent is his treatment of the buildings and gardens of Vauxhall. It is little wonder that Bramble should select Vauxhall for his most acrimonious, as well as his most lengthy and detailed, analysis of a London structure, for since its reopening in 1732 under the ownership of Thomas Tyers, it had become the most elaborate and popular recreational area in London. In fact, with its semicircular colonnades, dining pavilions, porticos, rotundas, triumphal arches, pillars, statues, painted perspectives, imitation ruins, tree-lined walks, and Temple of Neptune, it was probably the most frequently visited, written about, and talked about public place in the entire city. By attacking it, Bramble—and Smollett—was attacking a complex that reflected the taste and manners, sophistication and cultivation of contemporary London.

Bramble begins his criticism of Vauxhall by expressing the traditional humanist displeasure at excessive ornamentation and lack of unity: "Vauxhall is a composition of baubles, overcharged with paltry ornaments, ill conceived, and poorly executed; without any unity of design. . . ." Humanist architects insisted, as we have seen, upon completeness and oneness in their designs. While they did not oppose ornamentation (or mild diversity), they demanded that it be subordinated to the total design or controlling theme. As the various elements of the human body are subordinated and unified, according to Henry Wotton, so must be the various elements of any structure: "Each side, agreeing with the other, both in the number, in the qualitie, and in the measure of the Parts."[9] Ironically, although Vauxhall lacks tasteful and appropriate decorations as well as a unified design, it does support the humanist contention that a structure should be a reflection of the people who use it, for Bramble avers that there is a general lack of "taste and decorum" among the visitors to the area, as well as an absence of social or class unity among them. They are, according to him, a disagreeable mob who crowd together in the damp and insalubrious night air to hear songs that are inaudible to half their number; they are "possessed by a spirit, more

9. Wotton (note 7 above), p. 21.

absurd and pernicious than any thing we meet with in the precincts of Bedlam."

Bramble next criticizes Vauxhall for its uniqueness and oddness, for its generally bizarre appearance:

> It is an unnatural assembly of objects, fantastically illuminated in broken masses; seemingly contrived to dazzle the eyes and divert the imagination of the vulgar—Here a wooden lion, there a stone statute; in one place, a range of things like coffee-house boxes, covered a-top; in another, a parcel of ale-house benches; in a third, a puppet-shew representation of a tin cascade; in a fourth, a gloomy cave of a circular form, like a sepulchral vault half lighted; in a fifth, a scanty slip of grass-plat, that would not afford pasture sufficient for an ass's colt.

His description, while implying that Vauxhall fails to embody the order and logic of the natural world, would have also been understood by contemporary readers as reflecting the specific and well-known humanist prejudice against architectural "Novelty and Singleness."[1] To humanist architects, as to humanist writers such as Pope and Johnson, the novel and singular in art produce works which are modish and transitory, appealing to a limited audience for a limited time. Such works are the product, not of reason, but of an unbridled and uncontrolled imagination. It was theorized by Smollett's contemporaries that novelty and singleness in architecture was first introduced into Western society by the Goths and Vandals. John Gwynn, for instance, in *The Art of Architecture* (1742), a poem which consists of brief summaries of the major precepts of humanist architecture, asserted that

> The GOTHS first introduc'd the frantick Way
> Of forming Apes, or Monsters, wild as they
> Because the Tumult, fond of Tricks and Apes,
> Lov'd such Variety, and antick Shapes.[2]

To Gwynn the legacy of the Goths may be seen among our "Modern FOOLS" who, "Renouncing all the Rules the ROMANS had," build bizarre and tasteless structures.[3] Gwynn's opinion was shared by Morris, who averred that classical architecture was initially subverted by the Goths and Vandals, and that their grotesque creations "but too much resemble the unhappy Practices of our present Enemies to the Rules of the Ancients."[4] By viewing Vauxhall, then, in the context of these historical attitudes, contemporary readers would have been reminded, as they were with the Circus, of the degeneration of modern society from the classical

1. Morris, *Defence* (note 6 above), pp. 20, 28. Colin Campbell, a leading exponent of classical architecture, also criticized in his *Vitruvius Britannicus* (London, 1717-25) the "absurd Novelties [of modern architects], so contrary to those excellent Precepts in *Vitruvius*, and so repugnant to those admirable Remains the Antients have left us" (II, 2).

2. London, rpt. in Augustan Reprint Society, no. 144, ed. William A. Gibson (Los Angeles: University of California Press, 1970), pp. 24–25.
3. *Ibid.*, p. 26.
4. Robert Morris, *Defence* (note 6 above), p. iv. See also pp. 11, 21.

ideal. Vauxhall would have been seen as a modern counterpart of the "frantick" creations of the Goths, built and inhabited by contemporary barbarians whose taste and manners are no better than those of the hordes who invaded Rome.

In addition to implying that Vauxhall is comparable to the absurd and irregular creations of the Goths and Vandals, Bramble also describes the pleasure gardens in a manner that suggests an analogy between the physical structure and the society that visits it. The absence of "propriety of disposition" (the lack of proper arrangement of the parts), for instance, and the description (quoted above) of the grounds as a type of grotesque architectural great chain of being may be seen as the physical equivalent of the social chaos of contemporary London—the unnatural blending of classes and professions, the lack of hierarchy—that so disturbed Bramble as well as Smollett. "In short," writes Bramble immediately before his remarks on Vauxhall, "there is no distinction or subordination left—The different departments of life are jumbled together—The hod-carrier, the low mechanic, the tapster, the publican, the shop-keeper, the pettifogger, the citizen, and courtier, *all tread upon the kibes of one another* . . . they are seen every where, rambling, riding, rolling, rushing, justling, mixing, bouncing, cracking, and crashing in one vile ferment of stupidity and corruption." Furthermore, the primacy given to the imagination rather than the reason (Vauxhall is "seemingly contrived to dazzle the eyes and divert the imagination of the vulgar") suggests the inversion of the proper hierarchy in human nature as well as in art. The imagination's gaining ascendancy over the reason, it should be remembered, was thought in the eighteenth century to result in madness. Vauxhall, in its lack of rational design and in its imaginative excesses, thus becomes for Bramble (and Smollett) the embodiment of the madness of contemporary London, a London in which everyone appears "impelled by some disorder of the brain."

Although much of Bramble's attack is contained in his commentary on the architecture of Bath and London, his satiric use of architecture is not confined to those two cities. In a letter from Scarborough, for instance, he makes a lengthy pause in his description of the city to remark on the failure of British architects to adapt their designs to suit the characteristics of the British climate. Lord Burlington, who was instrumental in introducing the designs of Palladio to eighteenth-century England, recognized the need to modify designs employed in hot, dry climates for the rigors of the cold, damp air of his native country. Thus the porticos generally found on each side of a Palladian building were reduced by him at Chiswick House to a single portico in front, for while four porticos may be necessary to catch the breezes in warm Italian summers, they would provide too much ventilation for the English climate. Furthermore, he added a greater number of chimneys, which, while not enhancing the appearance of a building, were necessary to provide the inhabitants in a

420 • John F. Sena

colder climate with warmth. In the context, then, of the theory and practice of classical architects of making the plan—even the building materials[5]—of a structure conform to the locale, Bramble criticizes the use by British architects of the Gothic—or what he calls "Saracen" —design in English churches. Gothic or Saracen buildings, such as the Minster at York—"vast, narrow, dark, and lofty"—are appropriate to the hot and dry climates of Africa and Spain, according to Bramble, but "nothing could be more preposterous, than to imitate such a mode of architecture in a country like England, where the climate is cold, and the air eternally loaded with vapours; and where, of consequence, the builder's intention should be to keep the people dry and warm." Bramble's remarks on sacred architecture, then, alert the reader that not only is the new evangelicalism—as seen in Clinker's Methodism —threatening religion, but ignorant architects are as well, for by attending churches such as the Minster at York or the Abbey church at Bath one may, paradoxically, lose his life while trying to save his soul. Sacred architecture, which Vitruvius valued as the cornerstone of any society, has become a subversive element in English society.

In addition to attacking English society through his lengthy and detailed architectural analyses, Bramble often provides us with the means to evaluate contemporary society in his briefer references to architectural matters. He frequently complains, for instance, of the cramped, restricted rooms he is forced to stay in on his trip and of the pernicious effect they have on his health. In London, it will be recalled, he laments that he is "pent up in frowzy lodgings, where there is not room enough to swing a cat." The first topic he talks about after arriving at the inn at Harrogate is the small rooms; he complains that lodgers are "obliged to put up with dirty holes, where there is neither space, air, nor convenience," while his own apartment "is about ten feet square; and when the folding bed is down, there is just room sufficient to pass between it and the fire." In each case—at London and Harrogate—his description of his lodgings is followed immediately by complaints about his declining health.

While the rooms that Bramble describes would have reminded the reader of the failure of contemporary England to follow the architectural practices of the past,[6] they also have a metaphoric function in the novel. Small rooms may be seen as symbolic of a society grown too large, too

5. Ware, for instance, insisted that red bricks were not appropriate to the English climate: "in summer," he wrote, "it has an appearance of heat that is very disagreeable: for this reason it is most improper in the country" (*A Complete Body* [note 6 above], p. 61). The use of red bricks, it should be added, which during Queen Anne's reign had been the favorite building material for London structures, did in fact decline in favor of gray and yellow bricks by mid-century.

6. Bramble's remarks are in keeping with the philosophy of classical architects, who emphasized that rooms should be commodious and conducive to good health. Wotton, for example, who endorsed Vitruvius' love of "*Luminous rooms*," reiterated the notion that rooms should be airy and "spiritous" (*The Elements* [note 7 above], p. 68), while Colin Campbell praised "spacious and convenient" rooms throughout his *Vitruvius* (note 7 above), *e.g.*, I, 8, 10; II, 5,7.

flooded with people, to be able to accommodate them. The rapid expansion in urban population has caused a corresponding shrinkage of the space available for an individual to be by himself. Bramble's rooms, then, which should be a refuge from this over-crowding, become instead an architectural prison which imposes on him the same type of restriction and threats to his health that he seeks to escape. There is, in fact, no asylum, no sanctuary, in contemporary England.

Although Bramble's most famous and most detailed analyses deal with the architecture of England, he continues to evaluate buildings and cities in terms of classical architecture on his journey through Scotland. He finds, however, that in Scotland the principles of classical architecture have for the most part been observed. He remarks, for instance, that most of the ancestral mansions that he passes have been built on a proper situation, and give the impression of beauty and magnificence, while not sacrificing utility. The cities, too—especially Edinburgh and Glasgow —reflect the ideas of beauty and order valued by classical architects from Vitruvius through the eighteenth century. By conforming to the basic principles of humanist architecture, then, the buildings and cities of Scotland suggest a virtuous and moral people who have not, unlike the South Britons, allowed their pride and vanity to obscure the value of tradition and the wisdom of the past.

Since as a satirist Smollett is more concerned with delineating the general moral decay of England—the baleful effects of luxury, the ugly displays of vanity and pride, the disintegration of the great chain of being —than he is with establishing Scotland as an unequivocal ideal, it should not be surprising to find that his observations on the architectural achievements of the Scots are not as elaborate and comprehensive as his descriptions of English architecture. In fact, many of his most complimentary remarks about Scottish buildings are brief references which lack development or specific details. He writes, for instance, that from Dunbar to Edinburgh "there is a continual succession of fine seats, belonging to noblemen and gentlemen; and as each is surrounded by its own parks and plantation, they produce a very pleasing effect. . . ." He finds that Fife "exhibits a surprising number of fine seats, elegantly built, and magnificently furnished. There is an incredible number of noble houses in every part of Scotland that I have seen.—Dalkeith, Pinkie, Yester, and lord Hopton's, all of them within four or five miles of Edinburgh, are princely palaces, in every one of which a sovereign might reside at his ease." He tersely describes Hamilton as "a noble palace, magnificently furnished," while he despairs of being able to capture the beauty of the Castle of Drumlanrig for his correspondent: "I shall not pretend to enter into a description of this palace, which is really an instance of the sublime in magnificence, as well as in situation, and puts one in mind of the beautiful city of Palmyra, rising like a vision in the midst of the wilderness." Despite the brevity of these and other references, however, their cumulative effect is to inspire the admiration and respect of the reader, for through these allusions is suggested the presence of a noble and aristocratic people whose spirit and vitality, whose sense of distinction and grandeur, are no less visible and permanent than the buildings which they have created and inhabit.

Bramble's favorable impression of Scottish architecture is not confined to rural seats, but extends, as I have suggested, to Scottish cities as well. He commends, for instance, the beauty of Edinburgh's buildings, and, although he is less than enthusiastic about its situation, he insists to Dr. Lewis that the city's general "air of magnificence commands . . . respect." He praises the castle that dominates the city as "an instance of the sublime in scite and architecture." The palace of Holyrood-house is, he avers, "a jewel in architecture" despite its low situation which, he adds, is in no way the fault of the "ingenious architect" who built it. In addition to these magnificent edifices, the city boasts of "divers little elegant squares" on its south side, while the improvements that are being undertaken in the north sector "will add greatly to the beauty and convenience of this capital." For Bramble as for the reader, the grandeur and utility of Edinburgh's architecture is an appropriate counterpart to a city whose vitality and fame as a center of learning allowed it to be called the Athens of the North.

While Bramble is favorably impressed with Edinburgh, it is in his description of Glasgow that we are presented with a city that appears to be the architectural ideal of the entire journey. His initial remarks on Glasgow suggest the extent to which the city reflects the precepts of classical architecture, as well as the extent to which it differs from the English cities that he visited: "In short, it is a perfect bee-hive in point of industry. It stands partly on a gentle declivity; but the greatest part of it is in a plain, watered by the river Clyde. The streets are straight, open, airy, and well paved; and the houses lofty and well built of hewn stone. At the upper end of the town, there is a venerable cathedral . . . the college [is] a respectable pile of building. . . ." Instead, then, of the precipitous declivity which made the streets of Durham almost impassable,[7] we have here a city built, as Vitruvius advised, on a freely accessible site. The narrow, tortuous, and unpleasant streets of Bath and Durham have been replaced by streets that Palladio himself would find agreeable. Unlike the houses of Bath, which Bramble insisted were so flimsy that his hind could put his foot through their walls, the dwellings here are "lofty" and built of stone. Instead of the architecturally inappropriate churches at York and Bath or the "huge gloomy pile" where people worship at Durham, the cathedral at Glasgow is "venerable." Finally, the "confused heap of

7. "The city of Durham appears like a confused heap of stones and brick, accumulated so as to cover a mountain, round which a river winds its brawling course. The streets are generally narrow, dark, and unpleasant, and many of them almost impassable in consequence of their declivity. The cathedral is a huge gloomy pile. . . ."

stones and bricks" that affronted Bramble at Durham is here a "respectable pile of building." In short, virtually every detail cited by Bramble in this Scottish city is the antithesis of what he found in England. [8]

Unlike Bath and London, which, according to Bramble, resemble grotesque organisms—a "monster" with "growing excrescences" (36) and an "overgrown monster" (87), respectively—Glasgow is described as a "bee-hive" of industry, a metaphor which conveys preeminently the idea of order. As a beehive, Glasgow is not simply a place of great activity, but a city of ordered, systematic, and regulated activity. In a larger sense, the metaphor also implies a structural order, for a beehive is composed of symmetrical units harmoniously arranged in a total design that is logical and functional. It is an example of architectural principles found in the natural world which have been ignored, instead of imitated, by modern builders in England. Furthermore, as a social structure built upon the principle of hierarchy, a beehive embodies the idea of stratification or subordination—an entomological great chain of being—that Bramble failed to find in Bath and London. By comparing Glasgow to a beehive, then, he is able to imply that the Scottish city reflects architecturally and socially the order and harmony missing in the major cities of England.

Although Bramble generally approves of Scottish architecture, he also makes a number of negative observations. These faults are often attributed by him, however, not to vanity, bad taste, or general moral decay, as with the Circus and Vauxhall, but to the economic problems of Scotland. One instance of this may be found in his description of High Street in Edinburgh. He favorably evaluates—using criteria that appear in the section of Palladio's work dealing with town planning—the mile-long stretch of the street that runs from the lower part of the city to the castle that stands overlooking Edinburgh: "Considering its fine pavement, its width, and the lofty houses on each side, this would be undoubtedly one of the noblest streets in Europe." He quickly adds, however, that the beauty and convenience of the street is marred by a row of commercial shops called the Lucken Booths, "an ugly mass of mean buildings," which has "thrust itself . . . into the middle of the way." The intrusion of the Lucken Booths into an otherwise desirable street may be seen as an architectural manifestation of a dilemma Smollett saw Scotland facing. The desire for economic gain (as seen in the Lucken Booths), the "spirit of industry" that Smollett declared in *The Present State of All Nations* to be necessary for Scotland's prosperity, [9] is concomitantly threatening to destroy the traditional beauty—both physical and moral—of the country. The very force that can raise the Scottish standard of living can also undermine its ancient values: "a glut of wealth," as Lismahago observes

8. Smollett, who thought that "The people of the city (of Glasgow) are remarkable for their industry, their commercial spirit, their punctual observance of the presbyterian discipline," asserted in *The* *Present State of All Nations* (London, 1768–69) that "in a word Glasgow is the most beautiful town of Great Britain" (II, 106, 104).
9. *Ibid.*, II, 23.

424 • John F. Sena

in a statement with which Smollett would have been in sympathy, "brings along with it a glut of evils: it brings false taste, false appetite, false wants, profusion, venality, contempt of order, engendering a spirit of licentiousness, insolence, and faction, that keeps the community in continual ferment, and in time destroys all the distinctions of civil society; so that universal anarchy and uproar must ensue." Lismahago's solution—which reflects a moderate and reasonable position—is as applicable to architecture as it is to economics. Commerce must be "restrained" and controlled by "proper regulations," not allowed, like its physical expression in the Lucken Booths, to grow without plan or direction and destroy the native beauty of the country.

Bramble's disapproval of the landscape architecture in Scotland may also be seen as a manifestation of an economic—rather than a moral—problem. The gardens and parks, he tells us, "are not comparable to those of England . . . The pleasure-grounds are, in my opinion, not so well laid out according to the *genius loci*; nor are the lawns, and walks, and hedges kept in such delicate order." The rigid arrangement of trees also displeases him. In his indictment of Scottish landscape architecture, however, he also gives the reason for its inferiority to English landscape design: "almost all the gardeners of South-Britain were natives of Scotland." The migration of talented gardeners from Scotland to England is part of a larger problem that Bramble described in his discussion of Anglo-Scottish relations with Lismahago. Poor economic conditions and lack of opportunities have caused a migration of the most gifted Scots —those, both Bramble and Lismahago agree, who are "remarkably sober, orderly, and industrious"—to England where their "industry, œconomy, and circumspection" have allowed them to amass large fortunes. Since, according to Lismahago, it is a "hackneyed maxim" that "a supply of industrious people is a supply of wealth" to a nation, the migration southward has enriched England while reducing Scotland's ability to improve its economic climate and thus to halt the flow. The southward migration of gardeners, then, suggests that with people as with "the produce of our lands, and all the profits of our trade . . . the exchange between the two kingdoms is always against Scotland."

Upon re-entering England, Bramble employs an architectural concept to describe the first place where he is confronted with moral culpability —the Baynard estate. The vanity, egotism, and pride of Mrs. Baynard are portrayed by him largely in terms of her rejection of the precept of convenience, a precept stressed in their descriptions of country estates by poets as well as by architects.[1] Instead, for instance, of designing the

1. In Jonson's "To Penshurst," Carew's "To my friend G.N. from Wrest" and "To Saxham," Herrick's "A Panegerick to Sir Lewis Pemberton," and Marvell's "Upon Appleton House," for instance, the poet emphasizes that the grounds of an estate must be useful, capable of supplying the residents with all the necessities of life from food to mental relaxation, while the house itself must be conveniently constructed so that the social obligations of the owner may be met.

grounds of the estate so that they would provide her family with food, protection from the weather, and a place for contemplation, her plans have rendered them totally useless. The garden, which was once "well stocked with the best fruit which England could produce," has been devastated so that "there is not now the least vestige remaining of trees. . . . Nothing appears but a naked circus of loose sand. . . ." Trees and walls which had formerly acted as a wind screen have been torn down so that her family is now exposed to the east wind and its attendant melancholia. Tall oaks that had once given needed shade have been cut, while a stone gallery which furnished the inhabitants with a tranquil place for meditation has been replaced by "a screen of modern architecture." Nor is the interior of the house any more functional. The parlor, we are told, is so "fine and delicate, that in all appearance it was designed to be seen only, not inhabited. The chairs and couches were carved, gilt, and covered with rich damask, so smooth and slick, that they looked as if they had never been sat upon. There was no carpet on the floor; but the boards were rubbed and waxed in such a manner, that we could not walk, but were obliged to slide along them. . . ." Instead, then, of designing a residence like Burlington's Chiswick House, where the modesty, dignity, and good "Sense" of the owner may be seen in the priority given to convenience—"'Tis Use alone," Pope tells us, "that sanctifies Expence"[2]—the Baynard estate reflects the ostentation, pride, and foolishness of the Timon-like "builder [who] spent/ More cost in outward gay Embellishment,/ Then reall use. . . ."[3]

If the Baynard estate fails to conform to the precept of convenience, it also fails to embody the social obligations traditionally associated with country houses. Unlike, for instance, the estate of Wrest and the home of Saxham, celebrated by Carew, the Baynard residence is not a "house for hospitalitie" or a haven for the "weary Pilgrim,"[4] but is rather a "temple of cold reception" at which the visitor, Bramble, is offered as a sacrifice to the "inhospitable powers." Unlike country houses where the staff reflects the generosity and hospitality of the owners, so that there is no "currish Waiter to affright," no porter "who strikes" or who stands "at the doore/ T'examine, or keep back the poore,"[5] the servants at the Baynard residence literally and figuratively close the gates of the estate to

2. Alexander Pope, "Epistle IV. To Richard Boyle, Earl of Burlington," ll. 179–180, *The Poems of Alexander Pope*, ed. John Butt (New Haven: Yale University Press, 1966), p. 594.
3. Thomas Carew, "To my friend G.N. from Wrest," II.53–55, *The Poems of Thomas Carew*, ed. Rhodes Dunlap (Oxford: Clarendon Press, 1949), p. 87. After examining the major country-house poems of the seventeenth century, as well as Pope's "Epistle to Burlington," G. R. Hibbard concludes that "... the right and proper end of building is use, not show; and that the proper aim of the individual should be the subordination of

himself to the service of the community, not exploitation of the community for his own personal ends"—"The Country House Poem of the Seventeenth Century," *Journal of the Warburg and Courtauld Institutes*, XIX (1956), 174.
4. "To my friend G.N. from Wrest," l. 24, "To Saxham," l. 38, Carew, *op. cit.* (note 3), pp. 87, 28.
5. Robert Herrick, "A Panegerick to Sir Lewis Pemberton" ll. 47, 18, *The Poetical Works of Robert Herrick*, ed. F. W. Moorman (Oxford: Clarendon Press, 1915), pp. 146–147; "To Saxham," ll. 49–50, Carew, *op. cit.* (note 3), p. 28.

Bramble. They accost him, we are told, with "no civility" and keep him waiting a "considerable time in the coach" before telling him that the Baynards are not available. After entering the house, the valetudinarian is kept waiting an additional half-hour before either Baynard appears. Unlike Wrest, where "No sumptuous Chimney-peece of shining stone/ Invites the strangers eye to gaze upon/ . . . but cleare/ And cheerefull flames, cherish and warme him here,"[6] the "stove" of the Baynards provides no warmth or comfort to the visitor: "it was too bright and polished to be polluted with sea-coal, or stained by the smoke of any gross material fire." Instead, then, of embodying the traditional ideals of a country home—an edenic dwelling infused with the spirit of hospitality and altruism, administered by a virtuous man married to an equally virtuous woman[7]—the Baynard house is a wicked and pernicious place, inhabited by a vainglorious woman, a neurotic son, and a man who has become physically ill from the general moral decay.

In a sense, with Bramble's depiction of the Baynard estate we have come full circle, for the estate created by Mrs. Baynard seems spiritually akin to the architectural and social disorder of Bath and London. The vanity and pretension, the egotism and presumption, of the *nouveau riche* —those social interlopers who, according to Bramble, have little regard for propriety or the wisdom and practices of the past—that are partially responsible for the physical and social chaos of Bath and London have been transferred by Mrs. Baynard to the country.[8] Unlike the "fallen" cities of England, however, the Baynard estate is restored to order through the intercession of Bramble, whose pragmatic suggestions transform the estate to its former condition. By being brought into conformity with the Augustan ideal of a rural retreat, the Baynard estate becomes, like its urban counterpart, Glasgow, an emblem for the ordered and moral society valued by Bramble and his creator.

It is evident, then, that Bramble's architectural observations are not superfluous ornaments gratuitously added by Smollett to provide the novel with local color or a heightened sense of realism, but are instead central to the author's satiric vision. By allowing Bramble to evaluate and condemn structures in terms of a theory of architecture employed by the ancient Greeks and Romans, a theory which conceived of buildings as having moral as well as physical dimensions, Smollett has complemented his verbal indictment of contemporary England, as did Dryden and Pope, with graphic symbols of a world in decline. Although Scottish architec-

6. "To my friend G.N. from Wrest," ll. 25–28, *ibid*, p. 87.
7. For a discussion of the relationship between the ideals of a country house and the myth of the golden age, see William Alexander McClung, *The Country House in English Renaissance Poetry* (Berkeley: University of California Press, 1977), esp. pp. 7–17.
8. "Criticism of corrupted rural existence is," in *Humphry Clinker* as well as in the novels of Richardson and Fielding, according to David Evans, "centered primarily around the passivity, extravagance and uselessness which make the life of the gentry analogous to city life under the 'tide of luxury'"—"'Humphry Clinker': Smollett's Tempered Augustanism," *Criticism*, IX (1967), 258.

ture, and the morality it embodies, is seen as superior to England's, Bramble's architectural analyses provide the reader with a contrast not primarily between England and Scotland, or, for that matter, between the urban and the rural, but rather between the old and the new, between the heroism and virtue of the past and the foolishness and vice of the present. In the rejection of classical architectural practices, one may perceive the failure of Hanoverian England to reconstruct a society modeled after the ideals of Augustan Rome. Appropriately enough, Bramble, who expressed his desire—and doubtless Smollett's—to be like "Hogarth in these dull and degenerate times," has in fact succeeded in imitating the work of the pictorial satirist, for he has through his architectural commentary condemned contemporary society, not merely in words, but in visible metaphors.

CONNIE CAPERS THORSON

Smollett and *Humphry Clinker*:
A Bibliographical Essay

For the student interested in exploring *Humphry Clinker* and Tobias Smollett in greater depth, there are many essays, chapters of books, and books that can provide a wide variety of critical approaches and appraisals. This bibliographic essay will not attempt to present any analysis of all of the critical material about Smollett or *Humphry Clinker*; rather it will be selective in the inclusions, at the same time that it will provide objective and subjective commentary about those inclusions. Full bibliographical citations appear after the essay.

To look at biographical studies of Smollett is to watch a parade of studies stretching back to his own time, but the student need only to consult the masterful biography *Tobias Smollett, Doctor of Men and Manners* by the late Lewis M. Knapp to assure himself of the most accurate picture of the man and his career. Paul-Gabriel Boucé has surveyed "Eighteenth- and Nineteenth-Century Biographies" of Smollett in an essay of that name. Boucé also includes a good deal of biography in his *The Novels of Tobias Smollett*, but Knapp's earlier study remains definitive. Boucé and Knapp both note the dangerous tendency among students of Smollett to read the novels as veiled autobiography. Although a number of studies include excursions into Smollett's biography, most written since the Knapp biography are more or less heavily dependent on his work.

Smollett and *Humphry Clinker* have also attracted the attention of both analytical and enumerative bibliographers. Of the former, the most important work is that done by William B. Todd, who summarizes the work in his dissertation in a tightly packed article, "Bibliography and the Editorial Problem in the Eighteenth Century." A more expanded essay which comes to slightly different conclusions from Todd's is found in "A Consideration of the Bibliographical Problems Connected with the First Edition of *Humphry Clinker*" by Franklin B. Newman. O. M. Brack has made many contributions to the studies of bibliographical problems in Smollett's canon, including "'Of Making Many Books There Is No End': Editing Smollett." The major enumerative bibliographies are those by Donald M. Korte and Francesco Cordasco. Korte annotates his listing and restricts his scope to the scholarship published between 1946 and 1968. Cordasco tries to cover everything and must be handled with extreme care.

Of the many full-length studies of Smollett and his novels, in which *Humphry Clinker* always holds a position of importance, perhaps the most intelligently reasoned and tightly structured is John Sekora's *Luxury: The Concept in Western Thought, Eden to Smollett*. After a discussion of luxury in its classical contexts, Sekora analyzes the term as used in the eighteenth century. The discussion of luxury in Smollett's non-fiction is followed by a close analysis of *The Expedition of Humphry Clinker*, which Sekora regards as "the most successful conservative attack upon luxury written in any genre during the 1750's and 1760's, a pearl in a generation of sand" (p. 240). To complete the picture of how luxury informs the whole novel, the student will need to read, in addition to the chapter on politics included above, Sekora's discussion of the characters and the structure of the novel. This careful examination of the history of an idea and the way that idea prevails in the work of Smollett, particularly *Humphry Clinker*, is a fine addition to the canon of critical materials on Smollett.

Another reasoned and intelligent study that the student may wish to see for critical interpretation and evaluation is *Tobias Smollett: The Expedition of Humphry Clinker* by John Valdimir Price. Price discusses not only the structure and themes of the novel, but also the characters. He stresses Humphry's importance to the novel, addresses the problem of interpreting the novel as autobiography, and recognizes the many critical approaches that the student may take in thinking about the novel.

M. A. Goldberg, in *Smollett and the Scottish School: Studies in Eighteenth-Century Thought*, places Smollett squarely in the middle of the Scottish commonsense school, with an analysis of Smollett's five novels. He examines character, structure, and theme in each, though the thematic approach is the most obvious in the chapter on *Humphry Clinker*, in which he is primarily concerned with how primitivism and progress inform the novel, a somewhat simplistic view. *Smollett's Reputation as a Novelist* by Fred W. Boege is a useful compendium of critical responses from the appearance of *Humphry Clinker* until the mid-1940's. Louis L. Martz, in *The Later Career of Tobias Smollett*, examines

Smollett's work in compiling and editing between 1753 and 1756, finding that his many acts of literary drudgery during that period affected his later creative work, including *Humphry Clinker*. Martz presents detailed comparisons between observations of Scotland in *The Present State of All Nations* and those in *Humphry Clinker*, asserting, "The satire of England and encomium of Scotland may well represent Smollett's attempt to reconcile himself with those of his countrymen who were offended by *Present State*" (p. 130). In *Tobias George Smollett*, Robert Donald Spector attempts to make *Humphry Clinker* the final example of Smollett's use of the picaresque, but the argument is rather tenuous. He does not fully succeed in proving that Matt Bramble and Jery are picaros. Robert Giddings, in *The Tradition of Smollett*, also asserts that Smollett's tradition is the picaresque and maintains that *Peregrine Pickle* rather than *Humphry Clinker* is his best work. He also relates Smollett to Charles Dickens and John Barth. Alan Dugald McKillop's *The Early Masters of English Fiction* is a distinguished study of important novelists and novels in the eighteenth century. A student wishing a picture of how the early novel developed would be well advised to read all the essays in the book, not just the one on Tobias Smollett.

Win Jenkins' use of language is one element of *Humphry Clinker* that the student will deal with virtually from beginning to end. Of the many articles dealing with her language, some are concerned primarily with the words themselves, while others relate the language to the themes of the novel. W. Arthur Boggs has written many articles that are examples of the former: "Shakespeare and Win," in which several of her usages are related directly to Shakespeare's usage of the same words; "A Win Jenkins Lexicon," in which her strange usages are explicated; "Win Jenkins' Archaisms and Proverbial Phrases," in which her use of both proverbs and archaisms is explained; and "Smollett's Coinages In the Win Jenkins Letters," in which Boggs discusses a few words that are coinages by Smollett. Deborah D. Rogers, in "Further Shakespearean Echoes in *Humphry Clinker*," adds nine to Boggs' list of four malapropisms that resemble Shakespearean wordplay. Sheryl Barlow's "The Deception of Bath: Malapropisms in Smollett's *Humphrey Clinker*" (despite the misspellings in the title and throughout the article) establishes the connections between Smollett's themes and the malapropisms of Win and Tabby. Arthur Sherbo, in "Win Jenkins' Language," cogently disputes the findings in many of Boggs' articles.

Studies showing Smollett's indebtedness to others for ideas, themes, and characters abound. In "Voltaire and *Humphry Clinker*" by E. T. Helmick the influence of Smollett's having translated Voltaire before writing *Humphry Clinker* is analyzed. The satire of the two men is seen as closely akin. Robert B. Heilman, in "Falstaff and Smollett's Micklewhimmen," argues that Smollett borrowed greatly from Shakespeare's Falstaff in his characterization of Micklewhimmen. Smollett's debt to Richardson is discussed in "Fire-Scenes in Richardson's *Clarissa* and Smollett's *Humphry Clinker*" by Philip Mahone Griffith. Griffith argues reasonably that Smollett used the fire-scenes to satirize Richardson's over-developed moral sense. In "Verse Satire and Smollett's *Humphry Clinker*," Donald M. Korte's argument enlarges the apparent debt of Smollett to formal verse satire, especially that of Alexander Pope, by demonstrating the close ties between the episode of the Baynards and the fourth "Moral Essay." An essay devoting at least part of its argument to Smollett's indebtedness to Pope is G. S. Rousseau's "Beef and Bouillon: A Voice for Tobias Smollett, with Comments on His Life, Works, and Modern Critics." It is an essay that must be read very cautiously.

Three essays that examine *Humphry Clinker* as advocating country life as opposed to city life are Jeffry L. Duncan's "The Rural Ideal in Eighteenth-Century Fiction"; David L. Evans' "'Humphry Clinker': Smollett's Tempered Augustanism"; and Edward Copeland's "*Humphry Clinker*: A Comic Pastoral Poem in Prose?" All three essays, to varying degrees, argue that Smollett, in this late novel, came to the conclusion that the rural life is the ideal life. In differing ways, the essayists investigate how the rural ideal can become the vehicle for satiric sallies against the chaos and affectation of city life.

There are a surprising number of essays that deal with the historical and political backgrounds of *Humphry Clinker*. Robert C. Alberts, in "The Fantastic Adventures of Captain Stobo," and George M. Kahrl, in "Captain Robert Stobo," both investigate the life and adventures of Stobo, who, most agree, was the real-life forebear of Lieutenant Obidiah Lismahago. "Another Source for Smollett's Lismahago" by Michael Rymer shows Smollett's debt to Charles Johnston's *Chrysal, or The Adventures of a Guinea*. David Graham-Campbell presents fairly conclusive proof that Alexander Campbell was "The Original of Mr. Paunceford in *Humphry Clinker*."

While *Humphry Clinker* is not a novel that immediately strikes the reader as a political one, there are numerous characters, ideas, and incidents that can be interpreted as having political significance. For those interested in the political backgrounds of the novel, there are essays that should be read. "Smollett's *Humphry Clinker* as a 'Party Novel'" by Wolfgang Franke discusses in detail Smollett's propagandistic intent of vindicating the Scots as the organizing principle of the novel. Paul-Gabriel Boucé, in "The Duke of Newcastle's Levee in Smollett's *Humphry Clinker*," points out what he sees as Smollett's Tory bias by dissecting the Duke's patronage of the clergy, much to the detriment of the Duke. Obversely, Robin Fabel's "The Patriotic Briton: Tobias Smollett and English Politics, 1756–1771" takes the stance that Smollett, "far from being as so many have assumed in a Whig or Tory camp, understood the essential meaninglessness of the party labels and expressed consistently, in his latter years, nothing but contempt for the men that bore them" (p. 104). Byron Gassman believes that the praise of George III by Matt Bramble and Mr. Barton is truly complimentary, not satiric or ironic, given the social vision of the novel which supports a desire for reconstruction under the new monarch. Gassman's "'Humphry Clinker' and the Two Kingdoms of George III" is an intelligent examination of George's influence on the novel. Finally, the student who would like more information about some of the political characters and allusions in the novel should read "Some Political Figures in 'Humphry Clinker'" by John Sekora.

In Smollett's works satire is almost inevitable. For an examination of satire throughout his works, the chapter "Smollett: The Satirist as a Character Type" by Ronald Paulson in his book *Satire and the Novel in Eighteenth-Century England*, is a good place to begin. Paulson explains that Bramble is a good example of the satirist satirized, particularly because each of his letters to Dr. Lewis is a self-contained satire on Bramble himself. Paulson argues that Smollett's major aim in his novels is satiric and that Smollett's use of the epistolary form enables him to use both Juvenalian and Horatian modes of satire. There are, of course, many other essays that those interested in satire should read. G. S. Rousseau, in "Matt Bramble and the Sulpher Controversy in the XVIIIth Century: Medical Background of *Humphry Clinker*," argues that Smollett's knowledge of the subject enables him to write fine medical satire through Matt Bramble. In "Smollett's Matthew Bramble and the Tradition of the Physician-Satirist," John F. Sena asserts that Bramble reacts to physical discomforts on his journey because the physician-satirist, a sensitive person, always reacts badly to the corruption and decay of society. William West's "Matt Bramble's Journey to Health," B.L. Reid's "Smollett's Healing Journey," and Linda Pannill's "Some Patterns of Imagery in *Humphry Clinker*" argue for much the same kind of interpretation of the novel by relying on the journey to health as the frame. Thomas R. Preston approaches the satiric persona from a different viewpoint in "Smollett and the Benevolent Misanthrope Type." Preston thinks Bramble's combination of misanthropy and benevolence finally allowed Smollett to write the kind of amiable satire that he had been searching for for so long. Preston's reading of Smollett leads him to the conclusion that "this very world [the late 18th-century] which admires the man of feeling forces him into the posture of a misanthrope and a satirist to defend himself from it" (p. 57). Bramble is the man of feeling, the misanthrope, and the satirist.

Another approach to *Humphry Clinker* is through generic criticism. Charles L. Batten, Jr., in "*Humphry Clinker* and Eighteenth-Century Travel Literature," argues that the novel lacks the unity we have come to expect in the genre because it really is fictionalized travel literature. In "Smollett's Development as a Novelist," John M. Warner contends that

Smollett finally "achieves in *Humphry Clinker* the capacity to make telling comment on human life without injury to the conventions of his fictional world" (p. 161). In his insightful "*Humphry Clinker* as Comic Romance," Sheridan Baker argues that Henry Fielding's term *comic romance* is the appropriate generic classification for Smollett's novel. In "The 'Stage Passions' and Smollett's Characterization" Thomas Preston details the ways in which Smollett was influenced by the drama in his molding of characters. It is Preston's opinion, in this excellent account, that it is the outward reality of the characters, their stage passions, that becomes Smollett's realism. Tuvia Bloch argues for Smollett's development through the earlier novels in which he tried to use an ironic narrator like that of Fielding, and finds that Smollett found a more compatible form with the epistles that make up *Humphry Clinker*. Eric Rothstein, in his essay on *Humphry Clinker* in *Systems of Order and Inquiry in Later Eighteenth-Century Fiction*, obscures his dissection of the conceptual breadth and subtlety of the picaresque with verbose arguments. To Rothstein, it is the characters and their interactions that shape the novel and make it an orderly world for Matt Bramble. "The Smollettian View of Life" by Lance Bertelsen advocates that in order to deal with the "Smollett novel" the student come to grips with the episodic nature of the novels, that is, with how the dozens of episodes work together, in order to unearth the controlling ideas of the novels. Bridget Puzon, in "The Hidden Meaning in *Humphry Clinker*," presents her discovery that the novel belongs to a new sub-genre of fiction, the *Bildungsroman* of middle age. Finally, George M. Kahrl writes in "*Humphry Clinker*: The Story of the Last Journey" that the novel is a travel book based on Smollett's several trips to Scotland. He argues that the novel's being a travel book allows Smollett to show the characters in all the richness of their reactions to people and places and how these reactions ultimately allowed them to moderate many of their former prejudices.

Smollett is humorous. However, critics have interpreted this humor in varying ways. Robert Hopkins, in "The Function of Grotesque in *Humphry Clinker*," finds the grotesque an integral part of the comedy in the novel. His discussion of the texture and significance of the grotesque explains that it is the coupling of the grotesque and the comic that allows the extreme pessimism of the novel to work. In "*Humphry Clinker's* Humane Humor," Richard J. Dunn says that Smollett uses a more humane humor than in his previous works, allowing him to better emphasize "the tension between men of modest merit and a vicious world" (p. 229). The interplay of the perspectives of the characters is what Robert Folkenflik, in "Self and Society: Comic Union in *Humphry Clinker*," sees contributing the comic vitality of the novel.

Tobias Smollett and *Humphry Clinker* have long provided the critic and the scholar with much to think and write about. Those students who have had their curiosity piqued by the novel and/or by Smollett will find any of the articles and books discussed above very rewarding reading.

Bibliography

Alberts, Robert C. "The Fantastic Adventures of Captain Stobo." *American Heritage*, 14 (1963), 65–77.

Baker, Sheridan. "*Humphry Clinker* as Comic Romance." *Papers of the Michigan Academy of Science, Arts, and Letters*, 46 (1961), 645–54.

Barlow, Sheryl. "The Deception of Bath: Malapropisms in Smollett's *Humphrey* [sic.] *Clinker*." *Michigan Academician*, 2, no. 4 (1970), 13–24.

Batten, Charles L., Jr. "*Humphry Clinker* and Eighteenth-Century Travel Literature." *Genre*, 7 (1974), 392–408.

Bertelsen, Lance. "The Smollettian View of Life." *Novel*, 11 (1978), 115–27.

Bloch, Tuvia. "Smollett's Quest for Form." *Modern Philology*, 65 (1967), 103–13.

Boege, Fred W. *Smollett's Reputation as a Novelist*. Princeton: Princeton University Press, 1947.

Boggs, W. Arthur. "Shakespeare and Win." *American Notes and Queries*, 3 (1965), 149–50.

———. "Smollett's Coinages in the Win Jenkins' Letters." *Language Quarterly*, 2 (1963), 2–4.

———. "Win Jenkins' Archaisms and Proverbial Phrases." *Language Quarterly*, 4 (1965), 33–36.

———. "A Win Jenkins' Lexicon." *Bulletin of the New York Public Library*, 68 (1964), 323–30.

Boucé, Paul-Gabriel. "The Duke of Newcastle's Levee in Smollett's *Humphry Clinker*." *Yearbook of English Studies*, 5 (1975), 136–41.

———. "Eighteenth-and Nineteenth-Century Biographies." In *Tobias Smollett: Bicentennnial Essays Presented to Lewis M. Knapp*. Ed. G. S. Rousseau and P.-G. Boucé. New York: Oxford University Press, 1971, pp. 201–30.

———. *The Novels of Tobias Smollett*. London: Longmans, 1976.

Brack, O. M. "'Of Making Many Books There Is No End': Editing Smollett." In *Editing Eighteenth Century Novels*. Ed. G. E. Bentley, Jr. Toronto: A. M. Hakkert, 1975, pp. 91–115.

Butt, John. "Smollett's Achievement as a Novelist." In *Tobias Smollett: Bicentennial Essays Presented to Lewis M. Knapp*. Ed. G. S. Rousseau and P.-G. Boucé. New York: Oxford University Press, 1971, pp. 9–23.

Copeland, Edward. "*Humphry Clinker*: A Comic Pastoral Poem in Prose?" *Texas Studies in Literature and Language*, 16 (1974), 493–501.

Cordasco, Francesco. *Tobias George Smollett, a Bibliographical Guide*. New York: AMS Press, 1978.

Duckworth, Alistair M. "Fiction and Some Uses of the Country House Setting from Richardson to Scott." In *Landscape in the Gardens and the Literature of Eighteenth-Century England*, Los Angeles: Clark Memorial Library, 1981, pp. 89–128.

Duncan, Jeffrey L. "The Rural Ideal in Eighteenth-Century Fiction." *Studies in English Literature*, 8 (1968), 517–35.

Dunn, Richard J. "*Humphry Clinker's* Humane Humor." *Texas Studies in Literature and Language*, 18 (1976), 229–39.

Evans, David L. "*Humphry Clinker*: Smollett's Tempered Augustanism." *Criticism*, 9 (1967), 257–74.

Fabel, Robin. "The Patriotic Briton: Tobias Smollett and English Politics, 1756–1771." *Eighteenth-Century Studies*, 8 (1974), 100–114.

Folkenflik, Robert. "Self and Society: Comic Union in *Humphry Clinker*." *Philological Quarterly*, 53 (1974), 195–204.

Franke, Wolfgang. "Smollett's *Humphry Clinker* as a 'Party Novel.'" *Studies in Scottish Literature*, 9 (1971–72), 97–106.

Gassman, Byron. "'Humphry Clinker' and the Two Kingdoms of George III." *Criticism*, 16 (1974), 95–108.

Giddings, Robert. *The Tradition of Smollett*. London: Methuen, 1967.

Goldberg, M. A. *Smollett and the Scottish School: Studies in Eighteenth-Century Thought*. Albuquerque: University of New Mexico Press, 1959.

Graham-Campbell, David. "The Original of Mr. Paunceford in *Humphry Clinker*." *Scottish Literary Journal*, 4 (1977), 17–35.

Griffith, Philip Mahone. "Fire-Scenes in Richardson's *Clarissa* and Smollett's *Humphry Clinker*: A Study of a Literary Relationship in the Structure of the Novel." *Tulane Studies in English*, 11 (1961), 39–51.

Hames, Louise. "The Pronunciation of Tabitha Bramble." *Journal of English Linguistics*, 14 (1980), 6–19.

Heilman, Robert B. "Falstaff and Smollett's Micklewhimmen." *Review of English Studies*, 22 (1946), 226–28.

Helmick, E. T. "Voltaire and *Humphry Clinker*." *Studies on Voltaire and the Eighteenth Century*, 67 (1969), 59–64.

Hopkins, Robert. "The Function of Grotesque in *Humphry Clinker*." *Huntington Library Quarterly*, 32 (1969), 163–77.

Kahrl, George M. "Captain Robert Stobo." *Virginia Magazine of History and Biography*, 49 (1941), 141–51, 254–68.

————. "*Humphry Clinker*, the Story of the Last Journey." In *Tobias Smollett: Traveler-Novelist*. Chicago: University of Chicago Press, 1945, pp. 119–47.

Knapp, Lewis Mansfield. *Tobias Smollett, Doctor of Men and Manners*. Princeton: Princeton University Press, 1949.

Korte, Donald M. *An Annotated Bibliography of Smollett Scholarship, 1946–68*. Toronto: University of Toronto Press, 1969.

————. "Verse Satire and Smollett's *Humphry Clinker*." *Studies in Scottish Literature*, 7 (1970), 188–92.

Martz, Louis L. *The Later Career of Tobias Smollett*. Yale Studies in English, vol. 97. New Haven: Yale University Press, 1942.

McKillop, Alan Dugald. *The Early Masters of English Fiction*. Lawrence: University of Kansas Press, 1956.

Newman, Franklin B. "A Consideration of the Bibliographical Problems Connected with the First Edition of *Humphry Clinker*." *Papers of the Bibliographical Society of America*, 44 (1950), 340–71.

Niehus, Edward L. "Quixotic Figures in the Novels of Smollett." *Durham University Journal*, 71 (1979), 233–43.

Pannill, Linda. "Some Patterns of Imagery in *Humphry Clinker*." *Thoth*, 13 (1973), 37–43.

Paulson, Ronald. "Smollett: the Satirist as a Character Type." In *Satire and the Novel in Eighteenth-Century England*. New Haven: Yale University Press, 1967, pp. 165–218.

Preston, Thomas R. "Smollett and the Benevolent Misanthrope Type." *Publications of the Modern Language Association of America*, 39 (1964), 51–57.

————. "The 'Stage Passions' and Smollett's Characterization." *Studies in Philology*, 71 (1974), 105–25.

Price, John Valdimir. *Tobias Smollett: The Expedition of Humphry Clinker*. London: Edward Arnold, 1973.

Puzon, Bridget. "The Hidden Meaning in *Humphry Clinker*." *Harvard Library Bulletin*, 24 (1976), 40–54.

Reid, B. L. "Smollett's Healing Journey." *Virginia Quarterly Review*, 41 (1965), 549–570.

Rogers, Deborah D. "Further Shakespearean Echoes in *Humphry Clinker*." *American Notes and Queries*, 14 (1976), 98–102.

Rothstein, Eric. "*Humphry Clinker*." In *Systems of Order and Inquiry in Later Eighteenth-Century Fiction*. Berkeley: University of California Press, 1975, pp. 109–53.

Rousseau, G. S. "Beef and Bouillon: A Voice for Tobias Smollett, with Comments on His Life, Works, and Modern Critics." *British Studies Monitor*, 7 (1977), 4–56.

————. "Matt Bramble and the Sulphur Controversy in the XVIIIth Century: Medical Background of *Humphry Clinker*." *Journal of the History of Ideas*, 28 (1967), 577–89.

Rymer, Michael. "Another Source for Smollett's Lismahago." *Notes and Queries*, NS 21 (1974), 57–59.

Sekora, John. *Luxury: The Concept in Western Thought, Eden to Smollett*. Baltimore: Johns Hopkins University Press, 1977.

————. "Some Political Figures in 'Humphry Clinker.'" *Notes and Queries*, NS 24 (1977), 270–73.

Sena, John F. "Smollett's Matthew Bramble and the Tradition of the Physician-Satirist." *Papers on Language and Literature*, 11 (1975), 380–96.

Sherbo, Arthur. "Win Jenkins' Language." *Papers on Language and Literature*, 5 (1969), 199–204.

Spector, Robert Donald. *Tobias George Smollett*. New York: Twayne, 1968.

————. *Tobias Smollett: A Reference Guide*. Boston: Hall, 1980.

Todd, William B. "Bibliography and the Editorial Problem in the Eighteenth Century." *Studies in Bibliography*, 4 (1951), 41–55.

Thorson, James L. "Reflections of Oxford in *The Expedition of Humphry Clinker*." *Oxford*, 34 (1982), 34–44.

Warner, John M. "Smollett's Development as a Novelist." *Novel*, 5 (1971), 148–61.

West, William A. "Matt Bramble's Journey to Health." *Texas Studies in Literature and Language*, 11 (1969), 1197–1208.

NORTON CRITICAL EDITIONS

HOMER *The Odyssey* translated and edited by Albert Cook
HOWELLS *The Rise of Silas Lapham* edited by Don L. Cook
IBSEN *The Wild Duck* translated and edited by Dounia B. Christiani
JAMES *The Ambassadors* edited by S. P. Rosenbaum
JAMES *The American* edited by James A. Tuttleton
JAMES *The Portrait of a Lady* edited by Robert D. Bamberg
JAMES *The Turn of the Screw* edited by Robert Kimbrough
JAMES *The Wings of the Dove* edited by J. Donald Crowley and
    Richard A. Hocks
Ben Jonson and the Cavalier Poets selected and edited by Hugh Maclean
Ben Jonson's Plays and Masques selected and edited by Robert M. Adams
MACHIAVELLI *The Prince* translated and edited by Robert M. Adams
MALTHUS *An Essay on the Principle of Population* edited by Philip Appleman
MELVILLE *The Confidence-Man* edited by Hershel Parker
MELVILLE *Moby-Dick* edited by Harrison Hayford and Hershel Parker
MEREDITH *The Egoist* edited by Robert M. Adams
MILL *On Liberty* edited by David Spitz
MILTON *Paradise Lost* edited by Scott Elledge
MORE *Utopia* translated and edited by Robert M. Adams
NEWMAN *Apologia Pro Vita Sua* edited by David J. DeLaura
NORRIS *McTeague* edited by Donald Pizer
Adrienne Rich's Poetry selected and edited by Barbara Charlesworth Gelpi and
    Albert Gelpi
The Writings of St. Paul edited by Wayne A. Meeks
SHAKESPEARE *Hamlet* edited by Cyrus Hoy
SHAKESPEARE *Henry IV, Part I* edited by James J. Sanderson *Second Edition*
Bernard Shaw's Plays selected and edited by Warren Sylvester Smith
Shelley's Poetry and Prose edited by Donald H. Reiman and Sharon B. Powers
SOPHOCLES *Oedipus Tyrannus* translated and edited by Luci Berkowitz and
    Theodore F. Brunner
SPENSER *Edmund Spenser's Poetry* selected and edited by Hugh Maclean
    Second Edition
STENDHAL *Red and Black* translated and edited by Robert M. Adams
STERNE *Tristram Shandy* edited by Howard Anderson
SWIFT *Gulliver's Travels* edited by Robert A. Greenberg *Revised Edition*
The Writings of Jonathan Swift edited by Robert A. Greenberg and
    William B. Piper
TENNYSON *In Memoriam* edited by Robert Ross
Tennyson's Poetry selected and edited by Robert W. Hill, Jr.
THOREAU *Walden and Civil Disobedience* edited by Owen Thomas
TOLSTOY *Anna Karenina* (the Maude translation) edited by George Gibian
TOLSTOY *War and Peace* (the Maude translation) edited by George Gibian
TURGENEV *Fathers and Sons* edited with a substantially new translation by
    Ralph E. Matlaw
VOLTAIRE *Candide* translated and edited by Robert M. Adams
WATSON *The Double Helix* edited by Gunther S. Stent
WHITMAN *Leaves of Grass* edited by Sculley Bradley and Harold W. Blodgett
WOLLSTONECRAFT *A Vindication of the Rights of Woman* edited by
    Carol H. Poston
WORDSWORTH *The Prelude: 1799, 1805, 1850* edited by Jonathan Wordsworth,
    M. H. Abrams, and Stephen Gill
Middle English Lyrics selected and edited by Maxwell S. Luria and
    Richard L. Hoffman
Modern Drama edited by Anthony Caputi
Restoration and Eighteenth-Century Comedy edited by Scott McMillin